COMMERCIAL REPORTS

AREA STUDIES SERIES

EDITORIAL DIRECTOR   Professor J J O'Meara
RESEARCH UNIT DIRECTOR   T F Turley
ASSISTANT DIRECTOR   S Cashman

CHIEF EDITORIAL ADVISERS

P Ford
Professor Emeritus, Southampton University
Mrs G Ford

SPECIAL EDITORIAL CONSULTANT FOR THE UNITED STATES PAPERS

H C Allen
Commonwealth Fund Professor of American History, University College, London
Director of the London University Institute of United States Studies

RESEARCH EDITORS

Johann A Norstedt
Marilyn Evers Norstedt

This Series is published with the active co-operation of
SOUTHAMPTON UNIVERSITY

IRISH UNIVERSITY PRESS AREA STUDIES SERIES

BRISTISH PARLIAMENTARY PAPERS

UNITED STATES OF AMERICA

39

Embassy and consular
commercial reports
1897

IRISH UNIVERSITY PRESS
Shannon Ireland

PUBLISHER'S NOTE

The documents in this series are selected from the nineteenth-century British House of Commons *sessional and command papers*. All of the original papers relating to the United States of America are included with the exception of two kinds of very brief and unimportant papers. Omitted are (1) random statistical trade returns which are included in the larger and complete yearly trade figures and (2) returns relating to postal services, which are irregularly presented, of tangential USA relevance, and easily available in other sources.

The original documents have been reproduced by photo-lithography and are unabridged even to the extent of retaining the first printers' imprints. Imperfections in the original printing are sometimes unavoidably reproduced.

This reprint is an enlargement from the original octavo format.

© 1971 Irish University Press Shannon Ireland
Microfilm, microfiche and other forms of micro-publishing
© *Irish University Microforms Shannon Ireland*

ISBN 0 7165 1539 3

Printed and published by
Irish University Press Shannon Ireland
DUBLIN   CORK   BELFAST   LONDON   NEW YORK
T M MacGlinchey *Publisher*   Robert Hogg *Printer*

Contents

IUP Page Number

For ease of reference IUP editors have assigned a continuous pagination which appears on the top outer margin of each page.

Commercial Reports

F.O. annual series no. 1816: report on New Orleans, 1895–96
1897 [C.8277–34] XCIV 9

F.O. annual series no. 1842: report on the finances of the United States, 1895, 1896
1897 [C.8277–60] XCIV 29

F.O. annual series no. 1853: report on Chicago, 1896
1897 [C.8277–71] XCIV 55

F.O. annual series no. 1857: report on Charleston, 1896
1897 [C.8277–75] XCIV 125

F.O. annual series no. 1869: report on New Orleans, 1896
1897 [C.8277–87] XCIV 163

F.O. annual series no. 1883: report on Baltimore, 1896
1897 [C.8277–101] XCIV 197

F.O. annual series no. 1894: report on Galveston, 1896
1897 [C.8277–112] XCIV 211

F.O. annual series no. 1910: report on Philadelphia, 1895, 1896
1897 [C.8277–128] XCIV 241

F.O. annual series no. 1921: report on New York, 1896
1897 [C.8277–139] XCIV 265

F.O. annual series no. 1922: report on California, 1896
1897 [C.8277–140] XCIV 305

F.O. annual series no. 1930: report on Boston, 1896
1897 [C.8277–148] XCIV 373

F.O. annual series no. 1935: report on Portland, Oregon (including Astoria, Tacoma, and Seattle), 1896
1897 [C.8277–153] XCIV 411

As most commercial reports are extracted from larger papers, the reader should note that a particular report may lack a proper title page.

FOREIGN OFFICE.
1896.
ANNUAL SERIES.

No. 1816.
DIPLOMATIC AND CONSULAR REPORTS ON TRADE AND FINANCE.

UNITED STATES.

REPORT FOR THE YEAR 1895-96

ON THE

TRADE OF THE UNITED STATES.

Presented to both Houses of Parliament by Command of Her Majesty,
OCTOBER, 1896.

LONDON:
PRINTED FOR HER MAJESTY'S STATIONERY OFFICE,
BY HARRISON AND SONS, ST. MARTIN'S LANE,
PRINTERS IN ORDINARY TO HER MAJESTY.

And to be purchased, either directly or through any Bookseller, from
EYRE & SPOTTISWOODE, EAST HARDING STREET, FLEET STREET, E.C., and
32, ABINGDON STREET, WESTMINSTER, S.W.; or
JOHN MENZIES & Co., 12, HANOVER STREET, EDINBURGH, and
90, WEST NILE STREET, GLASGOW; or
HODGES, FIGGIS, & Co., Limited, 104, GRAFTON STREET, DUBLIN.

1896.

[C. 8277—34.]   *Price Three Halfpence.*

New Series of Reports.

Reports of the Annual Series have been issued from Her Majesty's Diplomatic and Consular Officers at the following places, and may be obtained from the sources indicated on the title-page:—

No.		Price.	No.		Price.
1698.	Jerusalem	1d.	1757.	Lisbon	1½d.
1699.	Cherbourg	2d.	1758.	Nagasaki	1d.
1700.	Leghorn	1½d.	1759.	Hamburg	2½d.
1701.	Boston	1½d.	1760.	Mozambique	2d.
1702.	Kiungchow	1d.	1761.	Cettinjé	1½d.
1703.	Naples	2½d.	1762.	The Hague	1½d.
1704.	Stockholm	2d.	1763.	Cephalonia	1d.
1705.	Corunna	2d.	1764.	Bahia	1d.
1706.	Rio de Janeiro	2½d.	1765.	Zanzibar	1½d.
1707.	San José	1d.	1766.	Pakhoi	1d.
1708.	Paramaribo	2d.	1767.	New York	2d.
1709.	Brest	1½d.	1768.	Chefoo	1d.
1710.	Montevideo	½d.	1769.	Caracas	½d.
1711.	Charleston	2½d.	1770.	Palermo	11½d.
1712.	Baltimore	1d.	1771.	Mombasa	½d.
1713.	Tripoli	1d.	1772.	Nice	1½d.
1714.	Callao	½d.	1773.	Bucharest	4½d.
1715.	Ningpo	1d.	1774.	Port Said	1½d.
1716.	Dunkirk	1½d.	1775.	Galatz	1½d.
1717.	Batoum	2d.	1776.	Madrid	2d.
1718.	Hankow	1½d.	1777.	Vienna	2d.
1719.	Foochow	3½d.	1778.	Canton	1d.
1720.	Syra	½d.	1779.	Yokohama	1½d.
1721.	Panama	1d.	1780.	Newchwang	1d.
1722.	Batavia	1½d.	1781.	Wuhu	1d.
1723.	Genoa	3d.	1782.	Athens	2d.
1724.	Cagliari	2½d.	1783.	Tonga	½d.
1725.	Chicago	7½d.	1784.	Smyrna	½d.
1726.	Trieste	1d.	1785.	Baghdad	1d.
1727.	Hakodate	1d.	1786.	Hiogo and Osaka	4½d.
1728.	Mannheim	1d.	1787.	Bangkok	1d.
1729.	Panama	1d.	1788.	Odessa	2d.
1730.	Caracas	1d.	1789.	Naples	2d.
1731.	Riga	6½d.	1790.	Beyrout	1d.
1732.	Tokio	1½d.	1791.	Tunis	1½d.
1733.	Tainan	1d.	1792.	Kiukiang	3d.
1734.	Portland	3d.	1793.	Bangkok	1d.
1735.	Fiume	1½d.	1794.	Rio Grande do Sul	1d.
1736.	Taganrog	2d.	1795.	Valparaiso	4d.
1737.	Swatow	1d.	1796.	Brindisi	2½d.
1738.	Chungking	1½d.	1797.	Bushire	2d.
1739.	Angora	1½d.	1798.	Christiania	5½d.
1740.	Shanghai	2½d.	1799.	Cadiz	2d.
1741.	Bilbao	3½d.	1800.	Meshed	2½d.
1742.	Tahiti	1½d.	1801.	St. Petersburg	4½d.
1743.	New Caledonia	1½d.	1802.	Batoum	1d.
1744.	Amoy	1½d.	1803.	Peking	3d.
1745.	Ichang	1d.	1804.	Samos	½d.
1746.	Berlin	½d.	1805.	Dantzig	2d.
1747.	Rio de Janeiro	5½d.	1806.	Antwerp	1½d.
1748.	Porto Rico	1½d.	1807.	Ajaccio	1½d.
1749.	Montevideo	1½d.	1808.	Stettin	3d.
1750.	San Francisco	3d.	1809.	Aleppo	1d.
1751.	Cayenne	½d.	1810.	Tangier	2½d.
1752.	Frankfort	3d.	1811.	Tokio	3½d.
1753.	Malaga	8½d.	1812.	Madeira	½d.
1754.	Söul	1d.	1813.	Vera Cruz	1d.
1755.	Copenhagen	3d.	1814.	Oporto	1d.
1756.	Nice	1d.	1815.	Hamburg	1½d.

No. 1816.

UNITED STATES.

NEW ORLEANS.

Acting-Consul Donnelly to the Marquis of Salisbury.

My Lord, New Orleans, September 9, 1896.

I HAVE the honour to transmit herewith enclosed a Statistical Report on the Commerce of the United States for the 12 months ending June, 1895–96, which I have compiled from the summary of the Bureau of Statistics, Treasury Department, Washington.

I have, &c.
(Signed) JAMES A. DONNELLY.

Statistical Report on the Commerce of the United States for the 12 Months ending June, 1895–96.

ABSTRACT of Contents.

	PAGE
General remarks	2
List of annexes	2
Total imports and exports	3
Bullion, tonnage and population	4
Imports—	
From United Kingdom	4
Twelve leading articles	5
Sugar, coffee, wool, other	5
From foreign countries compared	5
Exports—	
To the United Kingdom	7
Of twelve leading items	7
Increase and decrease of	7
To foreign countries compared	8
Annexes and supplements (nine) from A to G	10–18

(2268)

UNITED STATES.

General Remarks.

The following statistical report of the trade and commerce of the United States for 12 months ending June, 1896, has been exclusively compiled (and very much condensed) from the voluminous publication of the Bureau of Statistics, Treasury Department, Washington. It does not pretend to show the causes leading to an increase or diminution in either the imports or exports of the United States.

It embraces the following subjects in the order I have found it most expedient to place them, namely:—

Total of imports and exports of all merchandise; duties collected; and balances in warehouse.

Total imports and exports of gold and silver; tonnage, and population.

Imports, with Annexes A, C, and D, showing principal articles, with increase and decrease of, and comparative values of, from the different countries.

Exports, with Annexes B, C, and D, showing principal articles, with increase and decrease of, and comparative values of, from the different countries.

Annex A shows principal articles of imports and values. (Supplementary) Other articles.

Annex B shows the same for exports.

Annex C shows values of imports and exports by countries.

Annex C (supplementary) the same in respect of the European countries.

Annex D, imports and exports by United States customs districts, and by British Consular districts.

Annex E, imports of pounds of wool for 12 months ending June, 1896.

Annex F, exports of cotton (bales and value) from British Consular ports.

Annex G, table of principal articles of export of foreign merchandise to June, 1896.

The rate of exchange is taken at 4 dol. 85 c. per 1*l*. sterling.

NOTE.—The words and figures in *Italics* denote a *decrease* for 1896.

NEW ORLEANS.

UNITED States Commerce for 12 Months ending June, 1895 and 1896. — Total imports and exports.

	Value. 1895. £	Value. 1896. £
IMPORTS.		
Free	74,897,629	76,241,572
Dutiable	76,028,014	84,523,248
Total	150,925,643	160,764,820
Percentage of free	49·60	47·4
Duties collected	31,373,885	33,099,840
In warehouse, at end of month of June	8,188,190	10,609,133
EXPORTS.		
Domestic	163,585,970	177,979,337
Foreign	2,916,608	4,001,328
Total	166,502,578	181,980,665

	Value. 1895. £	Value. 1896. £
Of the above imports were brought in by—		
Rail and land vehicles	6,845,765	7,326,814
(a) American vessels	22,315,367	24,181,936
(b) Foreign vessels	121,764,511	129,256,070
And of the exports were carried out by—		
Rail and land vehicles	10,372,540	12,608,492
(a) American vessels	12,840,727	14,509,927
(b) Foreign vessels	143,289,311	154,862,246
	Per cent.	Per cent.
(a) Percentage of steam imports	65	68
,, ,, exports	65	68
(b) ,, imports	95	93
,, exports	92	92

NOTE.—Of the imports and exports by foreign vessels, British shipping enjoys an immense proportion.

(2268)

UNITED STATES.

Bullion.

GOLD AND SILVER.

	Gold.		Silver.	
	1895.	1896.	1895.	1896.
	£	£	£	£
Imports..	7,246,745	6,540,301	1,969,590	2,702,379
Exports..	13,635,284	23,156,504	9,737,584	12,342,868

Tonnage.

TONNAGE.

	1895.	1896.
Entered—		
Sailing	4,485,827	4,793,676
Steam	15,596,751	17,006,392
Cleared—		
Sailing	4,466,141	5,226,759
Steam	15,312,986	17,126,038

Population. Of the total imports and exports Great Britain and possessions sent in—

	Value.	
	1895.	1896.
	£	£
Imported from	48,953,845	53,356,893
Exported to	97,450,638	105,143,288

POPULATION.

	1895.	1896.
The population is given	69,878,000	71,390,000
Circulation per capita	22·96	21·15

Imports.

From United Kingdom. Of the total imports of merchandise (150,925,603*l*. in 1895, and 160,764,820*l*. in 1896) there arrived from Europe 79,102,165*l*. and 86,317,000*l*., of which the United Kingdom contributed 32,800,642*l*. and 35,043,876*l*. Including United Kingdom and possessions 48,953,845*l*. and 53,356,893*l*., or about one-third of the whole. For a list of the principal countries from which

NEW ORLEANS.

imports arrive, vide Annex C. Annex A contains a list of the principal items, with their values.

The Atlantic ports, as might be expected, hold the chief place in values of imports and exports (vide Annex D). While the Northern and Lake ports hold second place in total imports, they recede to third in exports, the Gulf ports being second in exports and fourth in imports. The Pacific ports hold third place in imports, and drop to fourth in exports (1896). New York takes the lead in the value of both imports and exports, being, indeed, the chief gateway of commerce, so to speak, of the United States. In imports of (raw) wool, however, she is excelled by Boston (vide Annex E), while in some items of export, cotton for instance, New Orleans leads.

In the values of the twelve leading articles of merchandise imports from all countries to June, 1896, sugar takes the first place this year instead of coffee (as in 1895), while coffee ranks second. Wool and manufactures of come third, silk and manufactures fourth, chemicals fifth, cotton and manufactures sixth, hides, &c., seventh, wood and manufactures eighth, indiarubber ninth, fruits and nuts tenth, leaf tobacco eleventh, and fibres and manufactures twelfth. As already noted, Annex A shows values for the two years. *Twelve leading articles of import.*

In sugar the decrease from Cuba is nearly 50 per cent. (8,276,675*l.* in 1895, and *4,423,990l.* in 1896), and naturally the deficiency has been increased by importations from the other principal sources of supply of this necessary commodity, namely, by the East Indies 978,715*l.*, West Indies 316,595*l.*, and Hawaiian Islands 812,490*l.* more than in 1895. *Sugar.*

Coffee imports decreased from 1895 to 1896, *2,338,190l.*, being from Brazil by *1,079,135l.*, from Central America by *950,130l.*, and from Mexico by *448,800l.* *Coffee.*

Wools and manufactures of increased from 13,215,725*l.* to 17,720,695*l.*, the bulk of this advance being from the United Kingdom. *Wools.*

Chemicals increased 976,130*l.*, cotton and manufactures of 227,775*l.*, hides, &c., 906,645*l.* (principally from South America). Wood and manufactures of 566,800*l.* (principally from Dominion of Canada), fruits 357,020*l.* (chiefly in lemons from Italy), while Indiarubber shows a net decline of *360,845l.* (Brazil sending *612,255l.* less, but United Kingdom 237,110*l.* more). Tin-plates show a decrease, from the United Kingdom, of *658,435l.* *Other.*

The increase (for 1896) in other articles of imports is in tobacco 362,355*l.* (Cuba sending 688,500*l.* more, while Netherlands *407,360l.* less). Earthenware 340,050*l.* (Germany and France largely contributing to this). Glass 184,430*l.*, art works, &c., 201,390*l.*, while the decrease is in fibres, &c., *64,900l.*, tea *96,275l.*, and furs, &c., *210,055l.*

The United Kingdom leads in wools 5,032,815*l.*, cottons 3,072,515*l.*, fibres (flax) 143,710*l.*, furs and skins 670,010*l.*, earthenware 1,009,180*l.*, nearly all the tin-plate 1,837,365*l.*, jewellery, &c., 517,045*l.*, tin bars, &c., 475,220*l.*, and paper *Imports from foreign countries compared. Great Britain.*

(2268)

stock (rags) 244,220*l.*; and sends largely hides and skins, indiarubber, cement, and art works.

Other countries. Brazil with 11,357,180*l.*, South America with 2,161,155*l.*, Central America with 1,394,000*l.*, Mexico with 782,380*l.*, and East Indies with 779,150*l.*, send nearly all the coffee.

Germany. Germany ranks next to the United Kingdom in total imports; in cotton manufactures with 1,724,035*l.*, woollen ditto (cloths) 1,757,375*l.*, furs and skins 421,500*l.*, and in earthenware, &c., 544,000*l.*; leads in cement 372,960*l.*, and gloves 596,790*l.*; and comes after France in wines 279,100*l.*, and silk manufactures 1,280,770*l.*

France. France holds third place in total imports; leads in wines with 883,185*l.*, art works, &c., 495,540*l.*, and silk manufactures 2,196,345*l.*; is next to Germany in wools, earthenware, firs, and gloves, this last with 512,645*l.*; is after Switzerland in cottons, taking fourth place, and after Netherlands in jewellery.

Belgium leads in cylinder glass, &c., 177,295*l.*, and holds third place in cement.

Brazil contributed 11,357,280*l.* of the 17,482,550*l.* import of coffee, and holds leading place also in indiarubber 2,108,420*l.*

South America, Central America, and Mexico follow Brazil in coffee. The first named leads in hides, &c., 2,558,965*l.*, an increase of 765,065*l.*; the second in bananas 316,225*l.*; Mexico in sisal 688,490*l.* South America also sends large quantities of wool, 825,375*l.*

Switzerland ranks third in cottons and silk manufactures (1,330,780*l.* and 814,810*l.*).

British North America leads in wood (boards and planks), 1,753,525*l.*; and also sends largely wools, fibres, hides, and skins.

British East Indies take second place in sugar with 2,185,810*l.*, and in tin bars, &c., 566,150*l.*, and sends largely fibres, and hides and skins, 528,290*l.*

British West Indies hold third place in sugar, 1,048,145*l.*, and second in bananas, 244,090*l.*

Spain's possessions show Cuba leading with sugar, 4,423,990*l.*, and tobacco, 2,165,315*l.* While the sugar decreased by *3,852,685l.*, the tobacco imports from this island increased from 1,476,800*l.* to 2,165,315*l.* Philippine Islands supplied Manilla fibre, 458,850*l.*

Italy sent nine-tenths of the lemons and three-fourths of the oranges, and holds third place in silk (raw) with 945,930*l.*

Netherland's position is second in jewellery, 312,600*l.*, tobacco, 971,140*l.*, and tin bars, &c., 258,465*l.*

Japan is first in silk (raw), 2,663,625*l.*, and fourth in silk manufactures, 506,520*l.*; second in tea, 1,002,825*l.*

China is first in tea, 1,399,750*l.*, and second in raw silk, 1,357,165*l.*

Hawaii holds second place in sugar, 2,337,480*l.*

Egypt supplied 1,058,135*l.* in cotton (raw).

Exports.

Of the total value of exports of domestic merchandise, 163,585,970*l*. in 1895, and 177,979,337*l*. in 1896, Europe receives the greater part (129,469,520*l*. and 138,750,270*l*.). Of this, the United Kingdom gets 79,747,845*l*. in 1895, and 83,633,575*l*. in 1896. Including United Kingdom and possessions, 97,450,638*l*. in 1895, and 105,143,288*l*., of the whole, or considerably more than half the total. {To the United Kingdom.}

The exports of foreign merchandise, amounting as a whole to but 2¼ per cent. of the total exports of merchandise (both domestic and foreign) are not quoted in the figures relating to exports (Annex B), but a separate list is appended in Table G.

For a list of the principal countries to which exports go, vide Annex C. Annex B is a table of principal articles and values.

As before-mentioned, the Atlantic ports of the United States hold the chief place in exports, as well as in the imports, New York taking the lead (vide Annex D). In some articles, however, notably cotton (vide Annex F), New Orleans, Galveston, and Charleston (including the ports within this last-named Consulate) naturally surpass her owing, presumably, to their nearness to the place of growth.

The order, in point of values, &c., of the 12 leading items of exports of domestic merchandise to all countries is as follows:—1st, cotton; 2nd, breadstuffs; 3rd, provisions; 4th, refined mineral oil; 5th, animals; 6th, iron and manufactures of; 7th, wood and manufactures; 8th, tobacco; 9th, copper (ore, &c.); 10th, leather and manufactures; 11th, coal; and 12th, chemicals. {Twelve leading articles of export.}

From the tabulated list (Annex B) it will be observed that the 1896 exports of cotton, provisions, tobacco, and coal decreased from 1895, while in the other articles quoted above there was a substantial increase. Breadstuffs head the list with an increase of 5,515,920*l*., and made up as follows: corn, by 4,780,635*l*. (of which the United Kingdom received more than in 1895 2,184,205*l*., Germany 711,140*l*., France 271,620*l*., and other Europe 1,211,740*l*.); barley by 481,050*l*., oats by 679,755*l*., and wheat flour 180,060*l*.; whereas there was a decrease in wheat by 842,495*l*. {Decrease in some.}

Mineral oil exports increased by 3,241,645*l*. The bulk of this is refined, and the increase is largely to Europe and to Asia. {Increase in others.}

Iron and manufactures of increased by 1,888,330*l*., machinery furnishing the chief item by 752,330*l*., hardware by 214,620*l*., and sewing machines by 181,260*l*.

Animals increased by 1,255,040*l*.; cattle, horses, and sheep principally, and nearly all to the United Kingdom.

Wood and its manufactures increased by 996,125*l*. Of these: logs, &c., 302,105*l*., lumber by 258,055*l*., staves, shingles, &c., by 179,850*l*., and household furniture and other manufactures by 242,010*l*.

Copper (ore, ingots, &c.) increase by 1,168,590*l*., all Europe, except the United Kingdom, taking the greater part. In ore, the increase of 194,270*l*. went to Great Britain; in ingots, 974,120*l*. to Europe.

Leather shows an increase of 954,295*l*.; of which: sole, 114,365*l*.; uppers, &c., 736,040*l*.; boots and shoes, 87,930*l*., the United Kingdom getting the increase.

Chemicals increased by 177,130*l*.; naval stores by 293,560*l*.; hides, &c., by 318,905*l*.; fish by 192,050*l*. (chiefly in canned salmon, 168,700*l*.); oilcake meal by 161,660*l*.; fruits by 145,830*l*.; paraffine and par. wax by 172,625*l*.; glucose by 42,075*l*.; paper, &c., by 108,890*l*.; instruments, &c., by 125,660*l*.; fibres, &c., by 30,115*l*.; and grease by 126,330*l*.

The decrease in values of exports (domestic) for 1896, compared with those of 1895, is as follows:—

Cottons show a net decrease in 1896, of *2,550,560l*. This is made up in the following way:—Unmanufactured really declined by *3,060,725l*. (say *2,278,515l*. to United Kingdom, *271,920l*. to Germany, *501,415l*. to France), while manufactured increased by 510,165*l*., principally to China.

Provisions declined by *439,340l*. Of some of the products under this heading are noted:—Fresh beef increased by 441,495*l*., salted beef by 83,025*l*.; bacon decreased by *893,495l*. (of which *263,460l*. for United Kingdom, *520,555l*. for Europe); hams increased by 352,410*l*. (the United Kingdom taking 169,300*l*., and all Europe, 161,210*l*. more); lard declined by *666,320l*. (to United Kingdom *160,850l*., Germany *59,610l*., France *113,455l*., other parts of Europe by *177,510l*., and Cuba *135,650l*. less). Dairy butter increased by 416,840*l*. (United Kingdom receiving 336,780*l*. of this increase). Cheese declined by *496,010l*. being by *385,940l*. less to United Kingdom, and *105,270l*. to British North America.

Leaf tobacco decreased by *251,035l*. (nearly all to United Kingdom).

Coal declined by *93,315l*.

Cotton-seed oil decreased by *275,635l*. (of which less to United Kingdom *60,910l*., to Germany *137,210l*., to Europe *180,030l*.; while France received 119,700*l*. more than in 1895.

Fertilisers, *276,425l*., furs, &c., *25,350l*. (to Great Britain), and hops, *81,170l*. (also to Great Britain), represent the decrease in other articles.

Exports to foreign countries compared. Great Britain.

Taking the exports for 1896 by countries, the United Kingdom leads in unmanufactured cotton, 19,185,650*l*.; breadstuffs (especially corn, 3,805,780*l*.; wheat, 8,187,595*l*.; and wheat flour, 10,726,840*l*.), all other Europe not taking one-fourth as much; provisions (such as canned beef, 748,300*l*.; fresh beef, 443,335*l*.; salted beef, 3,907,425*l*.; bacon, *5,721,000l*.; hams, 2,075,610*l*.; pickled pork, *163,090l*.; lard, *2,787,935l*.; butter, 364,630*l*.; and cheese, *513,625l*.); mineral oil (refined), 2,987,150*l*.; animals (cattle and sheep), 7,007,200*l*. and 545,900*l*.; iron manufactures; wood and manufactures; leaf tobacco and manufactures, 1,974,640*l*.; copper (ore, ingots, &c.) 755,360*l*.; leather (sole and upper), 2,955,160*l*.; **naval** stores (resin, spirits of turpentine, &c.), 708,290*l*.; oilcake meal, 723,035*l*.; fruits, nuts, &c., 447,400*l*.; paraffine and par. wax, 568,885*l*.; furs, 593,065*l*., and nearly all the hops.

Other countries in Europe receive, after the United Kingdom, the bulk of exports with a few exceptions, namely: British North America, British West Indies, Brazil, &c., receive wheat flour largely. The first-named also takes coal to the extent of 1,846,145*l*., machinery 301,875*l*.; also cotton manufactures in very considerable quantities. Europe. Other places.

Brazil, in addition to wheat flour, gets machinery to quite an extent.

Mexico gets coal and machinery.

Other South America, machinery and manufactured cottons to the extent of 653,300*l*.

Cuba receives coal, 126,475*l*.

China, manufactured cottons, 794,670*l*.

The West Indies, besides wheat flour, receive nearly all the pickled pork, 350,780*l*.

Annex A.—RETURN of Principal Articles of Import to the United States for 12 Months ending June in the Years 1895 and 1896.

Order of Values for 1896.	Articles. (*f.* means "Free of Duty.")		1895. Quantity.	1895. Value.	1896. Quantity.	1896. Value.
				£		£
22 (*f.*)	Art works	...	...	792,390	...	993,780
5	Chemicals, which include dyewoods, glycerine, gums, indigo, roots, waters, potash, soda, sulphur, &c.	...	...	8,984,860	...	9,960,990
24	Cements	Lbs.	1,059,871,593	703,080	1,195,838,653	791,610
2 (*f.*)	*Coffee*	"	642,208,975	19,821,750	*580,277,222*	*17,482,550*
6 (*f.*)	Cotton, unmanufactured	...	...	972,035	...	1,356,330
	Cotton, manufactured (dutiable)	...	...	6,844,660	...	6,688,140
15	Earthenware and stoneware	...	...	1,846,620	...	2,186,670
12	*Fibres* (nearly all free) flax, jute, Manila, sisal, hemp, &c	Tons	(236,711)	2,718,550	224,799	2,653,650
	(*Flax*)	...	...	(436,605)	...	(372,050)
	(*Jute*)	...	...	(567,620)	...	(412,620)
	(*Manila*)	...	...	(837,220)	...	(743,215)
	(*Sisal*)	...	...	(565,650)	...	(703,660)
	Manufactures, chiefly	...	...	5,420,820	...	5,591,675
(*f.*)	(Bagging of burlaps)	...	...	(228,950)	...	(319,970)
(*f.*)	(Burlaps)	...	...	(1,010,965)	...	(1,246,725)
	(*Other*, dutiable)	...	...	(3,799,075)	...	(3,775,925)
10	Fruits and nuts, all kinds, chiefly	...	...	3,139,600	...	3,496,620
(*f.*)	(*Bananas*)	...	...	(963,885)	...	928,560
	(Lemons)	...	...	(807,695)	...	1,039,245
	(Oranges)	...	...	(411,810)	...	555,490
14	*Furs and manufactures*	...	...	2,128,280	...	*1,918,225*
20	Glass, glassware, and cylinder glass	...	...	1,348,860	...	1,533,290
7 (*f.*)	Hides and skins (not furs)	Lbs.	236,575,745	5,386,170	219,398,011	6,292,815
9 (*f.*)	*Indiarubber, crude*	"	39,741,607	3,784,145	*36,774,460*	*3,423,300*
16	Tin-plates, &c.	"	508,038,938	2,503,930	*385,132,183*	*1,845,495*
17	Jewellery and precious stones	...	...	1,548,840	...	1,592,135
21	Gloves of kid and other leather	...	...	1,332,755	...	1,394,445
25	Paper, and manufactures of	...	...	590,420	...	653,500
4 (*f.*)	Silk, raw	Lbs.	7,974,810	4,542,075	8,000,621	5,411,825
	Manufactures (dutiable)	...	...	6,434,220	...	*5,495,415*
1	Sugars	Lbs.	3,574,510,354	15,765,520	3,896,328,557	18,395,820
	(Of this, *free of duty*)	...	...	(6,103,000)	...	(*2,337,480*)
	Dutiable	...	...	(9,662,520)	...	(16,058,340)
13 (*f.*)	*Tea*	Lbs.	97,253,458	2,715,745	*93,998,372*	*2,619,470*
19	Tin, in bars, blocks, pigs, &c. (*f.* and *d.*)	"	47,631,783	1,399,470	49,952,957	*1,394,170*
11	Tobacco (leaf)	"	26,662,261	3,040,350	32,925,016	3,402,705
18	*Wines* (of which champagne and other sparkling, more than half)	...	...	1,481,140	...	*1,465,360*
8	Wood, and manufactures of, chiefly *f.*	...	...	3,674,015	...	4,240,815
	(Of which boards, planks, &c.)	...	...	(1,406,700)	...	(1,753,525)
3 (*f.*)	Wools (clothing, combing, and carpet)	Lbs.	206,081,890	5,272,730	230,811,473	6,690,975
	Manufactures, of which	...	...	7,942,995	...	11,029,720
	(Cloths)	...	...	(3,363,145)	...	(4,512,685)
	(Dress goods)	...	...	(2,963,035)	...	(4,009,170)
	All other articles	...	...	28,789,618	...	30,763,320
	Total	...	...	150,925,643	...	160,764,820

NOTE.—*Italics* (words and figures) denote a decrease for 1896.

Annex A (Supplementary).—RETURN of other Articles of Import of Merchandise for 12 months ending June, 1896.

Articles.	Value.	Remarks.
	£	
Animals	87,860	
Breadstuffs	*573,360*	
Books	720,205	
Bristles	295,950	
Buttons and forms	293,590	
Clocks, watches and parts of	334,685	
Bituminous coal	*730,970*	From B.N. America 538,545*l.*
Cocoa	*492,080*	
Copper, &c.	264,455	
Feathers, downs, &c.	669,255	
„ fruits, &c., for millinery	381,840	
Fertilizers	228,230	
Fish	1,303,770	
Grease and tallow	*245,425*	
Hair	441,475	
Hats and bonnets	571,135	
Hay	576,740	
Lead	*501,700*	
Malt liquors	343,300	
Marble and stone	273,845	
Matting for floors	572,660	
Metals and manufactures	951,460	
Musical instruments	269,595	
Oils, animal and vegetable	1,132,650	
Paints	251,450	
Rice	*450,780*	
Salt	156,490	
Seeds (linseed, &c.)	*553,020*	A decrease of 794,525*l.*
Spices	*490,420*	
Spirits	634,670	
Toys	518,850	From Germany chiefly.
Vegetables	*519,875*	

NOTE.—*Italics* denote a *decrease* from 1895.

UNITED STATES.

Annex B.—RETURN of Principal Articles of Export (Domestic Merchandise) from the United States for 12 Months ending June in the Years 1895 and 1896.

Order of Values for 1896.	Articles.		1895. Quantity.	1895. Value. £	1896. Quantity.	1896. Value. £
5	Animals, which include	...	...	7,371,960	...	8,627,000
	Cattle	...	331,722	(6,310,055)	372,461	(7,125,910)
	Horses	...	13,984	(455,525)	25,126	(727,980)
	Sheep	...	405,748	(542,410)	491,565	(634,305)
2	Breadstuffs, and preparations	...	...	23,629,830	...	29,145,750
	Barley	Bushels...	1,563,754	(158,190)	7,680,331	(639,240)
	Corn	,, ...	27,691,137	(3,020,775)	99,992,835	(7,801,410)
	Oats	,, ...	569,977	(41,400)	13,012,590	(721,155)
	Wheat	,, ...	76,102,704	(9,030,090)	60,650,080	(8,187,595)
	Wheat flour	Barrels ...	15,268,892	(10,546,780)	14,620,864	(10,726,840)
12	Chemicals, drugs, dyes, &c.	...	...	1,688,480	...	1,865,610
11	*Coal* (anthracite and bituminous)	Tons ...	3,772,192	2,288,375	3,640,665	2,195,060
9	Copper and ore	,, ...	10,281	225,010	15,935	419,280
	Ingots, bars, and old	Lbs. ...	148,446,039	2,870,500	175,580,762	3,844,620
1	Cotton, *unmanufactured*	Bales ...	6,965,358	42,247,595	4,659,765	39,186,870
	Manufactures, cloth	Yards ...	184,258,061	2,160,660	225,139,365	2,670,825
25	Cycles, and parts of	...	...	(Not enumerated)	...	391,340
19	*Fertilizers*	Tons ...	638,586	1,183,765	514,143	907,340
17	Fish, all kinds	...	...	885,525	...	1,077,575
	Of which canned salmon	Lbs. ...	24,662,923	(467,360)	32,823,962	(636,060)
26	Fibres, and manufactures of	...	...	355,165	...	385,280
15	Fruits and nuts, of which	...	...	1,025,110	...	1,170,940
	Apples, dried	Lbs. ...	7,085,946	(95,095)	26,692,529	(276,745)
	Do. green or ripe	Barrels...	818,711	(402,950)	359,436	(191,460)
	Canned fruit	...	...	(179,685)	...	(283,770)
21	*Furs and fur skins*	...	...	808,890	...	783,540
22	Glucose, or grape sugar	Lbs. ...	133,808,329	529,540	171,231,650	571,615
27	Grease, scraps, and soap stocks	...	...	186,405	...	312,735
20	Hides and skins (not furs)	Lbs. ...	36,002,859	476,335	39,545,324	795,245
28	*Hops*	Lbs. ...	17,523,388	386,100	16,765,254	304,930
24	Instruments, and scientific appliances	...	...	394,385	...	520,045
6	Iron and steel, and manufactures of, chiefly	...	...	6,598,140	...	8,486,470
	Builders' hardware, saws, and tools	...	...	(921,295)	...	(1,135,915)
	Machinery, including locomotives and fire engines	...	...	(2,985,220)	...	(3,737,550)
	Sewing machines, and parts	...	...	(466,010)	...	(647,270)
10	Leather, and manufactures of, chiefly	...	...	3,219,465	...	4,173,760
	Sole	Lbs. ...	45,364,349	(1,426,670)	41,818,503	(1,541,035)
	Uppers	...	...	(1,385,800)	...	(2,121,840)
	Boots and shoes	Pairs ...	822,412	(208,295)	1,036,735	(296,225)
13	Naval stores	...	...	1,529,850	...	1,823,410
	(Resin, tar, turpentine, and pitch)—principally resin	Barrels ...	1,897,532	(705,465)	2,208,119	(872,110)
	Spirits of turpentine	Gallons...	14,652,738	(824,385)	17,431,566	(951,300)
14	Oil-cake, and oil-cake meal	Lbs. ...	733,652,495	1,477,440	798,366,723	1,639,100
4	Mineral oils, *crude*	Gallons...	111,285,264	1,064,265	110,923,620	1,262,235
	Refined	Gallons...	773,079,310	8,553,665	779,310,414	11,597,360
16	*Oil, cotton-seed*	Gallons...	21,187,728	1,404,810	19,445,848	1,129,175
23	Paper, and manufactures of	...	...	450,670	...	559,560
18	Paraffin, and paraffin wax	Lbs. ...	95,076,165	736,000	105,882,575	908,625

NEW ORLEANS.

RETURN of Principal Articles of Export (Domestic Merchandise) from the United States for 12 Months ending June in the Years 1895 and 1896—continued.

Order of Values for 1896.	Articles.		1895. Quantity.	1895. Value.	1896. Quantity.	1896. Value.
				£		£
3	Provisions, chiefly	...	...	27,553,460	...	27,114,120
	Beef, canned	Lbs.	64,102,263	(1,180,570)	63,698,180	(1,162,260)
	„ fresh	,,	191,338,487	(3,470,690)	224,783,225	(3,912,185)
	„ salted, &c.	,,	63,294,998	(748,825)	71,223,512	(831,850)
	Bacon	Lbs.	452,549,976	(7,788,920)	425,352,187	(6,895,425)
	Hams	Lbs.	105,494,123	(2,259,910)	129,036,351	(2,612,320)
	Pork, pickled	,,	58,266,893	(853,275)	69,498,373	(819,270)
	Lard	,,	474,895,274	(7,592,055)	509,534,256	(6,925,735)
	Oleomargarine (oil)	,,	78,098,878	(1,465,465)	103,276,756	(1,667,610)
	Butter (dairy)	,,	5,598,812	(188,770)	19,373,913	(605,610)
	Cheese	Lbs.	60,448,421	(1,133,510)	36,777,291	(637,510)
8	Tobacco, and manufactured	...	...	6,134,455	...	5,969,420
	Leaf	Lbs.	293,805,855	(5,283,140)	287,700,301	(5,032,005)
	Cigarettes	1,000	464,636	(243,445)	633,785	(290,475)
7	Wood, and manufactures	...	...	5,590,905	...	6,587,030
	Sawn, hewn, and logs	...	...	(1,217,900)	...	(1,520,005)
	Lumber (boards, planks, &c.)	M. feet	588,781	(1,826,850)	694,800	(2,084,865)
	Staves and headings	...	...	(647,100)	...	(670,225)
	Shingles, shooks, &c.	...	...	(548,500)	...	(705,225)
	Other manufactures	...	...	(1,288,620)	...	(1,530,630)
	Of which household furniture	...	...	(628,845)	...	(672,415)
	All other articles	...	...	9,859,215	...	11,553,472
	Total	...	...	163,585,970	...	177,979,337

NOTE.—*Italics* (words and figures) denote a decrease for 1896. In sole leather the *weight* largely *decreased*, but the values increased. In mineral oil (crude) the gallons *decreased*, but the values increased. In *pork* and *lard*, the weight largely increased, but the *values decreased*.

UNITED STATES.

Annex C.—TABLE showing Imports and Exports by Countries for the 12 Months ending June in the Years 1895-96.

Exports, by Countries.	Imports. 1895.	Imports. 1896.	Exports. 1895.	Exports. 1896.
	£	£	£	£
All Europe*	79,102,165	86,314,940	129,469,520	138,740,270
Dom. of Canada	7,541,090	8,427,865	10,897,880	12,307,125
British West Indies	2,015,965	2,227,590	1,600,860	1,800,510
British Guiana	519,940	706,045	348,675	361,660
British East Indies	4,384,740	4,198,075	588,445	668,200
Hong Kong	160,100	292,710	876,915	967,255
British Australasia	952,750	1,562,735	1,858,610	2,626,465
British Africa	160,025	357,145	1,072,860	2,328,040
All other British	418,610	492,865	383,980	449,465
Central American States	2,387,785	1,881,740	1,353,610	1,617,500
Mexico	3,223,870	3,599,220	3,093,995	4,010,360
Cuba	10,901,280	8,240,160	2,640,750	1,563,065
Haiti, San Domingo and Porto Rico	1,203,635	1,419,480	1,708,745	1,564,475
Brazil	16,253,900	14,651,335	3,126,915	2,939,830
Venezuela	2,077,100	1,989,670	771,230	791,495
Argentina	1,582,530	1,919,520	918,795	1,232,790
Chile	920,735	981,625	576,105	707,590
Colombia	365,705	1,024,660	535,320	679,420
Uruguay	556,630	668,540	260,205	307,085
Dutch East Indies	1,593,250	3,062,690	236,560	321,835
China	4,236,190	4,540,930	743,090	1,427,485
Japan	4,885,760	5,265,240	955,610	1,585,240
Turkey	637,105	673,445	26,855	9,020
Hawaiian Islands	1,626,590	2,424,270	767,640	821,795
Philippine Islands	975,540	1,027,390	24,590	33,495
Egypt	748,135	1,620,665	28,390	44,440

(Grouped for easier reference.)

* This is specified in another table.

The order of the leading places of import is:—United Kingdom, Germany, Brazil, France, Cuba, Dominion of Canada, Japan, Italy, China, British East Indies, Mexico, Dutch East Indies, Switzerland.

And of the exports:—United Kingdom, Germany, Dominion of Canada, France, Netherlands, Belgium, Italy, Mexico, Brazil, British Australasia, Spain, British Africa.

NEW ORLEANS.

Annex C (Supplement).—TABLE showing Imports and Exports by Countries (in Europe) for the 12 Months ending June in the Years 1895–96.

European Countries.	Imports. 1895.	Imports. 1896.	Exports. 1895.	Exports. 1896.
	£	£	£	£
United Kingdom	32,800,642	35,043,876	79,747,845	83,633,575
Germany	16,703,920	19,431,060	18,980,140	20,195,850
France	12,686,990	13,663,460	9,309,095	9,685,345
Italy	4,299,335	4,465,380	2,372,940	3,947,130
Netherlands	3,130,425	2,741,395	6,394,195	8,045,955
Belgium	2,091,025	2,840,415	5,204,650	5,514,235
Russia (Baltic and Black Sea)	737,195	747,820	1,228,420	1,545,705
Austria-Hungary	1,342,335	1,534,975	438,305	516,295
Denmark (b)	66,975	68,995	716,560	1,369,920
Portugal	348,590	465,100	612,660	650,915
Switzerland (a)	3,090,505	2,903,100	3,625	6,795
Spain	736,930	851,790	2,253,000	2,368,285
Sweden and Norway	521,915	684,600	959,300	1,038,515
Turkey in Europe (a)	432,515	549,510	8,605	7,200

(a) The exports to Switzerland and to Turkey are small as compared with the imports from these countries, while (b) on the other hand Denmark presents a reversed condition.

Annex D.—THE Imports and Exports, by Customs Districts.

Customs Districts.	Imports. 1895.	Imports. 1896.*	Exports. 1895.	Exports. 1896.*
Atlantic ports (a)	126,543,675	133,032,940 (I)	121,730,365	131,161,275 (I)
Northern and lake ports (b)	10,518,915	11,578,000 (II)	10,305,370	12,451,455 (III)
Pacific ports (c)	8,364,630	10,240,345 (III)	7,603,965	9,280,990 (IV)
Gulf ports (d)	3,889,790	4,273,930 (IV)	{ 26,860,830 2,048 }	29,088,162 (II)
Interior ports	1,608,633	1,639,605 (V)	...	83 (V)

SUBDIVIDED into British Consular Districts.

Consular Districts.		Imports. 1895.	Imports. 1896.*	Exports. 1895.	Exports. 1896*.
(a)	New York	98,503,245	103,078,840 (I)	67,129,855	73,046,320 (I)
	Boston	13,791,560	16,325,730 (II)	17,629,920	19,763,075 (II)
	Philadelphia	10,062,400	9,039,340 (III)	7,225,375	8,162,340 (V)
	Baltimore	2,527,980	2,778,685 (VI)	12,770,915	13,690,485 (IV)
	Charleston S.C.	137,475	103,570 (IX)	2,208,755	1,751,910 (VIII)
(b)	Chicago	3,103,740	3,205,320 (V)	321,250	266,610 (IX)
(c)	San Francisco	7,478,270	8,536,140 (IV)	5,128,480	6,511,935 (VII)
(d)	New Orleans	2,858,040	2,787,000 (VI)	14,105,835	16,698,295 (III)
	Galveston	76,190	124,290 (VIII)	8,636,415	7,504,548 (VI)

* The Roman numerals show their relative positions for 1896. Of the consular districts New York, Boston, San Francisco, Baltimore, increased in both imports and exports. Philadelphia and New Orleans increased their exports, while Galveston, Charleston and Chicago decreased.

(2268)

UNITED STATES.

Annex E.—IMPORTS of Wool (Raw) for 12 Months ending June, 1896; by Weight.

	Quantity.
	Lbs.
Into Boston	118,263,666
„ New York	82,247,659
„ Philadelphia	25,426,997
Total	225,938,322

And arrived from—

	Quantity.
	Lbs.
British Australasia	72,995,090
Argentina	32,281,341
China	26,084,232
Turkey (all)	18,298,173
United Kingdom	14,229,059
Russia	13,148,509
British East Indies	9,897,531
Uruguay	9,048,350
All other countries	9,956,037
Total	225,938,322

Annex F.—TABLE showing the Exports of Cotton for the 12 Months ending June, 1896, from Principal Places of Export, and to what Countries sent.

From—	Total. Quantity.	Total. Value.	United Kingdom. Quantity.	United Kingdom. Value.	Germany. Quantity.	Germany. Value.	France. Quantity.	France. Value.	Italy. Quantity.	Italy. Value.	Belgium. Quantity.	Belgium. Value.	Spain (a). Netherlands (b). Quantity.	Spain (a). Netherlands (b). Value.
	Bales.	£	Bales.	£	Bales.	£	Bales.	£	Bales.	£	Bales.	£	Bales.	£
New Orleans	1,615,835	18,204,650	737,070	6,755,391	286,592 / 27,444	2,583,260	312,722	2,560,480	184,988	1,093,050	15,237	123,260	...	...
Ports in Consular district of	122,903	987,230	92,736											
Galveston	746,952	6,544,210	475,697	4,135,590	153,405	1,346,840	100,032	901,745	5,913	53,730	7,769	68,750	...	...
Charleston, &c.	200,715 / 657,874	7,256,585	27,174 / 197,571	1,961,580	96,480 / 234,911	2,790,370	28,169	255,960	53,165	433,200	4,275	36,700	a 45,321 / 90,264	1,121,985
New York	684,458	5,875,135	346,756	3,068,700	155,148	1,251,290	31,217	288,250	60,786	506,800	48,437	...	b 16,211	133,700
Boston	262,813	2,307,130	259,321	2,277,610	...	...	...	...	...	...	5,110	...	...	...
Baltimore	146,421 / 67,926	1,696,380	58,666 / 51,371	917,802	76,330 / 9,955	638,560	2,014	15,425	...	...	4,900	...	b 4,301 / 1,700	445,425
Other ports of														
Philadelphia	11,096	89,825	9,072	72,025	...	...	...	...	...	...	2,023	...	...	...
Other ports	138,573	5,945,018	...	...	...	...	...	...	...	...	...	...	...	...
Total	4,650,565	39,186,870												

UNITED STATES.

Annex G.—TABLE of the Principal Articles of Export of Foreign Merchandise for 12 Months ending June, 1896.

Articles.	Value.
	£
Wheat	321,120
Chemicals	202,880
Gums	43,770
Coffee	259,540
Cottons	83,160
Fibres	163,690
Fish	108,240
Fruits	113,810
Hides and skins	206,820
Indiarubber (unmanufactured)	298,750
Lead, pigs, &c.	219,270
Oils, chiefly vegetable	31,795
Rice, rice flour, &c.	42,480
Seeds	24,160
Silk and manufactures	135,285
Spices	38,470
Spirits	25,900
Sugar, &c.	29,860
Tea	24,475
Tobacco	561,830
Wines	26,450
Wood and manufactures	196,125
Wools "	309,020
All other	534,428
Total	4,001,328

LONDON:
Printed for Her Majesty's Stationery Office,
By HARRISON AND SONS,
Printers in Ordinary to Her Majesty.
(75 10 | 96—H & S 2268)

FOREIGN OFFICE.
1897.
ANNUAL SERIES.

No. 1842.

DIPLOMATIC AND CONSULAR REPORTS ON TRADE AND FINANCE.

UNITED STATES.

REPORT FOR THE YEARS 1895 AND 1896
ON THE
FINANCES OF THE UNITED STATES.

REFERENCE TO PREVIOUS REPORT, Annual Series No. 1285.

Presented to both Houses of Parliament by Command of Her Majesty,
FEBRUARY, 1897.

LONDON:
PRINTED FOR HER MAJESTY'S STATIONERY OFFICE,
BY HARRISON AND SONS, ST. MARTIN'S LANE,
PRINTERS IN ORDINARY TO HER MAJESTY.

And to be purchased, either directly or through any Bookseller, from
EYRE & SPOTTISWOODE, EAST HARDING STREET, FLEET STREET, E.C., and
32, ABINGDON STREET, WESTMINSTER, S.W.; or
JOHN MENZIES & Co., 12, HANOVER STREET, EDINBURGH, and
90, WEST NILE STREET, GLASGOW; or
HODGES, FIGGIS, & Co., Limited, 104, GRAFTON STREET, DUBLIN.

1897.

[C. 8277—60.]   *Price Threepence.*

New Series of Reports.

Reports of the Annual Series have been issued from Her Majesty's Diplomatic and Consular Officers at the following places, and may be obtained from the sources indicated on the title-page:—

No.		Price.	No.		Price.
1722.	Batavia	1½d.	1782.	Athens	2d.
1723.	Genoa	3d.	1783.	Tonga	½d.
1724.	Cagliari	2½d.	1784.	Smyrna	½d.
1725.	Chicago	7½d.	1785.	Baghdad	1d.
1726.	Trieste	1d.	1786.	Hiogo and Osaka	4½d.
1727.	Hakodate	1d.	1787.	Bangkok	1d.
1728.	Mannheim	1d.	1788.	Odessa	2d.
1729.	Panama	1d.	1789.	Naples	2d.
1730.	Caracas	1d.	1790.	Beyrout	1d.
1731.	Riga	6½d.	1791.	Tunis	1½d.
1732.	Tokio	1½d.	1792.	Kiukiang	3d.
1733.	Tainan	1d.	1793.	Bangkok	1d.
1734.	Portland	3d.	1794.	Rio Grande do Sul	1d.
1735.	Fiume	1½d.	1795.	Valparaiso	4d.
1736.	Taganrog	2d.	1796.	Brindisi	2½d.
1737.	Swatow	1d.	1797.	Bushire	2d.
1738.	Chungking	1½d.	1798.	Christiania	5½d.
1739.	Angora	1½d.	1799.	Cadiz	2d.
1740.	Shanghai	2½d.	1800.	Meshed	2½d.
1741.	Bilbao	3½d.	1801.	St. Petersburg	1½d.
1742.	Tahiti	1½d.	1802.	Batoum	1d.
1743.	New Caledonia	1½d.	1803.	Peking	3d.
1744.	Amoy	1½d.	1804.	Samos	½d.
1745.	Ichang	1d.	1805.	Dantzig	2d.
1746.	Berlin	½d.	1806.	Antwerp	1½d.
1747.	Rio de Janeiro	5½d.	1807.	Ajaccio	1½d.
1748.	Porto Rico	1½d.	1808.	Stettin	3d.
1749.	Montevideo	1½d.	1809.	Aleppo	1d.
1750.	San Francisco	3d.	1810.	Tangier	2½d.
1751.	Cayenne	½d.	1811.	Tokio	3½d.
1752.	Frankfort	3d.	1812.	Madeira	½d.
1753.	Malaga	8½d.	1813.	Vera Cruz	1d.
1754.	Söul	1d.	1814.	Oporto	1d.
1755.	Copenhagen	3d.	1815.	Hamburg	1½d.
1756.	Nice	1d.	1816.	New Orleans	1½d.
1757.	Lisbon	1½d.	1817.	Bengazi	½d.
1758.	Nagasaki	1d.	1818.	Marmagao	½d.
1759.	Hamburg	2½d.	1819.	Gothenburg	2d.
1760.	Mozambique	2d.	1820.	Dar-al-Baida	3d.
1761.	Cettinjé	1½d.	1821.	Erzeroum	½d.
1762.	The Hague	1½d.	1822.	Munich	2½d.
1763.	Cephalonia	1d.	1823.	Samoa	½d.
1764.	Bahia	1d.	1824.	Chinkiang	1d.
1765.	Zanzibar	1½d.	1825.	Jeddah	1d.
1766.	Pakhoi	1d.	1826.	Sofia	1½d.
1767.	New York	2d.	1827.	Mexico	2d.
1768.	Chefoo	1d.	1828.	Teneriffe	3½d.
1769.	Caracas	½d.	1829.	Batoum	1d.
1770.	Palermo	11½d.	1830.	Cadiz	1d.
1771.	Mombasa	½d.	1831.	Martinique	1d.
1772.	Nice	1½d.	1832.	Odessa	1d.
1773.	Bucharest	4½d.	1833.	Ghilan	1d.
1774.	Port Said	1½d.	1834.	Old Calabar	6½d.
1775.	Galatz	1½d.	1835.	Tamsui	1d.
1776.	Madrid	2d.	1836.	Copenhagen	½d.
1777.	Vienna	2d.	1837.	Salonica	1½d.
1778.	Canton	1d.	1838.	Honolulu	½d.
1779.	Yokohama	1½d.	1839.	Buenos Ayres	2d.
1780.	Newchwang	1d.	1840.	Para	1d.
1781.	Wuhu	1d.	1841.	Bolivia	2d.

No. 1842.

Reference to previous Report, Annual Series No. 1285.

UNITED STATES.

WASHINGTON.

Sir Julian Pauncefote to the Marquis of Salisbury.

My Lord,   *Washington, January* 11, 1897.

I HAVE the honour to transmit herewith to your Lordship a Report by Mr. Reginald Tower, Second Secretary in this Embassy, upon the Finances of the United States for the Fiscal Years ended June 30, 1895 and 1896, together with some remarks upon the financial issues of the recent electoral campaign.

This comprehensive Report will, I doubt not, be read with particular interest at the present time and meet with your Lordship's approval.

I have, &c.
(Signed)   JULIAN PAUNCEFOTE

Mr. Tower to Sir Julian Pauncefote.

Sir,   *Washington, January* 11, 1897.

I HAVE the honour to transmit herewith a Report which I have drawn up on the Finances of the United States for the Fiscal Years ended June 30, 1895 and 1896.

Exceptional interest in finance has been taken in the United States during the last few months owing to the currency and tariff questions involved in the Presidential election, and on that account, in presenting a brief report on the finances of the country, I have added some remarks upon the financial issues of the electoral campaign of 1896, particularly with reference to the desire for currency reform.

As regards the main issue of the election, viz., that between the advocates of the gold standard and of the free coinage of silver, the result of the elections has been conclusive in giving the Republican candidate, Major McKinley, 272 votes in the electoral college, against 175 for Mr. W. J. Bryan,[*] the nominee

[*] The figures are approximate, the exact results not being yet officially made known, owing to disputes as to the elections in Kentucky and Wyoming, and a question as to legal qualification in Kansas.

(2300)

UNITED STATES.

of the Democratic Convention of Chicago, while it is claimed that the composition of Congress will show a preponderance in both the Senate and the House of Representatives in favour of "sound money."

The question of an increased protective tariff, with which the President-elect is identified, took a secondary place to that of the metals in the late contest, and it would be rash to hazard any prediction as to future legislation on this subject during the incoming administration.

The information and statistics given in this report are mainly taken from the report of the Secretary of the Treasury, and from reports prepared in the Bureau of Statistics.

I have, &c.
(Signed)   REGINALD TOWER.

Report upon the Finances of the United States for the Fiscal Years ended June 30, 1895 and 1896, together with some Remarks upon the Financial Issues of the recent Electoral Campaign.

Table of Contents.

	Page
Revenues and expenditures, 1895	3
Redemption of bonds, 1895	4
Revenues and expenditures, 1896	5
Redemption of bonds, 1896	6
Estimates for 1897 and 1898	6
Operations of the Treasury, 1895	8
Pensions	9
Foreign commerce	10
Exports and imports of gold and silver	12
Course of silver	13
National banks—	
Total number organised, liquidation and means of ameliorating	13
United States public debt	15
Circulation	16
Currency reform—	
Declarations of Republican, Democratic (Chicago) and National Democratic Conventions as to free coinage of silver	16, 17
Paper currency reform	18
"Greenbacks." Legislation since 1862	18
Gold reserve	18
Defects in currency system, and reform as suggested by Director of Mint	20
Protective Tariff: sugar, wool and merchant marine	21

Revenues, 1895.

The ordinary revenues of the United States from all sources during the 12 months ended June 30, 1895, amounted to 78,074,640*l*.,* and the expenditures during the same period to 86,635,685*l*., leaving a deficit of 8,561,045*l*.

---

* The rough calculation of 5 dol. to the 1*l*. sterling has been taken throughout this Report.

WASHINGTON.

The different items of revenue were:—

From—	Amount.
	£
Customs duties	30,431,724
Internal revenue	28,684,334
District of Columbia	731,610
Fees—Consular, letters patent, and land	531,059
Sinking fund for Pacific railways	347,177
Tax on national banks	342,510
Profits on coinage, bullion deposits, and assays	328,116
Sales of public lands	220,669
Navy pension and Navy hospital funds	201,908
Repayment of interest on Pacific railways	196,483
Customs fees, fines, penalties, and forfeitures	128,193
Miscellaneous sources	122,016
Sales of Indian lands	108,164
Reimbursement for cost of water supply, District of Columbia	76,412
Immigrant fund	61,045
Sales of lands and buildings under special Acts	44,042
Soldiers' home, permanent fund	42,493
Sales of Government property	35,624
Deposits for surveying public lands	32,521
Depredations on public lands	3,547
Bequest of General Cullum	1,719
Sales of condemned naval vessels	188
Tax on sealskins	140
Sale of ordnance material	6,321
Postal service	15,396,625
Total receipts	78,074,640

The expenditures for the same period were:— *Expenditures, 1895.*

For—	Amount.
	£
The civil establishment, including foreign intercourse, public buildings, collecting the revenues, deficiency in postal revenues, refund of direct taxes, bounty on sugar, District of Columbia, and other miscellaneous expenses	18,655,946
The military establishment, including rivers and harbours, forts, arsenals, and sea coast defences	10,360,952
The naval establishment, including construction of new vessels, machinery, armament, equipment and improvement at navy yards	5,759,559
Indian service	1,987,950
Pensions	28,279,046
Interest on the public debt	6,195,606
Postal service	15,396,626
Total expenditures	86,635,685

In addition to the ordinary revenues collected during the year, the cash in the Treasury was increased by the following sums:—
From the sale of 50 million 5 per cent. 10 year bonds issued under Act of January 14, 1875, 11,707,700*l.*; by the purchase of 13,023,249*l.* gold coin at a cost in 4 per cent. 30 year bonds of

(2300)

UNITED STATES.

12,463,080*l.*; and from the issue of 4 per cent. bonds in liquidation of interest accrued on refunding certificates converted during the year, 494*l.*, making a total of 24,731,443*l.*

Redemption of bonds, 1895.

The securities redeemed during the year on account of the sinking fund, were as follows:—

Description.	Amount.
	£
Redemption of—	
Loan of July and August, 1861	1,480
Loan of 1863	600
Funded loan of 1881	620
Funded loan of 1881 continued at 3½ %	500
Loan of 1882	1,470
Funded loan of 1891	19,240
Fractional currency and notes	924
National bank notes	202,439
Total	227,273

As compared with the fiscal year 1894, the receipts for 1895 increased 3,514,161*l.*, of which the more important items are as follows:—

Description.	Amount.
	£
Increases—	
Customs show an increase for 1895 of	4,068,017
Profits on coinage, bullion deposits	154,112
Sale of lands, Indian and other	72,243
Decrease—	
Internal revenue	737,912

There was a decrease of 2,265,996*l.* in the ordinary expenditure, of which the chief items are:—

Description.	Amount.
	£
Decreases—	
Treasury department—	
Bounty on sugar	2,226,811
Debentures or drawbacks, customs	211,158
Military establishment—	
Ordnance department	234,615
Naval establishment—	
Increase of navy	603,425
Increases—	
Deficiency in postal revenues	553,308
Legislative, salaries and expenses	209,974
Interest on public debt	627,325

WASHINGTON.

Fiscal Year, 1896.

The different items of revenue were:—

Revenue, 1896.

From—	Amount.
	£
Customs duties	32,004,350
Internal revenue	29,352,573
District of Columbia	769,287
Profits on coinage, bullion deposits, and assays	579,418
Fees—Consular, letters patent, and land	563,050
Sinking fund for Pacific railways	377,816
Tax on national banks	352,699
Navy pension and Navy hospital funds, &c.	227,442
Miscellaneous sources	222,353
Sales of public lands	201,106
Repayment of interest by Pacific railways	191,099
Customs fees, fines, penalties, &c.	124,401
Sales of Indian lands	114,322
Immigrant fund	89,134
Reimbursement for cost of water supply, district of Columbia	72,011
Sales of Government property	52,639
Deposits for surveying public lands	52,034
Soldiers' home, permanent fund	25,875
Depredations on public lands	10,421
Sales of land and buildings under special Acts	7,289
Sales of ordnance material	5,701
Tax on sealskins	220
Postal service	16,499,841
Total receipts	81,895,081

The expenditures for the same period were:—

Expenditure, 1896.

For—	Amount.
	£
The civil establishment, including foreign intercourse, public buildings, collecting the revenues, deficiency in postal revenues, bounty on sugar, District of Columbia, and other miscellaneous expenses	17,443,247
The military establishment, including rivers and harbours, forts, arsenals, and sea coast defences	10,166,184
The naval establishment, including construction of new vessels, machinery, armament, equipment and improvements at navy yards	5,429,546
Indian service	2,433,106
Pensions	27,886,800
Interest on the public debt	7,077,006
Postal service	16,499,842
Total	86,935,731

showing a deficit of 5,040,650*l.*

The above tables for 1896 show an increase in the receipts,

as compared with 1895, of 3,820,441*l.*, due chiefly to increases in customs receipts of 1,572,626*l.* and internal revenue of 668,239*l.*

Ordinary expenditure shows a decrease of a little over 300,000*l.* as compared with 1895, this reduction being effected upon various branches of the civil establishment.

In addition to the ordinary revenue collected during the year ended June 30, 1896, the cash in the Treasury was increased by the following sums:—

From the sale of 100 million 4 per cent. 30 year bonds issued under Act of January 14, 1875, 22,233,249*l.*, and from the issue of 4 per cent. bonds in liquidation of interest accrued on refunding certificates converted during the year, 826*l.*, making a total of 22,234,075*l.*

Redemption of bonds, 1896.

The securities redeemed during the fiscal year 1896, on account of the sinking fund, were:—

Description.	Amount.
	£
Loan of 1882	640
Loan of July and August, 1861	100
Loan of July and August, 1861, continued at 3½%	400
Loan of 1863	100
Funded loan of 1881	640
Funded loan of 1891	11,630
Oregon war debt	10
Fractional currency and notes	1,656
National bank notes	1,051,493
Total	1,066,669

Fiscal Year 1897.

Estimates for 1897.

The revenues of the Government for the current fiscal year are thus estimated upon the basis of existing laws:—

From—	Amount.
	£
Customs	29,600,000
Internal revenue	30,000,000
Miscellaneous sources	4,000,000
Postal service	17,958,624
Total estimated revenue	81,558,624

The expenditures for the same period are estimated as follows:—

For—	Amount.
	£
The civil establishment	21,400,000
The military establishment	11,200,000
The naval establishment	6,200,000
The Indian service	2,300,000
Pensions	28,000,000
Interest on public debt	7,400,000
Postal service	17,958,624
Total	94,458,624

or a deficit of 12,900,000*l.*

Fiscal Year 1898.

It is estimated that, upon the basis of existing laws, the revenues of the Government for the fiscal year 1898 will be:— *Estimates for 1898.*

From—	Amount.
	£
Customs	30,000,000
Internal revenue	31,000,000
Miscellaneous sources	4,000,000
Postal service	19,245,415
Total	84,245,415

The estimates of appropriations required for the same period, as submitted by the several executive departments and offices, are as follows:—

Description.	Amount.
	£
Legislative establishment	875,964
Executive establishment, including Executive proper, State, Treasury, War Navy, Interior, Post Office, Agriculture, Justice, and Labour Departments	3,973,190
Judicial establishment	181,424
Foreign intercourse	416,546
Military establishment	4,858,527
Naval establishment	6,486,954
Indian affairs	1,455,905
Pensions	28,265,716
Public works	6,287,412
Miscellaneous	7,268,844
Post Office, including deficiency in postal revenues	19,503,083
Permanent annual appropriations—	
Interest on public debt	7,230,000
Refunding—customs, internal revenue, &c., collecting revenue from customs, and miscellaneous	6,585,644
Total estimated appropriations, exclusive of sinking fund	93,389,209

or an estimated deficit of 9,143,794*l.*

UNITED STATES.

The foregoing estimates of receipts and expenditures for the fiscal year 1898 are made upon the assumption that there will be no substantial change in existing business conditions, and that the present scale of public expenditures will not be reduced. The difficulty of reaching satisfactory conclusions, especially as to the amount of receipts, is greatly increased at the present time by the unsettled condition of business, and the impossibility of seeing the changes that may occur before and during the year beginning on July 1, 1897. Should ordinary business activity be resumed, and should the consumption of articles subject to taxation increase to its normal proportions, the Secretary of the Treasury reports that the receipts for 1898 will, of course, be much larger than the foregoing estimates, and that there may, in fact, be no deficiency in the revenues.

Summary.

The revenue of the 4 years 1895–98 therefore are:

Year.	Amount.
	£
1895	78,074,640
1896	81,895,081
1897 (estimated)	81,558,624
1898 (estimated)	84,245,415

and the expenditures:—

Year.	Amount.
	£
1895	86,635,685
1896	86,935,731
1897 (estimated)	94,458,624
1898 (estimated)	93,389,209

Operations of the Treasury, 1895.

The Report of the Treasurer of the United States, dated December 1, 1895, shows that the total assets of the Treasury on June 30, 1895, were 162,525,544*l*., against 155,062,112*l*. on June 30, 1894, being an increase of 7,463,432*l*. during the fiscal year.

The amount of gold, silver, and United States' notes on deposit on account of outstanding certificates and Treasury notes decreased during the year from 123,231,164*l*. to 115,849,572*l*., being made up as follows:—

Description.	Amount.	
	June 30, 1894.	June 30, 1895.
	£	£
Gold coin and bullion	13,277,580	9,693,992
Silver dollars and bullion..	97,946,584	94,996,580
United States notes	12,007,000	11,159,000
Total	123,231,164	115,849,572

The remaining assets, being those available for the general uses of the Treasury, have been increased from 30,030,948*l.* to 46,675,971*l.*

According to the revised estimates, the total stock of money at the close of the fiscal year 1895 was 479,721,484*l.*, of which 159,327,789*l.* was in the Treasury and mints, and 320,393,695*l.* in circulation.

The only important changes reported in the composition of the currency was in the stock of gold, which is affected by the domestic production and consumption, as well as by exports and imports, and in the Treasury notes issued under the Act of 1870, which have been cancelled and retired since August, 1893, when redeemed in silver dollars.

The Army Pension List for the fiscal year 1895 amounts to 27,489,195*l.*, and the Navy List to 735,223*l.*, forming a total of 28,224,418*l.*

Pensions.

The following items may be noted:—

	Amount.
	£
War of 1812—	
Survivors	716
Widows	108,100
Total	108,816
Mexican War (1845–48)—	
Survivors	286,738
Widows	130,406
Total	417,144
Indian wars—	
Survivors	61,673
Widows	93,832
Totals	155,505

That this generous system is not to be curtailed is seen from the following:—

In the Republican platform of St. Louis which nominated

Major McKinley for President in the last election, it is stated:—
"We denounce the practice in the Pension Bureau, so recklessly and unjustly carried on by the present Administration, of reducing pensions and arbitrarily dropping names from the pension roll, as deserving the severest condemnation of the American people."

The Chicago Convention (Bryan-Democratic) "heartily endorse the rule that no names be arbitrarily dropped from the pension roll, and the fact that enlistment and service should be deemed conclusive evidence against disease and disability before enlistment."

And, lastly, the National Democratic Convention "favours a liberal policy of pensions to the deserving soldiers and sailors of the United States."

In addition to the pension fund are found the following items of expenditure:—

Description.	Amount.
	£
Military establishment—	
National Home for disabled soldiers	424,912
State homes for disabled soldiers	115,500
Soldiers' Home (Washington) permanent fund	15,000
Soldiers' Home, interest account	15,492

The number of pensioners on the rolls at the close of the fiscal year 1895 was 970,678, the largest number ever reported.

Foreign Commerce.

A comparison between 1894 and 1895 shows that the former year was one of large exports and diminished imports, the latter was one of large imports and diminished exports.

The smallness of imports in 1894 is accounted for by the uncertainty of tariff legislation in that year, while the improved crop conditions in other countries account largely for the diminished exports of domestic produce in 1895, which were 15,162,467*l.* less than in 1894, and the imports were 15,395,068*l.* greater in 1895 than in 1894.

WASHINGTON.

Trade Returns for Fiscal Years 1894 and 1895.

Description.	1894.	1895.	Increase or Decrease.
	£	£	£
Imports.			
Merchandise—			
Dutiable	55,039,817	73,747,234	+ 18,707,417
Free	75,959,107	72,646,759	− 3,312,348
Total	130,998,924	146,393,993	+ 15,395,069
Per cent. dutiable	42·0	50·4	
Gold	14,489,824	7,276,952	− 7,212,872
Silver	2,657,310	4,042,236	+ 1,384,926
Exports.			
Merchandise—			
Domestic	173,840,987	158,678,520	− 15,162,467
Foreign	4,587,127	2,829,113	− 1,758,014
Total	178,428,114	161,507,633	− 16,920,481
Gold	15,395,612	13,293,696	− 2,101,916
Silver	10,090,253	9,459,057	− 631,196
Imports for consumption	127,322,884	146,232,418	+ 18,909,534
Duties paid	25,736,373	29,580,243	+ 3,843,870

During the fiscal year 1896 the returns were:—

Description.	Amount.
	£
Imports.	
Merchandise—	
Dutiable	73,951,494
Free	81,993,440
Total	155,944,934
Per cent. dutiable	47·4
Gold	6,705,013
Silver	5,755,437
Exports.	
Merchandise—	
Domestic	172,640,097
Foreign	3,881,290
Total	176,521,387
Gold	22,481,989
Silver	12,108,334
Imports for consumption	151,938,817
Duties paid	31,220,920

UNITED STATES.

By this table it is seen that the excess of exports over imports, being respectively 172,640,097*l.* and 155,944,934*l.*, amounts to 16,695,163*l.*

So large an excess prepared the way for foreign exchange more favourable to the United States, and contributed largely to the recent heavy movement of gold from Europe to the United States in settlement of trade balances. While the export of gold during the fiscal year 1896 was greatly in excess of the import, the import in 1897 promises, according to the latest report of the Secretary of the Treasury, to more than turn the scale in favour of the United States.

Exports and imports of gold.

The net gold exports for the fiscal year 1895 were 6,023,476*l.*, as against 834,533*l.* for the previous year, being an increase of 5,188,943*l.*

The export of gold from the United States for the year 1895 was as follows:—

Description.	Amount.
	£
Domestic bullion	158,731
,, coin	11,019,328
Gold contained in copper matte	6,731
Domestic ores	65,602
Total domestic	11,250,392
Foreign coin and ores re-exported	2,050,035
Total gold exports	13,300,427

Of this amount the value of the domestic gold bullion exported to England was 1,662,453*l.*, and to France 5,350,680*l.*

The import of foreign gold bullion into the United States during 1895 amounted to 2,385,586*l.* Of this amount 1,341,882*l.* came from England, and about 330,000*l.* from France and Mexico.

Foreign gold coins were imported to the value of 2,493,225*l.*, of which amount about one-half came from France. Foreign gold ores of the invoiced value of 247,605*l.* were imported for reduction, of which two-thirds came from Mexico, and one-third from British Columbia.

Gold Imports, 1895.

Description.	Amount.
	£
Foreign bullion	2,385,586
,, coins	2,493,225
,, ores	247,605
Total foreign gold	5,126,416
United States' coin	2,150,535
Total gold imports	7,276,951

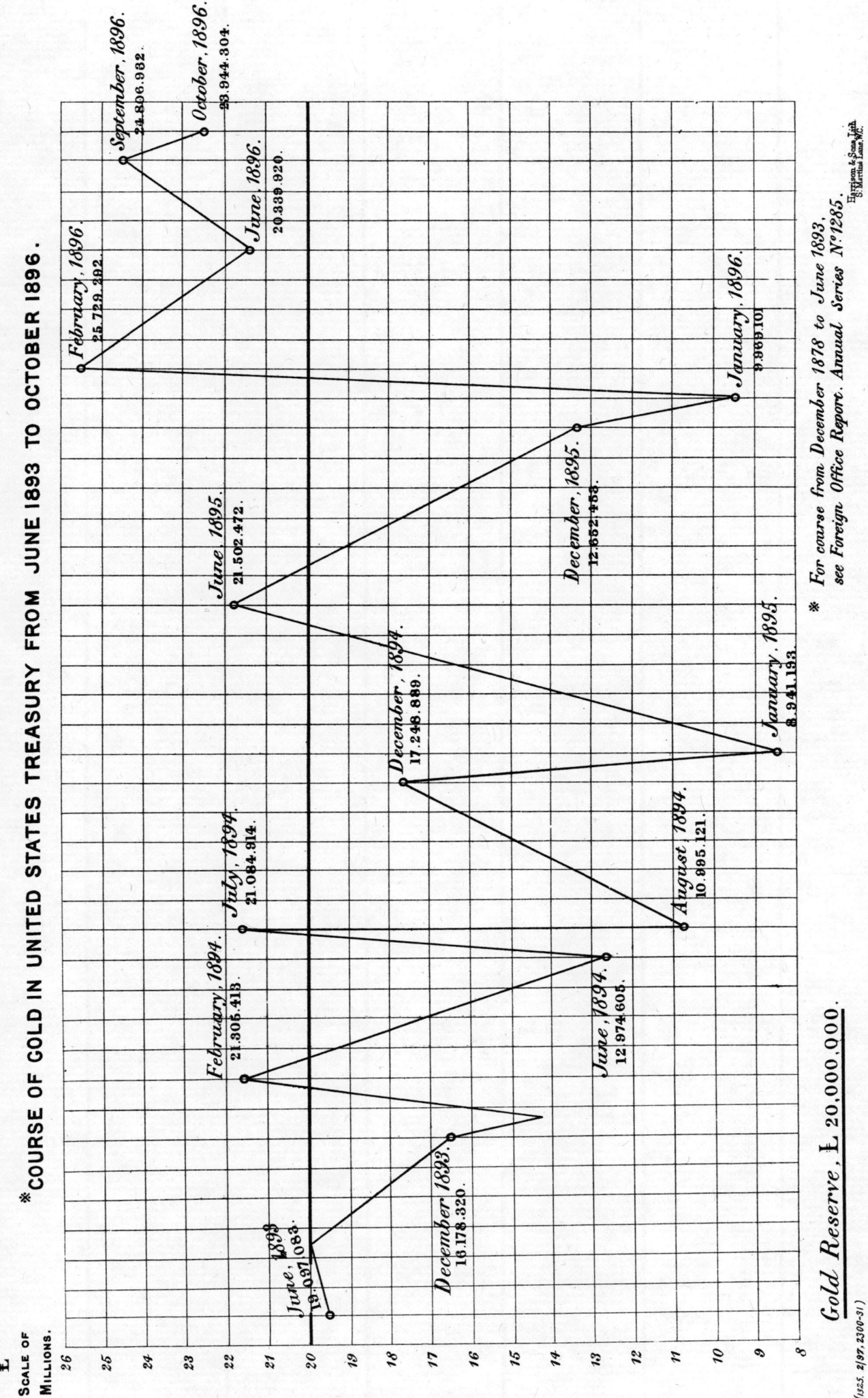

*COURSE OF GOLD IN UNITED STATES TREASURY FROM JUNE 1893 TO OCTOBER 1896.

£ Scale of Millions.

Date	Amount (£)
June, 1893	19,097,083
December, 1893	13,178,320
February, 1894	21,305,413
June, 1894	12,974,605
July, 1894	21,084,814
August, 1894	10,995,121
December, 1894	17,248,889
January, 1895	8,941,193
June, 1895	21,502,472
December, 1895	12,652,453
January, 1896	9,969,101
February, 1896	25,729,292
June, 1896	20,339,920
September, 1896	24,806,932
October, 1896	23,944,304

Gold Reserve, £ 20,000,000.

* For course from December 1878 to June 1893, see Foreign Office Report. Annual Series N° 1285.

The export of gold during the first 9 months of 1896 has amounted to 11,114,084*l.*, while the import of that metal during the same period has risen to 19,977,771*l.*, of which 6,831,826*l.* is during the month of September alone, a turn having occurred in foreign exchange in favour of the United States, which had the effect first of arresting the outflow of gold, and subsequently of causing a rapid current in the opposite direction.

The value of the exports during the fiscal year 1895 of domestic silver bullion, containing 62,783,792 ozs., was 8,006,522*l.*, of which 6,163,418*l.* went to England.

The imports of silver were as follows:—

Description.	Amount.
	£
Foreign bullion (commercial value)	696,157
Silver in foreign ores ,, ,,	2,131,732
Foreign silver coin	1,194,160
Total foreign	4,022,049
United States silver coin	20,187
Total silver imports	4,042,236

During the first 9 months of 1896 silver has been exported to the value of 8,288,208*l.*, and imported to the value of 1,690,927*l.*

Course of silver.

At the average price of silver bullion during the fiscal year 1895 the ratio of gold to silver was 1 to 32·5. The number of grains of pure silver purchasable with a United States silver dollar was 754·65, equivalent to 1·572 oz. fine, and in 1896 the number of grains was 710·06, equivalent to 1·479 oz. fine.

National Banks.

Total number organised.

Since the granting of the first certificate of authority in 1863, the total number of national banks organised has been 5,051, making an average for each year of 153. Of this number, there were in active operation on October 31, 1896, 3,679, having an aggregate capital of 130,002,979*l.*

During the year 1895, 43 banks were organised in 20 different States, with an aggregate capital of 978,000*l.*, and 28 banks were organised in 1896, with a capital of 649,000*l.*

The total amount of circulating notes outstanding on October 31, 1895, was 42,777,525*l.*, of which amount 38,036,192*l.* was secured by United States bonds, and 4,741,333*l.* by lawful money deposited with the Treasurer of the United States. The net increase in the amount of circulation secured by bonds during the year was 2,155,919*l.*, and the gross increase in the total circulation was 1,264,508*l.*

On October 31, 1896, the total circulation of all national banks was 46,910,761*l.*, of which 41,797,634*l.*, was secured by the United

UNITED STATES.

States bonds deposited by active banks, and the remainder by bonds held and lawful money deposited for account of insolvent and liquidating banks and banks reducing circulation.

The net increase in the amount of circulation secured by bonds during the year 1896 was 5,265,810*l.*, and the gross increase in the total circulation 4,219,885*l.*

Liquidation. Fifty-one banks went into voluntary liquidation during the year ended June 30, 1895, with an aggregate capital of 1,218,620*l.*, and circulation amounting to 230,400*l.* Receivers were appointed for 36 banks during the year, an increase of 15 upon the previous year.

The number of active banks, as compared with 1894, decreased 41 in 1895, with a corresponding decrease in capital of 1,287,622*l.* The number organised was seven less than in 1894, and the number going into voluntary liquidation 28 less.

The number of banks incorporated under the laws of the various States for the year was 5,066, and in 1896 this number had reached 5,708.

The number of national banks leaving the system in 1896 through voluntary liquidation was 37, having a capital stock of 729,000*l.*, and circulation of 252,563*l.* Receivers were appointed for 27 banks with an aggregate capital stock of 761,000*l.*, and circulation of 152,300*l.*

A comparison of the data of 1896 with 1895 shows that the number of active banks decreased 36.

Mr. Carlisle, the Secretary of the Treasury, in his report for 1895, defending the national banking system, states that "the most serious charge against the existing system is that the national banks are limited to the larger centres, and that the smaller centres of local trade, particularly those involving agricultural interests, have no facilities for utilising them." As the law stands at present, the organisation of any banking association is prohibited with a capital less than 10,000*l.*, and this only when the population does not exceed 6,000, and, if the population exceeds 6,000, the capital must be 20,000*l.*, and this must be not less than 100,000*l.* if the population exceeds 50,000.

Mr. Carlisle suggests in this connection that the law should be amended so as to permit national banking associations to establish branches which should be legally, and in fact simply, adjuncts of the main association. This recommendation is based upon examination of the banks and banking systems of 25 countries, all of which permit the establishment and operation of branch banks, one of which, France, makes their establishment compulsory.

Amelioration. As a means of placing the national banks on a better footing, the Comptroller of the Currency* recommends that—

(1) He should be empowered to remove officers and directors of such banks for violations of law and mismanagement.

(2) That once a year the directors should be required to submit

---

* In his report dated December 2, 1895.

to the Comptroller an annual report upon the affairs of such banks.

(3) That he should be authorised to issue to national banking associations circulating notes to the par value of the bonds deposited by them to secure such notes.

(4) That the semi-annual duty on the circulating notes of national banks be reduced so as to equal one-fourth of one per cent. per annum.

The redemptions of national bank-notes during 1896 were nearly 21,600,000*l.*, the largest in ten years, and, with the exception of three years, the largest since 1879.

Loans and Currency.

The interest-bearing debt of the United States was increased during the year ended November 1, 1895, by 22,463,740*l.*, consisting of:—

United States public debt.

(i.) 10,000,000*l.* of 5 per cent. bonds, of February 1, 1894, redeemable in coin at the pleasure of the Government after 10 years from that date.

(ii.) 4 per cent. bonds of the United States, dated February 1, 1895, and redeemable in coin at the pleasure of the United States after 30 years from that date, in payment for 3,500,000 ozs. of gold coin, amounting to 12,463,080*l.*

(iii.) The 4 per cent. loan of 1907 was increased by 660*l.*, issued in settlement of interest on refunding certificates of the Act of February 26, 1879.

During the same period 472,400*l.* of the 6 per cent. bonds issued in aid of Pacific railways, known as Currency sixes, have matured and ceased to bear interest. Of this amount, 472,000*l.* have been presented for payment and redeemed,

The amount and character of the public debt on June 30, 1894 and 1895, are shown in the following table:—

Class.	Amount. June 30, 1894.	Amount. June 30, 1895.
	£	£
Interest-bearing loans	127,008,378	143,240,412
Matured loans	370,248	344,318
Old demand loans	10,969	10,969
United States notes	69,336,204	69,336,204
Fractional currency (estimated)	1,379,427	1,378,824
National bank notes (redemption account)	5,274,337	5,071,897
Treasury notes of 1890	30,516,884	29,217,680
Certificates of deposit	92,554,280	86,623,892
Total	326,450,727	335,224,196

With regard to the condition of payment, the debt may be classified under five general heads, the Treasury notes being included with the certificates of deposit:—

(2300)

Description.	Amount.
	£
At maturity, future dates..	138,167,512
At option of the United States	5,072,900
On demand, without re-issue	6,806,009
,, for re-issue	98,553,883
,, out of deposits	86,623,892
Total	335,224,196

The interest bearing debt, exclusive of the bonds issued in aid of the Pacific railroads, was increased during the 12 months ended November 1, 1896, by the sum of 20,000,580*l.* consisting of:—

(i) 20,000,000*l.* bonds of the United States, dated February 1, 1895, and redeemable in coin at the pleasure of the United States after 30 years from that date.

(ii) The 4 per cent. loan of 1,907*l.* was increased by a further sum of 580*l.*

Circulation. The following table shows the changes in the amounts of the several kinds of money in the United States, outside the Treasury, during the year ended November 1, 1895. It is estimated that the population of the United States on that date was 70,378,000, and upon this basis the per capita supply of money outside the Treasury was 22 dol. 72 c., as compared with a population and per capita supply on November 1, 1894, of 68,887,000, and 24 dol. 27 c. respectively.

On November 1, 1896, the population was given as 71,902,000, and the per capita supply of money outside the Treasury was 22 dol. 63 c.

TABLE showing the comparison between Amounts of the several kinds of Money in the United States, outside the Treasury, in 1894, 1895, and 1896.

Description.	November 1, 1894.	November 1, 1895.	November 1, 1896.
	£	£	£
Gold coin	100,036,276	95,036,319	103,268,196
Standard silver dollars	11,288,734	11,670,818	11,638,160
Subsidiary silver	12,048,600	12,766,552	12,234,347
Gold certificates	12,850,414	10,083,531	7,639,462
Silver certificates	66,228,660	66,691,247	71,555,424
Treasury notes (Act July 14, 1890)	24,543,079	22,905,334	16,791,953
United States notes	56,094,941	47,797,256	51,390,065
Currency certificates (Act June 8, 1872)	10,809,000	11,348,000	6,493,000
National Bank notes	40,518,980	41,472,806	44,400,515
Total	334,418,684	319,771,863	325,411,122

Currency Reform.

Declaration of Republican Party for 'sound money.' In the Republican platform adopted by the St. Louis Convention which nominated Major McKinley as Presidential candidate, it is stated:—

"The Republican Party is unreservedly for sound money . . . .

We are unalterably opposed to every measure calculated to debase our currency or impair the credit of our country. We are, therefore, opposed to the free coinage of silver except by international agreement with the leading commercial nations of the world, which we pledge ourselves to promote, and, until such agreement can be obtained, the existing gold standard must be preserved. All our silver and paper currency must be maintained at a parity with gold, and we favour all measures designed to maintain inviolably the obligations of the United States and all our money, whether coin or paper, at the present standard of the most enlightened nations of the earth."

The Chicago Convention which nominated Mr. W. J. Bryan for President, declared in its platform :— *Democratic Party (Chicago Convention) for free silver.*

"Recognising that the money question is paramount to all others at this time, we invite attention to the fact that the Federal Constitution names silver and gold together as the money metals of the United States, and that the first coinage law passed by Congress under the Constitution made the silver dollar the monetary unit, and admitted gold to free coinage at a ratio based upon the silver unit. We declare that the Act of 1873 demonetizing silver without the knowledge and approval of the American people has resulted in the appreciation of gold and a corresponding fall in the prices of commodities produced by the people. . . . .

"We demand the free and unlimited coinage of both gold and silver at the present legal ratio of 16 to 1 without waiting for the aid and consent of any other nation. We demand that the standard silver dollar shall be a full legal tender equally with gold, for all debts, public and private, and we favour such legislation as will prevent for the future the demonetization of any kind of legal tender money by private contract. We are opposed to the policy and practice of surrendering to the holders of the obligations of the United States the option reserved by law to the Government of redeeming such obligations in either silver or gold coin.

"We are opposed to the issuing of interest-bearing bonds of the United States in time of peace, and condemn the trafficking with banking syndicates, which, in exchange for bonds and at an enormous profit to themselves, supply the Federal Treasury with gold to maintain the policy of gold monometallism. Congress alone has power to coin and issue money. . . . We denounce the issuance of notes as money for national banks as in derogation of the Constitution, and we demand that all paper which is made legal tender for public and private debts, or which is receivable for dues to the United States, shall be issued by the Government of the United States, and shall be redeemable in coin."

The National Democratic Convention which nominated General Palmer, denounced protection and free silver as schemes for the personal profit of the few at the expense of the masses, and denounced equally "the present costly patchwork system of national paper currency as a constant source of injury and peril. *National Democratic Party against free silver.*

(2300)

UNITED STATES.

We assert," it continues, "the necessity of such intelligent currency reform as will confine the Government to its legitimate functions, completely separated from the banking business, and afford to all sections of our country a uniform, safe, and elastic bank currency under governmental supervision measured in volume by the needs of business."

Paper currency reform.

As soon as the result of the election of November 3, 1896, in favour of Major McKinley, the Republican candidate, was made known, a campaign commenced against the paper currency at present in force. This movement is chiefly directed against the United States notes, commonly called "greenbacks," and is now assuming definite shape by the inauguration by the Indianapolis Board of Trade of a Convention of the Representatives of Boards of Trade in the Central West, to prepare for a larger Convention this month. The object of this movement is to "attain a banking currency based on specie, amply secured, redeemable in coin always and everywhere at full face value, replacing Government paper, which should be entirely abolished, by elastic bank notes resting solely on the reserves of gold held by the national banks."

Greenbacks. Legislation since 1862.

It may be well to endeavour briefly to trace the history of the "greenbacks."

During the Civil War, Acts were passed on February 12 and June 11, 1862, authorising issues of 60,000,000*l.* in notes—30,000,000*l.* by each Act—these notes being "legal tender for all debts, public and private, except duties or imposts and interest on the public debt and exchangeable for United States 6 per Cent. Bonds, redeemable at the pleasure of the United States after 5 years."

An Act of March 11, 1862, gave power to the Secretary of the Treasury to purchase coin with any bonds or notes of the United States authorised by law, at such rates and upon such terms as he may deem most advantageous to public interest. On January 13, 1863, 20,000,000*l.* more of legal tender notes were issued. Treasury notes, bearing interest at 5 and 6 per cent. with a definite term for payment were also issued during the war.

At the conclusion of the war, the total amount of greenbacks issued was 80,000,000*l.* By virtue of an Act of 1865, this amount was reduced to a little over 70,000,000*l.* when the law was repealed. By the Resumption Act of January 7, 1875, the Secretary of the Treasury was authorised to sell bonds without restriction for the purchase of the necessary coin. No less than 19,100,000*l.* in gold was obtained during 1877 and 1878 in this way, and use was again made of the Act in 1895 (see below).

Gold reserve.

In 1882, a fund of 20,000,000*l.* was ordered by Congress as a special reserve for redeeming the greenbacks, and 3 years later that sum was placed in a separate fund by the Treasurer of the United States for that purpose.

Under the law of July 14, 1890, known as the Sherman Act,

the United States Government purchased silver at the rate of 4,500,000 ozs. per month, to be paid for in Treasury notes payable in coin, which might be re-issued and were to be legal tender. Section 2 of this Act* states that " upon demand of the holder of any of the Treasury notes herein provided for, the Secretary of the Treasury shall, under such regulations as he shall prescribe, redeem such notes in gold or silver coin, at his discretion, it being the established policy of the United States to maintain the two metals on a parity with each other upon the present legal ratio or such ratio as may be provided by law." The silver bullion purchased under this Act was paid for in gold and was stored in the Treasury vaults.

Efforts were made in 1891 and 1892 to pass a bill for the free coinage of silver, but without success.

From July 1, 1890, to June 30, 1893, the loss in gold by export was 37,200,000*l*., and on June 27 of that year, India closed her mints to the free coinage of silver. In April, 1893, the Treasury reserve had fallen to 13,000,000*l*. and a panic was imminent. An extraordinary session of Congress was convened and the purchasing clause of the Sherman Act was repealed on November 1, 1893.

Attached to this Repeal Act was the following provision:— "It is hereby declared to be the policy of the United States to continue the use of both gold and silver as standard money and to coin both gold and silver into money of equal intrinsic value, such equality to be secured through international agreement or by such safeguards of legislation as will ensure the maintenance of the parity in value of coins of the two metals, and the legal power of every dollar at all times in the markets and in the payment of debts. And it is hereby declared that the efforts of the Government should be steadily directed to the establishment of such a system of bimetallism as will maintain at all times the equal power of every doller coined or issued by the United States in the markets and in the payment of debts."

Under the public notice of November 13, 1894, 10,000,000*l*. of 5 per cent. bonds were issued and sold. These were dated February 1, 1894, redeemable in coin at the pleasure of the United States after 10 years from that date.

The gold reserve rose in July, 1894, to 21,084,914*l*., but fell in the January following to 8,941,193*l*. (see chart annexed).

There were issued and delivered to the parties to a contract executed on February 8, 1895,† in payment for 3,500,000 ozs. of gold coin, 4 per cent. bonds of the United States, dated February 1, 1895, redeemable in coin after 30 years from that date, amounting to 12,463,000*l*. These bonds were made payable in coin and

* Under this Act, 168,764,682 ozs. of fine silver had been bought at a cost of 31,186,200*l*., and the total amount, together with that purchased under a former Act (Bland Act, 1878) was 459,946,701 ozs. at a cost of 92,842,052*l*. (For the text and further explanations of the Sherman Act see Foreign Office Report, Annual Series, 1893, No. 1285, page 35.)

† These operations were conducted by Mr. Carlisle, the Secretary of the Treasury, by virtue of the Act of January 7, 1875, above-mentioned.

taken at a premium to yield about 3¾ per cent. per annum. The question as to the meaning of the word "coin" was raised, and President Cleveland recommended to Congress that a specific undertaking should be made that the bonds should be paid in gold, to yield 3 per cent. interest instead of 3¾. This was, however, rejected on February 14, 1895.

The value of the United States notes on June 30, 1895, was 69,339,204*l.*, and of Treasury notes (Act of 1890) 29,217,680*l.*

Defects in currency system.

In his report for 1894 the Secretary of the Treasury pointed out the radical defects in the United States currency system in the following words:—

"(1) The circulation of the United States notes as currency and their current redemption in coin on demand.

"(2) The compulsory re-issue of such notes after redemption.

"(3) The excessive accumulation and coinage of silver and the issue of notes and certificates against it, upon a ratio which greatly overvalues that metal as compared with the standard unit of value in this and other principal commercial countries."

Further, in his report for 1895, the Director of the Mint endorses the above, and states that, before the United States can have a reasonably safe currency, these three defects must be remedied by appropriate legislation carried into practical effect. He adds that the "currency legislation of the United States, especially after 1873, has been to leave it a monetary system as inconsistent, illogical, dangerous, and expensive as can well be imagined. . . . Its reform is one of the most important and most urgent political and financial questions of the hour."

The following words were used in the message addressed to Congress by President Cleveland on December 7, 1896:—

"I cannot refrain from again earnestly presenting the necessity of the prompt reform of a system opposed to every rule of sound finance, and shown by experience to be fraught with the gravest perils and perplexity. . . . I am more convinced than ever that we can have no assured financial peace and safety until the Government currency obligations upon which gold may be demanded from the Treasury are withdrawn from circulation and cancelled. . . . The entire case may be presented by the statement that the day of sensible and sound financial methods will not dawn upon us till our Government abandons the banking business, and the accumulation of funds, and confines its monetary operations to the receipt of the money contributed by the people for its support, and to the expenditure of such money for the people's benefit."

Reform.

The practical shape which such reform should take is indicated by the Director of the Mint, as follows:—

"The legal tender notes definitively redeemed, and the Treasury notes issued under the Act of July 14, 1890, out of the way, both having been exchanged dollar for dollar in gold, the currency of the United States would consist of gold and silver, which are merely certificates of deposit payable in gold and silver, as the case may be, on presentation of national bank notes and currency certificates.

"The United States have the option of adopting the single gold standard and limiting the legal tender power of silver," or of "continuing the present system of free coinage of gold with the suspension of the coinage of silver and the limitation of the total amount of full legal tender silver currency in such a way as not to expel gold from circulation or menace the country with the single silver standard."

Lastly, in his report for 1896, the Secretary of the Treasury states:—

"Without a reformation of our currency, we cannot safely rely upon permanent accessions to our stock of gold from abroad in settlement of trade balances in our favour, nor can we hope ever to retain permanently the stock already in the country, as is conclusively shown by the experience of the last 4 years. During the 4 years from 1893 to 1896, both inclusive, our exports of merchandise and silver exceeded our imports by the amount of 376,408,057 dol. (75,281,611*l.*), and yet during the same time our net exports of gold amounted to 201,003,708 dol. (40,200,742*l.*); or, in other words, we paid during this time to the people of other countries 577,411,765 dol. (115,482,353*l.*) in merchandise and in silver and gold. Being a debtor nation, our favourable balances of trade will not bring us gold or any other form of money so long as we maintain a currency of doubtful value or stability, or continue an agitation which alarms foreign investors, and induces foreign creditors to demand the payment of their claims. Under these circumstances all our balances are absorbed by the withdrawal of previous investments and the collection of previous debts."

In the Republican platform adopted by the St. Louis Convention it was stated, "We renew and emphasise our allegiance to the policy of protection as the bulwark of American industrial independence and the foundation of American development and prosperity. The true American policy taxes foreign products and encourages home industry; it puts the burden of revenue on foreign goods, it secures the American market for the American produce; it upholds the American standard of wages for the American working man; it puts the factory by the side of the farm and makes the American farmer less dependent on foreign demand and price; it diffuses general thrift and founds the strength of all on the strength of each. In its reasonable application it is just, fair, and impartial; equally opposed to foreign control and domestic monopoly, to sectional discrimination and individual favouritism. . . . We demand such an equitable tariff on foreign imports which come into competition with American products as will not only furnish adequate revenue for the necessary expenses of the Government, but will protect American labour from degradation to the wage level of other lands. . . . The ruling and uncompromising principle is the protection and development of American labour and industry. The country demands a right settlement and then it wants rest.

Tariff.

UNITED STATES.

". . . Protection and reciprocity* . . . go hand in hand. Protection for what we produce, free admission for the necessaries of life which we do not produce. . . . Reciprocity builds up foreign trade and finds an outlet for our surplus."

Sugar.

"The Republican Party favours such protection as will lead to the production on American soil of all the sugar which the American people use, and for which they pay other countries more than 100,000,000 dol. (20,000,000*l.*) annually."

Wool and woollens.

"To all our products—to those of the mine and the fields as well as to those of the shop and the factory—to hemp, to wool, the product of the great industry of sheep husbandry, as well as to the finished woollens of the mill, we promise the most ample protection."

Merchant marine.

"We favour the American policy of discriminating duties for the upbuilding of our American merchant marine, and the protection of our shipping in the foreign carrying trade."

---

* The word "reciprocity" is probably used in the special technical sense of "discrimination." On page 47 of the Report of the Committee on Ways and Means concerning Reciprocity and Commercial Treaties, submitted to the House of Representatives on June 6, 1896, it is stated:—"Reciprocity was an endeavour . . . to secure for the farmer and manufacturer of the United States advantages which their rivals in other countries may not enjoy," and, on page 122, upon the Japanese tariff question, the Hon. W. E. Curtis, Assistant Secretary of the Treasury, states: "It will be difficult for the United States to negotiate a reciprocity treaty with Japan for the reason that the most-favoured nation clause appears with unusual breadth in all the treaties. In terms Japan agrees to impose no other or higher duties upon the same articles imported from any of the most-favoured nations." Lastly, on page 85, in a statement by Mr. Curtis upon the trade with the Argentine Republic, the following words occur:—"Although we may compete in the Argentine markets with either Great Britain, France, Germany, or Belgium, on even terms, the conditions are such that it is absolutely necessary for our exporters to have some advantages to offset those already enjoyed by their European competitors, and the advantages they require can only be obtained through legislation of our Congress and diplomatic negotiation."

LONDON:
Printed for Her Majesty's Stationery Office,
By HARRISON AND SONS,
Printers in Ordinary to Her Majesty.
(75 2 | 97—H & S 2300)

FOREIGN OFFICE.
1897.
ANNUAL SERIES.

No. 1853.

DIPLOMATIC AND CONSULAR REPORTS ON TRADE AND FINANCE.

UNITED STATES.

REPORT FOR THE YEAR 1896

ON THE

TRADE OF THE CONSULAR DISTRICT OF CHICAGO.

REFERENCE TO PREVIOUS REPORT, Annual Series No. 1725.

Presented to both Houses of Parliament by Command of Her Majesty,
MARCH, 1897.

LONDON:
PRINTED FOR HER MAJESTY'S STATIONERY OFFICE,
BY HARRISON AND SONS, ST. MARTIN'S LANE,
PRINTERS IN ORDINARY TO HER MAJESTY.

And to be purchased, either directly or through any Bookseller, from
EYRE & SPOTTISWOODE, EAST HARDING STREET, FLEET STREET, E.C., and
32, ABINGDON STREET, WESTMINSTER, S.W.; or
JOHN MENZIES & Co., 12, HANOVER STREET, EDINBURGH, and
90, WEST NILE STREET, GLASGOW; or
HODGES, FIGGIS, & Co., Limited, 104, GRAFTON STREET, DUBLIN.

1897.

[C. 8277—71.] *Price Fourpence Halfpenny.*

New Series of Reports.

Reports of the Annual Series have been issued from Her Majesty's Diplomatic and Consular Officers at the following places, and may be obtained from the sources indicated on the title-page:—

No.		Price.	No.		Price.
1731.	Riga	6½d.	1792.	Kiukiang	3d.
1732.	Tokio	1½d.	1793.	Bangkok	1d.
1733.	Tainan	1d.	1794.	Rio Grande do Sul	1d.
1734.	Portland	3d.	1795.	Valparaiso	4d.
1735.	Fiume	1½d.	1796.	Brindisi	2½d.
1736.	Taganrog	2d.	1797.	Bushire	2d.
1737.	Swatow	1d.	1798.	Christiania	5½d.
1738.	Chungking	1½d.	1799.	Cadiz	2d.
1739.	Angora	1½d.	1800.	Meshed	2½d.
1740.	Shanghai	2½d.	1801.	St. Petersburg	4½d.
1741.	Bilbao	3½d.	1802.	Batoum	1d.
1742.	Tahiti	1½d.	1803.	Peking	3d.
1743.	New Caledonia	1½d.	1804.	Samos	½d.
1744.	Amoy	1½d.	1805.	Dantzig	2d.
1745.	Ichang	1d.	1806.	Antwerp	1½d.
1746.	Berlin	½d.	1807.	Ajaccio	1½d.
1747.	Rio de Janeiro	5½d.	1808.	Stettin	3d.
1748.	Porto Rico	1½d.	1809.	Aleppo	1d.
1749.	Montevideo	1½d.	1810.	Tangier	2½d.
1750.	San Francisco	3d.	1811.	Tokio	3½d.
1751.	Cayenne	½d.	1812.	Madeira	½d.
1752.	Frankfort	3d.	1813.	Vera Cruz	1d.
1753.	Malaga	8½d.	1814.	Oporto	1d.
1754.	Söul	1d.	1815.	Hamburg	1½d.
1755.	Copenhagen	3d.	1816.	New Orleans	1½d.
1756.	Nice	1d.	1817.	Bengazi	½d.
1757.	Lisbon	1½d.	1818.	Marmagao	½d.
1758.	Nagasaki	1d.	1819.	Gothenburg	2d.
1759.	Hamburg	2½d.	1820.	Dar-al-Baida	3d.
1760.	Mozambique	2d.	1821.	Erzeroum	½d.
1761.	Cettinjé	1½d.	1822.	Munich	2½d.
1762.	The Hague	1½d.	1823.	Samoa	½d.
1763.	Cephalonia	1d.	1824.	Chinkiang	1d.
1764.	Bahia	1d.	1825.	Jeddah	1d.
1765.	Zanzibar	1½d.	1826.	Sofia	1½d.
1766.	Pakhoi	1d.	1827.	Mexico	2d.
1767.	New York	2d.	1828.	Teneriffe	3½d.
1768.	Chefoo	1d.	1829.	Batoum	1d.
1769.	Caracas	½d.	1830.	Cadiz	1d.
1770.	Palermo	11½d.	1831.	Martinique	1d.
1771.	Mombasa	½d.	1832.	Odessa	1d.
1772.	Nice	1½d.	1833.	Ghilan	1d.
1773.	Bucharest	4½d.	1834.	Old Calabar	6½d.
1774.	Port Said	1½d.	1835.	Tamsui	1d.
1775.	Galatz	1½d.	1836.	Copenhagen	½d.
1776.	Madrid	2d.	1837.	Salonica	1½d.
1777.	Vienna	2d.	1838.	Honolulu	½d.
1778.	Canton	1d.	1839.	Buenos Ayres	2d.
1779.	Yokohama	1½d.	1840.	Para	1d.
1780.	Newchwang	1d.	1841.	Bolivia	2d.
1781.	Wuhu	1d.	1842.	Washington	3d.
1782.	Athens	2d.	1843.	Berlin	2d.
1783.	Tonga	½d.	1844.	Uganda	1d.
1784.	Smyrna	½d.	1845.	Belgrade	1½d.
1785.	Baghdad	1d.	1846.	Dakar	½d.
1786.	Hiogo and Osaka	4½d.	1847.	Florence	1½d.
1787.	Bangkok	1d.	1848.	Copenhagen	2d.
1788.	Odessa	2d.	1849.	Havre	2d.
1789.	Naples	2d.	1850.	Serajevo	1d.
1790.	Beyrout	1d.	1851.	Madrid	2d.
1791.	Tunis	1½d.	1852.	La Rochelle	1½d.

No. 1853.

Reference to previous Report, Annual Series No. 1725.

UNITED STATES.

CHICAGO.

Mr. Vansittart to the Marquis of Salisbury.

(Received at Foreign Office, March 12, 1897.)

My Lord,

I HAVE the honour to transmit herewith my Report on the Trade and Commerce of Chicago during the year 1896, together with the Reports of the British Vice-Consuls at Denver, Kansas City, and St. Louis.

Mr. P. E. Burrough, at my request, has reported on the Trans-Mississippi and International Exposition, which is to be held next year, for a period of six months, at the City of Omaha, in the State of Nebraska. Statistics relating to Nebraska will be found in his Report, and, should any further information be required respecting the forthcoming Exposition, I would suggest that communications be addressed to the British Vice-Consul in Kansas City, Mo., who is in a position to answer all questions on the subject.

I venture to think that Mr. Burrough's suggestions and advice to British merchants in general, are worthy of their closest scrutiny.

There can be but little doubt that British trade is gradually but surely giving way to German competition, and in sundry branches such as crockery, earthenware, Portland cement, &c., the increased volume of German trade, to the detriment of Great Britain, is most marked throughout the Western States of this country.

The reasons assigned by Mr. Burrough in his Report, appear to me likewise to be worthy of close attention.

I have, &c.
(Signed) A. G. VANSITTART.

(2318)

UNITED STATES.

Report on the Trade and Commerce of the Consular District of Chicago for the Year 1896.

Table of Contents.

	Page
Chicago trade report for year 1896	2
Introductory and general review	2
Trade of Chicago	4
Produce trade of Chicago	8
Wholesale trade	9
Manufacturing trade	17
Tin-plate business	21
Shipping and freights	21
Strikes and labour situation	24
Railroads	26
Denver trade report	28
Kansas ,,	35
St. Louis ,,	58

Note.—Exchange is taken at the rate of four dollars and 85 cents to the pound sterling.

Chicago.

Introductory and General Review.

The year just closed has been one of great vicissitudes, and far from satisfactory from a financial point of view, and its financial history closely follows its political history.

The year began in depression and apprehension resulting from President Cleveland's Venezuelan message. Incident thereto were large gold exports, and early in the year to replenish the vanishing gold reserve the Government advertised for bids to the amount of 20,618,500*l.* 4 per cent. bonds. Bids were opened February 5, and showed a very large over subscription. The outlook then seemed brighter, and there was a considerable improvement running well into the spring. Then the free silver agitation began, and with many variations exerted a very depressing influence, until, early in August, it culminated in a condition bordering on panic. New York banks came to the relief of the threatened gold reserve, the political outlook grew clearer, heavy excesses of exports over imports diverted European gold this way, and there was a decided improvement, continuing until immediately after the Presidential election. For a few weeks after the election there was revival in certain manufacturing industries, and more activity in trade. But, although over some 300 manufactories in different parts of the country resumed business, the effect of this was not perceptible in general trade. Unfortunately the last month of the year witnessed the downfall of the second largest national bank in the west, and dragged with it the usual number of smaller concerns. It has, however, been demonstrated that the recent bank failures were not due to the pressure of hard times growing harder, but were the inevitable consequences of bad management, which left them too weak to rally. The strength exhibited by associated institutions, and business houses, in withstanding the shock is looked upon as a favourable sign, and, on the whole, business men reason that these bank failures have cleared the atmosphere.

Perhaps the most noticeable financial feature of the year was the extraordinary speculation in Diamond Match Stock, which advanced from 120 to 248, and, later, collapsed in a downfall that carried the Stock Exchange with it. That institution was closed from August 3 to November 5 as the result of the way in which its members became involved in the Diamond Match speculation, and, to a less extent, in the Street Railway situation.

In manufacturing, the year in Chicago does not compare favourably with previous years either in volume of output or in profits realized.

In the dry goods trade there was a decrease in the volume of business, and a falling-off in prices.

In live-stock, receipts of cattle were somewhat larger than in 1895, with a large increase in sheep, and a decrease in hogs and horses. Prices were lower, and conditions were not satisfactory either to producers or buyers. There was, during the year, a large trade in groceries, particularly in the closing months of the year, and clothing merchants report a good business despite the low prices.

It is noted that the tendency in most branches last year was to put out a cheaper grade of goods. The market for these was, on the whole, fairly satisfactory, but the margin of profits in many cases was small.

Briefly, therefore, the condition of business in 1896, so far as Chicago wholesale dealers, jobbers, and manufacturers are concerned, may be summed up in the statement that, while the volume compares favourably with that of 1895, prices were reduced to such an extent that the actual receipts range from 10 to 25 per cent. lower.

One of the most favourable indications of an early revival of trade is to be found in the condition of country stocks. These are reported from all quarters to be extremely low, and it seems almost safe to assume that, from now on, the tendency will be to make more liberal purchases.

The movement of farm produce was uniformly heavy. There is no increase in railway construction to report upon, and the year has been one of disappointed expectations, and new railway enterprises were among the chief sufferers by the continuance of the financial depression.

Real estate men speak of a steadier tone in their line, and assert that loans can be made now on easier terms than has been the case for a long time past, and that there are signs in the building trades that the spring will bring something like the usual activity in brick, and lumber, and mortar, and iron.

In conclusion, it may be said that the year 1896 closed with a good feeling in manufacturing and trade circles, and with a

(2318)

UNITED STATES.

better feeling in financial circles, despite the bank failures of December.

It is admitted that, after four to five years of great depression prosperity should come gradually; and business men are of opinion that the revival in trade can hardly be expected to show itself in any marked manner before the spring, and that booms should then not be looked for, and not be encouraged under any circumstances.

Trade of Chicago.

The following short comparative table illustrates the story of the year for all the commercial interests of the city of Chicago:—

		1896.		1895.	
		Quantity.	Amount.	Quantity.	Amount.
			£		£
Bank clearings	...	...	909,908,000	...	951,542,103
Board of Trade clearings	...	...	16,868,800	...	16,109,937
Grain, cars inspected	...	295,132	...	223,077	...
Flour and grain received	Bushels	253,802,133	...	189,432,919	...
Flour and grain shipped	,,	219,710,781	...	171,464,137	...
Live stock received	Head	14,101,018	...	13,921,927	...
Stock Exchange transactions	Shares	1,725,000	...	1,421,000	...
Stock Exchange transactions	Bonds	...	764,900	...	1,876,000

Banks and bank clearings.

If bank clearings are the best reflection of the general business situation, the year 1896 was not as prosperous a one for Chicago as 1895.

Their total, as seen by above table, was 41,634,103*l.* under the previous year. Compared with the business of 1895 it is a decrease of 4½ per cent. These figures tell the truth of the 12 months just closed. They were months of conservatism, of curtailment of consumption, of drawing in of enterprises, of husbanding of resources. Manufacturers in 1896 saw to it that old stocks were worked up before new ones were purchased; merchants that shelves were cleaned off before other goods were contracted for. The speculator, all through the year, kept within closer limits, and bankers narrowed their lines of credits.

The failure of the National Bank of Illinois towards the end of December came as a shock to the business and financial community, as well as to the general public, and carried down with it some five other financial concerns, nearly all of which were indebted to the National Bank of Illinois in considerable amounts. The failure was a revelation of injudicious management.

An analysis of the official bank reports made during the year give a pretty clear idea of the situation, and the conditions that have presented themselves.

On December 13, 1895, the loans and deposits of the 24

national banks in Chicago stood at 18,898,000*l*. and 26,889,300*l*. respectively. The first call by the Comptroller of the Currency in 1896, made on February 28, disclosed the fact that there had been a loss in the former item of about 618,500*l*., and in the latter of about 1,030,000*l*. The next statement, on May 7, showed a sharp gain in both items; on that date loans were reported at 19,547,000*l*., and deposits at 26,155,700*l*. These were the highest points touched during the year. On October 6, a month before the Presidential election, loans had dropped to 17,304,000*l*. and deposits to 22,623,600*l*. Twenty-three banks (the National Bank of Illinois having been closed a few days previous to the call) reported on December 17. The reports of these 23 banks showed a large gain in the item of cash means, the total being equal to nearly 55 per cent. of the total deposits. Loans showed an increase of only about 103,092*l*., indicating that the dividing up of the reserves had been the main consideration during the previous three months.

The returns made by the State banks were much the same. The National and State banks of Chicago number 48.

Board of Trade clearings. The huge crops of oats and corn made the grain movement in and out of Chicago far ahead of 1895, and up almost to the phenomenal year of 1892. The Board of Trade clearings, 16,868,800*l*., show that the whole volume of exchange transactions, spot and speculative, were ahead of any year since 1891.

The business at the stockyards was up to about the same (perhaps a trifle better) as that of last year, and last year was considered a good one.

Stock Exchange. The sales of shares on the Chicago Exchange for 1896 exceeded the 1895 record by 300,000 shares. But the bond transactions on the Exchange were the smallest for many years. The heavy stock business was due entirely to the Diamond Match and New York biscuit speculations, over 1,000,000 shares having changed hands. The crash, however, came after a period of great activity, and, as a consequence, the Stock Exchange remained closed from August 3 to November 5.

Building trade. The number of buildings put up in 1896 has been fully 30 per cent. less than last year. Activity in building operations cannot be expected until rents become firmer, and thereby offer better inducements for the erection of new buildings. There are, however, indications for a revival of building in the spring. Statistics of building permits issued during the year by the city building department show 4,686,700*l*. as the cost for 1896, as compared with 7,218,500*l*. for 1895.

Real estate. The year 1896 did not come up to the expectations of the sanguine real estate broker, and the early indications of a return of confidence were not realised, and commissions in the real estate market a rarity.

The real estate transfers for 1896 (21,541,300*l*.) were much less in the aggregate than for 1895. The difference amounts to 5,721,600*l*.

It is thought that one of the most hopeful features for the

(2318)

Insurance affairs.

increase of real estate values is that the rate of interest which money commands is steadily growing lower. Investments in real estate which heretofore were considered good when yielding 6 to 8 per cent., will soon be sought after when yielding only 4 to 5 per cent., and this should have a considerable bearing on future values.

Premium receipts on insurance policies showed a sharp decline in 1896, as compared with 1895. Wholesale and retail dealers, as a rule, carried light stocks, and reduced the necessary amount of insurance to a minimum. The losses by fire in 1896 aggregate 23,043,100*l.*, as compared with 27,129,000*l.* in 1895, a decrease of 4,085,900*l.* The year brought large German companies to the western States, viz., the Thuringia, Aachen and Munich, and the Magdeburg, the first and the last named coming in for the first time to this country in 1896. Affairs in the life insurance market have been very quiet during the year.

Union Stock Yards and Transit Company.

During the past year this company expended on improvements nearly 100,000*l.* The yards were first opened for business on December 25, 1865, and at that time could only accommodate a few cars of stock. At present they have a capacity for 75,000 cattle, 300,000 hogs, 50,000 sheep, and 5,000 horses.

The following figures show the receipts of live-stock at the Union Stockyards for the year 1896:—

	Head.
Cattle	2,599,138
Calves	139,010
Hogs	7,690,231
Sheep	3,589,134
Horses	105,680
	Number.
Total number of cars	277,775

Chicago horse market.

The horse business during the last year has been generally unsatisfactory. Something like 80,000 horses have been thrown out of employment owing to street car companies having engaged further in the equipment of their lines with electricity. Bicycles have likewise continued to play havoc with the trade in driving horses, and the general depression in business and low prices of farm products have all had a very depressing effect on the useful classes known as streeters, light-drivers, and farmers.

During the year about 10,000 horses were consigned to England and Scotland, 4,500 to France, and 3,500 to Germany. Buyers from Belgium, Italy, and Mexico took out upwards of 2,000 head, the number being about equally apportioned among the three countries. Most of the purchases for these latter three countries were drivers, with quality, shape, and action for private sale or use. It is stated here that a large number of the finest coach and carriage horses, trotters with good record and high-steppers, have been exported to London and Paris with satisfactory results, some taking blue ribbons at their annual exhibitions, others winning stake races, and obtaining good records.

Of the 105,680 horses received at the Union Stockyards, 97,314 head were exported to eastern, northern, or southern markets, about 8,360 having been taken by customers in this city and neighbourhood. The receipts show a falling-off of 7,633 head, and exports have decreased 11,832 head as compared with 1895. It may be said that breeding is almost at a standstill throughout the west, there being only about 7½ to 10 per cent. as many colts raised as in 1892–93.

The prices during the last half of 1896 have been about 20*l*. 12*s*. 6*d*. per car of 20 horses lower than in 1895 on common and medium grades. Good horses have averaged very favourably with the prices of 1894–95. Horses perfectly mannered, of good style and action, colour, size, and soundness, command good prices, and will sell on this market as high as 371*l*., and teams as high as 515*l*. to 618*l*. both at auctions and private sales.

Brewing trade. The year 1896, although not entirely satisfactory, has, at least, been a great improvement on the preceding year, the latter having been the most disastrous to the brewing business of this city. The sales show a decrease over 1895 of about 10 per cent. Beer may be called the poor man's luxury, and the fact that so many labouring men are unemployed is the direct cause of the decrease in the consumption of beer.

Several new breweries are now in course of construction, adding again to the capacity of Chicago breweries, which is already about three times as large as the output. It is feared that these buildings may be a useless expenditure. The beer war, which largely affected prices during 1895, was not a factor in the business of last year, having been ended to the satisfaction of the brewers. The price of supplies remained steady until the close of the year, when an advance came in almost all products used in the business.

About 1,500 saloons closed during the year owing to the depression of trade.

The spirit trade for the year has been fairly good, and at remunerative prices. There is but one distillery in Chicago, but the report of the Collector shows that there were 474,000*l*. worth of stamps sold.

The report of the internal revenue department, which is a good index to the beer trade, gives a fair indication of the beer business for 1896. It is as follows, showing the output by barrels by months for the years 1896–95 :—

UNITED STATES.

Months.	Quantity.	
	1896.	1895.
	Barrels.	Barrels.
January	196,202	156,157
February	184,307	163,582
March	210,215	205,045
April	280,242	249,163
May	320,285	311,691
June	305,200	326,057
July	341,362	339,548
August	316,305	360,465
September	250,070	309,640
October	225,460	240,457
November	203,572	223,722
December	208,891	225,820
Total	3,042,111	3,111,347

As to the prospects for 1897, it is hoped the spring will bring renewed activity, employment to labour, and, consequently, prosperity to the brewing trade.

Produce Trade of Chicago.

The following were the receipts and shipments of the leading articles of produce. The figures are those given by the Board of Trade, except live-stock, cheese, butter, and eggs:—

Principal Articles.		Receipts.		Shipments.	
		1896.	1895.	1896.	1895.
Flour	Barrels	2,531,995	3,005,460	2,854,832	2,532,000
Wheat	Bushels	19,933,402	20,637,642	25,888,647	22,775,780
Corn	,,	92,722,348	59,527,718	87,713,321	59,964,265
Oats	,,	109,725,689	79,890,792	82,119,852	66,839,596
Rye	,,	2,530,336	1,657,216	1,374,509	1,168,252
Barley	,,	17,496,381	14,194,981	9,767,708	9,322,244
Grass seeds	Lbs.	123,870,583	63,868,526	94,212,310	65,566,528
Flax seeds	Bushels	10,299,525	8,525,237	5,734,054	4,726,818
Broom corn	Lbs.	16,227,885	10,834,015	11,670,021	7,336,551
Cured meats	,,	159,931,671	172,203,523	714,666,394	698,210,341
Canned meats	Cases	14,245	7,584	1,261,593	1,143,131
Dressed beef	Lbs.	111,746,930	109,351,714	980,930,688	910,339,175
Beef packages	,,	994	3,641	86,093	102,660
Pork	Barrels	7,985	9,672	258,266	300,026
Lard	Lbs.	67,191,567	53,936,324	413,447,968	387,437,699
Cheese	,,	73,122,200	59,012,937	52,613,050	52,226,151
Butter	,,	236,776,450	185,453,997	220,975,300	176,846,168
Dressed hogs	Number	2,079	44,262	44,127	53,136
Live hogs	,,	7,660,678	7,901,883	1,895,707	2,103,244
Cattle	,,	2,599,500	2,599,422	818,617	789,925
Sheep	,,	3,590,236	3,420,622	562,893	476,587
Calves	,,	138,668	...	6,418	...
Horses	,,	106,052	...	97,653	...
Hides	Lbs.	96,195,328	90,822,102	171,069,994	174,807,918
Wool	,,	44,894,651	51,371,694	54,078,833	63,441,329
Coal	Tons	6,322,773	6,092,284	861,600	985,158
Lumber	Met. feet	1,286,643	1,638,130	599,920	773,983
Salt	Barrels	2,017,982	1,994,058	997,454	806,144
Hay	Tons	327,263	267,599	104,637	36,040
Potatoes	Bushels	4,290,772	4,934,391	864,234	1,123,556
Eggs	Cases	2,298,950	2,146,040	1,465,550	1,207,373
Shingles	Met. feet	265,205	352,313	577,329	298,835

CHICAGO.

The following are the totals of the value of produce received for the last year, and corresponding totals for 1895:—

Principal Articles.	Value. 1896.	Value. 1895.
	£	£
Flour	1,543,917	1,948,453
Wheat	2,700,000	2,594,639
Corn	4,659,381	4,894,845
Oats	4,064,329	3,946,391
Rye	160,000	163,917
Barley	1,050,927	1,068,865
Mill-stuffs	162,886	309,278
Total bread-stuffs	14,341,440	14,926,388
Butter	8,543,505	7,773,608
Cheese	1,221,237	1,082,061
Hides	1,195,463	936,082
Wool	1,020,206	1,588,865
Flax seed	1,592,783	2,143,298
Other seed	401,443	455,670
Broom corn	110,309	82,474
Salt	180,412	206,185
Potatoes	194,432	223,711
Other vegetables	121,649	123,711
Tallow and grease	223,711	185,567
Hay	618,556	642,473
Apples	84,536	103,092
California fruits	412,370	515,462
Other fruits	577,318	876,288
Hops	109,690	87,628
Eggs	1,838,762	2,177,113
Poultry and game	567,010	568,041
Live-stock	39,145,360	42,102,474
Beef	1,507,628	1,793,814
Pork, barrelled	12,164	20,412
Lard	625,154	679,318
Meats (hog)	1,329,896	1,947,422
Dressed hogs	2,474	91,340
Total	75,977,508	81,332,497

Grain trade. The grain trade makes a most satisfactory report. Receipts of flour and grain aggregated 53,802,133 bushels, an increase of 33·9 per cent. Receipts of corn were the largest on record, and oats beat all previous years. There were 295,132 cars of grain received, an increase of 72,442 cars over 1895. The receipts of corn increased 35 per cent., and oats 28 per cent., but receipts of flour decreased 15 per cent., and wheat 3 per cent. Exports of flour and grain were equal to 219,710,781 bushels, an increase of 21·9 per cent. The exports of flour alone increased 11 per cent., the other grains being 12 per cent. in wheat, 21 per cent. in corn, and 18 per cent. in oats.

Wheat and flour. The average price of No. 2 wheat during the year was 2s. 8¾d. a bushel, against 2s. 7d. in 1895. The highest price reached was

UNITED STATES.

in the month of November, viz., 3s. 8½d. per bushel, and the lowest in August, viz., 2s. 2¼d. per bushel. The flour millers have had a good year, particularly in the last four months, when prices advanced from 15s. to 1l. 1s. 3d., in sympathy with wheat and on the heavy export demand.

Corn. Corn touched the lowest price ever recorded in Chicago, No. 2 cash selling at 9¾d. per bushel on September 5. The highest price reached of No. 2 corn in the year was in April, viz., 1s. 3d. per bushel. The average price was 1s. 0½d. per bushel, as against 1s. 7½d. per bushel in 1895. The crop was the largest on record: 2,208,134,000 bushels, or 56,995,420 bushels in excess of 1895. The quantity held over from the latter year was heavy. The market was on a cash basis all the year, speculation was light, and the heavy exports 113,633,000 bushels, or 63,000,000 bushels more than for the 11 months in 1895, combined with the advance in wheat, prevented prices from going lower.

Oats. In oats it was a year of excessive stocks and extremely low prices; the latter declining to 7¼d. in September, making the range for the year on No. 2 cash 7¼d. to 10½d.; the close being at about intermediate figures. Prices have not been so low since 1861, when they sold at 6¼d. A feature of the trade was the increased demand for clipped oats, especially for export. The quality of the new oats was very poor.

Rye and barley. Rye prices ruled unusually low, owing in part to the fact that many distillers had shut down the previous year, and also because of the low values in other cereals, particularly corn. The average price of No. 2 rye throughout the year was 1s. 5½d. It sold at the lowest price on record, viz., 1s. 1¾d. The highest figure was 1s. 9¼d. Exports were 5,446,000 bushels, the largest for years.

The crop of barley decreased 11,125,846 bushels, being 75,946,898 bushels. Exports were about the largest in the history of the trade, but the quality sent abroad was mainly low grade to feed stock in the British Isles, Holland, South Africa, and other countries, some of which have never bought barley in this market before.

The average price of the latest crop was 1s. 2½d. The best came from Minnesota, Wisconsin, and North-Western Iowa. The choicest came from the bluffs of the Mississippi, being secured plump and sound. Barley sold for feed on the average at 11d. to 1s.

Flax seed. Flax seed disappointed both growers and speculators by selling at the lowest figures on record, 2s. 7¼d. for No. 1 cash, the range being 2s. 7¼d. to 3s. 10d. The crop of 1896 was a good average one. Business in timothy, clover, and other seeds was slow, timothy selling at the lowest prices for years, the average being 10s. 9d. The crop was ample for all requirements. Clover was damaged by rains at harvest; the average for the year was 1l. 6s. 9½ per 100 lbs.

Provisions. The market for hog products was remarkable for its narrowness, the volume of speculation being small, and the fluctuations confined within a range of 13s. 9½d. for pork, 11s. 6½d. for lard, and 9s. 5¾d. for short ribs. Supplies of hogs were more than ample, stocks of cured products were the largest for years, and of lard have never been exceeded. This caused lard to sell for less than tallow, and induced soapmakers to buy in preference. During the closing months of the year lard and ribs sold at 12s. 4¾d., and pork at 1l. 2s. 8d. There were heavy losses of hogs by cholera in the autumn. The export business was large.

Business with the packers was generally good, and profits part of the time better. The number of hogs slaughtered was 5,700,000, a decrease of 50,000 from the previous year. The weight was 15 lbs. heavier, and quality never better. The value of the hogs killed was 10,103,000l., or 2,680,400l. less than in 1895, the reduction being due largely to the fact that prices averaged 4s. 1½d. per 100 lbs. lower. The business, however, was large, and gave employment to between 16,000 and 18,000 hands. *Packers.*

The consumption of canned meats has largely increased. Export sales were heavy, and Chicago dressed meats are now to be had in all parts of the country at reasonable prices. The sale of beef extract has increased considerably, and more largely for culinary purposes than for medicinal, as formerly. A number of improvements in machinery have been adopted, notably that in the curing of what is commercially known as curled hair. Formerly this product was spread upon the ground, and allowed to bleach through the action of the elements; but under new and improved processes this is effected within a few days at present, and where formerly there were 12 different grades, there are now 45 upon the market.

The soap business is fairly established, and the Chicago packing-houses, which are utilising their tallow, are active competitors with the older soap manufacturers of the country. A new and important industry for the better utilization of animal products was put into operation during the year—that is, the manufacture of felt, in which wool and cattle hair are extensively used. The felt manufactured is used for insulating and for saddlery.

In point of volume the aggregate receipts of live stock in Chicago in 1896 were not the largest in the history of the trade, but were large enough to be highly satisfactory to both exporters and producers, when all the circumstances are taken into consideration. The supply totalled to 2,600,000 cattle, 7,700,000 hogs, and 3,600,000 sheep, which, compared with 1895, shows a gain of 12,000 cattle, a loss of 185,000 hogs, and a gain of 200,000 sheep. Stated in money, it represents a valuation of 41,237,100l. Prices, however, were not altogether satisfactory. *Live stock.*

The outlet was not up to expectations, hard times having thrown many persons out of employment, and so lessening the general consumption of meats.

When the year opened native beef cattle sold at 12s. 11¾d. to 18s. 11½d. The range at the close was 14s. 5d. to 1l. 2s. 8d.

In the export line business was good. In the course of the year 243,000 cattle were exported abroad alive. The average weight of cattle for the year was 1,118 lbs., the heaviest on record.

The supply of Texas and Western range cattle decreased nearly 200,000. The quality of Texas cattle was better, while Western rangers were poorer than in 1895. The average price of native cows and heifers was 10s. 11¼d., or 10d. lower than the previous year.

Hogs. The year 1896 will be on record as being the lowest in hog prices of any year since 1879. This was not brought about by excessive supplies, but by a lack of demand on the part of the packers. The stringency of the money market was the principal cause. Hog cholera had much to do with the lessening of receipts. The beginning of the year opened with sales at 14s. 0½d. to 15s. 3½d., and reached 16s. 1d. to 17s. 9d., but declined on August 1 to the low point, viz., 10s. 6d. to 14s. The average weight of hogs was 246 lbs., the second heaviest since 1883. Receipts of hogs at Chicago for 1896 were about 220,000 smaller than 1895, yet were the fourth largest on record, being 1,640,000 larger than in 1893, and over 900,000 smaller than the receipts of 1891, when 8,600,800 arrived.

Sheep. The receipts of sheep were the largest known; almost without interruption there has been a steady increase in the supply of sheep for 20 years. Formerly they were raised chiefly for wool, but now the demand is as pronounced for mutton as for beef or pork. This has caused not only an increase in supply, but in a better quality, and more well-bred sheep were noticed than before. Prices ruled low for inferior grades, and high for the best.

The year opened with sheep at 6s. 2¼d. to 16s. 6d., and lambs 10s. 4d. to 1l. 0s. 7½d. The highest price was paid in June, when sheep sold at 18s. 11¾d., and lambs up to 1l. 7s. 3¼d. Nearly 3,600,000 sheep were received in 1896, or nearly 200,000 more than were recorded in 1895. The weight of sheep and lambs averaged 88 lbs., against 90 lbs. for 1895.

Wool. The wool trade was dull and depressed. Domestic unwashed wools ranged from 7d. to 7½d. Territory wools from 4d. to 6½d. according to quality and condition.

The failure of the Senate to pass the Dingley Bill, which placed a duty of 3d. per 1 lb. on wool, checked operations. With diminished consumption, and large stocks on hand, values declined until in August they had reached the lowest point in the history of the trade. In October the result of the election having been to a certain extent discounted, a marked improvement took place, but in December the trade again fell off. Orders for goods were disappointing, and while some machinery was started, fully 50 per cent. remained idle. The year closed with prices from ½d. to 1d. per 1 lb. lower than at the beginning.

Hides, pelts, and tallow. Trade in hides was fairly prosperous. No. 1 opened in January at 3¾d., but declined to 2½d. in August. The close of the year was better, when prices reached 4½d.

The pelt market was fairly steady. The consumption of mutton in this country is increasing considerably, and the supply of pelts is becoming a far more important item in the hide trade than formerly.

Prices in tallow were the lowest ever quoted in the market. The enormous crops of corn for two years made large supplies of fat cattle, which, in turn, produced heavy supplies of tallow, and the only relief for the surplus was in exporting to France and England at a price which, though very low, kept the supply moving. The average year's price was 1½d. Higher prices are not anticipated for 1897, as farmers must continue to use large supplies of corn for feed.

Sales ran about 500,000 barrels more than for 1895, but prices declined fully 20 per cent., so that the volume of business done was not equal to that of the preceding year. At producing points prices were demoralised through over-production, and were from 35 to 40 per cent. lower than those of 1894. The trade from the north and north-west during 1896 was larger than for the previous year, but the demand from southern points was about equal to that in 1895. In Chicago the prices ranged for first three months of the year at 2s. 10¾d. per barrel, then, up to August 15 at about 2s. 6d., and at the close of the year 2s. 3d. *Salt.*

Some remarkable features appeared in the hop trade. During July and August the lowest prices for 20 years was reached, quotations ranging from 2¼d. to 2½d. per lb. At this time reports concerning the English and German crops began to arrive, the unfavourable features of which caused a continual advance in the home-grown products of 1896. The first sales were at from 2½d. to 3d. per lb., but a continual advance brought the price of Oregon hops up to 6¾d., and choice Otsego County, New York, hops were held firm at 8d. per lb. at the close of the year. Exports were about the same as for 1895, the equivalent of near 80,000 bales. The outlook is good. Another favourable feature is that the brewers have bought little of the new crop. They will thus be enabled to use up the large accumulation on hand, and become competitors with the export trade for the crop of 1897. *Hops.*

The potato crop was 240,330,000 bushels, a decrease of 57,000,000 bushels from 1895. Prices were unusually low, sales being made at an average of 11d. per bushel throughout the year. *Potatoes.*

The lumber trade was unsatisfactory throughout the greater part of the country, the cut of the Michigan, Wisconsin, and Minnesota mills was estimated at 25 per cent. less than 1895, and of yellow pine in the south 10 to 15 per cent., and of hardwood 15 to 25 per cent. There was a decrease in receipts of all kinds of lumber of 23 per cent., and in shingles of 29 per cent. The exports show a decrease of 10 per cent. on lumber, and 7 per cent. in shingles. The range of prices in long wide joists was 2l. 1s. 3d. to 2l. 9s. 6d. Total receipts of lumber for 1896 were 1,324,954,000 feet compared with 1,637,389,000 feet in 1895, and 2,205,337,000 feet in 1892, the last being the year of the World's Fair. Total exports for 1896 were 598,620,000 feet. Receipts of shingles were 287,879,000, and exports 266,342,000. Short price stuffs sold at 2s. 0¾d. to 8s. 3d. lower than in 1895. The highest point reached was 2l. 5s. 4½d. *Lumber.*

The statistics published by the Bureau of Coal statistics show *Coal trade.*

a total increase in receipts of all varieties of coal in Chicago market from January 1 to November 30, 1896, of 363,436 tons, but this increase is entirely in anthracite and Eastern bituminous coal, anthracite showing about 260,000 tons increase, and Eastern bituminous about 100,000 tons. Illinois bituminous coals showed an increase of 163,000 tons, while Indiana bituminous coal showed a decrease of 166,000 tons. Pennsylvania coal has increased moderately, showing the depression at industrial works, and the same may be said of Ohio coal, due to strikes, and manipulation in freight rates. The loss in the Indiana product was due to strikes in the bituminous fields of that State. Michigan and Iowa both developed large coal areas during 1896.

There was an increase in lake receipts of about 130,000 tons during the season of navigation, compared with the preceding year. All rail receipts showed an increase of 160,000 tons over 1895. One drawback of the trade was the vast strides made by gas, for, notwithstanding danger and cost, a large amount of anthracite was displaced by its use.

The year 1896 in bituminous business was the counterpart of what the last year was in the anthracite business, namely, the lowest prices ever recorded. The anthracite trade has been greatly improved in regard to prices, which ranged from 6s. 2d. to 8s. 3d. per ton over last year, but the sales were not satisfactory, and large stocks are on hand at present.

The nominal price at retail for the last sales of the year was 1l. 7s. 10d. delivered. Prices at the beginning of the year were low at about 1l. 0s. 7½d. and 1l. 1s. 8d. on cars.

The outlook for the coming year is brighter, and when the merchants get over the pressure of the last six months a gradual increase is to be expected in all lines of the coaling business. Taking it in all, the year 1896 has been a disastrous one for the coal trade.

Coke. On account of the restriction in demand for crude, and manufacturing uses, coke felt the depression in business. The receipts were about 375,000 tons, the price of which was from 6s. 6¾d. to 8s. 3d. at the furnace.

Eggs, butter, and cheese. The produce trade was the largest in volume for many years. In value, though, it does not make as good a return, owing to the unprecedentedly low prices. The average prices were, butter 9¼d. per 1 lb., cheese 4½d., eggs 6½d. per dozen, and 3¾d. per 1 lb. for poultry. Chicago is rapidly becoming the leading distributing point for butter; the storage demand was limited only by the storage capacity, and this would have been undoubtedly larger had there been additional cold storage facilities. Much of the over-production of butter found a ready sale in foreign markets. The export trade of this product is growing, as is shown by the fact that in 1895 the United States exported 15,647,500 lbs., and in 1896 sent abroad 26,320,000 lbs.

The supply of poultry has been smaller, proportionately, than in past years. It is estimated that the crop of turkeys was one-third less than in 1895.

On the whole the fruit market of 1896 was not satisfactory, Fruit. either to growers or dealers. Perhaps the feature of the 1895-96 apples was the change in the relative values of the Eastern and Western varieties. In the autumn of 1895 the Eastern were the favourites, and sold from 1s. to 2s. per barrel more than the standard Western varieties, but in May, 1896, this had not only been recovered, but an additional 1s. 5d. to 2s. in favour of the Western fruit was being obtained. Good fruit in carload lots, towards the end of the year, sold at 3s. 1d. to 3s. 8¾d. At retail from 7½d. to 1s. more was paid.

In the early part of the year oranges came from Jamaica. Mexican oranges, owing to the almost entire absence of Florida oranges, did well, and sold at 13s. 4d. Californian oranges came late in the year. In December there were received in Chicago about 50 to 75 cars of California oranges, prices ranging from 13s. 4¾d. to 16s. 6d. for navels, and 10s. 4d. to 12s. 4½d. for seedlings. There was a good demand for tangerines from Japan.

It is interesting to note that the freight and duty from Japan to Chicago are only a few pence more per box than the freight alone from California. The same applies also to oranges from Italy, freight and duty from Italy to Chicago being 3s. 3¾d. per box on oranges and lemons, and freight alone from California to Chicago on oranges 3s. 9d. per box, and on lemons 4s. 1½d. per box.

The Illinois crop of strawberries was not heavy, and the quality poor The first prices were 10s. 4d. to 12s. 4½d. for 24 quarts, but they soon declined to 4s. 1½d. to 5s. 1¾d.

The lemon business was unsatisfactory.

The supply of peaches was abundant. Prices opened at 6s. 1¾d. to 8s. 3d., rapidly declining to 2s. Michigan peaches came in immense quantities. The crop appears to have been the largest ever known. So great was the yield that to find a market New York and Boston were invaded for the first time, Western peaches coming into competition with the product of New Jersey and Maryland. Bushel baskets sold at 4s. 1½d., but prices afterwards reached 1s. 8d. to 2s. per bushel.

Wholesale Trade.

The following table gives the totals for last year, with corresponding figures for 1895, of the business done in the wholesale trade :—

(2318)

UNITED STATES.

Principal Articles.	Value.	
	1896.	1895.
	£	£
Dry goods and carpets	16,701,030	18,556,700
Groceries	13,402,061	13,608,247
Lumber	5,360,824	7,216,494
Manufactured iron	3,092,783	3,298,969
Clothing	3,402,061	4,020,618
Boots and shoes	7,938,144	7,422,680
Drugs and chemicals	1,525,773	1,701,033
Crockery and glassware	979,381	1,206,185
Hats and caps	1,494,845	1,649,484
Millinery	824,742	927,835
Tobacco and cigars	3,195,875	3,092,783
Fresh and salt fish and oysters	1,340,206	1,443,298
Oil	793,814	876,288
Dried fruits	752,577	876,288
Building material	659,793	824,742
Furs	649,484	721,649
Carriages	309,278	371,134
Pianos, organs, and instruments	1,546,391	1,701,033
Music books, sheet music	1,340,206	123,711
Books, stationery, and wall-paper	4,123,701	5,061,855
Paper	4,845,360	5,412,370
Paper stock	824,742	927,835
Pig-iron	3,144,329	3,453,607
Coal	3,814,432	3,628,865
Hardware and cutlery	3,938,144	4,432,989
Wooden and willow ware	979,381	1,144,329
Liquors	2,886,597	3,402,061
Jewellery, watches, and diamonds	3,608,247	4,226,803
Leather and findings	721,649	773,195
Pig-lead and copper	979,381	1,113,402
Iron ore	463,917	515,463
Miscellaneous	1,134,020	1,237,113
Totals	96,773,168	104,969,058

Wholesale and retail. During the first six months the volume of business exceeded corresponding periods in 1895, and was fully up to expectations. The change, however, came with the summer, when business men everywhere began to manifest the greatest care and concern in the management of their affairs. Among buyers there existed a marked feeling of economy, and the least expensive merchandise was almost universally selected. Individual sales, while numerous in dry goods, were comparatively small in amount.

As during the last six months of 1896 the country merchants, as well as those of the great cities, did not venture to increase their stocks extensively, they are, consequently, at the present time very low.

Groceries. The grocery business showed a marked improvement towards the end of the year. Luxuries were not so much in demand as necessities. Sales were small though generally numerous.

Sugars are being kept down by the large importations of beet sugar from Europe.

Coffees, syrup, and rice sold lower.

The importations of tea into Chicago fell off some 5,000,000 lbs. from those of 1895, owing to the shortage of crop in China and Japan. The comparative scarcity of tea leads many grocers to expect an increase of price. Chicago is now about the largest importing centre of Japan tea in the United States. In addition to the direct importation, there passed through the Chicago office over 2,000,000 lbs. of tea imported at other places, and sent to Chicago for examination and classification.

During the year ending June 30, it is stated that 275,353 packages of tea, weighing 15,573 tons, were invoiced at the port of Chicago.

The consumption of low grade coffees is increasing. The price of granulated sugar reached 1*l.* 4*s.* 2½*d.* in April, but the year closed with the market at 19*s.* 1¼*d.*

The domestic rice crop was almost a complete failure. A good deal from foreign countries was imported, particularly from Japan, Patna, Bassein, and Rangoon. The cheapest stock sold from 1*d.* to 1¼*d.* per lb., and the higher grades from 2*d.* to 2¾*d.*

The imported Havana cigar has almost entirely disappeared from the market, and, as no new leaf will be available for some two years to come, prices are likely to advance.

Prices remained about the same as during 1895, with the exception of beef, which advanced almost 1*d.* per lb. on all cuts, selling from 8*d.* to 11¼*d.* for the very best and choicest steer beef. Mutton sold for from 4*d.* to 6¼*d.* per lb. Veal had about same range. Pork brought from 3*d.* to 4*d.* per lb., and smoked meats ranged the same as formerly. *Price of meat.*

Manufacturing Trade.

The demand for pig-iron from England was the feature of the trade. On the whole the year closed has been one of disappointment. During the first half of the year prices remained steady, but during the last half prices for pig-iron declined from 8*s.* 3*d.* to 12*s.* and 4*d.* a ton, and there was practically no business in iron ore. The production of pig-iron in Chicago was about 50 per cent. less than last year. The capacity of the furnaces is 1,000,000 tons per annum. As the furnaces only run about half of the time, the production was estimated at 500,000 tons. No. 1 foundry coke-iron brought 2*l.* 13*s.* 7¾*d.* to 2*l.* 17*s.* 8¾*d.*, but towards the end of the year declined to 2*l.* 5*s.* 4½*d.* *Iron and steel.*

Prices for steel rails ruled at 5*l.* 19*s.* 8*d.* a ton at Chicago all the year, but there has been a falling off of 12*s.* 4*d.* a ton for this year. Billets sold at an average of 4*l.* 6*s.* 6*d.*

During 1896 all the pools, except that of bar-iron, were broken up. It is believed that this will be of advantage to all connected with the iron industry. The demand for merchant iron has probably been the smallest for many years. Construction of railways, buildings, railway cars, and bridges has

(2318)

Hardware business.

about reached a minimum. In view of the dearth of new enterprises, there is great hesitation on the part of owners of large manufacturing plants to incur the expense of repairs, and equipment of the same.

During the year, the wholesale shelf hardware business has been affected by the general depression prevailing throughout the country, but the break up of the nail pool and the advances in the price of farm products seem to point to an increased trade, and better profits, in the year 1897. Never before have prices been so low, in some instances not reaching the cost of production. The range for the year was 9s. 1d. to 11s. 1¾d.

Stove sales.

The stove business decreased 25 per cent. It is, perhaps, not generally known that Chicago is the largest stove market in the country. Of the 7,216,400l. worth of stoves manufactured, over 30 per cent. are made in this city. There are about 51 houses engaged in the wholesale stove, range, and furnace business, and a proportionately large number of retail houses. Stocks are at present very light.

Agricultural implements.

The business in the Central Western States has been fair, but otherwise poor. There has been a good trade in small tools, and a fair trade in thrashers, engines, and clove hullers. As implements are generally sold on long credit, a depression of a few months is not as effective as it is on other branches of business. Corn harvesters appear to have been of little use this autumn, owing to the fact that corn fields have been very wet at the season when harvesters could be used. There have not been many failures, and as stocks are light the outlook is fairly promising.

The foreign trade was of about the usual proportions, Chicago-made implements going to Australia, South America, Russia, and other European countries. It is noted that the great wheat fields of India have not yet been invaded, the reason given is that farmers of that country do not possess sufficient means to purchase self-binders, but still retain the primitive methods of harvesting their grain that have prevailed for centuries.

Furniture.

The year 1896 was not as good a year as 1895. The sales were about up to the average, but very largely in the cheaper grades. In the better and higher priced grades there was a marked falling-off. On the whole the city has been fairly free from failures, and few manufacturers, or dealers of any size or importance, have gone out of business, either voluntarily or involuntarily. There are some 250 factories in Chicago, employing 25,000 people, and a capital of over 4,123,700l. in the furniture line alone, or about 4,742,000l. in furniture and kindred lines.

Carpets.

The year was only a moderately successful one. Prices have ranged a little lower than in 1895. Almost all the wool used in carpets is imported from Russia and South America, the wool being longer and coarser than the kinds in this country. A certain number of large carpet mills are closed at present, but will open as soon as the demand for goods warrants. Those that are running, are only running on orders. Rugs of nearly all sizes, and many qualities, are now being made in this country, which compare quite favourably with imported ones, they being cheap and servicable.

Copper. Manufacturers of copper goods had a falling-off in demand amounting to fully 25 per cent. The prices ranged from 4½d. in January to 5¾d. at the close of November, when, under the cheering outlook, manufacturers at once ordered from dealers 800,000 lbs. Prices were sustained by reason of shipments to foreign countries, the European market being so active as to cause the supply to run light at the close of the year. Fair average price for the pig for the entire year was about 5¼d. per lb.

Drugs and chemicals. The last two years in the drug trade have been very poor. Prices were very low, particularly in the way of manufacturers' supplies; and staples such as opium and quinine averaged lower.

Glass, crockery, &c. Plate declined fully 25 per cent., and window-glass from 7½ to 10 per cent. Retail dealers bought 50 per cent. less this year. Stocks throughout the country are light, and perhaps never before has the stock of glass in the United States been so low as at present.

Although the prospects for 1897 are considered satisfactory, it is considered necessary by dealers that some legislation in the way of tariff reform be adopted, in some part restoring the reduction made by the Wilson Bill of from 33 to 40 per cent. on glass. The American dealers ask for an increase of about 15 per cent. over present duty, and it is said without this increase the glass business cannot live in competition with Belgian glass. The demand throughout the year was for the cheaper grades of crockery and glassware; the low prices cut down the profits materially. There are prospects for a better demand for high-class goods.

Pianos and organs. The number of pianos and organs sold was larger than that of 1895, but the profits received from them was not as large. The end of the year developed a demand for the better grades of instruments, and the tendency is towards lighter-coloured goods, fully 70 to 80 per cent. of the pianos and organs being of that character. There is also an increased demand for the parlour grand.

Carriages and waggons. Bicycles are chiefly responsible for the distressed condition of the carriage business. The fine trade is not affected to a very great extent, but the heavy wagon business had fallen-off 50 per cent. in volume. During the past year 60 failures have been reported of prominent manufacturers. The feature of the trade is the increase of rubber tyres and ball bearings. Fewer men were employed by the firms, and the wages of those who continued at work were in many instances cut down. This reduction, though, did not result in any trouble between employers and employés, the workmen not having the support of unions.

Bicycles. The bicycle business for the year 1896 was the largest on record, and it is believed that more bicycles will be sold in 1897 than in any year in the past. This city is perhaps the largest bicycle market in the world, and it is computed that 65 per cent. of the bicycle tyres sold in the country are made here by one firm.

The tendency at the present time is towards a cheaper machine, without in any way deteriorating from its usefulness. A number of the larger manufacturers have adopted the policy of replacing the wheels in use this year with the new and improved modern wheels, upon the payment of a very small sum, in addition to the old wheel. There have been a number of failures in the bicycle business, but this was due to the fact that a larger number of manufacturers entered the field than the demand warranted. Prices averaged from 4*l*. 2*s*. 6*d*. to 30*l*. 18*s*. The average-priced bicycles, for which kind there is an enormous demand, cost 5*l*. 12*s*. At the present moment wheels of medium weight, heavy tread tyres, and an equipment that will be productive of comfort whilst riding constitute the public taste.

Boots and shoes.

A falling-off of 25 per cent. in the leather business marked the past year. Oak-tanned leather sold at remarkably low figures. In upper leather the situation was no better.

The average price of packers' hides during the year was $4\frac{1}{4}d.$, and for country $3\frac{1}{4}d.$ Grain leather, the great bulk of which is made in Milwaukee and Sheboygan, Wisconsin, sold at 6*d*. per foot. During the year chrome-tanned upper leather gained rapidly in popularity.

The most pronounced feature of the wholesale shoe trade is the increase of manufacturing. Formerly the large firms were almost exclusively jobbers of New England-made shoes, but in recent years they have become large manufacturers. There are to-day four houses in Chicago that manufacture a total of 1,649,500*l*. worth of shoes a year. It is estimated that, perhaps, three-fifths of the shoes sold by the wholesale firms are goods of local manufacture, and the remaining two-fifths are Eastern goods.

During the year customers bought cash goods in larger volume than previously, and the cash system appears now to be furnishing the needed element of safety, and whilst the abolition of long-time credits has curtailed profits, it has at least diminished the risk of losses by bad debts.

Oil market.

The year in the oil market was uneventful. The most notable increase was in the export business in cotton-oil, due to the failure of the nut crop in Southern Europe. The demand for oil for mixing fell off on account of the low price of lard. Prices for crude oil ranged between $7\frac{1}{2}d.$ and 10*d*., and refined at 9*d*. to $11\frac{1}{2}d.$ at the mill. Carbons sold between $4\frac{1}{4}d.$ and $4\frac{3}{4}d.$, opening at the highest and closing at the lowest for water-white 150 degrees test. The demand for turpentine fell off 20 per cent., and prices were without material alteration.

Paper.

The amount of paper sold was about 5 per cent. less than during 1895, and prices declined from 5 to 10 per cent. The mills had a hard struggle, demand being slow, prices off, and competition fierce. Manufacturers appear to have made but small profits, and many met serious losses.

Clothing trade.

The tariff laws were considered unfavourable to the conduct of the business on a paying scale. Revision, it is claimed, would prevent the flooding of the country with cheap foreign goods, which, rightly or wrongly, it is thought would be the inevitable result of a delayed attempt at tariff legislation. Country dealers have hitherto refrained from stocking up for the spring trade, reserving their purchases for the period at which they will be needed. The wholesale trade of the city fell off fully 15 to 20 per cent., as compared with the business done in 1895. There was little reduction in the price of material, medium domestic goods being the only grade to show a diminution in value.

It is expected that business will continue in 1897 on a conservative, cautious basis, and that a moderately increased tariff on woollens would prove beneficial. It is argued it would encourage the American manufactures of the better class of woollens, and people who insist on having their garments made from foreign fabrics would probably accept the situation, and pay without murmuring the difference in cost.

Tin-plate Business.

Sales of tin-plate were light, and profits small, owing to competition among American manufacturers. This business has made great strides within the last five years, and where the imports of tin-plate largely exceeded the products of the United States, the conditions are materially changing. The production of American tin is on the increase, and many manufacturers look to its being exported to Europe in the near future. The Chicago collections were good, and the losses from bad debts small.

It is not believed that important changes will be made in the existing tariff, nor is it thought by tin-plate manufacturers that any action is necessary, the business being in a healthy condition, and prospects bright.

The production of tin-plate for the fiscal year ending June 30, 1896, was 212,598,181 pounds, while the imports for the same period were 385,139,183 pounds. The imports for 1895 were 436,780,713 pounds, against 534,514,907 pounds in 1894.

The average price of tin-plate ranged from 14*s.* 2½*d.* per 100 lbs. in May to 15*s.* in October. Prices are being maintained, and it is believed that the coming year will show better prices, and more unanimity of action between manufacturers.

Shipping and Freights.

Business on the whole was in reality better than much of the preceding year, and comparatively few vessels were compelled to lay up; while in 1895 a considerable part of the tonnage was forced out of business during the early part of the season, simply because there was nothing to carry. Boats well managed have made a small per cent. of profit, but those out of date have not done so well. Lake transportation charges have gone to a lower level, and the time has apparently passed when

General remarks.

(2318)

vessels can make a third, or a half, they were worth in a single season. The introduction of steel into vessel construction, the approaching completion of the 20-feet channel, and the entrance into the field of the big mining corporations with their own fleets are accountable for this change. Larger size of boats has had much to do with it, but this is the result of the first-named causes, rather than a direct cause itself.

The year witnessed the increase in the draught of water to Lake Superior, which has been placed on an equal plane with Lake Michigan in this respect. Freight rates from Lake Superior at once dropped to correspond with the increase in the size of cargoes.

The season was remarkably free from fog and severe gales. As a result the losses were light. It is stated that the loss of life of seamen has been the smallest for the past 10 years.

The excursion lines from Chicago did a larger business than ever before, and indications are that the increase is permanent.

The following table gives a comparative statement of the entrances and clearances at the six principal American ports during the fiscal year ending June 30, 1896 :—

Ports.	Number of Vessels. Entered.	Number of Vessels. Cleared.	Totals.
Baltimore	1,810	2,683	4,493
Boston	3,019	3,243	6,262
New York	7,174	6,788	13,962
New Orleans	1,212	1,189	2,401
Philadelphia	1,846	2,064	3,910
San Francisco	1,105	1,395	2,500
Totals	16,166	17,362	33,528
Chicago	9,263	9,424	18,687

It will be seen that Chicago has a record of over half of the entire total.

The tonnage entries of the coasting trade for Chicago in 1896 carried by 7,076 steam and sailing vessels was 4,756,307 tons, of which only 603,578 tons were carried by 1,810 sailing vessels.

In the foreign trade 78 steam and sailing vessels carried 30,943 tons. Of these only 13 were steamers, carrying 11,965 of the tonnage.

For South Chicago 805 steamers, and 475 schooners in the coasting trade, carried 1,185,150 and 449,965 tons respectively.

The foreign trade was only represented in South Chicago by five steamers and eight sailing vessels.

The clearances were about the same amount, carried by nearly the same number of steamers and schooners, as regards the coasting trade for both ports. But in the foreign trade 93 steamers and 122 schooners took 83,375 and 133,350 tons respectively from Chicago; while 50 steamers and 34 schooners took 42,021 and 18,264 tons from South Chicago.

The grand total of entrance tonnage was 6,481,115, and of clearance tonnage 6,591,203 tons.

The following table shows the exports by Lake in 1896:—

EXPORTS, by Lake, in 1896.

Commodities.		Quantity.	Value.
			£
Wheat	Bushels	549,500	67,300
Corn	,,	5,276,550	288,500
Oats	,,	575,668	22,800
Rye	,,	42,000	3,100
Steel rails	Tons	21,608	98,500
Angle bars	,,	1,499	7,100
Steel billets	,,	306	800
Wire rods	,,	3,563	13,900
Pig and scrap iron	,,	1,497	3,100
Machinery	Pieces	10	103
Merchandise	Packages	3	1,237
Total			506,440

The following table shows the shipment to Chicago by Lake for the last two years, in grain, &c.:—

Commodities.		Quantity.	
		1896.	1895.
Flour	Barrels	1,006,951	791,620
Wheat	Bushels	13,232,818	13,258,440
Corn	,,	74,379,206	47,857,550
Oats	,,	23,798,409	17,674,345
Rye	,,	971,603	57,000
Barley	,,	5,451,824	5,322,531
Flax seed	,,	3,351,518	1,868,036
Pork	Barrels	38,760	3,377
Lard	Lbs.	53,210,200	12,860,100

The port of South Chicago is rapidly becoming a formidable rival of her older sister, especially in the grain trade.

The value of the imported goods warehoused at the port of Chicago during the year amounted to 1,028,500*l*. The duties on those goods amounted to 669,400*l*.

The amount of drawback on merchandise intended for export with the benefit of such stipulation amounted to 17,200*l*.

The value of imported goods intended for consumption amounted to 2,566,600*l*. The duties thereon amounted to 937,300*l*.

UNITED STATES.

Vessels owned in Chicago.

Exactly 329 vessels, with a total net tonnage of 57,611, are owned in the district of Chicago. Over 257,700*l*. was expended in building new vessels during the last year alone; four vessels were lost on the lakes. Their total value was 3,290*l*., insured for 1,230*l*. Eleven lives were lost.

Chicago Shipbuilding Company and Rockfeller vessels.

During 1896 the Chicago Ship-building Company did a large and satisfactory business, having constructed and sent out from its yards six steel ships of the most modern type. Within the year the company added to its plant machinery and buildings, and all the necessary equipment for the construction of marine engines, and kindred machinery, and has now under contract one of the largest engines of this class on the lakes. The close of the year finds the company with five modern steel ships of the latest types and most improved class under contract. The number of men employed at the yards was about equal to the working force of the year previous, and the value of the ships built a little in excess of the returns for 1895. The modern steel schooners belong to what is known as the 6,000 tons class.

Mr. Rockfeller's Lake fleet of cargo ships are designed to furnish the maximum carrying capacity at the minimum expense. They are 432 feet long, 48 feet beam, 28 feet deep, and drawing 14 feet of water. They can take a cargo of 4,000 tons, which may be increased to 6,000 tons, with a draught of 18 feet, as the Lake canals are deepened to accommodate them; but a draught of 15 feet is the limit at present. They are built for a speed of 12 miles an hour, but can make 15 with a little more coal. They cost 55,600*l*. each. The new ships of the Great Northern Company, the North West, and the Northland, which were built by the Globe Ironworks at Cleveland, cost 154,600*l*. each. They are 386 feet long, measure 5,000 tons, have 7,000 horse-power engines, can make a speed of 21 miles an hour, and are able to carry some 550 passengers.

The cost of constructing a 6,000-ton ship of steel is computed at 56,000*l*.; one of 3,000 tons of the same material at 36,000*l*.; one of 2,000 at 32,900*l*.; and one of 1,000 tons at 20,600*l*.

The Rockfeller vessels carry ore principally, and it is estimated that the fleet will be capable next season of carrying from Lake Superior to Lake Erie and South Chicago as much ore as was produced in the entire region but a few years ago. The Government work in making the 20-feet channel from Chicago, Duluth, and Buffalo has materially aided the plans of corporate capital. By the machinery now in use, a vessel carrying 4,000 tons of ore can be loaded in 8 hours and unloaded in 12.

Strikes and Labour Situation.

The labour situation in Chicago has, on the whole, been fairly free from strikes and other disturbing influences, and although it was a hard one, there have been employed in manufacturing and industrial pursuits in the city something like 152,806 persons in 5,455 establishments. Of this number 2,358 were girls under 16 years of age, and 3,472 boys under 16 years. There are 25,036 females employed, and 121,940 males, together with 5,830 children under 16 years. This list includes those employed in candy factories, groceries, and manufactories of food products, garment workers, leather manufactories, metal workers, paper bags and envelopes, printing offices, wood-working trades. The largest number of males over 16, viz., 48,180, are employed in the metal-working trades; the largest number of females over 16, viz., 13,439, in the manufacture of garments, while the metal-working industry employs the larger number of boys 1,086, and the garment-workers employ 1,334 girls, 16 years of age and upwards.

It is pleasing to note that child labour in the State of Illinois is not only being reduced to a minimum, but, as far as it exists, is being carefully regulated, with a view to guarding the health of the girls and boys under 16 who are compelled by circumstances to seek employment in either factory or workshop.

Child labour

Miss Kelly, as Chief Factory Inspector, in her annual report to Governor Altgeld, gives some interesting statistics. She shows that in the 6,607 factories and workshops inspected, 7,340 children under 16 were found employed in a total of 200,140 employés. In percentage the number of children was 3·7 as against 4·5 in 1895, 6·2 in 1894, and 8·5 in 1893. This decrease is the more marked because the Inspectors covered 2,067 more establishments than in previous years.

It would seem reasonable to believe that the enforcement of the law by prosecution of all violations, and the growing efficiency of the Inspectors in finding workshops, and detecting violations, have contributed largely to reduce the amount of child labour in the manufacturing establishments of Illinois. This view is strengthened by the fact that the fines and costs paid by reason of 656 convictions of violation of child labour sections of the law amounted to 840l. in 1896.

Outside the stockyards and the sweating-shops the standard of size and health of the children employed improves. The change in this respect is conspicuous when comparison is made with the children employed in laundries and department stores, where the minimum age is not yet prescribed by law. There is no decrease in the number of children in the stockyards. On the contrary, the number of girls, 5, remains unchanged, and the boys are 242 in 1896, an increase of 5 over 1895. There is no improvement in the conditions under which these children work, nor has any officer of the State power to prescribe or require any improvement.

The conditions under which the children work in the sweating-shops are, unfortunately, incomparably worse than other departments.

The educational status of the children found at work shows no improvement. From garment and cigar shops children are still taken into court as witnesses in factory cases who speak no English, some of them having lived several years in the State in foreign colonies, going to school, if at all, where English is not taught.

Railroads.

Railroad building in 1896 was insignificant compared to that of most years in the last decade, but was about the same as in 1895. Altogether 163 lines in the States and territories laid 1,802·39 miles of track. The total railway mileage of the United States is now about 182,800 miles.

The following figures show the mileages of new tracks laid down during the past ten years, and are interesting for comparison sake:—

Year.	Mileage of Tracks Laid Down.
1887	12,983
1888	7,106
1889	5,230
1890	5,670
1891	4,281
1892	4,192
1893	2,635
1894	1,949
1895	1,803
1896	1,802

From the above figures it will be seen that for 10 years the railway builder has travelled a steadily descending road of activity from 13,000 down to 1,800 miles.

The year 1896 has been one of disappointment and losses in all lines of business, and as the railroads can hardly prosper when other interests suffer, they have painfully reflected the general depression. Compared, though, with either 1894, 1893, or 1892, the year just closed has not been altogether unfavourable.

It is estimated that 34 railroads, with 5,441 miles of line, and a bond and stock capitalisation of about 56,824,700l. joined the list of railways operated by receivers.

The most important failure of the year was that of the Baltimore and Ohio, with 2,094 miles of road, and over 25,567,000l. of bonds and stocks, besides heavy floating debt and arrears of interest. The bankruptcy of this old and formerly profitable company was discouraging evidence of the effects of unlimited competition.

The other notable failures include the Louisville, New Albany, and Chicago, 501 miles, and 5,927,800l.; the six railroads forming the Vandalia system, aggregating nearly 600 miles, and 4,948,400l. of bonds and stock; the Pittsburg and Western, involved in the embarrassment of the Baltimore and Ohio, 352 miles, and 3,814,400l.; and two Eastern railroads, the Central Vermont and Ogdensburg, and Lake Champlain, covering 778 miles of road, and nearly 3,505,100l. of investment.

The two prominent features that have attracted attention

during the year were the putting into effect on January 1 of the joint traffic agreement governing the Eastern lines, and the strength shown by the Gulf ports in getting traffic away from the old established lines leading to the North Atlantic ports, and at present it looks very much as if the export of grain would, to a large extent, be viâ the Gulf of Mexico, New Orleans, and Galveston, the two Gulf ports having shown large gains in their export grain business.

Most of the Western railroads, especially those that have been recently reorganised, have been spending a large amount of money in improvements, and in time these improvements will, no doubt, permit greater economies.

The most important railway construction that has taken place in the West during the year has been the extension of the Kansas City, Pittsburg, and Gulf Railroad, which company, in extending its road, and building connecting links, has constructed 219 miles of track.

In the State of Illinois only 58½ miles of track were built. The States where the greatest amount of construction was done were California, Louisiana, and Michigan.

For the locomotive and car builders the past year has not been a very fortunate one. The actual number of engines built during the period was 1,175, which exceeds by 74 locomotives the output of 1895, and is 74 more than the output of 1894. All the railroads have done a good deal in the way of rebuilding.

An interesting feature of locomotive building in this country during the year has been the growing importance of export orders. Two years ago the number of engines built for export was only 80, while in the past year the number increased to 309.

The passenger situation at the close of the year can be summed up briefly by saying that there was a fair amount of passenger traffic between the cities of the West, and considerable excursion travel to California. The holiday travelling was disappointing, falling far short of the year 1895.

It can be said that the Western railways have of late made considerable headway in getting together and harmonising their differences in the question of rates.

There was a large increase in the number of foreclosures in the last year, when it is computed that no less than 58 railroads were sold for their creditors, representing 13,730 miles of lines, and the enormous capitalisation of over 237,134,000*l*. Many great companies have helped to swell this list of foreclosure sales, which, in respect to number of railroads, has only been equalled in one previous year, while in mileage and capital involved, it far exceeds any other year in the history of railways.

Finally, it is believed that the year 1897 will see a clearing-up of most of the wreckage of this long period of financial disaster, and that better times are coming in the near future.

DENVER.

Mr. Vice-Consul Pearce reports as follows:—

The commercial aspect of the State of Colorado, and the city of Denver, has changed but little since my report for 1895.

Value of new buildings. The total number of building permits granted during the year was 526, and the value of the buildings erected 223,440*l*., showing a decrease of 3,582*l*. from 1895. Building operations were limited to the residential part of the city, and a great many substantial houses were constructed.

Real estate. The transactions in real estate for the year were 1,469,841*l*., showing a falling-off of 966,259*l*. as compared with 1895.

Clearing house record. The record of the Bank clearing-house of Denver for 1896 was 24,273,600*l*., a decrease from 1895 of 3,494,792*l*.

Banks. At the close of the year there were but four national banks doing business in Denver. The following is a summary of the condition of these banks at the close of the year's business:—

	Amount.
	£
Resources	4,327,755
Loans and discounts	2,013,255
Deposits	3,555,899

As compared with 1895 this shows a decrease as follows:—

	Amount.
	£
Resources	492,723
Loans and discounts	438,073
Deposits	361,323

Custom-house. The receipts at the custom-house for duties on the various classes of goods imported into Denver during the year were 11,811*l*., an increase of 2,703*l*. over 1895. One-fourth of the amount collected represents the tax on silver-lead ores imported from Mexico and British Columbia.

Internal revenue. An internal revenue tax of 1 dol. per barrel is levied on beer, 3 dol. per 1,000 on cigars, and 6 c. per 1 lb. on tobacco, and 81,115*l*. was collected from this source during the year, which is a considerable gain over 1895.

Post-office. The total receipts at the Denver post-office for the year were 75,974*l*.

Manufacturing. The value of the products of the manufacturing industry for the year shows a small increase over that of 1895. This is attributed principally to the increased demand for mining machinery, caused by the great activity in mining throughout the State. 75 per cent. of the mining machinery used in the State is manufactured in Denver and other districts in Colorado.

Manufacturers are turning their attention to Denver as a convenient centre for the manufacture of various supplies. During the year the Griffin Car Wheel Company has inaugurated a large branch establishment for the manufacture of car wheels, and it is reported that already 20,579 car wheels have been turned out of their Denver works, the approximate value being 28,000*l*. This new industry furnishes employment to about 70 men, the total wages paid during the year being about 7,000*l*.

The Overland Cotton Mills, a comparatively new industry in Denver, produced during the year 8,471,834 yards of cotton goods, a gain of 358,110 yards over the previous year. The value of the product was 76,000*l*. The mills keep 484 looms in steady operation, and employ 250 hands. About 18,000*l*. was paid out in wages during the year. The material manufactured at these mills finds a ready sale throughout the Western States and in British Columbia.

The Denver Paper Mills product for the year is valued at 60,000*l*. This industry gives steady employment to about 140 people of both sexes.

The following is a summary of the manufacturing industry, including the product of the smelting companies, for the years 1895 and 1896:—

	1895.	1896.
Number of men employed	12,866	13,103
	£	£
Amount of wages paid	1,201,263	1,305,140
Value of product	8,059,472	8,113,400

The total assessed valuation of taxable property in Colorado for the year was 41,313,712*l*., an increase of about 1,000,000*l*. over 1895. {Value of taxable property.}

Grazing and coal lands and cattle show an increased valuation, while agricultural land, horses, &c., show a decrease.

The records of the office of the Secretary of State show that 1,690 mining and other companies have been registered during the year, representing an aggregate capitalization of 260,000,000*l*. Of these 90 per cent. are mining incorporations. These figures indicate that the mining excitement, referred to in my last report, is still in a very active condition. {New companies.}

Farming, or in fact all forms of agriculture in Colorado, can only be carried on successfully with the aid of irrigation, and several large irrigation companies exist for the purpose of furnishing water to farmers and fruit growers at a small cost. These companies have about 12,000 miles of canals and ditches, which, under favourable conditions, are capable of supplying water sufficient to irrigate approximately 4,000,000 acres of land. At the present time, however, only about one-half of this is under actual cultivation. {Agriculture.}

UNITED STATES.

The estimated value of the agricultural produce for the year is as follows:—

Articles.	Value.
	£
Wheat	500,000
Alfalfa	900,000
Clover and timothy	180,000
Native grass	380,000
Corn, oats, barley, and other grains	1,000,000
Potatoes	280,000
Garden produce	890,000
Dairy and poultry	370,000
Total	4,500,000

This shows an increase of 428,700*l.* over 1895.

Fruit. Colorado is rapidly advancing in importance as a fruit-growing State. 15 years ago the growth of fruit was comparatively insignificant, and was confined to two districts, viz., Fremont and Jefferson counties. It has been found, however, that other districts, such as Montrose, Delta, Mesa, and Garfield counties, on the western slope, possess all the necessary conditions, as regards climate and soil, for the growth of fruit of all kinds.

The present area devoted to fruit-growing may be roughly estimated at 75,000 acres, an increase over the previous year of 8,000 acres. The value of the entire fruit product of the State is estimated at 581,112*l.*, showing an increase over 1895 of 40,380*l.*

Excellent qualities of apples, peaches, pears, cherries, grapes, apricots, nectarines, and all small fruits are grown in abundance in 17 counties in the State.

This industry has become a very important source of revenue, and it may be conducted with comparative safety, as irrigation and the favourable condition of the climate make crop failures a rare occurrence.

It is estimated that there are 800,000 acres of land in Colorado adapted to fruit-growing.

Live-stock. The State board of cattle inspection estimates the total number and value of live-stock in the State as follows:—

	Number.	Value.
		£
Cattle	650,000	2,700,000
Horses	200,000	1,000,000
Sheep	750,000	400,000
Hogs	40,000	24,000
Mules	20,000	40,000
Total	1,660,000	4,164,000

This shows a decrease in value of 36,000*l.* from 1895.

There are 25 lines of railway in Colorado, with a total mileage of 4,770. No new railroad construction during the year is reported, and the business done has not been as satisfactory as in previous years. *Railroads.*

The total assessed valuation of railroads in Colorado for the year 1896 is 6,251,501*l.*, which is 101,134*l.* more than in 1895.

Denver's cable and electric street railway system has the reputation of being one of the finest in the country for the size of the city. There are 159 miles of track, and for one fare of 5 c. all parts of the city and suburbs can be reached. Of the trackage 30 miles is cable and the rest electric. There are 206 cars in use, 812 men are employed, and the wages paid for the year were 146,120*l.* *Street railways.*

The following table shows the production and value of the iron and steel industry of the State for the year :— *Iron and steel.*

Articles.	Quantity.	Value.
	Lbs.	£
Pig-iron	90,032,905	144,051
Spiegel	11,001,630	27,525
Steel rails	87,616,937	271,923
Merchant-iron	31,674,891	126,659
Castings	6,897,698	27,591
Cast-iron pipe	2,949,086	8,845
Spikes	3,624,160	14,496
Angle bars	1,477,777	5,292
Iron ore	175,217,800	70,125
Total	..	696,507

This shows a falling-off in value from 1895 of 122,186*l.*

This statement is furnished by the Colorado Fuel and Iron Co., the only company engaged in this business in the State.

During the year considerable manganese iron ore was sent from the Leadville district to Chicago, and contracts have been made in the past three months for further supplies during the coming year.

The coal production of the State for 1896 did not vary from that of the previous year to any great extent; an increase of but 32,138 tons is shown. *Coal and coke.*

(2318)

TABLE showing Output of Coal by Counties for 1895 and 1896

Counties.	Quantity.	
	1895.	1896.
	Tons of 2,000 lbs.	Tons of 2,000 lbs.
Arapahoe	540	398
Boulder	432,333	504,947
Dolores	2,500	2,100
El Paso	49,938	32,016
Fremont	383,441	282,459
Gunnison	234,839	269,875
Garfield	221,549	227,280
Huerfano	415,597	365,648
Jefferson	38,460	18,105
Las Animas	1,213,898	1,331,115
La Plata	103,807	99,116
Montezuma	2,000	..
Mesa	19,236	20,457
Park	41,881	33,887
Pitkin	123,928	162,071
Weld	55,548	22,159
Total	3,339,495	3,371,633

TABLE showing Coke Production for the Years 1895 and 1896.

Counties.	Quantity.	
	1895.	1896.
	Tons of 2,000 lbs.	Tons of 2,000 lbs.
Gunnison	39,793	50,440
Las Animas	190,459	195,091
La Plata	1,900	2,851
Pitkin	65,617	76,312
Total	297,769	324,694

Stone. The value of the output from the stone quarries of the State for the year is estimated at 100,000*l*. The quarries supply a large part of the west with marble of all colours, granite of the best quality, and sandstone of all textures and colours.

Oil. The total product of the oil-fields of the State for the year was 500,000 barrels, valued at 100,000*l*. 25,000*l*. was paid out in wages in this industry.

TABLE showing the Value of the Output of the Mines in Colorado Mining. for the Year 1896.

Articles.	Value.
	£
Gold	2,600,000
Silver	2,680,000
Lead	443,744
Copper	213,400
Total	5,937,144

This shows a total decrease of 694,656*l.* as compared with last year, and is accounted for by the prolonged strike in Leadville (referred to below) and some slight interruption in the yield of one of the principal mines at Cripple Creek.

The average price of silver for the year was 67 c. per ounce, as against 65$\frac{2}{10}$ c. in 1895.

There has been no fresh discovery of any new district of importance, either for gold or silver, during the past year.

The Cripple Creek district, which has produced so much excitement during the last two years, continues to be prosperous, the further developments of its principal mines indicating beyond a doubt that the future of the district is assured as a gold producer.

It is difficult to procure at this time any reliable data in regard to the value of the Cripple Creek gold product for last year; it has been estimated at 2,000,000*l.*, but in all probability this is too high, 1,600,000*l.* being perhaps nearer the mark. In all the reports which are furnished to the public at the end of the year, mainly through the local newspapers, there is a tendency to exaggeration, and in giving these figures it must be understood that they are only approximately correct.

It is estimated that the Cripple Creek district produces 700 tons of ore per day. A small portion of this is treated by local mills, the larger portion going to the smelters at Denver and Pueblo and the cyanide and chlorination works of Florence and Colorado City.

The other mining districts in the State have been fairly prosperous during the year, except the most important ore-producing district at Leadville, which for the greater part of the year has suffered from a strike of the miners. Colorado has been comparatively free from labour troubles until last year, when an attempt was made by the members of the miners' union to force wages to a higher point, viz., from 2 dol. 50 c. to 3 dol. per day. The latter price ruled in Leadville before the heavy fall in the price of silver in 1893. An agreement was made at that time between the mine-owners and miners that, in view of the serious decline in the price of silver, the miners would be satisfied to accept 2 dol. 50 c. per day, as long as silver remained below 85 c. per ounce, and this price has not been realised up to the

(2318)

present time. The mine-owners showing no inclination whatever to accede to the demands of the miners, the result was that a general strike was declared on June 19, 1896. The proprietors, finding that all efforts towards a satisfactory settlement were of no avail, arranged to procure miners from Eastern points, mainly from the zinc and lead mines of Missouri. The arrival of these new men was the signal for a general outbreak; rioting and general disorder prevailed for a short time, and the State militia had to be summoned to protect property and the lives of the men who filled the places of the strikers.

Several of the mines have now resumed work under the protection of a small body of troops.

An attempt has been made by the new Governor of the State to bring about a reconciliation between the mine-owners and miners, but after an exchange of various propositions, no adjustment of the trouble has been accomplished.

Health.

The records of the health bureau of Denver show the mortality to be the lowest in 10 years, being 10·18 per 1,000 in a population estimated at 150,000.

The highest death-rate reached in the 10 years was in 1890, when it was 23·71 per 1,000.

STATEMENT of Values of Imports from Great Britain entered at the Port of Denver during the Year 1896.

Articles.	Value.
	£ s.
Gutta-percha and celluloid	79 0
Iron and steel	313 12
Manufactures of metal, jewellery, &c.	448 12
,, wood	34 16
,, glass	46 0
,, earthenware	123 0
,, leather	110 12
,, cotton, flax, hemp	243 8
,, wool	937 4
,, paper, including books	59 16
,, tobacco	65 16
Spirits	674 16
Wines	1,512 16
Ale and stout	260 0
Tin and terne-plates	1,528 0
Tea	191 16
Effects (personal)	170 4
Church regalia	23 4
Toys	75 12
Paintings	17 8
Gelatine	184 16
Olive oil	23 8
Chemicals	64 0
Rugs	156 8
Chamois skins	12 12
Manufacture of bone	8 12
White lead	0 12
Lye of wood ashes	0 4
Manufacture of horn	0 8
Total	7,366 12

CHICAGO.

RECORD of Imports from Great Britain for the past 10 Years.

Year.	Value.
	£ s.
1887	5,053 12
1888	8,109 12
1889	17,585 7
1890	32,512 4
1891	26,008 16
1892	9,357 4
1893	6,603 16
1894	4,984 4
1895	6,481 4
1896	7,366 12

During the year a large quantity of silver-lead ore has been received by the Colorado smelting companies from British Columbia, the value of which is given, on the authority of the custom-house officials here, at 26,300*l.*, and the indications are that for the year 1897 the importation of this material will be largely increased.

KANSAS CITY.

Mr. Vice-Consul Burrough reports as follows :—

The Consolidated Kansas City Smelting and Refining Company Smelting. smelted during 1896 one-third of the silver product of the United States, one-fourth of the lead, and 10 per cent. of the gold product. The following comparison of the Company's output of refined metals for the last three years is given :—

Year.	Gold.	Silver.	Lead.	Copper.
	Ounces.	Ounces.	Tons.	Lbs.
1894	93,438·71	9,498,366·00	28,871	2,031,294
1895	133,162·90	11,243,490·00	33,385	3,392,500
1896	198,348·14	15,099,748·00	41,206	4,438,700
	£	£	£	£
Cash value	816,246	2,019,510	466,255	89,077
Total cash value	£3,391,088			

The "Engineering and Mining Journal" reports that the lead Lead. business in this country in 1896 showed a remarkable degree of activity. The production from domestic ores was large, amounting in all to 175,717 tons, of which 137,478 tons were desilverised lead, 33,803 tons were soft lead, chiefly from the Missouri and Kansas district, and 4,912 tons were hard or antimonial lead. The domestic consumption showed an increase; as estimated it amounted to 206,102 tons, or less by 26,052 tons than in 1895. There was, however, a very large increase in exports, the total reported being 52,590 tons, as against 18,130 tons in 1895.

(2318)

UNITED STATES.

Aluminium.

Aluminium goods are fast spreading in this country, and it looks as though we shall see many new uses made of it at an early date. The output of this article for the past three years is as follows:—

Year.	Quantity.
	Lbs.
1894	550,000
1895	920,000
1896	1,400,000

Experiments are being made to substitute knives, forks, spoons, canteens, and seaboard cups for use in the United States Army, in place of articles made of other material; ovens, frying pans, kettles, and cooking utensils are also being made and tested.

Results are satisfactory from tests made with bits, spurs, rings, buckles, saddle-trees, stirrups, horseshoes, and other articles in army use.

Wholesale trade.

The wholesale trade for Kansas City for 1896 was larger than for 1895, on account of new country to the west being opened up so fast, and which will continue, without a doubt. The following is a list of goods sold by wholesale:—

Articles.	Value.
	£
Binding twine	1,065,047
Agricultural implements	3,372,285
Groceries	3,107,061
Dry goods	6,007,901
Coal	1,209,229
Lumber	1,212,980
Fruits	1,119,787
Drugs	401,929
Hardware	692,710
Tobacco	495,922
Jewellery	437,101
Tea, coffee, spices	387,007
Boots and shoes	407,219
Harness, saddlery	281,009
Hats, caps, gloves	304,060
Notions	191,069
Miscellaneous	1,923,672
Total	22,615,988

Labour and wages.

Wages in this city decreased about 4 per cent. during 1896. This includes all kinds of work, with but few exceptions. All kinds of labour are being formed into unions, and yet wages decrease. There have been only a few small strikes during 1896, and in nearly all instances with loss to the striker.

Bank clearings.

Bank clearings for Kansas City for the past four years are as follows:—

Year.	Amount.
	£
1893	97,870,675
1894	99,910,580
1895	107,617,899
1896	103,991,871

The decrease for 1896 is owing to the depreciation of the value of goods in general, and not to the amount of goods sold. One bank failed here, November 30, 1896, the Missouri National Bank, capital stock, 50,000*l*.

Land frauds. During 1896 a few young men came to the west under false pretences, through unreliable employment agencies in London, who obtained from them sums ranging from 30*l*. to 50*l*. to place them upon ranches and learn stock farming. Upon arrival here they were put upon small farms and deserted. In some cases they are not provided with work, but are left to the mercy of strangers, and being in a foreign land they would naturally appeal to the Vice-Consul for advice.

Such agencies do exist in London, and at present are sending cadets to Oklahoma and Indian Territory, and into North and South Dakota. This is done because so many complaints have been made from this Vice-Consulate, and cases investigated by the authorities, they (the agencies) have been compelled to seek other fields less settled than Kansas. Stringent measures should be taken, and persons who are connected with this practice of fraud should be punished.

Australian meat. The introduction and the outlook for the Australian meat and meat products in Great Britain and Europe is causing no small alarm among the packers in the west. They are beginning to realise that they have a strong competitor in Australia, and on account of lower prices the United States packers lost valuable orders in 1896.

Binding twine. Millions of pounds of binding twine are contracted for annually, and the British merchants do not enjoy a share of the trade; in my last report I mentioned it, and the Canadian merchants took advantage of the situation and sold large quantities here and throughout the West, and contemplate a larger trade this year, for a much larger amount will be required, as the average of wheat sown is larger than ever before.

Emigration. Do not emigrate to the West is my advice; no encouragement can be given you; the country is badly overdone with labouring classes.

Immigration from Great Britain still continues to come West, and settling mostly in Kansas and Missouri; they do not seem to go to Nebraska or States north of it. In the locality of coal, lead, and zinc mines can be found a great many. A great many American families are leaving here for British Columbia; those who have emigrated before write back very encouragingly.

Animal products. A large trade is done here in hides, horns hair hoof bones, tallow, bristles, stearine, and fertilizer; much of it is exported. The first shipment of black hoofs was made in 1896, direct to Genoa, Italy. Importers of articles mentioned might do well to look into these; the quantities can hardly be estimated when a person bears in mind that in 1896 the packers killed as follows:—

	Number.
Cattle	894,537
Calves	58,331
Hogs..	2,226,143
Sheep	685,727

It must be understood that while some of the localities show an increase of business and wonderful activity, yet as a whole, the financial and commercial state of business is in a most deplorable condition. Commercial failures were larger for 1896 than the year previous. A large number of bank failures occurred, National, State, and private, which is always a serious loss to depositors.

Carpets. The carpets arriving here from Great Britain are giving universal satisfaction, and are finding ready and profitable sale. The same can be said of mattings, oilcloths, and linoleums; they are so much more substantial than any other make, and patterns more tasty and satisfactory.

Matting. Several shipments of matting have arrived direct from Japan, and they are making a great effort to shut out all competitors.

Firearms. In 1896 several large shipments of firearms were received here from England; the dealers handling them were well pleased, and contemplate an increasing trade in these goods.

Seeds. Great Britain and Holland are both enjoying trade in this Western country in many garden and field seeds; from inquiry made the trade is steadily increasing, and bids fair for a bright future in this line of commerce.

Glassware. The bulk of glassware imported comes from Bohemia, and gives satisfaction. No other country seems to be anxious to secure a share of this trade, and this is a good field for same.

Tea. A considerable amount of tea arrives here from Japan; most of it comes viâ the Pacific Coast, and part of it viâ Vancouver; the Japanese tea trade is increasing rapidly in this section of country.

Tin-plate. Receipts of tin-plate at Kansas City for the past four years are as follows:—

Year.	Quantity.
	Lbs.
1893	4,127,065
1894	4,823,919
1895	6,774,851
1896	480,927

The production of tin-plate in this country is increasing, and bids fair to become an important competitor. American plate is to-day worth 14s. 2d. per box delivered Kansas City. Welsh tin is worth 18s. 1d., including duties, which is $1\frac{1}{5}$ c. per lb. Bear in mind that all British tin is used in re-exportation, and duty is paid back to the consumer; this being the case, the British tin only costs the consumer 12s. 10d. per box. The majority of imported tin is used by the packing houses for tinning goods for foreign order.

The oatmeal industry is increasing, and it is very fast becoming a more pronounced healthful food by all classes; export trade in this article is also getting larger.

During the past year large amounts of furs were received from Great Britain.

Earthenware. The crockery earthenware trade is increasing fast, all of it coming in bond to Kansas City. The amount from England was far below last year, but the amount from Germany has increased 300 per cent. The British merchants must be careful or the Germans will capture all the earthenware trade in this Western country. This same state of affairs exists in St. Joseph, Omaha, and all over the West.

Land investments. Persons contemplating investing in this country should well consider same before investing; various States have alien laws, and some of the States are now considering new laws, which, if passed, will be very detrimental to investments; in other words, there are no absolutely safe investments in this Western country under the present conditions, and I do not recommend same.

Portland cement. The British Portland cement is fast losing ground in this western country, on account of being badly adulterated. The German Portland cement is rapidly gaining ground here, and is used and liked very much by the contractors.

State of health. The general health of this Western country is very good; there has been one epidemic, and that was diphtheria, but it was mild in its form.

German competition with British trade. During the past year many goods of German make are finding their way to the West, and taking the place of British goods. Among the goods noticed are: chemicals, quinine, ammonia, caustic soda, crockery, earthenware, plate-glass, Fuller's earth, Portland cement, cutlery, needles, musical instruments, surgical instruments, paints, oils, lithographs, brac-a-brac, paintings, and Christmas toys; everything, as near as can be, is marked "Germany" or "made in Germany."

It is a well-known fact that German exporters have been striving for the past year to push their goods into this country, and certainly have met with some success. It cannot be said that the German goods, as a class, are as good as British make, but they are striving to get a foothold with their wares, which, if followed with perseverance, must result in their obtaining some trade.

German cotton prints are noticeable among the large houses, but so far they are not pleased with them, as the patterns do not suit the trade as do British patterns.

UNITED STATES.

German trade methods.

The question now confronts us: How does Germany push her trade in this country? It is on account of several reasons namely:—

1. They send commercial travellers through the country to see what others are doing, examine closely the prices and grades.
2. They select the largest dealers, and make prices that will secure the orders, placing upon the market an inferior grade or an adulterated article at a lower price, at the same time claiming for them the best quality.
3. They keep their customers well posted as to prices, furnishing the most complete catalogue, all printed in English language.
4. The German Government has 19 Consuls in the United States, as compared with 8 Consuls for Great Britain, and the German exporters use their consuls for the furtherance of their trade in every way conceivable; owing to the large number of consuls, they can cover the ground more thoroughly, and keep their Government closer in touch with the general trade.
5. They have been shipping their goods to the west, viâ the Gulf of Mexico ports, and thus obtaining cheaper rates of transportation than could be secured viâ the the Atlantic coast points.

The following are a few suggestions to the British exporters, which might be of some benefit.

Suggestions to British traders.

1. Don't be afraid to ask your Consular officer for information.
2. Send them your catalogues, so that they can be used, should occasion require it.
3. The Chambers of Commerce should send their business directory to the Consular officers; it is often needed.
4. Bear in mind that during the past 15 years the trade and population of the United States has moved West, and the wholesale trade can be as easily transacted as in the East; one-third of the population of this country now lives in the Mississippi Valley, and west of it. Banking facilities in this Western country are adequate.
5. Rates on transportation of goods from Great Britain to cities on the Mississsippi river and west can be secured much cheaper viâ the Gulf of Mexico ports than viâ Atlantic Coast ports, and should be well considered.
6. A good opportunity will be given to the exporters who desire to push their goods at the Trans-Mississippi and International Exposition at Omaha, Nebraska in 1898.

Woollens.

Experts estimate that the sale of British woollen goods has increased over 200 per cent. in the past three years in the West. Some German goods are also creeping in at present.

Agricultural implements.

This city still remains the largest agricultural implement market in the world; foreign trade is getting larger and more satisfactory; the trade for 1896 was about the same as 1895, no material change taking place. This is also the largest hay press market in the world.

From table below it can be seen that the oils of Wyoming possess nearly double the heating capacity of the coal. In the use of oil for steaming purposes the chief advantages are ease with which firing can be controlled (simply turning a valve will adjust the heat to the desired degree), economy of storage room, freedom from dirt and refuse from firing.

In several of the States in the West immense wells of oil are full, but as yet not developed.

The use of oil in iron manufacture is increasing rapidly. In the Ohio iron manufactories oil is considered cheaper at 1d. per gallon than coal at 8s. per ton for heating furnaces in making bolts, spikes, chain, and other small work.

Wyoming Petroleum and Asphalt.

Rank.	Location.	Mine.	Calories per Gram.	Foot-pounds per 1 lb. Oil.	Lbs., Water at 212° F. evaporated by 1 lb. Oil.
1. Petroleum	...	Bonanza	10,927	...	...
2. Petroleum*	Shoshone Reservation	...	10,883	15,204,000	22·24
3. Petroleum*	Salt Creek, Natrona Co.	...	10,813	15,106,000	20·11
4. Petroleum*	Oil Mountain, Natrona Co.	...	10,743	...	...
5. Petroleum*	Newcastle, Weston Co.	...	10,447	14,595,000	19·43
6. Petroleum*	Little Popo-Agie, Fremont Co.	Murphy Wells	10,430	14,571,000	19·40
7. Asphalt	...	...	9,532	...	...
8. Asphalt*	Wallace Creek, west of Garfield Park	...	6,307	...	...

* Collected by Prof. Knight.

Kansas City, Pittsburg, and Gulf Railroad. The construction work on the Kansas City, Pittsburg, and Gulf Railroad has been pushed steadily throughout the year. At the beginning of 1896, of a total length of 767 miles, 318 miles were in operation, at the close, 520 miles, and including the track not under operation, a total of 260 miles was laid during the year.

Port Arthur. This season has demonstrated irrefutably the necessity for Port Arthur, as the harbour facilities at Galveston and New Orleans have shown themselves to be quite inadequate for the traffic; roads leading into both points have been more or less blocked by the corn movement during the last four or five months.

Freights from New Orleans, Port Arthur, or Galveston to the Western States. A matter that it might be well for English importers not to overlook is the fact that the north and south railroads of the West are at times embarrassed to provide freight north bound with which to fill the empty cars which have been hauled south loaded with grain, and if English importers doing business in the northern part of the United States would look more fully into the matter, it is not to be doubted that they would be able to have their goods delivered at much cheaper freight rates if they were shipped by way of New Orleans, Port Arthur, or Galveston, than by way of New York, or any of the Eastern or Southern Atlantic ports.

UNITED STATES.

The time required for transportation by water from Liverpool or Manchester to these ports would be perhaps a few days longer, but that would be easily balanced by the difference in transportation charges.

The short line rail distances from Kansas City to the various Gulf ports, South Atlantic, and Atlantic ports are as follows:—

	Miles.
Baltimore, Md.	1,198
Boston, Mass.	1,468
Brunswick, Ga.	1,165
Charleston, S.C.	1,194
Galveston, Texas	799
Mobile, Ala.	871
New Orleans, La.	878
Newport News, Va.	1,208
New York, N.Y.	1,303
Philadelphia, Pa.	1,228
Pensacola, Fla.	993
Port Arthur, Texas	767
Port Royal, S.C.	1,104
Savannah, Ga.	1,159
Tampa, Fla.	1,035

Corn crops. The corn crop of Kansas in 1896 was 239,781,000 bushels; of Nebraska, 296,224,000 bushels; of Iowa, 310,986,000 bushels; and of Missouri, 172,186,000 bushels. The surplus of each State was large enough to supply the entire export demand, and have a few hundred thousand bushels left for inland consumption.

Wheat crops. The wheat crop in this territory in 1896 was below the average, but in an average year the surplus is equal to the entire exports of the United States. In 1892 Kansas alone shipped out of the state as wheat, 55,000,000 bushels, to say nothing of that shipped as flour from the mills.

Exports. While there was a falling-off in the shipments of canned beef in 1896, New Orleans had 1,078,456 lbs., as compared with 221,627 lbs. the previous year. There was a gain of salted beef of 20,378,965 lbs., of which 386,107 lbs. went from New Orleans. Total exports of tallow, 1895, 23,581,908 lbs.; and 1896, 84,327,980 lbs. New Orleans, 1895, 393,034 lbs.; and 1896, 4,451,715 lbs, showing the greatest percentage of increase of any American ports. Bacon and ham both show a market increase through New Orleans. Lard, total exported in 1895, 501,880,718 lbs.; and 1896, 486,723,804 lbs.; lard through New Orleans in 1895, 817,056 lbs.; and in 1896, 25,853,745 lbs. Oleo oil through New Orleans, 1895, 918,773 lbs.; 1896, 4,674,014 lbs., ending December 31, 1896.

The comptroller of Texas compiled returns in December of 1896, showing in the State 5,042,538 cattle, 1,804,875 hogs, 2,140,498 sheep, and 1,544,336 horses; a gain over 1895 of 168,685 cattle, 309,858 hogs, and 43,213 horses, and a decrease of 245,932 sheep.

The trade in mules is beginning to attract the attention of foreign governments for use in tropical countries; it has been proved that they will endure more and live much hardier and longer than horses. The Spanish Government has bought in Kansas City large numbers of mules in 1896; all were shipped to Cuba.

The sheep-rearing industry is assuming wonderful proportions; every market shows a very great increase of receipts, and bids fair to continue. There is an opportunity for the British breeders to dispose of their blooded sheep for breeding purposes if they will direct their attention to that end.

Sheep rearing.

With the increase of sheep, of course, will follow the increase of clipped wool, which was very large for 1896 ; the bulk of the wool is exported.

Kansas in area is about equal to Great Britain; it is 408 miles long and 208 miles wide. Kansas, like its twin sister, Nebraska, is a prairie State. Farm products reach the value of 28,000,000*l.*; the average yearly corn crop of 1877–78–79 was 88,000,000 bushels, which rose in 1884 to 191,000,000 bushels; in 1896 the corn crop was 239,781,000 bushels. The enormous amount of farm products in 1896 is shown in the following table:—

Articles.		Quantity.
Winter wheat	Bushels	27,153,365
Corn	,,	239,781,000
Oats	,,	19,314,772
Rye	,,	998,897
Barley	,,	1,169,539
Irish potatoes	,,	7,778,097
Sweet potatoes	,,	292,784
Sorghum	Gallons	1,415,820
Caston beans	Bushels	34,701
Cotton	Lbs.	44,950
Flax	Bushels	1,581,397
Hemp	,,	42,224
Tobacco	Lbs.	169,400
Broom corn	,,	16,580,000
Millet and Hungarian	Tons	691,197
Milo maize	,,	33,698
Kaffir corn	,,	1,323,172
Jerusalem corn	,,	27,599
Timothy hay	,,	2,100,700
Clover	,,	723,000
Blue grass	,,	1,217,000
Alfalfa	,,	571,067
Prairie grass, fenced	,,	1,592,447
Wool clip	Lbs.	793,936
Cheese	,,	1,141,869
Butter	,,	35,007,334
Wine, manufactured	Gallons	115,825
Honey and beeswax	Lbs.	321,692

UNITED STATES.

Kansas produced live-stock as follows :—

	Head.
Horses	846,841
Mules and asses	93,448
Milch cows	515,075
Other cattle	1,305,307
Sheep	182,236
Swine	1,833,091
Total	4,775,998

The total yield of winter wheat in Kansas was 27,153,365 bushels, or 11,641,124 bushels more than 1895, value 3,000,000*l.*, the average per acre being 8½ bushels.

The corn crop is 221,419,414 bushels, or 19,962,018 bushels more than last year, the average being 28·03 bushels per acre; value 7,141,000*l.*, as against 9,147,623*l.* for last year's crop.

The yield of oats is 19,314,772 bushels, against 31,664,748 bushels for 1895; the yield was 13·06 bushels per acre, and the value of the crop 562,074*l.* Spring wheat shows a yield of but 601,523 bushels in 1896.

The combined value of winter and spring wheat, corn, and oats raised in 1896 is 10,723,047*l.*, and of the same crops in 1895 was 12,007,912*l.*

Although the whole crops were larger in 1896 than in 1895, the difference in values is on account of the much lower prices of grain.

The total acreage of winter wheat now sown in Kansas is reported as 3 per cent. less than 1896. The average price for the year is given as 2*s.* 8*d.* per bushel. Prospects and conditions of this year's seeding are quite invariably reported excellent; perhaps never more satisfactory at this time of year.

The price of corn in Kansas now being contracted to feeders and others is about 7½*d.* per bushel. 30 per cent. of the crop was sold at this price by January 1, 1897. The number of cattle to be fattened is about the same as 1896.

Zinc.   The production of zinc in 1896 was 77,084 short tons.

The production of zinc oxide in the United States in 1896 was 16,799 short tons, which compares with 22,690 tons in 1895, showing a decrease of 5,891 tons, or 25 per cent. for the year.

There are zinc and lead mines in Cherokee county, with 23 smelters at Pittsburg. The exports of these materials exceed 200,000*l.* per year. The coalfields cover 17,000 square miles; Kansas coal is bituminous, nearly free from sulphur, and has a value for smelting and gas making. Gas wells are found in the coal country.

Salt is produced from salt wells; beds of rock salt over 100 feet thick underlie the central counties; there are salt marshes, covered with a brilliant white incrustation of salt, for thousands of acres.

Nebraska.   Nebraska is pre-eminently an agricultural State. The greater part of its surface is rolling prairie and level table-land; the richness of soil, mildness of climate, and the long seasons of growth are especially favourable to cereal crops, and in fact, all the products of the temperate zone. In the Western semi-arid section of the State a vast system of irrigation has been built up within the past five years; more than 300,000*l*. have already been expended in the construction of irrigation canals and ditches, which have a capacity for watering nearly 1,000,000 acres, and have an aggregate length of 2,250 miles.

With a total area of 49,000,000 acres, of which 33,000,000 acres are arable, the area under cultivation in Nebraska in 1896 is computed at only 18,091,936 acres, whose value is 12,000,000*l*.; the cultivated area is subdivided into 65,000 farms. The yield of corn in 1896 is estimated at about 300,000,000 bushels, and the yield of wheat in 1896 is computed at 18,000,000 bushels. In 1895 the wheat acreage was 1,232,252 acres, which yielded 14,787,024 bushels. The area planted in oats in 1895 was 1,676,962 acres, yielding 30,911,696 bushels. Barley, rye, buckwheat, potatoes, flax, hemp, and millet are also extensively cultivated, and hay is one of the most profitable crops in Nebraska. The hay crop for 1895 aggregated 1,811,454 tons.

Nebraska has become the second sugar-beet raising State in the United States, its soil being especially adapted to beet culture; the average yield of sugar-beets per acre is from 12 to 15 tons. Two extensive sugar-beet factories have been in operation for the past five years at Grand Island and Norfolk. Sugar-beet culture is, however, only in its infancy in Nebraska. Co-operative associations are being organised for the establishment of new factories, and eastern and foreign capitalists are negotiating for factories and refineries, which will be erected at no distant day. With its demonstrated advantages over all other Western States for raising sugar-beets as its most profitable crop, Nebraska can readily keep 100 factories supplied and in full operation. *Beet culture.*

The raising of chicory has become a profitable industry in Nebraska. Within the past two years two chicory factories have been established, where the root is fabricated into a merchantable commodity, for which there is a constantly increasing demand. *Chicory.*

Nebraska ranks among the leading cattle-raising States in the West; its vast prairies and nutritious grasses have attracted stock-raisers in large and increasing numbers. Western Nebraska offers almost unlimited facilities for stock-raising; large droves of the better grades of beef, cattle, hogs, and sheep are annually shipped to market from the older settled portions of the State; in fact, many of the farmers have made fine stock-raising a speciality, and have met with uniform success. Sheep-raising throughout the Eastern counties has increased in recent years; in one locality alone it is estimated that over 150,000 head of sheep are being wintered. The number of cattle in the State is 1,596,666; the number of swine, 1,289,726; and the number of sheep 1,926,210. The dairy interest has assumed very extensive proportions, and is steadily growing; the annual creamery products exceed 10,000,000 lbs.

Nebraska has no extensive mineral deposits; coal exists, but is mined only for local use; the saline lands are quite extensive, but have not been developed. Limestone of several varieties, sandstone, kaolin, and mineral paint have been found in various sections; extensive Portland cement beds exist near the Nicobrara River; valuable stone quarries have been opened; good building stone is also found in abundance.

At present the railroad mileage of the State is 5,547 miles. According to the census of 1890, Nebraska has a population of 1,058,910.

The following table shows the amount of corn, oats, and wheat produced in Nebraska from 1886 to 1896:—

Year.	Quantity.		
	Corn.	Wheat.	Oats.
	Bushels.	Bushels.	Bushels.
1886	106,129,000	17,449,000	21,865,000
1891	167,652,000	18,080,000	48,599,000
1895	176,034,600	13,107,600	35,342,400
1896	296,224,000	19,000,600	23,000,400

Trans-Mississippi and International Exposition at Omaha.

Situated 200 miles north of Kansas City is Omaha, Nebraska, and it is here that the Trans-Mississippi and International Exposition is to be held during 1898. The United States Government passed an Act, which was approved June 10, 1896, authorising and encouraging the holding of this Exposition, and appropriating 45,000*l.* for Government participation, 11,000*l.* for building, and 35,000*l.* for exhibit. Government officials consider that this is not enough for a proper recognition on the part of the Government of the great territory represented in this Exposition, and a Bill has been introduced in the present Congress increasing the amount to 70,000*l.*—25,000*l.* for building and 35,000*l.* for exhibit.

In due time the necessary papers will be forwarded to the ambassadors and ministers of foreign countries residing at the national capital inviting the co-operation and participation of the various foreign Governments. The Act passed by Congress provides that all goods for exhibition shall be entered duty free, and the Customs-house Department has issued regulations constituting the Exposition a bonded store, and a customs officer will be present, and in charge of this part of the Government business. This will be a golden opportunity for the British merchants who desire to push their wares into this broad expanse of Western country; the manufacturers of ropes, twine, and more especially binding twines, should not fail to take advantage of this Exposition. The State of Nebraska has appropriated 75,000*l.* for the Exposition.

Any information desired can be procured by addressing John A. Wakefield, Secretary, **Trans-Mississippi and International**

Exposition, Omaha, United States of America, or Philip E. Burrough, British Vice-Consul, Kansas City, Missouri, U.S.A.

Omaha has one of the largest smelting and refining plants in the world; it transacts a volume of business. Note business from Mexico and British Columbia.

The live-stock business at Omaha, Nebraska, although it ranks third in the list of packing centres of the world, fluctuates.

The present capacity of the yards is estimated as follows:—

	Head.
Cattle	13,000
Hogs	20,000
Sheep	12,000
Horses	1,000

Omaha has four packing houses, and a daily killing capacity of 5,000 cattle, 12,000 hogs, and 3,000 sheep. Omaha is the youngest of the four large packing points in the United States. The four establishments cover about 30 acres of ground, and give employment to about 3,200 men. The four houses killed, during 1895–96, as follows:—

	Number.	
	1895.	1896.
Cattle	318,146	303,382
Hogs	1,082,859	1,110,474
Sheep	87,310	197,492

Omaha is the largest city in Nebraska, but it is not the commercial city one would expect, considering its position. It has a population of about 140,000 people, has a number of railways entering the city, but it has never recovered from the severe depression and failure of real estate boom of years ago.

The crops of Missouri have been very good for 1896, and, owing to its lying between several good markets, it is indeed a very prosperous State. It is the third State in the number of farms, and third in the number of acres of improved land, having over 17,000,000 acres under cultivation. Missouri produced in 1896 nearly 50,000,000 lbs. of poultry, not being equalled by any State. It produced last year 936,808 horses and 351,599 mules. It also produced 4,040,084 lbs. of wool, and its tobacco crop was nearly 10,000,000 lbs. Its south-eastern counties raised an excellent crop of cotton of excellent quality.

Missouri.

The immense forests embrace pine, poplars, ash, oaks of 18 different kinds, hickories, walnut, linden, cottonwood, sweet, black and yellow gum cypress, sycamore, locust, elm, birch, tupelo, and every kind of timber required in manufactories of wood. During 1896 Missouri not only supplied the wants of her people with timber, but exported 300,000,000 feet of lumber, in addition to millions of railroad ties and 40,000,000 feet of logs not manufactured into lumber.

Missouri produces more lead ore than any other State, except Colorado, and, owing to the decreased output of silver in that State (much of the lead accompanying that production), the prospect is that Missouri will soon be the first State in the production of lead. It has a lead mine, the St. Joe Mine at Bonne Terre, in St. François county, which is thought to be the largest producer in the world, the estimated daily production being in the neighbourhood of 1,500 pigs. In addition to lead and zinc, Missouri has iron, silver, copper, pyrites, and glass sand, the latter in great quantities, and used by plate glass works.

The State possesses a great abundance of clays suitable for pottery, tilling, fire-brick, retorts, &c. These clays have a high reputation, and, besides their use at home, have been shipped to all parts of the world. In addition to these Missouri has 33 coal-producing counties, which in 1892 yielded 3,017,000 tons.

In the coal industry the output for 1896 was 2,420,147 tons, an increase of 137,066 tons over 1895.

Missouri exported in 1896 about 700,000 cattle, 2,200,000 hogs, 70,000 horses, 300,000 sheep, 3,000,000 lbs. of wool, 50,000,000 lbs. of poultry, 25,000,000 dozen eggs, 250,000,000 feet of lumber, 2,500,000 railroad ties, 4,000,000 feet of piling, 7,000,000 lbs. of pickles, 35,000,000 lbs. of canned goods, and 7,000,000 lbs. of hides.

Iowa is in the great prairie belt, and between the Missouri and Mississippi rivers, and at one time transacted all her business with Eastern cities, but as the great cattle, hog, and grain markets opened in the West they now look to the West for a share of the business, more especially since the great change of transportation of products has taken place to the Gulf of Mexico ports.

More than half the inhabitants of Iowa are farmers, and the product of their labour amounts to nearly 107,000,000*l.* annually. The corn crop of 1893 was 214,804,758 bushels, and in 1895 it was 285,000,000 bushels. The crop of oats for 1895 was 201,600,000 bushels. Immense crops of rye, barley, and potatoes are produced. The fruit crop annually is worth over 600,000*l.* The value of the annual apple product is 240,000*l.*, there being 135,545 acres devoted to apple orchards. Mills county alone produced in 1895 102,742 bushels of apples. The annual production of grapes is 4,350,721 lbs. In Iowa corn is king. The State produces more corn than any other State. The canneries of Iowa put up yearly more than 7,000,000 cans of corn, and nearly 2,000,000 cans of tomatoes. In 1895 the State produced as follows :—

		Quantity.
Corn	Bushels	285,000,000
Wheat	,,	9,500,293
Oats	,,	201,600,000
Potatoes	,,	7,869,321
Cattle in the state	Number	3,197,584
Hogs	,,	5,044,577
Sheep	,,	492,875
Creameries in the state	,,	732
Butter produced	Lbs.	520,914
Cheese	,,	4,628,240
Value of manufacturing establishments	Value £	5,000,000
Total annual wages	£	5,000,000

Along the Mississippi extend the great sawmills, of which Iowa has 300, with a yearly product exceeding 1,240,000*l*. Clinton possesses one of the largest sawmills in the world, capable of sawing 60,000 feet of lumber an hour. There are flour mills with a yearly product of 40,000,000*l*.; meat-packing establishments yielding 2,000,000*l*. yearly, and manufactories of agricultural implements, wagons, furniture, woollen goods, and boots and shoes.

There are 20,000 square miles of bituminous coal deposits; the veins are from 3 to 8 feet thick, and within 100 feet of the surface. In the north-west great quantities of lead and zinc are found in pockets in the limestone. At one time 200,000*l*. worth of lead was shipped yearly, but this industry is now nearly quiescent.

GENERAL Crop Report of Iowa for 1896.

Products.	Number of Acres.		Total Products.
Winter wheat	197,150	Bushels	3,351,550
Spring ,,	542,059	,,	7,047,233
Corn	8,043,390	,,	313,692,210
Oats	2,825,000	,,	73,450,000
Rye	121,670	,,	1,946,720
Barley	547,642	,,	15,881,618
Buckwheat	8,740	,,	147,850
Flax-seed	199,128	,,	1,891,716
Potatoes	170,000	,,	14,814,895
Sweet potatoes	3,650	,,	288,360
Timothy seed	170,000	,,	646,000
Clover seed	61,000	,,	122,000
Sorghum	19,000	Gallons	1,710,000
Hay (tame)	2,250,960	Tons	3,376,440
,, (prairie)	1,550,000	,,	2,325,000

Hog cholera was very bad in Iowa, and did a vast amount of damage to farmers. The epidemic raged from 8 per cent. to 27 per cent. in the different districts. The loss was about 1,800,000

Hog cholera.

hogs in 1896; the indirect loss is also very heavy on account of the shipment and slaughter of vast numbers of young animals in various stages of immaturity. The aggregate loss to the State, direct and indirect, cannot fall much short of 3,110,000*l*. for 1896.

The area of forests in Wyoming covers not far from 10,000,000 acres, mainly on the high mountains, and includes large yellow and white pines, white spruce and red cedar; only one-sixth of Wyoming's soil can be cultivated, and this portion has a sandy loam which, when irrigated, produces cereals, vegetables, and fruits.

Grazing is the chief industry of Wyoming, where cattle and sheep find capital nutriment in the bunch grass; the number of cattle exceeds 1,500,000; more than 1,000,000 sheep are grazing all the year out on the plains. Horse-raising is growing rapidly, and the State has 150,000 head; the live-stock interests represent an investment of 22,000,000*l*.

Mining employs several thousand men in Wyoming, although the larger part of the State remains undeveloped. The coal mines dispose of most of their products to the railroads; it is a lignite, containing 50 per cent. of carbon; the Wyoming coal mined exceeds 2,000,000 tons yearly, valued at 1,000,000*l*.; the coal region covers 30,000 square miles.

Petroleum has been developed over a belt 300 miles long, but the wells are plugged, awaiting the coming of better transportation facilities. Vein tin and stream tin are found, and copper and tin mines are in operation. On the Laramie plains occur sodium lakes, with deposits of sodium sulphide; these products are manufactured into merchantable soda at chemical works in Laramie. Among other mineral treasures are gypsum and mica, marble and granite, graphite and cinnabar, limestone and magnesium, kaolin and fireclay, glass sand and asbestos.

Wyoming. Wyoming has a total area of 62,645,120 acres, of which the greater portion is adapted to grazing and agriculture. It is estimated that between 12,000,000 and 15,000,000 acres can be successfully cultivated, and that nearly 10,000,000 acres are covered with timber. The soil is generally a rich, sandy loam, and where it is irrigated below 7,500 feet produces abundantly all the cereals, vegetables, and fruit common to the North-western States. Farming is not yet carried on in many places, the chief industry being stock-raising. A marked change, however, is rapidly taking place in the combination of pastoral and agricultural pursuits. The stock-raising industry comprises nearly one-half the total wealth of the State; but five years ago this industry represented more than three-fourths the entire valuation of property. Other industries have increased faster than live-stock raising, and the extension of railroads will give greater prominence to other interests.

The mineral resources of Wyoming are exceedingly varied and extensive, but so far in the history of the State but little attention has been paid to their development, with the exception of the coal mines. Although located in the midst of the Rocky Mountains, and nearly surrounded by States that count their annual output of the precious metals by the millions of dollars, Wyoming has never been known as a producer of gold and silver of any importance.

In Crook, Big Horn, Albany, Laramie, and Carbon counties there are lead properties that will assay from 30 to 350 ounces of silver to the ton.

There are several other mining enterprises that are of much more importance to the State than mining for gold at the present time. Coal mining has been the leading mineral industry of the State since the completion of the Union Pacific Railroad. Coal exists and is mined in every county in the State, with one exception. The productive measures cover an area of 21,400 square miles. There are upwards of 30 coal mines opened that produce about 2,500,000 tons of coal annually, and employ about 3,500 men. The coal veins that are of commercial importance vary in thickness from 3 to 75 feet, an average being about 6 feet.

The coal mined is bituminous, coking and non-coking, semi-bituminous and lignite. The only coking coal that is manufactured into coke is found at Cambria.

Wyoming has a vast area of oil land; there are eighteen known oil districts in which oil exists, and has been found in oil sand, or in springs. As in all other enterprises of the State, the development of these fields has been very slow. The output for the year 1896 will exceed 10,000 barrels, valued at 1*l*. 16*s*. per barrel f.o.b. Casper, for crude.

There are immense deposits of iron ore known in many places in the State; the ore is usually hematite, very pure, and would make excellent Bessemer steel. The production for 1896 has been about 9,000 tons. The ore is in blanket form, and varies in thickness from 1 to 25 feet. The run of the mines will average about 60 per cent. metallic iron. In one mine, at a depth of over 100 feet, a sample was taken across the deposit, a distance of 90 feet, and the metallic iron contents was nearly 62 per cent. The deposits, as a rule are very large, and as soon as the Bessemer ores are worked out in the East, Wyoming will have an opportunity to open her iron mines.

The natural soda deposits of the State can be divided into two classes; those that are nearly pure sulphate, and those that are a mixture of nearly equal percentages of sulphate and carbonate. These deposits vary in thickness, from a few inches to 12 feet; the area of the deposits varies from 20 to 100 acres. Several attempts have been made to manufacture the soda compounds from these natural deposits, but so far the only successful work has been in preparing the soda for glass-making. Besides the deposits of soda, there are wells that furnish water rich in carbonate of soda; two of the wells contain over 98 per cent. carbonate, and the water contains 24 per cent of sal soda. There is also a deposit of Epsom salts, covering an area of 90 acres. The salt is from a few inches to several feet in thickness, and is pure; there is enough of this salt in one deposit to control the

(2318)

Epsom salt trade of the world, if it were possible to secure transportation at a reasonable figure.

There are two kinds of plaster manufactured at the present time; one from gypsum and the other from disintegrated beds of gypsum that are associated with a carbonate of lime and sand. The gypsum beds are found in the Triassic rocks, and vary in thickness from 10 to 100 feet. These beds are so numerous that Wyoming could supply the demand for the entire world for centuries, and then not miss the gypsum. They manufacture high grades of plaster of Paris, and land plaster. At Laramie they manufacture a plaster that is taking the place of common lime in mortar-making, and is also being utilised for mortars for brick and stone. The analysis of the Laramie plaster proves that it is practically the same as the Egyptians used in the construction of the great Cheops pyramid.

Deposits of asbestos have been found on the Grand Encampment and in the Seminoe mountains, along the Sweetwater River, on Casper Mountain, and near Laramie Peak. With the exception of Casper Mountain, there has been but little development; small shipments have been made, but there was no product in 1896. The asbestos is of various grades that could be utilized for pulping and packing, but so far there has been but little found that would be suitable for weaving.

Mica (Muscovite) that is of a commercial quality, has been opened up at Whalen Cañon; it occurs in large pegmatite veins, and in sheets six inches by nine, that are almost water-white, and without a flaw. These mines have shipped some mica, but are not in operation now.

Grazing, which was at one time the great industry of the State, has dwindled to an industry of but little importance, with the exception of sheep-raising, and cannot again be what it has been, on account of the lack of range and water.

Montana. Montana is in two diverse sections, the eastern two-thirds consisting of rolling plains, clothed mainly with sage, brush, and bunch grass; the western third is the mountain region, covering 50,000 square miles of ranges. The State's area includes 30,000,000 acres of farm lands, 38,000,000 acres of grazing land, and 26,000,000 acres of woods and mountains. The total area is 146,080 square miles. There are forests of pine and cedar along the mountains and down the great valleys. Tongue River has valuable growth of black ash, and Hell Gate River flows through forests of yellow pine. Private enterprise has built up many irrigating canals; the Sun River canals are over 100 miles long, with immense reservoirs. The country north of the Mississippi is an immense rolling prairie, 18,000,000 acres in extent. In 1880 millions of buffalo were wantonly slaughtered in this region, and in 1884 the last great herd of buffalo, numbering 75,000, wintered in the Bad Lands.

Wheat of a superior grade, oats, and corn are raised in these valleys; the stock-raising interest has assumed great prominence in Montana, the vast plains affording pasturage for millions of domestic animals. The State contains 1,500,000 head of cattle, 200,000 horses, and 1,300,000 sheep. The latter produce yearly 10,000,000 lbs. of wool, and 440,000*l.* worth of mutton. There are a number of large horse ranches. Thousands of two-year-old steers from Texas and New Mexico are bought by the Montana stockmen, and kept on the ranches for two years, and then sold for beef; over 100,000 head are sent eastward yearly. The local production of hay amounts to 240,000 tons.

The farm products for 1896 were as follows:—

Products.		Quantity.
Corn	Bushels	33,275
Wheat	,,	1,065,223
Oats	,,	2,446,071
Barley	,,	142,525
Potatoes	Tons	292,657

Mining is the foremost industry of Montana, which has already added 84,000,000*l.* to the nation's wealth. Nearly one-third of the gold, silver, copper, and lead mined in the United States come from Montana. During 10 years 28,000,000*l.* in gold was taken out, yet little mining was done until 1860. Alder Gulch (Virginia City district), opened in 1863, has yielded 10,000,000*l.* Last Chance Gulch (Helena), opened in 1865, has produced 3,100,000*l.* Quartz mining was begun after 1870, and now vast and costly plants are perpetually at work. The smelters at Helena, Great Falls, and Castle alone cost 2,100,000*l.* The Granite Mountain mine has produced 2,710,000*l.* since 1880; 800 men are employed in it. The Drum Lummon mine has sent out upwards of 1,310,000*l.* There are immence deposits of copper at Butte and other points. Butte and Anaconda have sent out 120,000,000 lbs. in a year, their products being one-fourth of the world's supply. Coal fields underlie 60 square miles along the Missouri and Yellowstone; the coal fields east and south from San Coulee cover 360 square miles; 1,000 tons are mined daily. Large deposits of black-band iron ore are found in the Belt region, and bog and magnetic ores occur elsewhere. The mountains yield inexhaustible supplies of pale, pink porphyry. Grey granite, green-coloured sandstone, white and tinted marbles, limestone, and fire-clay, plumbago, and quicksilver, zinc, and other minerals have been found. The annual product of Montana is over 13,000,000*l.*, one-half in metal, one-third in live-stock, one-sixth in farm land and lumber. No other country in the world can show an equal product for its population.

(2318)

UNITED STATES.

PRODUCTS of 1896.

		£
Gold	.. ..	998,100
Silver	.. ..	4,762,000
Copper	.. ..	4,893,062
Lead	.. ..	127,092
Total	.. .. ..	10,780,254
		£
Agricultural products—		
Wheat	.. ..	100,000
Rye	.. ..	1,041
Barley	.. ..	47,092
Corn	.. ..	2,812
Oats	.. ..	15,710
Field peas	.. ..	8,009
Potatoes	.. ..	47,023
Hay	.. ..	309,927
Alfalfa	.. ..	32,041
Total	.. .. ..	563,665
		Number.
Livestock—		
Beeves marketed	.. ..	254,864
Sheep marketed	.. ..	640,000
		Lbs.
Wool clip	.. ..	21,790,289
Lumber products—		
Feet, rough, lumber cut	.. .. ..	122,647,039
Finished lumber produced	.. ..	17,066,000
Lath and shingles produced	.. ..	3,666,350

North Dakota has an area of 70,795 square miles; its population in 1890 was 182,719, and its estimated population to-day is 225,000.

The farm products for 1896 were as follows:—

Articles.		Quantity.
Corn	Bushels ..	658,979
Wheat	,, ..	61,057,710
Oats	,, ..	8,839,286
Buckwheat	,, ..	1,530
Potatoes	,, ..	5,119,448
Hay	Tons.. ..	585,377

Upon the vast extent of grazing lands, hundreds of thousands of cattle are fattened; the State now has nearly 500,000 sheep.

There are 50,000 farms in South Dakota, valued at 3,400,000*l.* The annual farm productions of the State are about as follows:—

Articles.		Quantity.	
		Annually.	1896.
Corn	Bushels ..	25,000,000	12,423,442
Wheat	,, ..	20,000,000	29,423,088
Oats	,, ..	15,000,000	39,911,699
Barley	,, ..	2,000,000	2,543,678
Potatoes	,, ..	2,500,000	4,037,054
Flax	,, ..	2,500,000	..
Hay	Tons	..	1,547,678

The wild prairie grasses yield 1,500,000 tons of hay yearly, and the tame grasses 120,000 tons. The cultivation of flax is an important industry.

The State has about as follows at present:—

	Head.
Swine	400,000
Cattle	600,000
Horses	200,000
Sheep	200,000
	Lbs.
Wool clipped, per year .. (about)	5,000,000

The Black Hills cover about 3,500 square miles, and embrace the richest 100 miles in the world. There are rich gold mines in this State, which will no doubt show great development in the near future. Following are productions for 1896, compared with 1895:—

Year.	Tons of Ore milled.	Value.
		£
1895	833,800	1,010,000
1896	1,013,560	1,823,000
Increase	179,760	813,000

The above figures do not include the value of silver and copper saved by the various reduction plants in the treatment of the ore, which will swell the total wealth produced to at least an additional 209,000*l.*

Both lode tin and stream tin are found in enormous quantities. The Hills contain saline, petroleum, and natural gas, and many other valuable minerals; there is white and red variegated sandstone; white and purple limestone, granite, and marble.

The trade of Arkansas, from Kansas City, is rapidly increasing, and, of course, must continue; the great railway system of

Arkansas.

this city brings within her grasp a large share of the Arkansas trade, for four of the railways from here traverse that State. The following statistics refer to the State of Arkansas :—

Area in square miles	53,840
Population in 1896	1,600,000
Assessed valuation £	39,000,000
Total number of acres	33,500,000
Acres under cultivation	5,000,000
Value of farms £	18,500,000
Annual live stock products £	7,400,000
Total value of farm products per annum £	8,900,000
Acres of timber land	19,000,000
Acres of coal land	2,500,000
Acres of iron ore land	1,500,000
Railway mileage	2,424
Value of annual products of manufactories £	4,172,000
Number of operatives	15,972
Yearly wages £	1,219,000

Farm products for 1895 were as follows :—

Articles.		Quantity.
Corn	Bushels	50,359,558
Wheat	,,	1,452,000
Oats	,,	8,306,486
Rye	,,	24,129
Potatoes	,,	1,476,300
Hay	Tons	214,396
Cotton	Bales	875,000

As a fruit-producing State it ranks among the first, having taken premiums over all competitors at the Expositions of New Orleans, California, St. Louis, and Chicago. The staple products are cotton, tobacco, sorghum, live stock, and fruit. The manufactures are cotton-seed oil, lumber, tobacco, and cigars.

The coal fields are very extensive, covering 2,347 square miles, and where coal mining is most largely prosecuted, the vein averages a thickness of 4 feet; the lignite coal bed comprises a larger area, it is said, than any other coal field in the United States; the output is 1,250,000 tons per annum.

Iron deposits of inexhaustible quantities are found: magnetic, hematite, carbonate, and specular iron ore abounds; large deposits of manganese are also found, and during the past 12 years vast quantities of this mineral have found a market north and east; this metal is also found in other parts of the State. Zinc ore in great abundance is also found, and has attracted large capital; the ore from some of the mines assays as high as 67 per cent metal. The zinc industry is the most profitable. Arkansas took the first award at the Chicago Columbian Exposition for its zinc ore; among its exhibits there was one piece of ore weighing over 12,000 lbs. According to a recent geological survey, the State has a distribution of 216 square miles of zinc ore, and overlying it, and surrounding it are 2,199 square miles of marble. Lead ore is found in the mountainous sections of the State; copper, in the form of carbonate and sulphuret, is one of the rich deposits of Arkansas. Among the other minerals are antimony, porcelain clay, extensive beds of gypsum, chalk, green sand, and bauxite, from which aluminium and alum are manufactured. Deposits of marble are greater than any other State; the marble is pink, grey, and white, all capable of high polish. A very valuable quality of lithographic stone has been discovered. Nitre and paint earths are found in great quantities, yielding many shades and colours. large quantities of roofing slate are being quarried, and granite of superior quality is found, and hone stone is found in inexhaustible quantities. petroleum and natural gas have been found, and there are also beds of soapstone.

A large portion of the land of Arkansas is heavily timbered; there is almost every variety of valuable and useful timber.

The varieties of lumber sent to market are chiefly pine, white, red, and post oak, gum, and ash. It is estimated that over 100,000,000 feet of lumber are shipped out of Arkansas annually.

Oklahoma Territory has made great strides in development during the past year, especially in educational and commercial matters. On January 18, 1897, the United States Senate passed a Bill releasing the settlers from paying their indebtedness to the Government for lands bought, which amounted to 7,200,000*l*. *Oklahoma Territory.*

Oklahoma has an area of 38,830 square miles, and a population of 275,587; the Territorial Board of Equalization gives the total valuation of property 8,172,000*l*.

There is a great diversity in the crops of the Territory. Wheat, Indian corn, cotton, castor beans, Kafir corn, oats, barley, sorghum, and the foliage plants, alfalfa, clover, and timothy are the principal products. Horticulture has made extraordinary progress in recent years; 1,500,000 fruit trees have been planted, while several millions of smaller fruits are thriving under the peculiar climatic influences. The corn crop for 1896 is estimated at 25,000,000 bushels, and about 25,000,000 bushels of Kafir corn were raised. In 1896 Oklahoma produced the greatest crop of cotton and castor beans of its history.

The Indian Territory is fast developing, and shows great promise of producing live-stock and grain for export purposes that will eventually surprise the most sanguine. One of the chief natural endowments of the Territory is its coal measures, covering 13,600 square miles, producing a valuable bituminous coal. Iron and lead, copper and gold, marble and sandstone are found; and salt appears in springs. *Indian Territory.*

Fully 400,000 acres are under cultivation in the domain of the five civilised tribes, producing yearly over 4,500,000 bushels of corn, wheat, and oats, 400,000 bushels of vegetables, 60,000 bales of cotton, and 175,000 tons of hay, amounting to nearly 1,230,000*l*. a year. They also own 800,000 head of live-stock. Among other products are 1,000,000 feet of lumber, maple sugar, wild rice, hemlock bark, and wool. The timber lands are very

ST. LOUIS.

Mr. Vice-Consul Bascome reports as follows:—

At the close of the year 1895 hopes were entertained of a speedy improvement in the general business of the city of St. Louis and State of Missouri, as well as of the country at large; but this has not been realised.

A general falling-off in business, increased failures, the closing of manufactories and business establishments, throwing out a large number of operatives, the working only of half-time in many that kept running, bore testimony to the hard times and the expedients used to keep going under the great pressure and want of confidence.

Depreciation of values. The great depreciation in all property, especially in securities which citizens of Great Britain were jointly largely interested in, equalled, if not exceeded, the loss occasioned by the panic of 1893. This was reflected locally in all classes of securities and property, particularly the breweries in which an English syndicate have a controlling interest. The one fact on which we can congratulate ourselves was the staunchness and steadiness of all our financial institutions. No banks failed, and they hold an exceptionally large average reserve, having abundance of money to loan, but the industrial conditions were such that there were comparatively few borrowers for legitimate purposes, loans for speculative account being declined.

Staunchness of financial institutions.

Effect of storms in May, 1896. During the month of May St. Louis and 35 other cities and towns were visited by cyclones, the loss being about 300 killed and 550 wounded.

Immediate effect on business. This calamity was in a measure a blessing in disguise, for it gave employment to the army of unemployed mechanics in the building line, and a market for building material, furniture, and furnishings, making business in that line active during the summer. Repairing and rebuilding were prosecuted with such vigour that at the close of the year 90 per cent. of the damage was repaired. The blight, however, has been sorely felt this winter, for the charitable societies report the calls for aid from the sick, suffering, and poor to be trebled in number and helplessness. The Provident Association reports 1,500 calls from poor families, against less than 500 last year to same date.

Poverty and suffering consequent.

Wheat prices fluctuated in 1896. There has been a singular and confusing fluctuation in prices during 1896. Wheat advanced from 2s. 9¼d. a bushel in December, 1895, to 3s. 4½d. on February 8, 1896; fell to 2s. 6d. in June, and rose to 3s. 10d. in Decembr last.

Cotton. Cotton started at 4¼d. per lb. in December, with stories of scanty supply; fell to 3·81d. on March 5, 1896; rose to 4⅓d. on May 7, 1896; dropped to 3½d. on July 15, a heavy surplus then pressing; rose to 4·43d. on November 10; fell to 3·53d. and closed at 3·56d. in December, 1896.

CHICAGO.

Wool advanced to an average of 7·37d. per lb., February 1, 1896; fell to 6·08d. September 1; rose to 6·83d. December 1, and since declined.

Wool.

Iron and its products rose 3 per cent. to April 1, 1896, then declined every month to December 1, in all about 20 per cent., rising slightly since.

Iron.

Boots and shoes fell 13 per cent. in the spring, against leather declining 18 per cent., and hides 21 per cent. Then shoes rose gradually 20 per cent. to December, and leather 17 per cent., but has since fallen 3 per cent., while hides rose 25 per cent. to June 3, dropped 22 per cent. to July 8, rose 50 per cent. to November 4, and have since declined 13 per cent.

Boots and shoes.

Cotton goods were at their highest January 1, fell 17 per cent. to August 16, rose about 7 per cent. to November 9, and have since declined about 2 per cent. This incongruity in prices indicates the obstacles business has had to face in 1896. The trade journals give little information on the aggregate business done in their various commodities.

Cotton goods.

Bradstreet's report of sales of boots and shoes in 1896 are 4,600,000l., against 4,540,000l. in 1895, an increase of 60,000l., but I think the trade of both years to be over-estimated, although this has been a leading and constantly-increasing traffic in years past.

Sales of boots and shoes.

Hides handled in 1896 were—

Hides.

	Number.
Received	46,505,880
Shipped	81,581,130

The year 1896 was a record breaker in every one of the four departments of the business—cattle, hogs, sheep, horses, and mules. The total gain was 793,773 head, of which 58,776 were in cattle, 533,516 in hogs, 136,175 in sheep, and 65,306 in horses and mules. The record of receipts for the last five years shows interesting figures:—

St. Louis stockyard.

Year.	Head.			
	Cattle.	Hogs.	Sheep.	Horses and Mules.
1892	653,337	847,703	298,532	14,920
1893	756,485	777,433	350,041	11,799
1894	663,657	1,146,925	292,223	12,689
1895	733,526	1,084,574	454,858	27,615
1896	792,302	1,618,000	591,033	92,921

The total receipts of horses and mules at the St. Louis market in 1896 were 121,662 head. Of these 92,921 were

UNITED STATES.

Average number of mules always on hand.

received by the national yards. One can judge of the vast business by the fact that 3,000 mules are always on hand to select from. Receipts of horses and mules at Chicago for November were 5,521 head; at Kansas City, 5,374 head; at St. Louis, 15,607 head. It will be seen that St. Louis received 4,712 head more than Chicago and Kansas City combined.

Dry goods.

Dry Goods.

Bradstreet reports sales of dry goods for 1896 to have been 6,000,000*l*., and an increase of 8 per cent. over 1895.

Freight Tonnage in 1895 and 1896.

	Receipts.		Shipments.	
	1895.	1896.	1895.	1896.
	Tons.	Tons.	Tons.	Tons.
By rail	10,489,344	10,760,881	5,349,327	5,864,918
By river	508,830	671,765	303,355	572,410
Total	10,998,174	11,432,646	5,652,682	6,437,328
Increase	..	434,472	..	784,646

Grain.

Grain.

Receipts and Shipments of Grain, including Flour, reduced to Wheat.

	1895.		1896.	
	Receipts.	Shipments.	Receipts.	Shipments.
	Bushels.	Bushels.	Bushels.	Bushels.
Total	37,410,330	29,339,368	42,141,145	34,392,229
Increase	..	..	4,730,815	5,052,861

Flour and grain exports.

Flour and Grain Exports.

Bulk Grain Exported from St. Louis by Rail.

	Viâ Eastern Ports.	In Bulk, viâ New Orleans.
	Bushels.	Bushels.
Flour reduced to wheat	374,621	..
Wheat	267,500	1,732,363
Corn	2,739,187	8,766,616
Oats	180,100	436,558

CHICAGO.

Groceries.

The trade papers do not give a general résumé of the business for the year. The receipts and shipments of the following articles were:—

		Quantity.	
		Receipts.	Shipments.
Sugar	Hogsheads	1,298	856
,,	Barrels	448,105	293,759
,,	Bags	253,919	223,217
Tea	Chests	16,157	..
Coffee	Sacks	403,288	262,759
Rice	..	87,690	64,616
Tobacco	Hogsheads	35,907	3,959
,, leaf	Packages	10,135	..
,, manufactured	Lbs.	15,139,840	64,114,500

Provisions.

St. Louis receipts and shipments of provisions for the years 1895–96 were—

Articles.		1895.		1896.	
		Receipts.	Shipments.	Receipts.	Shipments.
Pork	Barrels	2,965	15,186	4,235	17,492
Hams	Lbs.	14,270,300	33,714,082	11,614,300	40,756,230
Meats	,,	173,425,900	208,100,011	16,035,100	171,407,470
Lard	,,	26,939,100	94,731,066	23,707,600	84,875,547

St. Louis receipts and shipments of live stock for the years 1895–96 were—

		1895.		1896.	
		Receipts.	Shipments.	Receipts.	Shipments.
Cattle	Head	...	...	955,613	350,037
Hogs	,,	...	...	1,997,895	885,462
Sheep	,,	...	...	632,872	254,602
Horses and mules	,,	...	...	121,722	121,200
Fresh beef	Lbs.	42,895,470	238,966,600	17,847,900	248,746,200

UNITED STATES.

Receipts and Shipments of Sundry Articles at the City of St. Louis for 1896.

Articles.		Quantity.	
		Receipts.	Shipments.
Ale and beer	Packages	..	3,435,885
Barbed wire	Lbs.	17,166,200	48,040,225
Beef	Barrels and tierces	..	1,512
Fresh beef	Lbs.	17,847,900	248,746,200
Canned beef	,,	..	5,299,940
Boots and shoes	Cases	881,287	..
Cordage and rope	Coils	90,208	..
Cement	Sacks	730,563	..
,,	Barrels	262,095	..
Cotton-seed meal	Tons	5,004	6,672
Cranberries	Barrels	9,790	..
Candles	Boxes	..	155,685
Eggs	Packages	796,490	404,830
Fish	,,	43,427	..
Fertiliser	Tons	..	34,061
Hops	Bales	6,144	..
Iron and steel	Tons	107,416	..
Leather	Rolls	80,186	..
Malt	Sacks	77,915	132,900
Nails	Kegs	353,123	394,203
Oils	Barrels	45,124	..
,,	Tanks	8,547	..
Oilcake	Tons	..	211
Oranges and lemons	Packages	444,539	..
Ore, iron	Tons	15,086	3,637
,, zinc	,,	28,020	19,599
Pig-iron	,,	99,073	34,776
Railroad iron	,,	26,262	..
Staves	M.	236	..
,,	Cars	5,264	..
Soap	Boxes	..	656,009
Tallow	Lbs.	18,225,000	13,212,800
Tin	Boxes	49,455	..
Wines and liquors	Barrels	15,019	..
,,	Boxes and cases	37,237	..
Zinc and spelter	Slabs	516,589	1,104,563

Cotton receipts. The receipts of cotton in St. Louis for 1896 were 554,391 bales, and the shipments were 556,884 bales.

Coal. The receipts of bituminous coal in 1896 were 87,677,600 bushels; of anthracite coal, 218,955 tons; of coke 5,395,900 bushels; a falling-off in bituminous coal and coke.

Wool. The receipts of wool in St. Louis for 1896 were 15,139,840 lbs., and the shipments were 15,939,579 lbs.

Zinc and spelter. The receipts of zinc and spelter in 1896 were 516,589 slabs, and shipments were 1,104,563 slabs.

Lead. The receipts of lead in 1896 were 1,946,139 pigs, and shipments were 1,406,327 pigs.

White-lead. The shipments of white-lead in 1896 were 40,259,600 lbs.

CHICAGO.

The clearing-house statement for the year 1895 and 1896 shows a decrease during the year 1896 as follows:— *Bank clearings and balances.*

Year.	Amount.	
	Clearings.	Balances.
	£	£
1895	248,864,730	137,433,775
1896	231,720,472	130,498,488
Decrease in 1896 ..	17,144,258	6,935,287

The failures in the State of Missouri were in number 505 in 1895, and 661 in 1896, an increase of 156 in 1896. *Failures in Missouri.*

In assets, 216,293*l.* in 1895, and 1,151,902*l.* in 1896, an increase of 935,609*l.*—an increase of four times the amount in 1896.

In liabilities, 680,881*l.* in 1895, and 1,754,485*l.*, an increase of 1,073,604*l.* in 1896.

The failures in the city of St. Louis are comparatively small, but it has been impossible for me to obtain the figures for the year.

The biennial report of the auditor of the State of Missouri showed the condition of the State Debt on January 1, 1895, to be as follows:— *State debt.*

	Amount.	
	Dollars	c.
6 per cent. bonds	930,000	0
3½ per cent. option bonds..	5,086,000	0
6 per cent. school fund certificates	2,909,000	0
5 ,, ,, ,, ...	231,000	0
6 ,, seminary fund certificates	122,000	0
5 ,, ,, ,, ...	1,076,955	0
Total debt, January 1, 1896	10,354,955	0

(2318)

UNITED STATES.

Cancelled bonds.

During the last two years the Fund Commissioners took up and cancelled the following bonds:—

	Amount.	
	Dollars	c.
January 1, 1896, paid 6 per cent. State funding bonds maturing..	409,000	0
April 1, 1895, paid 6 per cent. penitentiary indemnity bonds maturing.	24,000	0
July 1, 1895, paid 6 per cent. Hannibal and St. Joseph renewal bonds maturing	94,000	0
January 1, 1895, paid 6 per cent. Hannibal and St. Joseph renewal bonds maturing	55,000	0
July 1, 1896, paid 6 per cent. Hannibal and St. Joseph renewal bonds maturing	837,000	0
December 31, 1896, purchased 6 per cent. Hannibal and St. Joseph renewal bonds due July 1, 1897, on basis of 3½ per cent.	11,000	0
December 31, 1896, called in 3½ per cent. option bonds for redemption	86,000	0
Reduction of bonded debt in 1895-96 ..	1,016,000	0

Present State debt.

During the last two years certain bonds have been taken up and cancelled, and the State debt on January 1, 1897, consists of the following:—

	Amount.	
	Dollars	c.
3½ per cent. option bonds due in 1907 and 1908, and subject to redemption at the pleasure of the State ..	5,000,000	0
6 per cent. school certificates ..	2,909,000	0
5 ,, ,, ,, ..	231,000	0
6 ,, seminary certificates..	122,000	0
5 ,, ,, ,, ..	1,107,840	14
Total debt, January 1, 1897 ..	9,369,840	14

It will be readily seen that the debt is in a satisfactory condition.

Products of the State of Missouri, 1896.

Missouri produced in 1896 200,000,000 bushels of corn, 13,000,000 bushels of wheat, 22,000,000 bushels of oats, 3,500,000 tons of hay, 14,000,000 lbs. of cotton, 7,000,000 lbs. of tobacco, 500,000 bushels of flaxseed, 8,000,000 bushels of potatoes.

The estimated annual value of the fruit crop is:—Apples, 10,000,000 dol.; strawberries, 500,000 dol.; grapes, 1,000,000 dol.; raspberries, blackberries, peaches, plums, and other fruit, 1,000,000 dol., or a total of 12,500,000 dol.

The dairy business of this State, exclusive of the investments of farmers and their products, and including only the creameries and dairies that have made reports, requires for its support the products of 132,000 acres of land, valued at 4,000,000 dol.; had 300,000 dol. invested in dairy buildings; owns 30,000 cows, valued at 900,000 dol., and annually produces for market 2,000,000 lbs. of butter, 600,000 lbs. of cheese, and 10,000,000 gallons of milk, or a total investment of over 5,000,000 dol., making a gross annual return in dairy products of 1,500,000 dol.

The review of the agricultural condition and the productions of Missouri indicates the unlimited possibilities of the State. She has an area of about 44,000,000 acres, the largest iron mountain in the world, twenty counties with an unlimited supply of iron, 23,000 square miles of coal area, and an annual output of 3,000,000 tons; lead mines operated in twenty-six counties, and the most productive single mine in America, and a total annual production of 61,000 tons of pig-lead. She also leads in zinc production, with an annual output of 131,000 tons. She has extensive quarries of red and grey granite; red, grey, cream-coloured and mottled marble, onyx, limestone, and sandstone. She has the largest stock-feeding farm, producing its own grain, the largest nursery, the largest orchard, and the largest jack-breeding and importing establishment in the world.

Among breeders of live-stock, her improved hogs, cattle, sheep, horses, and mules are winners in competition with the best animals in the world, and are widely drawn upon for breeding in other States and countries. Our live-stock is enumerated and assessed as follows :—Horses, 918,000 head, value 23,000,000 dol.; mules, 231,000 head, value 7,000,000 dol.; cows, 723,000 head, value 17,000,000 dol.; other cattle, 1,686,000 head, value 1,475,000 dol.; swine, 3,169,000 head, value 12,363,000 dol.; or total assessed valuation of 69,700,000 dol. *Live-stock.*

Noting the probable increase or reduction in commodities, as reported by correspondents and other reliable sources, we have shipped from the State in 1896, approximately, 700,000 cattle, 2,200,000 hogs, 70,000 horses, 300,000 sheep, 3,000,000 lbs. of wool, 50,000,000 lbs. of poultry, 25,000,000 dozen eggs, 250,000,000 ft. of lumber, 2,500,000 railroad ties, 4,000,000 ft. piling, 7,000,000 lbs. of pickles, 35,000,000 lbs. of canned goods, and 7,000,000 lbs. of hides.

Custom-House Transactions.—Condensed Classification of Commodities Imported into St. Louis during the Year ending December 31, 1896, showing Foreign Value and Duty Paid.

Commodities.	Value.	Duty.
	£ s. d.	£ s. d.
Ale and beer	18,300 0 0	548 17 0
Anvils	2,192 16 0	582 6 0
Books and printed matter	1,152 12 0	280 2 0
Brushes	921 0 0	322 7 0
Bone and horn manufactures	104 4 0	27 17 0
Carpets and carpeting	2,754 0 0	1,062 15 0
Cement	1,278 12 0	255 6 0
Chemicals and drugs	30,263 12 0	8,114 14 0
China and earthenware	31,229 8 0	10,421 7 0
Corks, and manufactures of corks	7,789 0 0	1,557 2 0
Cutlery	21,946 8 0	10,191 11 0
Fancy goods	9,794 0 0	3,368 6 0
Fish	86,460 4 0	..
Free goods	5,677 8 0	1,780 16 0
Glass and glassware	19,327 4 0	5,651 10 0
Guns and firearms	10,671 8 0	3,201 16 0
Hops	5,070 8 0	1,336 19 0
Jewellery merchandise	586 4 0	293 2 0
Lead	2,360 8 0	1,085 16 0
Marble	67,684 0 0	31,900 9 0
Manufactured cotton	22,037 12 0	7,704 1 7
,, linen	1,856 0 0	690 7 0
,, iron	616 4 0	169 15 0
,, leather	10,148 8 0	3,503 6 0
,, metal	4,119 16 0	1,015 3 0
,, paper	4,941 0 0	2,425 17 0
,, silk	29,532 16 0	14,331 9 0
,, wool	925 0 0	232 1 0
,, ,,	170 8 0	58 1 0
Musical instruments	287 12 0	137 9 0
Nuts and fruits	1,391 0 0	322 15 0
Oils	5,446 16 0	1,018 7 0
Paints and oils	1,058 16 0	267 10 0
Granulated rice	5,588 0 0	1,370 6 0
Rubber goods	397,212 1 0	115,229 5 0
Sugar	1,033 8 0	486 2 0
Dressed skins	2,540 0 0	508 0 0
Steel bars	1,337 4 0	343 17 0
,, wire	22,996 0 0	10,023 11 0
Tin and terne plates	23 12 0	10 18 0
Spirituous liquors	7,928 8 0	8,945 1 0
Tobaccos, cigars, &c.	40,249 12 0	46,795 7 0
Varnishes	90 12 0	22 13 0
Vegetables	2,146 12 0	523 2 0
Wine, sparkling, &c.	19,646 16 0	8,284 15 0
Window-glass	52,679 12 0	7,259 6 0
Miscellaneous merchandise	3,100 8 0	849 17 0
Collections from all other sources	..	2,772 7 0
Total	550,884 5 0	202,054 1 0

TRANSACTIONS at the Custom House, St. Louis.—General Exhibit of Merchandise brought into St. Louis in Bond from below-mentioned Ports of Entry during Year ending December 31, 1896, showing Foreign Values and Duties paid thereon.

Port.	Value. £ s. d.	Duty. £ s. d.
New York	216,175 0 0	90,893 8 0
Newport News	143,743 12 0	50,079 14 0
Baltimore	103,102 0 0	34,716 19 0
Philadelphia	17,794 12 0	7,341 10 0
New Orleans	28,793 4 0	12,451 16 0
Boston	3,713 12 0	1,851 14 0
San Francisco	1,870 4 0	175 7 0
Portland, Me.	2,569 8 0	1,143 12 0
Tacoma	3,633 16 0	86 2 0
Portland, Oregon	14,475 8 0	37 5 0
Detroit	6,213 8 0	3,118 1 0
Seatle	51 12 0	16 3 0
Port Huron	438 4 0	48 0 0
Total	537,604 0 0	201,219 11 0

(2318)

LONDON:
Printed for Her Majesty's Stationery Office,
By HARRISON AND SONS,
Printers in Ordinary to Her Majesty.
(75 3 | 97—H & S 2318)

FOREIGN OFFICE.
1897.
ANNUAL SERIES.

No. 1857.
DIPLOMATIC AND CONSULAR REPORTS ON TRADE AND FINANCE.

UNITED STATES.

REPORT FOR THE YEAR 1896
ON THE
TRADE OF THE CONSULAR DISTRICT OF CHARLESTON.

REFERENCE TO PREVIOUS REPORT, Annual Series No. 1711.

Presented to both Houses of Parliament by Command of Her Majesty,
APRIL, 1897.

LONDON:
PRINTED FOR HER MAJESTY'S STATIONERY OFFICE,
BY HARRISON AND SONS, ST. MARTIN'S LANE,
PRINTERS IN ORDINARY TO HER MAJESTY.

And to be purchased, either directly or through any Bookseller, from
EYRE & SPOTTISWOODE, East Harding Street, Fleet Street, E.C., and
32, Abingdon Street, Westminster, S.W.; or
JOHN MENZIES & Co., 12, Hanover Street, Edinburgh, and
90, West Nile Street, Glasgow; or
HODGES, FIGGIS, & Co., Limited, 104, Grafton Street, Dublin.

1897.

[C. 8277—75.]   *Price Twopence Halfpenny.*

New Series of Reports.

Reports of the Annual Series have been issued from Her Majesty's Diplomatic and Consular Officers at the following places, and may be obtained from the sources indicated on the title-page:—

No.		Price.	No.		Price.
1737. Swatow		1d.	1797. Bushire		2d.
1738. Chungking		1½d.	1798. Christiania		5½d.
1739. Angora		1½d.	1799. Cadiz		2d.
1740. Shanghai		2½d.	1800. Meshed		2½d.
1741. Bilbao		3½d.	1801. St. Petersburg		4½d.
1742. Tahiti		1½d.	1802. Batoum		1d.
1743. New Caledonia		1½d.	1803. Peking		3d.
1744. Amoy		1½d.	1804. Samos		½d.
1745. Ichang		1d.	1805. Dantzig		2d.
1746. Berlin		½d.	1806. Antwerp		1½d.
1747. Rio de Janeiro		5½d.	1807. Ajaccio		1½d.
1748. Porto Rico		1½d.	1808. Stettin		3d.
1749. Montevideo		1½d.	1809. Aleppo		1d.
1750. San Francisco		3d.	1810. Tangier		2½d.
1751. Cayenne		½d.	1811. Tokio		3½d.
1752. Frankfort		3d.	1812. Madeira		½d.
1753. Malaga		8½d.	1813. Vera Cruz		1d.
1754. Söul		1d.	1814. Oporto		1d.
1755. Copenhagen		3d.	1815. Hamburg		1½d.
1756. Nice		1d.	1816. New Orleans		1½d.
1757. Lisbon		1½d.	1817. Bengazi		½d.
1758. Nagasaki		1d.	1818. Marmagao		½d.
1759. Hamburg		2½d.	1819. Gothenburg		2d.
1760. Mozambique		2d.	1820. Dar-al-Baida		3d.
1761. Cettinjé		1½d.	1821. Erzeroum		½d.
1762. The Hague		1½d.	1822. Munich		2½d.
1763. Cephalonia		1d.	1823. Samoa		½d.
1764. Bahia		1d.	1824. Chinkiang		1d.
1765. Zanzibar		1½d.	1825. Jeddah		1d.
1766. Pakhoi		1d.	1826. Sofia		1½d.
1767. New York		2d.	1827. Mexico		2d.
1768. Chefoo		1d.	1828. Teneriffe		3½d.
1769. Caracas		½d.	1829. Batoum		1d.
1770. Palermo		11½d.	1830. Cadiz		1d.
1771. Mombasa		½d.	1831. Martinique		1d.
1772. Nice		1½d.	1832. Odessa		1d.
1773. Bucharest		4½d.	1833. Ghilan		1d.
1774. Port Said		1½d.	1834. Old Calabar		6½d.
1775. Galatz		1½d.	1835. Tamsui		1d.
1776. Madrid		2d.	1836. Copenhagen		½d.
1777. Vienna		2d.	1837. Salonica		1½d.
1778. Canton		1d	1838. Honolulu		½d.
1779. Yokohama		1½d.	1839. Buenos Ayres		2d.
1780. Newchwang		1d.	1840. Para		1d
1781. Wuhu		1d.	1841. Bolivia		2d.
1782. Athens		2d.	1842. Washington		3d.
1783. Tonga		½d.	1843. Berlin		2d.
1784. Smyrna		½d.	1844. Uganda		1d.
1785. Baghdad		1d.	1845. Belgrade		1½d.
1786. Hiogo and Osaka		4½d.	1846. Dakar		½d.
1787. Bangkok		1d.	1847. Florence		1½d.
1788. Odessa		2d.	1848. Copenhagen		2d.
1789. Naples		2d.	1849. Havre		2d.
1790. Beyrout		1d.	1850. Serajevo		1d.
1791. Tunis		1½d.	1851. Madrid		2d.
1792. Kiukiang		3d.	1852. La Rochelle		2d.
1793. Bangkok		1d.	1853. Chicago		1½d.
1794. Rio Grande do Sul		1d.	1854. Berlin		1d.
1795. Valparaiso		4d.	1855. Cherbourg		2½d.
1796. Brindisi		2½d.	1856. Beira		1d.

No. 1857.

Reference to previous Report, Annual Series No. 1711.

UNITED STATES.

CHARLESTON.

Consul Coëtlogon to the Marquess of Salisbury.

(Received at Foreign Office, March 26, 1897.)

My Lord,
 I HAVE the honour to forward, herewith, my Annual Trade Report and those of the Wilmington, Port Royal, and Brunswick Vice-Consulates for the year 1896, but the Savannah Report, I regret to say, I have not as yet been able to get on account of severe illness of Mr. Vice-Consul Robertson at that port.

I have, &c.
(Signed)   H. DE COËTLOGON.

Report on the Trade and Commerce of the Consular District of Charleston for the Year 1896.

TABLE of Contents.

	PAGE
General remarks..	2
Cotton	5
Fertilisers and phosphates	10
Rice	16
Naval stores and lumber	17
Shipping and navigation	23
Miscellaneous	24
Brunswick	26
Wilmington	29
Cape Fear River..	29
Port Royal	35

(2326)

UNITED STATES.

General Remarks.

Business conditions. Charleston has perhaps felt the commercial depression that prevailed throughout the country to a more appreciable extent, during the last business year, than at any time since the commercial panic which commenced in 1893. Railroad discriminations and unfavourable political conditions in this State have seriously injured the business of the port, and have retarded the development in several respects of the interests of this community, which has not yet wholly recovered from the injurious effects of the severe storm that three years ago devastated so large a section of country contributing to this market. In spite, however, of all drawbacks the credit of Charleston has been well maintained, and city and state stocks and bonds command ready sale and fairly good prices in the money markets of the country.

Total trade. From the regular annual statistics it appears that, during the commercial year ending August 31, 1896, the business of this port amounted altogether, in round numbers, to 67,265,000 dol., about (13,453,000*l.*), compared with 67,246,000 dol. (13,449,000*l.*) for the year before, showing a very small increase last year; say 19,000 dol., or 3,800*l.*

The principal branches of trade here consist of cotton, phosphate rock and fertilisers, rice, naval stores and lumber, shipping, and a variety of miscellaneous industries of lesser value, but which amount in the aggregate to an important total. Figures **Details.** and details with respect to these above-named departments of trade, for the year under review, are given further on in this report, in the order and under the headings stated.

Increase and decrease. The official figures show that during last year there was a marked increase, compared with the previous season, in the following branches of trade, namely, cotton, rice, phosphates and fertilisers, lumber, and the wholesale and retail trade, while a decrease is shown in turpentine and resin, cotton goods, domestic articles, &c., and in general manufactures, exclusive of fertilisers.

The jetties. The system of jetties for the deepening of the channel on Charleston bar is now practically completed, and has given the port a good passage way from the docks to the sea for vessels drawing from 22 to 23 feet; these works having already cost the United States Government over 3,000,000 dol. (about 600,000*l.*). **Terminal facilities.** The terminal facilities which have undergone considerable improvements within the last few years, have, during the past year, been still further increased by two new docks and a grain elevator that was built by the South Carolina and Georgia Railway Company for the accommodation of the new direct line of British steamers organised last season for direct trade with Liverpool and Manchester, which line was inaugurated by the arrival of the steamship "Casos" that reached Charleston on Sunday, December 6, **Direct British trade.** 1896; this being the initial ship of the new line. The establishment of this line has been brought about through an arrangement entered into by Messrs. William Johnston and Co., Limited,

CHARLESTON.

steamship owners of Liverpool, and the South Carolina and Georgia Railway Company and its western connections, who found that in order to secure contracts for freights from interior points on equal terms with competing ports, it had become an absolute necessity to have fixed and regular dates for the departure of vessels to England which would be independent of fluctuations in rates and the supply of tonnage for foreign freights; the heavy demand for grain vessels at the northern ports last autumn having caused a great scarcity of ships at the cotton ports during September and October.

The new line, however, appears to have failed, and after despatching one ship with unsatisfactory results, has undertaken no further operations. *Charleston Shipping Company failed.*

The whole scheme was merely an effort, but it was believed a highly important one, towards ultimately building up at Charleston a grain-exporting business of western products with Europe, in addition to her present established trade which consists almost solely of the produce of southern farms and forests, and it is to be hoped that the matter will be taken up again next season with more success. Up to three or four years ago it was useless for Charleston to make any especial efforts to handle grain or to build elevators to lie idle and rot away from long disuse, as was the case with grain elevators built at Savannah and Port Royal 15 or 20 years ago, which furnish well known and conspicuous instances of the folly of sinking money in grain elevators before it was possible either to secure the grain or to have loaded grain ships, had the cereal been obtainable, for want of sufficient water in the channel. Grain is a deep loading cargo, and there is now ample water on the bar for this business with an elevator just completed and ready for work as soon as the grain is brought to it. *Grain exporting.*

The headquarters of the new line will be at the docks and newly-constructed terminals of the South Carolina and Georgia Railway, situated on the upper eastern part of the city on Cooper river, where a warehouse and storage room has been prepared with a capacity for holding 50,000 bales of cotton, with further prospective improvements. Two new piers have also been completed, and are numbered respectively 1 and 4; other piers and additional improvements to the terminal facilities remaining to be finished as required with the development of business. *New terminals.*

The grain elevator above referred to was completed during the early part of last November, and its machinery, &c., is said by experts to work perfectly; it is designed to handle 50,000 bushels of grain daily, and has a storage capacity of 250,000 bushels. *Grain elevator.*

The promoters of the new line appear to be confident that their enterprise will not only result in attracting to this port a considerable amount of western products for export to Europe, but that it will also eventually bring about an import business from foreign countries direct to Charleston, particularly in such articles as salt, cement, plate, &c., together with, perhaps, other cargoes, the character of which will depend on the combined *Imports.*

(2326)

activity in the matter of Charleston and Western merchants and European exporters. The latter might find it to their interest to make a note of the above indicated changes in trade channels.

Some idea of the importance of the American grain crop and the possibilities of future business in this direction at Charleston and the other ports in this Consular district, if they can obtain a moderately fair share of the same, may be seen from the fact that the American wheat crop for this year is estimated to be from 420,000,000 to 456,000,000 bushels, and that the total corn crop would range from 1,500,000,000 to 2,000,000,000 bushels. It is, therefore, perhaps safe to say that the United States can produce, when conditions are favourable, about 2,500,000,000 bushels of grain annually, which would give an average of, say, 168 bushels a year to each family in a population of 70,000,000. But inasmuch, however, as the actual yearly consumption of each family in this country is only about 17 bushels of wheat, and of corn—so small a proportion of the average yield as to allow an almost unlimited quantity to spare above home requirements—it can readily be seen how vast the grain trade is, and what apparent prospects Charleston would seem to have, with good management, of getting a fair share of it under the favourable conditions now existing. This view is all the more emphasised by the growth of this business at Galveston and New Orleans; the former place immediately after getting 20 feet of water on her bar the year before last having received up to February, 1896, 3,997,687 bushels of corn alone (maize), and New Orleans having exported 145,000,000 bushels of wheat and corn during the season of 1894-95, compared with almost no exports of this kind a few years ago.

In addition also to the crop of cereals this country produces over 200,000,000 bushels of potatoes, together with immense quantities of provisions, fruit, sugar, and other food stuffs. The consideration of such statistics and the fact that a large part of these products is surplus and must find its way to other countries must, in the future, as in the past, act as a powerful stimulant to the efforts at the South Atlantic ports now being made to establish an export commerce with foreign lands on a larger and more direct basis than heretofore.

Two new features of the past year's business that may be of interest to British manufacturers has been the export of South Carolina manufactured cotton goods from the Darlington Mills to China, and the export of Alabama pig-iron direct from Charleston to Europe. A number of shipments of cotton cloths were made throughout the year from the above-named Carolina Mills, satisfactory freight rates having been made by railways to San Francisco, and thence by steamer to Chinese ports.

The first shipment of pig-iron that has ever figured in exports from here was made in October last, when the Italian steamer "Citta di Messina" took 1,000 tons of Birmingham (Alabama) pig-iron bound for Spanish and Italian ports; this shipment being followed by the British steamer "Elton," which cleared December 15 last with 830 tons for Barcelona, and the British steamer "Casos," a little later, bound for Liverpool and Manchester. In each of these cases the iron formed only a part of the cargo, designed to give stability to the vessels in a sea way and taken in sufficient quantity to answer that purpose, the remainder consisting of cotton, a comparatively light cargo in proportion to bulk.

Taken altogether, the combined China shipments and pig-iron exports do not amount to a very large item in last year's trade, but they may be important as indications of new tendencies in trade channels, and moreover they may increase in volume in the future.

There was a good demand for foreign shipping on the opening of the new season (September 1, 1896), and from that date until near the end of the year freights were good and vessels were loaded and despatched, as a rule, with promptness, no claims for demurrage having been reported on account of inability to obtain cargoes within time specified in charter-parties. There was a slight increase in the arrivals of British vessels during the last four months of the year, as also for the whole year, as compared with the previous season, with only two cotton fires reported for the year on British vessels, one of which was a small fire in the forepeak of the ss. "Axminster" at this port last spring, and the other a more serious one that occurred on the ss. "Otterspool" after leaving this port in the autumn. *British shipping.* *Cotton fires.*

Several instances have occurred within the past few months in which shipmasters and agents or charterers have not been able to agree as to the construction that should be placed upon certain clauses or terms in charters of ships signed by owners in Europe who have stipulated therein for conditions, binding upon masters here, which apparently admit of a different interpretation at the loading port from that placed on them by owners and masters, particularly in respect to the usual "customs of the port" provision generally contained in lump-sum cotton ship charters, and also the owners guarantee in regard to the 110 (as a minimum) or more feet per registered ton, as the case may be, which lump-sum charterers require before closing contracts for ships; the result of such misunderstanding has been a resort to, in some instances, expensive litigation and arbitrations, which ship-owners might be able to avoid in great measure for the future by more care in the wording and specifications of charters, and also by having a clearer understanding on the part of masters as to the rights and obligations of owners and charterers respectively in the matter. *Charters.*

Detailed statements of the year's trade are herewith given:—

Cotton.

The total crop of cotton produced in the United States during the commercial year ending August 31, 1896, amounted to 7,157,346 bales, which, compared with the previous year, shows a decrease of 2,743,905 bales. The greatest falling-off occurred *Total American crop.*

(2326)

UNITED STATES.

Decrease. in Texas and the Indian territory, where the decrease was 1,286,376 bales; while the decrease in the five States of North Carolina, South Carolina, Georgia, Florida, and Alabama was 619,771 bales; and in the four other cotton States of Tennessee, Mississippi, Louisiana, and Arkansas, the decrease reported was 837,758 bales.

Better prices. Prices, however, were better last year, and taking the American crop as a whole, the fluctuations in value ranged between $9\frac{3}{16}$ c. for middling cotton, as the maximum figure per pound, and $6\frac{1}{2}$ c. the minimum price during the season, which would make $8\frac{1}{8}$ as about a fair average price for the last crop, equal to a gain of, say, $2\frac{1}{4}$ c. per pound, or about 11 dol. per bale, over the average market price for the preceding year, the average commercial value per bale being 41 dol. last season, and 30 dol. during the previous year.

Total crop value. On this basis the total value of last season's crop of 7,157,346 bales would be about 294,095,347 dol., compared with the crop for the year before of 9,901,251 bales, valued at 297,037,530 dol.; thus showing a shortage in last year's crop of 2,743,905 bales, and a decrease in actual value of 2,942,183 dol.

Of the above-mentioned total crop the product of the three principal cotton-raising States in this Consular district was as **State product.** follows:—South Carolina, in 1895–96, 664,000 bales, and in 1894–95, 800,000 bales; North Carolina, 384,000 bales in 1895–96, and 465,000 bales in 1894–95; Georgia, 1,079,000 bales in 1895–96, and 1,300,000 bales in 1894–95.

Reduced weights. Two other interesting features in reference to last year's crop were the average reduction in weight of 6·8 pounds per bale, compared with the previous season, and also the unusually early marketing of new cotton in the month of August, **Early receipts.** 1896, when the total receipts at all ports and interior points were 165,909 bales, compared with 7,656 bales for the same month of the previous year; the past year's August receipts being without precedent in the history of the American cotton market.

Charleston's receipts. The receipts of all classes of cotton at the port of Charleston during the commercial year ending August 31, 1896, were 292,336 bales, compared with 425,552 bales received the season before, showing a falling-off during the past year of 133,216 bales. This decrease is attributed in part to the smaller crop produced last year in the section of country tributary to this port, and also to **Causes of decrease.** the large demand of the domestic mills, which maintained prices at a figure higher than exporters could afford to pay; the consumption of the South Carolina cotton mills alone having been nearly one-half of the crop grown in the State.

Uplands exports. The exports of upland cotton from here during the year ending August 31, 1896, compared with the same period of the previous season, were as follows:—

CHARLESTON.

Comparative Exports—Uplands.

Foreign Exports.

To—	Quantity.	
	1895-96.	1894-95.
	Bales.	Bales.
Liverpool	20,016	119,663
Havre	..	2,100
Continental ports	172,288	215,633
Total	192,304	337,396

Coastwise Exports.

To—	Quantity.	
	1895-96.	1894-95.
	Bales.	Bales.
New York	76,686	59,735
Philadelphia	..	5,748
Interior, by rail	120	1,300
Total	76,806	66,783

Grand Total.

	Quantity.	
	1895-96.	1894-95.
	Bales.	Bales.
Grand total, foreign and coastwise	269,110	404,179

The prices for uplands at Charleston during the past year were as follows:—For middling grades, $7\frac{1}{2}$ c. a pound was quoted at the opening of the cotton year September 1, 1895; on October 4 the quotations had advanced to $8\frac{1}{2}$ c. A slight decline in values took place after this, and throughout the rest of October and November there were moderate fluctuations ranging between 8 and $8\frac{3}{8}$ c. In December there was a decline to $7\frac{3}{4}$ c. From January 1, 1896, to June, prices averaged from $7\frac{5}{8}$ to 7 c., with a downward tendency. On July 17 the lowest point of the year was reached, when $6\frac{3}{8}$ c. was bid. After this figures advanced slowly until the close of the cotton year, August 31, 1896, when the ruling price at the close of the market was $7\frac{11}{16}$ c. per pound, with a steady tone and an upward tendency.

UNITED STATES.

Sea Island Cotton.

Quotations. The quotations for medium fine grades of sea island Carolinas at the opening of the market, October 1, 1895, were 19 c. per pound, but owing to fears occasioned by the prospect of short crops, there was an advance to $23\frac{1}{2}$ c. by the middle of December. From that time, however, under the influence of heavy receipts, the market declined to 20 c., and sales were even made as low as 18 c. for good stapled but not very bright medium fine qualities. Extra fine sea islands sold at 35 to 40 c. per pound early in the season, but lower prices prevailed later on. Extra choice Georgias opened in September at 16 c., then declined to $15\frac{1}{2}$ c.; advanced again in November to 16 c., and in December were quoted at 17 c. In January, however, prices began to decline, and in February extra choice had fallen to $14\frac{1}{2}$ c. East Floridas were of especially good quality, and opened at 19 to 20 c. per pound; advanced to 22 c., and further on in the season declined again to 19 c. for the best selections.

Receipts, exports, &c. The receipts, exports and stock of sea islands at Charleston during the past cotton year ending August 31, 1896, as compared with the previous season, were as follows :—

	Quantity.	
	1895-96.	1894-95.
	Bales.	Bales.
Receipts of Carolinas	9,851	5,383
Georgias and Floridas	123	61
Texas	645	..
Stock on hand, Sept. 1, 1895	2	463
Total	10,621	5,907

Comparative exports. The comparative exports from Charleston of sea island cotton during the year ending August 31, 1896, and for the same period of the year before were as follows :—

FOREIGN.

To—	Quantity.	
	1895-96.	1894-95.
	Bales.	Bales.
Liverpool	7,198	3,407
Havre	1,191	1,021
Continental ports	64	53
Total	8,453	4,481

CHARLESTON.

Coastwise.

To—	Quantity.	
	1895–96.	1894–95.
	Bales.	Bales.
New York	1,576	1,424
Savannah	20	..
Total	1,596	1,424

Grand Total.

	Quantity.	
	1895–96.	1894–95.
	Bales.	Bales.
Grand total of foreign and coastwise	10,049	5,905

Total American crop. The total production of sea island cotton in the United States last year for the season of 1895–96 amounted to 92,698 bales, of which 9,970 were Carolinas, 82,083 Georgia and Floridas, and the remainder, 645 bales, of Texas growth.

In comparison with these figures, the crop of the previous season of 1894–95 was as follows:—Carolinas, 5,891 bales; Georgia and Floridas, 68,737 bales; total crop, 74,628 bales.

Additional figures. In addition to the foregoing, the following facts with reference to the cotton trade of Charleston will give some idea of the business from September 1 to December 31, 1896, which four months will be included in the next annual trade report for the season of 1896–97.

Receipts. The total receipts of uplands cotton at this port, from September 1 to December 31, 1896, were 297,351 bales, compared with 199,093 bales for the same four months of the previous year; and the receipts of sea islands were 9,413 bags during the last four months, compared with 1,328 bags for the same period a year ago.

Exports. The exports during the four months ending December 1, 1896, were 268,165 bales of uplands, compared with 153,307 bales for the corresponding period of 1895; and the exports of sea islands were 3,819 bags for the last four months, in comparison with 6,654 bags the year before. Of the total amount exported, 63,487 bales went to Liverpool and Manchester, and the remainder to other European countries—mostly Germany, Italy, and Spain.

UNITED STATES.

Fertilisers and Phosphates.

American phosphates. The variety and extent of the American phosphate business has now grown to be very large, being divided into three principal classes, known to the trade as Carolina land and river rock, Florida hard rock and pebble, and Tennessee black rock, each possessing its own peculiar advantages, viewed from a commercial standpoint.

Low prices. During the past year, prices for the various kinds of American rock have been very low, and it is perhaps doubtful if any money has been made by phosphate miners in any section of the country, with the possible exception of some few of the Carolina miners, who report moderate profits realised on their year's work; the

Carolina phosphates. miners of this State having enjoyed a somewhat advantageous position throughout the season owing to the low freight rates they secured, which enabled them to deliver their products on favourable terms to railways, local manufacturers, or vessels for foreign and home shipment. It is on account of the exceptional advantages possessed by the Carolina miners that they were able to mine and sell rock at lower prices than any of their competitors in the United States, and also to under-sell the products of the phosphate mines in Algeria; the best informed French journals reporting that it costs about 30 fr. to pay the cost of mining and delivering Algerian rock at port, in addition to which must be added 2 fr. per ton royalty exacted by the Algerian Government, making the total cost 32 fr., or say 6 dol. 40 c. in American currency. These figures practically put the Algerian article out of competition with the Carolina or Florida rock, inasmuch as dry rock can be delivered at South Carolina ports at 3 dol. 25 c. per ton, and river rock at even lower prices. It is evident from these figures that American miners, with the low freight rates obtainable, can sell to buyers in ports in the United Kingdom with fair prospects of defying all present competition.

Mining operations. More rock was mined and sold during the past year than in the previous one; the necessities of the country have become greater, with its steady growth, and commercial manures and fertilisers are more used by the modern farmers than was the case with their predecessors a few years ago. Rock miners were very conservative last year; they were in such a condition that they felt that they could afford to shut down their operations if deemed advisable, reasoning that it costs nothing to allow the rock to remain undisturbed in the phosphate beds. Mining operations are not at present being pushed with any great energy, particularly in Florida. In South Carolina the production is strictly limited to the demand, and the miners are accumulating no stock. In Tennessee mining companies are comparatively few in number, and the extent of operations are small in comparison with South Carolina and Florida.

Phosphate miners appear to think that this will result in higher prices next season, and they expect that the new year's business will be considerably expanded in volume, and that operations will be conducted under an improved system. During last year this business, in common with most other branches of industry, suffered from the general depression that prevailed throughout the country; the out-put was limited, and investments in phosphate territory were small; but, nevertheless, in spite of unfavourable conditions, a number of new companies were organised for mining rock, of which the following is a list, the last three mentioned not, as yet, having made any shipments of rock, viz.:— Dutch River Company, of Tottey's Bend, Nashville, Tennessee; South Western Phosphate Company, of Fall Branch, Aetna, Tennessee; Tennessee Phosphate Company, Swan Creek, Baltimore; Swan Creek Company, Nashville, Tennessee; Standard Company, Blue Falls, Centreville, Tennessee; Hickman Phosphate Company, Swan Creek, Tennessee; and Lewis Phosphate Company, Summerton, Tennessee.

New companies.

Carolina Phosphate Rock.

Carolina rock is found along the margins of the navigable rivers in this State, and also in the beds of the rivers, much of it being convenient to the main railway lines; it is quickly mined, and can be delivered cheaply alongside of steamers and sailing vessels for shipment abroad; it is also easy to load on cars for interior points by railway and home consumption.

Exports of South Carolina phosphate rock to foreign and domestic points during the year ending August 31, 1896, were as follows:—

Exports.

From—	Quantity.	
	Foreign.	Domestic.
	Tons.	Tons.
Charleston	2,240	126,779
Beaufort	82,376	5,044
Total	84,616	131,823

Of the above-mentioned shipments of 126,779 tons to domestic points, from Charleston, 118,761 tons were crude rock, and 8,018 ground rock; compared with which, shipments for the previous season were 114,838 tons, of which 112,838 tons were crude, and 2,000 tons ground rock.

Comparative figures.

The shipments of Carolina rock from Beaufort for the season before last were 134,597 tons, of which 117,445 tons went to foreign and 17,152 to domestic points, showing that in last year's shipments of 87,420 tons of foreign and domestic rock from that port, as already stated, there was a falling off during last season of 47,177 tons in the total shipments.

Florida Phosphate Rock.

Character of rock, &c.

Although Florida, strictly speaking, is not in this Consular district, a few words relative to the phosphates of that State may not be out of place, inasmuch as the Florida product is the most powerful competitor with the Carolina article, and a comparison, briefly stated, will show the relative importance of the two industries, and the commanding influence which the combined phosphate business of the two States must exert in the regulation of prices in this and other countries.

Phosphate deposits in Florida are found in nearly every part of that State, the hard high grades, however, being confined to the northern, central, and western sections, and the pebble rock being found in the old and new river beds. The character of the rock is about the same in average quality and variety as that found elsewhere, although a large part of it is difficult to handle, many of the deposits being situated more or less remotely from ports and railways. The pebble mines are reported to be in good condition, having been operated steadily and marketing their product in the face of low and fluctuating prices, without over production. Florida hard rock is of a high grade, and the combination formed by miners to control the output, has exercised a good effect on the business in checking several abuses that threatened disaster to the trade. During the past season buyers for foreign houses secured some marked advantages, and were enabled thereby to secure some cheap purchases.

Improved conditions.

Hard rock mining.

Hard rock mining companies did not do so well as was expected, and most of last year's shipments were made from old stock carried over from the previous season, the output being small last year. It was unfortunate for the trade that the Phosphate Company of France was embarrassed during the past year, as that company had invested large sums in the development of phosphate enterprises in Florida, but French capitalists still appear to have greater faith in Florida phosphates than those of Algiers and Tunis, their investments being much greater in Florida phosphate deposits than in Africa. This is shown by the recent reorganisation of the Compagnie Générale des Phosphates de France, with M. Paul Girard as president.

Shipments.

The total shipments of Florida rock last year from all ports were 516,460 tons, compared with 515,878 tons during the previous season; of last year's shipments 31,092 tons went from Brunswick, and 67,581 tons from Savannah, both ports in this Consular district.

Tennessee Phosphates.

Character of rock.

The phosphate discoveries in Tennessee during recent years show the rock to be of different quality from the Carolina and Florida deposits. In appearance it is of darker colour, denser, and does not need washing or grinding; it is of good grade, but is generally found at remote interior points, so distant from railway stations and shipping places as to require considerable

CHARLESTON.

expense getting it to market. The nearest water outlet for Tennessee rock is at Pensacola, situated on the extreme western Gulf coast of Florida, a distance of about 400 miles from the phosphate beds. There have been some recent discoveries in Maury County, and also some good deposits in Cheatham County near Mount Pleasant, Tennessee, that are said to present encouraging indications for future operations, but as yet the business in this State has not become very extensive, and last year's industry was small. *Limited business.*

North Carolina Phosphate Rock.

No new phosphate discoveries have been reported in North Carolina since the finding of those near Castle Haines, in Prince George County, at a point near the Weldon Railroad. The fertiliser manufacturers of North Carolina use a considerable quantity of rock mined in South Carolina, and are good customers of the miners in this State. It is also reported that farmers of North Carolina now use commercial fertilisers on a large and steadily increasing scale. *No new discoveries.*

The use of Canadian apatite in this country has been materially checked of late years by the competition for foreign business of the French rock from Algiers and Tunis, and it is believed that the depression in the demand for apatite is most likely to be permanent. Indeed, it seems quite probable that in time the Algerian mines will yet become an important competitor in European markets with the American miners of Carolina and Florida. The Algerian rock being low in iron and aluminium, is easy to work, and with cheap freights could compete with any phosphate of the same grade in European markets. Good business conditions, however, and rigid economy will be necessary on the part of Algerian miners during next season in order to avert disaster to many of them, as the French Government, in addition to the 2 fr. (about 40 c. or 1s. 8d.) royalty now exacted per ton, are also considering the question of placing a duty of 8 fr. (1 dol. 60 c. or 6s. 8d.) per ton on the product of the mines in Algiers and Tunis. This, compared with 50 c. per ton State royalty on Florida rock, would, in the event of the proposed French duty being established, have the effect of placing Algerian rock at a manifest disadvantage in competing for European business with the American product. *Canadian apatite. Algerian competition. Future prospects.*

Sales of Algerian and Tunisian rock in 1895 amounted to 80,000 tons, compared with 45,000 tons for the year before, showing a decided increase on a comparatively small total output.

Large amounts of British capital have been invested in the phosphate industries of South Carolina during the past 15 or 20 years, and the above observations with reference to present and probable future conditions of foreign products may be useful to prospectors' investors, inasmuch as they may shed a little light on, and perhaps lead to a better understanding of, trade influences likely to hereafter effect Carolina rock mining. *British investors.*

14 UNITED STATES.

Fertilisers.

Yearly sales. The sales of commercial fertilisers at Charleston during the past business year ending August 31, 1896, were 257,715 tons, compared with 159,526 tons for the year before, and 316,611 tons during the previous season, showing that while the trade of last year did not come up to the figures three years ago, it was a marked improvement over the year before last. It was expected that, owing to generally improved conditions, there would be an increase in last season's business, and in order to conduct matters in a more satisfactory manner than formerly an agreement was entered into by the fertiliser companies having for its object such control of the output as would prevent the injurious effects of over-production. For some reason, however, which does not appear to be very clearly understood, the arrangement did not result so satisfactorily as was hoped, and the aggregate business of the year was not so large as conditions at first promised. Nearly all, however, of the fertiliser companies situated in the interior of the State did well and made money, having their resources at the end of the year well in hand and ready for next year's business.

Trade conditions. Some of the companies at Charleston also did a remarkably good business last season, and paid their stockholders satisfactory dividends, but several of the local companies made the mistake of carrying over stock until next year that should have been sold last season.

Low prices. Prices were very low for fertilisers during the season, and many northern parties bought large quantities of acid phosphate instead of using crude rock as usual heretofore. The south produced a moderately large crop of cotton, and it is expected that this will result in renewed activity in the business of manufacturing fertilisers, the latter industry being to a considerable extent the handmaid of the cotton trade.

The largest consumer of commercial fertilisers in the Southern States is Georgia, which used last year 310,000 tons of phosphate manures and 25,000 tons of cotton-seed meal, and although Georgia now manufactures a considerable quantity of fertilisers herself she is still a good customer for the acid phosphate, ammoniated goods, and the unrivalled phosphate rock of South Carolina.

Consumption of fertilisers. North Carolina also shows marked increase in consumption, having spent 2,500,000 dol. (500,000*l*.) for fertilisers last season, a gain of 50 per cent. over the year before, and an increase of fully 30 per cent. over the previous season of 1894.

Sales. The total sales of fertilisers at Port Royal, South Carolina, last year were 35,000 tons, compared with 19,000 tons the year before, and at Savannah 90,000 tons last year in comparison with 77,000 tons during the season before, which figures, added to the sales before mentioned at Charleston, would make the grand total of fertiliser sales at Charleston, Port Royal, and Savannah for last year amount to 382,715 tons, compared with 255,526 tons for the previous year of 1895.

There are now practically no shipments of manufactured **Shipments.**
fertilisers from this district to other countries, and imports of
foreign manures, which in former years were considerable, now
amount to little or nothing. The shipments for last year, and
also for the year previous, to domestic ports and places in the
United States from Charleston, Port Royal, and Savannah correspond identically both as regards details and totals with the
figures given for sales at the three ports respectively named.

The total amount of commercial fertilisers used in the United **Total**
States last year was 1,355,000 tons, compared with 1,128,000 tons **consumption.**
for the previous year. Of last year's consumption Georgia used
310,000 tons; South Carolina, 140,000 tons; North Carolina,
100,000 tons; Alabama, 75,000 tons; Florida and Virginia, each
50,000 tons; the Northern States of the Union, 220,000 tons;
the Western States, 125,000 tons; North Eastern States, 100,000
tons, and the remainder was distributed in amounts ranging from
20,000 to 35,000 tons each among the States of Tennessee,
Kentucky, Mississippi, Louisiana, Arkansas, Texas, and West
Virginia.

Chemicals.

The amount of chemicals used at Charleston during the year, **Chemicals**
ending August 31, 1896, required in the manufacture of the **and value.**
different grades of phosphate fertilisers, together with their values,
are given in the following table:—

Items.	Quantity.	Value.
	Tons.	Dollars.
Kainit	21,563	139,696
Sulphur	7,980	96,116
Muriate potash	2,527	92,148
Pyrites	12,272	27,935
Nitrate soda	799	24,406
Manure salt	51	1,101
Sulphate potash	47	1,996
Sulphur ore	13,700	50,002
Total	58 939	433,400

The comparative export of crude phosphate rock from **Later exports.**
Charleston during the period from September 1, 1896, to December
31, 1896, amounted to 31,044 tons, in comparison with 30,927
tons for the corresponding time of the year before. Of last year's
exports only 1,200 tons were shipped to foreign countries, the
remainder going coastwise and by railway to American ports and
interior places; New York, Baltimore, Philadelphia, and Richmond
getting the most of it. There were no shipments of ground rock
reported during the above-mentioned four months of last season,
and the fertiliser business for the new year had not yet begun.

(2326)

Rice.

Crop conditions.
The greater part of the rice crop of 1895–96 was harvested in fairly good condition, the grain, however, maturing somewhat later than usual, but, as a rule, coming to market well cured.

The season was a favourable one on the rivers to the southward of this city, but on the long rivers situated northward of Charleston planting operations, during the preceding spring, were greatly retarded by excess of water which prevented land drainage and made it impossible to properly prepare for early planting; much of the rice along these rivers could not be planted until June, and the quality of a good deal of the product was inferior.

Throughout the past season of 1895–96 there was a good demand for the better grades and remunerative prices were realised by sellers; but low grade rice was too plentiful, and in many instances had to be sold at ruinous prices.

Prices.
Prices for good qualities of rice averaged from $3\frac{1}{2}$ to 4 c. per lb., while a few choice lots sold as high as $4\frac{3}{4}$ c., but the selling rates for lower grades averaged generally from $2\frac{1}{2}$ to 3 c. and in some cases even as low as 2 c. was paid.

Receipts.
The receipts of rough rice at the South Carolina mills during the year ending August 31, 1896, were 959,118 bushels, as compared with 790,484 bushels during the previous season, showing a gain last year of 168,634 bushels. The receipts of rough rice at the mills situated at Charleston during the same period were 168,314 bushels more than for the year before, practically the bulk of the South Carolina milled rice coming to Charleston.

Early arrivals.
The first receipts of last year's crop were 18 barrels of rice that reached Charleston from the Waverly Mills, Georgetown, on August 30, 1895; followed the next day by 25 barrels more from the same mills; the next arrival being a cargo of rough rice from Ashepoo River, received on September 2 and sent to Bennett's Mill, but not pounded until the 10th of the same month; on the 20th, however, several cargoes came to market, and by the end of the month shipments became general, and the market was fully opened.

Crop of 1895–96.
One year later the crop matured much earlier than usual, and the first receipts were 30 barrels from the Waverly Mills that reached this city on August 18, 1896, and 18 barrels more from the same source two days later; a cargo of 1,500 bushels of rough rice from Pon Pon River arrived on August 22, was pounded at West Point Mills on the 24th and sold on the 27th of the same month. Other and heavier arrivals soon followed, and shipments became general early in September. The harvesting of Carolina rice was from two to three weeks earlier than in the previous season, and progressed rapidly after it had fairly commenced without any serious drawbacks or other disasters, and planters did their utmost to protect their crops from unfavourable weather which they might have to encounter later in the season; the indications being that fairly good prices would probably be obtained for the Carolina crop this year, as its principal competitor, the

Louisiana crop, was reported to be much smaller than for the year before, less rice having been planted in that State and unfavourable weather greatly decreasing the expected yield. At the opening of the new season the indications appeared to be that the new Carolina crop would be marketed at a value that would largely depend on the price of the better grades of foreign rice coming into competition with the home product during the next season.

Total crop.
The total rice crop produced in the United States during the year ending August 31, 1896, amounted to 798,497 barrels of milled rice, averaging 300 lbs. each, net weight; of which 128,392 barrels were raised in the Atlantic Coast States of South and North Carolina and Georgia; the remaining 670,105 barrels being the Louisiana crop for the season. Of the coast crop South Carolina produced 87,192 barrels, Georgia 32,700 barrels, and North Carolina 8,500 barrels.

Exports, &c.
The comparative exports of rice from Charleston during the past two seasons, as well as the shipments to interior points by railway and the home consumption, were as follows:—

Exports and Home Consumption.

To—	Quantity.	
	1895–96.	1894–95.
	Barrels.	Barrels.
North, by steamer..	20,894	14,712
Interior, by rail ..	30,606	32,678
Total exports ..	51,500	47,390
City consumption ..	25,000	20,000
Grand total exports and home consumption	76,500	67,390

Later figures.
The receipts of rice from September 1 to December 31, 1896, at this port were 39,344 barrels, in comparison with 31,592 for the same period of the year before, showing an increase last season of 7,752 barrels.

Exports for the four months ending December 31, 1896, were 24,663 barrels, as compared with 20,285 barrels for the same period of the previous year; the stock on hand at the close of the past year being 10,681 barrels, in comparison with 6,607 one year ago. Of the above-mentioned exports no shipments of rice went to foreign countries, the greater portion going to New York and inland places by railway.

Naval Stores and Lumber.

Resin and turpentine.
The business done at Charleston last season in resin and spirits of turpentine was not of a very encouraging nature, owing to the

(2326)

UNITED STATES.

Receipts, exports, &c.

gradual exhaustion of the yellow pine forests in the territory that is naturally tributary to this place. Indeed, for a number of years this industry has been a steadily declining one as has been shown, from time to time, in the annual trade reports from this Consulate. Receipts are gradually diminishing, and exports have been as a natural consequence small; but such little business, however, as was done, proved to be fairly satisfactory to dealers. Prices were tolerably good, especially for the lower grades of resin; B, C, and D resin selling, at the end of the year, at 1 dol. 30 c. per barrel, equal to a trifle over 5s. But for spirits of turpentine figures were very low, owing principally to over-production in other States; the selling figures at the end of the season for spirits being $21\frac{1}{2}$ c. per gallon, about 11d.

The following comparative statement shows the receipts and exports from this port of resin and turpentine from September 1, 1895, to August 31, 1896, and also for the same period during the previous season of 1894-95:—

	1895-96.		1894-95.	
	Spirits.	Resin.	Spirits.	Resin.
	Casks.	Barrels.	Casks.	Barrels.
Stock on hand at beginning of season	1,970	9,405	2,685	10,239
Receipts	8,910	59,530	11,939	74,492
Total	10,880	68,935	14,624	84,731

The coastwise and foreign exports of naval stores from Charleston during the year ending August 31, 1896, as compared with the previous year, were as follows:—

COASTWISE.

To—	1895-96.		1894-95.	
	Spirits.	Resin.	Spirits.	Resin.
	Casks.	Barrels.	Casks.	Barrels.
New York	5,651	25,452	6,337	28,572
Philadelphia	..	..	1	223
Interior by rail	525	124	1,932	3,576
Total	6,176	25,576	8,270	32,371

CHARLESTON.

Foreign.

To—	1895–96. Spirits. Casks.	1895–96. Resin. Barrels.	1894–95. Spirits. Casks.	1894–95. Resin. Barrels.
Rotterdam	..	2,404	..	3,000
Hamburg	300	3,000	..	..
Trieste	..	2,378	..	2,692
Glasgow	1,000	909	3,300	2,640
London	1,896	1,542	..	..
Liverpool	..	5,107	..	4,816
Harburg	..	..	..	3,656
Newcastle	..	..	275	7,169
Bremen	..	2,000	..	1,500
Europe, viâ Savannah	..	6,891	..	9,619
Bristol	941	6,114	809	4,463
Middlesboro'	..	..	..	3,400
Cardiff	..	2,961	..	..
Manchester	..	2,400	..	..
Total	4,137	35,706	4,384	42,955

Lumber Trade.

During the past year the lumber trade shared, to some extent, in the general depression that prevailed throughout the country; but, nevertheless, the total shipments were somewhat in excess of any previous year. Prices, however, were too low as a rule to make the business profitable to manufacturers, and it was only by the strictest economy that any margin above cost of production could be secured. But, notwithstanding all drawbacks, lumber dealers were energetic enough to keep the business up to such a footing as would enable them to take advantage of any rise that might take place in the market. Local trade was very light last year, comparatively few new buildings were erected, and stocks of lumber are reported to be exceedingly light at the close of the season. *Trade conditions.*

Very good facilities now exist at this port for the shipment of lumber from interior mills of the State direct, by water and railway, to this market, enabling Charleston dealers to be in a favourable position to compete with prices at any other southern port. Indeed, the saving effected in the water method of transportation has made it possible in some instances for merchants here to secure orders which more southerly markets were unable to obtain, owing to their being dependent solely on railway communications; this applying more particularly to square-edged and round quality of lumber and sawn trolley railway ties. All things considered it appears clear that, in the event of any further expansion of capital and increase in demand and prices, the trade here will likely be in a good condition to handle all business offered; at the same time it must be admitted that the immediate outlook is not *Good port facilities.*

(2326)

very encouraging, although stocks at northern markets are reported very light, which would seem to indicate brighter prospects for the coming year in that part of the country where any improvement in demand and prices is sure to immediately and favourably affect southern markets.

Comparative exports.

The comparative exports of lumber, timber, and cross-ties from the port of Charleston during the year ending August 31, 1896, as well as for the same period of the year before, were as follows:—

	Quantity.	
To—	1895–96.	1894–95.
	Feet.	Feet.
Coastwise—		
American ports	75,107,094	74,029,966
Foreign—		
West Indies	2,190,685	878,623
Total coastwise and foreign ..	77,297,779	74,908,589

Later receipts and exports.

The naval stores market opens April 1 each year, and the following figures will show the amount of this business done from that date to the close of 1896:—

Receipts of spirits of turpentine and resin at this port from April 1 to December 31, 1896, were 7,471 casks of turpentine and 38,354 barrels of resin, in comparison with 10,296 casks of turpentine and 57,269 barrels of resin received during the same time the previous year.

The total exports from April 1 to December 31, 1896, were 6,822 casks of turpentine and 38,955 barrels of resin, compared with 9,018 casks of turpentine and 48,045 barrels of resin during the corresponding period of the year before; the stock remaining on hand at the end of 1896 was 816 casks turpentine and 6,437 barrels resin, compared with 1,321 casks turpentine and 15,845 barrels resin at the close of 1895.

Total shipping.

The total number of vessels of all nationalities that arrived at Charleston during the year ending December 31, 1896, were 742, with a total tonnage of 813,553 tons, in comparison with 784 vessels arriving during the previous year having a tonnage of 850,484 tons; showing a falling-off last year of 42 vessels and 36,931 tons.

Of last year's arrivals the nationalities and tonnage were as follows:—

CHARLESTON.

Nationality.	Number of Vessels.	Tons.
American	656	709,673
British	55	78,859
Norwegian	1.	14,652
Italian	8	6,250
Spanish	2	933
German	1	735
Austrian	1	2,295
Columbian	1	176

Although, as above stated, there was a decrease in the total shipping business of this port it is gratifying to be able to report that the proportion carried in British vessels shows an increase of about 20 per cent. last year over the previous one, the figures being 55 arrivals during 1896, compared with 46 in 1895. *British shipping increased.*

There are 30 skilled full branch pilots here with three well-equipped pilot boats that regularly cruise in order to furnish inward bound vessels with pilots. *Pilots.*

There are also, for the accommodation of shipping, a number of suitably adapted tugs engaged in the bar and harbour service, these tugs being in charge of capable and experienced masters.

One of Charleston's new water front industries is the Pregnall Marine Railway which was completed last July; it is situated at the foot of Hasel Street. The cradle on which vessels are placed is 168 feet 10 inches long and 37 feet wide, and can accommodate a vessel of 600 tons. This establishment now does nearly all the repair work on boats around Charleston harbour besides bringing to this port a considerable amount of business from other places. *Marine railway.*

Cotton freight rates to foreign ports were very low during the greater part of last year, as was also the case at all of the other American ports, but a decided improvement in rates took place about the middle of August, when the increased demand for tonnage at northern grain exporting ports caused a scarcity of vessels and higher freight rates at the cotton exporting ports of the south, which also had the effect of creating something of a blockade for several weeks in September and October along the railways near Charleston, owing to the inability to unload cars promptly for want of ships to receive cargoes. Foreign freight rates on October 1, 1896, when the new cotton season opened, were as follows:—Cotton, by steam, viâ New York to Liverpool, 51 c. per 100 lbs. net; Havre, viâ New York, 51 c. per 100 lbs. net; Bremen, viâ New York, 54 c. per 100 lbs. net; sail freights to Mediterranean ports, viâ Cork for orders, 2s. 6d. for resin and 3s. 9d. for spirits of turpentine per barrel, and on turpentine to Genoa 2s. 3d., and to Trieste 2s. 6d. per barrel. *Freights.*

Coastwise freights ruled as follows:—Yellow pine lumber rates were firm, but not active, with the quotations for lumber to New York at 4 dol. 38 c. to 4 dol. 50 c. per 1,000 feet, and proportionate figures for cross-ties (railway sleepers) averaging about

(2326)

14 to 14½ c. each. Phosphate rock per ton to New York, 1 dol. 90 c.; to Philadelphia, 2 dol.

The jetties. The jetties at the entrance to Charleston, which were practically completed a year ago, have so far given good satisfaction, and appear to serve the needs of the harbour very well. From recent reports of the United States engineers in charge of the work it is learned that no disappointing effects or faults have been developed, and it is stated in the official survey for June, 1896, that at that time the new channel afforded a "straight and safe" passage across the bar of 18½ feet at low water and 23½ feet at high water. Although these figures give the depth at the shallowest point, the engineer's report adds that the general depth is considerably more, and the originally projected depth of 21 feet at low water and 26 feet at high water now actually exists straight through the channel, with the exception of about 700 feet of shoal, which is steadily disappearing under the combined action of the scour of the powerful jetty water currents and the operations of the dredging that is being steadily carried on. There are said, however, to be indications that the Old Pumpkin Hill Channel entrance to Charleston Harbour is gradually deteriorating, but this was not unexpected, and that channel can be spared, as it is seldom used, except now and then by American coasters going southward.

Completing channel work. Captain Abbot, the United States Engineer in charge of the jetties, does not state when in his opinion the final work on the channel will be completed, but the inference to be drawn from his report is that the present scene of active operations is well outside the area of the space between the jetty walls, and that, with the removal of the comparatively small amount of material remaining there, the whole improvement will be finished.

The expenditure so far on the work has been about 400,000 dol. (80,000*l.*) less than the estimated cost, and cash enough still remains on hand to maintain the jetties and continue the dredging until the outer shoal is so far removed as to occasion no more inconvenience to shipping; and if Congress further appropriates the amount of 253,000 dol., needed to complete the amount authorised to be expended under the plan of continued contract, the work can be maintained for at least 10 years.

CHARLESTON.

RETURN of British Shipping at the Port of Charleston in the Year 1896.

Direct Trade in British Vessels from and to Great Britain and British Colonies.

Entered.

Total Number of Vessels.			Total Tonnage.			Total Number of Crews.	Total Value of Cargoes.
With Cargoes.	In Ballast.	Total.	With Cargoes.	In Ballast.	Total.		£
9	13	22	6,627	19,224	25,851	429	7,927

Cleared.

Total Number of Vessels.			Total Tonnage.			Total Number of Crews.	Total Value of Cargoes.
With Cargoes.	In Ballast.	Total.	With Cargoes.	In Ballast.	Total.		£
10	1	11	12,190	161	12,351	225	395,908

Indirect or Carrying Trade in British Vessels from and to other Countries.

Entered.

Countries whence Arrived.	Number of Vessels.			Tonnage.			Number of Crews.	Value of Cargoes.
	With Cargoes.	In Ballast.	Total.	With Cargoes.	In Ballast.	Total.		£
Brazil	...	1	1	...	606	606	17	...
Germany	7	...	7	12,088	...	12,088	172	39,860
Italy	3	...	3	3,828	...	3,828	69	26,480
Portugal	6	...	6	6,297	...	6,297	123	11,200
Spain	7	2	9	8,437	4,950	13,387	148	29,900
United States	1	7	8	1,068	15,734	16,802	239	30,000
Total	24	10	34	31,718	21,290	53,008	768	137,440

Cleared.

Countries to which Departed.	Number of Vessels.			Total Tonnage.			Number of Crews.	Value of Cargoes.
	With Cargoes	In Ballast.	Total.	With Cargoes.	In Ballast.	Total.		£
France	1	...	1	1,068	...	1,068	21	40,000
Germany	16	...	16	28,770	...	28,770	413	916,000
Russia	1	...	1	1,575	...	1,575	25	58,000
Spain	9	...	9	8,487	...	8,487	171	308,600
United States	1	6	7	2,018	7,549	9,567	157	5,000
Total	28	6	34	41,918	7,549	49,467	787	1,322,600

UNITED STATES.

Miscellaneous.

Manufactures. Charleston's general manufacturing interests did not enjoy that degree of prosperity during the past commercial year ending September 1, 1896, which was expected at the beginning of the year. What appeared to be at that time the rising tide of returning prosperity was again checked by the agitation of the silver question throughout the country, and the uncertainty as to the financial future resulting therefrom, until the matter was fortunately settled by the Presidential election in November, with the defeat of the advocates of an extreme silver policy. Nearly all business interests languished, and manufactures shared in the general depression.

Cotton mill. The Charleston Cotton Mill did a moderately fair business during the early part of the year, the product turned out being about the same as the previous season, but operations were suspended and the mill closed down in June, and work has not yet been resumed.

Bagging. The bagging factory turned out about the same quantity of goods last year as for the previous one, but as prices averaged about 1 c. a yard higher last year, the value of the whole year's product was considerably greater than for the season of 1894–95, the estimated increase being about 20 per cent.

Ice factories. Two ice factories had all the business they could well handle during the year, prices obtained being 10 c. higher per 100 lbs. last season, as compared with the previous one, equivalent to an advance in wholesale prices of $33\frac{1}{3}$ per cent.; the cost, however, to consumers who buy at retail was considerably more than shown by these figures, and there has, perhaps, never before been a season in which so many complaints have been heard about ice dealers' prices.

The daily capacity of the two ice factories here combined is about 135 tons.

Fertiliser manufactures. By far the most important of Charleston's manufacturing industries is the making of phosphate fertilisers, which are already treated of in detail under the head of phosphates and fertilisers in this report. The total output for the year ending August 31, 1896, was 200,000 tons, including 70,000 tons on hand September 1, 1896, sold but not then delivered, which was an increase of about 60 per cent. over the previous year. The large sales, however, were more than set off last season by the lower prices prevailing, and the value of the total product was less by 120,000 dol. (24,000*l*.) than for the year before. Of this decrease in value, 90,000 dol. was due to the falling-off in prices for acid phosphates, and 30,000 dol. to ammoniated goods.

Failures. During the past year the most unfortunate feature to report in connection with this trade was the failure of the Ashley Phosphate Company, which was put up for sale at auction and bought in by the creditors, it being expected that the works would be again offered for sale when conditions were more favourable.

The basket and veneer works and also the Brewery Company

went into the hands of receivers since the last annual report, but both enterprises continued operations until they were reorganised under new management.

The mortgage on the Charleston City Waterworks was foreclosed last summer, and the Company was reorganised, but as the officers declined to announce the annual value of the product, exact figures for last year cannot be given; the capital stock, however, is said to consist of 100,000 dol. of stock, and 600,000 dol. of bonds. *Waterworks.*

The Charleston Knitting Company is a new enterprise started here last year; it is being managed by energetic and successful young business men, but it is too soon yet to give any figures as to its progress. *Knitting Company.*

Charleston's jobbing trade last year has a little more than held its own, the increase of business reported for the 12 months ending August 31, 1896, being little over half a million dollars, or to be more exact 541,000 dol. (108,000*l.*). In some departments of the wholesale trade there was a decline, while in other cases there were lines in which the proportionate increase was greater than that indicated by the above-mentioned total figures. There were comparatively few failures, and their number was probably equalled by the new houses established. The new season opened well in September, and throughout the early part of the autumn good accounts were given of the wholesale business, and collections were very good, but as the holidays approached, however, there was less demand for goods, and the year closed dull and quiet. *Wholesale trade. Few failures.*

Some attention was given last year to the general subject of cotton spinning in the Southern States, most of the mills being situated in the States of South and North Carolina and Georgia, which form part of this Consular district; as the industry seems to be on the whole an important and growing one, some further facts with reference to the business during the year now under review may not be uninteresting to British readers. *Southern cotton spinning.*

It appears that notwithstanding the unfavourable trade conditions last year, in southern mills, the industry is on the increase, a large number of new mills have been built, many old ones have materially increased the number of their spindles, and the building of new mills is reported to be progressing more actively than a year ago, notwithstanding the fears entertained by some investors, who, having regard to local conditions only, have been apprehensive that the business was being overdone. Conservative opinion seems to be that the unfavourable monetary and trade conditions existing should be regarded as temporary, and that confidence is fully justified by facts as to the ability of southern mills to ultimately consume a large percentage of the American cotton crop.

The total number of southern mills a year ago was 438, of which 15 have been "crossed out" and merged into other concerns, and 3 were burned, reducing the number to 420. To this, however, must be added 55 new mills last year, making the total number now 475 The number of spindles now in the *Mills and spindles increased.*

south is 3,698,238, compared with 3,177,310 a year ago, an increase of 520,928 during the past year. Of the above-named total, only 162,542 are reported idle at the close of the year.

Consumption capacity. The consumptive capacity of all the southern cotton mills at the present time, including old, idle, and new mills now building, is estimated to be 1,303,000 bales of cotton annually; this being an average of about 164·45 lbs. of the staple to the spindle.

Actual consumption. The actual consumption for the year ended September 1, 1896, was 904,701 bales, compared with 862,838 for the previous year, an increase last year of 41,863 bales, of which increase 26,731 bales are credited to South Carolina mills, 5,290 to North Carolina, and 4,726 to Georgia.

North Carolina mills. From reports issued by the North Carolina State Board of Agriculture, it is learned that the most notable feature in cotton manufacturing in that State last year was the improvement in equipment that took place, no less than fifty mills having thrown out old machinery and put in new; there has also been a decided tendency shown to manufacture less yarn, and unbleached warpings, and to increase the production of finer qualities of bleached goods and manufactured garments. At least ten mills that heretofore only spun yarn, are now making garments, and three years ago there was not a bleachery in the State. One mill is now making calico, the first one so far, and many mills are preparing to manufacture cordage, twine, &c., thus showing a disposition to greater diversity of product in this industry for the future.

Tobacco crop. Official statistics relative to the South Carolina tobacco crop during the past year, have not yet been published, but may be issued later on, and if they are of sufficient interest to justify it, a short special report on the subject will be made to the Foreign Office for publication.

Sufficient information, however, is available now to warrant the statement that the tobacco crop produced last year in this State was, on the whole, a good one, and much larger than for the previous season, although prices have ruled lower than the year before last.

BRUNSWICK.

Mr. Vice-Consul Torras reports as follows:—

Commercial situation. In relation to the commercial situation at this port, I beg to report that, in sympathy with the apparent general improvement in the country, and consequent upon the notable increase in the volume of transactions through the port for the year just closed, the feeling prevails that normally prosperous conditions have returned.

Improvement of channel at entrance. The new channel over the outer bar has been further deepened, and all uncertainty as regards its permanency is removed.

Depth on bar. The pilots will now take out a draft of 24 feet on average

CHARLESTON.

good tides. Prior to 1892 the port was rated at 18 feet maximum draft.

The British steamship "Saint Enoch" sailed in December drawing over 23 feet, and the British steamship "Maroa," of 6,802 tons, one of the largest cargo ships afloat, has since sailed with 21,274 bales of cotton, the second largest cargo ever leaving an American cotton port. The port now justly ranks as one of the deep water ports of the globe. *Unusually large cargo.*

The aggregate value of commodities passing over the bar during 1896 was 15,665,407 dol., as against 12,295.962 dol. for 1895, an increase of more than 25 per cent., and attributable, in a measure, to the feasibility of using heavy draft ships at advantageous rates, on account of the deepening of the channel. *Increase of commerce.*

Health conditions have continued excellent, and the official health report shows a further reduction in the annual death rate. *Health.*

This city possesses a most elaborate and efficient sewerage and subsoil drainage system, coupled with a modern waterworks' plant supplying excellent artesian water, and together with its municipal "Incinerator" for destroying all garbage, carcases, and street sweepings, is considered by sanitary experts as exceptionally well equipped for maintaining its excellent health record. *Sanitation.*

The National Government maintains a quarantine station in this harbour, removing ballast, and fumigating gratis all vessels arriving from suspected or infected ports. *Free quarantine.*

This feature exists at no other southern port.

The local authorities have abolished the fees of the harbour master and substituted therefor a small tonnage fee, which makes a more equitable tax, and provides for actual services of harbour master only when required by masters. *Harbour master's fee bill abolished.*

A new feature of the exports of 1896 was the direct shipments of Alabama pig iron and cotton to Manchester, viâ the Canal. *Pig iron to Europe.*

NATIONALITY and Tonnage of Vessels arriving at Brunswick during 1896.

Nationality.	Number of Vessels.	Tons.
American	349	266,634
British	49	58,199
Norwegian	51	32,645
Spanish	39	16,679
German	3	2,133
Russian	5	3,401
Swedish	3	1,450
Dutch	1	487
Italian	1	535
Portuguese	2	757
Brazilian	1	537
French	1	767
Total	505	384,224
" 1895	480	334,084

UNITED STATES.

Return of British Shipping at the Port of Brunswick, Ga., in the Year 1896.

Direct Trade in British Vessels from and to Great Britain and British Colonies.

	Entered.							Cleared.					
Total Number of Vessels.			Total Tonnage.			Total Number of Crews.	Total Value of Cargoes.	Total Number of Vessels.			Total Tonnage.			Total Number of Crews.	Total Value of Cargoes.
With Cargoes.	In Ballast.	Total.	With Cargoes.	In Ballast.	Total.			With Cargoes.	In Ballast.	Total.	With Cargoes.	In Ballast.	Total.		
2	15	17	424	26,402	26,826	460	£183	22	...	22	28,388	...	28,388	539	£687,775

Indirect or Carrying Trade in British Vessels from and to other Countries.

	Entered.									Cleared.							
Countries whence Arrived.	Number of Vessels.			Tonnage.			Number of Crews.	Value of Cargoes.	Countries to which Departed.	Number of Vessels.			Tonnage.			Number of Crews.	Value of Cargoes.
	With Cargoes.	In Ballast.	Total.	With Cargoes.	In Ballast.	Total.				With Cargoes.	In Ballast.	Total.	With Cargoes.	In Ballast.	Total.		
United States	...	15	15	...	19,494	19,494	355	£	Russia	1	...	1	1,063	...	1,063	13	£ 2,800
Brazil	...	2	2	...	1,254	1,254	23	...	Germany	9	...	9	15,429	...	15,429	225	154,451
West Indies	...	6	6	...	3,162	3,162	69	...	Roumania	1	...	1	1,361	...	1,361	23	5,000
Germany	...	1	1	...	324	324	8	...	Brazil	7	...	7	6,179	...	6,179	81	12,550
Canary Islands	...	2	2	...	2,572	2,572	46	...	Holland	3	...	3	4,407	...	4,407	72	25,550
Costa Rica	...	1	1	...	1,068	1,068	31	...	Hayti	1	...	1	109	...	109	5	250
Holland	...	1	1	...	1,063	1,063	13	...	Belgium	1	...	1	1,260	...	1,260	18	5,200
Total	...	28	28	...	28,937	28,937	545	...	Total	23	...	23	29,808	...	29,808	437	206,801

WILMINGTON.

Mr. Vice-Consul Sprunt reports as follows:—

Navigation.

In the year 1761, during a heavy storm, the Atlantic Ocean broke across the narrow sand beach which divided the sea from the river some 7 miles above the mouth, which from that time became known as the New Inlet, and which caused a rapid shoaling of the old channel, there being then two outlets instead of one as formerly.

Cape Fear River.

The Cape Fear River, from its mouth nearly to Wilmington is properly a tidal estuary of about 38 square miles. The river and its branches drain an area of about 8,000 square miles. The amount of fresh water passing out at the mouth, though large, is insignificant when compared with the tidal flow which alternately fills and empties this great reservoir. The mean fresh water discharge of the river does not exceed 9,000 cubic feet per second, while the tidal flow at the entrance averages about 175,000 cubic feet per second. This is the real force which creates and preserves the channel across the shifting sands of the coast at the mouth of the river. No demonstration is needed to prove the importance of concentrating this force. It is also apparent that such a force would be most efficient in preserving a passage across a bar and shoals which are in a position sheltered from the prevailing winds and heaviest storms of the coast. This we have at the natural mouth of the river which is wholly sheltered from northerly, north-easterly, and, in a great measure, from easterly winds by its position in the bay, protected by Cape Fear and Frying Pan Shoals.

Congress was accordingly petitioned to appropriate the necessary means for increasing the depth of water on Cape Fear bar and river; and after careful surveys and estimates by the Corps of Engineers, U.S.A., it was decided to undertake the entire closure of New Inlet under the direction of Colonel W. P. Craighill. This important and difficult work was begun in 1875. A continuous line of mattresses composed of logs and brushwood sunk and loaded with stone, was laid entirely across the New Inlet from October, 1875, to June, 1876. This was the foundation of the dam. The work was continued from year to year by piling small stone rip rap on and over this foundation, bringing it up to high water, and then covering it with heavy granite stones on the top and slopes to low water. The closure was completed successfully in 1881, and was the occasion of much rejoicing in Wilmington, for its failure would have completely ruined the port of Wilmington, which depends for its life upon deep water and successful competition with Norfolk and Charleston.

The length of the dam from Federal Point to Zeke's Island is 1 mile, but the extension of Zeke's Island jetties to Smith's Island makes the line much longer. The rock foundation of this wall is from 90 to 120 feet wide at the base, and for three-fourths of the line the average depth of stone wall is 30 feet from the top of the dam. In some places it is 36 feet deep. The stone used in this structure would build a solid wall 8 feet high, 4 feet thick, and 100 miles long. The cost of the work was 480,000 dol., a small sum when the magnitude and difficulty of the undertaking are considered. The sea-wall is one of the best planned and most successful engineering feats in the south.

Lieut.-Colonel D. P. Heap, Corps United States Engineers, who is now in charge of this work, reported recently to the Chief of Engineers, United States Army, as follows:—

The United States began to improve the river between the bar and Wilmington in 1829, and the channel on the bar in 1853. In 1829 the river was so obstructed that vessels drawing more than 10 feet were obliged to anchor 14 miles below Wilmington and discharge a part of their cargo into lighters. In 1853 at low-water on the bar the least mid-channel depth was 7 feet in the western channel, $7\frac{1}{2}$ feet in the eastern channel, and 8 feet at New Inlet, 7 miles above the mouth.

The original project of 1827 was to deepen the channel through the shoals in the 8 miles next below Wilmington by contracting it by jetties and by diverting into it water from Brunswick River and from Fishing and Rodman's Creeks.

The project of 1853 was to straighten and deepen the channel on the bar by building jetties and a wing dam, by dredging, by diverting water through it from New Inlet, by building a jetty at Federal Point, and by closing two small breaches in Zeke's Island.

The project of 1870 was to deepen the bar channel by closing the breaches between Smith's and Zeke's Islands, with the ultimate closure of New Inlet in view.

The project of 1873 was to deepen the channel through the bar, added to that of 1870, to dredge the Baldhead (eastern) Channel, to extend across Zeke's Island, and beyond it into the river, the dam then being built to close the breaches between Smith's and Zeke's Islands, and to close New Inlet, commencing with the building of a jetty from Federal Point.

The project of 1874 was to "get 12 feet at low-water as high as the City of Wilmington," by dredging a channel 100 feet wide through Horseshoe Shoal, below New Inlet, and through three other shoals near Wilmington.

The project of 1881 was to dredge a channel $2\frac{3}{4}$ miles in length through Horseshoe Shoal, and through eight other shoals above it, 270 feet wide and 16 feet deep at mean low-water from deep water at Smithville (Southport) to Wilmington.

February 28, 1889, pursuant to a requirement of the River and Harbour Act of August 11, 1888, the cost of obtaining a channel 20 feet deep at mean low water from Wilmington to the ocean was reported to be 1,800,000 dol. In the annual report for 1889 it was reported that an additional appropriation of 25,000 dol. would be required to complete the project of 1881, and obtain a channel 16 feet deep from Wilmington to the ocean. By the River and Harbour Act of September 19, 1890, Congress appropriated 170,000 dol. for improving the Cape Fear River at and below Wilmington, and dredging to the depth of 20 feet, commenced at Wilmington January 19, 1891, and ceased at Brunswick River Shoal, 4½ miles below Wilmington, September 7, 1892.

Since September 7, 1892, work has been in progress to obtain a channel through the shoals between Wilmington and the bar, and on the latter 18 feet at mean low water.

On June 30, 1895, a channel had been obtained 18 feet deep at mean low water, of variable width, but nowhere less than 148 feet, through all the shoals between Wilmington and the ocean, except that at Snows Marsh, where the depth was 16·7 feet, and on the bar, where there was a narrow straight channel 14·2 feet deep, and a narrow crooked channel 15 feet deep. A training dike 5,692 feet in length had been built at Snows Marsh, a suction dredging steamer had been built under contract and placed in operation on the bar and at Snows Marsh Shoal, and a breach made by the sea in the east bank of the river around the end of New Inlet Dam had been closed by the deposit of 1,353 tons of granite.

The work of the past fiscal year ending June 30, 1896, has been carried on by hired labour and use of the Government plant.

The United States dredging-steamer "Cape Fear" removed 318,636 cubic yards of material from the ocean bar during 142 working days, and 155,250 cubic yards from Snows Marsh Channel during 118 working days.

1,788 piles were driven, and 1,533·15 cords of brush fascines were used in extending the Snows Marsh Dike 2,992 feet up stream, and 556 feet down stream, and 1,417·17 cords of brush fascines were used in making needed repairs to the dike.

Minor repairs were made to the Swash Defence Dam, in which 25 tons of stone were used. A break 125 feet long in the New Inlet Dam, near Federal Point, the place where a similar break occurred last year, has been undergoing repair; 1,822 bags of sand, 175 tons of stone, and 85·10 cords of brush in fascines have been so far used in repairing this break, which work is at date unfinished.

A survey of the river for the establishment of harbour lines for the city of Wilmington was made, and three hydrographic surveys each were made of the ocean bar and Snows Marsh Channel and vicinity.

26 of the triangular stations along the river were made permanent by means of concrete.

The United States plant was repaired and kept in condition to perform the work required of it.

The condition at the close of the fiscal year ending June 30, 1896, is that a channel nowhere less than 148 feet wide and 18 feet deep at mean low water exists from Wilmington to the ocean.

(2326)

except at Snows Marsh Shoal, where the depth is only 16·7 feet, as it was last year.

The Snows Marsh Dike is now 9,240 feet long, and has by scour arrested the shoaling at this place.

The New Inlet Dam is intact and in good condition except at the place near Federal Point, where the break by undermining of 125 feet has occurred around its shore end.

The Swash Defence Dam is intact and in excellent condition.

The work on the river has been under the immediate charge of Mr. Charles Humphreys, assistant engineer.

The sum of 25,000 dol. will be required annually for maintenance of this improvement.

Carrying Trade.

The increased depth of water to 20 feet on Cape Fear Bar, and in Cape Fear River to Wilmington 18½ to 19 feet (average tide), has changed the class of tonnage to and from this port. In former years, for example, 10 years ago, in 1886, the British carrying trade employed only three or four steamers of 800 to 1,100 tons net register, and about 35 sailing vessels of 250 to 900 tons for the cotton, lumber, and naval stores trade. In 1896 there were employed 24 British steamers averaging about 1,800 tons each net register, and 16 sailing vessels of about the same class as formerly.

A line of American steamers sailing twice weekly has absorbed largely the coasting trade, which formerly employed several hundred American schooners.

10 years ago a large business was done in Scandinavian and German sailing bottoms. During the year past, 1896, this trade has been reduced by at least one-half, owing to the increase of American and British steam tonnage.

Products.

Turpentine &c. The trade of Wilmington has decreased in spirits of turpentine, resin, and tar, owing to the fact that the pine trees in the States of North Carolina and South Carolina have been gradually reduced in number by felling, and by depletion by tapping, and the operations of turpentine distillers have extended to Georgia and Florida, where there is a greater extent of virgin forest. It appears, however, that Wilmington trade in these products is not very far behind the volume of 10 years ago, as the following comparison of 1886 and 1896 will show:—

	Spirits, Turpentine.	Resin.	Tar.
	Casks.	Barrels.	Barrels.
Receipts, 1886	60,738	289,164	67,043
,, 1896	46,553	205,137	67,198

Cotton. In cotton receipts and exports there has been a very large increase, and it is worthy of remark that this development may be largely attributed to the enterprise and industry of a firm which was established in 1886 by two Scotchmen who became identified with the progress of Wilmington, and whose efforts have been marked in its development. They own one of the most extensive of cotton press plants in America, and their shipments to all cotton ports abroad now aggregate two-thirds of the entire Wilmington trade in raw cotton.

The total Wilmington receipts in cotton in 1886 were 137,357 bales, and those in 1896 will probably exceed 250,000 bales.

Fruit, &c. It may be mentioned that a large area of hitherto waste land on the lines of railways in North Carolina has been taken up for the cultivation of early small fruits and vegetables for supplying the markets of Baltimore, Philadelphia, and New York in the spring months of the year. This occupation has been most successful and remunerative, especially in the cultivation of strawberries, and the volume of trade in these products has increased from probably 5,000*l.* in 1886 to 50,000*l.* in 1896. At times when the supply from Florida and Southern Georgia is waning, the demand for Carolina fruit and vegetables is active, and the prices obtained leave large profits over the cost of production.

Fisheries. The fisheries in this State are extensive and profitable; hundreds of thousands of barrels of herring, shad, mullet, and other food fishes are shipped from the coast to the interior, and also to markets in the Northern States. The recent developments in deep sea fishing have largely increased this trade. It had been supposed that the food fish which are most numerous in September and October along the coast migrated to warmer seas on the approach of winter, but it has been found that such is not the case, and that in cold weather the fish seek the greatest depths which afford feeding ground within a few miles of the coast; large nets are now spread upon the floor of the ocean, and by a simple arrangement of blocks similar to that of the patent reefing appliance are drawn to the surface laden with almost incredible numbers of fish in fine condition.

RETURN of British Shipping at the Port of Wilmington, N.C., in the Year 1896.

Direct Trade in British Vessels from and to Great Britain and British Colonies.

Entered.

Total Number of Vessels.			Total Tonnage.			Total Number of Crews.	Total Value of Cargoes.
With Cargoes.	In Ballast.	Total.	With Cargoes.	In Ballast.	Total.		£
1	7	8	131	11,096	11,227	162	300

Cleared.

Total Number of Vessels.			Total Tonnage.			Total Number of Crews.	Total Value of Cargoes.
With Cargoes.	In Ballast.	Total.	With Cargoes.	In Ballast.	Total.		£
19	...	19	21,439	...	21,439	342	704,312

Indirect or Carrying Trade in British Vessels from and to other Countries.

Entered.

Countries whence Arrived.	Number of Vessels.			Tonnage.			Number of Crews.	Value of Cargoes.
	With Cargoes.	In Ballast.	Total.	With Cargoes.	In Ballast.	Total.		£
Spain	1	6	7	149	2,936	3,085	67	800
Portugal	...	1	1	...	1,695	1,695	24	...
United States ports	...	24	24	...	25,348	25,348	423	...
Total	1	31	32	149	29,979	30,128	514	800

Cleared.

Countries to which Departed.	Number of Vessels.			Tonnage.			Number of Crews.	Value of Cargoes.
	With Cargoes.	In Ballast.	Total.	With Cargoes.	In Ballast.	Total.		£
Germany	11	...	11	17,100	...	17,100	252	601,075
San Domingo	4	...	4	929	...	929	29	1,663
Hayti	3	...	3	634	...	634	21	1,033
Spain—Cuba and Porto Rico	2	...	2	595	...	595	15	1,600
Belgium	1	...	1	658	...	658	16	19,113
Total	21	...	21	19,916	...	19,916	333	624,484

CHARLESTON.

PORT ROYAL.

Mr. Vice-Consul Kessler reports as follows:—

Since my last annual report I beg to say that the condition of this port remains about the same, except that the phosphate rock industry has fallen-off about one-third, owing to the low price of rock and the competition of other countries which can mine the rock as cheaply and have no State royalty to pay.

The large Government dry dock is now completed and ready to take in any sized vessel.

We also have a coaling station at this port, and vessels can obtain coal day and night with quick despatch. Pilot's rates are cheaper than at Charleston or Savannah, so it would pay British steamers in want of coal to call at this port, and save time and the dangers of going round Cape Hatteras.

The general health of this port is very good.

Our exports consist of cotton, cotton-seed, cotton-seed meal flour, grain, lumber, phosphate rock, naval stores.

Imports: salt, kainit, meat, meal, sulphur, blood, soda.

EXPORTS to England from the Port of Beaufort, S.C., for Year ending December 31, 1896.

Month.	Nationality.	Commodities.	Quantity (Bales.)	Quantity (Tons.)	Quantity (M. feet.)	Value (Dol.)
January	British steamships	Cotton	3,492	...	...	141,356
,,	,, ,,	Lumber	...	...	27,000	816
February	,, ,,	Phos. rock	...	5,688	...	20,042
,,	,, ,,	Cotton	16,779	...	...	641,288
,,	,, ,,	Lumber	...	...	73,000	2,603
March	,, ,,	Cotton	11,539	...	...	453,705
,,	,, ,,	Phos. rock	...	5,127	...	19,048
,,	,, ,,	Lumber	...	...	125,000	4,893
April	,, ,,	Phos. rock	...	11,412	...	41,161
May	,, ,,	,, ,,	...	2,582	...	10,328
,,	,, ,,	Cotton	1,813	...	...	74,406
,,	,, ,,	Lumber	...	...	128,000	3,768
June	,, ,,	Phos. rock	...	5,777	...	21,333
,,	,, ,,	Cotton	269	...	...	9,035
,,	,, ,,	Lumber	...	...	148,000	5,418
July	,, ,,	Phos. rock	...	7,267	...	27,868
August	,, ,,	,, ,,	...	8,601	...	28,753
,,	,, ,,	Lumber	...	...	126,000	6,218
,,	,, ,,	Cotton	2,183	...	...	76,711
September	,, ,,	Phos. rock	...	4,932	...	19,728
October	,, ,,	,, ,,	...	3,491	...	11,773
,,	,, ,,	Cotton	7,743	...	...	303,526
,,	,, ,,	Lumber	...	...	11,000	326
November	,, ,,	Phos. rock	...	2,435	...	7,305
,,	,, ,,	Cotton	10,600	...	...	415,520
,,	,, ,,	Lumber	...	...	415,000	15,369
December	,, ,,	Phos. rock	...	9,035	...	26,075
,,	,, ,,	Cotton	20,300	...	...	796,027
,,	,, ,,	Lumber	...	...	132,550	883

RETURN of British Shipping at the Port of Port Royal in the Year 1896.

Direct Trade in British Vessels from and to Great Britain and British Colonies.

Entered.

Number of Vessels			Total Tonnage			Total Number of Crews.	Total Value of Cargoes.
With Cargoes.	In Ballast.	Total.	With Cargoes.	In Ballast.	Total.		£
8	9	17	17,600	18,450	36,050	425	5,750

Cleared.

Total Number of Vessels			Total Tonnage			Total Number of Crews.	Total Value of Cargoes.
With Cargoes.	In Ballast.	Total.	With Cargoes.	In Ballast.	Total.		£
36	4	40	90,150	5,000	95,150	11,020	632,540

Indirect or Carrying Trade in British Vessels from and to other Countries.

Entered.

Countries whence Arrived.	Number of Vessels			Tonnage			Number of Crews.	Value of Cargoes.
	With Cargoes.	In Ballast.	Total.	With Cargoes.	In Ballast.	Total.		£
United States	...	25	25	...	553,350	553,350	685	...
France	...	...	...	...	...	...	...	...
Germany	4	...	4	8,350	...	8,350	96	33,450
Spain	...	...	...	...	...	...	...	...
Brazil	1	...	1	850	...	850	12	3,250
Portugal	...	...	...	...	...	...	...	...
Total	5	25	30	9,200	553,350	562,550	793	36,700

Cleared.

Countries to which Departed.	Number of Vessels			Tonnage			Number of Crews.	Value of Cargoes.
	With Cargoes.	In Ballast.	Total.	With Cargoes.	In Ballast.	Total.		£
United States	...	4	4	...	6,185	6,185	104	...
France	1	...	1	2,750	...	2,750	23	8,100
Germany	2	...	2	47,306	...	47,306	52	16,200
Spain	1	...	1	2,700	...	2,700	24	8,350
Brazil	...	...	...	...	...	...	...	...
Portugal	...	...	...	...	...	...	...	...
Total	4	4	8	52,756	6,185	58,941	203	32,650

(75   4 | 97—H & S   2326)

FOREIGN OFFICE.
1897.
ANNUAL SERIES.

N°· 1869.
DIPLOMATIC AND CONSULAR REPORTS ON TRADE AND FINANCE.

UNITED STATES.

REPORT FOR THE YEAR 1896
ON THE
TRADE OF NEW ORLEANS.

REFERENCE TO PREVIOUS REPORT, Annual Series No. 1688.

Presented to both Houses of Parliament by Command of Her Majesty,
APRIL, 1897.

LONDON:
PRINTED FOR HER MAJESTY'S STATIONERY OFFICE,
BY HARRISON AND SONS, ST. MARTIN'S LANE,
PRINTERS IN ORDINARY TO HER MAJESTY.

And to be purchased, either directly or through any Bookseller, from
EYRE & SPOTTISWOODE, EAST HARDING STREET, FLEET STREET, E.C., and
32, ABINGDON STREET, WESTMINSTER, S.W.; or
JOHN MENZIES & Co., 12, HANOVER STREET, EDINBURGH, and
90, WEST NILE STREET, GLASGOW; or
HODGES, FIGGIS, & Co., Limited, 104, GRAFTON STREET, DUBLIN.

1897.

[C. 8277—87.] *Price Twopence Halfpenny*

New Series of Reports.

Reports of the Annual Series have been issued from Her Majesty's Diplomatic and Consular Officers at the following places, and may be obtained from the sources indicated on the title-page:—

No.		Price.	No.		Price.
1749. Montevideo	.. ..	1½d.	1809. Aleppo	.. .. ..	1d.
1750. San Francisco	.. ..	3d.	1810. Tangier	.. .. ..	2½d.
1751. Cayenne	.. .. ..	½d.	1811. Tokio	.. .. ..	3½d.
1752. Frankfort	.. .. ..	3d.	1812. Madeira	.. .. ..	½d.
1753. Malaga	.. .. ..	8½d.	1813. Vera Cruz	.. .. ..	1d.
1754. Söul	.. .. ..	1d.	1814. Oporto	.. .. ..	1d.
1755. Copenhagen	.. ..	3d.	1815. Hamburg	.. .. ..	1½d.
1756. Nice	.. .. ..	1d.	1816. New Orleans	.. ..	1½d.
1757. Lisbon	.. .. ..	1½d.	1817. Bengazi	.. .. ..	½d.
1758. Nagasaki	.. ..	1d.	1818. Marmagao	.. .. ..	½d.
1759. Hamburg	.. ..	2½d.	1819. Gothenburg	.. ..	2d.
1760. Mozambique	.. ..	2d.	1820. Dar-al-Baida	.. ..	3d.
1761. Cettinjé	.. ..	1½d.	1821. Erzeroum	.. .. ..	½d.
1762. The Hague	.. ..	1½d.	1822. Munich	.. .. ..	2½d.
1763. Cephalonia	.. ..	1d.	1823. Samoa	.. .. ..	½d.
1764. Bahia	.. .. ..	1d.	1824. Chinkiang	.. ..	1d.
1765. Zanzibar	.. ..	1½d.	1825. Jeddah	.. .. ..	1d.
1766. Pakhoi	.. .. ..	1d.	1826. Sofia	.. .. ..	1½d.
1767. New York	.. ..	2d.	1827. Mexico	.. .. ..	2d.
1768. Chefoo	.. .. ..	1d.	1828. Teneriffe	.. .. ..	3½d.
1769. Caracas	.. .. ..	½d.	1829. Batoum	.. .. ..	1d.
1770. Palermo	.. .. ..	11½d.	1830. Cadiz	.. .. ..	1d.
1771. Mombasa	.. ..	½d.	1831. Martinique	.. ..	1d.
1772. Nice	.. .. ..	1½d.	1832. Odessa	.. .. ..	1d.
1773. Bucharest	.. ..	4½d.	1833. Ghilan	.. .. ..	1d.
1774. Port Said	.. ..	1½d.	1834. Old Calabar	.. ..	6½d.
1775. Galatz	.. .. ..	1½d.	1835. Tamsui	.. .. ..	1d.
1776. Madrid	.. .. ..	2d.	1836. Copenhagen	.. ..	½d.
1777. Vienna	.. .. ..	2d.	1837. Salonica	.. .. ..	1½d.
1778. Canton	.. .. ..	1d.	1838. Honolulu	.. .. ..	½d.
1779. Yokohama	.. ..	1½d.	1839. Buenos Ayres	.. ..	2d.
1780. Newchwang	.. ..	1d.	1840. Para	.. .. ..	1d.
1781. Wuhu	.. .. ..	1d.	1841. Bolivia	.. .. ..	2d.
1782. Athens	.. .. ..	2d.	1842. Washington	.. ..	3d.
1783. Tonga	.. .. ..	½d.	1843. Berlin	.. .. ..	2d.
1784. Smyrna	.. .. ..	½d.	1844. Uganda	.. .. ..	1d.
1785. Baghdad	.. ..	1d.	1845. Belgrade	.. .. ..	1½d.
1786. Hiogo and Osaka	..	4½d.	1846. Dakar	.. .. ..	½d.
1787. Bangkok	.. ..	1d.	1847. Florence	.. .. ..	1½d.
1788. Odessa	.. .. ..	2d.	1848. Copenhagen	.. ..	2d.
1789. Naples	.. .. ..	2d.	1849. Havre	.. .. ..	2d.
1790. Beyrout	.. .. ..	1d.	1850. Serajevo	.. .. ..	1d.
1791. Tunis	.. .. ..	1½d.	1851. Madrid	.. .. ..	2d.
1792. Kiukiang	.. ..	3d.	1852. La Rochelle	.. ..	1½d.
1793. Bangkok	.. ..	1d.	1853. Chicago	.. .. ..	4d.
1794. Rio Grande do Sul	..	1d.	1854. Berlin	.. .. ..	1d.
1795. Valparaiso	.. ..	4d.	1855. Cherbourg	.. ..	2½d.
1796. Brindisi	.. .. ..	2½d.	1856. Beira	.. .. ..	1d.
1797. Bushire	.. .. ..	2d.	1857. Charleston	.. ..	2½d.
1798. Christiania	.. ..	5½d.	1858. Saigon	.. .. ..	½d.
1799. Cadiz	.. .. ..	2d.	1859. Suakin	.. .. ..	1d.
1800. Meshed	.. .. ..	2½d.	1860. Rouen	.. .. ..	2d.
1801. St. Petersburg	.. ..	4½d.	1861. Patras	.. .. ..	1½d.
1802. Batoum	.. .. ..	1d.	1862. Barcelona	.. ..	2d.
1803. Peking	.. .. ..	3d.	1863. Amoy	.. .. ..	2½d.
1804. Samos	.. .. ..	½d.	1864. Trebizond	.. ..	1d.
1805. Dantzig	.. .. ..	2d.	1865. Lisbon	.. .. ..	2½d.
1806. Antwerp	.. .. ..	1½d.	1866. Callao	.. .. ..	2d.
1807. Ajaccio	.. .. ..	1½d.	1867. Pernambuco	.. ..	5d.
1808. Stettin	.. .. ..	3d.	1868. Naples	.. .. ..	1½d.

No. 1869.

Reference to previous Report, Annual Series No. 1688.

UNITED STATES.

NEW ORLEANS.

Consul St. John to the Marquess of Salisbury.

(Received at Foreign Office, April 3, 1897.)

My Lord,

I HAVE the honour to transmit herewith my Annual Trade Report for 1896, as well as those from Mr. Howe, Her Majesty's Vice-Consul at Pensacola, and Mr. Barnewall, British Vice-Consul at Mobile.

I have, &c.
(Signed)   C. L. ST. JOHN.

Report on the Trade and Commerce of the Consular District of New Orleans for the Year 1896.

TABLE of Contents.

	PAGE
New Orleans—	
General remarks	2
Street electric tramways	4
Finance, clearing-house returns	4
Commerce	4
Free wharves	4
Cotton	5
„ prices	5
„ growth	5
„ exports	6
„ mills	6
„ spindles	7
Grain trade	7
Flour	7
Coal	8
Hardware	8
Small-pox epidemic of 1895–96	8
Principal exports	10
British shipping returns	10
Shipping returns	11

(2340)

UNITED STATES.

Table of Contents—continued.

	PAGE
Pensacola—	
Trade	11
Pitch pine freights, &c.	12
New trade to Mexican ports, Cuba, &c.	12
L. and N. railroad in connection with same	13
Imports	13
Seamen	13
Quarantine	14
Agriculture	14
Annexes—	
A.—Return of rates of freight	15
B.— „ principal articles of export	16
C.— „ imports and exports by countries	17
D.— „ shipping	17
Mobile—	
Trade and commerce largely increased	18
Cotton trade receipts and prices	20
„ exports	21
Fruit trade	21
Corn exports	22
Lumber and timber	22
Hardwoods	24
Staves	25
Wool	25
Vegetables	25
Receipts of leading articles	26
Mobile Harbour	26
Returns of shipping	31

General Remarks.

General remarks.

The past season has been the most important New Orleans has ever experienced, and has seen more accomplished than any previous five years. It has not been in every respect a fortunate season as there has been loss in some lines. New Orleans has felt the shrinkage in values from depressions throughout the country—results of hard times.

The competition exercised by neighbouring ports such as Mobile, Pensacola, and Galveston, has been taken as a warning that if this port is to hold its own, many improvements must at once be undertaken in the direction of improving the town in its appearance, health, and commercial facilities.

While the trade of New Orleans has increased in tonnage, it has decreased in valuation about 15 per cent. Commercially it has advanced, losing nothing, and gaining several new lines of business, or materially increasing those it already possessed. It has made an important step forward in its cotton and grain trades.

Owing to free wharfage at Chalmette, outside the city limits, and to the Stuyvesant Docks—so-called, though they are only wharves—which are free and within the city limits, wharfage dues are being considerably diminished, and the charges reduced by about 40 per cent., thus bringing to this port a great deal of cotton and grain which hitherto went elsewhere.

During the season ended August 31, 1896, New Orleans, it is said, succeeded in passing New York, Baltimore, and other eastern ports in the amount of grain handled; now standing the first grain port in the Union.

The railroad business has increased rapidly. During the season of 1886-87 the tonnage of goods coming to New Orleans amounted to 2,000,756, at present it stands at 4,516,193 tons.

The value of the product handled by the railroads has shown some fluctuations. In 1895, for instance, the value was 219,260,272 dol. (in round numbers 44,000,000*l*.), which in 1896 showed 201,115,620 dol. (about 40,000,000*l*.). Though there was a considerable increase in the amount of produce brought to New Orleans, the freight carried out showed a large decline, not only at New Orleans, but in all the great towns. This is owing to farmers and small country merchants having of late been less prosperous, and consequently having to put up with less than they were accustomed to.

The ocean trade shows the same characteristics as that of the railroads. The number and tonnage of vessels entering and clearing from this port was the largest in its history. The best record in the past was in 1892, when the total tonnage of the port was 3,333,658 tons. During the season ended August 31, 1896, it reached 3,335,636 tons, a considerable increase over the previous (1895), which showed 3,222,467 tons.

Though the imports during the past season have increased in tonnage, they have remained stationary in value; but there has been an increase both in tonnage and value of exports. The value of imports and exports for the season ended August, 1896, including coastwise, amounted, the former to 80,072,650 dol. (16,000,000*l*.), the latter to 122,409,616 dol. (24,500,000*l*.). This shows a total ocean trade of 202,482,206 dol. (40,500,000*l*.) for the past season, against 193,191,698 dol. (38,640,000*l*.) for 1895, which is a great improvement considering the decline in values.

The following figures show the total value of the trade of all kinds done by New Orleans during the last season :—

	Quantity.	Value.
	Tons.	£
Total tonnage of shipments	3,334,315	41,874,047
„ receipts	4,941,580	42,042,135

This, however, does not compare very favourably with the commerce of 1892-93, the value of which amounted to 105,566,126*l*., so far as values go, though the tonnage shows an increase. The difference is simply due to the decline in the price of farm products.

While there have been fluctuations in the trade of New Orleans, its manufactures have advanced. How greatly they have extended is shown by the fact that in 1870 there were only 63 different industries enumerated; last year 186.

(2340)

UNITED STATES.

Street electric tramways.

New Orleans has one of the best street tramways in the country. Since 1893, 158 miles of electric tramways have been laid down and used, and considerable extensions are yet to be made.

Finance.

The clearing-house gives the best returns since 1892, the bank clearances amounting to 99,763,236*l*., as compared with 89,442,267*l*. last year.

Commerce.

Compared with other ports of the United States, New Orleans holds this year, as last, the third place in exports, and has advanced to the fifth place in imports; the values for 1896 are as follows:—

	Value.	
	Currency.	Sterling.
	Dollars.	£
Exports	95,875,928	19,768,235
Imports	13,188,098	2,719,195

As compared with 1895 the imports show a decrease of 437,135*l*., but the exports an increase of 4,582,879*l*.

Annexed will be found a return of the principal articles of export carried in British ships during the year. No record of the values is obtainable, but the values of the exports to Great Britain is given by the customs returns as 8,455,878*l*., or about one-half the total exports.

Free wharves.

There can be no doubt that the hitherto exorbitant wharf dues have driven the commerce of this town to other ports; but the building during 1896 of free wharves, such as those of Chalmette, situated below the city, and the Stuyvesant dock within the city limits, have caused the Wharf Company, who hold a lease till 1901 to moderate their charges. It is only a question of time when these will be brought out by the town, and free wharves established all along the riverside, by which vessels will be greatly benefited.

With regard to the "Stuyvesant Docks," the wharf is owned by the Illinois Central Railway, of which Mr. Stuyvesant Fish is president. This company has made it a free wharf within the city limits, and has erected enormous elevators by which wheat can be shot into a ship's hold. It is stated that this free wharf will be a saving of 100*l*. to 200*l*. to every ship.

The wharf is situated within easy reach of Louisiana Avenue.

Agents of British liners have long been complaining of the heavy charges they have been put to by private wharf companies, and they have been compelled to send their ships to other ports for cargoes in preference to New Orleans. It is, however, possible that, owing to the inroads made in their business by the free wharfage at Southport, Port Chalmette, and the Stuyvesant Docks, the lessees may deem it advisable to sell at a reasonable price before the expiration of their term in 1901.

When reporting on cotton from New Orleans, the most important export market for that article, it would be unsatisfactory to confine one's self to that grown exclusively in this Consular district. This report, therefore, must allude, though in a limited degree, to the whole crop of the Southern States, by which only a proper estimate can be made. *Cotton.*

The cotton crop of the United States for the year ending August 31, 1896, amounts to 7,157,346 bales, showing a decrease under the crop of 1894–95 of 2,743,905 bales, and an increase over that of 1892–93 of 456,981 bales.

The greatest falling-off, as compared with last year, has been in Texas, the drop from the yield of the previous season having reached 1,286,376 bales, but the yield that year had been a phenomenal one.

As a whole, the year has been a most unsatisfactory one to the trade, but to the producing interests the shrinkage of the crop has been almost made up by the improvement in price.

Based on a fair average for the United States, the highest point touched was $9\frac{3}{16}$ c. per lb. for middling, and the lowest $6\frac{1}{2}$ c.; the average for the entire season being 8·18 c., a gain on the crop over last year's average of 2·26 per lb., or, say, in round figures, 11 dol. per bale. *Cotton prices.*

The average commercial value of the crop has been 41·09 dol. per bale against 30 dol. last year, and 37 dol. 50 c. the year before.

The actual growth can only be arrived at approximately. This year's commercial crop contains part of the growth of other seasons. Usually the quantity of new cotton marketed in August is not large; this year, however, it exceeds all precedent. *Cotton growth.*

As stated by Mr. Hester, secretary of the New Orleans Cotton Exchange, the calculation is as follows:—

	Quantity.
	Bales.
Commercial crop of 1895–96	7,157,000
Less old cotton crop left over, 1894–95	215,000
	6,942,000
Plus growth not marketed in 1895–96	166,000
Actual growth of 1895–96	7,108,000

An item in this connection is the reduced weights of bales, which average 6·80 lbs. less than last year, so that if calculated on last year's weights, the result, says Mr. Hester, would be slightly more than 95,000 bales less. In other words, the commercial crop of the year is equal in round figures to but 7,062,000 bales of last year's crop, and the approximate actual growth of to but 6,846,000.

(2340)

UNITED STATES.

New Orleans, export of cotton.

New Orleans in 1895–96 exported the following amount of cotton in bales:—

	Quantity.
	Bales.
Great Britain	715,699
France	306,951
Continent	596,418
Total	1,619,068
„ 1894–95	2,053,831

TOTAL Exports of the United States.

Year.	Quantity.			
	Great Britain.	France.	Continent.	Total.
	Bales.	Bales.	Bales.	Bales.
1895–96	2,299,182	465,870	1,861,116	4,626,168
1894–95	3,443,574	774,476	2,500,911	6,718,961
1893–94	2,859,114	587,299	1,775,784	5,222,197

Included under Continent are exports to Mexico and Japan, not, however, from New Orleans, but from Galveston, Mobile, and other ports.

Cotton consumption of the south, mills, &c.

As a report on cotton consumption in this Consular district only would be of very little use, I continue to comprise the other Southern States in order to enable the reader to form an idea of competition in the cotton industry.

The cotton milling industry of the South has continued to increase. A large number of new mills have been added, and many of the old establishments have materially increased their spindles. Building of new mills is still going on at a rate even exceeding the activity in that respect mentioned in former reports from this Consulate.

MILLS.

	Number.
Total number of mills last year	435
Ceased working and burnt	15
	420
New mills added	55
Total actual working mills	475

SPINDLES.

	Number.
In the South, operating	2,956,396
Idle	162,542
New, not complete	574,300
Total	3,693,238
„ last year	3,177,310
Increase of spindles	515,928

The total consumption in all the mills, old and new, for the year was 904,701 bales, against 862,838 for the season 1894-95.

	Quantity.
	Bales.
Consumption of Southern States	904,701
„ Northern States	1,600,271
Total consumption by United States	2,504,972

The grain trade. New Orleans it appears now leads as the largest exporter of corn in America. December shipments exceeded, it is said, 3,000,000 bushels, and run the total for the year up to 27,000,000 bushels, or nearly 5 times what it was in 1895. The business was a new one, and it was only during the year that New Orleans secured those facilities that have enabled it to handle the trade satisfactorily.

With regard to wheat there has not been the same increased exportation, owing to that product being grown further away from New Orleans than corn. But, nevertheless, there has been an increase, as shipments up to the end of November, 1896, amounted to 3,648,694 bushels, as compared to 739,372 in 1895.

The total export of grain for the year 1896, including 204,934 bushels of oats and some rye, is computed at 31,500,000 bushels, of which the value is 2,640,000*l*. This is the beginning, as the grain trade may be said to have started only in 1895.

Flour. There has been a marked increase in the exports of all leading products. New Orleans shipped 240,000 barrels of flour during the 11 months of 1896, as compared with 87,600 barrels in 1895; and 23,500,000 lbs. of lard, as compared with 673,000 lbs. last season.

These shipments were made direct to thirty-one ports, including England, Scotland, Ireland, France, Germany, Russia, Italy, Spain, Holland, Sweden, Norway, Denmark, Belgium, Mexico, and Jamaica. The grain trade has brought New Orleans into communication with countries with which, hitherto, it had little trade.

UNITED STATES.

Coal.

No coal is exported from New Orleans, but the following table shows the amount and value of that article exported from Mobile to different countries during 1896.

Country.	Quantity.	Value.
	Tons.	Dollars.
Guatemala	525	1,305
Haiti	1,493	3,747
Colombia	20	60
Cuba	1,013	2,464
British Honduras	114	500
Mexico	610	2,765
Nicaragua	53	144
Total	3,828	10,986
Equiv. in sterling	..	2,200*l.*

NOTE.—Average price, 12*s.* per ton.

From Pensacola the trade is more considerable, as the annexed report from that place shows.

Hardware.

With regard to iron manufactured goods from Sheffield, Birmingham, and other places in the United Kingdom, there is no great demand in the Southern States; nor is there much imported from Germany. Those engaged in the trade tell me that Germany cannot compete in cheap goods of this class, owing to a 40 per cent. tariff; and that this is also applicable to the best class of English goods, which undoubtedly, they say, are the best, and made cheaper than in the United States; but again the tariff steps in and makes competition impossible.

Knives of a cheap kind and of very inferior quality from Germany find their way into these markets with "Sheffield" stamped on them. On my asking how it was that such inferior goods were offered, I was told that they, the merchants, had to please the public, not themselves, and that all they had to look to was a sale. Moreover, American goods of that kind are beautifully finished, pleasing to the eye, and stand next to British made goods in quality, but I was shown articles of so inferior a quality, made in the States, that after very little wear they became useless; and yet these, on account of their cheapness, find a ready sale.

British made saws are acknowledged to be the best; Philadelphian are the next, and owing to the tariff, can be sold cheaper though the cost of making is greater.

Sanitary state of New Orleans.

The report of the Board of Health giving the usual mortality reports and other statistical matter will not be published in time for this report, but the following statement on small-pox in New Orleans, 1895–96, its introduction and suppression, by Mr. Woods, M.D., Chief Sanitary Inspector, may be of interest:—

"In February, 1895, a man came here from Arkansas, and afterwards developed a well marked case of variola. At that time the disease existed all over the Eastern Arkansas and

Western Tennessee counties. Otherwise than in a very general manner we could not further or more definitely trace the origin of the disease. From this case others in due season developed. In February, one; in March, four; April, three; and in May it reached the alarming proportion of 58 cases; in June there were 36 cases. After the first case in February, the authorities vaccinated all parties living in the infected localities, that is, all who would accept vaccination. The clothing, bedding, and wearing apparel, except those worn by the patient when sick, and the bed upon which he slept, were subjected to boiling water for 30 minutes, and afterwards left over night in a bichloride solution of 1–1000. Those articles and fabric coming in direct contact with the patient were destroyed by fire. All carpets and mattings in the patient's room were also destroyed by burning. The walls, floors, all furniture and fixtures, the galleries, and even walks, yards and outhouses, were sprayed or otherwise washed down with a bichloride solution of 1–1000. The interior of the house, after thoroughly closing the openings and chinking all cracks, was subjected to sulphur fumes for 9 hours, with from 5 to 7 lbs. of sulphur candles to 1,000 cubic feet of air space. With these rigid measures observed in every instance of the disease, the outbreak was in a manner controlled during the summer months of 1895, but, with the advent of winter, the disease seemed to take a fresh start, having been re-introduced from time to time from the country parishes where it existed to quite an extent. In the fall of 1895, a very rigid vaccination campaign was inaugurated by the Board of Health, and the work was not stopped until the entire city had been canvassed by a large and efficient corps of physicians who systematically, by districts, went from house to house offering and urging free vaccination. During this campaign, 53,437 people were vaccinated and re-vaccinated. After this systematic vaccination campaign was over, and the influx of darkies from the country parishes had ceased, the disease steadily decreased. In March, 1896, we had the greatest number of cases of any month during its prevalence, reaching a total of 334 cases. Since the introduction of the disease in February, 1895, we have had 1,126 cases with 291 deaths, making a death-rate of 25·84 per cent."

UNITED STATES.

RETURN of Principal Exports Carried in British Ships during the Year 1896.

Articles.		Quantity.
Cotton	Bales	1,418,029
,, seed	Sacks	138,841
,, ,, oil	Barrels	46,805
,, ,, cake	Sacks	290,767
,, ,, meal	,,	511,493
,, ,, soap stock	Barrels	2,226
Corn	Bushels	18,139,979
Wheat	,,	2,922,386
Flour	Sacks	236,281
Staves	Pieces	6,518,646
Timber	Logs	9,448
,,	Pieces	260,623
,,	Tons	22
,,	Car loads	72
Lumber	Feet	4,863,964
Lard	Tierces	23,977
,,	Pails	183,547
,,	Tubs	13,670
,,	Barrels	6,308
,,	Cases	5,100
,,	Firkins	3,530
,,	Boxes	1,450
,,	Car loads	47

Compared with 1895, British shipping returns for 1896 show a large increase:—

ENTERED.

Year.	Steam.		Sailing.		Total.	
	Number of Vessels.	Tons.	Number of Vessels.	Tons.	Number of Vessels.	Tons.
1896	395	784,833	4	4,977	399	789,810
1895	291	541,000	2	1,514	293	542,514

CLEARED.

Nationality.	Steam.		Sailing.		Total.	
	Number of Vessels.	Tons.	Number of Vessels.	Tons.	Number of Vessels.	Tons.
1896	391	773,016	2	2,746	393	775,762
1895	310	580,559	3	3,075	313	583,634

NEW ORLEANS.

Annex A.—RETURN of all Shipping at the Port of New Orleans during the Year 1896.

ENTERED.

Nationality.	Steam. Number of Vessels.	Steam. Tons.	Sailing. Number of Vessels.	Sailing. Tons.	Total. Number of Vessels.	Total. Tons.
British	395	774,833	4	4,977	399	779,810
American	169	117,237	28	8,802	197	126,039
Norwegian, &c.	270	127,317	1	548	271	127,865
Spanish	59	129,317	8	5,145	67	134,462
German	27	42,355	7	8,915	34	51,270
Italian	2	3,503	6	3,364	8	6,867
French	12	21,096	...	...	12	21,096
Danish	11	20,735	...	...	11	20,735
Mexican	4	1,141	...	...	4	1,141
Dutch	5	11,420	...	...	5	11,420
Portuguese	1	1,509	13	9,794	14	11,303
Austrian	1	1,856	...	...	1	1,856
Russian	...	...	1	431	1	431
Nicaraguan	...	...	1	45	1	45
Total	...	...	...	...	1,025	1,294,340
„ for the year preceding	...	...	...	...	867	975,930

NOTE.—The above figures do not include American coastwise tonnage: 253 vessels of 498,116 tons.

CLEARED.

Nationality.	Steam. Number of Vessels.	Steam. Tons.	Sailing. Number of Vessels.	Sailing. Tons.	Total. Number of Vessels.	Total. Tons.
British	391	773,016	2	2,746	393	775,762
American	151	86,818	5	1,032	156	87,850
Norwegian, &c.	258	137,419	...	...	258	137,419
Spanish	57	124,588	8	5,174	65	129,762
German	33	50,676	7	7,897	40	58,573
Italian	2	4,721	5	3,017	7	7,738
French	12	20,658	...	...	12	20,658
Danish	14	26,581	...	...	14	26,581
Mexican	4	807	...	...	4	807
Dutch	5	11,420	...	...	5	11,420
Portuguese	1	1,509	15	9,971	16	11,480
Austrian	7	13,693	...	...	7	13,693
Russian	...	...	1	431	1	431
Nicaraguan	1	45	...	...	1	45
Guatemalan	1	52	...	...	1	52
Total	...	...	...	...	980	1,282,271
„ for the year preceding	...	...	...	...	828	1,004,552

NOTE.—The above figures do not include American coastwise tonnage: 284 vessels of 524,582 tons.

PENSACOLA.

Mr. Vice-Consul Howe reports as follows:—

In this report of the trade of Pensacola for the year 1896, which exceeded in volume that of any previous year to my knowledge, and in looking particularly to the business of the port in which shipowners and other capitalists of the United Kingdom are interested, I will first go into, and show by the

Trade and British capitalists.

tables following, what was done here during the year so far as British interests were concerned.

British steamers. British steam tonnage at Pensacola during the year was about 33 per cent. beyond the largest amount of British steam tonnage arriving here in any one year preceding; and, in fact, beyond the combined steam tonnage of British and other foreign flags loading in any one year at this port.

British sailing vessels. British sailing vessels at Pensacola during the year exceeded in tonnage similar arrivals here in the past several years since the increase of steam carriers at Pensacola.

Pitch-pine freights. Pitch-pine freights for steam and sailing vessels averaged fairly well during the year from Pensacola to the United Kingdom and Continent. Steam charters for this business are mostly from the spring to summer months inclusive. To South American ports and other places the rates of freight were proportionately good. At the end of the year freights increased, as vessels became scarcer. See table of freights hereto annexed.

In proportion to other carriers of pitch-pine, shipments of cargoes by British vessels far exceeded the exports in vessels of other foreign flags loaded at Pensacola during the year. British steamers averaged a carrying capacity of not less than 2 tons to each net ton of their measurement. The total shipments from Pensacola of pitch-pine during the year amounted to about 700,000 tons; of that quantity British steamers carried about 286,000 tons, and British sailing vessels about 64,000 tons; therefore, it will be seen that of the total shipments of pitch-pine cargoes from the port during the year, British bottoms carried about one-half.

Besides the regular trade of Pensacola in pitch-pine wood, in which British tonnage was engaged during the past year, several British steamers have been plying between this port and Liverpool, and ports in Mexico—the latter vessels mostly on time charters—loaded with assorted cargoes, principally of products of the Western States of this country. This large export business is referred to in another part of this report.

Pig-iron. Among the late new departures from Pensacola's staple wood trade, pig-iron is being exported to Europe and the United Kingdom. This article is brought here from the works at Birmingham, Alabama, and promises to develop greatly.

Other exports. In addition to the regular business of the port in shipments of pitch-pine wood in various manufactures within the past two years, branchings out in other exports have been largely commenced. Steamers sail semi-monthly from Pensacola to Liverpool, taking Western products, in corn, flour, tobacco, and other articles up to large values. Also cotton and other products from these Southern ports go forward to Liverpool by the same line.

Pensacola and Cuba trade, &c. A business between Pensacola and Cuba, which was opened some few years ago—also in shipments of goods from the Western States—continues although the former activity in this business has languished owing to the troubles in that island. And, lately, in addition to the Cuba and Liverpool trade in goods different to Pensacola's staple wood trade, quite a business has been commenced between Pensacola and Mexican ports, as referred to elsewhere in this report in shipments of Western products, grain, flour, &c., &c. Besides all of which the large coal exports from Pensacola to Mexican and other ports actively continue. See table annexed.

All the export business to Liverpool, Mexico, and Cuba, as last above referred to, is managed by the Louisville and Nashville Railroad Company. The business is done through this powerful corporation as receivers and shippers under the style and management of "The Gulf Transit Company," having its headquarters at Louisville and Pensacola. *Louisville and Nashville Railroad Company.*

The railroad company have made immense outlays in improving their wharves at Pensacola, and establishing electric lights, erecting large store-houses, and other buildings, elevators, and other necessary appliances for a large export trade, and continue to add improvements, looking toward the increased development of an export trade for commodities from the interior of the country to be brought in by their road for exportation through Pensacola to foreign ports.

The Gulf Transit Company own a steamer of 1,069 tons net, which vessel makes quick trips to Mexican ports and ports in Texas, loaded with coal from Pensacola. This steamer was built and formerly owned in the United Kingdom, but having met with a casualty in American waters, was condemned and sold, and became the property of this Company, and has been for some time past successfully operated in the trade above given under the American flag. She has been named "Pensacola." The Gulf Transit Company, in connection with its coal exports, also own wooden and iron barges, and the barges loaded with coal are towed by tugs and the steamer "Pensacola" (the latter always coal loaded) to ports in Mexico and Texas. A table annexed to this report gives the quantity of coal exported from Pensacola—received here from the mines in Alabama—during the year 1896. This is quite an immense and increasing industry through Pensacola. *A former British steamer under American flag.*

With reference to the new trade between this place and ports in Mexico as well as the trade with Liverpool and Cuba, I must not omit to mention that British steamers are largely employed. Some of these vessels, as stated elsewhere in this report, being engaged for long periods on time charters. *New trade.*

The imports of articles at Pensacola during the year, other than chief articles for every day domestic trade, are fruit, from the islands of the British West Indies; hemp (in transit), tobacco, and cigars, &c., from Mexico; salt from Liverpool; articles for manufacture of fertilisers from Germany; sugar from Cuba (in transit); steel pyrites from Portugal, for manufacture of pig-iron, &c., at Birmingham. *Imports.*

In connection with shipping, I am pleased to be able to report that the lot of the sailor at Pensacola has very much improved within the last couple of years. A Corporation has been formed by some benevolent members of the city, termed "The Seamen's Friend *Seamen.*

Society of Pensacola." The object of the society as set forth in their Articles of Incorporation is for the promotion of the welfare of sailors by providing suitable houses or boarding houses to which they can repair when desiring to do so, and to help all seamen in matters tending to their welfare. Religious services are held at stated times weekly at the home already established.

The Corporation distinctly sets forth that its workings are to be simply in a philanthropic spirit, and that no profit is in view in connection with their supervision of the undertakings in keeping with the beneficial objects they have in view for seafaring persons.

Since the commencement of the work of the society, I have observed that the seamen I have to deal with always appear to be satisfied with their expense accounts at the Home provided for them by the society, and that their advance wages are always in keeping with their own wishes, and only in amount to cover their liabilities at the Home. Before leaving the Home accounts are furnished to them.

Desertions. The desertions from British vessels at this port, as reported to this office during the year, were 140; of this number 100 were from 32 sailing vessels, and 40 from 98 steamers; which strengthens my remarks made in a former report on this subject, showing how much better satisfied the seamen on steamers appear to be than on sailing vessels.

Health of port. The health of the port was good throughout the year with no epidemics. Since the year 1882 yellow fever has not appeared at Pensacola. Small-pox appeared during the year, but was kept within limited bounds, although not entirely eradicated at the year's end.

Quarantine. Quarantine regulations are very strict at Pensacola, and hardships therefrom are very often complained of by shipowners and others concerned, who allege that some of the extreme measures adopted in this respect are unnecessary and unwarranted.

Local trade and population. Business at Pensacola during the year in all branches of the port's usual local trade has been well maintained in comparison with former years, and the people here appear to move along as comfortably as ever in their domestic and other every day affairs without suffering or hardship. In short, Pensacola is a generous contributing place in its facilities for providing the ways and means towards its merchants, mechanics, and all other classes of its people in the upper and lower walks of life. The population of Pensacola is increasing, and is now about 17,000.

City advancing. The city is moving onward in trade and improvements generally. A new line of street railway to be operated by electricity or compressed air is being established here.

Agriculture. As regards agriculture, as this industry at Pensacola does not give material enough for a separate report on such subject, I shall just here remark that the productions of every day articles, in garden products as well as poultry, sheep, milch cows, beef, cattle, pigs, &c., for immediate supply of the town, still continue without stint.

The returns in connection with the foregoing report now follow:—

Annex A.—RETURN of Rates of Freight at Pensacola during the Year 1896.

Month.	Sailing. United Kingdom and Continent. Per Standard. From—	To—	Buenos Ayres and Monte Video. Per Supl. M. From—	To—	Rio de Janeiro and Ports in Brazil. Per Supl. M. From—	To—	Steam. United Kingdom. Per Standard. From—	To—	Continent of Europe. Per Standard. From—	To—
	£ s. d.	£ s. d.	Dol. c.	Dol. c.	Dol. c.	Dol. c.	£ s. d.	£ s. d.	£ s. d.	£ s. d.
January	4 10 0	4 12 6	11 00	.. ..	14 50	15 00	.. ..	.. ..	.. ..	.. ..
February	4 10 0	4 15 0	11 00	11 50	14 50	15 50	5 2 6	5 5 0	5 5 0	5 7 6
March	.. ..	.. ..	11 50	12 50	15 00	.. ..	4 17 6	5 0 0	5 0 0	5 2 6
April	4 12 6	4 17 6	.. ..	.. ..	.. ..	.. ..	4 15 0	4 17 6	4 17 6	5 0 0
May	.. ..	.. ..	.. ..	.. ..	.. ..	.. ..	.. ..	.. ..	.. ..	.. ..
June	.. ..	.. ..	13 50	14 50	.. ..	.. ..	.. ..	.. ..	.. ..	.. ..
July	4 15 0	5 0 0	13 50	14 00	.. ..	.. ..	4 12 6	4 15 0	4 15 0	4 17 6
August	4 17 6	5 2 6	13 25	13 75	.. ..	.. ..	4 15 0	4 17 6	4 17 6	5 2 6
September	4 15 0	5 0 0	.. ..	.. ..	.. ..	.. ..	5 10 0	5 12 6	5 10 0	5 12 6
October	5 0 0	5 5 0	.. ..	.. ..	.. ..	.. ..	5 12 6	5 15 0	5 15 0	3 0 0
November	4 15 0	5 2 6	13 00	13 25	.. ..	.. ..	5 15 0	6 0 0	.. ..	.. ..
December							5 2 6	5 5 0	5 5 0	.. ..

(2340)

UNITED STATES.

Annex B.—RETURN of Principal Articles of Export from Pensacola during the Years 1896-95.

		1896. Quantity.	1896. Value. £ s. d.	1895. Quantity.	1895. Value. £ s. d.
Pitch pine lumber	Super. feet	157,961,584	394,903 13 6	152,851,000	382,127 9 8
Sawn pitch pine timber	Cubic feet	11,375,608	284,390 4 0	11,078,165	276,954 3 4
Hewn " "	"	526,224	12,059 6 0	323,701	7,417 16 0
Cotton	Bales	51,878	540,395 16 8	6,915	72,031 5 0
Tobacco	Hogsheads	7,933	122,961 10 0	103	1,596 18 0
Coal	Tons	123,967	103,305 16 8	87,428	72,856 14 0
Corn	Bushels	373,334	38,888 19 2	80,505	8,385 16 0
Flour	Sacks	33,890	28,241 13 4	47,407	39,505 16 0
Pig-iron	Tons	6,091	12,689 11 8	4,082	8,504 3 4
Lard	Tierces	1,047	6,980 0 0	724	4,826 12 0
Bran	Sacks	17,987	5,056 15 2	...	...
Hay	Bales	21,496	4,478 6 8	...	...
Cedar	Cubic feet	55,991	4,082 13 6	...	...
Oak timber	"	29,576	2,772 15 0	16,840	1,578 14 0
Rosin	Barrels	4,167	2,604 7 6	2,093	1,308 0 0
Oak staves	...	84,800	1,060 0 0	...	...
Poplar and ash	Cubic feet	3,344	250 16 0	...	...
Cypress	"	...	...	81,062	5,910 16 4
Coke	Tons	...	...	2,200	2,062 10 0
Turpentine	Barrels	...	...	30	75 0 0
Other articles	...	...	20,000 0 0	...	607 5 3
Total	...	...	1,585,122 4 10	...	885,748 18 11

NOTE.—The following, as regards the foregoing table of exports, is descriptive of the quantities, values, weights and measures; the conversion of money into sterling being at the rate of 4 dol. 80 c. per 1l.; lumber at average of 2l. 10s. per 1,000 superficial feet, board measure; sawn timber at an average of 6d. per cubic foot, basis 40 feet average; hewn timber at an average of 5½d. per cubic foot, basis 100 feet average; cotton at an average of 5d. per lb., in bales of 500 lbs. average weight each bale; coal, 16s. 8d. per ton; cypress at 1s. 5½ per cubic foot; flour at 16s. 8d. per sack of 200 lbs.; corn at 2s. 1d. per bushel; rosin at 12s. 6d. per barrel; pig-iron at 2l. 1s. 8d. per ton; oak at 1s. 10½d. per cubic foot; coke at 18s. 9d. per ton; lard, 6l. 13s. 4d. per tierce; tobacco at 15l. 10s. per hogshead; bran at 5s. 7½d. per sack hay at 4s. 2d. per bale; cedar at 1s. 5½d. per cubic foot; poplar and ash at 1s. 6d. per cubic foot; oak staves at 12l. 10s. per 1,000.

NEW ORLEANS.

Annex C.—TABLE showing Total Value of all Articles Exported from and Imported to Pensacola from and to Foreign Countries during the Years 1896-95.

Countries.	Exports. 1896.	Exports. 1895.	Imports. 1896.	Imports. 1895.
	£ s. d.	£ s. d.	£	£
United Kingdom	892,621 10 5	312,870 0 0	825	4,696
British possessions	19,017 5 0	10,507 0 0	90	200
Mexico	128,140 0 0	1,833 6 0	15,203	2,000
Brazil	104,547 2 3	55,579 3 6	...	...
France	67,695 4 1	62,814 10 0	...	...
Netherlands	57,752 6 0	53,259 7 7	...	...
Argentine Republic	55,751 5 4	59,186 4 0	...	...
Italy	51,764 0 0	55,379 3 5	21	...
Spain and colonies	28,441 6 5	70,099 11 6	2,963	...
Belgium	27,934 8 0	25,502 0 0	...	...
Germany	12,175 3 2	17,947 18 0	5,021	2,380
Egypt	9,730 0 0	8,129 3 5	...	...
Austria	9,257 1 6	7,699 0 0	...	...
Uruguay	5,165 2 0	7,545 0 0	...	...
Portugal	3,560 0 0	6,493 10 0	...	...
Denmark	2,758 6 8	589 12 0	...	...
Tunis	2,496 0 0	...	...	...
Venezuela	503 4 0	786 0 0	...	...
Russia	...	1,088 10 0	...	...
Turkey	...	806 13 6	...	...
Total to foreign countries	1,479,309 4 10	758,115 12 11	...	...
,, to ports in the United States	104,808 0 0	126,632 10 0	...	...
Grand total	1,584,117 4 10	884,748 2 11	24,123	9,276

Annex D.—RETURN of all Shipping at the Port of Pensacola during the Year 1896.

ENTERED.

Nationality.	Sailing. Number of Vessels.	Sailing. Tons.	Steam. Number of Vessels.	Steam. Tons.	Total. Number of Vessels.	Total. Tons.
British	36	39,046	96	150,983	132	190,029
American	77	35,657	42	32,401	119	68,058
Swedish and Norwegian	87	86,563	6	5,535	93	92,098
Italian	60	39,225	...	...	60	39,225
Spanish	3	2,012	17	28,190	20	30,202
Russian	22	14,949	...	...	22	14,949
German	6	5,739	3	1,996	9	7,735
Austrian	6	3,156	2	3,265	8	6,421
Danish	3	1,847	2	2,633	5	4,480
French	4	3,063	...	...	4	3,063
Portuguese	2	1,252	...	...	2	1,252
Netherlands	1	491	...	...	1	491
Total	307	233,000	168	225,003	475	458,003
,, for the year preceding	481	312,207	88	126,732	569	438,939

(2340)

UNITED STATES.

Cleared.

Nationality.	Sailing. Number of Vessels.	Sailing. Tons.	Steam. Number of Vessels.	Steam. Tons.	Total. Number of Vessels.	Total. Tons.
British	39	42,261	97	153,361	136	195,622
American	77	44,221	38	33,080	115	77,301
Swedish and Norwegian	84	83,182	7	7,197	91	90,379
Italian	63	42,417	...	...	63	42,417
Spanish	3	2,002	14	24,149	17	26,151
Russian	28	20,037	...	...	28	20,037
German	5	4,855	4	2,880	9	7,735
Austrian	5	2,498	2	3,264	7	5,762
Danish	3	1,846	2	2,632	5	4,478
French	3	1,816	...	...	3	1,816
Portuguese	2	1,252	...	...	2	1,252
Total	312	246,387	164	226,563	476	472,950
,, for the year preceding	472	316,257	87	126,831	559	443,088

Note.—Of the American steamers given above as entered and cleared, the ss. "Pensacola," referred to elsewhere in this report, made 28 trips.

Mobile, Alabama.

Mr. Vice-Consul Barnewall reports as follows:—

Trade and commerce of Mobile. Mobile has done exceedingly well this year; she has gone onward despite the hard times, and has made progress where other places have been well content to hold their own. The record is one of which we may well be proud.

Foreign trade. Foreign trade increased at the rate of 100 per cent.; the largest exports on record.

Custom-house Receipts for the Fiscal Year ended June 30, 1896.

	Amount. 1892–93. Dollars.	1893–94. Dollars.	1894–95. Dollars.	1895–96. Dollars.
Duties on imports	15,109	9,990	18,642	19,210
Tonnage tax	8,610	6,982	8,402	11,207
Forfeitures, &c.	168	..	141	433
Miscellaneous	430	570	931	731
Storage, &c.	62	57	125	153
Fees	2,053	2,491	3,115	2,900
Total receipts	26 432	20,090	31,356	34,634

The receipts for the last fiscal year were not only the largest on record, but exhibit an increase of 75 per cent. over those of two years previous in 1893–94; this clearly shows that the ocean trade of Mobile has been making a very satisfactory progress, and in proof of this the following figures taken from the custom-house records giving the total value of the exports of the port for the same four years before referred to :—

NEW ORLEANS.

VALUE of Exports for Four Years.

	Value.			
	1892–93.	1893–94.	1894–95.	1895–96.
	Dollars.	Dollars.	Dollars.	Dollars.
Domestic commodities..	3,319,381	2,822,887	5,111,716	6,985,876
Foreign ,, ..	..	330	61,317	10,203
Total	3,319,381	2,823,217	5,173,033	6,996,079

Reducing these statements to a comparative form, it will be seen that the export trade of the port for the last fiscal year exceeded that of 1892–93 by 3,676,000 dol., or 110 per cent.; it also more than doubled the export trade of 1893–94, exceeding that year by 4,173,000 dol., or 148 per cent., and exceeded last year's exports by 1,823,000 dol., or 35 per cent.

The value of imports for the two last fiscal years at the port of Mobile were as follows:—

Imports value.

Country.	Value.	
	1894–95.	1895–96.
	Dollars.	Dollars.
Germany..	21,158	19,157
England..	19,800	28,975
Scotland..	..	13
Italy ..	13,047	19
France ..	..	1,229
Sweden and Norway ..	..	221
Netherlands ..	89	..
Total Europe ..	54,094	49,614
Honduras ..	101,367	120,947
Nicaragua ..	175,955	78,524
Mexico ..	304,622	393,956
British West Indies ..	16,055	5,177
Cuba ..	9,998	12,959
Colombia..	304,393	190,419
British Honduras ..	41,919	59,108
Guatemala ..	..	29,833
Venezuela ..	820	..
Brazil ..	58	4
British Guiana ..	..	21
Hayti ..	..	17
Total America ..	955,187	890,965

(2340)

UNITED STATES.

RECAPITULATION.

	Value.	
	1894-95.	1895-96.
	Dollars.	Dollars.
Total Europe	54,094	49,614
Total America	955,187	890,965
Total imports	1,009,281	940,579

The totals show a slight decline both from European countries and from American countries to the South. The deficit of 60,000 dol. for the year 1895–96 was caused by a falling-off in the banana trade, yet with a deficit in the import trade, the exports to the same countries for the last fiscal year show a considerable increase, as will be seen by the following comparative statement:

Exports to—	Value.	
	1894-95.	1895-96.
	Dollars.	Dollars.
Europe	3,850,528	5,376,048
America	1,261,375	1,609,828
Other countries	61,400	10,203
Total	5,173,303	6,996,079

In the foregoing statement as to the exports of this year, for the two fiscal years it will be seen that the exports increased from 1,261,000 dol. in 1894–95, to 1,600,000 dol. in 1895–96 to American countries in the South; this increase of nearly 30 per cent. to the countries mentioned was done in the face of a slight decline in the imports from same countries.

Cotton trade.

In the local market, on a short cotton crop, there naturally occurred a decrease in receipts, but the reverse as to value.

Receipts and prices.

Last year's receipts of 253,178 bales averaged 5·56 c. per lb. on a total crop of 9,901,251 bales, and brought a total value to 7,150,000 dol. For the season just closed the net receipts are 209,876 bales on a total crop of about 7,200,000 bales. The average value per lb. is 7·84 c. or a total of 8,220,842 dol.

	Quantity.	
	1895–96.	1894–95.
	Bales.	Bales.
Great Britain	72,060	92,175
Continent	27,444	20,194
Mexico	2,503	10,626
Total foreign	102,007	122,995
New Orleans	100,007	114,579
North East	9,129	22,711
Other points	565	803
Total United States	109,701	138,093
„ foreign	102,007	122,995
Grand total	211,708	261,088

RECEIPTS of Bananas and Cocoanuts.

Articles.	Quantity.	
	1895–96.	1894–95.
Bananas	1,887,059	2,261,088
Cocoanuts	3,398,714	4,923,832

RECEIPTS of Miscellaneous Fruit.

Articles.		Quantity.	
		1895–96.	1894–95.
Pineapples	Bulk	4,964	20,224
„	Barrels	3,066	4,000
Oranges	Bulk	67,300	653,100
„	Boxes	18,487	22,701
„	Barrels	791	659
Lemons	Boxes	1,016	2,620
Limes		17,500	45,700
Plantains		71,950	173,925

Owing to a large portion of the fruit trade which this port enjoyed last season being diverted to New Orleans, the above figures show a very considerable falling-off in receipts; still, owing to certain facilities which cannot be taken from us, we are certain to handle a large quantity of fruit at this port.

(2340)

UNITED STATES.

Corn.

The shipments for two years ending August 31 compare as follows:

Year.	Quantity.	Value.
	Bushels.	Dollars.
1895–96	1,536,587	585,195
1894–95	103,161	52,917
Increase	1,433,426	532,278

This shows a remarkable increase in the corn trade for one year. In August there were 5 cargoes, each of which was larger than the entire shipments for the year 1894–95.

Lumber and timber.

The compilation of the figures of the lumber and timber trade of Mobile for the past year shows that there has been no falling-off in this branch of Mobile's commerce. The total trade in lumber and timber shows an increase on last year of 33,783,745, against an increase last year over the previous year of something over 1,000,000 feet. There has been an increase all along the line, except in the exports of hewn timber, which were greater last year than this by 800,000 feet. There has been an increase in the amount of local consumption and shipments by river, in lumber towed to Ship Island, and in railroad shipments.

Prices.

At the beginning of the season just closed the shipments were rather small, and lumber and timber seemed to be somewhat of a drug. At the close of last season the contracting price for timber was 9 c. in round numbers, while at the close of this season it is a fraction more than 3 c. better, and there is a good demand for contracts. During the past 12 months the price of timber has been gradually rising, and there has been an increase in the demand, till at the present time there is no accumulation of stock in Mobile, and most of the timber that is brought to market is taken immediately at market price.

NEW ORLEANS.

Shipments.

Destination.	Quantity. 1895-96.	1894-95.
	Super. feet.	Super. feet.
FOREIGN.		
United Kingdom	8,859,124	10,438,245
France	396,322	754,648
Germany	2,173,290	1,010,891
Holland	1,607,318	461,298
Nicaragua and U.S. Colombia	1,577,582	2,608,173
British West Indies	335,230	1,403,002
Mexico	2,752,467	3,536,652
Cuba	4,309,978	9,806,797
Jamaica	1,165,451	2,552,904
Trinidad	..	1,593,259
Africa	3,901,720	888,403
Hayti	882,663	1,825,840
River Plate	..	1,053,821
Argentine Republic	20,429,756	8,402,932
Uruguay	4,572,165	967,899
Austria	125,067	62,967
Denmark	..	216,841
Italy	..	628,188
Paraguay	..	360,000
Costa Rica	..	213,038
Venezuela	1,137,322	..
Dutch Guiana	318,000	..
Porto Rico	930,165	..
Brazil	2,053,998	..
Spanish Honduras	125,500	..
British Honduras	1,064,480	..
Guatemala	229,946	..
Various	..	4,271,487
Total	58,947,544	53,057,305
COASTWISE.		
New York	790,000	1,799,023
Boston	466,966	1,434,000
Philadelphia	1,221,456	997,709
Portland	520,000	300,000
Various	460,000	..
Total	3,458,422	4,530,732
Grand total	62,405,966	57,588,037

UNITED STATES.

Timber.

Country.	Quantity.	
	Hewn.	Sawn.
	Cub. feet.	Cub. feet.
United Kingdom	1,038,103	2,952,689
France	41,247	174,814
Holland	84,252	596,640
Africa	30,015	322,860
Germany	30,137	86,358
Austria	38,087	93,863
Mexico	2,876	33,400
Argentine Republic	..	44,008
Cuba	..	20,048
Total	1,264,717	4,324,680

Comparative Table.

Year.	Hewn.	Sawn.	Total.
	Cub. feet.	Cub. feet.	Cub. feet.
1894–95	1,319,377	3,162,325	4,481,702
1895–96	1,264,717	4,324,680	5,589,397

Summary. The following summary of lumber and timber business done in this port shows the standing of 1895–96 as compared with 1894–95. The timber is reduced to superficial feet for the sake of comparison:—

Description.	Quantity.	
	1895–96.	1894–95.
	Super. feet.	Super. feet.
Lumber, total foreign and coastwise	62,405,966	57,588,037
„ railroads	14,024,376	3,650,900
„ towed to Ship Island	3,000,000	500,000
„ local and river	15,000,000	12,000,000
Timber, direct in vessels—		
Hewn	15,176,604	15,832,524
Sawn	51,896,160	37,947,900
Towed to Ship Island—		
Hewn	300,000	450,000
Sawn	600,000	650,000
Total	162,403,106	128,619,361
Increase	33,783,745	..

Hard woods, shipments. Shipments of hard woods the past season show a heavy increase as compared to the season previous, both in quality and variety. The following is the statement:—

NEW ORLEANS.

Articles.	Quantity.	
	1895–96.	1894–95.
	Cub. feet.	Cub. feet.
Oak	194,927	162,145
Cedar	24,451	2,873
Poplar	107,531	252,797
Ash	20,248	5,504
Whitewood	65,128	..
Gum	50,107	..
Walnut	83,392	..
Assorted	29,565	44,547
Total	575,349	467,866

There was also exported to foreign parts 87,261 lineal feet piling, 35,814 fence pickets, 1,221 telegraph poles, 14,000 posts, and 9,750 round pine logs.

The past season's business was below the average, as shown by the following figures :— **Staves.**

Year.	Quantity.
1895–96	147,978
1894–95	335,000

The receipts show a heavy falling-off this season, as compared to last season :— **Wool receipts.**

Year.	Quantity.	Value.
		Dollars.
1895–96	175,000	21,000,000
1894–95	410,000	60,000,000

The following figures show the season's growth brought to market, as compared with last season :— **Vegetables.**

Articles.		1896.		1895.	
		Quantity.	Value.	Quantity.	Value.
			Dollars.		Dollars.
Cabbages	Crates	58,200	86,978	34,439	60,268
Potatoes	Barrels	80,720	141,260	108,528	162,795
Beans	Boxes	65,000	...	53,421	...
Peas	,,	1,500	...	4,100	...
Tomatoes	,,	500	...	2,500	...
Cucumbers	Barrels	168	...	...	...
Beets	Crates	285	...	...	...
Various		1,200	...	2,000	...

UNITED STATES.

RECEIPTS of Leading Articles from September 1, 1895, to August 31, 1896.

Articles.		Quantity.			
		1896.	1895.	Decrease.	Increase.
Bagging	Pieces	21,775	11,869	...	9,906
Iron ties	Bundles	37,325	21,000	...	16,325
Bacon	Casks	6,301	6,575	274	...
Hams	Tierces	2,506	2,106	...	400
Butter	Kegs	5,079	4,619	...	460
Bran	Sacks	67,566	57,209	...	10,357
Cotton seed meal	,,	129,230	108,327	...	20,903
Coffee	,,	10,768	8,645	...	2,123
Corn	,,	751,378	255,222	...	496,156
Cheese	Boxes	8,647	8,147	...	500
Coal (Alabama	Tons	163,176	159,616	...	3,560
,, (foreign)	,,	...	2,066	...	...
Candles	Boxes	1,310	665	...	645
Flour	Barrels	164,176	153,148	...	11,028
Hay	Bales	84,331	69,273	...	15,058
Lard	Tierces	7,803	7,099	...	704
Lime	Barrels	8,015	10,015	2,000	...
Fertilizers	...	18,705	13,600	...	5,105
Molasses	Barrels	1,537	1,350	...	187
Oats	Sacks	113,369	100,328	...	13,041
Potatoes	Barrels	13,815	10,427	...	3,388
Pork	,,	2,754	492	...	2,262
Rice	,,	5,110	4,085	...	1,025
Salt	Sacks	71,760	77,344	5,584	...
Soap	Boxes	63,633	59,045	...	4,588
Sugar	Barrels	18,602	16,617	...	1,985
Tobacco	...	5,080	3,650	...	1,430
Whiskey	Barrels	2,495	2,646	151	...
Wool	Sacks	2,540	5,245	2,705	...

Mobile Harbour.

Over the outer bar there has been no diminution in depth since the steamship "Mendota" crossed drawing 24 feet 11 inches.

To sum up, our city has a safe and commodious harbour with railroad facilities on her wharves to and from which are shipped in large and increasing quantities cotton, lumber, coal, iron, grain, tropical fruits, sisal grass, and manufactured articles of all kinds.

During the past year we have to chronicle in this connection two events which, while small in themselves, are, we believe, the harbingers of great things to come. First, in December, there arrived from the Warrior coalfields a barge load of coal brought entirely by water through the Warrior, Tombigbee, and Mobile Rivers. This practical demonstration of the feasibility of bringing coal of good quality cheaply to our city was made possible by the completion of three locks in the Warrior River above Tuskaloosa. Second, during this season a shipment of pig-iron from here to Manchester, England. With regard to the shipment of coal the general government has during the past year begun the construction of the first lock and dam to give slack water navigation during the entire year between Tuskaloosa and our city.

When all the locks needed for this improvement shall have been completed great benefit to all concerned must come. Our port, it is believed, will be the great depôt for the supply of coal to all the Gulf steamships and for export.

Mobile, from its position on the Gulf of Mexico, should have the great part of the export and import business of the United States through the Gulf. For many years this was denied the city on account of lack of depth to the channel. In 1827, when first the work was done by the general government for the improvement of the channel, the depth of water through Choctaw Pass was $5\frac{1}{2}$ feet, and there was only 8 feet on Dog River bar. Since that time, with many delays and many intermissions, work has been going on.

It was not, however, until 1888 that systematic work was begun to gain a channel of 23 feet at mean low water from the mouth of Chickasabogue Creek to the deep water of the Gulf. From then till now has this work been going on by dredging. During this long time the immense amount of 18,000,000 cubic yards of material has been excavated and redeposited where it does not interfere with the navigation of the channel. To-day vessels drawing more than 23 feet load to their full capacity at our wharves and go to sea without delay or danger.

An idea of the magnitude of the work is shown by the length of the channel, more than 33 miles, and the amount of material, 18,000,000 cubic yards, which, if piled solidly on a base 1 acre in extent, would rise to a height of more than 2 miles.

The result to commerce and business has been most flattering as will be seen from the table below.

Much work to increase our harbour capacity has also been done by the owners of the river front. Dredging has been going on in front of the city wharves and those of the different railroads.

UNITED STATES.

COMPARATIVE statement of Number and Draft of Vessels passing up and down the Dredged Channel during the Fiscal Year ending June 30, 1896.

Draft (in feet).	Steamships. Up. 1896.	Steamships. Up. 1895.	Steamships. Down. 1896.	Steamships. Down. 1895.	Square-rigged Vessels. Up. 1896.	Square-rigged Vessels. Up. 1895.	Square-rigged Vessels. Down. 1896.	Square-rigged Vessels. Down. 1895.	Schooners. Up. 1896.	Schooners. Up. 1895.	Schooners. Down. 1896.	Schooners. Down. 1895.	Total. Up. 1896.	Total. Up. 1895.	Total. Down. 1896.	Total. Down. 1895.
Under 13	255	271	131	182	98	51	8	2	7	135	...	90	360	457	139	274
13 to 14	16	18	32	17	30	24	1	3	94	...	30	3	140	42	63	23
14 15	16	29	16	50	30	23	5	9	...	...	39	10	46	52	60	69
15 16	12	8	24	19	15	13	12	6	...	4	20	15	27	25	56	40
16 17	11	13	20	42	5	4	15	6	...	2	5	17	16	19	40	65
17 18	1	...	16	7	1	1	15	6	...	...	...	2	2	1	31	15
18 19	...	...	38	7	...	1	20	5	...	...	...	2	...	1	58	14
19 20	...	1	5	1	2	...	11	16	...	...	...	...	2	1	16	17
20 21	...	...	3	4	...	...	23	17	...	...	...	...	...	...	26	21
21 22	...	...	6	4	...	...	13	10	...	...	...	...	...	...	19	14
22 23	...	...	9	3	...	...	34	24	...	...	...	...	...	...	43	27
23 23-7	...	...	3	...	...	...	19	6	...	...	...	...	...	...	22	6
Total	311	340	303	336	181	117	176	110	101	141	94	139	593	598	573	585

NEW ORLEANS.

Mobile, Ala., September 1, 1896.

To the Editor of "The Register":—

I herewith hand you my report of the number of large sea-going vessels of different rigs that have arrived and departed from this port, commencing September 1, 1895, and ending August 31, 1896; also showing the maximum draught that has passed up and down the channel in that time, and other matters applicable to the port:—

The harbour master's report.

Description.	Number of Vessels.
Steamships up channel, drawing up to and including 16 feet 6 inches ..	288
Steamships down channel, drawing up to and including 23 feet	260
Ships and barks up channel, drawing up to and including 19 feet ..	201
Ships and barks down channel, drawing up to and including 23 feet 5 inches..	197
Brigs up channel, drawing up to and including 9 feet..	11
Brigs down channel, drawing up to and including 17 feet 10 inches..	11
Schooners up channel, drawing up to and including 16 feet 6 inches ..	7
Schooners down channel, drawing up to and including 17 feet	96
Total vessels up channel	597
,, down channel	564
Total vessels up and down	1,161

From the above it will be seen that the deepest draught vessel that has passed up or down the channel was 23 feet 5 inches, which shows conclusively that the channel holds its own, that is, a depth of 23 feet.

There are quite a number of smaller, though sea-going vessels, that ply between this port and the fruit islands, and also between this port and the near-by domestic coastwise ports that are not included in the above list. They constitute, however, quite a fleet, and the money they leave here, both for incoming and outgoing cargoes, is very considerable at this port.

Referring to the above-mentioned deep-draught vessels, they have all passed up and down the channel without any serious detention, except one, viz., the ship "Frank Carvill," sunk by an unseen obstruction, supposed to be a deadhead in the channel of the river, which necessitates her discharging cargo, repairing, and reloading.

We have a natural depth of water on Mobile bar of between 25 and 26 feet, and if it continues to increase naturally in the future as in the past we will have deeper water on the bar than any other on the Gulf. This is a natural and not an artificial depth.

The chances now are, after a long and weary wait, that in a short time the channel will be lighted from end to end with the

Pintsch gas lights, as the beacons for the same are now here, and only await the contractor to start putting them up. In the meantime the channel has been lighted with oil lamps, except the two lower ones, these being the two Pintsch gas buoys, and these have given general satisfaction. When the channel is lighted all the way with gas, we will have a brilliantly lighted route to the Gulf. We will then be enabled to better navigate the same at night.

There is one matter to which I wish to call the public attention, and that is our facilities for hauling out vessels. The Mobile Marine Ways were built for a capacity of 1,000 tons. They now have out the bark "Sleipner," of 1,267 tons, which they hauled out with the greatest ease. Captain Eitzen, an old ship master, and at present located at Pensacola, as the representative of the Norwegian Board of Underwriters, who was here superintending the hauling out of the "Sleipner," expressed to the writer the greatest satisfaction with the manner in which the bark was hauled out, and said he would not hesitate to haul out a vessel of 1,500 tons on these ways, and would in future, as to all vessels in which he was interested, recommend them to come here of that tonnage.

We have also a sectional dry dock, of six sections, capable of taking out vessels of 1,000 tons, and it will compare favourably with any dock of its size in the United States.

These two docks have attached shipyards, with first-class ship carpenters and other mechanics, who can do as good work as can be done anywhere. We have also here several first-class foundries, machine and boiler shops, and can turn out as good a class of work as any of their kind in the United States or elsewhere.

The size of vessels that come here now is much larger than in the past. There are two vessels loading here now, one with grain and the other with timber, viz., the American steamship "Miami" and the British sailing four-masted ship "King's County," which are the largest ships of their kind ever in this port.

In conclusion, I beg to say that we have the longest dredged channel in the world, and for its length, the best.

Very respectfully,
R. SHERIDAN, Jun.,
Harbourmaster, Port of Mobile.

Annex A.—Return of all Shipping at the Port of Mobile during the Year 1896.

Entered.

Nationality.	Sailing. Number of Vessels.	Sailing. Tons.	Steam. Number of Vessels.	Steam. Tons.	Total. Number of Vessels.	Total. Tons.
British	73	44,343	87	109,536	160	153,879
Norwegian	80	75,352	109	46,336	189	121,688
American	43	15,638	3	5,222	46	20,860
Swedish	4	3,505	...	...	4	3,505
Russian	14	7,863	...	...	14	7,863
Mexican	1	200	...	...	1	200
Dutch	3	3,624	...	...	3	3,624
Danish	2	926	...	...	2	926
Italian	17	13,641	...	...	17	13,641
Colombian	1	157	...	...	1	157
German	5	4,581	7	4,684	12	9,265
Total	243	169,830	206	165,778	449	335,608
Coastwise	...	...	...	...	29	19,839
Grand total	...	...	...	...	478	355,447
Total for the year preceding	...	...	...	...	542	339,398

Cleared.

Nationality.	Sailing. Number of Vessels.	Sailing. Tons.	Steam. Number of Vessels.	Steam. Tons.	Total. Number of Vessels.	Total. Tons.
British	70	42,557	85	106,429	155	148,986
Norwegian	95	89,448	116	49,848	211	139,296
American	42	16,744	2	4,584	44	21,328
Swedish	4	3,946	...	...	4	3,946
Russian	14	7,913	...	...	14	7,913
Dutch	2	2,173	...	...	2	2,173
Mexican	1	200	...	...	1	200
Danish	1	476	...	...	1	476
Italian	16	11,768	...	...	16	11,768
Colombian	1	157	...	...	1	157
German	4	3,229	8	5,307	12	8,536
Total	250	178,611	211	166,168	461	344,779
Coastwise	...	...	...	...	21	15,564
Grand total	...	...	...	...	482	360,343
Total for the year preceding	...	...	...	...	527	311,291

(2340)

LONDON:
Printed for Her Majesty's Stationery Office,
By HARRISON AND SONS,
Printers in Ordinary to Her Majesty.
(75 4 | 97—H & S 2340)

FOREIGN OFFICE.
1897.
ANNUAL SERIES.

Nº 1883.
DIPLOMATIC AND CONSULAR REPORTS ON TRADE AND FINANCE.

UNITED STATES.

REPORT FOR THE YEAR 1896
ON THE
TRADE OF THE BALTIMORE CONSULAR DISTRICT.

REFERENCE TO PREVIOUS REPORT, Annual Series No. 1712.

Presented to both Houses of Parliament by Command of Her Majesty,
MAY, 1897.

LONDON:
PRINTED FOR HER MAJESTY'S STATIONERY OFFICE,
BY HARRISON AND SONS, ST. MARTIN'S LANE,
PRINTERS IN ORDINARY TO HER MAJESTY.

And to be purchased, either directly or through any Bookseller, from
EYRE & SPOTTISWOODE, East Harding Street, Fleet Street, E.C., and
32, Abingdon Street, Westminster, S.W.; or
JOHN MENZIES & Co., 12, Hanover Street, Edinburgh, and
90, West Nile Street, Glasgow; or
HODGES, FIGGIS, & Co., Limited, 104, Grafton Street, Dublin.

1897.

[C. 8277—101.] *Price One Penny.*

New Series of Reports.

Reports of the Annual Series have been issued from Her Majesty's Diplomatic and Consular Officers at the following places, and may be obtained from the sources indicated on the title-page:—

No.		Price.	No.		Price.
1763. Cephalonia		1d.	1823. Samoa		½d.
1764. Bahia		1d.	1824. Chinkiang		1d.
1765. Zanzibar		1½d.	1825. Jeddah		1d.
1766. Pakhoi		1d.	1826. Sofia		1½d.
1767. New York		2d.	1827. Mexico		2d.
1768. Chefoo		1d.	1828. Teneriffe		3½d.
1769. Caracas		½d.	1829. Batoum		1d.
1770. Palermo		11½d.	1830. Cadiz		1d.
1771. Mombasa		½d.	1831. Martinique		1d.
1772. Nice		1½d.	1832. Odessa		1d.
1773. Bucharest		4½d.	1833. Ghilan		1d.
1774. Port Said		1½d.	1834. Old Calabar		6½d.
1775. Galatz		1½d.	1835. Tamsui		1d.
1776. Madrid		2d.	1836. Copenhagen		½d.
1777. Vienna		2d.	1837. Salonica		1½d.
1778. Canton		1d.	1838. Honolulu		½d.
1779. Yokohama		1½d.	1839. Buenos Ayres		2d.
1780. Newchwang		1d.	1840. Para		1d.
1781. Wuhu		1d.	1841. Bolivia		2d.
1782. Athens		2d.	1842. Washington		3d.
1783. Tonga		½d.	1843. Berlin		2d.
1784. Smyrna		½d.	1844. Uganda		1d.
1785. Baghdad		1d.	1845. Belgrade		1½d.
1786. Hiogo and Osaka		4½d.	1846. Dakar		½d.
1787. Bangkok		1d.	1847. Florence		1½d.
1788. Odessa		2d.	1848. Copenhagen		2d.
1789. Naples		2d.	1849. Havre		2d.
1790. Beyrout		1d.	1850. Serajevo		1d.
1791. Tunis		1½d.	1851. Madrid		2d.
1792. Kiukiang		3d.	1852. La Rochelle		1½d.
1793. Bangkok		1d.	1853. Chicago		4d.
1794. Rio Grande do Sul		1d.	1854. Berlin		1d.
1795. Valparaiso		4d.	1855. Cherbourg		2½d.
1796. Brindisi		2½d.	1856. Beira		1d.
1797. Bushire		2d.	1857. Charleston		2½d.
1798. Christiania		5½d.	1858. Saigon		½d.
1799. Cadiz		2d.	1859. Suakin		1d.
1800. Meshed		2½d.	1860. Rouen		2d.
1801. St. Petersburg		4½d.	1861. Patras		1½d.
1802. Batoum		1d.	1862. Barcelona		2d.
1803. Peking		3d.	1863. Amoy		2½d.
1804. Samos		½d.	1864. Trebizond		1d.
1805. Dantzig		2d.	1865. Lisbon		2½d.
1806. Antwerp		1½d.	1866. Callao		2d.
1807. Ajaccio		1½d.	1867. Pernambuco		5d.
1808. Stettin		3d.	1868. Naples		1½d.
1809. Aleppo		1d.	1869. New Orleans		2½d.
1810. Tangier		2½d.	1870. Vera Cruz		2½d.
1811. Tokio		3½d.	1871. Madeira		1d.
1812. Madeira		½d.	1872. Jerusalem		1d.
1813. Vera Cruz		1d.	1873. Ningpo		1d.
1814. Oporto		1d.	1874. Rio de Janeiro		2½d.
1815. Hamburg		1½d.	1875. Trieste		1d.
1816. New Orleans		1½d.	1876. Curaçoa		1d.
1817. Bengazi		½d.	1877. Goa		1d.
1818. Marmagao		½d.	1878. Cagliari		1d.
1819. Gothenburg		2d.	1879. Guayaquil		1d.
1820. Dar-al-Baida		3d.	1880. Havana		1½d.
1821. Erzeroum		½d.	1881. Reykjavik (Iceland)		1d.
1822. Munich		2½d.	1882. Milan		1½d.

No. 1883.

Reference to previous Report, Annual Series No. 1712.

UNITED STATES.

BALTIMORE.

Acting-Consul Coates to the Marquess of Salisbury.

(Received at Foreign Office, April 21, 1897.)

My Lord,

I HAVE the honour to transmit herewith to your Lordship a Report drawn up by me on the Trade and Commerce of Baltimore for the year 1896, together with similar Reports from the Vice-Consuls at Norfolk, Va., and Richmond, Va.

I have, &c.
(Signed)   A. G. COATES.

Report on the Trade and Commerce of the Consular District of Baltimore for the Year 1896.

TABLE of Contents.

	PAGE
Trade of Baltimore	2
Channel approaches	2
Local finance	2
Shipping	2
Marine disasters	2
Ship-building	2
Breadstuffs	2
Dry goods	3
Canned goods	3
„ oysters	3
„ peaches	3
Coffee	3
Tobacco	3
Cotton	3
Wholesale clothing	4
Coal	4
Bicycles	4
Manufactures of straw	4
Immigration	4
Annexes—	
A.—Return of shipping	5
B.—Exports	5
C.—Imports	6
D.—Value of exports and imports	6
Trade report of Norfolk Vice-Consulate	7
„ Richmond „	10

(2364)

UNITED STATES.

Trade of Baltimore.
The trade of Baltimore, taken as a whole, was dull during 1896. (The grain trade, however, formed a notable exception.) This dulness is, to a large extent, attributable to the detrimental influence of a succession of national and international questions of grave importance to commerce which arose during the year. The closing months of 1896 were somewhat better, and there are grounds for expecting more prosperity in the next twelve months.

Channel approaches.
Congress was petitioned for funds to deepen and improve the channel approaches of Baltimore, so as to enable the city to maintain her place among the leading seaports on the Atlantic coast. 2,500,000 dol. was asked for this purpose, but only 400,000 dol. was granted. That sum, with 50,000 dol. already allowed for annual maintenance, gives in all 450,000 dol. to be expended. It is expected that the judicious outlay of this comparatively small sum will produce good results.

The lighting of the Chesapeake Bay is considered inadequate, and efforts were made to secure an appropriation from Congress for its improvement, but, so far, without success. A lightship or gas-buoy is more particularly needed for the middle ground inside Cape Henry.

Local finance.
The bank clearances for the year were 720,089,733 dol.—a greater amount than for any year since 1893.

Shipping.
The tonnage movement of the port shows the large increase of about 45 per cent. over that of the previous year. 565 British vessels arrived, against 388 in 1895.

Steamship lines.
A number of important additions were made to the steamship lines trading between Baltimore and foreign ports.

The Johnston Line, trading to Liverpool, added the new steel vessel "Vedamore," of 4,122 tons (net), and the "Ikbal," of 3,490 tons, was chartered for a year, but will, I am informed, be permanently employed by the Company. Two large vessels, now in course of construction, will also shortly be chartered.

The Puritan Line, trading to Antwerp, added the "Scottish King," of 2,147 tons.

The Donaldson Line, running to Glasgow, added the "Orthia," of 2,694 tons.

New vessels have also been acquired by some of the lines not under the British flag, which trade regularly with this port.

Marine disasters.
Thirty-nine reports of marine disasters were filed with the collector, showing a loss of 30 lives, besides 134,122 dol. in vessel, and 50,733 dol. in cargo property.

Shipbuilding.
Thirty-one vessels were built at local shipyards (27 sail and 4 steam) valued at 232,220 dol.

Breadstuffs.
The trade in breadstuffs was active, especially during the latter part of the year, notwithstanding depressing influences which affected trade generally. It showed an increase of about 50 per cent. Indeed, the volume of grain and flour dealt with has never been exceeded in the history of this port.

Exports, which were dull in 1895, have been very large, and would probably have been one-third larger had there been sufficient elevator accommodation.

For practical purposes, the present elevators can scarcely be said to hold more than 3,500,000 bushels; but merchants hope that additional elevators will soon be built—at least one more at Locust Point for the Baltimore and Ohio Railroad Co., and one at Canton for the Northern Central Railroad trade.

The trade in wheat, though satisfactory, did not keep pace with that of other cereals, owing to the comparative failure of the winter crop.

Dry goods. Prices for wholesale dry goods were lower than in 1895— cottons averaging 10 per cent. lower, and woollens 15 to 20 per cent. lower. An early upward movement in prices is not expected, and consequently there may be increased purchases during the spring.

In retail dry goods business was fair at first, and sales during the early months of the year were larger than in 1895. Later, however, business was hampered by the political campaign, and prices were low.

Canned goods. The canned goods trade was somewhat better than in 1895, and during the latter part of 1896 there was considerable demand for this class of goods. The comparative few failures among packing firms indicates that the trade was not unprofitable. That circumstance, combined with the relatively small quantities packed, give hope for an improvement in 1897.

Oysters. An average quantity of oysters was packed, and the supply equalled the demand. However, the cold weather of September and October caused the yield to diminish and values to be maintained. Prices for good stock ranged from 60 c. and 70 c. to 1 dol. and 1 dol. 10 c. per bushel.

Peaches. The peach crop was abundant, but only a relatively small quantity was put up. The late fruit was too costly to admit of profitable packing.

Coffee. The coffee trade was exceptionally dull, especially during the last months of the year. Receipts show a falling-off of 114,403 bags. That falling-off, however, was partly made up by merchants having imported considerable quantities of coffee by way of New York. They had to adopt that course owing to the absence at Rio and Santos of vessels bound for Baltimore at the time of purchase. As the year advanced prices steadily declined from $14\frac{1}{2}$ c. per lb. for No. 7 Rio to $10\frac{1}{8}$ c., in consequence of the extent of the Brazilian crop.

Tobacco. The Maryland crop of tobacco was somewhat larger than that of 1895. Part was of a better quality than usual and brought excellent prices—from 10 c. to 11 c. per lb. The greater portion, however, consisted of inferior grades, and the large supply of these supplemented by the quantity on hand at the beginning of the year had a depressing effect on the prices of the common kinds, which were as low as $1\frac{1}{2}$ c. and 1 c. per lb., and such figures attracted large purchases from Europe.

The French Government contracted for its usual supply of 11,000 hgds., and Germany bought about half that quantity.

Cotton. The cotton trade was dull, and prices fell from $8\frac{7}{8}$ to 7 c. per lb.

(2364)

UNITED STATES.

at the end of the year, owing to the heavy receipts, which amounted to 263,889 bales. The total crop is estimated at 8,500,000 bales. Foreign exports were 56,057 bales less than in 1895. The usual quantity of about 65,000 bales was consumed by local mills, and 99,000 bales were sent coastwise.

Wholesale clothing. The output in the wholesale clothing trade was about 33⅓ per cent. less than in 1895. Sales also were much less than during that year, and were chiefly confined to the cheaper qualities. Prices were 20 to 25 per cent. lower. The aggregate volume of business amounted to some 9,000,000 dol., against 12,000,000 dol. in 1895. About 75 firms are engaged in this industry, which is one of the most important of Baltimore.

Coal. Shipments of coal were more considerable than for many years past, but the amount exported abroad was less than in 1895. Prices were low. The coal which supplies the Baltimore market is mined chiefly at Georges Creek, in Maryland, and in the Cumberland region of West Virginia. The outlook of the trade is considered satisfactory.

Bicycles. The manufacture of and trade in bicycles has of late been of some importance, and Baltimore is becoming a centre for supplying the south. About nine firms are engaged in the manufacture.

Manufactures of straw. The straw plait trade was unsatisfactory. The volume of business only amounted in value to 1,500,000 dol., against 2,000,000 dol. in 1895.

Immigration. In the number of immigrants there was an increase of 3,247 over the previous year, and they are considered to be of a more desirable type than the immigrants under the old immigration laws. They were of the following nationalities.

Nationality.	Male.	Female.	Total.
England	38	7	45
Scotland	5	..	5
Ireland	7	..	7
British West Indies	18	11	29
Austria	1,638	783	2,421
Hungary	1,224	506	1,730
Germany	1,800	1,867	3,667
Russia	2,534	1,248	3,782
Various	20	12	32
Total	7,284	4,434	11,718

BALTIMORE.

Annex A.—RETURN of all Shipping at the Port of Baltimore during the Year 1896.

ENTERED.

Nationality.	Sailing. Number of Vessels.	Sailing. Tons.	Steam. Number of Vessels.	Steam. Tons.	Total. Number of Vessels.	Total. Tons.
British	10	1,943	555	1,044,230	565	1,046,173
American (foreign)	100	32,402	38	20,573	138	52,975
German	1	712	107	370,580	108	371,292
Italian	8	6,299	...	...	8	6,299
Norwegian	...	...	52	31,945	52	31,945
Swedish	1	241	1	1,325	2	1,566

CLEARED.

Nationality.	Sailing. Number of Vessels.	Sailing. Tons.	Steam. Number of Vessels.	Steam. Tons.	Total. Number of Vessels.	Total. Tons.
British	10	1,943	565	1,061,528	575	1,063,471
American (foreign)	105	46,272	37	17,863	142	64,135
German	1	712	108	374,300	109	375,012
Italian	10	7,948	...	...	10	7,948
Norwegian	...	...	52	31,945	52	31,945
Swedish	1	241	1	1,325	2	1,566

Annex B.—RETURN of Principal Articles of Export from Baltimore during the Years 1896-95.

Articles.		Quantity. 1896.	Quantity. 1895.
Wheat	Bushels	6,589,856	4,033,922
Flour	Barrels	3,065,845	2,485,360
Maize	Bushels	26,382,182	9,515,021
Oats	,,	6,919,518	134,318
Cloverseed and timothy	,,	50,221	75,003
Cattle	Head	59,833	40,111
Sheep	,,	43,118	107,325
Canned goods	Cases	229,071	321,619
Lard	Lbs.	91,127,738	69,257,241
Petroleum (refined)	Gallons	45,276,588	45,689,227
Coal	Tons	51,826	80,880
Coke	,,	35,595	53,920
Copper	Lbs.	84,293,837	39,294,155
Lead	,,	9,854,872	..
Lumber	Feet	46,654,756	26,488,000
Logs	,,	56,149	68,392
Tobacco	Hogsheads	61,347	60,929
Oilseed cakes	Lbs.	127,296,125	57,258,880
Cotton	Bales	167,524	223,581
Resin	Barrels	85,798	115,355
Horses	Head	894	961
Hay	Tons	196	823

(2364)

Annex C.—RETURN of Principal Articles of Import into Baltimore during the Years 1896-95.

Articles.		Quantity.	
		1896.	1895.
Iron ore	Tons	368,561	249,163
Salt	,,	20,301	16,819
Manure salt	,,	40,941	34,246
Chemicals	Packages	116,623	267,306
Brimstone	Tons	13,721	9,526
Phosphate	Bags	17,275	18,890
Nitrate of soda	,,	9,500	23,804
Cement	Casks	303,603	331,916
Whisky	Barrels	8,291	7,481
Bananas	Bunches	1,104,449	899,458
Pineapples	Dozens	270,550	315,416
Cocoanuts		2,379,000	1,945,000
Coffee	Bags	134,552	262,011
Rice	,,	46,701	82,546
Sugar	,,	322,321	196,462
,,	Cases	2,080	..
Matting	Value (Dol.)	104,289	106,962
Liquorice-root	Lbs.	3,401,771	2,288,731

Annex D.—TABLE showing Total Value of all Articles Exported from and Imported to Baltimore during the Years 1896-95.

Country.	Exports.		Imports.	
	1896.	1895.	1896.	1895.
Great Britain	Dollars. 40,686,306	Dollars. 30,644,356	Dollars. 2,936,221	Dollars. 4,927,113
	£ 8,354,476	£ 6,087,136	£ 652,201	£ 1,011,111
	Dollars.	Dollars.	Dollars.	Dollars.
Belgium	5,653,637	3,934,335	135,570	120,562
Brazil	2,138,223	2,852,144	1,962,745	4,579,526
Cuba and Spain	53,888	105,109	437,844	414,694
France	4,987,694	3,166,127	114,765	132,516
Germany	12,810,187	10,322,494	2,309,491	1,953,694
Netherlands	13,572,224	8,385,045	393,958	217,267
Mexico	217,653	398,046	27,102	7,945
Italy	161,471	3,865	652,898	443,987
Other countries	1,227,553	360,070	1,356,000	1,212,827

NORFOLK, VIRGINIA.

Mr. Vice-Consul Myers reports:—

As predicted in my report for the year 1895, the transfer of the deep-water terminus of the Southern Railway from West Point, Virginia, to Norfolk, has largely increased the trade and volume of business of the port.

While this applies to all branches of business, it is more noticeable in the unprecedented increase in the variety and value of the exports and of the shipping.

The exports for this year being nearly three times that of last, while the number of vessels entered and cleared has about doubled.

Quite a large number of vessels entering at this port, however, are from the Southern ports, and merely call in here for bunker coals, and as this is supplied to them in from four to six hours, the volume of business is not proportionate to the tonnage shown in the accompanying statement of shipping. The statement of imports shows only a slight increase in value over that of last year, which is surprising, in view of the fact that at least two of the foreign transportation companies have regular boats to and from the United Kingdom. With the present large transportation facilities, which are constantly being added to by the numerous railroads entering here, this should be a good distributing point for British merchants who are exporting to the Southern and Western States.

While the city has not yet recovered from the financial depression, so prevalent all over this country, the following returns of the balances paid in the clearing-house for the years 1885, 1890, and 1896, indicate a steady growth under adverse circumstances:—

	Amount.
	Dollars.
Balance paid in the clearing house, 1885	5,958,128
,, ,, 1890	7,255,898
,, ,, 1896	8,079,647

The cotton receipts show a large gain over the past three years as will be seen from the following statement:—

	Quantity.
	Bales.
Receipts for year ending December 31, 1893	456,940
,, ,, 1894	476,120
,, ,, 1896	721,376

The following table, which embraces the principal public and private enterprises in Norfolk, gives a concise view of the commercial importance of the place:—

UNITED STATES.

	Number.
Manufactories of fertilisers	13
Cigar manufactories	30
Cotton knitting mills	6
Manufactories of barrels and boxes	12
Oyster packers	25
Hosiery mills	1
Flour and corn mills	2
Candy manufactories	6
Peanut oil and meal factory	1
,, cleaning factories	6
Carriage manufactories	2
Furniture factories	2
Paper box factory	1
Ironworks	7
Manufactories of agricultural implements	3
Creosote works	2
Ice factories	2
Banks	2
Hospitals	2
Sanitariums	2
Cotton pressing companies	3
Hotels	6
Telephone companies	2
Telegraph companies	2
Printing establishments	11
Business colleges	3
Daily newspapers	7
Weekly newspapers	4
Monthly newspapers	1
Wholesale fruit dealers	5
,, grocers	11
,, druggists	4
Broom factories	2
Brick yards	4
Ship yards (including U.S. Government yard)	4
Electric car lines	3
Saw mills	12

BALTIMORE.

TABLE showing Principal Articles of Export and Import at the Port of Norfolk during the past Year.

EXPORTS.

Articles.	Value.
	Dollars.
Corn, bushels	4,478,044
Cotton, bales	6,847,905
Logs and lumber	1,392,486
Staves and headings	124,050
Splint coal	240,481
Bituminous coal	175,201
Coke	66,352
Coal (Pocohontas)	43,479
Flour, barrels	190,712
Leaf tobacco	255,865
Cattle	198,440
Mowers and reapers	127,092
Lard	559,538
Steel and copper bars	372,178
Oats	18,785
Meal	26,000
Gunpowder	13,200
Bark	288
Cotton seed meal	700
Miscellaneous articles	413,060
Total	15,543,856

IMPORTS.

Articles.	Value.
	Dollars.
Sulphate of ammonia	55,095
Kainit	49,093
Manure salt	39,896
Brimstone	27,273
Fruits	890
Wearing apparel	869
Wines	1,250
Miscellaneous articles	17,238
Fertilisers	24,669
Total	216,273

UNITED STATES.

TABLE showing the Movement of all Shipping at the Port of Norfolk during the Year 1896.

ENTERED.

Nationality.	Sailing. Number of Vessels.	Sailing. Tons.	Steam. Number of Vessels.	Steam. Tons.	Total. Number of Vessels.	Total. Tons.
British	9	11,180	413	727,230	422	738,410
German	...	...	28	48,266	28	48,266
Norwegian	...	...	18	28,208	18	28,208
Spanish	...	...	36	59,079	36	59,079
American	27	8,944	3	2,755	30	11,699
Italian	7	3,910	...	...	7	3,910
Danish	...	...	5	10,381	5	10,381
Dutch	1	2,180	...	...	1	2,180
Total	44	26,214	503	875,919	547	902,133

CLEARED.

Nationality.	Sailing. Number of Vessels.	Sailing. Tons.	Steam. Number of Vessels.	Steam. Tons.	Total. Number of Vessels.	Total. Tons.
British	13	11,430	421	736,832	434	748,262
German	...	...	31	55,094	31	55,094
Norwegian	1	381	17	26,662	18	27,043
Spanish	...	...	35	57,113	35	57,113
American	50	30,776	5	3,098	55	33,874
Italian	5	2,856	...	...	5	2,856
Danish	...	...	4	8,190	4	8,190
Dutch	1	2,180	...	...	1	2,180
Total	70	47,623	513	886,989	583	934,612

RICHMOND, VIRGINIA.

Mr. Vice-Consul Brine reports:—

General trade. Despite the prevailing depression in trade—which has been felt in a greater or less degree in all quarters of the globe—and in the face of the Presidential campaign and the consequent stagnation of business, the records of the public offices and the personal testimony of business men go to show that the volume of business transacted here during the past 12 months has exceeded what could have been expected.

There has been an agreeable absence of the nervous conditions which prevailed in 1894 and 1895, and although the number of commercial failures has been considerable, none of them have been very large, and it has been a process of weeding out, and the survival of the fittest.

Manufacturing. The number of manufacturing enterprises has increased from 889 in 1895 to 984 in 1896, but there has been a falling-off in the number of operatives—18,133 being employed in 1895, and only 16,886 last year. The amount of capital invested has increased from 16,163,000 dol. to 16,275,750 dol., but the aggregate sales were only 31,569,665 dol., or 456,335 dol. less than in 1895.

Jobbing trade. The jobbing trade shows a falling-off in the annual sales of

303,462 dol., and there has been a slight increase in the amount of capital invested in this branch. The falling-off is due undoubtedly to the great drop in the prices obtainable, for the year 1896 will long be remembered as a year of low prices and small profits, the total sales amounting to 29,886,062 dol., as compared with 30,189,524 dol. for the previous year. The failures for the year were 66, as against 69 in the previous year, and represented assets to the amount of 576,170 dol.; liabilities, 1,009,581 dol.

Banks. The banks' clearings show a decided decrease. In 1894 clearings were 113,327,889 dol.; in 1895 the amount was 121,545,780 dol.; while in 1896 the amount was 114,378,841 dol.; a decrease of 7,166,939 dol. on last year.

Tobacco. The tobacco trade in 1896 reflects in a general way the dulness incident to all other branches of business. There is very little complaint, however, among manufacturers. Business has been fairly steady with nearly all; profits have been small, but this had been expected; no firms of any note have discontinued or failed. The trade in granulated tobacco has been dull. The larger cheroot factories have done well. In smoking mixtures business was not bad. The local plug trade has been good for the times. The cigarette trade has been very fair in volume, but profits will probably be smaller than heretofore. Several of our leading plug and export factories show no diminution in business, but have a steady, good trade in standard brands, with very satisfactory profits and better prospects ahead.

The manufacturing tobacco-supply firms, representing the trade at large in the State, report a decline in business, but with good returns on what has been sold. In the retail trade there are many evidences that business has been prosperous.

Leaf-tobacco statistics. Private sales for the year ending December 31, 1896:— Wrappers, 2,687 hogsheads; smokers, 2,461; fillers, 7,068; cutters, 1,388; dark leaf, 8,514; scrap, 1,187; Burley, 1,038; lugs, 2,962; stems, 525; Western, 335; sun-cured, 39; total, 28,204 hogsheads, against 35,317 hogsheads last year, 39,703 hogsheads in 1894, and 27,463 hogsheads in 1893.

Dark loose sales for year 1896, 2,200,490 lbs., with 18 c. per lb. highest price paid. Average price for all sold, $3\frac{3}{4}$ c. per lb., making the past year's sales amount to 82,518 dol. 42 c. Sales in 1895 were 2,412,310 lbs., thus showing a decrease of 211,820 lbs. in 1896, which deficit is accounted for by last year's small crop, and the lateness in marketing the present one.

Bright loose sales for the year, 1,966,100 lbs., 8 dol. 15 c. per 100 lbs. average price for all sales, representing in money 160,237 dol. 10 c. Sales last year (1895) 3,632,405 lbs., showing a decrease in 1896 of 1,666,305 lbs.

Total bright and dark loose sales for year, 4,166,590 lbs., worth in money, 242,755 dol. 52 c.

James River improvement. The work of deepening the James River channel now being carried on by the United States Government, has been steadily proceeded with during the year, and it is safe to say that we now have $17\frac{1}{2}$ feet of water at low tide between Richmond Bar and Hampton Roads.

UNITED STATES.

Export trade. Richmond has undoubtedly increased her export trade, but as the export takes place at other ports principally Norfolk and Newport News, Virginia, it will be credited to those ports, this port and its sub-port West Point being, practically, no longer ports of entry or clearance for foreign-going vessels.

TABLE of Articles Imported into Richmond, Virginia, during the Year 1896.

Articles.	Value.
	Dollars.
Farm and garden seeds	30,957
Guano	25,250
Tin-plate	18,782
China and earthenware	8,375
Tobacco and cigars	6,052
Salt	5,870
Matches	3,221
Wines and spirits	2,789
Miscellaneous	5,260
Total	106,556

RETURN showing Value of Articles Imported into Richmond, Virginia, during the Year 1896.

Country.	Value.
	Dollars.
Great Britain	48,692
Orchilla, W.I.	25,250
France	14,677
Germany	12,667
Cuba	3,078
Other countries	2,192
Total	106,556

LONDON
Printed for Her Majesty's Stationery Office,
BY HARRISON AND SONS,
Printers in Ordinary to Her Majesty.
(75 5 | 97—H & S 2364)

FOREIGN OFFICE.
1897.
ANNUAL SERIES.

Nº 1894.

DIPLOMATIC AND CONSULAR REPORTS ON TRADE AND FINANCE.

UNITED STATES.

REPORT FOR THE YEAR 1896

ON THE

TRADE OF GALVESTON.

REFERENCE TO PREVIOUS REPORT, Annual Series No. 1687.

Presented to both Houses of Parliament by Command of Her Majesty,
MAY, 1897.

LONDON:
PRINTED FOR HER MAJESTY'S STATIONERY OFFICE,
BY HARRISON AND SONS, ST. MARTIN'S LANE,
PRINTERS IN ORDINARY TO HER MAJESTY.

And to be purchased, either directly or through any Bookseller, from
EYRE & SPOTTISWOODE, East Harding Street, Fleet Street, E.C., and
32, Abingdon Street, Westminster, S.W.; or
JOHN MENZIES & Co., 12, Hanover Street, Edinburgh, and
90, West Nile Street, Glasgow; or
HODGES, FIGGIS, & Co., Limited, 104, Grafton Street, Dublin.

1897.

[C. 8277—112.] *Price Twopence.*

New Series of Reports.

Reports of the Annual Series have been issued from Her Majesty's Diplomatic and Consular Officers at the following places, and may be obtained from the sources indicated on the title-page:—

No.		Price.
1776. Madrid	.. ..	2d.
1777. Vienna	.. ..	2d.
1778. Canton	.. ..	1d.
1779. Yokohama	.. ..	1½d.
1780. Newchwang	.. ..	1d.
1781. Wuhu	.. ..	1d.
1782. Athens	.. ..	2d.
1783. Tonga	.. ..	½d.
1784. Smyrna	.. ..	½d.
1785. Baghdad	.. ..	1d.
1786. Hiogo and Osaka	..	4½d.
1787. Bangkok	.. ..	1d.
1788. Odessa	.. ..	2d.
1789. Naples	.. ..	2d.
1790. Beyrout	.. ..	1d
1791. Tunis	.. ..	1½d.
1792. Kiukiang	.. ..	3d.
1793. Bangkok	.. ..	1d.
1794. Rio Grande do Sul	..	1d.
1795. Valparaiso	.. ..	4d.
1796. Brindisi	.. ..	2½d.
1797. Bushire	.. ..	2d.
1798. Christiania	.. ..	5½d.
1799. Cadiz	.. ..	2d.
1800. Meshed	.. ..	2½d.
1801. St. Petersburg	..	4½d.
1802. Batoum	.. ..	1d.
1803. Peking	.. ..	2d.
1804. Samos	.. ..	½d.
1805. Dantzig	.. ..	2d.
1806. Antwerp	.. ..	1½d.
1807. Ajaccio	.. ..	1½d.
1808. Stettin	.. ..	3d.
1809. Aleppo	.. ..	1d.
1810. Tangier	.. ..	2½d.
1811. Tokio	.. ..	3½d.
1812. Madeira	.. ..	½d.
1813. Vera Cruz	.. ..	1d.
1814. Oporto	.. ..	1d.
1815. Hamburg	.. ..	1½d.
1816. New Orleans	.. ..	1½d.
1817. Bengazi	.. ..	½d.
1818. Marmagao	.. ..	½d.
1819. Gothenburg	.. ..	2d.
1820. Dar-al-Baida	.. ..	3d.
1821. Erzeroum	.. ..	½d.
1822. Munich	.. ..	2½d.
1823. Samoa	.. ..	½d.
1824. Chinkiang	.. ..	1d.
1825. Jeddah	.. ..	1d.
1826. Sofia	.. ..	1½d.
1827. Mexico	.. ..	2d.
1828. Teneriffe	.. ..	3½d.
1829. Batoum	.. ..	1d.
1830. Cadiz	.. ..	1d.
1831. Martinique	.. ..	1d.
1832. Odessa	.. ..	1d.
1833. Ghilan	.. ..	1d.
1834. Old Calabar	.. ..	6½d.

No.		Price.
1835. Tamsui	.. ..	1d.
1836. Copenhagen	.. ..	½d.
1837. Salonica	.. ..	1½d.
1838. Honolulu	.. ..	½d.
1839. Buenos Ayres	.. ..	2d.
1840. Para	.. ..	1d.
1841. Bolivia	.. ..	2d.
1842. Washington	.. ..	3d.
1843. Berlin	.. ..	2d.
1844. Uganda	.. ..	1d.
1845. Belgrade	.. ..	1½d.
1846. Dakar	.. ..	½d.
1847. Florence	.. ..	1½d.
1848. Copenhagen	.. ..	2d.
1849. Havre	.. ..	2d.
1850. Serajevo	.. ..	1d.
1851. Madrid	.. ..	2d.
1852. La Rochelle	.. ..	1½d.
1853. Chicago	.. ..	4d.
1854. Berlin	.. ..	1d.
1855. Cherbourg	.. ..	2½d.
1856. Beira	.. ..	1d.
1857. Charleston	.. ..	2½d.
1858. Saigon	.. ..	½d.
1859. Suakin	.. ..	1d.
1860. Rouen	.. ..	2d.
1861. Patras	.. ..	1½d.
1862. Barcelona	.. ..	2d.
1863. Amoy	.. ..	2½d.
1864. Trebizond	.. ..	1d.
1865. Lisbon	.. ..	2½d.
1866. Callao	.. ..	2d.
1867. Pernambuco	.. ..	5d.
1868. Naples	.. ..	1½d.
1869. New Orleans	.. ..	2½d.
1870. Vera Cruz	.. ..	2½d.
1871. Madeira	.. ..	1d.
1872. Jerusalem	.. ..	1d.
1873. Ningpo	.. ..	1d.
1874. Rio de Janeiro	.. ..	2½d.
1875. Trieste	.. ..	1d.
1876. Curaçoa	.. ..	1d.
1877. Goa	.. ..	1d.
1878. Cagliari	.. ..	1d.
1879. Guayaquil	.. ..	1d.
1880. Havana	.. ..	1½d.
1881. Reykjavik (Iceland)	..	1d.
1882. Milan	.. ..	1½d.
1883. Baltimore	.. ..	1d.
1884. Cettinjé	.. ..	½d.
1885. Bilbao	.. ..	2½d.
1886. Florence	.. ..	1½d.
1887. Brest	.. ..	1½d.
1888. Marseilles	.. ..	1½d.
1889. Wuhu	.. ..	1d.
1890. Chinkiang	.. ..	1d.
1891. Malaga	.. ..	1d.
1892. Antwerp	.. ..	½d.
1893. Amsterdam	.. ..	1d.

No. 1894.

Reference to previous Report, Annual Series No. 1687.

UNITED STATES.

GALVESTON.

Consul Nugent to the Marquess of Salisbury.

(Received at Foreign Office, April 23, 1897.)

My Lord,

I HAVE the honour to transmit my Annual Report on the Trade and Commerce of Galveston for the year 1896, together with the Report of Mr. Vice-Consul Roland on Sabine Pass.

I regret that, owing to the extreme pressure of official business, my Report has been delayed and is forwarded later than usual.

I have, &c.
(Signed) HORACE D. NUGENT.

Report on the Trade and Commerce of the Consular District of Galveston for the Year 1896.

TABLE of Contents.

	PAGE
Galveston—	
Introductory remarks—	
Remarkable year for Galveston	3
Increase in trade	3
Satisfactory increase of British trade	4
Remarks as to increasing import business	4
List of imports required	4
General foreign trade, total value of	5
Imports—	
Value of direct imports	5
Imports free of duty	5
„ subject to duty	5
„ from Great Britain	5
Remarks on imports from Great Britain	5
Imports from Germany	6
„ France	6
„ other countries	6

UNITED STATES.

Table of Contents—continued.

	PAGE
Galveston—continued—	
Exports—	
Total value of exports	6
Cotton	7
Cotton-seed oilcake and meal	7
„ oil	7
Wheat	7
Maize	7
Wheat flour	7
Lumber and logs	7
New exportations	7
Exports to Great Britain	7
„ Germany	8
„ France	8
„ the Netherlands	8
„ Denmark	8
„ Belgium	8
„ other countries	8
Shipping and navigation—	
Total tonnage of shipping	9
Tonnage of foreign shipping	9
British shipping	9
Cargoes of British vessels	9
Freights	10
Immigration—	
Immigration from Germany	10
Texas as a field for immigrants	11
Advice to immigrants	11
Railroads—	
Figures as to Texas railroads	11
Lines into Galveston	12
Grain trade—	
Increasing importance of Galveston as a grain port	12
Exports of wheat and maize	12
Additional elevators being built	12
Grain-laden British vessels	12
Table of exports of grain	12
Cotton business, 1895-96—	
United States crop for season	13
Decrease in Texas	13
Average price of crop	13
„ commercial value of crop	13
Details of Texas crop	13
Percentage of deliveries from various groups of cotton-growing States	14
Receipts of cotton at various United States ports	14
Exports of cotton from various United States ports	15
Cotton business, 1896-97—	
Estimated total crop	15
„ Texas crop	15
Increased receipts at Galveston	15
Prospects at Galveston	16
Receipts at, and exports from, Galveston	16
Cotton prices for 1896	18
Public Works	19
Plan to utilise Pelican Island	19
Harbour improvements—	
Four feet added to depth of channel	19
Jetties practically completed	19
Sabine Pass—	
Prosperity of Sabine Pass	20
Exports of lumber	20
Sabine Pass as a port	20

GALVESTON.

Table of Contents—continued.

	Page
Sabine Pass—continued—	
British shipping	20
Channel over bar	20
Tables of shipping	20
Exports of lumber to foreign ports	21
" " coastwise ports	21
Exports, table of	22
Imports, "	24
Shipping returns	26

Note.—Calculations are made throughout this report at 5 dol. to the 1*l.* sterling.

Introductory Remarks.

In common with the rest of the Union, Texas suffered considerably during 1896 from unsettled business conditions and financial depression.

The effect of these adverse features is forcibly demonstrated by the failures in the State during the year, which numbered 751, with liabilities of 10,486,435 dol., as against 551, liabilities of 4,949,406 dol. in 1895.

It is hoped by many that 1896 will prove the clearing-out year following the disastrous year of 1893, just as 1878 cleared away nearly all the remaining wrecks caused by the panic of 1873.

Better times are now looked for, following the settling down, after the late presidential election.

However unkind 1896 may have been to the rest of Texas, the year was a remarkable one for the port of Galveston.

Remarkable year for Galveston. Increase in trade

For some years past it has been evident that trade, especially export trade, was being deflected from the eastern ports, notably from New York, and was being absorbed by the Southern and Gulf ports.

This deflection was more marked than ever in 1896, and during the first 10 months of the year the gain at the Southern ports in export business was 33 per cent., as against 20 per cent. gain in the total value of exports from the entire country.

Owing to her recently acquired deep water, Galveston was enabled to take full advantage of the change of methods, and the result has been most striking.

Imports have doubled; exports increased nearly 60 per cent. in value, *i.e.*, from 7,106,425*l.* to 11,148,978*l.*; shipping has increased 80 per cent. in tonnage; a large and satisfactory cotton and grain exporting business has been done, the increase in the latter being something phenomenal, and many new articles of export have found their way through this port. In short, 1896, the first year that this port has actually enjoyed the benefits of an unimpeded deep channel to and from the sea, has demonstrated beyond cavil the immense advantage deep water is to Galveston. Nor has the full extent of the advantage been yet thoroughly

(2365)

employed. Trade is constantly growing here, and it may be confidently asserted that whilst 1896 shows a gain of 60 per cent. over 1895, in its turn 1897 will show an increase over 1896.

Satisfactory increase of British trade.
It is especially satisfactory to note that British trade has largely participated in the increased business here, and has risen from 4,139,857*l.* in 1895 to 6,781,349*l.* in 1896, an increase of nearly 64 per cent.

The great disparity between the imports and exports at Galveston will be noticed, the latter being a little over 70 times the value of the former.

Remarks as to increasing import business.
Whilst the imports are slowly increasing, it is very certain that they are out of all proportion, at present, to the exports.

No less than 95 British vessels arrived direct from Great Britain during 1896 in ballast, whilst the railways running into Galveston are compelled to send away train after train empty out of here for want of freight.

It would seem that some re-adjustment of present conditions is necessary if Galveston is to do the import business she should. Her geographical position should give her a large proportion of the import trade for the States of Texas, Kansas, and Colorado, and even for that of California.

If New Orleans can do an import business equal to 25 per cent. of her export trade, surely Galveston can increase hers in this direction.

Almost any rate of freight, no matter how small, would probably pay better than to run ships out here in ballast, and any freight, no matter how little, would repay the railways better than to run full trucks into Galveston and empty ones out.

In my report for 1895 I gave a list of articles which could be imported with profit into Galveston, and for which there is a constant demand. I think it advisable to repeat this list, which was drawn up by a practical merchant here:—

List of imports required.
"From Europe: cement, earthenware, crockery, tinplate, salt, glassware, patented goods of every kind, beer, ale, porter, wines, and other goods of a similar character can be imported with profit; bottled goods, and especially the bottled waters of the famous springs of Europe, tinned goods not put up in this country, firebrick, anthracite coal, potash, lemons (from Italy), and fabrics of every kind in the textile department, especially the cheaper goods of Germany, and Irish linens, hosiery, &c.

"From the West Indies and South and Central America, could be obtained coffee, sugar, hard-woods, and all kinds of tropical fruits, including bananas, cocoanuts, pineapples, oranges, lemons, limes, &c.

"In addition to these commodities, hides and alligator skins, leaf-tobacco, sisal, Trinidad asphalt, vanilla, cocoa, &c., could with advantage also be imported through this port, as well as every other product of the tropics."

GALVESTON.

General Foreign Trade.

The total value of the trade to and from Galveston during the year 1896, amounted to 56,539,798 dol., equal to 11,307,959*l*., as against 35,869,285 dol., equal to 7,173,857*l*. in 1895, thus showing an increase of very nearly 60 per cent. Of this amount 158,981*l*. represented the value of imports, and 11,148,978*l*. that of exports.

Imports.

The total value of the direct imports from foreign countries during the year 1896 was 158,981*l*., as compared with 67,422*l*. in 1895, thus showing an increase of over 100 per cent.

Of this amount of 158,981*l*., 82,440*l*. represented the value of commodities imported free of duty, whilst 76,541*l*. represented that of articles subject to duty.

The principal articles imported free of duty were coffee, cotton ties, paper stock, salt, sisal grass, and jute butts, whilst amongst those subject to duty the following were most important, viz., cement, earthenware, preserved fruits, manufactures of iron and steel, and beetroot sugar.

In nearly all the above quoted articles an increase was shown.

The imports from Great Britain and colonies were valued at 77,153*l*. during 1896, as against 43,182*l*. in 1895.

The following table shows the value of the principal imports from Great Britain and colonies during the years 1896-95:—

Articles.	Value. 1896.	Value. 1895.
	£	£
Cotton ties*	32,155	3,906
Paper stock (old bagging)*	4,140	1,246
Salt*	6,909	9,930
Jute and jute butts*	16,417	5,750
Chemicals (sheep-dip)	1,825	3,650
Earthenware (plain and decorated crockery)	4,218	2,655
Flax and hemp (manufactures of jute)	1,740	2,722
Iron and steel, manufactures of	2,185	720
Ale and porter	1,520	1,985
Tin-plates	..	3,904
All other articles	6,044	6,714
Total	77,153	43,182

* Free of duty.

From the figures given in the foregoing table it will be seen that the major part of the imports from Great Britain and colonies came under the heading of merchandise free of duty.

Since 1895 the duty on cotton ties has been removed, and in

(2365)

consequence nearly nine times the value was imported in 1896 over that of 1895. As, however, it seems to be the intention of the incoming Administration at Washington to re-impose the McKinley duty on cotton ties it would seem advisable to exporters in England to take advantage of existing conditions, as there is, no doubt, a very large demand for English cotton ties in Texas as long as they can be imported free of duty.

Similar remarks apply to salt, on which it is also proposed to re-impose the duty.

A large increase will be noticed in the importations of jute butts from India, owing, no doubt, to deeper laden vessels being able to enter Galveston. This jute goes largely to St. Louis.

The importations of earthenware also increased materially during 1896, and Galveston supplies a great part of the country lying back of this port; some of the crockery goes as far as Salt Lake City.

There is no foreign competition to speak of with English crockery in Galveston, and the business might, therefore, be made much more extensive than it is.

The quantity of ale and porter imported into Galveston has decreased of late years, as there is a more general demand for a lighter beer in this semi-tropical climate.

Several articles have disappeared from the list of importations from Great Britain.

It will be noticed that tin-plates to the value of 3,904*l.* were imported in 1895, and none at all in 1896.

Cement, too, is another article, which as recently as 1893 was largely imported from Great Britain, but the trade has practically passed into the hands of Germany and Belgium.

Imports from Germany. The imports from Germany during 1896 were valued at 50,369*l.*, as against 10,154*l.* in 1895. This large increase is chiefly due to the fact that the vessels of the North German Lloyd and Hamburg American steamship lines now come direct to Galveston. The chief items imported from that country are beetroot sugar valued at 39,108*l.*, and cement valued at 5,715*l.*

Imports from France. The imports from France were valued at 3,768*l.* in 1896, as compared with 2,174*l.* in 1895. These chiefly consisted of preserved fruits, sardines, preserved vegetables, and wines.

Imports from other countries. There was a considerable increase in the value of imports from Mexico during 1896, these being 15,117*l.*, as against 255*l.* in 1895. The chief items were coffee, 2,274*l.*; timber and logs, 2,208*l.*; and sisal grass, 10,010*l.* The only other items of importance amongst the imports during 1896 were cement from Belgium, value 7,858*l.*, and coffee valued at 1,940*l.* from Porto Rico.

Detailed tables of the imports are annexed.

Exports.

Exports, total value of. The total value of the exports from the port of Galveston during 1896 was 11,148,978*l.*, as against 7,106,425*l.* in 1895, or an increase of 60 per cent.

GALVESTON.

The leading commodity exported was, as usual, cotton. Cotton.

During the year 1896 the largest amount of cotton ever exported from this port left Galveston, viz., 1,182,601 bales, value 9,419,062*l.*

For 1895 the figures were 931,167 bales valued at 6,534,253*l.*

Next in importance to cotton was cotton-seed oilcake and meal, of which 136,648 tons, value 593,376*l.*, were exported in 1896, as compared with 97,752 tons, value 391,556*l.* in 1895. Cotton-seed oilcake and meal.

Besides these products of cotton, there was a large export business in cotton-seed oil, viz., 1,832,830 gallons, value 94,344*l.* in 1896, as against 452,268 gallons, value 37,443*l.* in 1895. Cotton-seed oil.

The exports of cereals showed a striking increase in 1896. During 1895 no wheat was exported, but during the past year 3,440,494 bushels, value 414,702*l.*, left Galveston. Wheat.

Maize to the amount of 6,222,282 bushels, value 402,615*l.*, was also exported, as compared with 1,233,477 bushels, value 78,152*l.* in the previous year. Maize.

The exports of wheat flour during 1896, also show an increase, these being 56,195 barrels, value 42,578*l.*, as against 53,244 barrels, value 37,536*l.* in 1895. Wheat flour.

Lumber was exported during 1896 to the value of 13,332*l.*, as against 9,857*l.* in 1895, whilst logs exported were valued at 10,120*l.* in 1896, compared with 15,010*l.* in 1895. Lumber and logs.

New exportations from Galveston during 1896 were as follows:— New exportations.

Articles.	Value.
	£
Spelter	88,663
Lead	13,196
Copper and copper-matte	14,876
Borax	23,153
Lard	5,433

As usual Great Britain was the best customer for the commodities exported from Galveston. Exports to Great Britain.

The total value of the exports to Great Britain and colonies during 1896 was 6,704,196*l.*, as compared with 4,096,675*l.* in 1895, or an increase of 63 per cent.

The following table shows in detail the exports to Great Britain and colonies for 1896 and 1895:—

Articles.	Value.	
	1896.	1895.
	£	£
Cotton	6,118,165	4,001,918
Cotton-seed oilcake and meal	89,451	67,248
Maize	128,922	22,012
Wheat	210,924	..
,, flour	2,206	3,587
Lumber	2,106	..
Cotton-seed oil	13,894	2
Logs	880	..
Spelter	87,567	..
Lead	8,676	..
Copper and copper-matte	14,876	..
Borax	25,153	..
Sundries	1,376	1,908
Total	6,704,196	4,096,675

It will be seen from the foregoing table that there is a larger increase in almost every article of export, and that several new commodities have been added to the list, such as spelter, lead, copper, and borax, in which the trade has been heavy.

Exports to Germany. The export trade to Germany from Galveston was second in value, and rose from 1,715,332*l.* in 1895 to 2,418,614*l.* in 1896.

The values of the principal exports were cotton, value 1,705,764*l.*, cotton-seed oil and cake, value 422,625*l.*, wheat, value 113,577*l.*, maize, value 131,511*l.*, and cotton-seed oil, value 18,710*l.*

Exports to France. The export trade to France during 1896 was 1,350,982*l.*, as against 994,952*l.* in 1895.

The values of the principal articles taken by that country were cotton, value 1,327,947*l.*, and maize 9,144*l.*

Exports to the Netherlands. The export trade to the Netherlands largely increased during 1896, being valued at 281,193*l.*, as against 61,837*l.* in 1895.

The principal exports were cotton, value 62,966*l.*, cotton-seed oilcake and meal, value 51,385*l.*, wheat, value 82,361*l.*, maize, value 28,631*l.*, and cotton-seed oil, value 48,830*l.*

Exports to Denmark. The exports to Denmark also show a striking increase in 1896, being valued at 149,151*l.*, as compared with only 7,140*l.* in 1895.

The principal items were maize, value 97,889*l.*, cotton, value 27,075*l.*, and cotton-seed oil and cake, value 23,030*l.*

Exports to Belgium. The exports to Belgium show a decrease during 1896, being valued at 65,968*l.*, as against 99,627*l.* in 1895.

The principal of these was cotton, value 54,360*l.*

Exports to other countries. As regards exports to other countries, Russia took cotton to the value of 81,305*l.* during 1896, as against 23,126*l.* in 1895, and Italy 35,880*l.*, as against 61,070*l.* in 1895.

Other important exports were wheat flour to the value of 21,335*l.* to Cuba, and to the value of 17,433*l.* to the West Indies, and cotton-seed oil to the value of 11,655*l.* to Mexico.

Tables showing the exports in detail are annexed.

GALVESTON.

Shipping and Navigation.

There was a very large increase in the shipping movement during the year 1896. Although the coastwise shipping somewhat decreased during the year, being only about 320,000 tons, yet the total tonnage entering the port was the largest ever recorded in one year, being slightly over 800,000 tons. *Total tonnage of shipping.*

The foreign shipping amounted to 485,747 tons entered, and 484,211 tons cleared. *Tonnage of foreign ships.*

Of the entries of foreign ships 230 were British, 26 Spanish, 24 Norwegian, and 10 German. The movement of British shipping was the largest ever recorded in the history of Galveston.

During 1896 there were 230 British vessels entered at Galveston, as compared with 145 in 1895. Their combined registered tonnage amounted to 395,607 tons, as against 223,519 tons in 1895, thus showing a gain of nearly 80 per cent. in tonnage over last year. The average tonnage per vessel was higher than ever before known, viz., 1,720 tons. *British shipping.*

Of these 230 vessels 34 brought full or partial cargoes, though only 21 brought cargoes direct to Galveston, the remainder having cargo in transit. *Cargoes of British vessels.*

The number of vessels arriving from Great Britain was 110, of which 15 brought cargoes. The remaining 120 vessels arrived from other countries as follows :—26 from Brazil, 25 from Cape Verde Islands, 17 from Las Palmas, 14 from Mexico, 14 from United States ports other than Galveston, 9 from United States of Colombia, 4 from Belgium, 4 from Monte Video, and 7 from other countries.

During 1896, 229 British vessels cleared from Galvaston, as against 163 in 1895, and 169 in 1894. Their combined registered tonnage was 391,934, compared with 253,202 in 1895, and 259,586 in 1894, thus showing an increase of 54 per cent. over last year.

The total value of the exports in British vessels during the year was 9,121,882*l*., or 1,889,400*l*. more than the highest total ever previously recorded of the whole foreign export trade of Galveston.

In 1895 the exports in British vessels were valued at 6,016,700*l*., so there has been during 1896 an increase of over 50 per cent. in value.

The values of the cargoes conveyed in British ships to Great Britain and other countries were as follows :—

Country	Value.
	£
Great Britain	5,170,762
Germany	2,128,184
France	1,380,035
Holland	184,165
Denmark	85,112
Belgium	65,968
Russia	53,332
Italy	41,891
Mexico	12,433

UNITED STATES.

The following is a list of the principal exports in British vessels during the year 1896:—

Articles.		Quantity.
Cotton	Bales	987,389
Cotton-seed meal	Sacks	1,964,010
,, oilcake	,,	186,962
Wheat	Bushels	2,886,159
Corn (maize)	,,	4,897,472
Cotton-seed oil	Gallons	1,097,983
Walnut lumber	Pieces	29,370
,, logs	,,	484
Spelter	Plates	2,097,386
Borax	Sacks	23,364
Copper matte	,,	28,261
Lead	Bars	35,987
Lumber	Feet	203,621
,,	Pieces	138,972
Cedar logs	,,	2,602
Staves	,,	101,015

Freights.

Freights.

The year 1896 opened with cotton freights at $\frac{7}{32}d.$ to $\frac{15}{64}d.$ per lb., and oilcake 15s. per ton. During the last half of January cotton rose to $\frac{1}{4}d.$, oilcake remaining at the same price. These figures remained in force during February. During March the cotton freights fell to $\frac{13}{64}d.-\frac{7}{32}d.$ During April and May they were from $\frac{3}{16}d.$ to $\frac{15}{128}d.$, which was the lowest ever recorded. During the earlier period of the year grain freights were 3s. 4½d. per quarter.

At the commencement of the season in August cotton rates opened at $\frac{7}{32}d.$, and only advanced one point until September, when, owing to a scarcity of tonnage, and an earlier movement of the cotton crop than anticipated, freights jumped to $\frac{9}{32}d.$ and $\frac{19}{64}d.$ In October rates went up to $\frac{5}{16}d.$, and in November to $\frac{21}{64}d.$, the grain rates advancing correspondingly from 3s. to 4s. per quarter, and the rates for cotton-seed cake from 16s. 6d. to 22s. per ton.

During December the rates gradually declined, and at the end of the month stood at $\frac{1}{4}d.$ for cotton, 3s. 4½d. for grain, and 17s. 6d. for oilcake.

Immigration.

Immigration from Germany.

The regular arrival at this port during the year 1896 of the steamers of the North German Lloyd and Hamburg American Lines has brought to Texas a fair number of high-class immigrants, chiefly, of course, Germans.

There are already several thriving German communities in Texas, and some districts are almost entirely inhabited by a population of German origin and with German ideas.

The communities are chiefly agricultural, though the merchants and traders are often German too.

There is no doubt that Texas to-day offers as good a field for a certain class of immigrant farmer as can be found in North America. *{Texas as a field for immigrants.}*

It is largely agricultural at present, and already produces one-third of the cotton crop of the United States, as well as large crops of cereals, fruits, and vegetables, for which there is a growing demand. In fact, almost anything can be grown in the State.

The climate is, on the whole, fairly healthy, though very warm in summer, and enervating for Englishmen.

Taxes are light and the land is cheap, with the soil rich enough to yield a good crop without the use of commercial manures, so that, given fair weather, a farmer ought always to make enough to live on comfortably, even if he cannot lay by much.

And there is room for much more immigration here. With an area of 260,000 square miles, an area greater than the German Empire, there is a population under 4,000,000.

A few words of caution to the would-be immigrant are necessary. It is of no use whatever for clerks, engineers, architects, &c., to come to Texas, unless to starve. The supply far exceeds the demand. *{Advice to immigrants}*

For farmers the prospect is much better, and there is also a demand for domestic servants in the towns at good wages—say 30*l*. to 50*l*. per annum, but no one should come without money enough to keep them some months, so as to look about.

Intending farmers should not buy land until here on the spot, or else they will be probably deceived.

Men with families should come alone at first, and then send for their families when familiar with the prospects and conditions.

On the whole, however, Texas is far more suitable as a field for immigration for Germans and Bohemians than for the ordinary English labourer.

Railroads

According to the figures issued by the Railroad Commissioners for the year ending June 30, 1896, there were 67 railways in operation in Texas. The total length of line was 9,437 miles, exclusive of yard tracks and sidings, and there was an addition of 147 miles of new line during the year. *{Figures as to Texas railroads.}*

The aggregate earnings amounted to 35,318,629 dol., and the aggregate expenses to 28,047,083 dol., or 79·41 per cent. of the gross earnings.

The gross amount of freight carried was 14,510,919 tons as against 15,591,262 tons in the previous year, or a decrease of 6·93 per cent.

The number of passengers carried was 6,226,077 against 6,537,250, a decrease of 4·76 per cent.

The gross amount of revenue decreased 10·33 per cent., and the working expenses decreased 2·83 per cent.

The net earnings of the Texas railroads for the year ending June 30, 1896, were 7,271,546 dol., a decrease of 3,351,328 dol., or 31·5 per cent.

Lines into Galveston. There are now five lines running into Galveston, and the prospects are that there will be one or two more ere long.

Grain Trade.

Increasing importance of Galveston as a grain port. The trade in grain, which at the end of 1895 was beginning to become of importance to the port of Galveston, has kept up a steady increase, and now bids fair to be a permanent and striking feature of this port.

Exports of wheat and maize. During the year 1896 the total amount of cereals exported was 9,662,776 bushels, as against 1,233,477 bushels in 1895 or an increase of some 800 per cent. Of this amount, 3,440,494 bushels were wheat and 6,222,282 bushels maize.

Now that Galveston has established herself as a permanent exporting point for grain, it has been found that the elevator facilities are insufficient for the business.

The present elevators, of which there are two, can accommodate 1,400,000 bushels at a time.

Additional elevators being built. It is now proposed to erect a new elevator which, at present, is in course of construction, to hold 600,000 bushels, and to enlarge the capacity of the elevator of the Texas Star Flour Mills from 400,000 to 700,000 bushels, thus giving Galveston a total storage capacity of 2,300,000 bushels.

It is expected that this capacity will be ready for use by July.

There are also plans proposed for the building of additional elevators by outside companies, but the schemes are not yet fully matured. The indications are that Galveston will before long become an extremely important grain exporting centre. Her geographical position is all in favour of this, and so far from grain deteriorating whilst in storage here, as used to be alleged as an argument against shipping at this port, it has been fully demonstrated that grain materially improves here, though exactly why cannot be ascertained.

Grain laden British vessels. Table of exports of grain. No less than 126 British vessels loaded full or partial cargoes of grain at Galveston during 1896.

The following table shows the exports of maize and wheat from the commencement of the present season, September 1, to February 26:—

GALVESTON.

Destination.	Quantity.	
	Maize.	Wheat.
	Bushels.	Bushels.
England	1,670,196	1,650,898
Germany	1,459,846	1,126,358
Holland	416,016	565,848
France	137,141	20,000
Belgium	29,000	50,000
Denmark	437,981	..
West Indies	7,800	..
Mexico	3,750	..
Total	4,161,730	3,413,104

Cotton Business, 1895–96.

The cotton crop of the United States for the year ending August 31, 1896, amounted to 7,157,346 bales, valued at 294,095,347 dol., as compared with 9,901,251 bales, valued at 299,037,530 dol. for the year ending August 31, 1895. The decrease for the season was 2,743,905 bales, and the greatest falling-off was in Texas, where the drop from the phenomenal yield of the season of 1894–95 was no less than 1,286,376 bales. {United States crop for season.} {Decrease in Texas.}

The season of 1895–96 was most unsatisfactory to cotton traders, but to producers the improvement in prices made up for the shortness of the crop.

The highest point touched was $9\frac{3}{16}$ c. per lb. for middling, which was reached in the middle of October 1895.

The lowest price was $6\frac{1}{2}$ c., the average for the entire season being 8·18 c. per lb., a gain of about 11 dol. per bale over the previous season. {Average price of crop.}

The average commercial value of the crop was 41 dol. 9 c. per bale, as against 30 dol. for the season of 1894–95. {Average commercial value of crop.}

The following table gives the details regarding the disposition of the Texas crop, which is taken to include the cotton grown in Indian Territory:— {Details of Texas crop.}

	Quantity.	
	1895–96.	1894–95.
	Bales.	Bales.
Receipts at Texas seaboard	1,055,094	1,660,591
Shipped inland to Mexico and points west of Mississippi River	71,355	86,749
Shipped by rail viâ St. Louis and Cairo (Kentucky)	234,511	460,014
Receipts at New Orleans (exclusive of Galveston)	586,442	1,025,334
Receipts at points on Mississippi River, north of St. Louis, bound eastward	42,180	43,270
Total	1,989,582	3,275,958

UNITED STATES.

Percentage of deliveries from various groups of cotton-growing States.

During the last two seasons the proportion of deliveries from the various groups of the cotton-growing States was as follows, viz.:—

	Quantity.	
	1895–96.	1894–95.
	Bales.	Bales.
Texas	1,990,000	3,276,000
Other Gulfs	2,162,000	3,000,000
Atlantic	3,005,000	3,625,000
Total	7,157,000	9,901,000

Receipts of cotton at various United States ports.

The following table shows the net receipts of cotton at the different United States ports during the seasons of 1895–96 and 1894–95, together with the exports for these seasons from the same ports. The great decrease, owing to the shortness of the crop, will be noticed, although Galveston held its place as the second cotton port in the United States:—

NET Receipts of Cotton at United States Ports.

Ports.	Quantity.	
	1895–96.	1894–95.
	Bales.	Bales.
New Orleans	1,809,864	2,584,115
Galveston	1,001,075	1,659,999
Mobile and Pensacola	227,379	253,187
Savannah	782,996	944,410
Charleston	292,288	425,487
Wilmington	176,447	234,621
Norfolk	344,124	472,540
Baltimore	45,038	118,872
New York	98,557	187,794
Boston	154,521	335,453
Philadelphia	45,414	121,573
West Point	143,838	285,937
Newport News	15,472	33,685
Brunswick	74,340	102,013
Port Royal	77,906	159,150
El Paso, Texas	300	9,156
Laredo, Texas	24,293	32,833
Eagle Pass, Texas	9,492	14,985
Texas City, Texas	54,019	..
Velasco	..	592
Other minor points	42,883	29,765
Total	5,420,246	8,006,177

GALVESTON.

TABLE showing Exports of Cotton from United States Ports for 1895–96.

From—	Great Britain.	France.	Continent and Channel.	Total.	Total, 1894–95.
	Bales.	Bales.	Bales.	Bales.	Bales.
New Orleans	715,699	306,951	596,418	1,619,068	2,053,831
Galveston	445,976	95,480	164,634	706,090	1,348,561
Mobile and Pensacola	89,563	...	29,947	119,510	122,995
Savannah	35,386	26,399	304,331	366,116	545,627
Charleston	27,174	...	173,543	200,717	339,853
Wilmington	40,053	1,770	90,708	132,531	202,270
Norfolk	36,715	...	17,107	53,822	188,324
Baltimore	58,321	2,017	87,069	147,407	274,506
New York	380,593	28,654	289,069	698,316	809,419
Boston	275,716	...	...	275,716	290,137
Philadelphia	7,419	...	1,550	8,969	64,129
West Point	8,930	...	...	8,930	107,308
Newport News	14,629	...	...	14,629	33,363
Brunswick	50,381	...	23,959	74,340	103,808
Port Royal	73,007	...	4,899	77,906	159,150
El Paso, &c.	...	...	400	400	11,176
Laredo	...	...	24,293	24,293	32,833
Eagle Pass	...	...	9,492	9,492	14,985
Texas City	39,620	4,599	8,800	53,019	...
Velasco	...	...	...	...	592
San Francisco, &c.	...	...	34,897	34,897	16,094
Total	2,299,182	465,870	1,861,116	4,626,168	...
Last year	3,443,574	774,476	2,500,911	6,718,961	6,718,961

Cotton Business, 1896–97.

Estimated total crop. Early in the present season the cotton crop for 1896–97 was estimated at 15 per cent. increase over that of 1895–96, which would give, in round figures, a total of 8,230,000 bales.

Of late, however, cotton has been coming into sight so much more freely than was anticipated that present conservative estimates now place the crop at 8,400,000 to 8,500,000 bales.

Estimated Texas crop. The average production of the State of Texas is now generally a little below one-third of the total crop.

This would give 2,800,000 bales as the amount of the Texas crop, but it is doubtful whether it will reach 2,500,000 bales during the peresnt season.

Increased receipts at Galveston. In spite of this Galveston has largely gained in receipts and in export business during the present season, as compared with other United States ports.

The difference between the amount of cotton handled here and at New Orleans is very much less marked than is usually the case.

Very much more Texas cotton is now being exported, by way of Galveston, than has hitherto been the case.

It is usual for this port to receive and handle about 50 per cent. of the Texas crop, the greater part of the remainder going to New Orleans.

This season, up to now, Galveston has handled 65 per cent. of the cotton brought into Texas, and it is confidently expected that henceforth this port will receive at least 75 per cent. of the Texas crop.

As it was, during the first two months of the season, viz.,

(2365)

UNITED STATES.

Prospects at Galveston.

September and October, the shipments at Galveston were the largest in the United States.

It is quite within the bounds of possibility that before many years have passed Texas will produce 4,000,000 bales of cotton, of which 3,000,000 bales will pass through Galveston.

The following table gives the receipts at Galveston during the last seven seasons up to February 22:—

Year.	Receipts to Date.	Receipts, Season.	Texas Crop.
	Bales.	Bales.	Bales.
1890-91	881,286	1,023,599	2,111,092
1891-92	1,024,465	1,154,208	2,406,108
1892-93	947,253	1,047,910	2,025,060
1893-94	930,233	1,021,724	1,824,922
1894-95	1,500,672	1,659,999	3,275,938
1895-96	806,250	1,001,075	1,989,582
1896-97	1,223,817	..	..

The receipts at Galveston thus far this season and those during last season are compared in the following table, as well as those for the same periods at new Orleans, Savannah, and Charleston, showing the percentage of increase at each port up to the present this season.

Galveston's gain will be noticed:—

	Galveston.	New Orleans.	Savannah.	Charleston.
	Bales.	Bales.	Bales.	Bales.
Receipts to February 22, 1896	806,250	1,484,927	631,180	251,735
Receipts to February 22, 1897	1,223,817	1,801,850	734,543	369,529
Percentage of increase	51·8	25·3	16·3	46·7

Receipts and exports at Galveston.

The following table gives the receipts, exports (foreign and coastwise) and stocks, from the beginning of the cotton season on September 1 up to and including February 22 of each year for the last seven years.

The marked increase of foreign exports is particularly noticeable, these being greater than in any year within the period covered by the table, with the exception of 1894-95, when the crop was about 1,500,000 bales larger than the present estimated crop:—

GALVESTON.

Year.	Receipts, Net.	Exports. Foreign.	Exports. Coastwise.	Stock, February 22.
	Bales.	Bales.	Bales.	Bales.
1890-91	881,286	552,198	285,990	61,427
1891-92	1,024,465	710,042	244,881	85,594
1892-93	947,253	681,230	201,227	87,783
1893-94	930,233	710,061	148,544	85,958
1894-95	1,500,972	1,165,168	196,653	145,067
1895-96	804,901	546,845	172,515	95,994
1896-97	1,223,817	1,050,528	156,529	112,803

The following tables show the standing of Galveston this season, as compared with other cotton exporting ports of the United States, up to February 22, and further the exports of cotton in detail up to the same date.

Ports.	This Season.	Last Season.
	Bales.	Bales.
Galveston	1,223,817	806,250
New Orleans	1,801,850	1,484,927
Mobile	264,067	185,549
Savannah	734,543	631,180
Charleston	369,529	251,735
Wilmington	234,317	155,534
Norfolk	626,765	266,506
Baltimore	51,059	35,293
New York	98,139	82,452
Boston	135,989	95,054
Philadelphia	29,583	28,913
West Point	50	136,933
Brunswick	87,260	66,774
Newport News	9,845	9,917
Port Royal	60,202	51,764
Texas City	45,796	49,205
Other ports	44,171	9,414
Total	5,816,982	4,347,400
Last year	4,347,400	..
Difference	1,469,582	..

TABLE of Receipts and Exports at Galveston, 1896-97, up to February 22, 1897.

RECEIPTS.

Receipts.	This Season.	Last Season.
	Bales.	Bales.
Net	1,223,817	806,250
Other ports in district	42,107	1,510
Gross total	1,265,924	807,760

(2365)

UNITED STATES.

Exports—Foreign.

Destination.	This Season.	Last Season.
	Bales.	Bales.
Great Britain	668,538	330,493
France	157,148	90,916
Continent	223,981	134,258
Channel	861	2,610
Total	1,050,528	558,277

Exports—Coastwise.

Destination.	This Season.	Last Season.
	Bales.	Bales.
New York	147,957	153,685
Morgan City	485	2,215
Other domestic ports	8,050	15,812
North, by rail	37	803
Total	156,529	172,515

Cotton Prices.

Cotton prices, 1896. The following table shows the range of prices of spot middling cotton in Galveston for each month in 1896:—

Month.	First Day.	High.	Low.	Last Day.
January	8	$8\frac{1}{16}$	$7\frac{13}{16}$	8
February	8	8	$7\frac{9}{16}$	$7\frac{9}{16}$
March	$7\frac{9}{16}$	$7\frac{13}{16}$	$7\frac{3}{8}$	$7\frac{5}{4}$
April	$7\frac{3}{4}$	$7\frac{3}{4}$	$7\frac{11}{16}$	$7\frac{3}{4}$
May	$7\frac{3}{4}$	$7\frac{7}{8}$	$7\frac{1}{2}$	$7\frac{5}{16}$
June	$7\frac{3}{8}$	$7\frac{3}{8}$	$6\frac{9}{16}$	$6\frac{9}{16}$
July	$6\frac{9}{16}$	$6\frac{9}{16}$	$6\frac{3}{8}$	$6\frac{1}{2}$
August	$6\frac{9}{16}$	8	$6\frac{9}{16}$	$7\frac{1}{4}$
September	$7\frac{1}{2}$	$8\frac{1}{4}$	$7\frac{1}{2}$	$7\frac{3}{8}$
October	$7\frac{3}{4}$	$7\frac{11}{16}$	$7\frac{1}{4}$	$7\frac{3}{8}$
November	$7\frac{3}{8}$	$7\frac{9}{16}$	$7\frac{1}{4}$	$7\frac{5}{16}$
December	$7\frac{5}{16}$	$7\frac{7}{16}$	$6\frac{11}{16}$	$6\frac{3}{4}$

Public Works.

Improvements. Nothing notable in the way of public improvements has taken place in Galveston during 1896; though the general standard of business facilities, wharves, docks, and sheds has been maintained.

One or two of the large wharves and sheds were destroyed by fire last summer, but these have either already been replaced or are in course of re-construction.

A new railway station is now about to be built and the old one, together with some adjacent sheds and wooden buildings, will be torn down; thus making room for additional railroad facilities to the wharves.

The recent impetus given to the export trade of Galveston by the deflection of business to this port, owing to deep water, was so sudden and so unexpected that in the minds of many the accommodation for shipping has not been adequate even this season and certainly will not be so, should the anticipated increase of business next season take place. A scheme has accordingly been mooted by several influential persons here to utilise Pelican Island, which lies in the channel opposite the town of Galveston, for additional wharfage accommodation for ships. This scheme, however, has not yet been fully matured, but there is no doubt that if Galveston's trade continues to increase at the present rate further docks for ships will very soon be necessary. *Plan to utilise Pelican Island.*

Harbour Improvements.

During 1896 the gain in depth of water in the channel where the bar once was has been steadily maintained.

During the year some 4 feet have been added to the depth of this channel. *Four feet added to depth of channel.*

At the beginning of 1896 the depth of the channel at mean low tide was 21 feet. At present it is about 25 feet at mean low tide or 26½ feet at high water.

This increased depth has been partly accomplished by the system of jetties, combined with the natural action of the water, and partly by dredging.

During the year the Government dredge boat, "General Comstock," removed 715,305 cubic yards of sand, &c.

As regards the jetties, by which the channel is confined, it may be stated that they are very nearly complete, and that by March or April it is expected that work on them will cease for the present. *Jetties practically completed.*

During the year the north jetty was completed from the 21,200 feet mark to the 24,400 feet mark, a gain of 3,200 feet; whilst the south jetty was completed from the 32,000 feet mark to the 34,100 feet mark, or a gain of 2,100 feet.

SABINE PASS.

Mr. Vice-Consul Roland reports as follows:—

The inhabitants of Sabine Pass are in the best of circumstances, and have not felt the depressing financial panic of last year. Prosperity is a general rule. *Prosperity of Sabine Pass.*

The health of Sabine Pass is splendid, and there have been no epidemics during the past year.

The farming of the adjacent country is limited mostly to vegetable farming. Cattle-raising is the chief occupation of the neighbourhood, although rice is grown quite extensively.

Exports of lumber.

The exportation of lumber, which is the chief business at Sabine Pass, is as yet only in its infancy. There was, however, a marked increase in this respect over 1895.

The large mill companies are beginning to realise the vast opportunity for trade here, and they all stand ready to promote any measures that will aid its development.

Sabine Pass as a port.

Shipowners at home and abroad can now look upon this port as a safe one for business, and with sufficient water to allow the entry of vessels of heavy draught with safety and without detention.

At present the whole of the trade of Sabine Pass is in exports, there being no imports except by rail.

As regards exports, the lumber and timber trade, which is the chief one, is increasing monthly with a steady market, and a heavy tonnage will be required to move the visible supply of long-leaf yellow pine.

British shipping.

British shipping is not so prominent at Sabine Pass as it should be, but it still shows an increase for 1896 over 1895.

Two of the largest cargoes, however, were taken away by British steamers.

The fact that water of sufficient depth to accommodate heavy draught vessels was not officially announced until the year was nearly half gone, resulted in shipowners not availing themselves of Sabine Pass to the full extent.

Channel over bar.

The available water over the bar is now over 20 feet, and the bar itself is composed of soft mud, and contains no dangerous obstruction.

Foreign and coastwise shipping.

The following tables give details as to foreign and coastwise shipping during 1896:—

FOREIGN.

Nationality.	Steam. Number of Vessels.	Steam. Tons.	Sailing. Number of Vessels.	Sailing. Tons.	Total. Number of Vessels.	Total. Tons.
British	2	6,111	9	3,618	11	9,729
Norwegian	6	2,219	7	4,879	13	7,098
American	1	431	38	12,774	39	13,205
Total	9	8,761	54	21,271	63	30,032

COASTWISE.

Rig.	Number of Vessels.	Tons.
Steamships	1	1,069
Barques	2	987
Schooners	8	5,582
Total	11	7,638

GALVESTON.

Lumber, including sawn timber, railroad ties, sashes, doors and blinds, to the value of 262,911 dol., was shipped to the following ports, and of which three-fourths were furnished by mills at Beaumont, or north of that place:— *Exports of lumber, &c., to foreign ports.*

Destination.	Quantity.
	Feet.
Tampico, Mexico	8,769,219
Vera Cruz ,,	4,602,703
Tuxpan ,,	378,555
Lazuna ,,	221,856
Frontera ,,	113,141
Tecolutha ,,	103,236
Montevideo, Uruguay	564,149
Buenos Ayres, Argentine Republic	969,554
Rosario, Argentine Republic	445,533
Kingston, Jamaica	1,470,811
Bahia, Brazil	429,107
Castries, West Indies	151,219
Mayaques, P.R.	329,278
Havannah, Cuba	257,862
Port Natal	500,637
London, U.K.	2,977,810
Greenock, U.K.	900,886
Total	23,185,561

The total amount of coastwise exports in lumber and railroad ties, valued at 83,680 dol., was as follows:— *Exports of lumber to coastwise ports.*

Destination.	Quantity.
	Feet.
New York	5,331,296
Boston	683,000
New Haven	332,398
Texan ports	2,021,378
Total	8,368,072

UNITED STATES.

Exports from Galveston for the Year 1896.

Destination.	Cotton. Quantity. Bales.	Cotton. Value. £	Cotton-seed Oilcake and Meal. Quantity. Tons.	Cotton-seed Oilcake and Meal. Value. £	Wheat. Quantity. Bushels.	Wheat. Value. £	Maize. Quantity. Bushels.	Maize. Value. £	Wheat Flour. Quantity. Barrels.	Wheat Flour. Value. £	Lumber. Quantity. Feet.	Lumber. Value. £
Great Britain and colonies	765,217	6,118,165	21,428	89,451	1,714,936	210,924	1,963,246	128,922	4,060	2,206	821,000	2,106
Germany	216,239	1,705,764	95,051	422,625	953,082	113,577	2,086,689	131,511	141	90	687,000	6,016
France	168,734	1,327,947	1,712	6,325	20,000	2,240	142,556	9,144	...	...	85,000	250
Netherlands	8,027	62,966	12,277	51,385	702,476	82,361	442,070	28,631	2,195	952	1,136,000	4,960
Denmark	3,325	27,075	5,980	23,030	...	...	1,506,073	97,889	895	482	...	...
Belgium	6,788	54,360	200	760	50,000	5,600	29,000	2,204	...	...	...	...
Russia	9,786	81,305	...	...	...	...	...	...	...	...	...	...
Italy	3,785	35,880	...	...	...	...	...	...	...	...	...	...
Spain and colonies	700	5,600	...	...	...	...	441	42	27,379	21,335	...	...
West Indies (including Cuba and Porto Rico)	...	...	...	...	...	...	7,000	558	21,425	17,433	...	...
Mexico	...	...	...	...	...	...	45,207	3,714	100	80	...	...
Total for 1896	1,182,601	9,419,062	136,648	593,576	3,440,494	414,702	6,222,282	402,615	56,195	42,578	2,729,000	13,332
,, 1895	931,167	6,534,253	97,752	391,556	...	...	1,233,477	78,152	53,244	37,536	1,048,000	9,857

GALVESTON.

Exports from Galveston for the Year 1896—continued.

Destination.	Cotton-seed Oil. Quantity. Gallons.	Cotton-seed Oil. Value. £	Logs. Value. £	Lard. Value. £	Spelter. Value. £	Lead. Value. £	Copper Matte. Value. £	Borax. Value. £	Sundries. Value. £	Total, 1896. £	Total, 1895. £
Great Britain and colonies	285,300	13,894	880	...	87,567	8,676	14,876	23,153	137,648	6,838,468	4,096,675
Germany	304,946	18,710	8,706	2,391	808	2,540	...	...	9,224	2,421,962	1,715,322
France	12,500	675	333	...	288	1,980	...	...	4,068	1,353,250	994,952
Netherlands	909,425	48,830	...	...	...	...	...	...	1,108	281,193	61,837
Denmark	10,100	580	...	...	...	...	...	...	95	149,151	7,140
Belgium	...	...	...	2,798	...	...	...	...	246	65,968	99,627
Russia	...	...	...	...	...	...	...	...	...	81,305	23,126
Italy	...	...	...	...	...	...	...	...	409	36,289	61,070
Spain and colonies	...	...	...	...	...	...	...	...	303	27,280	33,857
West Indies (including Cuba and Porto Rico)	...	...	...	244	...	...	...	...	109	18,344	212
Mexico	310,559	11,655	201	...	...	...	...	...	6	15,656	12,607
Total for 1896	1,832,830	94,344	10,120	5,433	88,663	13,196	14,876	23,153	153,216	11,288,866	...
,, 1895	452,268	37,443	15,010	...	...	...	...	...	2,618	...	7,106,425

(2365)

UNITED STATES.

IMPORTS at Galveston during the Year 1896, Free of Duty.

Commodities.	Quantity.	Value. Great Britain.	Germany.	France.	Mexico.	British East Indies.	Belgium.	All other Countries.	Total, 1896.	Total, 1895.
		£	£	£	£	£	£	£	£	£
American manufactures (re-Imported)	...	...	2,209	...	...	...	...	...	2,209	1,480
Art, works of	...	...	104	...	...	...	...	...	104	...
Books and printed matter	...	...	20	116	...	...	...	...	136	55
Coffee	Lbs.	117,461	...	...	2,274	...	...	1,940	4,214	1,383
Cotton ties (iron and steel)	,,	11,341,309	32,155	...	...	...	...	...	32,155	3,906
Fertilizers	...	...	...	214	...	...	...	...	214	...
Fruits and nuts	...	...	...	...	...	...	...	...	...	391
Household and personal effects	...	...	132	398	...	...	...	...	530	598
Mineral waters (natural)	...	...	...	74	...	...	...	...	74	137
Paper stock (old bagging)	...	...	4,140	...	...	...	...	...	4,140	1,247
Salt	Lbs.	24,277,572	6,909	...	...	...	...	...	6,909	9,930
Scientific apparatus	...	...	...	237	...	...	...	31	268	322
Timber and logs	Tons	867	...	...	2,801	...	...	...	2,801	...
Vegetable fibres (sisal grass)	,,	5,632	...	...	10,010	...	...	...	10,010	...
„ „ jute and jute butts	...	...	...	...	...	16,417	...	...	16,417	5,750
Miscellaneous articles	...	...	1,791	1	7	2	5	452	2,259	1,337
Total value of free imports for 1896	...	...	45,127	3,257	123	15,087	16,418	5	2,423	82,440	...
„ „ „ 1895	...	...	16,977	1,374	8	130	5,750	...	2,401	...	26,536

GALVESTON.

Imports at Galveston during the Year 1896, Paying Duty.

Commodities.	Quantity.	Great Britain.	Germany.	France.	Mexico.	British East Indies.	Belgium.	All other Countries.	Total, 1896.	Total, 1895.
		£	£	£	£	£	£	£	£	£
Asphalte	...	...	...	...	...	...	...	...	...	1,946
Books and printed matter	...	70	...	...	...	...	1	...	71	101
Breadstuffs and preparations of food	...	18	...	8	...	...	...	...	26	81
Cement, Portland (in barrels)	Lbs.	...	5,715	...	...	...	7,858	...	13,573	10,821
Coal bituminous	Tons	765	...	...	...	...	...	...	765	944
Chemicals (sheep dip)	...	1,825	...	...	...	...	...	...	1,825	3,650
,, (other compounds)	...	163	...	...	...	...	...	...	163	333
,, dead oil creosote	...	...	...	...	...	...	...	...	...	924
Cotton, manufactures of	...	315	134	11	...	256	...	21	737	161
Earthenware (plain and decorated, crockery)	...	4,218	...	...	...	...	...	...	4,218	2,714
,, all other, and bricks and tiles	...	325	141	...	...	...	...	...	466	298
Flax and hemp, manufactures of	...	1,233	...	...	...	...	...	...	1,233	2,722
,, other manufactures of	...	507	10	...	...	...	...	...	517	7
Fruit and nuts, green and ripe	...	5	...	102	...	...	...	18	23	121
Fruits, preserved and prepared	...	218	...	...	...	...	...	...	3:0	135
,, (in spirits)	...	76	...	2,048	...	...	...	...	2,124	1,960
Fish (sardines in oil)	...	...	...	280	...	...	...	...	280	321
,, all other	...	30	92	245	...	...	...	10	285	417
Glass, all kinds of	...	30	1	132	...	...	691	...	945	184
Iron and steel, manufactures of, and machinery	...	2,185	33	...	...	...	571	2	2,757	210
Metals, manufactures of	...	29	9	...	...	...	...	...	64	549
Malt liquors (ale and porter in bottles)	Gallons	1,520	...	137	...	...	...	284	1,529	1,985
Oils (vegetable, olive)	,,	153	15	14	...	...	...	44	574	122
Provisions (dairy products and prepared meats)	...	6	...	...	...	1	...	...	79	11
Rice (free of outer hull)	Lbs.	...	1,311	...	...	4	...	...	1,311	1,954
Sugar (beet)	,,	...	39,108	...	...	...	...	...	39,108	2,458
Spirits (distilled)	Gallons	103	8	35	...	19	...	20	166	106
Tin and turn plates	...	...	3	...	...	...	...	...	...	3,903
Vegetables, preserved and prepared	...	522	224	220	...	...	...	6	751	827
Wines, still and sparkling	...	42	74	309	...	...	...	197	772	390
Wood, manufactures of	...	3	20	...	...	...	...	7	85	43
Wool, ,,	...	179	...	...	30	...	...	59	262	29
Miscellaneous (all other dutiable articles)	...	788	214	104	...	...	172	183	1,512	355
Subject to duty for 1896	...	15,328	47,112	3,645	30	280	9,293	853	76,541	40,782
Free of duty for 1896	...	45,127	3,257	123	15,087	16,418	5	2,423	82,440	26,640
Total imports for 1896	...	60,455	50,369	3,768	15,117	16,698	9,298	3,276	158,981	...
,, ,, 1895	...	37,266	10,154	2,174	255	5,916	6,975	4,682	...	67,422

UNITED STATES.

Table of Shipping engaged in the Foreign Trade at Galveston during the Year 1896.

Entered.

Nationality.	In Ballast. Number of Vessels.	In Ballast. Tons.	With Cargo. Number of Vessels.	With Cargo. Tons.	Total. Number of Vessels.	Total. Tons.
American	...	...	5	529	5	529
Belgian	1	2,191	...	...	1	2,191
British	196	335,427	34	60,187	230	395,614
Dutch	1	887	...	...	1	887
German	1	1,938	9	18,649	10	20,587
Mexican	...	...	...	...	...	...
Norwegian	17	22,360	7	4,213	24	26,573
Spanish	25	37,244	1	2,122	26	39,366
Total	241	400,047	56	85,700	297	485,747

Cleared.

Nationality.	In Ballast. Number of Vessels.	In Ballast. Tons.	With Cargo. Number of Vessels.	With Cargo. Tons.	Total. Number of Vessels.	Total. Tons.
American	2	680	3	1,021	5	1,701
Belgian	...	...	1	2,191	1	2,191
British	5	8,925	224	383,009	229	391,934
Dutch	...	...	...	...	...	...
German	...	...	10	20,557	10	20,557
Mexican	...	...	1	177	1	177
Norwegian	...	...	23	26,550	23	26,550
Spanish	...	...	27	41,101	27	41,101
Total	7	9,605	289	474,606	296	484,211

GALVESTON.

RETURN of British Shipping at the Port of Galveston in the Year 1896.

Direct Trade in British Vessels from and to Great Britain and British Colonies.

Entered.

Total Number of Vessels.			Total Tonnage.			Total Number of Crews.	Total Value of Cargoes.
With Cargoes.	In Ballast.	Total.	With Cargoes.	In Ballast.	Total.		£
15	95	110	26,762	164,258	191,020	2,901	...

Cleared.

Total Number of Vessels.			Total Tonnage.			Total Number of Crews.	Total Value of Cargoes.
With Cargoes.	In Ballast.	Total.	With Cargoes.	In Ballast.	Total.		£
103	...	103	183,723	...	183,723	2,899	5,170,762

Indirect or Carrying Trade in British Vessels from and to other Countries.

Entered.

Countries whence Arrived.	Number of Vessels.			Tonnage.			Number of Crews.	Value of Cargoes.
	With Cargoes.	In Ballast.	Total.	With Cargoes.	In Ballast.	Total.		£
America, U.S.	5	9	14	6,500	17,221	23,721	356	...
Spain and colonies	2	15	17	4,028	23,772	27,800	421	...
Mexico	3	11	14	5,961	16,342	22,303	380	...
Belgium	3	1	4	5,421	1,977	7,398	97	...
Colombia, U.S.	5	4	9	9,623	6,517	16,140	312	...
Portugal and colonies	...	25	25	...	40,231	40,231	607	...
Uruguay	...	4	4	...	7,912	7,912	110	...
Brazil	...	26	26	...	48,898	48,898	756	...
Other countries	1	6	7	1,885	8,299	10,184	194	...
Total	19	101	120	33,418	171,169	204,587	3,235	...

Cleared.

Countries to which Departed.	Number of Vessels.			Tonnage.			Number of Crews.	Value of Cargoes.
	With Cargoes.	In Ballast.	Total.	With Cargoes.	In Ballast.	Total.		£
America, U.S.	...	5	5	...	8,925	8,925	189	...
Germany	70	...	70	120,274	...	120,274	1,784	2,128,184
France	25	...	25	41,080	...	41,080	651	1,380,035
Holland	11	...	11	16,840	...	16,840	264	184,165
Denmark	8	...	8	12,394	...	12,394	184	85,112
Belgium	2	...	2	2,601	...	2,601	44	65,968
Russia	1	...	1	1,569	...	1,569	23	53,332
Italy	1	...	1	1,224	...	1,224	20	41,891
Mexico	3	...	3	3,304	...	3,304	63	12,433
Total	121	5	126	199,286	8,925	208,211	3,172	3,951,120

(2365)

LONDON :
Printed for Her Majesty's Stationery Office,
By HARRISON AND SONS,
Printers in Ordinary to Her Majesty.
(75   5 | 97—H & S   2365)

FOREIGN OFFICE.
1897.
ANNUAL SERIES.

N⁰. 1910.
DIPLOMATIC AND CONSULAR REPORTS ON TRADE AND FINANCE.

UNITED STATES.

REPORT FOR THE YEARS 1895 AND 1896
ON THE
TRADE, &c., OF PHILADELPHIA.

REFERENCE TO PREVIOUS REPORT, Annual Series No. 1397.

Presented to both Houses of Parliament by Command of Her Majesty,
MAY, 1897.

LONDON:
PRINTED FOR HER MAJESTY'S STATIONERY OFFICE,
BY HARRISON AND SONS, ST. MARTIN'S LANE,
PRINTERS IN ORDINARY TO HER MAJESTY.

And to be purchased, either directly or through any Bookseller, from
EYRE & SPOTTISWOODE, EAST HARDING STREET, FLEET STREET, E.C., and
32, ABINGDON STREET, WESTMINSTER, S.W.; or
JOHN MENZIES & Co., 12, HANOVER STREET, EDINBURGH, and
90, WEST NILE STREET, GLASGOW; or
HODGES, FIGGIS, & Co., Limited, 104, GRAFTON STREET, DUBLIN.

1897.

[C. 8277—128.]   *Price Three Halfpence*

New Series of Reports.

Reports of the Annual Series have been issued from Her Majesty's Diplomatic and Consular Officers at the following places, and may be obtained from the sources indicated on the title-page:—

No.		Price.	No.		Price.
1790.	Beyrout	1d.	1850.	Serajevo	1d.
1791.	Tunis	1½d.	1851.	Madrid	2d.
1792.	Kiukiang	3d.	1852.	La Rochelle	1½d.
1793.	Bangkok	1d.	1853.	Chicago	4d.
1794.	Rio Grande do Sul	1d.	1854.	Berlin	1d.
1795.	Valparaiso	4d.	1855.	Cherbourg	2½d.
1796.	Brindisi	2½d.	1856.	Beira	1d.
1797.	Bushire	2d.	1857.	Charleston	2½d.
1798.	Christiania	5½d.	1858.	Saigon	½d.
1799.	Cadiz	2d.	1859.	Suakin	1d.
1800.	Meshed	2½d.	1860.	Rouen	2d.
1801.	St. Petersburg	4½d.	1861.	Patras	1½d.
1802.	Batoum	1d.	1862.	Barcelona	2d.
1803.	Peking	3d.	1863.	Amoy	2½d.
1804.	Samos	½d.	1864.	Trebizond	1d.
1805.	Dantzig	2d.	1865.	Lisbon	2½d.
1806.	Antwerp	1½d.	1866.	Callao	2d.
1807.	Ajaccio	1½d.	1867.	Pernambuco	5d.
1808.	Stettin	3d.	1868.	Naples	1½d.
1809.	Aleppo	1d.	1869.	New Orleans	2½d.
1810.	Tangier	2½d.	1870.	Vera Cruz	2½d.
1811.	Tokio	3½d.	1871.	Madeira	1d.
1812.	Madeira	½d.	1872.	Jerusalem	1d.
1813.	Vera Cruz	1d.	1873.	Ningpo	1d.
1814.	Oporto	1d.	1874.	Rio de Janeiro	2½d.
1815.	Hamburg	1½d.	1875.	Trieste	1d.
1816.	New Orleans	1½d.	1876.	Curaçoa	1d.
1817.	Bengazi	½d.	1877.	Goa	1d.
1818.	Marmagao	½d.	1878.	Cagliari	1d.
1819.	Gothenburg	2d.	1879.	Guayaquil	1d.
1820.	Dar-al-Baida	3d.	1880.	Havana	1½d.
1821.	Erzeroum	½d.	1881.	Reykjavik (Iceland)	1d.
1822.	Munich	2½d.	1882.	Milan	1½d.
1823.	Samoa	½d.	1883.	Baltimore	1d.
1824.	Chinkiang	1d.	1884.	Cettinjé	½d.
1825.	Jeddah	1d.	1885.	Bilbao	2½d.
1826.	Sofia	1½d.	1886.	Florence	1½d.
1827.	Mexico	2d.	1887.	Brest	1½d.
1828.	Teneriffe	3½d.	1888.	Marseilles	1½d.
1829.	Batoum	1d.	1889.	Wuhu	1d.
1830.	Cadiz	1d.	1890.	Chinkiang	1d.
1831.	Martinique	1d.	1891.	Malaga	1d.
1832.	Odessa	1d.	1892.	Antwerp	½d.
1833.	Ghilan	1d.	1893.	Amsterdam	1d.
1834.	Old Calabar	6½d.	1894.	Galveston	2d.
1835.	Tamsui	1d.	1895.	Piræus	2½d.
1836.	Copenhagen	½d.	1896.	Stettin	2½d.
1837.	Salonica	1½d.	1897.	Martinique	1½d.
1838.	Honolulu	½d.	1898.	Corunna	2½d.
1839.	Buenos Ayres	2d.	1899.	Calais	1d.
1840.	Para	1d.	1900.	Honolulu	1d.
1841.	Bolivia	2d.	1901.	Riga	2d.
1842.	Washington	3d.	1902.	Tripoli	2d.
1843.	Berlin	2d.	1903.	Batoum	2d.
1844.	Uganda	1d.	1904.	Lorenzo Marques	2d.
1845.	Belgrade	1½d.	1905.	Batavia	2½d.
1846.	Dakar	½d.	1906.	Corfu	1½d.
1847.	Florence	1½d.	1907.	Foochow	1½d.
1848.	Copenhagen	2d.	1908.	Montevideo	5½d.
1849.	Havre	2d.	1909.	China	5½d.

No. 1910.

Reference to previous Report, Annual Series No. 1397.

UNITED STATES.

PHILADELPHIA.

Consul Clipperton to the Marquess of Salisbury.

(Received at Foreign Office, May 11, 1897.)

My Lord,

I ENCLOSE herewith a Report on the Trade, Commerce, and Manufactures of this Consular District during the years 1895 and 1896.

I have, &c.
(Signed)   ROBT. CHAS. CLIPPERTON.

Report on the Trade, Commerce, and Manufactures of the Consular District of Philadelphia for the Years 1895 and 1896.

TABLE of Contents.

	PAGE
Introduction and general business outlook	2
Financial, monetary conference	2
Textiles	3
Iron and steel	5
Shipbuilding	7
Navigation	7
Winter load-line	8
Immigration	8
Imports and exports	9
Petroleum	11
Sugar	12
Grain	14
Tin-plate	15
Institutions—	
The Philadelphia Museum	16
,, Textile School	17
,, Savings Fund Society	18
Coal	19
Table of shipping	21

(2386)

UNITED STATES.

Introduction.

General depression in all business transactions has been experienced during the past two years in the States composing this Consular district, namely, Pennsylvania, Ohio, Indiana, and Michigan, which are four of the most important States of the Union for industrial and agricultural products, as also mineral deposits, and railway enterprises. But business conditions are now considered as becoming gradually more favourable, although actual trade is still by no means satisfactory. As proof of such being the case, it is cited that the failure list is decreasing, payments through banks are increasing, and the industrial output is enlarging.

Exports of merchandise continue large, while the imports do not increase, in the face of the prospect of increase of duties anticipated by many. There are still numerous failures, and many plants are either idle or running half-time.

Last January is reported as being the first month for years that has not witnessed net exports of gold from this country. The Treasury gold supply in that month increased 7,000,000 dol., in exchange for which, and to meet the accumulating revenue deficit, it paid out over 23,000,000 dol. in legal tender notes, which have gone into the general circulation of the country.

The generally improved conditions in business transactions are reported to have strengthened the stock market, and a more cheerful feeling pervades the Stock Exchange, usually referred to as "the Street," while evidence of preparations for spring trade are seen in various channels, so that the belief is growing strong that the lowest depression point has passed.

Financial.

Monetary conference at Indianapolis.

In the early part of this year a Monetary Convention was held at Indianapolis, when it was decided to create a Monetary Commission. Great care had been taken in the selection of delegates to this convention so as to secure leading business men, merchants, manufacturers, and bankers, and also to get representatives from all sections of the country. About 275 delegates attended who were chosen by the Boards of Trade, Chambers of Commerce, and other business and commercial organisations in their respective localities, representing over 100 cities and towns in about 30 States.

Everybody's plans and suggestions were given a hearing, and referred to a committee, and the report made therefrom laid down the method of practical action which was determined upon and adopted with marked unanimity.

This report set out the basis of the "consistent, straightforward, and deliberately planned monetary system which has become absolutely necessary." Neither in the report nor in the proceedings of the convention is there any reference to "free

received for bonds to the amount of nearly 527,000,000 dol., and the average price obtained was over 111.

The Treasury reserve, which had fallen below 45,000,000 dol. on February 10, was raised to over 123,000,000 dol. before the end of February, and to over 128,000,000 dol. in March.

In consequence of the special demand for gold to pay for these bonds that metal commanded a premium during the months of January and February, and during the former month the position was quite anomalous as gold was being exported in consequence of the rate of exchange, and imported at the same time in view of this demand.

In July the National Democratic Convention pronounced for free silver, this created an alarm and increased the drain on the Treasury gold reserve, the exports of gold having meanwhile continued since April. The banks and financial institutions, however, came to the assistance of the Treasury, and the foreign exchange houses made arrangements to stop the outflow of gold.

In the month of August the movement was reversed, and imports of gold commenced in consequence of the great excess of exports over imports of merchandise. From this time till the end of the year the gold reserve of the Treasury was never again in danger.

Depressing effect of silver agitation. — The action of the National Democratic Convention, alluded to above, had an extremely depressing effect on business; money, both gold and currency, was hoarded; gold again went to a premium, and borrowers found it very difficult to obtain loans on any terms.

The production of iron declined, and the railroad receipts showed a marked falling-off.

Agricultural produce. — The crops were decidedly good, more especially that of Indian corn which is returned, for the whole of the United States, at about 2,284,000,000 bushels, as compared with 2,151,000,000 bushels in 1895 which was considered an extremely large crop; oats, 707,000,000 bushels, although 117,000,000 bushels below that of 1895 is still a very large return; the wheat crop, 427,000,000 bushels, is 40,000,000 bushels below that of 1895, and rather below an average. In consequence of the two very heavy crops in succession, the price of Indian corn was again lower, and stood at 31 c. (1s. 3½d.) per bushel in the New York market at the end of the year. On the other hand the price of wheat again advanced in view of the short crops in other producing countries, and stood at about 97 c. (4s. 0½d.) at the same period.

The cotton crop was larger than that of the former year, and the price was on an average of the whole year higher than in 1895, but closed lower at a little under 7 c. (3½d.) per lb.

The average prices received by farmers and planters all over the whole country are, of course, lower than those given above. The following table shows these prices as reported by the Agricultural Bureau:—

(2396)

UNITED STATES.

Average Prices received by Farmers and Planters.

Articles.		1896.	1895.	1894.	1893.	1892.	1891.
		Cents.	Cents.	Cents.	Cents.	Cents.	Cents.
Wheat	Per bushel	72·6	50·9	49·1	53·8	62·4	83·9
Rye	,,	40·9	44·0	50·1	51·3	54·8	77·4
Oats	,,	18·7	19·6	32·4	29·4	31·7	31·5
Barley	,,	32·3	33·7	44·2	40·6	47·2	54·0
Indian corn	,,	21·5	26·4	45·7	36·5	39·4	40·6
Cotton	Per lb.	6·6	7·59	4·6	6·99	8·4	7·3

Production of pig-iron. The total production of pig-iron throughout the United States is given as 8,623,127 tons in 1896 being only 823,181 tons less than in 1895, when the output was the largest on record. On making a comparison between the two years, it is found that during the first six months the production exceeded that of 1895 by about 900,000 tons, while during the last six months it was 1,711,859 tons less than during the corresponding period of the previous year.

Railways. Whereas in 1895 the earnings of railways were rather poor during the first six months and very good during the latter half of the year, in 1896 the conditions were entirely reversed.

The receipts continued fairly satisfactory during the first six months, but compared very unfavourably with 1895 during the last six months. On the whole, however, the gross earnings in 1896 will probably show some slight increase over those of the former year. The grain movement was a very large one, and the North Western lines seem to have done better than the others, while the railroads in the middle and middle Western States were adversely affected by the industrial depression.

Imports and exports. The total exports of merchandise from the United States were the largest ever known, amounting to upwards of 1,005,000,000 dol. in value, 181,000,000 dol. more than in 1895. The imports on the other hand were restricted on account of the industrial depression, their value was about 680,000,000 dol. or 121,000,000 dol. less than in the previous year. The excess of exports of merchandise over imports thus amounted to 325,000,000 dol., of which 250,000,000 dol. accrued during the last six months. The better prices obtained for wheat and cotton, taking the average of the whole year, have contributed to swell the totals, but in each case there was a larger export, in the case of wheat, including flour, 154,500,000 bushels in 1896, against 132,000,000 bushels in 1895, and of cotton about 6,000,000 bales, as against 5,500,000 bales in 1895.

The imports of gold exceeded the exports by about 47,500,000 dol., whereas in 1895 about 70,500,000 dol. were exported on balance.

The excess of silver exports over the imports of the same metal amounted to about 33,800,000 dol., as compared with about 30,000,000 dol. in 1895.

New York money market. The money market was more than usually disturbed during the year 1896, and there were times when loans and discounts were scarcely procurable on any terms.

NEW YORK.

As regards loans on the Stock Exchange, the panic of December was to a certain extent prolonged into the early part of January, but the rate which had been as high as 35 per cent. fell rapidly, and by the end of the month the fluctuations were within much narrower limits, the quotations being from 3 to 6 per cent. During the first two weeks of the month of February the rate again touched 7 and 8 per cent., but from that time forward until the month of August the range was only between 1½ and 4 per cent.

Early in the month of August there were many adverse influences, foreign exchange ruled high, gold was being withdrawn from the Treasury on domestic account, a heavy failure at Chicago led to the temporary closing of the Stock Exchange in that city, bank reserves were low, and credits were greatly curtailed.

The rate for call money varied between 5 and 15 per cent., and although at the end of the month the conditions had improved and gold was being imported, the market continued in a more or less strained condition until after the elections on November 4.

So great was the feeling of nervousness and anxiety in connection with the silver question that in the last few days of October and on November 2 loans were made at 96, 100, and 127 per cent., but immediately the result of the elections was known the rate dropped to 4 per cent., and from that point to 1½ to 2 per cent., which was the ruling rate in December.

The rate of discount for good commercial bills having 60 to 90 days to run was about 6 per cent. during January and February and slightly lower during March, April, May, June, and July; in August and September only the very best paper was negotiable at rates varying from 8 to 10 per cent., while in October it was difficult to obtain accommodation at any price. In November the rate was again 6 per cent., and declined to 3½ to 4 per cent. at the close of the year.

The following table shows the position of the New York Clearing-house Banks at different periods of the year; the rate of conversion being 5 dol. to the 1*l*.:— *New York banks.*

Week ending—	Loans.	Deposits.	Specie.	Legal Tenders.	Reserve to Deposits.	Surplus Reserve.
	£	£	£	£	Per cent.	£
January 4 ...	93,116,140	98,322,980	13,790,940	14,747,140	29·02	3,955,920
February 1 ...	89,428,540	98,089,440	13,369,180	17,077,860	33·07	7,924,680
March 7 ...	92,897,780	97,776,880	12,307,620	16,783,500	29·75	4,646,900
April 4 ...	93,044,980	96,359,140	11,850,320	15,640,660	28·52	3,401,180
May 2 ...	94,132,700	99,000,820	11,864,800	17,474,260	29·63	4,588,840
June 6 ...	95,363,820	99,436,000	12,361,700	16,194,560	28·71	3,697,260
July 3 ...	95,239,860	99,809,380	12,373,260	16,644,740	29·07	4,065,640
August 1 ...	93,907,180	97,002,800	9,250,940	18,545,480	28·67	3,585,720
September 5 ...	90,614,020	89,414,360	9,839,380	14,159,920	26·84	1,645,700
October 3 ...	90,633,200	90,946,620	11,160,220	14,881,640	28·63	3,305,200
November 7 ..	88,435,940	87,687,520	12,740,520	12,143,840	27·10	2,962,080
December 5 ...	94,488,360	100,409,200	15,135,580	16,459,800	31·46	6,492,880
,, 26 ...	97,534,660	105,167,440	15,353,600	17,800,240	31·52	6,861,980

The surplus reserve represents the excess over 25 per cent. of the deposits, and the returns give the average of each week, not the actual figures for the day mentioned.

(2396)

UNITED STATES.

The maximum and minimum of deposits were in 1896, maximum 105,167,440*l.* and minimum 87,687,520*l.*, as compared with 115,444,660*l.* and 100,164,500*l.* in 1895. The maximum and minimum of reserve 8,036,485*l.* and 1,645,710*l.* in 1896, and 9,176,090*l.* and 2,682,690*l.* in 1895.

New York Clearing-house returns. The New York Clearing-house returns show a decrease of 3·3 per cent. as compared with those of the previous year, the figures being 28,871,000,000 dol., or about 5,774,200,000*l.*, as compared with 29,842,000,000 dol., or about 5,968,400,000*l.* in 1895. These figures are considerably below the average of the last 15 years, although in both cases better than in 1894. It must, however, be borne in mind that since 1892 the greater part of the share sales of the New York Stock Exchange have been cleared through the Stock Exchange Clearing-house, and that in 1896 the Cotton Exchange began clearing its own transactions, the effect being in each case to diminish the figures of the Bank Clearing-house.

Clearings outside of New York. The clearings outside of New York amounted to about 22,304,000,000 dol., or, roughly, 4,461,000,000*l.*, a decrease of 4·8 per cent. as compared with 1895.

This is, with the exception of 1894, the smallest total since 1889, and as the number of clearing-houses has increased considerably of late years the comparison is all the more unfavourable.

Sterling exchange. Sterling exchange on London was lower than in 1895, more especially during the latter half of the year. The following table gives the posted rates, highest and lowest, for each month in the year. These are, however, fractionally higher than the rates at which the bulk of business is done :—

NEW YORK.

TABLE showing the Posted Rates of Sterling Exchange for the Year 1896.

Month.		At 60 Days.	At Sight.
		Dols.	Dols.
January	highest	4·89	4·90½
	lowest	4·87½	4·89
February	highest	4·88½	4·90
	lowest	4·87	4·88½
March	highest	4·89	4·90
	lowest	4·87	4·88½
April	highest	4·89	4·90
	lowest	4·88	4·89
May	highest	4·89	4·90
	lowest	4·88	4·89½
June	highest	4·88½	4·89½
	lowest	4·88	4·89
July	highest	4·89	4·90
	lowest	4·87½	4·88½
August	highest	4·89	4·90
	lowest	4·82½	4·84½
September	highest	4·84	4·85½
	lowest	4·82	4·84½
October	highest	4·84	4·86½
	lowest	4·80½	4·84
November	highest	4·84½	4·88
	lowest	4·81½	4·85
December	highest	4·85	4·88½
	lowest	4·84	4·87

Under ordinary circumstances the rate for bills payable on demand, which admits of the export of gold from New York to London, is about 4 dol. 88 c. for bars, and 4 dol. 89 c. for coin, and the rate at which gold coin can be imported without loss is about 4 dol. 83½ c.

The rate of exchange adopted in this report is the London Stock Exchange rate of 5 dol. to the 1*l*. As the true value of the 1*l*. sterling at par is 4·8665 dol., the Stock Exchange valuation is about 2¾ per cent. below par, and accordingly the present London quotations of American securities are about 2¾ per cent. higher than in New York, a bond worth 100 in the United States being quoted at 102¾ in London.

On the Stock Exchange the sales were only 54,654,096 shares, as compared with 66,583,232 shares in 1895, and the volume of business was small, even where prices fluctuated widely. The total is, with the exception of the year 1894, the smallest since 1878. There was a similar falling-off in the sales of railway bonds, the aggregate value being 363,158,820 dol. (72,631,764*l*.) in 1896, and 499,758,080 dol. (99,951,616*l*.) in 1895. {Stock Exchange}

Of cotton, the future sales were 426,727,800 bales in 1896, against 51,489,700 bales in 1895. {Cotton Exchange.}

On the Produce Exchange the total of sales was smaller than in any year since 1882. There was a large decrease in flour, wheat, maize, and oats, but an increase in barley and malt, and in {Produce Exchange.}

rye. Calculating the barrel of flour as equivalent to 4½ bushels of grain, the total sales amounted to about 1,286,000,000 bushels, as against over 1,899,000,000 bushels in 1895.

A certain amount of this loss of trade is attributed to the difference in the rates of the Railway Traffic Association for the transport of grain from Chicago and Buffalo to New York on the one hand, and to Philadelphia, Baltimore, Norfolk, Newport News, and Boston on the other hand, and complaints have been made in consequence. The rates from Chicago were, to New York, 20 c. per 100 lbs.; to Philadelphia, 18 c.; and to the other places named, 17 c.; from Buffalo, 11 c. to New York, and 10 c. to Philadelphia and Baltimore.

Failures.

The following taken from tables prepared by Messrs. R. G. Dun and Co. show the number of commercial failures in this Consular district, as well as those in the whole of the United States in 1896 as compared with 1895:—

	Number of Failures.		Amount of Liabilities.	
	1896.	1895.	1896.	1895.
			£	£
New York	2,173	1,940	9,322,428	9,045,107
Connecticut	290	254	419,864	488,596
New Jersey	193	182	640,966	722,500
Rhode Island	125	202	544,204	754,280
Delaware	57	68	128,220	92,020
Whole of United States	15,088	13,197	45,219,367	34,639,212

There was a certain increase in the number of failures, and in the amount of the liabilities in the State of New York, but if all the five States be taken together there is very little difference as compared with the previous year, the figures being 2,838 failures, with liabilities amounting to 11,055,682*l.* in 1896, and 2,646 failures, with liabilities 11,102,503*l.* in 1895. As regards the whole of the United States, the increase was very marked, and both the number of the failures and the amount of liabilities was larger in the second half-year than in the first. The impression is that many of these failures have occurred not because business was unduly extended, but rather from the restriction of operations and the curtailment of credit due to long depression and the fear of silver legislation; that there has been a disinclination to employ capital, and that even cautious business houses have suffered in consequence.

The tables published by Messrs. R. G. Dun and Co. now show the insolvencies by branches of trade, and while there is an increase in the number and in the amount of liabilities in almost every branch of manufacturing and trading, the most notable in number are carpenters and coopers among manufacturers of dry goods and carpets, and transporters and brokers in respect of trades.

The total amount received by the Commissioner for the head-tax during the fiscal year was 26,184 dol., while the expenditure for the same period amounted to 12,977 dol. 72 c., leaving a balance of 13,206 dol. 28 c. in favour of the United States Treasury.

Imports and Exports.

The imports to the port of Philadelphia during the past year, as compared with the two preceding years, have decreased, while the exports have increased as compared with 1895.

Imports.

The value of importations for the last three years is as follows:—

Year.	Value.
	£
1894	10,310,740
1895	9,454,287
1896	7,961,455

The imports of sugar made up a large portion of these figures, and the falling-off in the value of importations may be traced to present disturbances in the Island of Cuba.

TABLE, by Countries, showing the Values of Goods Imported into the Port of Philadelphia in American and Foreign Vessels during the Year ending December 31, 1896.

Country.	Free.	Dutiable.	American.	Foreign.	Total.
	Dollars.	Dollars.	Dollars.	Dollars.	Dollars.
Austria	201,371	491,316	3,966	688,721	692,687
Madeira Islands	...	1,818	...	1,818	1,818
Belgium	127,340	502,490	154,296	475,534	629,830
Denmark	2,747	6,202	77	8,872	8,949
France	489,904	1,646,757	155,886	1,980,775	2,136,661
Germany	934,561	7,858,474	331,874	8,461,161	8,793,035
Greece	11,091	5,149	...	16,240	16,240
Greenland	40,056	...	20,503	19,548	40,056
Italy	295,754	339,059	16,399	618,414	634,813
Netherlands	199,793	325,368	104,514	420,647	525,161
Portugal	10,270	4,498	1,675	13,093	14,768
Russia on the Baltic Sea	266,057	8	...	266,065	266,065
Russia on the Black Sea	93,342	196	...	93,538	93,538
Spain	188,497	160,248	9,520	339,225	348,745
Sweden and Norway	2,309	117,782	1,293	118,798	120,091
Switzerland	8,297	206,788	51,871	163,214	215,085
Turkey in Europe	177,586	34,586	21,968	190,204	212,172
England	3,426,537	5,185,846	772,716	7,839,667	8,612,383
Scotland	1,146,565	392,887	28,761	1,510,691	1,539,452
Ireland	2,015	233,140	29,202	205,953	235,155
Bermuda	400	...	...	400	400
Nova Scotia	51,514	6,693	43,564	14,643	58,207
Ontario	...	40	...	40	40
Newfoundland	59,543	1,960	...	61,503	61,503
Honduras	3,436	...	...	3,436	3,436
Nicaragua	4,200	...	...	4,200	4,200
Mexico	104,555	562	...	105,117	105,117
British West Indies	493,550	116,341	137,286	472,605	609,891
Danish West Indies	141	...	...	141	141
Hayti	68,358	...	...	68,358	68,358
Cuba	186,728	2,691,442	524,529	2,353,641	2,878,170
Puerto Rico	981	90,272	61,120	30,133	91,253
Argentine Republic	96,929	...	...	96,929	96,929
Brazil	80	608,864	63,932	545,012	608,944
Chili	199,400	...	33,554	165,846	199,400
Colombia	22,192	16,190	24,461	13,921	38,382
British Guiana	75	256,285	79,844	176,516	256,360
Peru	928	...	...	928	928
Uruguay	8,648	...	8,648	...	8,648
China	5,130	732	...	5,862	5,862
British East Indies	1,045,899	78,543	30,839	1,093,603	1,124,442
Dutch East Indies	24,908	5,644,698	...	5,669,606	5,669,606
Hong-Kong	3,632	12,503	422	15,713	16,135
Japan	17,881	90,121	7,837	100,165	108,002
Turkey in Asia	304,633	48,416	7,667	345,382	353,049
Arabia	57,422	...	1,002	56,420	57,422
British Possessions in Australasia	489,553	...	165,954	323,599	489,553
Philippine Islands	142,987	435,174	65,099	513,062	578,161
British Possessions in Africa	57,285	194,924	...	252,209	252,209
French Possessions in Africa	32,032	644	1,459	31,217	32,676
Turkey in Africa (Egypt)	118,556	764,912	23,100	860,368	883,468
Morocco	9,450	232	...	9,682	9,682
Total	11,235,118	28,572,160	2,984,843	36,822,435	39,807,278
Equiv. in sterling £	2,247,023	5,714,432	596,968	7,364,487	7,961,455

Exports.

The value of exports during the last three years was as follows:—

Year.	Value.
	£
1894	7,488,200
1895	7,349,023
1896	8,487,897

PHILADELPHIA.

The exports of petroleum during the past year were:—

Petroleum.

From—	Quantity.
	Barrels.
Philadelphia	6,370,699
Baltimore	935,435
New York	8,629,467
Total	15,935,601

Refined petroleum in cases is estimated at five to the barrel, and are included in the above figures.

TABLE showing the Value of Exports, the Growth and Produce of Manufactures of the United States, to Foreign Countries from the Port of Philadelphia during the Year 1896.

Countries to which Exported.	Value.
	£
Austria	143
Belgium	693,279
Denmark	148,279
France	383,645
Germany	661,035
Greece	19,403
Italy	250,143
Netherlands	141,814
Portugal	54,741
Russia	398,302
Spain	34,730
Sweden and Norway	152,213
England	3,626,665
Scotland	673,897
Ireland	302,258
Nova Scotia and New Brunswick	8,696
Quebec	2,454
Newfoundland	4,034
Guatemala	660
Honduras	50
Mexico	86,332
Nicaragua	133
British West Indies	8,534
Danish West Indies	25,546
French West Indies	14,956
Dutch West Indies	478
Hayti	1,406
San Domingo	808
Cuba	148,669
Porto Rico	25,421
Argentine Republic	41,987
Brazil	21,105
Colombia	4,395
Uruguay	2,500
Venezuela	2,611
British India	171,233
Japan	373,666
Total	8,486,221

UNITED STATES.

SUMMARY.

Carried in—	Value.
	£
American steam vessels	646,313
" sailing vessels	238,624
Foreign steam vessels	6,926,455
" sailing vessels	674,829
Total	8,486,221

Imports. The imports of sugar at Philadelphia during the past two years, and which show a decrease, were as follows :—

Year.	Quantity.	Value.
	Tons.	£
1894	473,392	5,107,455
1895	358,105	3,105,285
1896	343,149	2,166,899

The great falling-off in quantity and value is due to the condition of the Island of Cuba, whence the principal supply is derived.

The following table shows the quantities of sugar imported at the principal Atlantic seaports of the United States from 1890 until 1896 :—

TABLE of Sugar Importations during the Years 1890-96.

Port.	1890. Quantity.	1890. Per cent.	1891. Quantity.	1891. Per cent.	1892. Quantity.	1892. Per cent.	1893. Quantity.	1893. Per cent.	1894. Quantity.	1894. Per cent.	1895. Quantity.	1895. Per cent.	1896. Quantity.	1896. Per cent.
	Tons.		Tons.		Tons.		Tons.		Tons.		Tons.		Tons.	
Philadelphia	357,118	29·44	491,395	32·01	484,986	34·60	438,971	30·85	473,392	29·12	358,105	24·73	343,149	21·43
New York	704,507	58·08	824,082	53·69	727,190	51·87	810,716	57·00	980,821	60·32	915,120	63·18	1,056,377	65·98
Boston	151,285	12·48	193,661	12·62	189,603	13·53	170,856	12·00	171,747	10·56	165,584	11·43	183,992	11·49
Baltimore	...	...	25,849	1·68	...	...	2,200	·15	...	...	9,520	·66	17,377	1·10
Total...	1,212,910	100·00	1,534,987	100·00	1,401,779	100·00	1,422,743	100·00	1,625,960	100·00	1,448,329	100·00	1,600,895	100·00

14 UNITED STATES

Beet sugar.

The manufacture of beetroot sugar has made considerable progress in the United States since its first trial in 1830, when but a few pounds were manufactured, up to the present time.

There are now eight factories in operation: three in California, two in Nebraska, one in New Mexico, one in Utah, and one in Virginia. Four additional factories are approaching completion, namely, one at Rome in the State of New York, which has been removed from Canada, one at Menomenee Falls, Wisconsin, one at Alamatos, California, and the last at Salinas City, California.

So far it does not appear that the manufacture of beetroot sugar can be taken as one of the industries of Philadelphia. The trial was made to cultivate beetroot in Lancaster County in the State of Pennsylvania, but failed. The same may be said of the production of sugar from sorghum.

The following table shows the growth of the production of beetroot sugar in the United States from the year 1830 until 1896.

Year.	Quantity.
1830	A few hundred lbs.
1831–37	None
	Lbs.
1838–39	1,300
1839–62	None
1863–71	300 to 500 lbs. per annum
	Tons.
1872	500
1873	700
1874–77	Under 100 per annum
1878	200
1879	1,200
1880	500
1881–82	Under 500
1883	535
1884	953
1885	600
1886	800
1887	255
1888	1,910
1889	2,600
1890	2,800
1891	5,359
1892	12,091
1893	20,453
1894	20,443
1895	30,000
1896 (estimated)	40,000

Grain.

Grain.

Of late there has been a moderate increase in export sales of wheat, insufficient however to give good support to alues,v prices having declined 1 c. in all markets. Wet weather and bad roads have restricted the western movement of corn, and the reduced supplies have made it difficult to maintain an active export trade.

The following shows, in bushels, the quantities of wheat, corn, and oats exported from the port of Philadelphia to European ports since 1894:—

	Quantity.		
	1894.	1895.	1896.
	Bushels.	Bushels.	Bushels.
Wheat	4,487,496	1,885,598	4,902,181
Corn	2,577,540	3,140,920	8,934,402
Oats	169	59,420	438,824
Total	7,065,205	5,085,938	14,275,407

Tin-Plate.

The production of black and tin-plate has been rapidly pushed to the front, and is now one of the leading industries of Pennsylvania. Out of a total capacity in the United States of 175 hot-mills for the turning out of black plate for tinning purposes, Pennsylvania has 64, which represent some of the largest, best equipped, and most successfully operated tin-plate plants of any country. All the tin-plate works in this State, with the exception of two plants, are new works constructed on the most approved plan since the enactment of the McKinley law, while the works of the two old establishments have been so remodelled as to conform to the more modern plants.

The American manufacturers have adopted what is known as the single stand of hot rolls, and claim that their mills are more substantially built with much stronger foundations, and housings and rolls much heavier, their standard housings weighing about 11 tons.

The rolls used are from 22 to 24 inches in diameter, with neck of 18 to 19 inches in diameter. It is said that much heavier work is therefore accomplished in American mills, where nearly all packs are usually rolled 20 by 56 inches, and cut in two 20 by 28 inches.

With the exception of one in Philadelphia and one in Harrisburg, all the tin-works in Pennsylvania manufacturing black plate are situated in the western part of the State, and of the 19 dipping plants, 9 are in Philadelphia, 7 in Alleghany County, 1 in Armstrong County, 1 in Berks County, and 1 in Montgomery County.

The wages paid to the hands of every description connected with these works are said to be fully 100 per cent. higher in this country than are paid to the same hands in Great Britain.

Notwithstanding all the difficulties encountered it is now

(2386)

believed that with proper fostering the time is not far distant when the United States will produce all the tin-plate required for her consumption. Pennsylvania alone is prepared, should the condition of the market be such as to warrant it, to produce for the fiscal year ending June 30, 1897, from the steel billet to the finished product, 250,000,000 lbs. of tin-plate, fully one-third of the entire consumption of the United States.

It has been officially stated that the large falling-off since 1892 of the production of tin-plates in Great Britain, is due to the growth under protection of the manufacture of tin-plate in the United States.

Institutions.

The Philadelphia Museum. "The Philadelphia Museum" was first organised by ordinance of City Councils, with the approval of the Mayor of the city, June 15, 1894, with the object of making a special study of foreign commerce, and compile all facts relative thereto, so as to make them available in as concise and definite a form as possible to American business men and manufacturers.

This institution has, since starting, made very marked progress towards utility and development under the active administration and energy of Dr. William P. Wilson, who is secretary and director of the museum. In starting out, the originators of the museum were able to obtain some of the important exhibits made by foreign exhibitors at the Chicago World's Fair, at the Atlanta Exhibition, and also from the exhibitions held in Berlin and at Buda-Pesth. The administration was also fortunate in obtaining a vast, well-built, and suitable building, in which it was enabled to store and exhibit samples, in the original premises of the Pennsylvania Railroad, which had been vacated by the Company to occupy their new offices at the terminal situated in the centre of the city.

The object of the museums is to be in a position to show samples to manufacturers and dealers who desire to import raw products of foreign countries, advise them as to prevailing prices in the country of origin, the means and cost of transportation, quantity available, and conditions under which the particular products desired can be obtained. Those desiring to secure a wider market for their products can see samples of what is now being made for the trade of the countries where they might compete and learn the specific requirements of the market, and the tastes of the people, with full details of the competition likely to be met with; the character and variety of goods demanded in each market; the countries whence imported, together with the names and addresses of foreign manufacturers; the quantity imported annually; the manufacturer's price at factory; the retail price in each city where sold; the transport charges from Europe to each market, compared with similar charges from the United States; import duties; character of packing; the names and addresses of importers.

PHILADELPHIA.

The Bureau collects detailed information on all public improvements in progress or contemplated in Spanish America, South Africa, Australia, and other export countries of interest to the business men of the United States, and likewise collects all information concerning the state of foreign markets from which products are imported, such as wools, hides, skins, woods, fibres, dyestuffs, minerals, food products, &c., and all new products of the world obtained through constant communication with the museums' correspondents are immediately made known for the benefit of American commerce.

It is claimed that the exhibition of raw products contains over 50,000 objects, and is probably, therefore, the largest permanent collection in existence, coming from nearly all countries of the world, and renewed from time to time. Large exhibits of products from all countries and in all branches of trade are being secured so as to enlighten the manufacturer as to where American goods may profitably compete.

Philadelphia Textile School.

Among the institutions of Philadelphia which should be mentioned is the Philadelphia Textile School, which for some years past has held a very high position, and is spoken of as having no rival, great or small, upon this side of the Atlantic Ocean.

It was established in 1884, and to-day is recognised as being a model in its line.

For 13 years this institution stood alone in the United States, and claims to have as creditable a record as any of the similar institutions in Europe. This school forms one department of the school of industrial art of the Pennsylvania museum, which commenced in the year of the Centennial Exhibition (1876). The school at first was without the machinery, the apparatus, and even the teaching staff to give the necessary technical instruction, and everything was wanting which the charter, issued to the school, of the art industries of the State, called for.

In 1882 the President of the Philadelphia Textile Association saw the advisability of making this a school to train students to the practical knowledge of textile industries, and therefore undertook to carry out the project. In course of time the sum of 30,000 dol. (6,000*l*.) was obtained and placed at the disposal of the trustees, with which rooms were rented, teachers engaged, and a class of night students organised in 1884–85. In the following summer it was decided to erect an annex to the main school building for the special uses of the textile department.

The school has now a teaching staff of some 15 men and women, among whom are instructors in chemistry and dyeing, in weaving, in Jacquard sketching and designing, in carding and spinning, design and colour harmony, in dry and in wet finishing. Further, there are a lecturer on Patent law and teachers of French, German, Italian, and Spanish. Two separate three-year courses are arranged for, the one for day classes, the other for evening classes, the first being necessarily more

(2386)

Savings banks.

thorough than the second; also partial and special courses for students limited as to time. It is said that machinery valued at 50,000 dol. (10,000*l.*) is now in rooms of the school to which the students have free access.

There are eleven savings banks in operation in the city of Philadelphia, one of the most prominent and best patronised being the Philadelphian Savings Fund Society.

It is related that in the month of November, 1816, a Mr. Condy Raguet having noticed in recently received English journals an account of the establishment of savings banks in the United Kingdom, mentioned to some leading philanthropists of the city the propriety of instituting a similar society. Eventually it was decided to call a meeting to consider and act on the suggestions of Mr. Raguet. Five of the twelve gentlemen who attended had agreed to unite for the purpose of establishing a society after the plan of the savings banks of Great Britain, met and determined to establish a society under the direction of 12 managers, afterwards increased to 25, for the purpose of receiving and investing small deposits, and the 12 gentlemen each paid down the sum of 50 dol. to form a capital. The interest paid to depositors was first fixed at $4\frac{4}{5}$ per cent., but it has since been reduced to 3 per cent., at which rate it now stands.

In December, 1816, the office of the society was first opened for the transaction of business, and such had been the rapid increase in the number of depositors that it was found necessary, after numerous changes, to provide larger and additional accommodations for its office in order to facilitate the transaction of its business and to provide for its future wants.

From December, 1816, to November, 1888, 503,816 persons had opened accounts with the society, of which 126,545 remained open at that latter date, aggregating in amount 29,531,594 dol. 43 c., and averaging to each depositor, 233 dol. 36 c. Following is the financial statements made by the Philadelphia Savings Fund Society on January 1, 1897:—

	Amount.	
	Dol.	c.
LIABILITIES.		
Due to depositors, January 1, 1897	41,576,204	44
Contingent fund or surplus	4,973,033	24
Total	46,549,237	68
ASSETS.		
Bonds and mortgages	11,175,247	17
Real estate	330,500	90
Temporary loans	88,100	0
Public loans	31,464,987	45
Cash	3,490,402	16
Total	46,549,237	68

Anthracite Coal.

The reports made annually by the mine inspectors show that the producing companies were successful in restricting the output during the year 1896, when only 47,925,732 tons were mined as against 50,847,104 tons during the year 1895.

The number of working days in the anthracite mines during 1896 was 168, being 16 days less than the time worked in 1895, and the total number of men and boys employed in and around these mines last year was 149,390, an increase over the preceding year of 5,785.

The anthracite coal trade was and is dull, with a falling-off of orders owing to the stringency in manufacturing business, and the shutting down of many mills. The prices now quoted are the same as have been in force for some time past, but it is generally understood that the prices will not be maintained as dealers have received notice that there would be a reduction of 15 c. a ton on all sizes. So far it does not appear that the large companies have made any concessions, but it is understood that the individual coal operators are trying to get rid of their surplus stock, and therefore make a further concession in prices.

The price of stove coal at the mines is 2 dol. 70 c. (11s. 3d.) per ton; egg coal, 2 dol. 65 c. (11s.); chestnut, 2 dol. 50 c. (10s. 5d.), and broken, 2 dol. 25 c. (9s. 5d.) per ton.

The coal companies are selling their coal at 15 c. below these figures, but the individual operators are said to be selling stove coal at 2 dol. 25 c. (9s. 5d.), egg coal at 2 dol. 10 c. (8s. 9d.), chestnut at 2 dol. (8s. 4d.), and broken 2 dol. (8s. 4d.) per ton.

Even at these low figures orders are scarce with few enquiries being made, although coal mine owners claim that prices now are as low as they ever will be, and that the recent reduction was made to equalise prices.

UNITED STATES.

The accidents in the mines during 1896 exceed those of 1895 by over 100, as shown by the following table :—

	Number.			
	Total Accidents.	Fatal.	Widows.	Orphans.
First District— Scranton	186	45	17	50
Second District— Scranton	202	40	15	29
Third District*— Pittston	320	112	59	173
Fourth District— Wilkes-Barre	381	80	35	67
Fifth District— Hazleton	147	46	22	37
Sixth District— Shenandoah	179	60	26	57
Seventh District— Shamokin	206	71	28	19
Eighth District— Pottsville	183	48	23	71
Total, 1896	1,804	502	225	503
„ 1895	1,543	391	189	515
„ 1894	1,433	439	219	666

* It was in this district the terrible twin-shaft disaster occurred last June.

PHILADELPHIA.

RETURN of British Shipping at the Port of Philadelphia in the Year 1896.

Direct Trade in British Vessels from and to Great Britain and British Colonies.

Entered.

Total Number of Vessels.			Total Tonnage.			Total Number of Crews.	Total Value of Cargoes.
With Cargoes.	In Ballast.	Total.	With Cargoes.	In Ballast.	Total.		£
125	119	244	193,223	263,757	456,980	8,058	...

Cleared.

Total Number of Vessels.			Total Tonnage.			Total Number of Crews.	Total Value of Cargoes.
With Cargoes.	In Ballast.	Total.	With Cargoes.	In Ballast.	Total.		£
196	29	225	352,952	31,625	384,577	7,041	...

Indirect or Carrying Trade in British Vessels from and to other Countries.

Entered.

Countries whence Arrived.	Number of Vessels.			Tonnage.			Number of Crews.	Value of Cargoes.
	With Cargoes.	In Ballast.	Total.	With Cargoes.	In Ballast.	Total.		£
Spain	141	3	144	322,907	2,908	325,815	3,425	...
United States	...	62	62	...	90,854	90,854	1,500	...
France	1	16	17	2,620	35,418	38,038	513	...
Germany	26	4	30	25,957	6,440	32,397	826	...
Mexico	3	8	11	2,618	10,112	12,730	252	...
Denmark	2	...	2	1,933	...	1,933	59	...
Italy	4	1	5	4,890	2,102	6,992	115	...
Russia	2	...	2	2,784	...	2,784	48	...
Brazil	4	2	6	6,229	2,738	8,967	134	...
Argentine Republic	1	2	3	2,721	2,424	5,145	69	...
Netherlands	22	...	22	44,571	...	44,571	670	...
Japan	...	...	...	...	...	...	...	...
Portugal	...	...	...	...	...	...	...	...
United States of Colombia	...	3	3	...	4,130	4,130	55	...
Chili	3	...	3	4,130	...	...	...	...
Norway and Sweden	...	...	...	...	...	...	...	...
Belgium	6	...	6	11,747	...	11,747	181	...
Greece	1	...	1	1,449	...	1,449	23	...
Guatemala	1	...	1	822	...	822	27	...
Egypt	3	...	3	6,033	...	6,033	98	...
Uruguay	...	1	1	...	2,267	2,267	31	...
Peru	1	...	1	835	...	835	17	...
San Domingo	1	...	1	658	...	658	10	...
Total	222	99	321	442,904	155,263	598,167	8,053	...

Cleared.

Countries to which Departed.	Number of Vessels.			Tonnage.			Number of Crews.	Value of Cargoes.
	With Cargoes.	In Ballast.	Total.	With Cargoes.	In Ballast.	Total.		£
Spain	61	26	87	82,226	24,114	106,340	2,054	...
United States	...	113	113	...	182,378	182,378	2,919	...
France	59	...	59	202,882	...	202,882	1,712	...
Germany	4	1	5	6,523	1,264	7,787	109	...
Mexico	14	...	14	19,234	...	19,234	336	...
Denmark	22	...	22	31,959	...	31,959	582	...
Italy	5	...	5	9,197	...	9,197	138	...
Russia	9	...	9	14,972	...	14,972	217	...
Brazil	1	...	1	215	...	215	8	...
Argentine Republic	...	...	...	...	...	...	...	...
Netherlands	3	2	5	5,518	3,848	9,366	149	...
Japan	13	...	13	24,836	...	24,836	337	...
Portugal	1	...	1	348	...	348	8	...
United States of Colombia	3	1	4	3,966	540	4,506	97	...
Chili	...	...	...	...	...	...	...	...
Norway and Sweden	3	...	3	5,474	...	5,474	87	...
Belgium	...	...	...	...	...	...	...	...
Greece	2	...	2	2,424	...	2,424	45	...
Guatemala	...	...	...	...	...	...	...	...
Egypt	...	...	...	...	...	...	...	...
Uruguay	...	...	...	...	...	...	...	...
Peru	...	...	...	...	...	...	...	...
San Domingo	...	...	...	...	...	...	...	...
Total	200	143	343	409,774	212,144	621,918	8,798	...

RETURN of British Shipping at the Port of Philadelphia in the Year 1895.

Direct Trade in British Vessels from and to Great Britain and British Colonies.

Entered.

Total Number of Vessels.			Total Tonnage.			Total Number of Crews.	Total Value of Cargoes.
With Cargoes.	In Ballast.	Total.	With Cargoes.	In Ballast.	Total.		£
134	93	227	257,219	182,900	440,119	8,429	...

Cleared.

Total Number of Vessels.			Total Tonnage.			Total Number of Crews.	Total Value of Cargoes.
With Cargoes.	In Ballast.	Total.	With Cargoes.	In Ballast.	Total.		£
150	29	179	299,585	37,968	337,553	6,419	...

(75 5 | 97—H & S 2386)

Indirect or Carrying Trade in British Vessels from and to other Countries.

Entered.

Countries whence Arrived.	Number of Vessels.			Tonnage.			Number of Crews.	Value of Cargoes.
	With Cargoes.	In Ballast.	Total.	With Cargoes.	In Ballast.	Total.		£
Spain	190	11	201	253,163	4,053	257,216	4,608	...
United States	...	61	61	...	92,831	92,831	1,441	...
France	6	11	17	7,926	21,570	29,496	414	...
Germany	18	...	18	29,432	...	29,432	487	...
Mexico	4	6	10	5,405	6,320	11,725	242	...
Denmark	1	1	2	1,246	1,325	2,571	72	...
Italy	9	...	9	11,358	...	11,358	225	...
Russia	18	1	19	26,851	1,113	27,964	475	...
Hayti	11	...	11	9,182	...	9,182	218	...
Brazil	13	...	13	15,197	...	15,197	285	...
Argentine Republic	4	...	4	5,127	...	5,127	85	...
Netherlands	7	2	9	17,481	14,457	31,938	302	...
Japan	...	...	...	...	...	...	...	...
Portugal	...	2	2	...	2,486	2,486	44	...
United States of Colombia	5	...	5	2,200	...	2,200	80	...
Chili	4	...	4	4,932	...	4,932	69	...
Norway and Sweden	1	...	1	1,555	...	1,555	30	...
Belgium	2	2	4	3,473	2,998	6,471	83	...
Venezuela	...	...	...	...	...	...	...	...
Greece	1	...	1	1,567	...	1,567	23	...
Turkey	2	...	2	3,020	...	3,020	36	...
Total	296	97	393	399,115	147,153	546,268	9,219	...

Cleared.

Countries to which Departed.	Number of Vessels.			Tonnage.			Number of Crews.	Value of Cargoes.
	With Cargoes.	In Ballast.	Total.	With Cargoes.	In Ballast.	Total.		£
Spain	92	37	129	123,742	50,408	174,150	2,980	...
United States	...	149	149	...	216,666	216,666	3,888	...
France	49	4	53	89,548	1,446	96,988	1,441	...
Germany	1	1	2	1,403	...	2,849	44	...
Mexico	9	3	12	14,886	4,729	19,615	299	...
Denmark	20	1	21	27,319	588	27,907	516	...
Italy	6	2	8	8,576	3,082	11,658	194	...
Russia	2	...	2	3,494	...	3,494	52	...
Hayti	...	...	...	...	...	...	...	...
Brazil	5	1	6	5,595	1,921	7,516	118	...
Argentine Republic	3	1	4	3,189	1,842	5,031	72	...
Netherlands	2	...	2	3,530	...	3,530	55	...
Japan	5	...	5	9,894	...	9,894	159	...
Portugal	2	...	2	620	...	620	19	...
United States of Colombia	...	1	1	...	1,322	1,322	25	...
Chili	...	...	...	...	...	...	...	...
Norway and Sweden	2	...	2	3,539	...	3,539	61	...
Belgium	...	1	1	...	1,365	1,365	27	...
Venezuela	...	...	...	...	...	...	...	...
Greece	...	...	...	...	...	...	...	...
Turkey	2	...	2	3,018	...	3,018	51	...
Total	201	200	401	299,718	289,444	589,162	10,001	...

FOREIGN OFFICE.
1897.
ANNUAL SERIES.

N°. 1921.
DIPLOMATIC AND CONSULAR REPORTS ON TRADE AND FINANCE.

UNITED STATES.

REPORT FOR THE YEAR 1896
ON THE
TRADE OF THE CONSULAR DISTRICT OF NEW YORK.

REFERENCE TO PREVIOUS REPORT, Annual Series No. 1767.

Presented to both Houses of Parliament by Command of Her Majesty,
JUNE, 1897.

LONDON:
PRINTED FOR HER MAJESTY'S STATIONERY OFFICE,
BY HARRISON AND SONS, ST. MARTIN'S LANE,
PRINTERS IN ORDINARY TO HER MAJESTY.

And to be purchased, either directly or through any Bookseller, from
EYRE & SPOTTISWOODE, EAST HARDING STREET, FLEET STREET, E.C., and
32, ABINGDON STREET, WESTMINSTER, S.W.; or
JOHN MENZIES & Co., 12, HANOVER STREET, EDINBURGH, and
90, WEST NILE STREET, GLASGOW; or
HODGES, FIGGIS, & Co., Limited, 104, GRAFTON STREET, DUBLIN.

1897.

[C. 8277—139.] *Price Twopence Halfpenny.*

New Series of Reports.

Reports of the Annual Series have been issued from Her Majesty's Diplomatic and Consular Officers at the following places, and may be obtained from the sources indicated on the title-page:—

No.		Price.	No.		Price.
1799.	Cadiz	2d.	1860.	Rouen	2d.
1800.	Meshed	2½d.	1861.	Patras	1½d.
1801.	St. Petersburg	4½d.	1862.	Barcelona	2d.
1802.	Batoum	1d.	1863.	Amoy	2½d.
1803.	Peking	3d.	1864.	Trebizond	1d.
1804.	Samos	½d.	1865.	Lisbon	2½d.
1805.	Dantzig	2d.	1866.	Callao	2d.
1806.	Antwerp	1½d.	1867.	Pernambuco	5d.
1807.	Ajaccio	1½d.	1868.	Naples	1½d.
1808.	Stettin	3d.	1869.	New Orleans	2½d.
1809.	Aleppo	1d.	1870.	Vera Cruz	2½d.
1810.	Tangier	2½d.	1871.	Madeira	1d.
1811.	Tokio	3½d.	1872.	Jerusalem	1d.
1812.	Madeira	½d.	1873.	Ningpo	1d.
1813.	Vera Cruz	1d.	1874.	Rio de Janeiro	2½d.
1814.	Oporto	1d.	1875.	Trieste	1d.
1815.	Hamburg	1½d.	1876.	Curaçoa	1d.
1816.	New Orleans	1½d.	1877.	Goa	1d.
1817.	Bengazi	½d.	1878.	Cagliari	1d.
1818.	Marmagao	½d.	1879.	Guayaquil	1d.
1819.	Gothenburg	2d.	1880.	Havana	1½d.
1820.	Dar-al-Baida	3d.	1881.	Reykjavik (Iceland)	1d.
1821.	Erzeroum	½d.	1882.	Milan	1½d.
1822.	Munich	2½d.	1883.	Baltimore	1d.
1823.	Samoa	½d.	1884.	Cettinjé	½d.
1824.	Chinkiang	1d.	1885.	Bilbao	2½d.
1825.	Jeddah	1d.	1886.	Florence	1½d.
1826.	Sofia	1½d.	1887.	Brest	1½d.
1827.	Mexico	2d.	1888.	Marseilles	1½d.
1828.	Teneriffe	3½d.	1889.	Wuhu	1d.
1829.	Batoum	1d.	1890.	Chinkiang	1d.
1830.	Cadiz	1d.	1891.	Malaga	1d.
1831.	Martinique	1d.	1892.	Antwerp	½d.
1832.	Odessa	1d.	1893.	Amsterdam	1d.
1833.	Ghilan	1d.	1894.	Galveston	2d.
1834.	Old Calabar	6½d.	1895.	Piræus	2½d.
1835.	Tamsui	1d.	1896.	Stettin	2½d.
1836.	Copenhagen	½d.	1897.	Martinique	1½d.
1837.	Salonica	1½d.	1898.	Corunna	2½d.
1838.	Honolulu	½d.	1899.	Calais	1d.
1839.	Buenos Ayres	2d.	1900.	Honolulu	1d.
1840.	Para	1d.	1901.	Riga	2d.
1841.	Bolivia	2d.	1902.	Tripoli	1d.
1842.	Washington	3d.	1903.	Batoum	2d.
1843.	Berlin	2d.	1904.	Lorenzo Marques	2d.
1844.	Uganda	1d.	1905.	Batavia	2½d.
1845.	Belgrade	1½d.	1906.	Corfu	1½d.
1846.	Dakar	½d.	1907.	Foochow	1½d.
1847.	Florence	1½d.	1908.	Montevideo	5½d.
1848.	Copenhagen	2d.	1909.	China	5d.
1849.	Havre	2d.	1910.	Philadelphia	1½d.
1850.	Serajevo	1d.	1911.	Rio Grande do Sul	3½d.
1851.	Madrid	2d.	1912.	Quito	1d.
1852.	La Rochelle	1½d.	1913.	San José	1d.
1853.	Chicago	4d.	1914.	Dunkirk	1d.
1854.	Berlin	1d.	1915.	Samoa	1d.
1855.	Cherbourg	2½d.	1916.	Bordeaux	2½d.
1856.	Beira	1d.	1917.	Porto Rico	1½d.
1857.	Charleston	2½d.	1918.	Galatz	1½d.
1858.	Saigon	½d.	1919.	Christiania	½d.
1859.	Suakin	1d.	1920.	Copenhagen	3d.

No. 1921.

Reference to previous Report, Annual Series No. 1767.

UNITED STATES.

NEW YORK.

Consul-General Sanderson to the Marquess of Salisbury.

(Received at Foreign Office, May 20, 1897.)

My Lord,

I HAVE the honour to forward my Annual Report on the Trade and Commerce of the Consular District of New York together with a Report of a similar character which I have received from Mr. Vice-Consul Stockwell respecting Providence, Rhode Island.

I have, &c.
(Signed)   PERCY SANDERSON.

Report on the Trade and Commerce of the Consular District of New York for the Year 1896.

TABLE of Contents.

	PAGE
New York—	
General remarks	2
Situation of the Treasury	2
Agricultural produce	3
Production of pig-iron	4
Railways	4
Imports and exports	4
New York money market	4
New York banks	5
New York clearing-house returns	6
Clearings outside of New York	6
Sterling exchange	6
Stock exchange	7
Cotton exchange	7
Produce exchange	7
Failures	8
State banks of deposit and discount	12
Debt of State of New York	13
New York city debt	13
Freights	14
Shipping at New York	15

(2396)

UNITED STATES.

Table of Contents—continued.

	PAGE
New York—continued—	
Public works—	
Canals	15
Canal transport between New York and Cleveland	17
Deep water canal construction	17
Improvements of the North River	18
Projected bridge over the Hudson River	18
Harbour Channel of New York	18
Railroads	18
Vital statistics	19
Immigration	19
Strikes	21
Trade and commerce—	
Anthracite coal	22
Iron and steel	22
Comparative prices of staple commodities	22
Silk	23
Dry goods	23
Cotton goods	23
Woollen goods	24
Flax	24
Exports from New York	24
Cattle	24
Cheese	24
Scotch herrings	25
Export trade to South Africa	25
Return of principal articles of export	26
,, ,, import	27
Total value of imports and exports	28
Specie	29
Grain shipments	30
Return of shipping	31
,, number of seamen engaged and discharged	32
Providence, Rhode Island, trade report	33

General remarks. The year 1896 was one of depression and anxiety.

The improvement in the general condition of trade and industry which had been noted in 1895 was not maintained, for while there was no recurrence of the great strikes and labour troubles, heavy floods and extensive forest fires which marked the year 1894, reviving confidence was checked by the political situation, and above all by the silver agitation; as regards the former at the beginning of the year the markets were still under the depressing influence of the controversy as to the boundary between British Guiana and Venezuela, and although the apprehension on this account diminished very considerably as early as the months of January and February the incident was not finally closed till the end of the year. Cuban affairs may also be said to have presented an element of uncertainty of a disturbing character although in a minor degree, but the greatest apprehension dated from July when the silver agitation first assumed a really serious aspect.

Situation of the Treasury. In January a fresh loan was required to replenish the gold reserve of the Treasury; great opposition was manifested to another contract with a syndicate similar to that made in 1895, and a notice was issued inviting tenders for 100,000,000 dol. of 4 per cent. bonds. The loan proved a great success, bids being

silver" or "bimetallism," they being considered as a "past issue." The basis of the principles declared that "the present gold standard must be maintained; that steps should be taken to insure the ultimate retirement of all classes of United States notes by gradual and steady process, and that a banking system should be provided which shall furnish credit facilities to every portion of the country, and a safe and elastic circulation."

This plan is to be formulated into Bills enacting the necessary legislation by a Monetary Commission, which Congress will be requested to create; that failing, the Convention has provided for the appointment of an Executive Commission of 15 members to be appointed by the President of the body, Mr. C. Stewart Patterson, of Philadelphia, the chairman of which committee will probably be Mr. H. H. Hanna, of Indianapolis, who is considered to have unusual qualifications for the post. The number of this committee can be increased to 45, and is to urge upon Congress the enactment for the appointment of the Commission by the incoming President, Mr. McKinley. Should this step be unsuccessful, an independent commission will be appointed from the best available financial talent in the country.

The movement originated with business men in order to solve the most serious problem of the time, and is apart from party politics, or from any one preconceived plan or scheme of reform.

It is their intention to devote to the work all the necessary time and attention, as they desire to get at a practical solution which will give the currency system safety and permanency, and which will likewise insure against any danger during the process of the necessary currency changes which may eventually be decided upon. During the latter part of March, the executive committee appointed by the recent Indianapolis Monetary Conference had interviews with the President of the United States, Secretary of the Treasury, and Speaker of the House in Washington on the subject of creating a Monetary Commission to draft a plan for currency reform as instituted by the Conference. The Committee found them averse to taking up this subject before the disposal of the Tariff Bill in Congress, regarding the latter as more urgent. It is at present considered improbable that a Bill creating a Monetary Commission will pass during this session of Congress.

Textiles.

The knitted goods branch of this industry appears lately to have improved somewhat, the lower priced goods having steadily increased. Very little profit is, however, being made on this class of goods, but it is thought that, as there is an improvement in the trade, prices will also improve. In underwear there is a great competition in low-priced fleece goods, which are now offered from 15 to 25 per cent. below last year's quotations. *[marginalia: Knitted goods. Underwear.]*

While balbriggans are improving, hosiery goods in general *[marginalia: Balbriggans.]*

show poor signs of progress, although it is said that some manufacturers are behind their orders in certain novelties.

As a rule manufacturers are thought to be cautiously inclined even to an excess, experiencing much difficulty in convincing the retail merchant and jobber of the improvement, who simply point to surplus stock on their shelves which could not be replaced for less money. It appears to be a general opinion that a cut in wages is indispensable to the starting of the trade at present low prices, to be gradually increased as the demands creep up.

Dry goods. What is termed as dry goods showed some improvement during the early part of the year, prices having advanced 3·16 c. in consequence of the purchase of one block of 750,000 pieces of cloth by a large printing company, and as a result of the short time movements among the print cloth mills, but buyers have since shown less interest, and the market has receded 1·16 c. to 1·8 c.

In other lines of cotton goods the expectation of better business has been somewhat realised. There has been a larger aggregate business, but continued within conservative limits, and there has been little disposition shown to operate in advance of actual requirements.

Both manufacturers and buyers appear to be averse to making large contracts ahead, owing to the unsatisfactory prices. Free sellers of spot goods are reported at former rates, and in no branch of the trade has there been any material improvement in values.

Wool. A large business has lately been done in domestic wools by manufacturers and dealers, in addition to heavy buying of Australian, South American, and English wools on foreign markets. Prices of grease wools have advanced, and scoured wools have increased in proportionate value.

There has been some increase in consumption, but the buying has been far in excess of the normal requirements of the mills. Some manufacturers are reported as having already secured supplies for six months or a year ahead, while others with ample capital have covered their probable needs for considerably more than a year to come. It is thought that this advance of wool purchasing will have an important effect on checking the advance in prices which many expect to follow the enforcement of the new tariff schedules.

The wool markets are unquestionably strong, but by the time the tariff becomes effective, a new United States clip will be ready for sale, and the foreign markets, feeling the effect of the subsidence of the American demand, are likely to recede.

Yarns. In the yarn trade there has been a steady improvement. Manufacturers having received more orders for goods, have consequently given more orders for yarns. The demand has chiefly been for low and medium grades of worsted yarns, because these qualities of fabrics have been mostly in demand. Cotton yarns have been in fair demand. Prices have undergone no important change, but the market is steady, and spinners think that the situation is more encouraging.

PHILADELPHIA.

Iron and Steel.

At the close of the year 1896 the iron and steel market was favourable for enterprises and buyers. Prices of all kinds of iron and steel products were and still are low, in some branches lower than ever before known, considerably lower even than the prices prevailing in Europe. Machinery and all other kinds of materials can be had at correspondingly low cost, and with greater celerity than in any past period. Mechanical engineering establishments are anxious for business; labour, both skilled and unskilled, is abundant.

The steel rail pool formed in August, 1887, which consisted of 15 firms, and was reported as being the greatest combination in the iron trade, as well as to have enjoyed the longest life, has been broken. In the earlier days of this combination its career was decidedly chequered, while the ties which bound it together were exceedingly loose. In 1888 the pool appears to have been reduced to 13 firms, later the Duquesne Steel Company, the only important competitor of the pool, was purchased by the Carnegie Steel Company, the largest firm in the combination. In 1893 the smaller works gradually dropped out of the pool, which in February, 1897, was finally dissolved, leaving an open market. The causes of the breaking-up were various, but the chief reasons were the discovery that the agreement as to prices of the "combine" was not being respected, and that known customers of one member of the pool were removing their names to the books of another firm of the pool.

Machinery for a steel plant, a locomotive plant, and a pipe-making plant was bought and shipped to Russia during the previous year. The steel plant, valued at 73,000*l.*, was shipped hence to Mariupol; the locomotive plant, valued at 300,000*l.*, was to be landed at St. Petersburg, while the pipe-making plant, valued at 50,000*l.*, was shipped from Wilmington, on the Delaware, to Novorossisk.

The complete return sent in by manufacturers of pig-iron in the United States for 1896, and also the complete returns of unsold pig-iron in the hands of makers or their agents at the close of the year, show that the total production of pig-iron in 1896 was 8,623,127 gross tons, against 9,446,308 tons in 1895, 6,623,127 tons in 1894, 7,124,502 tons in 1893, 9,157,000 tons in 1892, 8,279,870 tons in 1891, and 9,202,703 tons in 1890. The production in 1896 was 823,181 tons, or about 9 per cent. less than in 1895. The production of pig-iron from 1894 to 1896 has been as follows in gross tons:—

	Quantity.		
	1894.	1895.	1896.
	Tons.	Tons.	Tons.
First half	2,717,983	4,087,558	4,976,236
Second half	3,939,405	5,358,750	3,646,891
Total	6,657,388	9,446,308	8,623,127

There was a great shrinkage in production in the second half of 1896, but it will be observed that in the 12 months embracing the second half of 1895 and the first half of 1896, 334,986 tons of pig-iron were produced. This large production was due to the boom of 1895. The greatly decreased production in the second half of 1896 was due to the reaction from that boom, and to the uncertainty and apprehension attending the presidential campaign of that year.

The production of Bessemer pig-iron in 1896 was 4,654,955 tons, against 5,623,695 tons in 1895, a decrease of 968,740 tons. The great increase in the total production of pig-iron in 1895 over 1894 was caused by the extraordinary demand for Bessemer pig-iron, which demand was in turn chiefly caused by the extraordinary demand for structural steel, but in 1896 there was a slackening in the demand for structural steel, and also in the demand for steel rails.

The production of basic pig-iron in 1896 amounted to 336,403 tons, distributed as follows:—New England, New York, and New Jersey, 22,692 tons; Alleghany County, Pennsylvania, 168,095 tons; other counties in Pennsylvania, 51,768 tons; Virginia and Alabama, 73,604 tons; and Ohio and Wisconsin, 20,244 tons. The production of charcoal pig-iron in 1896 was 310,344 tons, against 225,341 tons in 1895, an increase of 85,003 tons. The production of spiegeleisen and ferro-manganese in 1896 was 131,904 tons, against 171,724 tons in 1895.

The stocks of unsold pig-iron in the hands of manufacturers or their agents on December 31, 1896, and which were not intended for their own consumption, amounted to 711,649 tons, against 644,887 tons on June 30, 1896, and 444,332 tons on December 31, 1895. These figures of unsold stock of pig-iron do not include pig-iron sold but not removed from the furnace bank, nor pig-iron manufactured by rolling mill proprietors for their own use.

In addition to the stocks of pig-iron above noted as unsold on December 31, 1896, there should be added 136,037 tons which have passed out of the hands of the makers into the yards of the American Pig-Iron Storage Warrant Company, making 847,686 tons, which may be said to have been then on the market, against 705,847 tons, which were similarly held on June 30, 1896, and 506,132 tons on December 31, 1895. The total quantity of stocks in warrant yards on December 31, 1896, was 200,700 tons, against 106,200 tons on December 31, 1895, and 112,000 tons on June 30, 1896.

During the latter part of 1896 the pig-iron market showed a tendency to rise in the rate of reproduction, but this seems to have run its course, as in January, 1897, the increase was so small that the rate of output may be considered stationary.

A very large share is from furnaces directly connected with the steel works or rolling mills. This amounted in January to 375,000 tons. Taking into consideration the blowing in of some large furnaces during the month of January, it represents a capacity of about 87,000 tons per week, leaving about 70,000 tons to reach the open market weekly.

Shipbuilding.

The following is a list of the vessels turned out from the ship and engine building company, William Cramp and Sons, of this port since 1894:—

NAVAL VESSELS.

Name.	Tons Displacement.	Horse-Power.
U.S.S. "Minneapolis," protected cruiser	7,350	22,000
U.S.S. "Indiana" battle ship	10,400	10,000
U.S.S. "Massachusetts," battle ship	10,400	10,000
U.S.S. "Iowa," battle ship	11,300	12,000

MERCHANT VESSELS.

Name.	Net Tonnage.	Gross Tonnage.	Horse-Power.
S.S. "Lebanon"	1,157·37	1,485·98	1,032
S.S. "St. Louis"	5,893·73	11,629·21	20,000
S.S. "St. Paul"	5,874·14	11,629·21	20,000
S.S. "Comanche"	2,073·22	3,203·44	4,100
S.S. "Thespia"	170·04	311·74	800
S.S. "Curaçoa"	695·21	1,505·44	1,100
S.S. "Tamaqua"	383·80	564·41	921
S.S. "Atlanta"	1,399·30	2,094·50	2,320
S.S. "Pittsburg"	865·92	1,273·41	2,000

Navigation.

It has been decided to deepen, during the coming season, the channel of the River Delaware so as to permit vessels of the deepest draught to navigate the river at any state of the tide.

A breakwater or harbour of refuge is to be constructed at the entrance of the river. The work involves an expenditure of more than 4,660,000 dol., and was authorised by the River and

Harbour Act of last June, which empowered the Secretary of War to enter into a contract for the work, to be paid for as appropriations are made from time to time, not to exceed in the aggregate 4,660,000 dol.

The plans and specifications were prepared at the office of the United States Engineer in Philadelphia. The work is to be commenced at once, and the time for completion is fixed at December 31, 1901, depending upon the appropriations made by Congress.

The Winter Load Line.

Considerable feeling is expressed at the Maritime and Commercial organisations of this port against the present ruling of the Board of Trade on the North Atlantic winter freeboard, which is looked upon as prejudicial to shippers north of Cape Charles, and very much to the interests of shippers from Baltimore and Chesapeake Bay.

Immigration.

The Commissioner of Immigration at Philadelphia reports that during the fiscal year ending June 30, 1896, 28,694 persons arrived at this port, and were examined and inspected as required by the several immigration Acts of Congress. This number included cabin as well as steerage passengers, and 52 stowaways and 1 workaway. Of the total number of arrivals (28,694) 3,658 were citizens of the United States and alien visitors or aliens in transit, and 25,036 were alien immigrants; and of that number 59 were debarred, and 24,977 were permitted to land in the United States, a decrease on the previous year of 1,350 in the number of alien immigrants arrived, as shown by the following table:—

Month.	Number. 1894–95.	Number. 1895–96.
July	2,143	2,036
August	1,809	2,289
September	3,158	3,526
October	3,324	1,797
November	1,424	1,306
December	1,099	1,161
January	922	927
February	839	861
March	1,804	2,152
April	2,382	2,775
May	3,849	4,027
June	3,574	2,120
Total	26,327	24,977

The figures given by Bradstreets differ slightly from the above, and the tables they publish classifying these failures according to their primary causes are not without interest. The primary causes come under 11 heads, 8 of which refer to faults of those failing, viz., incompetence, irrespective of other causes; inexperience without other incompetence; lack of capital, including the trying to do too much business for the capital employed; granting of unwise credit; speculation outside of regular business; neglect of business due to doubtful habits; personal extravagance; fraudulent disposition of property. The remaining three heads refer to failures not due to the faults of those failing, viz., disaster (flood, fire, failure of crops, commercial crisis); failure of others, apparently solvent debtors; special or undue competition. The summaries are as follows:—

NUMBER of Failures in United States with Amount of Liabilities

	1896. Number.	1896. Liabilities.	1895. Number.	1895. Liabilities.	1894. Number.	1894. Liabilities.	1893. Number.	1893. Liabilities.
		£		£		£		£
Incompetence	1,892	6,867,114	1,781	3,104,309	1,794	3,054,586	2,546	5,681,705
Inexperience	688	767,905	518	556,382	538	855,144	940	936,273
Lack of capital	4,699	10,194,538	4,305	8,424,695	4,385	7,833,272	5,194	15,139,699
Unwise credit	653	1,905,452	603	1,637,407	532	1,060,509	726	2,630,118
Speculation	182	2,118,435	146	1,203,064	108	884,125	181	4,252,644
Neglect	345	435,255	333	430,556	321	389,297	481	784,229
Extravagance	140	539,616	128	425,108	135	309,070	198	750,185
Fraud	1,395	2,769,028	1,154	2,105,998	1,022	1,947,446	1,142	3,259,766
Disaster	4,153	18,444,749	3,229	10,677,113	3,295	11,694,960	3,463	34,708,546
Failure of others	397	4,499,445	299	2,569,468	317	1,876,472	446	7,616,252
Competition	550	842,266	462	611,438	277	404,823	191	671,339
Total	15,094	49,383,803	12,958	31,745,538	12,724	30,309,704	15,508	76,430,736

NEW YORK.

PERCENTAGE of Failures and Liabilities.

	1896. Number.	1896. Liabilities.	1895. Number.	1895. Liabilities.	1894. Number.	1894. Liabilities.	1893. Number.	1893. Liabilities.
Incompetence	12·5	13·6	13·7	9·8	14·1	10·4	16·4	7·4
Inexperience	4·6	1·6	4·0	1·7	4·2	2·1	6·1	1·2
Lack of capital	31·1	20·7	33·2	26·1	34·6	25·8	33·5	19·8
Unwise credits	4·4	3·5	4·6	5·1	4·2	3·5	4·7	3·4
Speculation	1·2	4·3	1·1	3·7	0·8	3·0	1·2	5·6
Neglect	2·3	0·9	2·6	1·3	2·5	1·3	3·2	1·0
Extravagance	0·9	1·1	1·0	1·6	1·1	1·0	1·3	1·0
Fraud	9·2	5·7	8·9	6·9	8·0	6·4	7·4	4·2
Disaster	27·5	37·4	24·9	33·6	25·9	39·0	22·3	45·2
Failure of others	2·7	9·2	2·3	8·1	2·5	6·2	2·9	10·0
Competition	3·6	2·0	3·6	2·0	2·1	1·3	1·2	1·0

UNITED STATES.

State banks of deposit and discount.
Suspension.

In his report for the fiscal year ended September 30, 1896, the Superintendent of Banks of the State of New York comments with satisfaction on the fact that notwithstanding all the adverse influences of that period he has only to report the insolvency of one bank and one building and loan association out of nearly 800 institutions under his supervision. He mentions that in addition to these suspensions four banks of deposit and discount went into voluntary liquidation, and one bank reduced its capital. On the other hand three new banks were organised under the State law during the fiscal year; the total number of State banks of deposit and discount transacting business at the close of the fiscal year was 213, a net decrease of two during that period, and the total amount of capital was about 6,244,000*l.*, showing a decrease of about 380,000*l.* The assets and liabilities amounted to about 54,759,000*l.*, about 5,891,000*l.* less than at the corresponding date in 1896.

Number.

Capital.
Assets and liabilities.

The total resources of all the institutions under the supervision of the department are given as follows:—

	Amount.
	£
Banks of deposit and discount .. (about)	54,759,000
Savings banks	161,350,000
Trust companies	79,384,000
Safe deposit companies	915,000
Foreign mortgage companies	5,115,000
Building and loan associations	10,034,000
Total	311,557,000

This shows an increase of nearly 4,000,000*l.* as compared with 1895. The securities and cash held in trust by the Superintendent for the protection of depositors amounted to about 800,000*l.*

Legislation.

The changes made in the Banking Law during 1896 comprise:

A provision specifically requiring foreign corporations (including building and loan associations) doing business in the State of New York, and receiving deposits in trust in that State, to deposit with the Superintendent securities to the amount of 100,000 dol. each as security for the depositors and creditors in the State;

A provision modifying in certain cases the prohibition of a loan or discount by a corporation or banker exceeding one-fifth part of the capital stock and surplus of such corporation or banker;

An obligation for directors of trust companies to affirm on oath their eligibility as defined by the statute, and assuming the obligations that attend the trust;

Establishing conditions for the incorporation of mortgage loan and investment companies, and defining the general powers of such companies;

NEW YORK.

Authorising a reduction or an increase in the number of trustees of savings bank corporations.

Recommendation. The Superintendent recommends that banks in general should manifest less anxiety to apply their profits as fast as earned to the payment of dividends, and should rather endeavour to build up a strong surplus. He recognises that a number of banks do proceed on this principle, but suggests that it might be wise to somewhat broaden the provisions of the law on the subject.

He further recommends that bank examiners should be selected by the head of the banking department, and that the examination by the Civil Service Commission be confined to candidates so selected; that co-operative savings and loan associations, foreign mortgage and investment companies, savings banks and safe deposit companies, which are now exempted, should be brought within the provisions of the law requiring a deposit of money or some approved security to the extent of 500 dol. to 1,000 dol., to be held in trust as security for depositors and creditors, or for application, if need be, to the payment of their respective charges for the support of the department. That the directors of every State bank be required by statute to create an examining committee who shall count the cash and examine all papers held by the bank at least once in six months, and that the law be amended so that no officer of a bank which has become so involved as to necessitate its being closed should be allowed to exercise any further controlling influence in its affairs.

Debt of State of New York. The indebtedness of the State of New York amounted on October 1, 1896, to 2,320,660 dol., or about 464,200*l.*, this being a portion of 9,000,000 dol., for which sum an issue of bonds has been authorised. The tax rate for the purposes of the State Government is 2 dol. 69 c. per 1,000 for the present fiscal year, as compared with 3 dol. 24 c. in 1895–6.

New York City Debt. The position of the funded and temporary debt of the City of New York on December 31, 1896, as compared with December 31, 1895, is given below:—

	December 31, 1896.		December 31, 1895.	
	Currency.	Sterling.	Currency.	Sterling.
	Dollars.	£	Dollars.	£
Funded debt	195,907,690	39,181,538	185,588,597	37,117,719
Sinking fund	77,630,491	15,526,098	75,703,087	15,140,617
Net funded debt	118,277,199	23,655,440	109,885,510	21,977,102
Temporary debt	2,433,327	486,665	2,564,510	512,902

The valuations of the year 1896 were:—real estate, 1,731,509,143 dol.; personal estate, belonging to residents, 245,883,488 dol.; belonging to non-residents, 46,468,081 dol.; belonging to shareholders of banks, 82,624,193 dol.; the total being 2,106,484,905 dol., or about 421,296,981*l.*, as compared with about 403,389,533*l.* in 1895. The increase has been almost entirely in the valuation of real estate. As regards personal property, that belonging to non-residents shows an increase which is nearly balanced by the decrease in the valuation of that belonging to residents; while personal property belonging to shareholders in banks remains about stationary. The total taxes were 44,900,330 dol. (8,980,066*l.*), as compared with 38,403,761 dol. (7,680,752*l.*) in 1895: and the rate of taxation was 2·14 per cent. on the assessed valuations of real and personal estate, and 1·8276 per cent. on the assessed valuation of the personal estate of such corporations, &c., as are subject to local taxation thereon. The rates for 1895 were 1·91 and 1·7278 per cent. respectively.

Freights. Business in general showed a marked improvement in the freight market, and during the autumn and winter months steamers usually employed in the trade to the East Indies were attracted to American ports by the better rates prevailing in consequence of the abundant crops.

Grain freights. Grain freights were maintained at the low level of the previous year till about August, when an active movement commenced embracing almost every kind of grain harvested in this country, and freights rose rapidly reaching their highest point in October, namely 4*s.* 6*d.* per quarter for Cork for orders and 4*s.* to 4*s.* 3*d.* for direct ports.

These rates are attributed largely to the fact that shippers had accepted orders on a basis of an average of the freight paid in former years, and found the market somewhat bare when the time came to execute these orders; the competition became all the more keen owing to the demand for tonnage at the cotton ports, where the season set in a month earlier than usual and found charterers there quite unprepared to meet the rush of cotton offering. One of the features of the grain business of 1896 is the large increase in shipments, especially maize, from southern ports. The diversion to Philadelphia and Baltimore mentioned in the report for 1895 has continued during the year under review, and the difference in railway rates has been made the subject of complaint; it has been stated, however, that high charges and want of facilities for loading and discharging at New York have a good deal to do with the diversion of grain shipments to other ports.

Cotton freights. Cotton freights closed at low figures at the expiration of the season of 1895–96, but opened high in September and ruled strong up to the close of the year.

The rates ranged from 34*s.* to 50*s.* per steamer's net register ton from the Gulf ports, and from 28*s.* to 45*s.* from the Atlantic ports. The crop, besides developing into a large one, matured about a month before the average period, charterers were unprepared with tonnage, and compelled to pay freight on a sharply advancing market.

A few cargoes of cotton were shipped late in the season by sailing vessels to Russian Baltic ports, but with this exception both grain and cotton have been sent by steamers as in the previous year.

Petroleum. Owing to temporary disturbances in the export trade from Batoum the Standard Oil Company increased its shipments of petroleum in all directions, but mainly that in boxes to the far East. This company continues to control the exports to Europe by its tank boats, and the number of sailing vessels taken to outports with oil in barrels is growing less from year to year. During the closing months of the year the better general demand for tonnage produced some increase in the rates of freight for petroleum, but the average was about the same as during the preceding year.

Timber. Timber has been carried by both steamers and sailing vessels, the tendency being rather in favour of steamers. Rates of freight were fairly satisfactory during the year, and better at the close in consequence of the demand in connection with the export of cotton.

Deal. Deal freights have been about the same as in 1895, leaving but a small margin of profit to carriers; the preference is given to sailing vessels.

Sugar. Sugar freights from Cuba have been but a small factor, the yield having been reduced to a mere percentage of the former export. The greater part came by boats of the regular lines.

Cattle. Cattle shipments were on a much more extensive scale than hitherto, but they were taken chiefly by steamers of the regular lines whose carrying facilities were enlarged.

Shipping at New York. The return of shipping at New York shows very little change, the total entries were 4,226 vessels of 6,959,925 tons in 1896 as compared with 4,406 vessels of 6,838,667 tons in 1895, and the clearances, 4,012 vessels of 6,698,508 tons in 1896, as against 4,186 vessels of 6,705,251 tons in 1895.

The British tonnage showed 2,087 vessels of 3,440,237 tons entered as compared with 2,163 vessels of 3,197,547 tons in 1895; United States, 907 vessels of 1,117,800 tons in 1896, and 1,068 of 1,184,651 tons in 1895; German, 485 vessels of 1,208,663 tons in 1896, and 461 of 1,275,338 tons in 1895. The next in order of importance are vessels flying the Netherlands flag, 317,027 tons, and the French flag, 305,758 tons.

Public works. Canals. The report of the Superintendent of Public Works of the State of New York shows that 3,714,894 tons (of 2,000 lbs. each) passed through the canals in 1896, as compared with 3,500,314 in 1895, and 3,882,560 in 1894; there is thus some slight improvement as compared with 1895, but the total is far below an average, and, in fact, it would be necessary to go back to 1859 to find totals so low as those of the last three years.

(2396)

The amounts carried by the several canals were as follows:—

	Quantity.
	Tons.
Erie Canal	2,742,438
Champlain Canal	802,579
Oswego Canal	57,245
Black River Canal..	57,953
Cayuga and Seneca Canal..	54,739

The total east bound tonnage was 2,605,012 tons, and the west bound 1,109,882 tons.

The classification was as follows:—

	Quantity.
	Tons.
Products of the forest	852,647
Products of agriculture	1,136,665
Manufactures	152,322
Merchandise	270,603
All other articles	1,302,837
Total	3,714,894

As compared with 1895 the chief increases were in wheat, oats, and flax seed, wood-pulp, and ice, the two latter being new items of over 100,000 tons. On the other hand there was a considerable decrease in wood, timber, and boards, and in a lesser degree of anthracite coal.

The total receipts of flour and grain at New York by all routes between May 1 and December 1, 1896 (the time during which the canals were open), amounted to 112,121,954 bushels, of which 32,107,888 bushels, equivalent to rather more than 28½ per cent., came by canal.

The report states that the delay to canal navigation from all causes has probably been as small as in any year, and that the water supply has been found adequate. The practice which had grown up during former years of allowing mill power owners, whose supply was supposed to be dependent on the surplus water of the canals, to control the gates or openings from waste weirs, or to determine the elevation of overflows from the canals, has been substantially abated. The control of the water is in the hands of the Superintendents, and private parties are absolutely prohibited from interfering with it in any way.

Boatmen are said to have done a comparatively prosperous business in 1896, although complaints were made of high charges and discrimination in favour of railway companies at Buffalo and New York.

The average price for the transportation of wheat between Buffalo and New York is given as 3·75 c. per bushel; the price reached 4·6 c. per bushel in 1893, but with this exception it is the highest since 1890, and compares with 2·2 c. in 1895.

A special appropriation of 375,000 dol. (about 75,000*l*.) was made by the legislature for such extraordinary repairs and improvements of the canals as could not be made under the terms of the Act passed in the previous year for improving the Erie, the Champlain, and the Oswego Canal, nor be provided for out of the limited amount provided for ordinary repair and maintenance. This has enabled the department to take prompt measures as any emergencies arose, and an appropriation of 360,000 dol. is recommended for the present year.

The Act above alluded to provides for the issue of bonds by the State to an amount not exceeding 9,000,000 dol. (1,800,000*l*.), of which 4,000,000 dol. (800,000*l*.) would be immediately available for the purpose of enlarging and improving the Erie Canal, the Champlain Canal, and the Oswego Canal; the Erie and Oswego Canals are to be deepened to not less than 9 feet, except over and across aqueducts, miter sills, culverts, and other permanent structures, where the minimum depth is to be 8 feet. The Champlain Canal is to be deepened to 7 feet, and in the case of all the canals the locks are to be lengthened and improved, and the walls strengthened. Contracts were entered into before the close of the navigation for the larger part of the work, and this was to be prosecuted in some cases both night and day, and in such a manner as not to interfere with navigation in 1897. It is anticipated that after the improvement has been made the cost of power will be greatly reduced, and that the carrying trade on the canals will be successfully maintained with a fair profit, in spite of any railroad competition.

Canal transport between New York and Cleveland. The system of canal transport between New York and Cleveland, Ohio, which was referred to in the report for the year 1895, proved sufficiently successful to encourage operations on a larger scale during 1896. The canal boats are made of steel, and a fleet consists of five boats and one steamer; they have successfully encountered heavy gales on Lake Erie during 1896, and this class of traffic seems likely to increase. The trip from Cleveland to New York is said to take from 10 to 12 days.

Deep-water canal construction. Attention has been directed to the ultimate construction of a deep-water canal connecting the Great Lakes with the ocean, and among projects that have been examined is a proposal to incorporate the Maritime Canal Company of America with a view to the construction of canals from a point near the head of the tide water navigation in the Hudson River to Lake Champlain, from Lake Champlain to Lake St. Francis, from the head of Lake St. Francis to the Long Sault Rapids on the St. Lawrence, and from Lewiston, on the Niagara River, to a point above the Niagara Falls. All these canals would have channels of 20 feet navigable depth, and be sufficiently wide for the largest vessels to pass.

Report of Commission of Enquiry. A Commission of Enquiry has been held to report on the feasibility of the construction of deep-water canals, and has reported in the following sense:—

(2396)

That it is quite feasible to construct such canals, and develop such channels as will be adequate to any scale of navigation that may be desired between the several great lakes and to the seaboard, and to conduct foreign and domestic commerce through the same. The navigable depth recommended is not less than 20 feet. That starting from the heads of Lakes Michigan and Superior, the most eligible route is through the several great lakes and their intermediate channels, and the proposed Niagara Ship Canal (Tonawanda to Olcott) to Lake Ontario; and that the Canadian seaboard may be reached from Lake Ontario by way of St. Lawrence River, or by way of Oswego, the Oneida, Mohawk Valley, and the Hudson River. That the alternative routes from Lake Ontario to the Hudson require complete surveys and further study; that the completion of the entire system on the basis of the largest useful capacity is fully justified, and that the Niagara Ship Canal should first be undertaken, and incidentally the broadening and further deepening of the intermediate channels of the lakes.

Improvements of the North River. The pier accommodation of the North River has been found for some time past to be inadequate, many of the piers being too short, and the water too shallow for the large vessels which cross the Atlantic. Plans for the construction of six new docks and five new piers were approved in 1894, the requisite appropriation was voted in the winter of 1896, and the work is now being commenced.

Projected bridge over the Hudson River. There is a project for building a bridge over the Hudson River to connect New York with New Jersey. The cost is estimated at about 5,000,000$l.$, and it is calculated that it would take five years to construct.

Harbour channel of New York. At the present time the channel of the harbour of New York has a minimum depth of 30 feet at low water, and as several vessels have now a draught of $30\frac{1}{2}$ feet, a survey of the harbour has lately been made with the view of estimating the cost of deepening the channel to 35 feet at mean low water, and of maintaining this depth.

Recommendations have been made to the United States Government that improvements should be carried out, providing for a channel 1,000 feet wide and 35 feet deep at mean low water from the Narrows to the sea. The depth of the channel was increased 10 years ago from $22\frac{1}{2}$ to 30 feet.

Railroads. Goods traffic. During the year 1896 the total tonnage of all classes of merchandise sent westward from New York City by rail and consigned to or beyond Buffalo, Salamanca, Pittsburg, Bellaire, &c., was 1,290,373 tons of 2,000 lbs.; that arriving in New York City from the places above noted, or from points to the west of them, amounted to 5,077,651 tons. The railroads carrying these goods are the New York, Central, and Hudson River; Erie; Pennsylvania; Baltimore and Ohio; West Shore; Delaware, Lackawanna, and Western; Lehigh Valley; New York, Ontario, and Western; and Chesapeake and Ohio.

These amounts show a decrease of about 150,000 tons in

NEW YORK.

the amount of goods sent westward, but an increase in the amount received from the west of about 500,000 tons, the figures in 1895 having been 1,446,495 tons sent, and 4,585,745 tons received.

The vital statistics of the city of New York for the past two years are given as follows :— *Vital statistics.*

	Number.	
	1896.	1895.
Births	55,632	53,731
Still-births	3,542	3,372
Marriages	20,513	20,612
Deaths	41,622	41,175

Of the deaths reported, 16,807 were of children under five years of age :—

Cause of Death.	Number.	
	1896.	1895.
Small-pox	1	10
Measles	714	793
Scarlet fever	402	468
Diphtheria	1,555	1,634
Croup	208	342
Whooping cough	435	496
Typhoid fever	297	322
Diarrhœal diseases	5,418	6,047
Puerperal fever	198	218
Cancer	1,141	1,030
Phthisis	4,994	5,205
Other tuberculous diseases	932	..
Congenital debility	2,710	2,670
Diseases of nervous system	3,358	3,429
Heart diseases	2,396	2,297
Bronchitis	1,292	1,636
Pneumonia	5,383	5,751
Diseases of digestive organs	3,040	3,181
Bright's disease	2,195	2,019
Acute nephritis	490	678
Accident	2,641	2,045
Homicide	71	76
Suicide	384	376

The cases of contagious diseases reported were diphtheria, 11,093; croup, 306; measles, 11,850; scarlet fever, 4,728; typhoid fever, 1,002; smallpox, 5.

The population was estimated on July 1, 1896, at 1,934,077, and the death-rate for the year is given as 21·52, as compared with 23·11 in 1895.

The immigration returns show a slight increase in respect of *Immigration.* the total number of immigrants over those of 1895, the numbers

(2396)

being 233,394, as compared with 229,370. There was a considerable decrease in the number from Great Britain and Ireland, as well as from Russia and Germany; on the other hand immigrants from Italy increased from 42,271 to 67,581; the countries and destination are noted below:—

Country.	Male.	male.	Total. 1896.	Total. 1895.
	Number.	Number.	Number.	Number.
Great Britain	5,707	2,999	8,706	16,592
Ireland	9,486	12,263	21,749	26,989
Austria-Hungary	26,743	15,411	42,154	42,185
Belgium	607	306	913	899
Denmark	1,362	986	2,348	3,477
France	1,080	846	1,926	2,587
Germany	11,873	10,022	21,895	24,545
Greece	1,593	43	1,636	1,113
Italy	50,321	17,260	67,581	42,271
Netherlands	801	551	1,352	1,229
Norway	3,518	2,002	5,520	6,995
Portugal	1,035	967	2,002	1,350
Roumania	376	337	713	633
Russia	19,562	10,842	30,404	36,347
Spain	175	27	202	154
Sweden	7,156	6,553	13,709	15,259
Switzerland	1,154	695	1,849	2,444
Turkey	75	22	97	4,024
Other countries	5,463	3,175	8,638	277
Total	148,087	85,307	233,394	229,370

Destination.	Number.
North Atlantic States	186,773
South Atlantic States	2,235
North Central States	35,383
South Central States	2,890
Western and Pacific	6,113
Total	233,394

In addition to the above, 2,549 immigrants were refused—1,920 as being paupers, or likely to become a public charge, 621 as contract labourers, 6 as insane, and 1 as an idiot; 1 on account of disease.

Total immigration into the United States. — In his annual report on the total immigration into the United States for the fiscal year ended September 30, 1896, the Commissioner-General gives the number landed during that period as 340,468, of whom there were among those over 14 years of age 5,066 who could not write, and 78,130 who could neither read nor write; of the latter 31,374 came from Italy, 12,816 from Russia proper, 12,154 from Hungary, 6,107 from Bohemia and Moravia, 5,281 from other parts of Austria-Hungary, 2,473 from Ireland,

1,566 from Arabia and Syria, and 1,589 from Portugal. From the data obtainable as to the number annually returning to their own country, the Commissioner-General doubts there having been any material increase in the foreign born population of the United States since 1893.

The report of the State Board of Mediation and Arbitration mentions that during the year ended October 31, 1896, the number of strikes and lock-outs was 246, as compared with 417 in 1895. This noticeable decrease is attributed mainly to the continuance of depression in business, and the consequent increase in the number of unemployed hands, but it is also considered to be in some measure due to conservative action on the part of the working men who have learned by experience that striking should not be resorted to till other means have been exhausted.

Strikes.

The most important labour disturbances were the house-smiths' strike in New York city; the coat-makers' strike in New York and Brooklyn; and the grain-shovellers' strike or lock-out in Buffalo.

The house-smiths' strike lasted about three weeks, and ended in the defeat of the workmen.

The coat-makers' strike began on July 21, when about 10,000 men in the employ of coat contractors in New York and Brooklyn went on strike in obedience to orders issued by the Brotherhood of Tailors; their demands were for higher wages and the abolition of task work. The Brooklyn contractors acceded to the demands of their men, but the strike continued in New York during the month of August. On September 1 the strike was practically at an end, although it had not been declared off, about 4,000 men had arranged with the contractors and returned to work, although not receiving the increased wages which they had demanded, and there was little employment for the remainder, as the clothing trade was unusually depressed.

In March, 1896, the grain-shovellers at Buffalo formed a Union, and they soon afterwards made a demand for higher wages and for the abolition of the "boss saloon." It appears that for many years it had been customary for the foreman of a gang to keep a drinking shop (boss saloon), which the men under his superintendence found it to their advantage to patronise. The contractor agreed to the abolition of the "boss saloon," but the Board of Mediation were satisfied after investigation that the differences between him and the new union on one side, and the local union on the other side, could not be adjusted, and the most that could be accomplished was to secure pledges for the future.

Nearly all the building strikes were in New York city, and many were caused by dissensions in the ranks of organised labour. The United Brotherhood of Carpenters and Joiners fell out with the other Carpenters' Union and with the Board of Walking Delegates; there was a quarrel during the greater part of the year between two unions of electrical workers, and the Painters' Union disagreed with the Progressive Varnishers' Union as to the jurisdiction in varnishing buildings, and refused to abide by the decision of the Board of Walking Delegates.

UNITED STATES.

Trade and Commerce.

Anthracite coal.

The amount of anthracite coal which was brought to market in 1896 was somewhat over 43,000,000 tons, whereas the corrected figures for 1895 were about 46,500,000 tons, the heaviest output in any calendar year in the history of the anthracite coal trade. Prior to 1896 every company mined without limit, the market was overstocked, prices ruled low, and in some instances mining was carried on at a loss. In January, 1896, the different companies came to an agreement to restrict the output of coal, but the result was only a partial success. During the five months from January to June inclusive, the production was reduced by about 2,500,000 tons, as compared with the previous year, but for the remainder of the year full normal amounts were mined, the depression in business consequent on the silver agitation reduced the demand, and stocks had again accumulated at the end of the year.

Iron and teel.

The average price of iron was, for almost all kinds, lower in 1896 than in 1895, and although on an average for the whole year both steel billets and steel rails show a slight advance, the prices of these as well as of all classes of iron were much lower at the end of the year, largely in consequence of the breaking up of a number of combinations in these trades. The average price of Bessemer pig-iron was 12 dol. 14 c. per ton, as compared with 12 dol. 72 c. in 1895; those of steel rails and steel billets 28 dol. and 18 dol. 83 c. per ton, as against 24 dol. 41 c. and 18 dol. 49 c. per ton respectively in 1895. In December, 1896, the price of steel rails was reduced to 25 dol. per ton, and on January 1, 1897, steel billets were 15 dol. 50 c., and Bessemer pig-iron 11 dol. 25 c. per ton.

Comparative prices of staple commodities.

The tendency of prices of staple commodities was unfavourable during the greater part of 1896, but showed some slight recovery during the last quarter if the whole of the 108 articles included in a table published in Bradstreets are taken into consideration.

A comparison of prices on January 1, 1897, with those ruling on January 1, 1896, shows 33 articles higher, 72 lower, and 3 practically the same. If the comparison be made with prices on October 1, 1896, the quotations show 40 articles higher, 40 lower, and 28 practically the same. As regards quotations which were higher on the 1st of January than at the same date in 1896, the most conspicuous advances were in flour, wheat, potatoes, leather, Australian wool, Bessemer pig-iron, and anthracite coal, while there was a noticeable rise in the prices of hops, nails, glass, opium, rubber, and live-stock; the decreases in price for most of the food products, for hides, cotton, wool, hemp, raw silk, flax, print cloths, sheetings, and ginghams, as well as for eastern and southern pig-iron, steel, tin-plates, silver, aluminium, lead, tin, and quicksilver, soft coal and coke, petroleum, linseed and cotton-seed oils, turpentine, brick, pine and spruce timber, tobacco, and paper, and almost all the drugs and chemicals noted in the list. A remarkable feature in this table is the price of bread taken in conjunction with that of flour and wheat. The following were the prices of these three articles :—

Articles.		April 1, 1896.	July 1, 1896.	October 1, 1896.	January 1, 1897.
		Dol. c.	Dol. c.	Dol. c.	Dol. c.
Wheat	Per bushel ...	0 79¼	0 64¾	0 78⅜	1 6¼
Flour	Per barrel ...	3 40	3 25	3 25	4 25
Bread	Per loaf ...	0 4	0 5	0 5	0 5

From the returns of the Silk Association of America, it Silk. appears that the imports of silk manufactures during the year 1896 shows a considerable decrease when compared with those of the former year, the total value being returned at about 3,947,000*l*., as compared with about 5,464,600*l*. in 1895. Piece-goods show a falling-off of nearly 900,000*l*. in value, the figures being about 2,141,400*l*. in 1896, and about 3,020,000*l*. in 1895. The diminution amounted to about 190,000*l*. in velvets, and to about the same in goods made of silk and cotton.

The only article in which there was any appreciable increase was laces, which were imported to the value of about 480,000*l*., as compared with about 412,000*l*. in 1895. These figures include imports amounting to about 6 per cent. of the whole at Boston, Chicago, and Philadelphia, in addition to those at New York. The imports of raw material, viz., raw silk, waste silk noils, and pierced cocoons at all ports in the United States, decreased in even a greater degree than that of manufactured silk goods, the figures being 5,661,630 lbs., valued at about 2,970,000*l*., as against 11,070,941 lbs., valued at about 6,240,000*l*. in 1895.

The total importation of dry goods at the port of New Dry goods. York shows considerable decrease as compared with 1895, although the value was somewhat greater than in 1894. The values for the three years are approximately as follows:—21,178,000*l*. in 1896; 29,370,000*l*. in 1895, and 18,800,000*l*. in 1894. The largest reductions are shown in manufactures of wool, 6,400,000*l*., as compared with close on 10,000,000*l*. in 1895—and manufactures of silk as noted above. Manufactures of cotton show 4,635,000*l*. in 1896, and 5,200,000*l*. in 1895.

There were considerable stocks of cotton goods on hand at the Cotton goods. commencement of the year, and further accumulations in January, when prices declined and trade was poor. There was a slightly better demand in February, but this was of a temporary character, and in March some of the leading coloured goods mills began to curtail their production. This action became more general later, and it was calculated that during four weeks of the months of July and August, out of a total capacity of 16,800,000 spindles in the country, nearly half had shortened their output. This led to a certain recovery in prices, but the tendency on the whole was downward in all staple descriptions of cotton goods. In brown sheets and drills, in bleached cotton and coarse coloured cotton, the opening prices of the year were the highest, and the closing prices show a decline varying from 5 to 12½ per cent.

The fall in the price of ginghams was as much as 40 per cent at one time, and so small was the demand that some mills abandoned the gingham trade altogether, and others diverted a large proportion of their looms to other purposes. It is stated that prints never were sold cheaper than last year, and that in indigo blues, shirtings, turkey-reds, &c., the spring and summer months saw business done at the lowest price ever recorded. It would appear that in cotton cloths the productive capacity has been increased while the consumption has fallen off, but there is a considerable increase in the export to China (73,250,000 yards), British North America (19,700,000 yards), and Africa (15,400,000 yards), in the fiscal year ended June 30, 1896. These figures show that the export to British North America has nearly trebled, and in the other cases nearly doubled. On the other hand there was a slight decrease in the exports to South America; about three-fourths of these exports are heavy brown goods. The imports at New York show a decrease of about 10 per cent. in manufactured cotton goods, and of about 30 per cent. in unmanufactured.

Woollen goods. The business in woollen goods is stated to have been even more unsatisfactory than that in cotton, the year to have been one of unbroken dulness in fabrics for men's wear, and of moderate results only for dress goods. The stoppage of machinery in woollen mills at one time in the late summer was estimated to amount to over 60 per cent. of the productive capacity of the country. Towards the close of the year there was an improvement, but on the whole stocks were ample during the year, and there was a steady depreciation in their value. The imports at New York show a decrease of about 30 per cent. in unmanufactured wool, and of about 38 per cent. in manufactured woollen goods.

Flax Increases and decreases in imports at New York. Free list. The value of the imports of manufactures of flax was about 2,576,000*l*., showing a reduction of nearly 20 per cent. as compared with 1895, but a considerable advance on the import of 1895. The imports into New York on the free list according to the present tariff show the following decreases:—chemicals, 22 per cent.; coffee, 14 per cent.; indiarubber, 20 per cent.; skins, 35 per cent.; and tin bars or pigs, 27 per cent.

Dutiable articles. In dutiable articles, chemicals show a decrease of 20 per cent.; furs, 60 per cent.; gloves and manufactured leather, 42 per cent.; tobacco, 41 per cent.; and tin-plates 26 per cent. The imports of sugar show an increase of 42 per cent., the value being over 10,250,000*l*.

Exports from New York. As regards exports from New York, there was a decrease in bacon and ham and in lard, but a considerable increase in the export of fresh beef. There were also large increases in the export of copper, machinery, manufactures of iron and steel. A return of the principal articles of export is given below.

Cattle. The export of cattle from New York amounted to 123,563 head, as against 98,288 in 1895. During the last two years the export has been larger from Boston than from New York; the other shipping ports are Philadelphia and Baltimore. The shipments have increased at all these ports, and the aggregate is about 100,000 head more than in 1895.

Cheese. The imports of cheese at New York have increased in a somewhat higher ratio than the exports, and the United States Department of Agriculture, in a study comparing the making of cheese in this country with that in Europe, draws attention to the fact that imports are increasing, and exports diminishing in a very marked degree. The reasons given are the competition with Canada, the Canadian cheese having a better reputation in England, and a decline in consumption in England, owing to the importation of Australian and South American fresh beef and mutton. In other quarters it has been pointed out that the manufacture of filled cheese is allowed in the United States, whereas it is prohibited in Canada.

Scotch herrings.

The trade in Scotch herrings has grown up almost entirely within the last eight or nine years, and it is said to be gaining ground in New York, the competition being chiefly with the Dutch herrings. Other sources of supply are Sweden and Norway and Canada. The total importation of pickled and salted herrings into the United States is about 30,000,000 lbs. per annum, of which about one-quarter comes from the United Kingdom. The demand for these fish is greatest in the months of July and August, but the market is often overstocked at this season, and it has been suggested that it might be of advantage to distribute the supplies more evenly over the whole course of the year.

Exports to South Africa.

The export trade to South Africa for the fiscal year ended June 30, 1895, amounted to about 1,000,000*l*., and the increase had been progressive since 1892. For the fiscal year ended June 30, 1896, the amount was about 2,000,000*l*., or double that of the previous year, the increase being due chiefly to direct steamer communication. No regular lines exist, but American firms now send from three to four steamers a month to South Africa, whereas formerly the trade was dependent on sailing vessels. Large quantities of bicycles, patent medicines, furniture, and farm implements have been sent out there lately, and as regards farm implements, some of the older patterns which had become difficult to sell here, in consequence of recent inventions, are said to have found a ready market. There is also a large export of hardware, doors, sashes, blinds, castings, &c., and, in fact, the cargoes sent out present a wonderful variety of goods. It takes on an average 30 days for a steamer to reach South Africa. Boston was at one time the chief port for shipping, the bulk of the business is now, however, done from New York.

UNITED STATES.

RETURN of Principal Articles of Export from New York during the Years 1896–95.

Articles.		1896. Quantity.	1896. Value.	1895. Quantity.	1895. Value.
			£		£
Agricultural implements	...	...	722,375	...	877,041
Bacon and ham	Tons	101,161	3,488,435	119,850	4,566,484
Beef—					
Fresh	,,	72,974	2,404,903	42,712	1,650,758
Canned	,,	13,218	470,983	15,612	566,911
Cured and salted	,,	16,766	393,679	17,004	441,513
Barley	Bushels	7,997,070	591,529	...	...
Books, maps, &c.	...	...	290,361	...	...
Butter	Tons	9,615	605,477	4,970	335,996
Carriages, and parts thereof	...	...	313,402	...	...
Cattle (live)	Number	123,563	2,417,616	98,288	1,935,860
Cheese	Tons	13,865	533,720	13,702	505,929
Copper	,,	92,942	4,056,417	48,142	1,898,633
Cotton—					
Raw	,,	169,574	6,215,434	162,349	5,249,070
Cloths	Yards	194,317,463	2,186,362	156,707,244	1,744,233
Cycles	...	...	557,983	...	...
Drugs and patent medicines	...	...	1,072,973	...	...
Flax (seed)	Bushels	3,849,979	623,587	...	...
Flour	Barrels	4,817,435	3,602,868	4,516,145	3,325,648
Fruit	...	...	655,745	...	...
Furs and hides	...	...	1,039,422	...	...
Hardware	...	...	581,778	...	...
Hops	Tons	5,764	257,026	7,186	313,585
Horses	Number	17,533	497,460	...	...
Indian corn	Bushels	19,100,058	1,398,357	19,626,817	1,843,687
Indiarubber (manufactures of)	...	...	222,535	...	...
Instruments (scientific)	...	...	418,343	...	...
Iron and steel manufactures	...	...	1,476,267	...	...
Lard	Tons	111,330	2,675,699	136,476	4,248,043
Leather	...	...	1,374,874	...	1,163,226
Machinery	...	...	2,586,186	...	1,545,441
Oats	Bushels	15,880,250	831,486	...	...
Oil—					
Illuminating	Gallons	491,260,824	6,263,139	421,988,543	5,398,822
Lubricating	,,	39,570,692	1,088,397	33,762,469	950,582
Cotton seed	,,	11,860,302	655,822	...	...
Oilcake and meal	Tons	90,686	366,620	92,473	419,605
Paper	...	...	289,340	...	...
Paraffin and paraffin wax	Tons	39,554	723,589	...	...
Pork	,,	18,108	407,470	20,774	588,406
Rye	Bushels	3,568,858	300,708	...	...
Sewing machines	...	...	546,352	...	554,747
Specie and bullion	...	...	20,807,283	...	27,990,391
Tallow	Tons	21,106	373,130	...	...
The oil	,,	32,401	920,247	28,512	1,050,537
Timber	...	...	517,106	...	...
Tobacco (leaf)	Tons	61,754	2,337,166	72,522	2,776,516
Wheat	Bushels	18,476,263	2,710,092	20,339,263	2,739,782
Wood (manufactures)	...	...	894,723	...	...

NEW YORK.

RETURN of Principal Articles of Import into New York during the Years 1896-95.

Articles.		1896. Quantity.	1896. Value. £	1895. Quantity.	1895. Value. £
FREE.					
Art works	...	...	605,281	...	686,037
Argols	Tons	9,183	431,116	12,760	438,224
Books	...	...	264,460	...	285,227
Burlaps	...	...	663,797	...	...
Chemicals	...	...	971,208	...	1,338,206
Cocoa, and shells of	Tons	10,948	476,522	11,567	554,350
Coffee	,,	245,035	13,799,762	236,553	15,934,519
Cork, wood, or bark	...	...	210,010	...	...
Cotton (unmanufactured)	Tons	3,565	197,115	5,199	255,365
Feathers and downs (crude)	...	...	390,187	...	413,053
Fruits	...	...	345,029	...	317,723
Gum	...	...	1,098,590	...	1,101,612
Indiarubber	Tons	14,422	2,982,145	17,299	3,602,982
Jute, manilla, and sisal grass	,,	103,549	964,367	118,069	903,487
Liquorice root	,,	32,463	231,513	32,619	238,968
Matting	...	...	441,074	...	...
Oils	...	...	465,609	...	531,571
Skins	...	...	3,673,925	...	5,656,595
Silk (raw)	Tons	486	806,536	1,456	1,703,452
Soda (nitrate of)	,,	79,133	491,654	75,391	488,779
Spices	,,	10,361	277,802	...	...
Sugar	,,	41,672	617,315	...	...
Tea	,,	25,768	1,485,529	22,151	1,664,001
Tin bars and pigs	,,	16,380	960,939	21,638	1,321,134
Wool	,,	26,313	1,274,555	38,114	1,784,630
DUTIABLE.					
Cheese	Tons	4,318	264,537	3,973	251,322
Chemicals	...	...	633,747	...	923,509
China	...	...	1,027,555	...	1,085,058
Coal-tar colours	...	...	488,845	...	506,984
Dry goods—					
Cotton (manufactured)	...	...	4,764,802	...	5,317,336
Silk	...	...	3,821,814	...	5,578,847
Woollen	...	...	5,907,775	...	9,634,406
Fish	...	...	440,730	...	454,774
Flax and hemp (manufactures)	...	...	2,765,473	...	3,205,712
Fruits and nuts	...	...	1,991,228	...	1,812,747
Furs	...	...	582,818	...	1,432,188
Glass	...	...	905,009	...	1,223,830
Gloves and manufactures of leather	...	...	991,013	...	1,726,466
Jewellery and precious stones	...	...	1,052,263	...	1,401,132
Metals, N.E.S.	...	...	573,874	...	637,003
Paper, and manufactures of	...	...	431,920	...	448,189
Specie and bullion	...	...	18,146,793	...	6,571,225
Sugar	...	...	10,251,232	...	7,272,873
Tobacco (leaf)	...	...	1,324,520	...	2,257,017
Tin-plates	Tons	59,789	591,999	83,112	848,153
Wines and spirits	...	...	1,172,060	...	1,301,659

UNITED STATES.

TABLE showing Total value of all Articles Exported from and Imported to New York from and to Foreign Countries during the Year 1896.

Country.	Exports.	Imports.
	£	£
Great Britain and Ireland	29,991,025	16,169,094
British possessions	7,253,288	5,720,143
Germany	7,518,312	13,654,122
France and possessions	3,809,385	9,112,100
Belgium	3,418,868	1,530,515
Spain and possessions	1,723,986	4,604,157
Netherlands	3,870,635	1,668,303
United States of Colombia	641,036	781,215
Central American States	630,291	1,055,482
Italy	1,907,514	3,101,196
Brazil	1,814,236	12,014,331
China	1,461,170	2,023,735
Denmark and possessions	580,886	109,019
Venezuela	698,693	2,036,125
Portugal	432,039	383,612
Argentine Republic	988,029	610,349
Mexico	889,897	1,671,027
Hayti	682,364	189,567
Sweden and Norway	714,540	363,779
Japan	863,430	1,217,700
Chile	491,709	749,574
San Domingo	177,925	552,483
Uruguay	200,090	355,464
Austria	410,766	1,200,459
Russia	432,603	326,066
Peru	183,251	102,922
Other countries	1,418,294	6,794,930
Total	73,204,262	88,097,469

NEW YORK.

Port of New York.

Table showing Countries to and from which Specie was Imported and Exported during the Years 1896-95.

Country.	1896. Imports. Currency. Dollars.	1896. Imports. Sterling. £	1896. Exports. Currency. Dollars.	1896. Exports. Sterling. £	1895. Imports. Currency. Dollars.	1895. Imports. Sterling. £	1895. Exports. Currency. Dollars.	1895. Exports. Sterling. £
Great Britain	47,865,419	9,573,084	59,267,462	11,853,492	13,389,193	2,677,839	97,760,123	19,552,025
France	18,713,535	3,742,707	11,696,008	2,339,202	8,498,889	1,699,778	13,999,173	2,799,834
Germany	3,683,571	736,714	28,536,172	5,707,234	1,319,297	263,860	13,113,704	2,622,741
Cuba	7,384,150	1,476,830	52,035	10,407	1,505,789	301,158	9,322,955	1,864,591
Mexico	8,226,005	1,645,201	66,641	13,328	5,309,482	1,061,896	399	80
Other countries	4,861,288	972,257	4,418,100	883,620	2,833,472	566,694	5,755,603	1,151,120
Total	90,733,968	18,146,793	104,036,418	20,807,283	32,856,122	6,571,225	139,951,957	27,990,391

UNITED STATES.

TABLE showing Shipments of Grain from the Port of New York to Great Britain and the Continent of Europe, with the Nationality of the Vessels, for the Years 1896-95.

Countries.	Steam Vessels.	Sailing Vessels.	1896. Total Number of Vessels.	1896. Total Number of Bushels.	1895. Number of Vessels.	1895. Number of Bushels.
Great Britain	623	8	631	46,601,698	499	28,509,783
Belgium	32	...	32	3,118,798	48	2,466,669
Netherlands	75	...	75	3,820,173	66	2,274,708
Germany	162	...	162	10,748,033	143	5,695,932
France	27	...	27	1,187,990	15	424,313
Portugal	16	1	17	1,215,592	16	1,266,141
Denmark	26	1	27	1,264,934	20	743,824
Italy	1	...	1	21,315	2	94,118
Spain	1	...	1	73,062	2	369,538
Norway	6	...	6	588,447	...	...
America	5	3	8	513,365	1	48,000
Austria	3	1	4	138,005	2	77,272
Nicaragua	...	1	1	50,550	...	...
Total	977	15	992	69,341,962	814	41,970,298

The grain shipments for 1896 were as follows :—

Name of Grain.	In— Steam Vessels.	In— Sailing Vessels.	Total Quantity. 1896.	Total Quantity. 1895.
	Bushels.	Bushels.	Bushels.	Bushels.
Wheat	21,340,781	253,635	21,594,416	22,981,970
Maize	15,944,449	236,570	16,181,019	17,966,126
Rye	3,438,708	..	3,438,708	..
Oats	15,673,414	7,681	15,681,095	878,377
Barley	7,634,933	108,997	7,743,930	11,200
Buckwheat	1,163,068	1,348	1,164,416	96,723
Flaxseed	3,538,378	..	3,538,378	..
Peas	..	..	..	35,902

NEW YORK.

RETURN of all Shipping at the Port of New York during the Year 1896.

ENTERED.

Nationality.	Number of Vessels.			Tonnage.		
	Sailing.	Steam.	Total.	Sailing.	Steam.	Total.
Great Britain and colonies ...	586	1,501	2,087	345,521	3,094,716	3,440,237
United States	578	329	907	292,874	824,926	1,117,800
Austrian	2	11	13	1,629	19,714	21,343
Belgian	1	53	54	834	178,356	179,190
Brazilian	1	...	1	834	...	834
Colombian	...	...	...	...	...	...
Dutch	9	139	148	7,502	308,393	315,895
Danish	12	31	43	6,610	54,854	61,464
French	1	103	104	1,225	286,191	287,416
German	39	446	485	47,706	1,160,957	1,208,663
Haytian	5	...	5	831	...	831
Hawaiian	1	...	1	989	...	989
Italian	55	4	59	43,414	5,666	49,080
Nicaraguan	...	...	...	...	...	...
Norwegian	41	213	254	35,906	144,470	180,376
Portuguese	1	16	17	442	29,301	29,743
Russian	1	2	3	1,085	1,298	2,383
Spanish	3	40	43	995	61,328	62,323
Swedish	2	...	2	1,358	...	1,358
Total	1,338	2,888	4,226	789,755	6,170,170	6,959,925

CLEARED.

Nationality.	Number of Vessels.			Tonnage.		
	Sailing.	Steam.	Total.	Sailing.	Steam.	Total.
Great Britain and colonies ...	686	1,382	2,068	388,749	2,934,446	3,323,195
United States	420	328	748	253,852	840,467	1,094,319
Austrian	2	4	6	1,629	6,668	8,297
Belgian	...	53	53	...	178,331	178,331
Brazilian	3	...	3	2,502	...	2,502
Colombian	1	...	1	157	...	157
Dutch	12	138	150	11,608	305,419	317,027
Danish	15	32	47	8,029	54,506	62,535
French	6	108	114	6,721	299,037	305,758
German	41	394	435	48,697	1,036,735	1,085,432
Haytian	5	...	5	866	...	866
Hawaiian	3	...	3	3,677	...	3,677
Italian	48	2	50	39,658	2,833	42,491
Nicaraguan	2	...	2	3,405	...	3,405
Norwegian	45	218	263	39,169	136,222	175,391
Portuguese	1	17	18	442	30,950	31,392
Russian	...	1	1	...	649	649
Spanish	3	40	43	996	61,282	62,278
Swedish	2	...	2	806	...	806
Total	1,295	2,717	4,012	810,963	5,887,545	6,698,508

(2396)

UNITED STATES.

Return of the Number of Seamen who have been Engaged, Discharged, Left Behind, Reported Dead, or Deserted, or who have been Relieved at the British Consulate-General, New York, and showing the Total Number of British and Foreign Sailors who were Engaged, Discharged, &c., from British Ships, with the Amount of Wages paid at the Consulate-General to Seamen on discharge from their Ships, and from Hospital or Jail; and also showing the Number of New Agreements entered into during the Year 1896.

Seamen.										Nationality.		Wages.			Agreements.
Engaged.	Discharged.	Left Behind.			Dead.			Deserted.	Relieved.	British.	Foreign.	Total Number of Seamen.	Paid on Discharge from Vessel.	Paid on Discharge from Hospital or Jail.	Total Wages Paid.	Number Opened.
		In Hospital.	In Jail.	Total.	At Sea.	On Shore.	Total.									
9,763	8,603	173	9	182	50	26	76	1,601	327	10,039	10,513	20,552	Dol. c. 399,766 09	Dol. c. 3,020 22	Dol. c. 402,786 31	174

PROVIDENCE, RHODE ISLAND.

Mr. Vice-Consul Stockwell reports as follows:—

During the year 1896 business was slow in all departments of trade and commerce. When politics lead as they do always in a presidential year all other interests fall behind.

The customs district of Providence includes the ports of Providence, Pawtucket, Pawtuxet, and East Greenwich. The total receipts for the year ending June 30, 1896, were 232,329 dol. 96 c. Arrivals from foreign ports, 107; tonnage of the port, 34,314 tons; duties collected from January 1 to December 31, 1896, 188,278 dol. 51 c. In the State are two other customs districts, namely, the district of Newport and the district of Bristol and Warren.

The bank clearings show the volume of trade. In 1895 the bank clearings amounted to 280,809,700 dol., and in 1896 256,286,200 dol. The largest amount that ever passed through the Providence Clearing-house was 290,908,500 dol. in 1892. The average rate of discount of commercial paper during the year was 6 per cent.

The print cloth market was not particularly active at any time during the year. The price of 64's at the beginning of the year was 3 c. the highest price of the year, the lowest being $2\frac{7}{16}$ c. The average price was the lowest for many years. At the close of the year the price was nominal at $2\frac{1}{2}$ c. The total stock of 64's in the country at the close of the year was 2,300,000 pieces.

The price of middling cotton in this market ranged from $7\frac{3}{16}$ c. to 9 c. The northern cotton mills used about 500,000 bales less than last year. The cotton mills in the State have been in operation about eight-tenths of the year. Wages generally remain unchanged. In some cotton and woollen mills there has been a slight reduction of wages as the result of the "re-adjustment of wages."

The wool market has been very dull, and without any new features. The following table, in the first column, shows the price of wool in January, 1896, and in the second column the price in December, 1896:—

	January, 1896.	December, 1896.
	Cents.	Cents.
Ohio XX and above	19 to 20	19 to 20
Ohio and Michigan	16 18	16 19
„ „ No. 1	20 22	19 20
Fine unwashed	12 14	11 13
„ unmerchantable	13 15	12 14
Half-blood, unwashed, combed	17 18	15 18
Three-eights and one-quarter blood, Ind. and Ky.	18 19	16 17
Spring Texas	10 13	8 11
Fine and medium Montana	11 14	9 11
„ „ Wyoming	8 11	8 10
North Spring California	12 15	12 13
Eastern Oregon	9 13	7 11
A super. ch. brushed	31 31	29 31
B super. ch. „	28 29	27 28
Australian combing	19 24	20 26
„ clothing	18 24	20 27
Crossbreds	22 24	22 23
Cape and Natal	14 16	14 17
Montevideo	15 16	15 16
Carpet wools—		
Angoras	9 11	9 11
Khorassans	16 17	15 17
Baghdad	14 17	14 17
Aleppos, washed	17 19	16 17
„ unwashed	9 13	8 9
China ball	9 13	8 13
Scotch wool	12 13	12 13

Harbour improvement. The improvement of Providence harbour is in progress. The Secretary of the Navy has authorised the expenditure of 174,500 dol. in making a ship channel 400 feet wide and 25 feet deep at mean low water from Sassafras Point to Conimicut Point. This channel will open this port to the deep draft shipping of the world.

Street improvement. The city of Providence has 207 miles of streets, of which 174 miles are paved either with granite, cobbles, brick, asphalte, vulcanite, or macadam. The amount expended in 1896 on streets was 220,044 dol. 53 c.

Parks. Roger Williams Park, the great breathing place of the city, has been enlarged to include 428 acres, of which 130 are water.

Sewers. An important improvement in sewerage has been made since my last report. Heretofore sewage was deposited by trunk sewers emptying into the river through which the tide ebbs and flows in the heart of the city. By a new system of sewerage the sewage is carried 3 miles below the city and emptied into the bay after passing through precipitation tanks. There is in consequence much less pollution of the river than formerly.

Fires. The total loss by fire in the city of Providence during the year 1896 amounted to 389,717 dol. 4 c. The amount of insurance paid was 326,503 dol. 76 c. The most disastrous fire was the burning of the Masonic Temple in March, causing a loss of 262,315 dol.

Terminal facilities. The question of terminal facilities for railways, referred to in this report for the last 10 years, is near solution. The work of providing facilities demanded by the increase of population and commerce may be completed in another year.

The new State House (in Providence) of marble is in process of construction. The State voted by popular vote to issue bonds to the amount of 1,500,000 dol. to pay the cost. It is believed that the State will be called upon to vote additional bonds before the marble palace is completed. *State House.*

In all the New England States, and in others, the attempt is made in the interest of public health to eradicate the disease among cattle known as tuberculosis. For five years the State through its Board of Agriculture (composed of 12 members) has expended 15,000 to 25,000 dol. annually in this work. A commissioner in each county is appointed, whose duty is to examine cattle and report for slaughter all diseased animals. The owner of the cattle receives half value, as determined by the State appraiser. During the year 1896 the Board caused 561 animals to be killed. In May a law was passed requiring all bovine animals imported into the State to be accompanied by a certificate showing that each animal had been subjected to the tuberculin test. This law is practically identical with laws in Connecticut and Massachusetts passed for a like purpose. *Public health.*

An important improvement for the benefit of general shipping was made at Block Island during the year 1896. On the northern end of the island is a body of water called Great Salt Pond. It was proposed to open the pond and to connect it with the sea. The work began on April 1, 1896, and a channel was made connecting the pond with the surrounding water. The south jetty has been extended into the sea 1,200 feet, and up to the close of the year, the total cost was 53,547 dol. Block Island is off Point Judith, 15 miles away in the deep sea, where the sea is as rough as anywhere on the Atlantic coast—where many vessels have gone to pieces. Great Salt Pond will be as intended a harbour of refuge, and as was anticipated all classes of vessels have already utilised it. The first month it was available, 551 vessels found harbour there. During eight months, 3,054 schooners, 2,379 sloops, 560 steamers, and 45 barges—a total of 6,038 vessels. During the year 1896 11,750 schooners, 926 steamers, 1,463 sloops, 25 ships, 28 barques, and 17 brigs—total, 14,209—passed the life-saving station on the east side of Block Island, and 6,433 schooners, 1,589 steamers, 1,200 sloops, and 51 barques passed the life-saving station on the west side of the island. This may show that in a time of storm, Great Salt Pond may be a convenient harbour of refuge. *Block Island. Harbour of refuge.*

The agitation of the "good roads" question, started by bicyclists, is bearing abundant fruit. The State is now building half-mile samples of improved road in different parts of the commonwealth. The question of wide tires, also, has invaded the halls of legislation. It is proposed to pass a law requiring all heavy teaming to be done on wide tires on wagons with rear axle longer than the front axle. Rhode Island has not yet ordered *Good roads.*

Convict labour.

its convicts to work on the highways, but, outside of New England, the example has been set, and the employment of convicts on highways may become more general.

Annex A.—RETURN of Shipping at the Port of Providence during the Year 1896.

ENTERED.

Nationality.	Sailing. Number of Vessels.	Tonnage.
British	79	8,240
American	16	3,902
Danish	1	476
Italian	2	1,029
Total	98	13,647
„ 1895	106	17,651

CLEARED.

Nationality.	Sailing. Number of Vessels.	Tonnage.
British	75	7,334
American	7	2,651
Total	82	9,985
„ 1895	81	11,448

Annex B.—RETURN of Principal Article of Export from Providence during the Year 1895.

Article.	Value.
Coal	£ 958

RETURN of Principal Articles of Import into Providence during the Years 1896–95.

Articles.	Value. 1896.	Value. 1895.
	£	£
Dry goods	39,514	48,922
Chemicals	15,809	26,506
Metals	22,229	45,220
Wool	..	31,628
Lumber	29,571	..
Liquors	3,566	3,293
Precious stones	34,556	..
All others	30,732	79,726
Total	175,977	235,295

Annex C.—TABLE showing the Total Value of all Articles Exported from and Imported into Providence from and to all Countries during the Years 1896–95.

Countries.	Exports. 1896.	Exports. 1895.	Imports. 1896.	Imports. 1895.
	£	£	£	£
Austria	..	..	8,600	2,336
Belgium	..	..	7,789	1,768
British East Indies	..	..	107	49
British West Indies	..	..	7,085	14,312
Canada	..	958	29,483	27,118
Cuba	..	..	2,819	2,813
Dutch West Indies	..	..	..	791
Egypt	..	..	..	35
England	..	..	47,277	102,729
France	..	..	38,335	32,781
Germany	..	..	16,677	19,071
Hayti	..	..	1,032	659
Ireland	..	..	310	123
Italy	..	..	1,987	4,506
Japan	..	..	262	924
Netherlands	..	..	550	339
Portugal	..	..	207	271
Scotland	..	..	3,699	3,536
Spain	..	..	6,306	588
Sweden and Norway	..	..	124	7,815
Switzerland	..	..	3,302	4,306
Turkey in Asia	..	..	..	30
Turkey in Europe	..	..	..	19
All others	..	..	25	8,441
Total	..	958	175,976	235,360

LONDON:
Printed for Her Majesty's Stationery Office,
By HARRISON AND SONS,
Printers in Ordinary to Her Majesty.
(75 5 | 97--H & S 2396)

FOREIGN OFFICE.
1897.
ANNUAL SERIES.

N°· 1922.
DIPLOMATIC AND CONSULAR REPORTS ON TRADE AND FINANCE.

UNITED STATES.

REPORT FOR THE YEAR 1896
ON THE
TRADE AND AGRICULTURE OF CALIFORNIA.

REFERENCE TO PREVIOUS REPORT, Annual Series No. 1750

Presented to both Houses of Parliament by Command of Her Majesty,
JUNE, 1897.

LONDON:
PRINTED FOR HER MAJESTY'S STATIONERY OFFICE,
BY HARRISON AND SONS, ST. MARTIN'S LANE,
PRINTERS IN ORDINARY TO HER MAJESTY.

And to be purchased, either directly or through any Bookseller, from
EYRE & SPOTTISWOODE, EAST HARDING STREET, FLEET STREET, E.C., and
32, ABINGDON STREET, WESTMINSTER, S.W.; or
JOHN MENZIES & Co., 12, HANOVER STREET, EDINBURGH, and
90, WEST NILE STREET, GLASGOW; or
HODGES, FIGGIS, & Co., Limited, 104, GRAFTON STREET, DUBLIN.

1897.

[C. 8277—140.] *Price Threepence Halfpenny.*

New Series of Reports.

Reports of the Annual Series have been issued from Her Majesty's Diplomatic and Consular Officers at the following places, and may be obtained from the sources indicated on the title-page:—

No.		Price.	No.		Price.
1806.	Antwerp	1½d.	1864.	Trebizond	1d.
1807.	Ajaccio	1½d.	1865.	Lisbon	2½d.
1808.	Stettin	3d.	1866.	Callao	2d.
1809.	Aleppo	1d.	1867.	Pernambuco	5d.
1810.	Tangier	2½d.	1868.	Naples	1½d.
1811.	Tokio	3½d.	1869.	New Orleans	2½d.
1812.	Madeira	½d.	1870.	Vera Cruz	2½d.
1813.	Vera Cruz	1d.	1871.	Madeira	1d.
1814.	Oporto	1d.	1872.	Jerusalem	1d.
1815.	Hamburg	1½d.	1873.	Ningpo	1d.
1816.	New Orleans	1½d.	1874.	Rio de Janeiro	2½d.
1817.	Bengazi	½d.	1875.	Trieste	1d.
1818.	Marmagao	½d.	1876.	Curaçoa	1d.
1819.	Gothenburg	2d.	1877.	Goa	1d.
1820.	Dar-al-Baida	3d.	1878.	Cagliari	1d.
1821.	Erzeroum	½d.	1879.	Guayaquil	1d.
1822.	Munich	2½d.	1880.	Havana	1½d.
1823.	Samoa	½d.	1881.	Reykjavik (Iceland)	1d.
1824.	Chinkiang	1d.	1882.	Milan	1½d.
1825.	Jeddah	1d.	1883.	Baltimore	1d.
1826.	Sofia	1½d.	1884.	Cettinjé	½d.
1827.	Mexico	2d.	1885.	Bilbao	2½d.
1828.	Teneriffe	3½d.	1886.	Florence	1½d.
1829.	Batoum	1d.	1887.	Brest	1½d.
1830.	Cadiz	1d.	1888.	Marseilles	1½d.
1831.	Martinique	1d.	1889.	Wuhu	1d.
1832.	Odessa	1d.	1890.	Chinkiang	1d.
1833.	Ghilan	1d.	1891.	Malaga	1d.
1834.	Old Calabar	6½d.	1892.	Antwerp	½d.
1835.	Tamsui	1d.	1893.	Amsterdam	1d.
1836.	Copenhagen	½d.	1894.	Galveston	2d.
1837.	Salonica	1½d.	1895.	Piræus	2½d.
1838.	Honolulu	½d.	1896.	Stettin	2½d.
1839.	Buenos Ayres	2d.	1897.	Martinique	1½d.
1840.	Para	1d.	1898.	Corunna	2½d.
1841.	Bolivia	2d.	1899.	Calais	1d.
1842.	Washington	3d.	1900.	Honolulu	1d.
1843.	Berlin	2d.	1901.	Riga	2d.
1844.	Uganda	1d.	1902.	Tripoli	1d.
1845.	Belgrade	1½d.	1903.	Batoum	2d.
1846.	Dakar	½d.	1904.	Lorenzo Marques	2d.
1847.	Florence	1½d.	1905.	Batavia	2½d.
1848.	Copenhagen	2d.	1906.	Corfu	1½d.
1849.	Havre	2d.	1907.	Foochow	1½d.
1850.	Serajevo	1d.	1908.	Montevideo	5½d.
1851.	Madrid	2d.	1909.	China	5d.
1852.	La Rochelle	1½d.	1910.	Philadelphia	1½d.
1853.	Chicago	4d.	1911.	Rio Grande do Sul	3½d.
1854.	Berlin	1d.	1912.	Quito	1d.
1855.	Cherbourg	2½d.	1913.	San José	1d.
1856.	Beira	1d.	1914.	Dunkirk	1d.
1857.	Charleston	2½d.	1915.	Samoa	1d.
1858.	Saigon	½d.	1916.	Bordeaux	2½d.
1859.	Suakin	1d.	1917.	Porto Rico	1½d.
1860.	Rouen	2d.	1918.	Galatz	1½d.
1861.	Patras	1½d.	1919.	Christiania	½d.
1862.	Barcelona	2d.	1920.	Copenhagen	3d.
1863.	Amoy	2½d.	1921.	New York	2½d.

No. 1922.

Reference to previous Report, Annual Series No. 1750.

UNITED STATES.

SAN FRANCISCO.

Consul-General Warburton to the Marquess of Salisbury.

(Received at Foreign Office, May 22, 1897.)

My Lord,

I HAVE the honour to inclose my Annual Report on the Trade, Commerce, Agriculture, and other matters of interest for the year 1896, together with Reports from the British Vice-Consuls at Los Angeles and San Diego.

I have not been able to complete this Report sooner, as much of the necessary statistical information has only just been issued.

I have, &c.
(Signed)   J. W. WARBURTON.

Report on the Trade, Commerce, Agriculture and other Matters of Interest of the Consular District of San Francisco for the Year 1896.

TABLE of Contents.

	PAGE
San Francisco—	
General remarks	2
Clearing-houses	3
Banking	3
Insurance	4
Failures	4
Shipping, &c.	5
Freights and charters	6
Seamen's wages	7
Pilotage dues	7
Whaling results	8
Ocean transport of timber	8
Exports	10
Imports	11
Manufactures and other industries	11

(2397)

UNITED STATES.

Table of Contents—continued.

	PAGE
San Francisco—continued—	
Building trades	14
Railway extension	15
Mining, precious metals, &c.	15
Agriculture, &c.	18
Grape and wine crop	19
Wheat, &c.	19
Tobacco growing experiments	19
Fibre growing experiments	20
Vital and social statistics, hygiene, &c.	21
Tuberculosis, great increase of	21
Adulteration of food	23
Tuberculosis among dairy cattle	24
Care of criminal and defective classes: its cost	25
Loss of British trade	27
Activity of Japanese	29
Tramways system	30
Redwood timber	32
Rights of aliens	32
Legislation	33
Labour market and the unemployed	33
Los Angeles—	
Introductory remarks	34
Clearing-houses	34
Mortgages and bonded indebtedness	35
Chino Ranch and beet-sugar industry	36
Mining and mines	36
Advice to emigrants	36
Land frauds	39
Reformatory and free schools	40
Harbour for Los Angeles	41
Mistakes of British importers	41
Industries: wine, spirits, fruit, &c.	42
Freights	43
Population and industries	44
Agricultural products and experiments	45
Social and vital statistics	46
Railway extension, &c.	47
Agriculture, &c.	48
San Diego—	
General remarks	52
Imports and exports	53
Shipping and navigation	54
Coal trade	55
Seamen's wages	55
Quarantine, &c.	55
Freights	56
Teredo-proof piles	57
Population and industries	57
Agriculture, fruit industry, &c.	59
Public works	63
Harbour defences and new jetty	63
Railroads and tramways	63

General remarks. The year 1896 at its opening gave considerable promise of improvements over 1895 but the promise was not fulfilled, and all that can be said is that it compares favourably with that year. The records of the clearing-house are the best indication of the state of business, but as they include speculative business, this must be eliminated in order to arrive at the results of legitimate business.

SAN FRANCISCO.

The monthly statements of the clearing-house for the two years are:— *Clearing-house returns.*

Months.	Amount. 1895.	Amount. 1896.
	Dollars.	Dollars.
January	52,227,411	56,481,993
February	47,926,126	53,371,343
March	56,250,690	56,555,653
April	54,270,043	56,378,886
May	54,618,182	55,009,730
June	59,333,554	54,997,742
July	58,881,368	54,525,646
August	57,462,098	53,608,617
September	54,403,900	55,168,413
October	67,306,667	63,126,138
November	66,006,501	62,371,642
December	63,392,297	61,628,796
Total	692,078,837	683,224,599

showing a decrease in 1896 of 8,854,238 dol. (about 1,770,847*l.**), but there was more speculation in wheat in 1895 than in 1896, and allowing for this, the figures for both years would be about equal.

For a while in the spring and again towards the close of the year there was a very fair amount of business, but the remainder of the year was dull.

The wheat crop was excellent in quality but in quantity fell short of the estimate, and there was an unusually good demand both for wheat and barley.

The condition of all the banks in California, *i.e.*, savings, commercial, private, and foreign, is thus given in the report of the Chamber of Commerce:— *Banking.*

Resources.	Amount. July 31, 1896.	Amount. June 17, 1895.
	Dollars.	Dollars.
Bank premises	6,088,372	6,097,042
Other real estate	10,805,562	7,845,968
Invested in stocks, bonds, and warrants	30,465,786	25,050,676
Loans on real estate	123,050,605	121,134,231
„ stocks, bonds, and warrants	19,191,591	20,505,487
„ other securities	45,460,293	48,238,780
Money on hand	17,570,477	23,329,712
Due from banks and bankers	14,829,278	20,516,307
Other assets	5,404,691	5,304,095
Total resources	272,866,655	278,022,298

* At 5 dol. to the 1*l.*, at which rate all calculations are made in this report.

(2397)

Liabilities.	Amount.	
	July 31, 1896.	June 17, 1895.
	Dollars.	Dollars.
Capital paid up	50,718,216	53,478,316
Reserve fund and profit and loss	23,682,277	24,458,114
Due to depositors	186,322,811	184,333,073
„ banks and bankers	6,804,579	2,977,427
Other liabilities	5,338,772	12,775,368
Total liabilities	272,866,655	278,022,298

NUMBER of California Banks.*

State.	Number.	
	July 31, 1896.	June 17, 1895.
Savings banks	57	59
Commercial banks	174	173
Private banks	20	18
Total	251	250

NOTE.—There were also 31 national banks on July 31, 1896, and the same number on June 17, 1895.

* Under the jurisdiction of the State Board of Bank Commissioners.

Insurance. In my report of last year (Annual Series, 1896, No. 1750) I referred to the war of rates among insurance companies. An agreement has now been come to among the fire insurance companies as to the rates to be charged, which will be those in force before the war began. Those rates, however, will be reduced 20 per cent. when the Municipal Fire Department (referred to in another part of this report) shall be established. The insurance companies have hitherto kept up the Fire Department.

The rate war began in March, 1895, and since then about 20 companies have withdrawn entirely from business on the Pacific Coast.

A Bill was introduced in the State Legislature this year to require all foreign insurance companies to make a deposit of 200,000 dol. (about 40,000*l.*) in bonds or mortgages with the State Treasury in order to qualify them to engage in business in the State. An amendment was moved to the Bill making it applicable to fire insurance only, as, owing to the fact that much of the marine insurance is done by foreign companies, the effect of the measure would have been to greatly put up rates. There was great opposition to the Bill, and it was finally thrown out.

Failures. The failures for the whole State in 1896 are reported as, liabilities, 5,025,223 dol. (about 1,005,044*l.*), with assets, 2,099,678 dol. (about 419,935*l.*).

SAN FRANCISCO.

The following table shows the number and nationality of Shipping. vessels which entered and cleared at this port during the past year:—

Annex A.—RETURN of all Shipping at the Port of San Francisco during the Year 1896.

ENTERED.

Nationality.	Sailing. Number of Vessels.	Sailing. Tons.	Steam. Number of Vessels.	Steam. Tons.	Total. Number of Vessels.	Total. Tons.
British	233	443,923	70	158,797	303	602,720
American, from foreign countries	297	197,477	193	381,163	490	578,640
American, from Atlantic ports of Union	25	52,294	...	...	25	52,294
Hawaiian	20	23,638	12	19,056	32	42,694
Norwegian	4	4,838	13	26,269	17	31,107
German	19	30,525	...	...	19	30,525
Nicaraguan	2	944	13	16,562	15	17,506
Italian	11	17,054	...	...	11	17,054
French	8	10,235	...	...	8	10,235
Others	4	2,509	1	272	5	2,781
Total	623	783,437	302	602,119	925	1,385,556
,, for the year preceding	551	728,346	317	563,029	868	1,291,375

CLEARED.

Nationality.	Sailing. Number of Vessels.	Sailing. Tons.	Steam. Number of Vessels.	Steam. Tons.	Total. Number of Vessels.	Total. Tons.
British	201	345,092	70	158,982	271	504,074
American, to foreign countries	273	211,000	213	378,205	486	589,205
American, to Atlantic ports of Union	10	18,743	...	...	10	18,743
Hawaiian	18	21,014	15	22,908	33	43,922
Norwegian	4	4,961	15	30,180	19	35,141
German	21	32,436	...	...	21	32,436
Nicaraguan	4	2,223	14	17,836	18	20,059
Italian	13	19,596	...	...	13	19,596
French	7	9,388	...	...	7	9,388
Others	5	4,260	1	272	6	4,532
Total	556	668,713	328	608,383	884	1,277,096
,, for the year preceding	503	632,527	311	551,757	814	1,184,284

NOTE.—The entrances and clearances of American ships do not include the coasting trade, whaling, or fishing voyages.

British shipping shows a substantial increase over 1895; 69 more vessels of 157,638 tons having entered and 42 more of 64,458 tons having cleared. The entries of American ships from foreign countries show a decline of 23 ships, as compared with 1895. There was no change in the clearances. Hawaiian, Norwegian, German, and Italian ships show a moderate increase, while Nicaraguan show a decrease. The activity in foreign

(2397)

shipping is accounted for by the increased demand for wheat in Europe, the great bulk of which is carried in foreign bottoms.

Freights and charters.

At the opening of the year grain freights had a declining tendency, and in March went down to 1*l*. From that point they gradually improved, but showed no great activity until the middle of August. On the 18th of that month a strong English wheat market which advanced in a few days nearly 2*s*. per quarter, brought shippers into the market and created a strong chartering demand, resulting in the chartering of about 25 vessels spot and to arrive at from 1*l*. 6*s*. 3*d*. to 1*l*. 7*s*. 6*d*. for orders. A feature of the business was the chartering of a number of steamers, these being willing to accept sailing vessel rates, and giving better options.

From September 1 to 20 there was very active chartering, from 35 to 40 ships having been closed at rates ranging from 1*l*. 6*s*. 3*d*. to 1*l*. 11*s*. 3*d*. according to size and position of ship. After that date chartering ceased owing to an advance in the English wheat market from 1*l*. 6*s*. 9*d*. to 1*l*. 10*s*. 9*d*. per quarter. Spot wheat advanced from 97½ c. to 1 dol. 20 c. per cental (100 lbs.) which was above the English parity.

October was the quietest month for chartering, only two charters for the United Kingdom having been reported. The English wheat market advanced from 1*l*. 10*s*. 6*d*. to 1*l*. 16*s*. 3*d*., which excited the local market to such an extent that prices were 1 dol. 50 c. to 2 dol. per ton above the English parity.

In November the freight market entirely collapsed. On the 9th a large vessel accepted 1*l*. 2*s*. 6*d*. f.o., and on the 16th a vessel was rechartered at 18*s*. 9*d*. f.o., these being the only charters reported for the United Kingdom. Several charters were reported for Australia at lower figures, and at the close of the month 15*s*. for Sydney and 19*s*. for Melbourne, Brisbane, or Adelaide were asked; 1*l*. was the nominal figure for the United Kingdom.

In December not a single charter was reported for the United Kingdom. The nominal rate was about 17*s*. 6*d*. though it was doubtful if 15*s*. could have been obtained. Several vessels were taken for Cape Town at from 1*l*. 1*s*. 3*d*. to 1*l*. For Sydney 12*s*. 6*d*. was asked.

At the close of the year a large number of ships remained in port awaiting better rates.

The following table shows the highest and lowest rates paid for iron wheat ships in each month of the past year, based on the prices paid for spot ships to Cork for orders to the United Kingdom, Havre, Antwerp, or Dunkirk:—

Month.	Lowest.			Highest.		
	£	s.	d.	£	s.	d.
January	1	2	6	1	7	5
February	1	1	3	1	1	3
March	1	0	0	1	2	6
April	1	1	3	1	2	6
May	1	3	9	1	3	9
June	1	4	6	1	8	9
July	1	5	0	1	6	3
August	1	6	3	1	7	6
September	1	6	3	1	11	3
October	1	5	0	1	6	3
November	0	18	9	1	2	6
December*	..	..	..	..	..	..

* No charters.

Seamen's wages. Seamen's wages opened at 4*l.* per month for A.B.'s, and fluctuated between that figure and 3*l.* 10*s.* during the greater part of the year. At the end of December they went down to 3*l.* owing to the dulness in shipping, and the large number of seamen in port.

Seamen's institute. Almost four years have elapsed since the Seamen's Institute was established, and it has proved a great benefit to seamen and apprentices visiting the port. The committee of management, however, finds it difficult to raise sufficient funds for the needs of the institute, and it is well worthy of the support of British shipowners.

Pilotage charges. In my report of last year (Annual Series No. 1750) I said (p. 6) that San Francisco was one of the most expensive ports in the world in regard to charges on shipping, and that an organised effort was being made to obtain a reduction of the port charges.

Among the heavy charges is that for pilotage. A Bill was recently introduced into the State Legislature to amend the pilot service, reduce the charges for pilotage, and abolish the charge of half-rates where pilots are not employed.

The port of San Francisco is a very easy one to enter, and it is alleged that any need there may be for a pilot is fully met by the tug boats, whose captains know the harbour perfectly well; and this opinion is borne out by the fact that insurance companies make no difference in rates between vessels which take pilots and those which do not.

The pilots are appointed for a term of one year, but the license is to be renewed annually unless there be good cause for withdrawing it.

The Bill was thrown out.

Quarantine. Up to last summer the boarding and inspection for health and quarantine purposes of ships entering the port of San Francisco was left to the local health authorities. But in June notices were issued by order of the Federal Government that all such vessels were in future to be inspected by a Federal quarantine officer. It appeared at first as though there would be friction between the Federal and the State officials, to the inconvenience of shipping, but they have worked harmoniously together, and ships are visited by the Federal and the State medical officers.

Catch of whaling fleet. The catch of the Arctic Whaling Fleet during the season of 1896 was:—

Articles.		Quantity.	
		1896.	1895.
Oil	Barrels	7,057	4,390
Bones	Lbs.	201,997	104,595
Ivory	,,	6,640	4,160

Ocean transport of timber. On August 27 last there arrived in this port from the Columbia River, nearly 600 miles north, a raft of logs. This was the second successful experiment of the kind on the west coast. The first successful raft arrived here in August, 1895. It was built by Messrs. Bains and Robertson, of Stella, Washington Territory, who also built the present one. The "Minneola" tug towed both rafts. The 1895 one was towed from bar to bar in $5\frac{1}{4}$ days. The 1896 raft took about the same time.

The shape of each raft was that of a flattened cigar, and both were about equal in size. The 1896 one measured 528 feet long, 52 feet wide, and 31 feet deep in the middle, and contained 6,000 M feet board measure. The value was about 37,000 dol.

The firm built rafts of the same kind on the Atlantic side, and after some disastrous losses made the system a success. The first one they built on this coast in March, 1894, was lost in a storm.

Trade and Commerce.

The following tables show the amount and principal articles of export and import for the years 1895 and 1896.

SAN FRANCISCO.

Annex B.—RETURN of Principal Articles of Export from San Francisco during the Years 1896-95.

Articles.		1896. Quantity.	1896. Value.	1895. Quantity.	1895. Value.
			£		£
Wheat and flour	Centals	15,722,825	3,734,010	13,897,288	2,636,103
Barley	,,	3,852,455	639,507	1,605,285	256,846
Tinned salmon	Cases	579,967	483,423	581,423	480,133
Tinned fruit and vegetables	,,	373,737	247,645	330,409	225,026
Timber	Feet	33,576,556	129,872	17,121,866	57,538
Wine	Gallons	937,874	91,610	707,129	70,517
Quicksilver	Flasks	9,494	63,515	4,265	32,627
Hops	Lbs.	1,350,180	15,276	804,115	11,201
Brandy	Gallons	42,492	8,593	37,294	5,959
Other articles	...	...	2,673,298	...	2,096,143
Total merchandise	...	...	8,086,749	...	5,872,093
Treasure	...	...	3,102,166	...	3,759,934
Grand total	...	...	11,188,915	...	9,632,027

RETURN of Principal Articles of Import to San Francisco during the Years 1896-95.

Articles.		1896. Quantity.	1896. Value.	1895. Quantity.	1895. Value.
			£		£
Sugar	Tons	163,159	2,432,414	122,996	1,465,949
Raw silk	Lbs.	2,067,379	1,218,007	3,782,898	2,230,108
Coal	Tons	898,000	898,000	983,600	1,032,780
Coffee	Lbs.	18,895,057	590,946	21,981,168	676,896
Tin-plates	Boxes	342,688	169,410	435,768	233,288
Rice	Tons	19,441	151,995	21,968	148,212
Tea	Lbs.	5,515,385	141,165	5,822,061	160,150
Cement	Barrels	343,013	90,943	289,624	78,262
Pig-iron	Tons	8,189	20,720	1,847	4,693
Other articles	...	...	1,569,372	...	1,704,783
Total merchandise	...	...	7,282,972	...	7,785,121
Treasure	...	...	2,372,885	...	686,859
Grand total	...	...	9,655,857	...	8,471,980

UNITED STATES.

Annex C.—TABLE showing Total Value of all Articles Exported from and Imported to San Francisco from and to Foreign Countries during the Years 1896–95.

Country.	Exports. 1896.	Exports. 1895.	Imports. 1896.	Imports. 1895.
	£	£	£	£
Great Britain	3,194,639	2,907,846	645,056	774,315
Australasia	1,028,468	271,471	134,520	176,416
Hawaiian Islands	737,412	691,099	2,384,651	1,396,574
Central America	683,892	637,745	488,837	564,582
China	655,793	465,664	1,067,222	1,198,022
Japan	495,304	361,099	1,097,905	2,086,944
Mexico	289,722	246,570	62,608	49,913
South Africa	209,790	20,637	..	..
East Indies	142,654	11,983	245,888	258,211
Belgium	120,740	..	132,037	124,403
Asiatic Russia	113,619	49,384	39,988	69,227
Canada	86,374	73,715	356,395	436,568
Pacific Islands	78,162	65,068	52,462	40,374
South America	53,443	23,072	113,182	141,669
France	18,621	2,777	153,192	162,112
Germany	15,427	17,480	213,047	188,362
Italy	..	..	29,616	27,298
Other countries	162,689	26,483	66,366	90,131
Total merchandise	8,086,749	5,872,093	7,282,972	7,785,121
Treasure	3,102,166	3,759,934	2,372,885	686,859
Grand total	11,188,915	9,632,027	9,655,857	8,471,980

NOTE.—The imports by rail, included in the above totals of merchandise amounted to 413,725*l.* in 1896; against 517,625*l.* in 1895.

Exports.

Not including treasure, the total value of exports showed an increase for 1896 over those of 1895 of 2,214,656*l.* Of this, the United Kingdom took 286,793*l.* more; British Colonies, 958,809*l.*, and the East Indies, 130,671*l.* The increase was chiefly in wheat, barley and timber.

The exports of grain, &c., to the United Kingdom and British Possessions were:—

To—	Quantity. Wheat.	Flour.	Barley.	Oats.
	Centals.*	Barrels.†	Centals.	Centals.
United Kingdom	8,672,923	85,025	2,853,800	..
Australasia	1,699,024	261,948	1,927	2,010
South Africa	776,151	2,070	6,712	2,626
India	480,937	..	..	..

* A cental is 100 lbs. † A barrel of flour is equal to 3 centals.

SAN FRANCISCO.

The United Kingdom took, in 1896, 7,520,839 feet of timber, against 3,758,600 feet in 1895. Among the other principal exports to the United Kingdom in 1896 were—

Articles.		Quantity.
Canned goods	Cases..	3,880
,, fruits	,,	267,836
Dried fruits	Lbs.	45,542
Canned salmon	Cases..	473,891
Wine	Gallons	130,736
,,	Cases..	202
Brandy	Gallons	3,760
Whiskey	,,	70

Australasia took—

Articles.		Quantity.
Canned fruits	Cases..	63,429
Dried fruit	Lbs.	496,716
Raisins	Packages	1,506
Salmon	Cases..	73,882
	Barrels	2,255
	Half barrels..	2,116
	Kits*..	17

* A kit is 56 lbs.

Imports. Of imports, excluding treasure, there was a decrease in 1896 of 502,149*l.* The United Kingdom lost 129,259*l.*, Australia and Canada 122,069*l.*, and the East Indies, 12,323*l.* The falling-off was chiefly in raw silk, coal, coffee, tin-plates, and tea.

There was a considerable increase in raw sugar from Hawaii, and increases in cement and pig-iron.

The imports are classified as follows:—Free goods, 5,117,403*l.*; dutiable, 2,165,564*l.*; entered for immediate consumption, 6,664,951*l.*; and for warehousing, 618,021*l.*

Manufactures. The past year was not a prosperous one in the manufacturing industries of San Francisco. While some have held their own, others have not, and there has not been any increase. Eastern competition has been intense. In articles of food, that is, necessaries, there was an increase. A considerable amount of structural iron has been turned out by the rolling mills and foundries, but a great deal of the iron used in the State has been imported from the East. There has been no increase in textiles, and there has been a falling-off in the amount of lumber planed, &c.

The value of manufactures in 1896 is given as follows:—

Articles.	Value.
	Dollars.
Food	41,000,000
Metal	10,000,000
Textiles, &c.	9,000,000
Lumber, &c.	7,000,000
Leather, &c.	7,000,000
Miscellaneous	20,000,000
Total	94,000,000
Or about .. £	18,800,000

Salmon pack. The following is the estimate of the total salmon pack of 1896:—

	Quantity.	Total.
	Cases.	Cases.
Columbia River—		
Spring	435,100	
Fall	66,100	
		501,200
Sacramento River—		
Spring	7,732	
Fall	6,740	
		14,472
Rogue and Klamath Rivers—		
Spring	15,000	
Fall	5,400	
		20,400
Oregon Rivers—		
Fall	..	95,000
Puget Sound and Points near Fraser River	..	206,000
Alaska	..	874,596
Fraser River	323,174	
Skeena River	99,280	
Rivers Inlet	107,300	
Other Northern Points	34,040	
Cohoes Pack (estimated)	25,000	
		588,794
Total	..	2,300,462

SAN FRANCISCO.

The estimate of the fruit pack is given as follows:— **Fruit pack.**

Articles.	Quantity.	Total.
	Cases.	Cases.
Apples	5,000	
Apricots	200,000	
Asparagus	15,000	
Cherries, white	30,000	
„ black	25,000	
Currants	5,000	
Gooseberries	4,000	
Nectarines	2,500	
Pears	150,000	
Peas	15,000	
Peaches	250,000	
Plums	55,000	
Grapes	10,000	
Raspberries	5,000	
Strawberries	5,000	
		776,500
Pie fruits	30,000	
Tomatoes	150,000	
Jams and jellies	15,000	
		195,000
Total		971,500

The amount of sugar refined in 1896 has not yet been announced, but the figures for 1895 are given as 719,700,263 lbs. **Sugar, refined.**

The tonnage of vessels, steam and sailing, built in California in 1896 and documented at San Francisco was: gross 3,392·74 tons, net 2,384·27. They were all of small tonnage, the largest steamer being 691 tons, and the largest sailing vessel 480. The steamer was built to carry oil from Ventura County to San Francisco. **Shipbuilding.**

The great Union Ironworks launched on the 18th March two gunboats for the United States Government, the "Marietta" and the "Wheeling," of 1,000 tons each. On the 11th of March the ceremony was performed of driving the first rivet of the American ship-of-war "Wisconsin," which is being built at these works. This ship will be of 12,500 tons, and 10,000 h.p. The firm was also about to commence a torpedo-boat, the "Destroyer," for the United States Government. **Union Ironworks. Ships of war.**

The following ships-of-war have been built by the firm at different times for the American Government:—

	Tons.
The "Charleston"	3,780
"San Francisco"	4,080
"Monterey"	4,000
"Olympia"	5,800
"Oregon"	10,800

UNITED STATES.

They are also building a cruiser of 5,000 tons for the Japanese Government.

Building trade.

The condition of the building trade in 1896 was not very satisfactory, nor is it just now. It would appear that the most prosperous year at this season for some years past was 1891, when during January and February 210 buildings were erected at a cost of 1,777,636 dol. The record for January and February of this year is 612,535 dol., but there is reason to believe that the prospects are brightening.

New buildings.

On the 27th of March the foundation-stone of the affiliated college buildings was laid, and among the new structures which are likely to be undertaken before long are the Hall of Justice, the Mission High School, the Menlo Park Academy of the Sacred Heart, the new Federal building, and the new post office.

Ferry building.

The new ferry building mentioned in Mr. Acting Consul-General Moore's report of 1895 (Annual Series No. 1576, p. 6) was commenced towards the close of last year, and is progressing rapidly.

The total length of the building is 661 feet, and the breadth 152. There is a projection in the middle of the land front for the main entrances, 146 feet wide, projecting 28 feet from the face of the building. There is a central tower about 30 feet by 32, the height from the pavement to the time ball at rest being 234 feet. The United States Hydrographer's office will locate their time ball system on the building.

There are three main entrances to the building, each 21 feet 6 inches in width. The first storey will be used for men's waiting rooms, station (district) post office, department baggage rooms and other offices. The second storey will contain the offices of the Harbour Commissioners and additional accommodation for the post office department. The above rooms are on the front of the building.

In the rear (water front) and running the whole length will be an open nave finished in marble, iron, and mosaic 45 feet wide and 24 feet high. At the rear of this nave and extending the whole length of the building are the waiting rooms for men and women, with a number of exits from the different ferry-boats. On the extreme rear of the building and extending throughout its entire length is an open passage way through which passengers can walk about and obtain access to the upper decks of the various ferry-boats.

Extending at right angles from the building at the rear between each ferry slip will be bridges made in the shape of the letter Y through which access will be had to the upper decks of the ferry boats.

The building will be of steel faced with stone. Of steel 2,500 tons (5,000,000 lbs.) will be used in the construction. This part is now nearly completed. The stone is a grey sandstone with slightly green tinge, of very fine quality, resting on a first course of very superior grey granite. The sandstone is said to be the finest in California, the grain is fine and even, there are no nodules, and it cuts perfectly. It comes from Colusa County. The cost of the building will be about 600,000 dol. (say 120,000*l*.) and it is expected to be completed in about a year from the present time.

During the past year about 275 miles of railway have been constructed. The chief work has been on the San Joaquin Valley Railroad, which now reaches from Stockton to Fresno, a distance of 125 miles. Of this about 100 were completed last year. As soon as the necessary rights of way shall have been secured, it will be carried on southwards to Bakersfield. Work on the first section of this extension, from Fresno to Hanford, a distance of 30 miles, has been commenced since the beginning of the present year, and is being rapidly carried on. New railways.

There is water communication between Stockton and San Francisco (as well as a railway, a portion of the Southern Pacific System), and this will give communication between Bakersfield and this city, in competition with the Southern Pacific. It is intended to extend the San Joaquin Valley line as soon as possible to this city, and surveys for the purpose are being made.

The promoters hope eventually to get access to the east from Bakersfield. This would give an additional line the whole way from San Francisco to the east, in competition with the Southern Pacific.

The remainder of the 275 miles consists of several small extensions or feeders, which have been made mostly by or in connection with the Southern Pacific System.

The State Mineralogist of California, in his biennial report for the two years ended September 30, 1896, says that considerable activity has prevailed during the past year, and still continues in nearly all lines of mining industry, and that a great deal of capital is seeking investment in legitimate mining enterprises, citizens of the State investing as much as non-residents. Mining industry.

He observes that "statistics show that of all industrial occupations mining is here the most profitable, the average annual product or earning per capita in California of persons engaged in farming being about 300 dol., in manufacturing, including bounties, about 1,000 dol., and in mining," with all its burdens and penalties, "nearly 1,500 dol."

The census of those engaged in mining occupations, including milling, quarrying, well boring, &c., show an increase for the two years of 40 per cent. over that of the two previous ones. The figures are (including Chinese):—

Year.	Number.
1893 and 1894	13,765
1895 and 1896	19,508

Petroleum is likely to become a very important industry in this State. Oil is said to have been first discovered many years Petroleum.

UNITED STATES.

ago in Palomares Cañon, Alameda County, and a shaft was sunk near Haywards, from which oil and salt water were both obtained. Both, however, disappeared after the earthquake of 1868. This earthquake caused a spring to flow which contained traces of oil and natural gas. Since then, at different times, borings have been made in different districts with increasing results.

Of late there has been a considerable amount of excitement in several portions of the State over the prospecting for both petroleum and natural gas—notably in the counties of Los Angeles, San Luis, Obispo, Alameda, Contra Casta, and San Bernardino. The most important operations, however, have been in Los Angeles County, where the total output for 1895 was 979,695 barrels. The price realised was 732,817 dol., and of this amount 729,695 barrels were yielded by the district of Los Angeles city. In the beginning of March, 1896, there were 330 wells in the Los Angeles oil field.

Coal mining. Most of the coal found in California is lignite of excellent quality. Bituminous and anthracite coal is found in Utah, Nevada, and Arizona, and a semi-anthracite in south-western Utah and north Arizona, but it is not worked to any great extent.

Corral Hollow mine opened. Great preparations have been made for mining coal in Corral Hollow, about 36 miles from Stockton, Contra Casta County, and the mine was publicly opened on the 20th of March. It is stated that several veins have been opened up, varying from 7 to 14 feet in thickness. The coal, I am informed, is a lignite of good quality, and it is estimated that 30,000,000 tons are within reach. The result of the opening of this mine will probably be to reduce very considerably the price of coal in the State.

Diamonds. Diamonds have been found in El Dorado County, and near Placerville, in the mining sluices, but the matrix has not yet been recognised. The last two stones found within the past two years weighed about ¾ carat each. It is not expected that any finds of value will soon be made.

Precious metals. The following returns of precious metals produced during 1896 in the states and territories within the jurisdiction of this Consulate-General have been issued by Messrs. Wells, Fargo, and Co.:—

States and Territory.	Gold Dust and Bullion Conveyed by Express.	Gold Dust and Bullion by other Conveyances.	Silver Bullion by Express.	Ores and Base Bullion by Freight.	Total.
	Dollars.	Dollars.	Dollars.	Dollars.	Dollars.
California	11,553,928	3,973,376	83,839	20,248	15,631,391
Nevada	1,081,656	950,000	478,814	248,894	2,759,364
Utah	777,698	1,163,122	1,050,348	7,392,591	10,383,759
Arizona	1,313,510	1,775,880	293,618	5,882,909	9,265,917
Total	14,726,792	7,862,378	1,906,619	13,544,642	38,040,431

Base metals. The returns of base metals produced in California in 1896 have not yet been made up, but the produce in 1895 as returned by the State Mineralogist is as follows:—

Articles.						Quantity.
Antimony	..	..	..	Tons ..	..	23
Copper ..	..	..	..	Lbs. ..	..	225,650
Lead ..	..	..	..	..	..	1,592,400
Manganese	..	..	..	Tons ..	..	880
Quicksilver*	..	..	..	Flasks	..	36,108

* The "Commercial Herald and Market Review" gives the number as 30,000.

Of platinum the production was 150 ozs.

Of petroleum 1,245,339 barrels were raised in 1895, and 79,858 tons of coal. *Petroleum.*

The total value of all metals, minerals, and mineral substances, such as stone, asphalt, and bituminous rock, petroleum, natural gas produced in 1895 was 22,844,664 dol. 29 c., against 20,203,294 dol. 44 c. in 1894. *Total value of all mineral substances.*

The mint coinage in San Francisco in 1896 was:—

	Amount.
	Dollars.
Gold	30 094,000
Silver	5,674,990
Total	35,768 990

The gold production of California in 1895, taken from the report of the State Mineralogist above referred to, is estimated at 15,334,317 dol. *Gold production, in 1895.*

The consumption of coal during the past year was more than 10 per cent. less than in 1895, which is an indication that the year was not prosperous for manufacturing industries. The prices of coal were unprecedentedly low. The cheap Australian coal has caused the diminution of the imports of British Columbia and Seattle (Washington State) coals by about 20 per cent. Crude oil has not been used to the same extent for fuel, owing to the cheapness of coal. *Coal supply and consumption.*

As stated in another place, the opening of the large mines at Corral Hollow is likely to still further reduce the price of coal. It will probably also further diminish the consumption of oil unless the development of the oil industry should cause a fall in the price of this article. This, however, is doubtful owing to the power of the Great Oil Trust.

The sources of coal supply, and the quantities for the last two years were:—

(2397)

UNITED STATES.

	Quantity.	
	1895.	1896.
	Tons.	Tons.
British Columbia	651,295	551,852
Australia	268,960	273,851
England and Wales	201,180	156,368
Scotland	4,098	8,356
Eastern (Cumberland and Anthracite)	26,863	17,907
Seattle (Franklin and Green River)	150,888	128,919
Carbon Hill and South Prairie	256,267	255,923
Mount Diabolo and Coos Bay	84,954	110,237
Japan, &c.	9,015	2,247
Total	1,653,520	1,505,660

Coke. The total arrivals of coke for the past year were 36,132 tons, or 50 per cent. more than in 1895. Of this, 75 per cent. came from England and Belgium. It is expected that shipments will soon come from British Columbia, where, as stated in my report of last year, large coking ovens have recently been erected, and this will cause a material reduction in the imports from the United Kingdom.

Agriculture. With reference to the remarks contained in my report (No. 423, Miscellaneous Series) relative to the beet sugar industry and the condition of the sugar-beet growers, I am able to give a copy of the contract which the Chino Sugar Factory exacts from the beet growers on the Chino Estate who grow beets for the factory; also of that which the Bixby Land Company of Los Angeles County compels those to whom it sells or rents its beet lands to execute for growing beets and supplying them to the Alamitos Sugar Factory.* The heading of the Company's prospectus describes it as "Owners of .... acres, Los Alamitos Rancho and Los Alamitos Townsite," &c., "Superior sugar-beet land for sale from $ .... per acre up, with contracts to raise sugar-beets for the Los Alamitos Factory." This is a new factory near Los Angeles, which will commence work this year.

Price of land. With reference to my remarks on the fall in the value of land, since the report was written another important sale has been effected, that of an estate known as the "Theodor Winters Ranch." This property consists of 19,000 acres, 10,000 in Lassen County, California, and 9,000 in Nevada adjoining. On the Nevada portion there is a debt of 1 dol. per acre, in all 9,000 dol. due to the State of Nevada. With this exception the estate is clear of all liability. It consists mostly of rough stock-raising land, but is at a considerable distance from a railway. About 2,000 acres are, I am informed, good bottom land, with a small stream running through them, and producing good grass, a portion of which is cut for hay every year. This part has more or less facilities

* These contracts have been sent to the Emigrants' Information Office.

irrigation. There were 14,000 head of sheep on the land, and these were included in the purchase. The price paid was 72,000 dol., added to which the charge of 9,000 dol. due to the State of Nevada makes 81,000 dol., or about 4¼ dol. per acre, including the sheep. The agents for the sale were Messrs. Bovee, Toy and Sonntag, who gave me the above information.

I mentioned that endeavours were being made to secure a Free market. free market for the sale of fruit, &c. A Bill has passed the Legislature, and become law, providing for the establishment of a free market in this city. Under this Law the Board of Harbour Commissioners are to set apart upon some convenient portion of the water front a sufficient number of docks and piers contiguous to each other for the reception of all perishable products arriving by rail, water, or otherwise, including fruit, vegetables, poultry, eggs, game, dairy produce, and fish, such goods to be sold for the account of the producers only. No rents are to be charged for the use of the market, which is to be connected by car tracks with the railroad. The expenses are to be provided for by tolls.

The grape crop of 1896 was much better than, owing to the Wine crop. sharp frosts of last May, was anticipated, and the wine crop is said to be of very good quality.

The California Wine Makers' Corporation, at a meeting held on November 18, unanimously adopted a resolution to fix the minimum price of standard dry wines at 20 c. a gallon. This is an advance of 5 c. over the price of 1895, and of 7½ c. over that of 1894. They informed me in December that the output of the whole vintage for 1896 was 14,000,000 gallons, valued at 4,000,000 dol., as against the same quantity, value 3,000,000 dol. in 1895. It is, however, stated in the "Commercial Herald and Market Review" that the product was 10,000,000 gallons.

The wine-makers paid this year 18 dol. to 22 dol. per ton for grapes, an increase of about 25 per cent. over 1895.

At a meeting of the trustees of the California Sweet Wine Association early in January last, a resolution was adopted fixing the price of sweet wines under its control at 33½ c. for port, and 35 c. for angelica per gallon "naked," being an advance of 25 and 27 c. a gallon respectively on last year's prices. The reason given for this advance is that the vintage of sweet wines is nearly 40 per cent. less than that of 1895, which was about 4,500,000 gallons. About one-half of this is port and angelica, and the rest sherry, muscat, and malaga. These three varieties are not in the combination.

The wheat crop of the State of California in 1896 was Wheat. 25,000,000 bushels, and the barley crop 12,000,000 bushels. The Barley. beet sugar crop for 1896 has not yet been announced, but for 1895 Beet sugar. it was 64,257,122 lbs.

The wool clip of the State for 1896 is estimated by two Wool. different leading authorities respectively at 29,000,000 lbs., and and 27,195,550 lbs.

Experiments have, during the last few years, been made in Tobacco. growing tobacco with varying success in this State. There is good reason to believe that certain districts are very well suited for tobacco growing, but as yet the matter has not been taken up with much energy.

Fibre growing.
As regards the possibilities of the State in the matter of fibre industry, Professor Hilgard, Director of the Agricultural Experiment Station of the College of Agriculture, University of California, in a letter to the chairman of the State Development Committee, says, "This department has always kept prominently in view the possibilities of the fibre industry in this State. We have grown experimental plots of the various more important fibre crops for many years at the several culture stations, and have distributed the seed or roots to farmers, receiving from them reports as to the results of their trials. Partly in this way, partly from outside trials, we have ascertained in a very definite manner the climate and soil regions within which the several fibre plants adapted to our State may be expected to succeed on a practical scale.

"We have also had tests made of the quality of the several fibres, partly in the State, partly in the East, with the result that in general they are of at least equal, and in the case of cotton of higher grade than when grown elsewhere. These results have been published both in our reports, and in the case of cotton in the United States Government publications. Among them the following may be mentioned.

"Jute does not make a sufficient growth for practical purposes in any part of the State, and the fibre is of too low value to be profitably grown and cleared here.

"Cotton can be successfully grown in the great valley, and produces a very superior fibre, for which the Oakland Cotton Mills have offered an advance of 2 c. per lb. over the price of Louisiana cotton delivered here.

"Ramie can be grown successfully in the great valley, and in the warmer valleys of the coast range, making from 3 to 4 c. annually on strong land.

"We have grown for many years a number of varieties of flax, both for seed and fibre, and we find for it a considerably wider range than for ramie, and excellent quality both of fibre and seed when grown for each separately.

"Hemp has at least an equally great range of successful cultivation with excellent quality.

"The same is true for New Zealand flax, and for esparto grass, which has been on our distribution list for many years.

"As for silk, its quality, as produced in California, has been repeatedly tested and found to be excellent.

"There is, therefore, no question as to the eminent adaptation of a large portion of the State for these fibre cultures, and doubtless more might be added from the leaf fibre class to which Pita and Sisal belong for the southern part of the State.

"These facts are widely known and appreciated, and the causes of the non-establishment of the fibre industry in this State is clearly to be sought elsewhere, as a matter of fact they lie in the main in the high cost of hand labour, and the cost of marketing."

SAN FRANCISCO.

Hygiene, Vital Statistics, &c.

The serious attention of the medical profession and the public has lately been drawn to the danger which menace the people of California from the prevalence and fatality of tubercular diseases. The beautiful climate of the greater part of the State has led to its becoming a resort for consumptives, and the medical profession are alarmed to find that the death-rate from tuberculosis is rapidly increasing, not only among those who arrive in the State diseased, but also among natives.

Tubercular diseases: danger to California from.

According to statistics published by the State Board of Health, there were 10,316 deaths reported in the whole State during the fiscal year ended June 30, 1887. Of these 1,617 were caused by tuberculosis pulmonalis, or consumption of the lungs, more than 15 per cent. During the next year the total number of deaths increased to 12,322, and those from consumption to 1,832. During the year ended June 30, 1892, the number of the latter had risen to 2,304. Of those who died of consumption in 1887, 309 were natives; in 1888, 355; in 1891, 436; and in 1892, 529.

The returns for the State for the years ended June 30, 1895 and 1896 respectively, are unfortunately not complete. The Board in their report for these two years recently issued, say that only 25 counties out of 53 have reported the number of deaths, births, and marriages.

Two sets of tables are given in this report. One is headed "Monthly review of deaths and prevailing diseases," and consists of returns for each month of the two periods of 12 months from a number of "towns, villages, and sanitary districts" ranging from 60 to 79, and aggregating a population varying from 432,023[*] to 791,223 per month for the first period of 12 months; and from 49 to 79 towns, &c., with a population varying from 716,806 to 778,017 per month for the second period of 12 months. This return shows a total number of deaths for the 12 months ended June 30, 1895, of 11,430, of which 2,041, or about $17\frac{3}{4}$ per cent. were due to "consumption," and for the 12 months ended June 30, 1896, 11,480, of which 1,998, or about 17 per cent. were from the same cause.[†]

The other set of tables headed "Number of deaths from all causes" reported to the State Board for the same periods gives the deaths for those periods as: total for 1894–95, 10,976, of which 1,790 were attributable to phthisis pulmonalis and 265 to tubercular meningitis; and total for 1895–96, 10,462, of which 1,534 were due to phthisis pulmonalis, and 305 to tubercular meningitis.

The nationality of the persons whose death is recorded in the second set of tables is given as follows:—

---

[*] For the month represented by this low number of the population no return was received by the State Board from San Francisco.

[†] The Secretary to the State Board of Health informed me in answer to an enquiry that "all tubercular diseases, tubercular meningitis for instance," were included under the head of consumption in this return.

	Pacific States.	Atlantic States.	Foreign.	Not ascertained.	Total.
	Number.	Number.	Number.	Number.	Number.
1894–95.					
Phthisis pulmonalis	407	432	819	132	1,790
Tubercular meningitis	120	64	58	23	265
1895–96.					
Phthisis pulmonalis	356	344	696	138	1,534
Tubercular meningitis	124	94	61	26	305

The report of the Health Department of the city and county of San Francisco for the fiscal year ended June 30, 1896, gives the deaths in the city during that period from tubercular diseases as 1,087, out of a total of deaths from all causes of 5,966, or over 18 per cent. Of the 1,087, those from phthisis pulmonalis were 1,003. The nationalities for the 1,087 are given as:—

Nationality.	Number.
Pacific States	325
Atlantic States	180
Foreign	579
Not ascertained	3
Total	1,087

A pamphlet published last year by Dr. Remondino, of San Diego, calls attention to this serious state of affairs. It is reprinted from the "Transactions of the Fourth State Sanitary Convention," held at Los Angeles in April last, and urges the necessity of strict sanitary regulations in order to protect the healthy from contagion.

It is the general opinion of physicians in the State that while the influx of afflicted persons contributes to the spread of phthisis, one of the main causes of the great increase of tubercular disease is the use of milk and meat from tuberculous cows and cattle.

Death rate, San Francisco. As stated above, the number of deaths in San Francisco city for the fiscal year ended June 30, 1896, was 5,966, or 18·07 per 1,000 of the population, which is estimated at about 330,000. The numbers for the last six years were:—

Year.	Number of Deaths.	Rate per 1,000 (About)
1890	6,378	21·26
1891	6,650	20·15
1892	6,911	20·94
1893	6,061	18·36
1894	6,060	18·36
1895	6,059	18·36

SAN FRANCISCO.

The rate has, therefore, fallen from about 21 per 1,000 in 1890, to about 18 in 1896, on an estimated population of 330,000. The reduction has been caused by a decrease in deaths from zymotic diseases. In 1891 these were answerable for 1,102 deaths; in 1892, for 1,002; in 1895, for 539; and in 1896 for 472. On the other hand deaths from constitutional diseases increased during the five years from 1,231 to 1,460. The record for diphtheria during the five years was 229, 153, 38, 21, and 19; for scarlatina, 45, 111, 14, 2, and 6. *[margin: Zymotic diseases.]*

The decrease in infant mortality is almost equally satisfactory. In 1891 the deaths of children under five years of age were 603; in 1892, 649. The number since then has decreased until last year, when it was 314, or less than half what it was four years ago. *[margin: Infant mortality, decrease in.]*

The decrease in infantile mortality is stated to have been largely the result of the inspection of milk. The same cause is also believed to have recently reduced the deaths from consumption, for although the deaths for the whole year from this cause were 1,003, those for the latter halves of the last three years were respectively, 522, 491, and 455.

Among other prominent causes of death given in the returns for the whole State and for San Francisco respectively during the fiscal year ended June 30, 1896, are:— *[margin: Other prominent causes of death.]*

	The whole State.	San Francisco.
	Number.	Number.
Apoplexy	..*	204
Bronchitis	237	178
Cancer	451	322
Convulsions	155	101†
Other diseases of the brain and nervous system	698	..*
Heart disease	956	707
Homicide	..*	148
Pneumonia	687	467
Suicide	228	148
Typhoid fever	194	101

* Not given.   † Of these 100 were infantile.

The number of marriages in San Francisco has been decreasing during the last few years. In 1891 it was 3,389; in 1892 it rose to 3,500. Since then it has been falling off each year till 1896, when it was 3,138. In 1891 the number was 11·7 per 1,000 of the population, and last year 10·4. *[margin: Marriages.]*

The registered births for the last five years have numbered —4,088, 3,889, 3,894, 3,755, and 5,020, but the actual number has probably not increased in proportion, for the registration was more thorough last year, greater attention having been given to the matter. *[margin: Births.]*

Attention has of late been drawn to the serious extent to which the adulteration of food is carried in this State, and the *[margin: Adulteration of food.]*

Board of Health has now taken up the matter vigorously. Out of 33 samples of currant jelly bought a few days ago for analysis from as many different grocers—some of them prominent and leading firms—only nine were found to be pure. Many had no currant juice at all in them; ten were found to be dangerous as food from the ingredients of which they were composed. The so-called currant jelly consisted either entirely or chiefly of glucose, apple jelly, starch, and acetic acid, coloured with aniline dyes. Of 26 samples of tomato catsup analysed during December, 10 were manufactured in San Francisco or its vicinity, and nine of these were impure. Yet the tomato is one of the most plentiful fruits grown in the State. The "Chronicle" of March 19 says that :—"Thousands of gallons of doctored wines are made in this city, as are gross after gross* of artificial honey. Spices are freely adulterated, and the revelations made by Chemist Wenzell about counterfeit jellies proves that their manufacture has become a large domestic business." At a meeting of the Retail Grocers' Association held on the 24th March, it was stated that "63 per cent. of the manufactured food products in the United States were adulterated."

It is not only in food that adulteration is found. The "Chronicle" warns the public against "potash, concentrated lye, and caustic soda," much of which is, it says, "abnormally adulterated." "The guarantee of '98 per cent.' which is upon the packages, is of no value whatever," the article says, as "some of the worst adulterations which have been found—testing only 20 or 30 per cent.—have been from packages marked '98 per cent.'" And it warns horticulturists that "many formulas" used by them "in which 98 per cent. potash is prescribed, will entirely fail of expected results" when a low grade article is substituted.

Tuberculosis among dairy cattle.

It was stated above that the increase of tubercular diseases among human beings in the State of California was attributed in a great measure to the use of milk and meat from tuberculous cows and cattle.

During the spring of last year public attention was called to the fact that tuberculosis existed to an alarming extent among dairy cattle in the city of San Francisco and surrounding districts. The health authorities, to whom I applied for information, furnished me with the following particulars in June last.

The number of dairies in the city district was 150. The number of animals in the dairies 7,000. Tuberculosis to a certain extent existed in all the dairy herds, but it was impossible to estimate the percentage of diseased cows until a complete inspection had been made. Of 34 cows examined at one dairy in the city 31 had been killed as being badly diseased. At a milk ranch outside the city 4 were killed out of 60.

The health authorities decided to inspect all the animals "according to the rules adopted by the United States Bureau of Animal Industry," but this inspection has not yet been completed.

* *Sic* in original.

SAN FRANCISCO.

Ducks are stated to have also been found infected with tuberculosis.

The population of California in 1890 according to the census taken in that year was 1,208,130. Of this number there were :—

	Number.
English born	35,503
Irish born	63,138
Scotch born	9,299
"British American" born	26,028

The population of San Francisco was then according to the census 298,997, of whom were :—

	Number.
English	9,828
Irish	30,718
Scotch	3,181
"British American"	4,371

The increase of the population of California by immigration in 1896 is stated to be 12,000.

610 divorce cases were brought in the local courts, of which 590 were granted. This is a little more than one-fifth of the number of marriages.

The attention of the public has recently been called to the heavy cost incurred by the State of California in its reformatories, penitentiaries, and various asylums. It appears that there are five asylums for the insane, two reformatory schools, two penitentiaries, a home for the feeble-minded, besides a home for the adult blind, a veterans' home, and an asylum for the deaf, dumb, and blind.

These institutions keep up a staff of 926 employés, and pay annual salaries amounting to 598,097 dol. The cost amounted last year to 1,366,076 dol., equal to a tax per head of the population of the State of about 1 dol. 12 c. California paid last year 407,076 dol. for the care of its criminals, while New York with a population seven times as great paid only 464,269 dol. Oregon, with one-third of the population, paid for the care of the insane 109,207 dol., while California paid 784,400 dol.

The tax per head for the care of the defective and criminal classes in New York amounted to 65 c., in Oregon to 77 c., and in California to 1 dol. 12 c.

The value of all property in the State of California, as returned by the State auditors, and altered by the Board of Equalisation for the years 1895 and 1896, is given in the official report of the Board of Equalisation as follows :—

Value of all Property in California.

Year.	Value of Real Estate and Improvements.	Personal Property, other than Money and Solvent Credits.	Money and Solvent Credits.	Total of preceding Columns.	After Equalisation.	Railroad Assessment.	Total Value of all Property.
	Dollars.	Dollars.	Dollars.	Dollars.	Dollars.	Dollars.	Dollars.
1895	964,600,571	135,519,290	26,270,813	1,126,390,674	1,089,694,034½	43,018,640	1,132,712,674
1896	972,205,051	131,729,224	45,623,195	1,149,557,470	1,220,548,592	43,223,344	1,263,771,936

The number of acres of land assessed and the valuation of real estate and improvements are given as—

Year.	Acres.	Value of Real Estate, other than City and Town Lots.	Value of City and Town Lots.	Value of all Real Estate.	Value of Improvements on Real Estate, other than City and Town Lots.	Value of Improvements on City and Town Lots.	Value of all Improvements.
		Dollars.	Dollars.	Dollars.	Dollars.	Dollars.	Dollars.
1895	38,784,480	386,301,045	325,870,824	712,174,869	66,217,482	184,160,520	250,878,902
1896	39,769,329	377,644,387	330,573,461	708,217,848	63,835,182	200,151,020	263,987,203

The total amount of all mortgages on real estate in California was in 1895, 194,902,872 dol., or about 20·20 per cent., and in 1896, 192,932,131 dol., or about 19·76 per cent.

The sales of real estate in San Francisco during 1896 amounted to 11,545,331 dol., against 15,947,361 dol. in 1895.

Loss of British Trade.

British Chambers of Commerce are continually complaining that Her Majesty's Consuls do not help them sufficiently in pushing British trade abroad. Her Majesty's Consuls on the other hand are constantly pointing out how British manufacturers, &c., fail to exert themselves to open out new channels of trade, or lose existing trade through supineness or neglect.

The following is an instance of loss of British trade through what would appear to be pure supineness, and in spite of repeated warnings.

Some ten years or so ago nearly all the cement used in the Western States was of British manufacture. Somewhere about that time Belgium and Germany made great efforts to compete with English cement. A member of one of the principal English mercantile firms here told me that at the time this competition began his firm warned the English makers through their English house of what was going on, and repeated the warning for several years till they gave it up as a hopeless task. The manufacturers at home ignored the warning, and said that Belgian and German cement could not possibly compete with the British article.

The Germans and Belgians, however, persevered, and they have now got such a firm hold of the market of this coast that it will in all probability be impossible for British makers to recover it, if, indeed, they do not lose altogether what is left to them.

The accompanying return (which I have had considerable difficulty in obtaining) of the imports of cement into all the ports of the Western States for the 12 years from 1885 to 1896 inclusive, will show what the loss of the trade of the United Kingdom in this article has been.

Towards the end of last year a contract was given for 10,000 barrels of Belgian cement for use in the construction of new forts which are about to be built for the defence of this harbour and city.

UNITED STATES.

RETURN, showing Imports of Cement, 1885 to 1896 inclusive San Francisco, California.

	Belgium.	Germany.	Total, Belgium and Germany.	United Kingdom.	Total, all Countries.
	Barrels.	Barrels.	Barrels.	Barrels.	Barrels.
1885	3,500	500	4,000	57,793	61,793
1886	\multicolumn{3}{c}{No particulars.}			146,607
1887	9,703	9,915	19,618	314,725	334,343
1888	\multicolumn{3}{c}{No particulars.}			353,238
1889	6,956	35,128	42,084	209,315	251,399
1890	43,682*	60,925	104,607	332,141*	436,748
1891	127,069*	75,394	202,463	365,372*	567,835
1892	47,902	4,645	52,547	145,592	198,139
1893	38,518	12,636	51,154	208,955	260,109
1894	53,850	23,147	76,997	234,575	311,572
1895	79,879	55,334	135,213	154,412	289,625
1896‡	71,641	94,973	184,156†	153,248	337,404

* The heavy imports in 1890-91 were due to low freights, and the result was an over-stocked market and heavy loss to all engaged in the trade. This explains the falling off in 1892.

† Including 14,992 barrels from France, and 2,550 from China. A portion of the consignment from France was in reality Belgian, but being shipped at Dunkirk it was entered as French.

‡ The figures for 1896 were obtained in the beginning of January. The figures now issued by the customs are as follows:—Belgium, 76,646; Germany, 94,973; France, 14,994; China and Japan, 2,554; United Kingdom, 153,847; total, 343,014.

LOS ANGELES, California.

	Belgium.	Germany.	Total, Belgium and Germany.	United Kingdom.	Total, all Countries.
	Barrels.	Barrels.	Barrels.	Barrels.	Barrels.
1885	\multicolumn{5}{l}{Returns for 1885 and 1886 were included in those for San Diego.}				
1886					
1887	...	...	...	...	...
1888	...	...	...	21,383	21,383
1889	...	...	...	...	...
1890	...	...	...	...	...
1891	5,200	...	5,200	7,000	12,200
1892	...	...	...	11,502	11,502
1893	8,770	...	8,770	21,827	30,597
1894	3,022	...	3,022	11,200	14,222
1895	7,000	15,691	22,691	11,320	34,011
1896	12,933	35,253	48,186	15,856	64,042

SAN DIEGO, California.*

	Belgium.	Germany.	Total, Belgium and Germany.	United Kingdom.	Total, all Countries.
	Barrels.	Barrels.	Barrels.	Barrels.	Barrels.
1885	...	...	...	No returns.	...
1886	...	...	...	,,	...
1887	...	...	...	23,006	23,006
1888	...	...	...	68,071	68,071
1889	...	...	...	57,645	57,645
1890	...	...	...	No returns.	...
1891	...	...	...	49,438	49,438
1892	...	...	...	45,940	45,940
1893	...	...	...	33,824	33,824
1894	...	...	...	55,927	55,927
1895	...	...	...	52,101	52,101
1896	...	10,100	10,100	44,875	54,975

* The reason why Belgian and German cement has not been able to obtain a footing in San Diego is that a certain family have enormous amounts invested there, which has enabled them practically to control the port so far as imports are concerned, and they have always confined their operations to British cement.

PORTLAND, OREGON, including Astoria.

	Belgium.	Germany.	Total, Belgium and Germany.	United Kingdom.	Total, all Countries.
	Barrels.	Barrels.	Barrels.	Barrels.	Barrels.
1885	...	No	returns.	...	...
1886	...	...	...	19,347	19,347
1887	...	...	...	26,427	26,427
1888	5,000	...	5,000	32,637	37,637
1889	...	...	...	24,579	24,579
1890	11,300	...	11,300	47,689	58,989
1891	19,296	...	19,296	73,734	93,030
1892	19,351	...	19,351	21,680	41,031
1893	13,124	...	13,124	56,911	70,035
1894	57,124	...	57,124	41,342	98,466
1895	49,371	5,600	54,971	23,620	78,591
1896	38,334	10,759	49,093	12,022	61,115

PUGET SOUND, State of Washington.

	Belgium.	Germany.	Total, Belgium and Germany.	United Kingdom.	Total, all Countries.
	Barrels.	Barrels.	Barrels.	Barrels.	Barrels.
1885	...	...	...	...	...
1886	...	...	...	...	...
1887	...	...	...	2,056	2,056
1888	...	...	...	7,594	7,594
1889	...	...	...	26,036	26,036
1890	...	...	...	71,130	71,130
1891	...	...	...	33,468	33,468
1892	...	...	...	17,940	17,940
1893	10,000	...	10,000	63,732	73,732
1894	...	...	...	35,498	35,498
1895	...	3,000	3,000	20,446	23,446
1896	15,335	18,100	33,435	18,702	52,137

Grand Totals for San Francisco, Los Angeles, San Diego, Portland, and Puget Sound.

	Belgium.	Germany.	Total, Belgium and Germany.	United Kingdom.	Total, all Countries.
	Barrels.	Barrels.	Barrels.	Barrels.	Barrels.
1885	3,500	500	4,000	57,973	61,793
1886	...	Full	particulars wa	nting.	165,954
1887	9,703	9,915	19,618	366,214	385,832
1888	...	Full	particulars wa	nting.	487,923
1889	6,956	35,128	42,084	317,575	359,659
1890	54,982	60,925	114,907	450,960	565,867
1891	151,565	75,394	226,959	529,012	755,971
1892	67,253	4,645	71,898	242,654	314,552
1893	70,412	12,636	83,048	385,249	468,297
1894	113,996	23,147	137,143	378,542	515,685
1895	136,226	79,649	205,875	261,899	467,774
1896*	138,243	169,085	324,870†	244,703	569,573

* Including France, in 1896, 14,992; and China, in 1896, 2550. † *See* †, p. 28.

On the other hand the Japanese are displaying much activity in endeavouring to capture some of the trade of the West Coast. Agents visit the country for the purpose, and there have been proposals for the establishment of a line of Japanese steamers between Japan and one of the Western ports.

Activity of Japanese.

Tramways.

The tramways system of San Francisco is said to be the most complete in existence, and I can well believe it. The ground on which the city stands is a series of hills and undulations. On many of the streets the grades are so steep that it is almost impossible for carriages drawn by horses to ascend or descend them and were it not for the cable and electric tramways many of the residential portions of the city which are now the most valuable, and where the finest private residences are situated, would probably have remained unbuilt over, and of little or no value. I cannot give a better idea of what most of the streets along which the lines run are like than by saying that they resemble a gigantic system of switchback railways.

The electric lines are not able to ascend grades as steep as the cable lines, and therefore on their very steep grades the former combine cable with the electric power.

The steepest grades on the two systems are—cable lines, 21·0, 19·4, 19·4, 18·7, 18·4, and 18·2 per cent.; electric lines, 14·5, 14·1, 12·9, 12·1, 12, and 11·8 per cent.; electric lines, with auxiliary cable construction, 25·4 and 24·0 per cent.

There is a uniform fare of 5 c. (about $2\frac{1}{2}d$.) for any distance covered by each company's system, and some of the companies transfer passengers to the systems of other companies without extra charge. For instance, a passenger can go from the ferries landing stage (to which most of the lines converge) to the Cliff House, at the mouth of the Golden Gates, a distance of about 8 miles over the systems of two or more sets of lines, for 5 c. He can also go from the ferries by the San Mateo line, a distance of about 8 miles direct, into the country for the same sum.

The cars are, with few exceptions, clean, airy, and comfortable, and at night well lit, especially on the electric lines, where they are brilliantly lit. Most cars have seats open to the air as well as inclosed.

There are altogether seven companies. The San Francisco and San Mateo system is partly suburban. The tracks of the Sutro Co. and of the Presidio and Ferries Co. extend beyond the city proper, but houses are springing up along these routes.

The following particulars relating to the different lines have been obligingly furnished to me by the respective companies. It will be seen that there are $38\frac{1}{4}$ miles of single, and $112\frac{3}{4}$ of double track, and that the amount of capital involved is 25,400,000 dol. (about 5,080,000*l.*), for a city whose population is about 330,000.

There are also tramways at Alameda and Oakland, on the opposite side of the bay, which run from the ferries.

The postal authorities run their own mail cars over any of the lines as they may require.

SAN FRANCISCO.

Name of Company.	Motive Power.	Miles of Single Track.	Miles of Double Track.	Miles of Streets Run Through.	Number of Cars, &c.*	Number of Power Stations.	Engine Capacity, H.-P.	Boiler Capacity, H.-P.	Number of Employees (about).†	Capital.
										Dollars.
Market Street Railway Company	Cable	6·0896	29·5421	...	Cable, 428	Cable, 6	5,700	5,505	...	...
	Electric	12·5063	32·7775	...	Electric, 211	Electric, 2	6,600	8,720	...	...
	Horse	7·0848	10·6800	...	Electric trail, 11		...	...	...	...
	Steam	1·2048	8·6569	...	Horse, 211		...	...	...	...
					Steam, 32		...	...	...	...
					Steam motors, 15		...	...	...	...
Total	...	26·8855	81·6565	106·5420	908	8	12,300	14,225	2,050	18,750,000
Geary Street, Park, and Ocean Railroad Company (worked by Market Street Company)	Cable	...	3·8350	3·8350	Grip, 30	...	...	...	...	...
					Trail, 30		...	...	...	...
					Combination, 10		...	...	...	...
Total	...	...	3·8350	3·8350	70	1	300	600	85	1,000,000
California Street Cable Railroad Company	Cable	...	5·5000	5·5000	All combination, 43	1	500	360	200	1,000,000
Sutter Street Railway Company	Cable	...	5·7500	...	Trail, 45	...	...	...	...	...
	Horse	...	0·7500	...	Grip, 45	...	...	...	...	...
Total	...	...	6·5000	6·5000	90	1	500	500	265	2,000,000
Presidio and Ferries Railroad Company ...	Cable	...	4·0000	...	Cable, 29	...	...	...	...	1,000,000
	Steam	...	0·5000	...	Steam, 5	...	...	...	...	Bonds, 250,000‡
	Horse	...	1·0000	...	Open, 4	...	...	...	...	...
					Steam motors, 4		...	...	...	...
Total	...	...	5·5000	5·5000	42	1	250	300	85	1,250,000
Sutro Railroad Company ...	Electric	0·6370	4·8750	4·7730	27	1	900	900	67	400,000
San Francisco and San Mateo Electric Railway Company	Electric	10·7290	5·0000	15·7290	37	1	1,000	1,000	150	1,000,000
Grand total	...	38·2515	112·8665	148·3790	1,217	14	15,750	17,885	2,902	25,400,000

* The majority of electric and cable cars have the motor or grip apparatus self-contained. For those that have not, separate motor or grip cars are used.
† The number of employés varies slightly with the season and amount of work. It is now at about the lowest.
‡ Of these bonds only 150,000 dol. have been issued.

(2397)

Redwood timber.

I desire to draw the attention of builders, decorators, and furniture makers at home to redwood timber, which is so extensively used in this country for building and decorative purposes, both out-of-door and in-door.

The redwood is the *Sequoia Sempervirens*,* the great tree of the coast belt of California. It attains a height of 250 feet or more, and, I am told, a girth of 60 feet. I have measured some trees 45 feet in circumference between 4 and 5 feet from the ground, but these were not in the finest groves.

The wood is said to stand any climate, from the dry heat of Australia, or the interior of this State, to the dampest climate, without being affected, after it has been thoroughly seasoned. The chief objection to its use is the difficulty of seasoning it. A board, say, 6 inches thick will not thoroughly season in the warmest part of California under about 2 or $2\frac{1}{2}$ years. This, of course, adds to the cost

Much of the wood is exceedingly handsome for internal use and decorative purposes, such as doors, panelling of rooms and ceilings, dados, mantelpieces, and over mantels, &c.; and once properly seasoned it never shrinks or cracks. I have carefully examined rooms the walls and ceilings of which were entirely panelled with it, as well as many doors, and have not been able to detect a crack. Another advantage is that boards of great width can be obtained entirely free from knots.

In colour the wood ranges from light to dark reddish brown. The varieties of graining are great. Some, especially the "curly" and the "burl" are very beautiful. The "curly" has a wavy pattern. I can best describe the "burl" as being in its markings something like Thuya wood, but with larger markings, English oak "burr," and the finest knot walnut. This wood, however, except the "burl," is soft and liable to be marked by blows. When properly prepared it takes polish and varnish well. Certain articles of furniture such as tables, &c., are made from the "burl."

The timber has been of late shipped to the United Kingdom, the annual shipments from this port being, I am informed, about 7,000,000 or 8,000,000 feet. But much of what has been sent to England has been of a very inferior quality, so that buyers at home must not judge of the quality of the timber by inferior specimens they may have seen.

The price here is just now about 3*l.* 10*s.* per 1,000 feet, f.o.b. The price at home can be calculated by adding freight, which, of course, varies.

Rights of aliens.

The question as to the effect on the rights of aliens in California, in regard to the "acquisition, possession, enjoyment, transmission, and inheritance" of real estate, of the Constitutional Amendment of 1894, referred to in previous reports (Annual Series Nos. 1576 of 1895 and 1750 of 1896), remains in the same

---

* This is of course not the same as the *Sequoia gigantea*, the giant tree of the Mariposa and Yosemite Valleys, which attains twice the size of the redwood.

state of uncertainty. But the more general opinion seems now to be that, as the legislature has not taken any action upon it, the amendment is practically a dead letter, and I am myself inclined to take this view.

Among the Acts passed this year by the State Legislature is one known as the "Torrens Land Act," borrowed from Australia which provides for the classification and registration of land titles, and the simplification of the transfer of land, and is to take effect from July 1 next. Under this law no adverse possession after registration will be possible, but persons defrauded will not lose their rights, and existing statutes governing probate, insolvency and equity will not be affected. {Torrens Land Act.}

Another Act passed in the Session which has lately closed provided for a Fire Department for San Francisco. Reference is made to this measure under the heading of insurance. {Municipal Fire Department.}

An Act has also been passed fixing a minimum wage rate of 2 dol. (about 8s.) per day for labour performed under the direction, control, or by the authority of any officer of the State, or of any municipal corporation within the State, and directing that a stipulation to that effect must be made a part of any contracts to which the State or any municipal corporation is a party. The Act does not apply to persons employed regularly in any of the public institutions, or by any city or county of the State. {Minimum wage for Government work.}

Another Act provides that passengers' bicycles shall be carried as luggage, and that no crate or other cover or protection shall be required. But no passenger shall be entitled to carry more than one bicycle as luggage. {Bicycles as luggage.}

The labour market has been in a very depressed state, and there has been much distress among the unemployed during the winter. Collections of food and money have been made for their relief, and a public collection has been and is still being made to provide as many as possible with employment. Many of them are homeless, and as many as possible of these have been given shelter in large halls and other places of the kind. {Labour market.}

The fund collected up to now has amounted to about 25,000 dol., but the greater portion has been spent. The work on which all for whom there is room are now engaged is the construction of roads beyond the city limits. Tools and materials for the work, which will be of great public utility, have also been contributed. The men are paid 1 dol. (about 4s.) a day, and they also receive car fares to and from their dwelling places. Up to the present time about 300 to over 400 men have been thus daily employed. The number of applicants for the work is said to have amounted at times to about four times that number. The fund is, however, not keeping pace with the necessities of the case.

The Salvation Army are endeavouring to start a scheme for settling the unemployed on farms of from 5 to 10 acres on reclaimable land, and for cultivating unoccupied lots in the city. The army do an immense amount of good in the city in relieving distress.

(2397)

There is much distress among British subjects in this State, and applications are constantly made at the Consulate-General for relief and for assistance in obtaining employment, not only from the labouring classes, but from persons of education of both sexes, teachers of music, governesses, &c. Such persons often come here from the United Kingdom, Australia, New Zealand, India, and even China and Japan, under the impression that employment is easily obtainable. This is a very great mistake, and I cannot too strongly warn British subjects not to come here in search of employment unless they have reason to know that they can obtain it.

Los Angeles.

Mr. Vice-Consul Mortimer writes:—

Introductory. In my report for 1895 I pointed out that owing to a variety of causes it was probable that the progress of this district would be temporarily arrested, and this view has proved to be correct. The figures given below, however, show that the depression in business has not been very marked, and I now incline to the opinion that a period of great prosperity for this city and district is about to commence. Some of the local conditions which point in this direction are briefly as follows:—An abundant rainfall this winter ensures good crops this season, and has replenished the sources of supply of the artesian wells, which, owing to insufficient rainfall in 1894, 1895, and 1896, were seriously diminished. Congress has appropriated 600,000l. for the construction of a breakwater at the port for this city, ensuring a good harbour, and, in all probability, a great increase in foreign shipping. As stated elsewhere in this report another transcontinental railway to Los Angeles has been commenced, and will open new markets to the fruit growers, and otherwise enrich this city. For these and other reasons I am of opinion that the steady growth of the past seven years will shortly culminate in another "boom," and, owing to the geographical position of this city, and the fact that it has two, and will shortly have three competing transcontinental lines in a few years' time Los Angeles will probably be the most important city on the Pacific Coast. The Oriental trade now controlled by San Francisco and Tacoma will probably be diverted to Los Angeles when the harbour is completed, owing to the fact that the railway journey from this city to the Eastern centres is more than a day less in time, and, as the grades are easier, freight can be taken to the Eastern States at much less expense. The decrease in business in 1896 referred to above is shown by the following comparative statements.

Clearing-house. The Los Angeles Clearing-house (which, however, represents less than half the banking houses in Los Angeles) reports clearing (in round numbers) as follows:—

SAN FRANCISCO.

Year.	Amount.
	£
1894	9,400,000
1895	12,400,000
1896	11,500,000

The considerations named in all deeds filed in the office of the Recorder here in 1896 aggregated 2,700,000*l*. This is 800,000*l*. less than the corresponding figures for 1895. It is, however, nearly 400,000*l*. more than the corresponding figures for San Francisco.

It is stated in the Los Angeles "Investor" (the principal financial paper of Southern California), that the investment on mortgage security for the past two years has been as follows:— **Mortgages.**

Year.	Amount.
	£
1895	2,128,000
1896	3,104,000

All property is valued annually by the assessor of each county for purposes of taxation. These valuations are about one-third to one-half the amount at which owners are willing to sell. The assessed value of all property in the counties of Los Angeles and San Bernardino for the past two years has been as follows:—

Year.	Value.	
	Los Angeles.	San Bernardino.
	£	£
1895	16,960,000	3,520,000
1896	20,100,000	3,680,000

The other counties in this district show a corresponding increase.

The bonded indebtedness of this city is about 300,000*l*., bearing interest at 7 per cent. to 4½ per cent., the lower rate being on the later issues. A new issue of 4½ per cent. bonds will shortly be made to take up 7 per cent. bonds. **Information for British capitalists.**

These bonds, and the school bonds referred to in my report for 1895, are payable in gold, and are an excellent investment for persons satisfied with 4 to 5 per cent. Some of the irrigation bonds referred to elsewhere in this report are also good.

Seven per cent. net can be obtained on the best first mortgage security.

(2397)

36 UNITED STATES.

Chino Ranch Company bonds.

In my report for 1895 I referred to a reported sale to an English syndicate of 39,000 acres of the Chino Ranch for 500,000*l.*, which sale was not completed however, the property being subsequently acquired by an American company with an English name, "The California Beet Sugar Estate and Land Company, Limited." The word "limited" at the end of the name of a company has no significance here, a shareholder in a joint stock company is liable for the debts of the company in proportion that the shares he owns bears to the whole of the subscribed stock of the company. A member of the California Beet Sugar Estate and Land Company, Limited, tells me that the company has taken an English name to facilitate the sale of bonds on the London market.

Sugar factories and industry.

Two English syndicates are negotiating the purchase of large tracts of land in this vicinity, with a view to building beet sugar factories. Persons interested in the matter would do well to read an article by the President of the San Francisco Produce Exchange published in the Los Angeles Daily Times of February 10, 1897.

It appears from this article that in Ventura County the percentage of saccharine is higher than at Chino. In some experimental plantings at Ventura County the following results were obtained:—"The average per cent. of saccharine matter was 18·21, and the average purity 83·68 per cent. . . . . the per cent. of saccharine matter averaged 3 per cent. higher, and 8 per cent. higher in purity, and over 3 tons per acre more than in Chino."

It is stated in a bulletin of the Department of Agriculture that "the area of soil suitable for beet cultivation in the County of Los Angeles is 1,480 square miles."

Reference is made to the sugar beet industry elsewhere in this report.

Iron and coal mines.

I am informed on unquestionable authority that there are inexhaustible deposits of the finest iron ore, with beds of coal in close proximity within 300 miles of this city on the projected road to Salt Lake City.

Street railway syndicate.

The Los Angeles "Investor" states that a syndicate of South African millionaires had an option last summer on the principal street car lines in this city (operated by electricity); that the price was about 800,000*l.*, and that the syndicate decided finally not to purchase, partly because recent experiments have demonstrated that compressed air motors are likely to supersede electricity as a motive power for street railways.

Trans-Siberian Railway.

Interest is taken here, and speculation indulged in, as to the effect on this district of the completion of the Trans-Siberian Railway. It is anticipated that steamship lines will be established between Los Angeles and the Pacific terminus of the railway; that the Chinese will come under the influence of European civilisation, and that greater and more profitable intercourse between them and the people of this country will result.

Advice to emigrants.

I am not at present prepared to advise English people to come to California, except invalids who have sufficient means for their support, and capitalists seeking investments. Recognising, however, that many English people who have a little capital will be tempted to come here, I wrote to an English gentleman, who has had five years experience in this State, and who is a member of a co-operative English company, asking his opinion on Southern California as a field for English emigrants, and as to the "farm pupil" system. I place implicit confidence not alone in the integrity of my correspondent, but also in his ability to advise, and so quote his reply in full as follows:—"Young men who have no capital beyond health and strength, and no certainty of commanding any in the future, should be advised to go where unskilled labour is less plentiful than here, and where the floating Englishman is not at a discount. Chances are, however, better for the settler with 250*l.* in cash and upwards. Here is an example. Mr. H., starting with 300*l.*, has for three years been working up a dairy business, has recently sold a part interest in it, and with the proceeds has purchased a neighbouring dairy farm of pure bred Jerseys, with a herd of registered hogs, first-class buildings, 10 acres of alfalfa, &c. Mr. H., while sole owner, attended to 12 cows, drove 40 or 50 miles daily delivering milk, besides doing his own housework. He says he has never felt better in his life, and that with his present experience he could have made 100*l.* go as far as 300*l.*

"If only such men as these could be induced to take pupils, the benefit of their experience would be cheap at 100*l.* for a year. The 'pupil,' however, would be more trouble than 10 cows, and not as profitable, and thus it is that a man running a good business like this, or a first-class citrus grove, will not risk the loss that a careless pupil might inflict, without a heavy premium for insurance. To find such homes, however, for boys fresh from school, ignorant of the A B C of agriculture, and dependent only in their own imaginations is surely a legitimate and useful business in duly qualified hands.

"Married couples with small resources should substitute for their own ideas of Western America a realisation of what it is. Except in certain specially desirable and limited areas demanding a capital of from 1,000*l.* to 2,000*l.*, and an income besides of 150*l.*, isolated ranch life and fruit farming entail much household bondage, and disappointing social surroundings, and above all much anxiety as to a refined education for the children. Yet a man and wife prepared to make sacrifices to escape the discomforts of a poverty stricken town or country life at home, will find what many consider ample compensation here, where a small income means affluence, and the charms of the climate, and free life in the open air, though much advertised, are real.

An English company, started about 18 months ago in San Diego County, and as yet partly in the pioneer stage, indicates a possible means of minimising the disadvantage of isolation, and the amount of necessary capital, while it offers a substitute for the pupil system. A club-house in this case offers an escape from household drudgery, and the system in working combines some good features both of private and joint ownership of land and plant. The vendors receive nothing in cash, and no salaries are paid. The well-watered ranch is adapted to most Californian outdoor industries, the products of which in the shape of cattle, honey, milk, butter, poultry, and fruit, can be handled better collectively. About 20 lots of 20-acres each are in the hands of shareholders, and others are surveyed for sale, the remainder of the lands being devoted to joint stock farming. The directors consider that the social lines of this settlement are sound and promising, and that if bogus land schemes have not diverted all investors from South California, financial success is also assured."

In my report for 1893, I commented on the "large numbers of people who were coming here from the eastern States at a time when the class required here was farmers with some little capital," and I added, "The expenditure of the large sums used in advertising Southern California, would be explicable did it result in attracting here rich farmers only; for one rich farmer, however, there are a dozen others who are soon in direct competition with many of those who contributed money to induce them to come here, and who are now suffering from the competition their presence causes."

The following cutting from a recent issue of the "Los Angeles Times," bears out the advice I have given, and now again give in this report as to the classes required here:—

"The very fact which has been widely advertised throughout the world, that Los Angeles is so attractive and progressive a city, has led thousands to come this way with expectations that could not, in the nature of things, be fulfilled. No matter how prosperous and progressive a city may be, no matter how rich the resources of its surrounding territory, it can only support a certain percentage of non-producers. Los Angeles has more than its due share of such people—of physicians, lawyers, music teachers, clerks and book-keepers, real estate agents, parsons, and amateur journalists. They come here with enough to live on for a few months; wait for 'something to turn up,' and then, as they see their hopes fade, they naturally grow discontented.

"This condition of affairs is aggravated by the number of people who come here for their health, or for the health of some member of the family. In many cases they have just enough to live on, and are able to do some light work in return for pocket money. This naturally tends to depreciate the rate of wages paid for such work, so that it is, perhaps, lower in Los Angeles than in the average American city.

"The manufacturing industry is in its infancy here. The mechanical and labouring classes are at present more than fully represented."

Unemployed. There are upwards of 1,200 men out of employment in this city at present. To relieve this distress a very large sum has been subscribed by private citizens, and about five hundred heads of families have been given employment in the park at a wage of

4s. per day. I am informed by a member of the relief committee that there are a number of lawyers, doctors, parsons, and other professional men working with pick and shovel for 4s. per day.

A recent advertisement for a music teacher produced 65 replies from persons willing to teach music from 7d. to 4s. per hour; many of these poor people were young English women, who had come here to "better themselves." {Music teachers.}

In response to an advertisement for a nursery governess, 40 replies were received in one day. Several of these replies were from thoroughly competent English governesses, some of whom offered to give their services gratis for board and lodging. {Governesses.}

In my report for the year 1890 (Annual Series No. 906, and in several subsequent reports) I commented at some length on the sugar beet industry, which had then just been commenced on the Chino Ranch about 40 miles east of this city. I pointed out that the owner of the ranch was willing to rent farms of 20 to 40 acres; that he stated that an industrious farmer could cultivate 20 acres of beets and make a minimum net profit of 6l. per acre; and that, as I always advise English farmers to rent land for a year or two before purchasing, I thought this a good opening for those who purposed settling here. Many English farmers have settled at Chino in the past six years, and many thousands of acres of the Chino Ranch are now cultivated in sugar beets by tenant farmers. The following is a description of the treatment of the farmers by the proprietors of the sugar factory :— {Sugar-beet growers on Chino estate.}

"Contracts are entered into annually between the tenant farmers and the proprietors of the factory, which reserve to the latter the privilege of calling in the crops at their own pleasure; that the beets are paid for in proportion to the amount of sugar they contain; that the maximum of sugar in the beets only remains for a short time; that the crops of the farmers who displease the managers are not called in until they are so depreciated as to be of little value; and that the 500 families at Chino only make about 40l. per annum for each family."

I am informed by an English farmer, who I consider both reliable and competent, that the tenant farmers at Chino are not making any money, and are dissatisfied, and that the farmers who have purchased land there affect to be well satisfied, but are anxious to sell their lands.

About 100 miles east of this city a portion of the Mojave Desert, known as the Minneola Valley, is being brought under cultivation; an agency for the sale of the lands has been established in London, and a newspaper is being published there to "boom" the colony. The land, with water for irrigation, is offered at 5l. 5s. per acre, and purchasers of 40 acres are given a free passage from London to Minneola. The San Francisco "Chronicle" has attacked this enterprise, characterising it as a swindle, and stating that "the land consists of sand and alkali, on which, under the burning sun, eggs can be fried without fire." I am informed by a number of persons here, in whom I place confidence, that the soil is as good as at Hesperia, a neighbouring colony, where alfalfa and deciduous {Minneola Valley.}

fruits are successfully grown, and that the colony has sufficient water for about 4,000 acres of land. It is not a suitable place for English people to settle, however, as the heat is almost unbearable for three or four months in the year. Apart from this, however, I cannot too strongly urge intending emigrants not to purchase land without seeing it, and not to purchase at all until they have lived here for at least a year. I have dissuaded many settlers from purchasing upon their arrival here, and in every case they have subsequently thanked me for giving them this advice.

Whittier Reform School.

In previous reports I have commented at some length on a reform school for juvenile offenders, established in 1891 at Whittier, about eight miles east of this city. The distinguishing feature of this school is that the inmates are treated with great kindness, are taught a trade, and can choose from 18 trades which one they wish to learn. The superintendent writes me that "it is not often necessary to inflict severe punishment, but we find it advisable for some of the pupils to know that such punishment may be inflicted in case of necessity."

The daily average number of inmates in 1896 was 400, and the cost per inmate was 55*l*. per annum. In the five years the school has been in operation, 1,069 children have been confined in it, 980 of whom were committed for the following offences:— Burglary, larceny, vagrancy, and incorrigibility. The parents of 517 of these children were native-born Americans, and 552 were of foreign birth. The percentage of Irish parents among those of foreign birth is remarkably large. I am assured by a former superintendent, that the school has made good citizens of numbers of embryo criminals.

Free schools.

There are now 54 free schools in this city attended by upwards of 20,000 pupils, for whose instruction there are 377 teachers.

The estimated value of the school property is 230,000*l*., and the bonded indebtedness, which is secured primarily on the school property, and is also guaranteed by the State, is 90,000*l*. These bonds bear interest at 8 to 5 per cent., the lower rate being on the later issues.

Owing to the large sums of money expended here annually in free education, the supply of professional men, clerks, typewriters, stenographers, &c., is out of proportion to the needs of the community. It is being recognised that it is a mistake to give a "Thousand dollar education to a ten cent boy," and interest is being taken in proposals to substitute free instruction in a trade in lieu of a free classical education.

Sales of land by the Southern Pacific Company.

In my report for 1884 I referred to the forfeiture of the land grant to the Atlantic and Pacific Railway. The Southern Pacific Railway claimed a portion of the forfeited lands, and conveyed large tracts in this district to private purchasers, who in many cases took possession and made valuable improvements. The Supreme Court of the United States has held that the lands comprised in the lapsed grant reverted to the United States, and did not inure to the benefit of the Southern Pacific Company under the terms of the land grant to that Company. Suits have been instituted by some of the purchasers against the Southern Pacific Company to recover the purchase-money they have paid to that Company, and the plaintiffs will probably succeed—after years of litigation. I mention the matter as I find that some of the victims are English people (more than one of whom has complained to me), and as a warning to emigrants not to buy land, even from a rich corporation, without having the title examined by a competent attorney.

Climate. The climate of this district is generally considered to be an exceptionally good one, more especially for persons suffering from affections of the lungs. After 15 years' experience I may say that it is a good climate for consumptives who are in a position to take great care of themselves, and who avoid the trying change of temperature at sunset, and it is also good for elderly people who desire to prolong their lives. On the other hand, owing to the sudden change of temperature at sunset, people who cannot stay in their houses at that time are very subject to bad colds, catarrh, and neuralgia. It is not a good climate for nervous people.

Harbour for Los Angeles. I stated in my report for 1895 that the ports for this city are San Pedro (22 miles south) and Port Los Angeles (18 miles west), and that representatives of these ports were trying to secure a Government appropriation. Congress appropriated 600,000*l.* to be expended in the construction of a breakwater at whichever port should be selected by a Commission appointed by the President of the United States. This Commission has decided in favour of San Pedro, and when the breakwater is completed wharves will be built, and the foreign shipping, which at present goes to the Southern Pacific Company's wharf at Port Los Angeles, will go to San Pedro.

I am indebted to the collector of customs for the return of shipping, Annex A, at the end of this report. It does not include the coast trade.

Mistakes of English exporters. In my report for 1895 I gave letters from the principal wholesale merchants here, stating that they handle English goods as little as possible, owing to the fact that they are dissatisfied with the manner of distribution adopted by the exporters in England. This is a matter of great importance to English exporters, as the amount of English goods used in this district is very large and could be greatly increased. The tables attached to this report do not give any idea of the business done here; the imports for Los Angeles being entered at San Francisco and New York, and brought here by rail. A firm of wholesale grocers writes me as follows:—

"To place staple goods on our market at reasonable prices is a main requirement, and as we stated when writing you a year ago, to place these goods in the hands of people who will distribute them through legitimate channels is another. We presume that on account of taxation English goods as a rule are so much higher than those of American manufacture that we have been in the habit of looking upon them as of a fancier character, and sold to the minority who have a fastidious taste rather than to the majority who consume a quantity. In our line we should imagine that if the English can successfully produce anything for our trade to consume, it would be in the preserve and pickle line. There is, of course, a very large demand for ale, stout, ginger ale, &c., but these are not within our province. Jams, marmalade, pickles, olive oils, sauces, catsups, chutneys, crackers, &c., are the goods that there would be a larger demand for on our part, and on the part of other grocers, both wholesale and retail."

Wine. A very pure good brandy is made here, and ought, I should think, to sell well in England. The sweet wines of this district, though pure and wholesome, are not adapted to the English market. Prices continue to be so low as to leave little, if any, profit to the producer.

Portland cement. Very large quantities of Portland cement are used in this district, and the demand is more likely to increase than to diminish. Competition has cut the price so low that the profit to the exporters must be quite small. W. P. Fuller and Co., manufacturers and importers of paints, oils, glass, &c., are the only direct importers here.

Walnuts. The product of walnuts is increasing rapidly, and the industry has been very profitable at Rivera, Los Nietos, and a few other places in the vicinity of this city. The area of lands in this district where the walnut will thrive, however, is quite limited.

Oranges. It is stated in the press that the California navel oranges have been sold this season in New York at an average price of 11s. per box, that the California seedlings realised 5s. to 7s. per box, and that seedlings from Italy realised at auction an average price of only 3s. 7d. per box. I wrote to "Bradstreets," the principal New York trade journal, in regard to the competition of oranges from Italy, and other matters, and have received from the Editor the following letter addressed to him by the Goodsell Fruit Company:—

"Replying to your favour, we would say that to all appearances there is a very large foreign competition in domestic oranges. The superior quality of the California fruit, however, both in flavour and colour, is such as to make it possible for us to obtain very much better prices for the Pacific Slope orange than for the fruit shipped from Sicily, Spain, or elsewhere. The Sicilian orange does not grow as large in size as the California fruit. It is packed very much better, however, being shipped in boxes of Bangor wood, which is a preferable package to the California package made of domestic wood.

"Quite an art is displayed in packing the foreign product which the domestic fruit grower has not yet succeeded in getting the knack of. In our opinion California's product, by reason of superiority in flavour and appearance and popular demand, make it unassailable by the foreign fruit. As a better evidence of this, a catalogue of our sales of California fruit during the past few days, together with a catalogue of foreign oranges, show that the latter are selling for about one-half the price of the home product, in spite of the fact that there are double the number of oranges in the foreign packages."

The Transcontinental Railways write me that the shipments of oranges and lemons from this district in the past three years have been as follows:—

Year.	Quantity.
	Tons.
1894	49,770
1895	77,000
1896	78,620

The Earl Fruit Company, the principal fruit shippers here, write me that the shipments of oranges and lemons in 1896 amounted to 6,647 carloads. This would be about 66,470 tons, more than 12,000 tons less than the figures given above. In the preliminary report of the State Agricultural Society for 1896 it is stated that the shipments of citrus fruit for 1895 aggregated 11,582 carloads, which is equivalent to 115,820 tons. I cannot reconcile the discrepancies in the foregoing returns for 1895 and 1896.

The imports of oranges into this country are increasing steadily, as shown by the following official returns:—

Year.	Value.
	£
1894	225,401
1895	399,453
1896	538,826

Lemons. Lemon culture is increasing here, and is likely to be a profitable industry, more so possibly than orange culture. The import of lemons into the United States in 1896 exceeded in value 1,000,000*l.*

Vegetables. The Earl Fruit Company write me that the shipments of vegetables in 1896 amounted to 7,770 tons, and the transcontinental railways report 9,590 tons.

Freight rates. The transcontinental railways are now carrying oranges and lemons to all points East for 5*s.* and vegetables for 3*s.* per 100 lbs.

Fruit for Europe. For some years unsuccessful efforts have been made to sell oranges and other California fruits in London. I have made some enquiry into the matter, and am inclined to think that it would be profitable to ship a limited quantity of the finest fruits if rolled in tissue paper, and packed separately in cardboard boxes to ensure arrival in a perfectly sound condition. There are many details, such as the style and size of packages of dried and green fruits, which must be attended to to please the English buyer, and with which shippers here are unfamiliar. I should think a wholesale fruit firm in London might with great profit establish an agency here to buy and ship carefully-selected fruits.

Dried fruits. Dried fruits from this district are being shipped to Europe in increasing quantities. The business would be much more profitable to the growers if they would pack their product here in the manner approved by European purchasers, and ship direct, viâ New Orleans or Panama. At present the bulk of the dried fruits is packed roughly in bags and shipped to Chicago, where it is re-packed to suit the European market, and the retail purchaser in Europe pays 1*s.* per lb. for fruit for which the grower has possibly received 3*d.*

General remarks.

I am indebted to the Collector of Customs for the statistics in Annexes B and C at the end of this report.

Manufactures.

The "Los Angeles Journal" gives an account of the manufactures of this city, embracing iron and metals, food and miscellaneous products, manufacture of brick, and production of oil. The aggregate capital invested amounts to 2,000,000*l.*, giving employment to 3,400 men, who receive in wages 300,000*l.* per annum. The value of the annual product is 1,700,000*l.*

Mining and Stock Exchange.

The rapid development of the mines of this district has resulted in the formation of the Los Angeles Mining and Stock Exchange. At the opening of this institution in May, 1896, a paper prepared by a committee of the Exchange was read, from which I extract the following statistics. There are 125 mills in Southern California of 850 stamp capacity, employing 6,000 miners, and representing capital to the amount of 3,100,000*l.* A committee of the Exchange has prepared a list of the principal mines in territory tributary to Los Angeles, and which mines are owned by foreign capitalists. The list comprises 26 mines, with an aggregate capital of 5,400,000*l.*

Mines.

Some mines on the San Jacinto Estate are now being worked by the Riverside Gold Mines, Limited, an English company, and the prospects so far are, I understand, very satisfactory. Very valuable gold mines have recently been discovered on the desert about 100 miles north of Los Angeles. A town of about 3,000 inhabitants named Randsburg has sprung up, and a large amount of gold has been mined. Owing to the absence of water, and the necessity of hauling the ore 15 miles to be milled, only 10*l.* ore is being worked at present. Kramer, about 26 miles distant on the Santa Fé route, is the nearest railway station. I am informed that a branch will shortly be constructed by the Santa Fé Railroad from Kramer to Randsburg.

Oil.

About 600 oil wells have been bored in this city in the past three years, averaging 900 feet in depth, and costing about 300*l.* each. Some of these wells have produced as much as 60 barrels of oil per day (42 gallons to the barrel), and others have proved to be valueless. The average production is about 10 barrels per well per day. The sales of oil produced from the Los Angeles wells amounted to about 350,000*l.* The price, which a year ago was for a time only 1*s.* 6*d.* per barrel, has increased steadily, and is now 6*s.* per barrel.

Mr. Watts, of the State Mining Bureau, writes me that the output of the wells in this city for 1896 was about 720,000 barrels, and elsewhere in the county about 250,000 barrels; total, 970,000 barrels.

In the last report of the State Mineralogist, it is stated that the output of oil in this county in 1895 was 979,695 barrels.

The local railways are now using oil for fuel, as it has been demonstrated that with coal at 1*l.* 6*s.* 6*d.* per ton, and oil at 5*s.* 4*d.* a barrel, a saving of 27 per cent. is effected by the use of oil.

Canaigre.

A great deal of interest is being taken in this district in the cultivation of canaigre. I am informed by the owners of three large ranches that they are in communication with, and are in expectation of effecting sales to, three different syndicates of British capitalists, who they tell me contemplate the cultivation of canaigre on a large scale. I am not aware whether it has been demonstrated that leather tanned with canaigre is as durable as that tanned with bark; it is beyond question, however, that the former process is very much cheaper, and that the cost of tanning with bark is increasing so much that a cheaper substitute will be welcomed. It was stated in the Press here in February, 1897, that a syndicate of English and American capitalists had purchased 22,000 acres about 50 miles east of this city for 100,000*l.*, for the purpose of cultivating canaigre. I am informed by the agent for the San Francisco Savings Union (the vendors), that the purchasers, the Anglo-American Canaigre Co., consist of an American and an English syndicate; that the American syndicate is taking over the land, and the English syndicate is interested only in the product. The vendors acquired the property under foreclosure, and are selling at cost price. The Company is planting 8,000 acres this season.

Sugar beets.

In some of the Western States the pioneer farmers destroyed forests which would now be priceless to clear the land for the plough, when, in adjoining States, the farmers were using corn for fuel. It is now stated that the American farmer exports the wheat raised on seven acres of land to pay for the sugar he could raise on one acre cultivated in sugar beets. In this State the percentage of saccharine is higher than in France or Germany; the climate admits of a succession of crops; labour is now plentiful, and reasonably cheap, and with enterprise and capital the bulk of the 2,000,000 tons of sugar now imported into this country might be produced here.

The beet sugar factory for this district is at Chino, about 40 miles east of this city. The product of this factory for the past two years has been as follows:—

Year.	Granulated Sugar.
	Tons.
1895	10,000
1896	8 000
1897 (estimated)	15,000

The decrease in 1896 was occasioned by unfavourable weather. To show the relative importance of the Chino factory I give the following statistics:—The product of sugar in California in 1896 was 32,250 tons, and in the United States 315,000 tons. The imports amounted to 1,948,169 tons, and the world's product was 4,320,000 tons. Persons interested in the sugar beet business should procure the report of the State Agricultural Society; 38 pages of the report for 1895 are devoted to the sugar beet. In that report it is stated that tests made by the United States Government in 1891, 1892, and 1893 demonstrated that at the Chino factory 6·56 tons of beets returned 1 ton of sugar, and that at Watsonville and Alvarado, in the northern part of the State, 8·40 and 9·09 tons of beets respectively were required to produce a ton of sugar.

Alamitos sugar factory. A large sugar beet factory, costing 80,000*l*., is being constructed on the Alamitos Ranch, about 20 miles south east of this city, by the Bixby Land Company. Contracts for the planting of sugar beets have been made with the farmers in the vicinity, and it is expected that about 4,800 tons of sugar will be produced this season. The farmers in the Alamitos district have for several years raised beet for the Chino factory; the percentage of saccharine is so much higher here than at Chino, that the additional price paid them has more than paid the freight to Chino. The Bixby Land Company is willing to rent land to farmers for one-fourth of the crop—that is, the tenant covenants to plant the land he rents in sugar beets, and, in lieu of paying a money rent, delivers to the landlord one fourth of the produce of the land. Newly arrived farmers are very unwise to purchase land until they have been at least a year here, and as under the foregoing system they will have an opportunity to acquire information about the country, and make some profit without risk, I think it worth the consideration of intending emigrants.

Borax. It is stated in the Press that a proprietor of borax properties in San Bernardino County, has recently borrowed 100,000*l*. from English capitalists, and has purchased two English borax refineries, with a view to introducing his borax into the European market.

Divorce. Decrees of divorce were granted by the Superior Court of Los Angeles County in the past three years as follows:—

Year.	Number.
1894	285
1895	312
1896	237

In 1896, 393 suits for divorce were commenced, but the decrease in the number of decrees granted is probably due to the fact that, owing to pressure of business in the Courts, many of these suits are still undetermined.

Inquests. The number of inquests held during the years 1895 and 1896, and the number of cases in which verdicts were returned, are as follows:—

SAN FRANCISCO.

	Number.
Murders during the year 1895	17
Inquests held during the year 1895	370
Murders during the year 1896	14
Inquests held during the year 1896	289

New buildings. The value of new buildings constructed in this city in the past three years (exclusive of Government buildings) has been as follows :—

Year.	Value.
	£
1894	465,000
1895	777,000
1896	550,000

Health. The City Health Officer reports that the total number of deaths in this city in 1896 was 1,366, and that the births numbered 1,661. As the population is 100,000, this gives a death-rate of 13·66, and a birth-rate of 16·61 per 1,000. The principal causes of deaths were as follows :—

	Number.
Infectious diseases	233
Diseases of respiratory system	384
Violence and accidents (including 36 suicides)	114

376 of the deceased had resided here less than a year. Out of 188 cases of diphtheria 9·57 per cent. proved fatal, and in 1895 out of 152 cases 18·42 per cent. proved fatal. The decrease of the death-rate from this cause is ascribed to the use of antitoxine. There are 387 registered physicians, and 115 dentists in this city.

Mountain railway. In my report for 1893 I referred to the construction of a cable-electric railway to a peak of the Sierra Madre Mountains, overlooking Los Angeles, about 6,000 feet above the sea. This railway issued bonds to the amount of 100,000l., of which few, if any, were taken by British capitalists; the undertaking has not proved financially successful, and it is now in the hands of a Receiver. Owing to an informality in the issue of the bonds it is possible that the bondholders will get nothing.

Salt Lake Railway. The proposed railway to connect Los Angeles and Salt Lake City, Utah, has practically been commenced at both ends, and will, I think, be completed in a few years' time. It will open up a very rich mining country, which will become tributary to Los Angeles, and it will open the north-western market to the fruit-

(2397)

growers, besides shortening the journey from Los Angeles to Chicago by nearly 24 hours. At the Salt Lake end of the line construction has proceeded as far as Milford, about 200 miles south-west of Salt Lake City, and the Secretary of the Salt Lake Chamber of Commerce is informed that 200 miles of iron has already been purchased, and bids are now being published for 100,000 ties. Information from reliable sources convinces him that the proposition has been financed, and that before the close of the year a good portion of the road will be in operation.

At the Los Angeles end of the line, a commencement was made a couple of years ago by the construction of a line from Blake (a station on the Santa Fé route, about 120 miles north-east of Los Angeles) to Manvel, near the Vanderbilt mines, about 30 miles north of the point of commencement. The California and Eastern Railway has acquired this line, and the manager informs me that his company will construct from Manvel to Goode Springs (about 50 miles) this year. This will leave a gap between Goode Springs and Milford of about 300 miles.

At the opening of the Los Angeles Mining and Stock Exchange in 1896 an address prepared by a committee of the Exchange was read. The following is an extract :—

" Probably the greatest mining country that ever will be known is close to Los Angeles, and is as yet almost entirely undeveloped owing to the lack of transportation facilities. This is Southern Utah and Nevada, and it is inevitable that within a very few years this great country will be opened to conquest by Los Angeles through the construction of the Salt Lake Railroad. The mineral products of this portion of the great south-west are simply wonderful. Gold, silver, and copper abound, and it is no exaggeration to say that there are mountains of excellent coal and the best iron only waiting for a means of transportation to reach a market. Added to these, asphalte and petroleum are found in large quantities."

Railway to San Francisco. The Southern Pacific Railway, connecting Los Angeles and San Francisco (487 miles), runs through the San Joaquin Valley at a considerable distance from the coast. The same company has now nearly completed another railway to San Francisco, which closely follows the coast line, and of which only 30 miles remain to be constructed. As, however, this 30 miles is through a very mountainous part of the country, it may not be completed for some time.

Orange-growing. I am indebted to Mr. Cayley, an Englishman who is engaged in orange growing at Riverside, for the following interesting letter on that industry :—

" The orange crop in Southern California this past season has been much smaller than was generally expected. This was largely owing to the excessive dropping of fruit in the spring of 1896. There are many theories as to the cause, the one most generally accepted being that a late frost nipped the fruit soon after it had first set. However the fruit dropped in many localities where there was no frost. I myself am inclined to think that it was caused by the sudden comparatively cold weather which followed the extreme heat we had in June. The cold would check the sap which was flowing so vigorously. The total crop of Southern California will probably be about 58,000 tons, of which amount Riverside will contribute 20,000 tons. Next season the crop for Riverside will be about 40,000 tons, and for the whole of Southern California 80,000, supposing there is no frost. I still think an Englishman may do well out here, but only in a very few localities. Land comparatively free from frost, with an ample supply of water, is absolutely essential to ensure success. I also think only the best varieties of oranges are likely to pay, as even with a possible tariff of ½d. per pound we cannot compete with Mexico and Europe in the inferior grades, owing to the high price of labour and transportation in the United States. There is a considerable risk in buying bare land and planting it, as by the time it comes into bearing, in addition to the probability of many of the trees not turning out to be of the variety desired, there is the further possibility of there being by then no protective tariff. I should add that prices on the whole have been fairly satisfactory this season, navels averaging about 5s. 7d. per box (70 lbs.) to the grower. Inferior varieties have, of course, commanded a lower price."

The Chamber of Commerce of this city has petitioned Congress to prohibit the importation of Mexican oranges, on the ground that they are so infected with the " Mexican orange worm " that importations will introduce that disease and so endanger the industry here. Official returns show that the imports of oranges from Mexico in 1896 nearly equal the aggregate imports from that country for three previous years.

The census of 1890 showed 12,400 acres in bearing trees in this district, and 700 acres elsewhere in this State. The latest figures I have received for this district are as follows:—

	Number.
Number of acres in bearing orange trees	18,000
Number of acres in orange trees coming into bearing	25,000
Total number of acres of orange trees	43,000

In the preliminary report of the State Agricultural Society for 1896, the following advice is given to fruit farmers:—

" Until new methods of handling our fruit crop are devised, we think further extension in tree-planting unwise, as there are in our State so many other resources which invite investment at this particular time, and which will prove more profitable in a much shorter period of time."

I am satisfied that the profits to be made in raising vegetables for the Eastern market, and in dairy farming, are much more stable and in the long run more satisfactory than fruit farming.

The cultivation of the olive is steadily increasing, and is, I Olives.

think, destined to be one of the most important industries in this State. In competing with the product of France and Italy, the California grower is heavily handicapped by the high wages paid here; labour-saving devices for picking the fruit, &c., have been patented, and American ingenuity may enable the growers here to capture the Eastern market. The olive is comparatively little used in the United States, and what the growers really need is to educate the people to save themselves from the pangs of dyspepsia by using pure olive-oil for cooking purposes, in preference to butter, lard, &c.

Official returns show that the imports of olive-oil into the United States have steadily increased for the past five years, from 175,322*l.* in 1892 to 221,410*l.* in 1896.

Walnuts.

It is stated in the Press that a disease has attacked the walnut trees, and that Professor Pierce of the Department of Agriculture has decided that it is of bacterial origin. He is reported to have said that it is extremely dangerous, and that unless checked it is likely to destroy the walnut industry.

Insect pests.

The Secretary of the State Board of Horticulture, writes me under date March 26, 1897, as follows:—

"The general condition of trees in California to-day is better than ever before; insect pests are now better understood; practical remedies are applied, and they do not do the injury they did in former years."

Mr. Scott, Horticultural Commissioner for this county, writes me as follows:—

"The fruit trees in Southern California are in splendid condition, and there is every prospect of an abundant crop of both citrus and deciduous fruits. 'Red scale' has not increased during the past year, nor can I say it has decreased to any extent. It is certainly the worst pest citrus fruit growers have to cope with. No damage has been done by frost in any of the orange groves in Southern California so far this season."

Irrigation Act.

In previous reports I have commented on an irrigation law of this State known as the "Wright Act," under which two-thirds of the freeholders in any district, capable of irrigation from a common source, may form an irrigation district, vote and sell bonds, and use the money in supplying their lands with water. The constitutionality of this Act was pronounced by the Supreme Court of California some years ago; in 1895, however, the United States Circuit Court held that it was unconstitutional, and the Supreme Court of the United States has now reversed the decision of the Circuit Court, and affirmed the constitutionality of the Act. One objection to the Act is that land included in an irrigation district is made too valuable for grain culture, and it is uncertain whether it will be profitable to plant more fruit trees. Many grain farmers have lost their property owing to their inability to pay their annual assessments to cover the interest on the bonds.

There are a great many irrigation districts in this vicinity, and the aggregate issue of irrigation bonds in this district approximates 2,000,000*l.*

SAN FRANCISCO.

In this report 2,000 lbs. is taken to be a ton, and dollars have been converted into pounds sterling at the rate of 5 dol. to the 1*l*.

Annex A.—RETURN of all Shipping at the Ports for Los Angeles California during the Year 1896.

ENTERED.

Nationality.	Sailing.		Steam.		Total.	
	Number of Vessels.	Tons.	Number of Vessels.	Tons.	Number of Vessels.	Tons.
British	7	11,640	2	4,050	9	15,690
American	2	82	16	29,923	18	30,005
Other countries	2	3,117	17	33,391	19	36,508
Total	11	14,839	35	67,364	46	82,203
,, for the year preceding	30	25,581	28	54,929	58	80,510

CLEARED.

Nationality.	Sailing.		Steam.		Total.	
	Number of Vessels.	Tons.	Number of Vessels.	Tons.	Number of Vessels.	Tons.
British	7	11,640	2	4,050	9	15,690
American	2	82	16	29,923	18	30,005
Other countries	2	3,117	17	33,391	19	36,508
Total	11	14,839	35	67,364	46	82,203
,, for the year preceding	16	19,792	28	54,929	44	74,721

Annex B.—RETURN of the Principal Article of Export from Los Angeles, California, during the Year 1896.

Article.	Quantity.	Value.
	Sacks.	£
Barley	40,538	6,077

RETURN of Principal Articles of Import to Los Angeles, California, during the Years 1895-96.

Articles.		1895.		1896.	
		Quantity.	Value.	Quantity.	Value.
			£		£
Coals...	Tons	128,249	84,620	118,833	83,554
Portland cement	Barrels	5,933	9,060	11,308	19,570
Other articles	...	3,236	7,577	...	26,300
Total...	...	...	101,257	...	129,424

(2397)

UNITED STATES.

Annex C.—TABLE showing Total Value of all Articles Exported from and Imported to Los Angeles from and to Great Britain during the Years 1895–96.

Country.	Exports.		Imports.	
	1895.	1896.	1895.	1896.
Great Britain	£ ..	£ 6,077	£ 101,257	£ 129,424

SAN DIEGO.

Vice-Consul Allen writes as follows:—

General business. San Diego is still feeling the effects of the general depression in business and uneasiness in financial affairs which has been noticed in the two previous years. The Presidential election and the "silver question" no doubt contributed largely to the situation.

Notwithstanding this, however, the city and county have maintained a steady growth, and some improvement in general business may be expected as the year advances.

Grain. Two cargoes of grain left for the United Kingdom in British vessels during the year, valued at 20,941*l*. 8*s*.

Coal. The oil wells at Los Angeles and other points have still continued to keep down the importations of coal. The oil, however, has advanced considerably in price since the previous year, and although the Santa Fé Railway still consumes it, some of the local railways and private engines, used for various purposes, have again taken to coal as being not only as cheap, but more reliable in general work, and an increase in coal importations may possibly result. With coal at present prices, the saving effected by using crude oil is but slight.

Cement. Cement importations stand a fair chance of showing an increase, as four large reservoirs will be built by the California Mountain Water Company, of which mention is made elsewhere. The contracts for the work all call for "Portland cement."

The city is also continuing its improvements in side-walks, for which large quantities of cement are required annually. The year 1896 showed a considerable increase in buildings, and it is confidently predicted that the coming year will make a far better showing.

Steel pruning shears. There appear to be no pruning implements of English manufacture in the California market, although the large amount of orchards would seem an inducement to make a venture in this line. Thousands of pairs of pruning shears alone must be sold annually, the demand being supplied by America, France, and Germany. If an English pair of shears made of the best Sheffield steel of sterling quality and thoroughly "practical pattern" were offered at the same or nearly the same price the demand would be good, and the market in this respect might be captured and held.

Most of the imports, with the exception of coal and cement, were received by sail and rail from the East.

The following tables show the imports and exports for the past two years:—

RETURN of Principal Articles of Import to San Diego, California, U.S.A., during the Years 1895-96.

Articles.		1895.		1896.	
		Quantity.	Value.	Quantity.	Value.
			£ s.		£ s.
Coals	Tons	70,809	36,264 12	46,352	23,227 16
Cement	Casks	52,100	13,712 8	73,025	14,278 0
Other articles	...	...	7,277 0	...	7,161 4
Stock	Number	3,455	7,968 0	2,583	4,388 12
Guano	Tons	1,405	3,505 12	1,509	1,387 16
Bullion	...	...	15,495 16	...	25,539 4
Total	...	...	84,223 8	...	75,982 12
Lumber received from domestic ports	Feet	20,612,000	...	15,000,000	...

RETURN of Principal Articles of Export from San Diego, California, U.S.A., during the Years 1895-96.

Articles.		1895.		1896.	
		Quantity.	Value.	Quantity.	Value.
			£ s.		£ s.
Barley	Bushels	1,316	128 8	} 272,270	20,841 8
Wheat	,,	179,709	20,132 16		
Agricultural implements	...	...	323 12	...	360 12
Fruit and nuts	...	...	194 12	...	535 8
Manufactured iron and steel	...	...	2,873 0	...	4,967 8
Wine	...	...	82 4	...	...
Powder and explosives	...	...	227 12	...	...
Lumber	...	...	1,099 4	...	...
Lime and cement	...	...	74 0	...	...
Coals	Tons	873	633 16	...	...
Other articles	...	...	7,843 16	...	14,020 12
Total	...	...	33,613 0	...	40,725 8

TABLE showing Total Value of all Articles Exported from and Imported to San Diego from and to Foreign Countries during the Years 1895-96.

Country.	Exports.		Imports.	
	1895.	1896.	1895.	1896.
	£ s.	£ s.	£ s.	£ s.
Great Britain and British possessions	20,398 16	20,841 8	53,613 4	36,709 8
Mexico	13,214 4	19,262 0	34,364 8	35,033 0
Not classified	..	..	29 16	4,482 8
Total	33,613 0	40,103 8	88,007 8	76,224 16

(2397)

UNITED STATES.

Customs Return for the Port of San Diego, California, for the Year ending June 30, 1896.

Articles.		Quantity.	Value.
			£ s.
Dutiable imports	..	..	56,368 2
Free imports	..	..	29,053 2
Coal	Tons ..	57,195	28,854 8
Cement ..	Casks..	75,302	19,136 2
Grain exports	Bushels	179,709	20,129 2

For the year ending June 30, 1896, the total value of merchandise was 64,489*l.* 6s.; duties collected thereon, 11,045*l.* 6s.

Shipping and Navigation.

Return of all Shipping at the Port of San Diego, California, U.S.A., during the Year 1896.

ENTERED.

Nationality.	Sailing.		Steam.		Total.	
	Number of Vessels.	Tons.	Number of Vessels.	Tons.	Number of Vessels.	Tons.
British	13	23,818	4	6,273	17	30,091
American	120	9,654	148	138,830	268	148,484
Other countries	1	1,592	81	16,684	82	18,276
Total	134	35,064	233	161,784	367	196,851
,, for the year preceding	169	59,352	249	162,302	418	221,654

CLEARED.

Nationality.	Sailing.		Steam.		Total.	
	Number of Vessels.	Tons.	Number of Vessels.	Tons.	Number of Vessels.	Tons.
British	13	23,818	4	6,273	17	30,091
American	120	9,654	148	138,830	268	148,484
Other countries	1	1,592	81	16,684	82	18,276
Total	134	35,064	233	161,784	367	196,851
,, for the year preceding	169	62,905	248	161,937	417	224,842

The number of vessels arriving during 1895–96 to end of fiscal year was 454, classified as follows:—

SAN FRANCISCO.

Nationality.	Number of Vessels.	Tons.
American (U.S.)	339	180,574
British	24	40,269
Nicaraguan	82	8,528
Mexican	1	58
Norwegian and German	8	15,065
Total for fiscal year ending June 30, 1896	454	244,494

I am indebted to the collector of customs for the information given in the preceding tables.

British Columbian coal trade. — The number of entries and clearings of British ships again shows a decrease. The Norwegian steamer, "Peter Gebsen," still continues to do the carrying trade in British Columbia coal to this port, there being no British steamer apparently willing or able to undertake it. The coal importations during 1896 from British Columbia amounted to 17,573 tons, valued at 14,058*l*. 4*s*.

Seamen's wages. — Seamen's wages ruled from 3*l*. 10*s*. to 4*l*. per month, during the year.

Quarantine station. — During the past year 1,000*l*. has been expended on a steam disinfecting plant at the quarantine station, and it is probable that an additional 400*l*. will soon be available for further improvements, the Secretary of the Treasury having recommended the expenditure of that sum for the purpose of completing the station according to the original plans. This would include another wharf, where disinfecting baths could be given to steerage passengers arriving on infected vessels.

Disinfecting plant. — The wharf and warehouse where vessels can be disinfected has a frontage of 125 feet, with a depth of 30 feet at mean low tide. About 300 feet off each end of the wharf and just inshore slightly are two larger iron mooring buoys attached by a heavy chain to 5,000 pound mushroom anchors. These mooring buoys each have a large iron ring at the top, to which may be secured the fore and aft lines of a vessel. The disinfecting pump consists of one vertical tubular steam boiler 42 inches in diameter, 9 feet high, containing 109 submerged tubes 2 inches in diameter. The boiler has all necessary steam fittings, connections, &c., and supplies steam to the Westinghouse engine.

The steam disinfecting chamber consists of a jacketed rectangular shell, 4 feet 4 inches by 5 feet 4 inches inside, 5 feet 10 inches long, with a door at each end; the inside and outside shell of jackets constructed of $\frac{3}{16}$ths-inch thick of C.H. No. 1 boiler iron, of an ultimate tensile strength of 50,000 lbs. to the square inch of section. An iron car provided with six movable trays is supplied for moving articles to be disinfected into the steam chamber. To prevent condensation coming in contact with clothing, &c., loaded on the car, the top of the disinfecting chamber is provided with copper diaphragm, or roof, made of 16-ounce sheet copper, properly wired at edges, and fastened in position as indicated. There is also a vacuum pump tank, and a are pump, the latter supplying the storage tank with salt water, find for fire and flushing purposes, also a bichloride pump, which is a Worthington steam pump for pumping a bichloride mixture from the storage tank and through hose to the different parts of a vessel as desired. There is also a sulphur disinfecting apparatus, consisting of furnace, receiver, exhaust fan, fan engines, connecting and discharging pipes, &c

Disinfecting a ship.

A ship to be disinfected is brought alongside the wharf, all clothing, bedding, hangings, mattresses, &c., are taken from the vessel, and placed in the steam disinfecting chamber, and allowed to remain 30 minutes, subject to a temperature of from 100° to 102° C. (212° to 216° Fahr.), which is believed to destroy all bacteria inimical to human life. The vessel is thoroughly washed down inside with bichloride of mercury solution. After an entire clearing up of the vessel, the hatches are covered over, and fumes of sulphur dioxide gas are forced in and the foul air driven out, until the vessel is thoroughly filled up with the disinfecting medium, which is allowed to remain from 24 to 48 hours. In case of decided infection or danger from yellow fever, the vessel and ship's company are kept in quarantine of observation for five days after these processes have been carried out.

Freight facilities.

This port has three large wharves, erected and maintained with almost constant additions and repairs, which do the bulk of the business. There are three or four smaller wharves accommodating lumber and guano schooners and other coasters. One of the best wharves is that of the Spreckels Bros. Commercial Company, which is 3,500 feet long. Its width increases as it goes out from the shore, commencing with 50 feet and terminating with 75 feet at the 26-foot water-line. Eight of the largest vessels may be accommodated at this wharf, which cost 18,000*l*. The coal bunkers on the wharf have a capacity of 15,000 gross tons. They are 650 feet long, 30 feet wide, and 30 feet in depth. The machinery is the best for the purpose, the wharf is situated at the foot of G Street, and has a track connecting it with the Southern California Railroad (Santa Fé). Ships are unloaded directly into the bunkers at a rapid rate, or into cars which carry the coal far into the interior and up the coast. In connection with the wharf is a fine grain warehouse, and a track scales for weighing cars. This wharf has received attention during the past year in the way of renewed pilings. On piles which were sound, but liable to attack from "teredos," a square of concrete was placed about the pile, running down to the bottom, and above high tide. The services of a diver were necessary to carry on this work, which is expensive, but is considered satisfactory and teredo-proof.

The Santa Fé Wharf at H and Atlantic Streets has two spurs, one 2,500 feet long, and the other 800 feet in length. It varies from 20 to 70 feet in width, and can accommodate eight sea-going ships, and six coasters. The track of the Southern California Road extends the entire length of the longer spur, and cargoes may be unloaded directly into the cars. The wharf cost about 16,000*l*.

It has been almost entirely rebuilt during 1896, new piling being driven, and a new floor laid. The new piles are partly those invented by Captain Polhamus, superintendent of Spreckles Bros. Commercial Company, and partly those of the Teredo Proof Pile Company of San Francisco.

Captain Polhamus' invention consists in boring a hole longitudinally in the pile, and filling it with creosote down to the level of the bottom. The creosote impregnates the wood, and the "teredo" working in, finds it growing stronger and stronger as he goes further, which discourages his energy as quickly as anything yet discovered. The piles are capped, and when the creosote has gone it may easily be replenished. The Teredo Proof Pile Company has taken advantage of the fact that the teredo will not cross a crack, however small. Many piles have been examined, but though honeycombed by teredo tunnels, none have ever been discovered where the holes crossed. The Company takes a 6 by 6 inch timber, coats it with asphaltum and tar paper, and builds it up by adding 1-inch boards alternating with asphaltum and tar paper, until the required size is secured. Though a new invention, this is claimed to be an absolute preventive of teredo ravages. The cost of these repairs to the Santa Fé Wharf was over 2,000*l*., besides 1,400*l*. expended on improvements on the ferry slip. {Teredo-proof piles.}

During the year important negotiations were held with representatives of Japanese steamship companies, with a view to the establishment of a line between Yokohama and San Diego viâ Honolulu. These negotiations are still in progress, but it is impossible to foretell their outcome. The outlook is favourable, however, for the early establishment of commercial relations with the Orient direct from San Diego Bay, inasmuch as the Santa Fé system, the only transcontinental line owning its own track direct from Pacific tide-water to the City of Chicago, has no connection with the Orient, and thus is unable to compete with its formidable rivals for international business. A steamship line at San Diego is a necessity to the Company, and self interest will no doubt cause it to hasten the plans made several years ago for the inauguration of such a line. {Japan steamship line.}

The development common to every city on lines of business growth, enlargement of manufacturing enterprises, opening up of new territory by road building, and extension of commercial relations, and street and side-walk improvements, has taken place in San Diego during 1896. During the year also the inhabitants have by more than two-thirds majority shown their strong faith in the future of the city by voting bonds in the sum of 300,000*l*. for a new water system, which will give a perpetual supply of 1,000 inches of water, or 13,000,000 gallons, daily. The city now uses about 150 inches daily, thus indicating that the new supply will be sufficient for all immediate needs of future growth. {Bonds voted by city.}

Great improvement has been made during the year 1896 in the streets and side-walks of the city of San Diego. Naturally, the thoroughfares of the city require but little attention as com- {Streets and side-walks.}

pared with cities in the east and north of this country, owing to the absence of storms and mud, and consequently, when the streets are once graded, or paved and kerbed, there is nothing to prevent them lasting almost for ever. Streets which a year ago were but little used now have side-walks their entire length made with fine cement, and the houses and other buildings along the streets have been improved to correspond with the changed conditions of the thoroughfare.

Gas and electricity. The San Diego Gas and Electric Light Company is one of the largest enterprises here. The Brush, Jenny, and Western systems are all used, and light and power are generated by Corliss engines of great capacity. The city is lighted at night by a number of masts, each 125 feet high, and placed at advantageous points, each mast holding six arc lights of 2,000 candle power each. There are also over 100 lights at prominent corners. During the past year 200 consumers have been added to the gas plant, most of the increase being the result of the tendency among residents of the city to use gas for fuel as well as for lighting purposes. The output of the works has been increased in consequence fully 25 per cent. The capacity of the gasholder is 150,000 feet, and the plant as a whole could supply many times more than at present required. During the year the mains throughout the city have been extended fully four miles.

Building. During the year 1896 the amount expended in building operations was over 100,000*l*. The number of permits issued during the year extended into the hundreds, the largest single amount being 30,000*l*., which represents the cost of the brewery erected near the southern boundary line of the city. Numerous other fine buildings were erected during the year in all parts of the city. In the suburbs many fine houses have been erected, and the activity of the year appears to have extended over the entire county.

San Diego brewery. The San Diego Brewery is situated south of the city, on the bay shore. The buildings and plant have cost 30,000*l*. It is of stone and brick, and furnished with the best brewing machinery obtainable. The capacity of the brewery is 150,000 barrels a year, with a storage capacity of 35,000 barrels. The main building is six stories in height, the bottling-house and office are under one roof, and the bottling works are sufficient to supply the whole coast. The ice factory in connection has a capacity for ten tons daily. The main trade of the brewery will be in Mexico and Central America, and later at Honolulu.

Citric acid. A factory for the manufacture of citric acid and oil of lemon was established during 1896. It takes from four to six weeks to condense the juice of 60 to 70 lbs. of lemons into 1 lb. of acid. The factory employs seven hands, has steam works, and a capacity for 40,000 lemons a week; only culls are used. The same company also makes oil of lemon.

Irrigation laws. A decision has been handed down from the Supreme Court that the Wright Irrigation Law is legal. It is at present undergoing revision, and when amended will be presented to the State legislature as a committee bill, and will pass in that form.

San Diego is building one of the largest irrigation systems in the United States. It is by far the largest in California. The heart of the southern California citrus country—Riverside, San Bernardino and Redlands—has 35,000 acres of trees. San Diego's new irrigation system will cover 100,000 acres, in addition to a complete water supply for the city of San Diego. The system now building, inside and outside the city, will call for an expenditure of 600,000*l*. Three dams will be constructed—one at Morena, another at Barretts', and the third at Lower Otay, the latter being practically completed. The total drainage area of the system is 375 square miles.

New water system.

Morena Dam is 43 miles east of the city. It will impound at 150-foot contour 3,219 inches, or 15,226,975,170 gallons of water. The city of San Diego will receive its supply from this source. A force is now at work there, and on December 26, 1896, the largest blast in the history of the United States was exploded, taking 100,100 lbs. of powder, and dislodging 150,000 tons of rock.

Lower Otay Dam is almost completed, being up to the 106-foot contour. It will be completed to 130 feet by April, and will impound 2,918 inches, or 13,766,328,500 gallons of water.

Barrett Dam is located 35 miles east of the city, 8 miles below Morena. The reservoir will impound at 175-foot contour 3,304 inches, or 15,630,000,000 gallons. Reduced to miners inches the three reservoirs will impound 9,441 inches. Yet in all three only 3,305 acres will be flooded, showing that the water will be in deep bodies.

The progress of the year is not confined to the city, as the back country has taken a good stride. The work of rendering productive lands that were formerly useless has gone steadily forward, and tree-planting has been carried on during 1896 on a scale equal to that of 1895. This has been especially the case with the lemon and the olive. In the former San Diego County leads the State, having in round numbers 500,000 lemon trees, of which between 90,000 and 100,000 are in bearing. The output is already heavy, and will amount to 2,000 or more car-loads annually in the course of two or three years, when the young trees come into bearing.

Horticultural progress.

The county now has 170,000 olive trees, and of these nearly 25,000 are in bearing. Many new groves have been planted during the past year. The Secretary of the County Board of Horticultural Commissioners gives the following report of fruit and nut trees which have been inspected and placed on the horticultural record of San Diego County. Up to December 1, 1896, there were inspected a total of 1,676,668 fruit and nut trees divided as follows :—

	Number.	Of which are Bearing.
		Per cent.
Oranges	212,991	40
Lemons	556,176	20
Apples	118,216	50
Apricots	94,691	70
Cherries	4,639	30
Figs	36,771	85
Nuts	58,264	20
Olives	170,053	15
Pears	42,388	50
Peaches	208,505	60
Prunes	168,889	40
Miscellaneous	5,085	60

Total acreage, 20,958. It is estimated that the tree planting of 1895-96 will reach 400,000 trees, which is not included in this report. Vines to the amount of 2,143,342 are planted, 96 per cent. in bearing; a total acreage of 5,358.

Raisins and olives. During the past year there have been shipped from San Diego County 98 car-loads of raisins, each containing 15 tons, or 2,940,000 lbs. There were 61 car-loads from El Cajon, 21 from Eccondido, and two each from Fallbrook and Poway. One shipment of 28 tons of El Cajon raisins was sent to Hamburg, Germany. Prices the past year were more than double those of 1895. The production of pickled olives and oil, and dried fruits, comprising apricots, peaches, and prunes, &c., amounted to several car-loads.

Citrus fruit. The citrus fruit crop was over 100 car-loads larger than in the previous year. However, owing to dull times everywhere, prices were not, as a rule, satisfactory. The oranges brought more than for two or three years, but the lemon market was low, except for about two months. The chief reason for the latter was the heavy importation of foreign lemons of low grade.

Report of State Board of Agriculture. The report of the State Board of Agriculture for 1896 offers many valuable suggestions. To wheat growers especially the report ought to be reassuring. Their industry during recent years has not been as profitable as formerly, and there has been a strong sentiment in favour of abandoning this branch of agriculture for some other that might promise more profit. The report notes the fact that at the beginning of 1896 the prospects of the wheat grower were gloomy, but says that the year has brought about a marked change for the better. Prices, says the report, for 1895 improved over 1894, while the great advance of 1896 showed a tendency to place wheat-growing upon the paying basis of the '70's. At the close of 1894 the price of wheat was 88 c. per cental; at the close of 1895, 1 dol. 2½ c. per cental; and at the close of 1896, 1 dol. 52½ c. per cental, at San Francisco, the latter price being from 3 to 5 c. lower than it has sold in the same market during the three months previous. The report adds:—"One year has brought about a marked change in the prospects of the wheat grower. At the beginning of 1896 his future looked extremely dark, and his noble vocation seemed to have passed into history as another one of the victims of over-production. But it must now be conceded by all that the production of wheat offers special inducements to the soil worker, as much as in the days past when the virgin land produced immense quantities, and the expense of harvest was three times as great as now."

One of the interesting topics treated in the report is the fruit industry, which is considered in a very practical manner. Allusion is made to the unremunerative prices for orchard products, and the view is advanced that the fault is to a great extent with the grower himself. The report declares that the check received by orchard growers during the past few years is mainly due to lack of business methods in the prosecution of their industry. The fruit is produced properly enough, study is given to the best methods of culture, but comparatively little attention is paid to the important question of marketing. On this subject the report says:— *Fruit industry.*

"The manufacturer of almost any article of commerce gives much of his attention to the disposition of his output before it is manufactured. In other words, he studies the market, and meets it. Why should not the fruit grower do his business in a like systematic manner? Under the present system it is the bright, quick, and energetic commission agent that keeps posted and handles the grower's product in the market, and his expenses in many cases cover the entire amount of the sale, which is a forced one, and his chief aim is to get his money just as quickly as possible, regardless of the outcome to the grower. The remedy for the present unsatisfactory condition of the fruit industry is offered in the following suggestion:—

"It is time the California fruit-grower awoke to the situation and took cognisance of methods used by other producers. Let them organise in their respective localities and properly prepare the fruit of that section for shipment, and then have a general organisation which should only look after the sales in the green, canned or dried state. Force a legitimate trade in this product, or stop producing it and get into some other business, otherwise in a few years natural consequences will result in the complete failure of all so engaged."

The report speaks very freely of the decline of the sheep industry in this State. In 1876, it says, there were 7,000,000 sheep on the various ranges, and there was a wool clip of 56,556,970 lbs., which brought an average of 15 c. per lb. in the grease at San Francisco, aggregating over 10,000,000 dol. in value. Since that time the industry has gradually declined, until now "we have only about 2,500,000 sheep in the entire State, with a wool product of 27,195,550 lbs., with nominal value." *Sheep and wool.*

UNITED STATES.

Beet sugar.

The report discusses the beet-sugar industry at some length saying:—

"There is without any question sufficient land in California that will yield 12 tons of sugar beets per acre per annum, of 15 per cent. saccharine matter, of 80 per cent. fine, to supply the United States with sugar. We pay to foreign countries over 100,000,000 dol. annually for sugar, and produce less than 300,000 tons. Here is an industry that opens up an avenue for investment of capital, that stands without precedent in the history of agriculture. . . . . The agricultural classes stand ready with a little assurance of partial success at the beginning to put them on their feet, to go into this business with a vim."

The foregoing are only a few of the leading topics considered in the report. Generally speaking, most of the agricultural industries of the State are shown to be in a healthy condition, and where they are not they can be made so.

Silk culture.

Like many other branches of industry, silk has suffered from the general disruption of business during the past years, but the friends to it and its advocates are certain of its final success, and that, too, in the near future. Thousands of mulberry trees are being planted, and calls for information as to the possibilities of the industry continue from all parts.

Tobacco.

Tobacco of good quality and flavour has been successfully grown in this country, and a factory is being established in the city for handling the product. The treatment of tobacco here is about the same as it is everywhere. Here, also, it has to be irrigated, and no doubt this matter of irrigation will affect the quality for better or worse, and will be a question to be determined only by experiment.

Pineapples.

About six years ago pine-apple culture was commenced here, at first in an experimental way. Eighteen varieties have been tested, and five of them have proved hardy and well adapted to cultivation in the open air, without protection, at an elevation of 80 to 100 feet above sea level. Their fruiting season seems to be much later than in other countries, and extends from September 1 to May 1.

Canaigre.

Canaigre is the American corruption of the Spanish "cana agria," sour cane. It is also called "Yerba-Colorado" in Mexico, localisms being "red dock," "tanner's dock," and "wild rhubarb." The best way to propagate the plant is by use of small roots rather than by seed. About 1,000 lbs. of tubers will plant an acre, and October and November are the best months for putting in the crop; though where irrigation can be practised, planting may be done at any time. The value of canaigre as a tanning agent, either alone or in connection with other tannins, has been proved beyond question. For light leather it gives great tensile strength, and is far better for split leather than gambier, oak, or hemlock. It is a quick tanner, and the yellow colour absorbed by the hide in the process of tanning is considered highly desirable for certain leathers. The sliced and dried tubers, containing an average of 30 per cent. of tannic acid are worth from 8*l*. to 9*l*. per ton. A yield of from 7 to 10 tons per acre, would give 2½ to 3½ tons of the dried product, for which there is a constant demand in Europe and America. Inasmuch as the plant grows wild in this vicinity, and the seed roots are readily obtained, the industry commends itself it to the farmer of small means, as it is harvested in such a short period after planting.

The final report of the International Boundary Commission, and the announcement of the completion of the work assigned to it, was submitted to Secretary Olney on November 28, 1896. The Commission was organised under the treaty between the United States and Meixco for the purpose of surveying and remarking the boundary between the two countries west of the Rio Grande. The original Convention was concluded July 29, 1882, and subsequently continued by a later Convention to October 11, 1896. *Mexican boundary.*

The report consists of nearly 700 pages of printed matter, accompanied by maps and photographic views. In brief, the report shows the complete marking by a series of stone and iron monuments of the entire divisional line from the Rio Grande to the Pacific Ocean, about 700 miles. The principal work performed was in restoring the original monuments wherever destroyed or displaced, erecting new ones where necessary. The line was formerly marked by about 50 monuments. The re-marking became necessary to put an end to constant disputes and controversies over territorial rights.

After a number of years of work on the part of the United States engineers, in surveying and urgently recommending appropriations for the work, the money is available for fortifying San Diego harbour, and work has actively begun. The plan of defence contemplates four 10-inch quick disappearing guns on Ballast Point, torpedo casements just inside Ballast Point, a battery of big guns on Point Loma's seaward side, and a battery of 16 12-inch mortars on the sand-spit south of Hotel del Coronado. Not all this work can be done at once, as Congress makes appropriations only occasionally, and then in a lump sum, which must be allotted by the War Department to the defences of all the harbours of the United States. San Diego's share of the last appropriation amounts to some 40,000*l*., and with this on hand contracts have been let for the construction of two emplacements for guns on Ballast Point, and for the torpedo casement on Point Loma's eastern side, just inside Ballast Point. Work has begun on certain portions of this work—building a wharf at Ballast Point, ordering materials, and putting in machinery, cranes, &c., and the excavating will begin in the early weeks of 1897. It is estimated that it will require eight months to complete the work. *Harbour defences.*

The railroad facilities of San Diego, while not so ample as they might be, meet all present necessities. It is conceded by everybody, however, that a direct transcontinental line is a probability in the near future, and that when it exists, in fact, the traffic over the road will be large and profitable from the start. This statement is not based upon the amount of commerce available in and *Railroads.*

about the city and county, but that which a transcontinental line would naturally attract to the harbour.

The Pacific Coast terminus of the Atchison, Topeka, and Santa Fé road is at San Diego, but the haul northward of several hundred miles before a direct eastern direction is taken is a loss of time that a road running straight eastward from this city would not incur. As it is, however, very good service is given to this region by the Santa Fé line, and the overland trains established during the past year make it possible to go to or from Chicago as quickly as over any other route reaching the Pacific Coast.

That portion of the Santa Fé connecting Los Angeles and San Diego is known as the Southern " California " Railroad, and is one of the most important branches of the main system.

The Southern " Pacific " main line traverses much of the eastern portion of San Diego county, but as yet has no connection with the city or harbour. It has been frequently said that the company desired to make a terminus here, and prevailing conditions in railroad affairs in this country make the statement credible.

Local railways. Penetrating the valleys directly eastward from the city of San Diego for a distance of 26 miles, the San Diego, Cuyamaca, and Eastern Railway Company operates a broad-gauge line that does a fair business. The road runs through Lemon Grove, El Cajon, and other communities, the products of which are becoming more and more difficult to handle. The increase in the production of lemons alone indicates that before many years hundreds of car-loads will be tributary to the Cuyamaca road. At present the eastern terminus of the road is at Foster, but a movement was lately instituted to build an extension to Santa Maria Valley, 15 miles beyond. It is more than likely that within a few months a great area of mountain country will be brought into closer connection with the city. Beginning at the foot of Fifth Street in this city, the Coronado Railway Company operates a substantial line which passes through National City, Chula Vista, and the head-of-the-bay region, and on around the bay to Hotel Coronado and the ferry landing. The road is of standard gauge, and 20 miles in length. The National City and Otay Railway, owned by the San Diego Land and Town Company, also traverses the National City and Chula Vista country, besides the Otay and Tia Guana Valleys and a good part of the Sweet Water Valley. The line is about 30 miles long, and well equipped. Pacific Beach and La Jolla, two attractive resorts in this part, are reached by the San Diego and Pacific Beach Company which en route passes through old San Diego. The line is well equipped, and maintained in good condition. The road does a very fair business with La Jolla, a pleasure resort.

Electric roads. The tracks of the San Diego Electric Street Railway Company are heavy and solidly laid. The system comprises over 15 miles of road, and every portion of the city is reached by the cars at brief intervals. The recent substitution of electricity for horse-power in the portions of the line where they were still used has resulted in the disappearance of horses for street car purposes in this city.

The Citizens' Traction Company line is over 5 miles long, beginning at the foot of Sixth Street, and passing through the heart of the city, and out through Fourth Street, Florence, and University Heights to the bluffs overlooking Linda Vista and the old Mission built in 1769.

LONDON:
Printed for Her Majesty's Stationery Office,
By HARRISON AND SONS,
Printers in Ordinary to Her Majesty.
(75   6 | 97—H & S   2397)

FOREIGN OFFICE
1897.
ANNUAL SERIES.

N°· 1930.

DIPLOMATIC AND CONSULAR REPORTS ON TRADE AND FINANCE

UNITED STATES.

REPORT FOR THE YEAR 1896

ON THE

TRADE OF THE CONSULAR DISTRICT OF BOSTON.

REFERENCE TO PREVIOUS REPORT, Annual Series No. 1701.

Presented to both Houses of Parliament by Command of Her Majesty,
JUNE, 1897.

LONDON:
PRINTED FOR HER MAJESTY'S STATIONERY OFFICE,
BY HARRISON AND SONS, ST. MARTIN'S LANE,
PRINTERS IN ORDINARY TO HER MAJESTY.

And to be purchased, either directly or through any Bookseller, from
EYRE & SPOTTISWOODE, EAST HARDING STREET, FLEET STREET, E.C., and
32, ABINGDON STREET, WESTMINSTER, S.W.; or
JOHN MENZIES & Co., 12, HANOVER STREET, EDINBURGH, and
90, WEST NILE STREET, GLASGOW; or
HODGES, FIGGIS, & Co., Limited, 104, GRAFTON STREET, DUBLIN.

1897.

[C. 8277—148.] *Price Twopence Halfpenny.*

New Series of Reports.

Reports of the Annual Series have been issued from Her Majesty's Diplomatic and Consular Officers at the following places, and may be obtained from the sources indicated on the title-page:—

No.		Price.	No.		Price.
1812.	Madeira	½d.	1871.	Madeira	1d.
1813.	Vera Cruz	1d.	1872.	Jerusalem	1d.
1814.	Oporto	1d.	1873.	Ningpo	1d.
1815.	Hamburg	1½d.	1874.	Rio de Janeiro	2½d.
1816.	New Orleans	1½d.	1875.	Trieste	1d.
1817.	Bengazi	½d.	1876.	Curaçoa	1d.
1818.	Marmagao	½d.	1877.	Goa	1d.
1819.	Gothenburg	2d.	1878.	Cagliari	1d.
1820.	Dar-al-Baida	3d.	1879.	Guayaquil	1d.
1821.	Erzeroum	½d.	1880.	Havana	1½d.
1822.	Munich	2½d	1881.	Reykjavik (Iceland)	1d.
1823.	Samoa	½d.	1882.	Milan	1½d.
1824.	Chinkiang	1d.	1883.	Baltimore	1d.
1825.	Jeddah	1d.	1884.	Cettinjé	½d.
1826.	Sofia	1½d.	1885.	Bilbao	2½d.
1827.	Mexico	2d.	1886.	Florence	1½d.
1828.	Teneriffe	3½d	1887.	Brest	1½d.
1829.	Batoum	1d.	1888.	Marseilles	1½d.
1830.	Cadiz	1d.	1889.	Wuhu	1d.
1831.	Martinique	1d.	1890.	Chinkiang	1d.
1832.	Odessa	1d.	1891.	Malaga	1d.
1833.	Ghilan	1d.	1892.	Antwerp	½d.
1834.	Old Calabar	6½d.	1893.	Amsterdam	1d.
1835.	Tamsui	1d.	1894.	Galveston	2d.
1836.	Copenhagen	½d.	1895.	Piræus	2½d.
1837.	Salonica	1½d.	1896.	Stettin	2½d.
1838.	Honolulu	½d.	1897.	Martinique	1½d.
1839.	Buenos Ayres	2d	1898.	Corunna	2½d.
1840.	Para	1d.	1899.	Calais	1d.
1841.	Bolivia	2d.	1900.	Honolulu	1d.
1842.	Washington	3d.	1901.	Riga	2d.
1843.	Berlin	2d.	1902.	Tripoli	1d.
1844.	Uganda	1d.	1903.	Batoum	2d.
1845.	Belgrade	1½d.	1904.	Lorenzo Marques	2d.
1846.	Dakar	½d.	1905.	Batavia	2½d.
1847.	Florence	1½d.	1906.	Corfu	1½d.
1848.	Copenhagen	2d.	1907.	Foochow	1½d.
1849.	Havre	2d.	1908.	Montevideo	5½d.
1850.	Serajevo	1d.	1909.	China	5d.
1851.	Madrid	2d.	1910.	Philadelphia	1½d.
1852.	La Rochelle	1½d.	1911.	Rio Grande do Sul	3½d.
1853.	Chicago	4d.	1912.	Quito	1d.
1854.	Berlin	1d.	1913.	San José	1d.
1855.	Cherbourg	2½d.	1914.	Dunkirk	1d.
1856.	Beira	1d.	1915.	Samoa	1d.
1857.	Charleston	2½d.	1916.	Bordeaux	2½d.
1858.	Saigon	½d.	1917.	Porto Rico	1½d.
1859.	Suakin	1d.	1918.	Galatz	1½d.
1860.	Rouen	2d.	1919.	Christiania	½d.
1861.	Patras	1½d.	1920.	Copenhagen	3d.
1862.	Barcelona	2d.	1921.	New York	2½d.
1863.	Amoy	2½d.	1922.	San Francisco	3½d.
1864.	Trebizond	1d.	1923.	Kiukiang	1d.
1865.	Lisbon	2½d.	1924.	Harrar	½d.
1866.	Callao	2d.	1925.	Berne	1½d.
1867.	Pernambuco	5d.	1926.	Mannheim	1d.
1868.	Naples	1½d.	1927.	Fiume	1½d.
1869.	New Orleans	2½d.	1928.	Oporto	1d.
1870.	Vera Cruz	2½d.	1929.	Hangchow	1d.

No. 1930.

Reference to previous Report, Annual Series No. 1701.

UNITED STATES.

BOSTON.

Consul-General Sir D. Colnaghi to the Marquis of Salisbury.

(Received at Foreign Office, May 25, 1897.)

My Lord,

I HAVE the honour to transmit to your Lordship herewith enclosed, my Annual Report on the Trade and Commerce of Boston for the year 1896, to which is annexed a Report on the Trade and Commerce of Portland for the same period, by Mr. Vice-Consul Keating.

I would add that I am greatly indebted to Mr. Vice-Consul Stuart for the help he has afforded me in the compilation of the present Report.

I have, &c.
(Signed) D. E. COLNAGHI.

Report on the Trade and Commerce of the Consular District of Boston for the Year 1896.

TABLE of Contents.

	PAGE
Boston—	
General review	2
City of Boston	3
Boston Harbour	6
Dock and terminal facilities	8
Business of Boston	9
Failures	10
Imports and exports—	
Cattle	13
Wheat	13
Corn	13
Oats	13
Flour	13
Hay	14
Provisions	14
Produce	14

(2400)

UNITED STATES.

Table of Contents—continued.

	PAGE
Boston—continued—	
Imports and exports—continued—	
Eggs	14
Poultry	14
Fruit	14
Cotton	15
Wool	15
Hides and leather	16
Metals	17
Fish, salt	18
Fish, fresh	18
Foreign and maritime trade	20
Money and sterling exchanges	21
Annexes—	
A.—Immigrants	23
B, C, D.—Shipping	24
E.—Steamship sailings	27
F.—Freights to Liverpool	28
G.—Exports	29
H.—Value of imports	30
I.—Value of exports	31
Portland—	
Trade report	32

NOTE.—The 1*l.* has been reckoned as equal to 5 dol.

General review.

[*] For a series of years the record in this Consular district has been one of general loss in both commercial and industrial business interests. With the past year, it may be trusted, that the time of depression is ended, as now, under changed conditions, business shows decided signs of a general and steady improvement, with which, it may be hoped, nothing will happen to interfere.

The depression of 1896, notwithstanding exports, showed large gains, but this was due, in the case of natural products, to the enormous crops in this country which the rest of the world needed owing to their own shortage in crops, and, in the case of manufactured goods, probably, to curtailed consumption in the United States, which led manufacturers to seek a market for their goods in foreign countries.

In the foreground of all other causes of trouble, during 1896, has been the great silver question, which gradually grew in importance until, in July, it culminated as the chief issue of the Presidential Campaign. The defeat of the Silver Party at the election has, undoubtedly, cleared the atmosphere and permitted merchants and manufacturers to resume and extend their operations with comparative confidence and safety.

Appearances, in many ways, indicate this extension of operations. Accumulated stocks having disappeared and importations

---

[*] For much of the information on the trade and commerce of Boston, the excellent Annual Report of the Boston Chamber of Commerce has been consulted. For the foreign shipping returns I am indebted to the courtesy of the United States Collector of Customs at this port.

of foreign manufactured goods having been so small, the situation is such as to tempt the manufacturers to go ahead and supply the immediate wants of the market with the least possible delay. Thus, under the new and healthier conditions now existing, capital may be expected to re-enter the channels of trade and develop new lines of industrial activity.

<small>City of Boston. Population.</small>

In 1638, the inhabitants of Boston numbered 158; in 1790, they had risen to 18,028; the increase continued with regularity until, in 1895, the population of Boston proper, *i.e.*, the city territory, exclusive of annexations, amounted to 160,349. At different dates, between 1804 and 1873, various outlying centres which contained, in 1895, 336,571 inhabitants were absorbed into the city government, thus the grand total of population included in the Municipality of Boston amounted, according to the census of 1895, to 496,890 souls (males, 239,666; females, 257,224).*

<small>Enlargement of area.</small>

While the population has thus increased, the area on which the city is built has been widely enlarged by the reclamation of marsh lands and flats, both on the western and eastern sides of its territory. Boston Neck has disappeared, the Charles River has been embanked, South Bay forms an inner harbour, and bridges have been built to connect the different points of the city and its vicinity, separated by water-ways, so that the original aspect of the territory has entirely changed.

<small>Back Bay.</small>

The quarter of the city on its south-western side, now known as the Back Bay, has, as its name points out, risen from the water, its buildings, in this respect resembling Venice, being erected on piles. The Back Bay which, 40 years ago, was inchoate, has become the favourite residential district of the city. The work of building is still extending into the country district, and the street improvements are being supplemented by a vast Park system,† which is being carried out, regardless of cost, to the great hygienic benefit of this beautiful city, the only drawbacks to which are the extremes of its variable climate, and the too constant prevalence of its east wind, pointing to the neighbourhood of the Atlantic.

The following figures will give an idea of the importance of the Back Bay improvements from a financial point of view:—

---

* "Census of the Commonwealth of Massachusetts, 1895." Prepared under the direction of Horace G. Wadlin, Chief of the Bureau of Statistics of Labour. Vol. 1. Part II. Boston. 1896.

† See p. 5.

(2400)

	Real.	Personal.	Total.
	£	£	£
In 1876 the total valuation of Boston, in round numbers, was	..	..	149,500,000
In 1889 the total valuation of Boston, in round numbers, was	..	..	159,000,000
Ward 11, in 1876..	9,400,000	6,000,000	
„ 1889..	15,200,000	9,500,000	
Ward 22, in 1876..	3,000,000	400,000	
„ 1889..	5,400,000	430,000	
Or, jointly, Wards 11 and 22 (Back Bay)—			
In 1889	..	..	30,530,000
1876	..	..	18,800,000
A gain of	..	..	11,730,000

or more than the total gain throughout the city between these two dates.*

Business quarter. The business quarter of Boston has, likewise, undergone considerable improvements. After the great fire of 1872, many streets were widened and straightened and fine stone and brick edifices, suitable for offices, some few of which tower high above their fellows, have been erected. With regard to these latter, however, a law has been passed regulating the height of buildings. Besides the general trade and industry, Boston is the great shopping centre for a district of some 30 miles round the city.

Electric cars. In addition to the footways, always crowded, to the heavy waggons, express carts, carriages, and cabs, to say nothing of bicycles, which often block the roads, the streets, not only in the business quarter, but throughout the city, are traversed by a rapid succession of electric cars, with overhead wires. The service of the cars extends to the neighbouring cities and towns, with the most important of which constant communication is maintained by night as well as by day. The fares are uniform, $2\frac{1}{2}d.$ for any distance with a system of transfers which cost $1\frac{1}{2}d.$ The pressure of the traffic, in the centre of the city, will shortly be relieved by the opening of a subway, now in course of construction, which runs beneath the principal thoroughfares from the public garden to the Union Station, and which may, not improbably, be supplemented in due course by a proposed elevated railroad.

uildings. The new Southern Union Railroad Station, which is now about to be erected, will cover an area of $12\frac{1}{2}$ acres. To secure the required area in the city necessitates the pulling down of 209 large buildings, of which 190 have already been levelled.

The class and value of new buildings completed in this city, during 1896, were as follows :—

* "Shurtleff's Topographical History of Boston." 3rd Edition. 1890. Prefatory Note by W. H. Whitmore.

BOSTON.

	Value.
	£
Classes I and II, brick and stone	1,598,200
Class III, wood	1,193,468
Increase in value, due to alterations	469,500

The Park system* of Boston, which is now in course of development, is twofold; 1. The City Park system; 2. The Metropolitan Park system.

1. City Park System.—In 1877 an appropriation of about 100,000*l.* was made, for the purchase of 100 acres of lands and flats in the so-called Full Bay Basin at Back Bay. By 1885, the sites of six parks had been secured, and the cost, for both land and construction, had reached 800,000*l.* The establishment, at this time, of a low tax and debt limit made the further carrying out of the Park scheme a difficult matter. But the work has been continued by means of long term loans outside of the debt limit. From 1885 to 1896, the number of Park sites, including Park ways and playgrounds, has increased from 6 to 19, and the cost has risen from 800,000*l.* to 2,600,000*l.*, the greatest advance having been made since 1890.

The Boston Park scheme includes two divisions. The Main Park and the Marine Park systems. The cost of the Main Park System to January 31, 1896, in round numbers, was as follows:—

	Cost.	Total Area.
	£	Acres.
Land	799,000	1,301
Construction	1,275,000	
Total	2,074,000	

The Marine Park system has cost to January 31, 1896:—

	Cost.	Total Area.
	£	Acres.
Land	406,000	861
Construction	157,000	
Total	563,000	

---

* City of Boston. Department of Parks. "21st Annual Report of the Board of Commissioners for the Year ending January 31, 1896." Printed for the Department. 1896.

Public Document, No. 48. "Report of the Board of Metropolitan Park Commissioners, January, 1897." Boston. Wright and Potter Printing Company. State printers. 1897.

(2400)

UNITED STATES.

With the addition of some 23,000l. for general account, park nursery, and betterment expenses, the total sum expended on the City Park system, up to January 31, 1896, amounted, in round numbers, to 2,660,000l., and the work is still going on. The total land area of the city parks is 2,162 acres, of the ponds and rivers, 129·9 acres. When the above system is completed, the length of the driveways will be 36·95 miles, the length of walks, 65·21 miles, and the length of rides, 7·8 miles.

Metropolitan park system. The Metropolitan Park system is managed by a Board of five Commissioners. The total appropriations thus far made to the use of the Board are 860,000l. Up to December 1, 1896, the total expenditure, including a provision for a sinking fund, was 632,235l., leaving a balance in hand of 227,765l.

The areas of the reservations now in the care of the Board are as follows:—

	Area.
	Acres.
Blue Hills	4,189·69
Middlesex Fells	1,799·60
Stony Brook	460·64
Charles River	188·88
Beaver Brook	53·08
Hemlock Gorge	24·68
Revere Beach	63·29
Total	6,779·86

In addition to the above, various reservations have been secured by different local authorities, among which may be mentioned the Lynn Woods (2,000 acres) acquired by the city of Lynn before the Board entered on its work, but which may, properly, be taken under its care.

Boston harbour. The harbour of Boston is thus described by Lieut.-Colonel Mansfield, United States Engineers, in his annual report for the fiscal year 1896 :—*

"Boston Harbour consists essentially of an inner and outer harbour united by a deep waterway, and each accessible from the sea by a distinct channel, widening into a deep and capacious roadstead.

"1. Inner harbour: This harbour lies to the north and west of Long Island, and has deep water and good anchorage in the President Roads, seaward of Lower Middle Bar, and also near the city, west of Upper Middle Bar.

"Four rivers discharge their waters into the basin—the Charles, Mystic, and Chelsea Rivers from the north, and the

---

* "Annual Report upon the Improvement of Rivers and Harbours in Eastern Massachussets in the charge of Lieut.-Colonel S. M. Mansfield, Corps of Engineers, U.S.A."—Extract from Annual Report of the Chief of the Engineers to the Secretary of State. Washington. 1896.

Neponset from the south. The direct entrance from the sea is by Broad Sound.

"2. Outer harbour: This harbour lies to the south of Long Island, and has a fine anchorage in Nantasket Roads, as well as in Hingham Bay—a well-sheltered harbour south-east of Paddock's Island. It connects with the inner harbour of the main ship channel, through the Narrows, and by secondary channels east and west of Long Island. It is reached from the sea by Nantasket Roads, which lie south of George's and Brewster Islands, and is marked at the sea entrance by Boston Light.

"Weymouth and Weir Rivers empty into the outer harbour.

"Both the inner and outer harbours are sub-divided into several minor harbours, and contain many islands, which shelter the anchorages from winds and storm waves.

"The range of the tides at the Navy Yard is 9 feet 8 inches, and at the entrance to the outer harbour 9 feet 4 inches."

From the same report are taken the following notes of the harbour works of preservation and improvement:—

The works of preservation of Boston Harbour consist of sea-walls, aprons, jetties, &c., which protect the shores of the islands and headlands, prevent additional wash into the channels, control tidal scour, and preserve the full height of anchorage shelter for vessels in the roadstead. Such have been built or repaired at Point Allerton and the Islands of Great Brewster, Lovell's, Gallops, Long, Deer, Rainsford, George's, and Castle.

The works of improvement have been by dredging and blasting, by which means many dangerous rocks and shoals have been removed, and the main ship channel enlarged from 100 feet wide and 18 feet deep at mean low water, so that it is now at least 625 feet wide and 23 feet deep at mean low water.

The following tributary channels have also been improved:—

(*a.*) Charles River: Widened, straightened, and deepened.

(*b.*) Fort Point Channel: An important branch of the main ship channel had a least depth of 12 feet at its entrance, and the channel was narrow and crooked. It has been widened to 175 feet and deepened to 23 feet at mean low water from its mouth to Congress Street Bridge, a distance of 1,900 feet.

(*c.*) Nantasket Beach Channel: Is now 150 feet wide and 12 feet deep at mean low water.

(*d.*) Channel between Nix's Mate and Long Island: A cut has been made through the bar 300 feet wide and 15 feet deep at mean low water.

(*e.*) Broad Sound: The Barrel Rock has been removed.

(*f.*) Jeffrey's Point Channel: This channel is an extension of the main ship channel from near Grand Junction Wharf (East Boston) toward Jeffrey's Point. It is now 400 feet wide from Grand Junction Wharf to just east of Simpson's Patent Dry Docks, and 18 feet deep at mean low water, thence gradually narrowing to 250 feet, and decreasing in depth of water to 15 feet at mean low water at a junction with the same depth off Jeffrey's Point.

The total amount of the appropriations by the United States Government for Boston Harbour, from 1825 to June 30, 1896, amounted to 574,855*l.*

I may note that two range lights have been erected on Spectacle Island to carry vessels up the main ship channel after passing No. 8 State Ledge Buoy. The lights are not yet in operation, but will be so before long. In the meantime the lighthouses serve as a day range.

South-east and north-east winds principally affect the anchorages of Boston Harbour.

Dock and terminal facilities.

By an Act of the Legislature of the State of Massachusetts (Chap. 291, 1895) a Board of three Commissioners was appointed to investigate the wants of the port of Boston for an improved system of docks and wharves, and terminal facilities in connection therewith. The Commissioners completed their report in January, 1897.*

At the present time the wharves and docks of Boston are entirely under railroad and private control. While not recommending interference with the present sytem in general, the Commissioners desire the introduction of the element of public ownership to counterbalance the other two and prevent the chance of a huge trust or monopoly being at any future time created. Their recommendations, therefore, include the creation of a model dock and pier on land belonging to the Commonwealth of South Boston, to be followed by the creation of further docks as occasion may arise, and the purchase of some 20,000,000 feet of private flats and marsh lands at East Boston and on Dorchester Bay to be used when and as future necessities may dictate. Their proposals further extend to (among others) the re-location of some of the railroad terminals and grade lines on streets; to forming a new channel for ocean steamers, and improving the anchorage in the harbour; to urging the United States Government to erect a second dry dock at the Navy Yard, and that the Commonwealth should do all in her power to foster waterways and basins wherever they can be utilised in the interest of economy in transporting necessaries to the citizens. The Commissioners also recommend that wharfage charges should be kept at invariable rates, and as low as possible, while pointing out that, although this is not always the case at present, the action of the great railroad corporations in promoting the export trade of Boston has enabled its merchants to enjoy low rates of freights for their imports. With regard to expenditure, the Commissioners believe that it may be limited at present to a total sum of from 200,000*l.* to 250,000*l.*, to include the erection of a dock and the purchase of the foreshores. These recommendations have not been received without some opposition, and it remains to be seen how far they will be adopted by the State Legislature.

Up to a recent date the main ship channel was adequate for

* "Report of the State Board on Docks and Terminal Facilities, January, 1897." Boston. Wright and Potter Printing Company.

the equipment of commerce. The increase of length and draught of the modern steamship now demands, however, wider and deeper waterways. Of the several good channels which Boston Harbour possesses, it is highly probable that the one which lighter draught vessels passing in and out have used, called Broad Sound Channel, by the removal of rocks and shoals can be made serviceable for vessels of the largest type. The proposed channel will be nearly in a direct course from Long Island Light out to sea, having a least width of 2,500 feet, and a depth at mean low water of not less than 30 feet. The dangerous cross currents which exist at the union of Black Rock Channel will be avoided. Vessels in approaching and entering between Nahant and the Grans, upon both of which adequate lights will be placed, will sail in a straight course through a buoy-lighted passage into President Roads. Thus, if the above plan is carried out, in addition to the main ship channel, Boston Harbour will, the Commissioners declare, have a magnificent thoroughfare, capable of accommodating the commerce of the future, and affording a safe and easy approach and entrance in any kind of weather, and at all stages of the tide.

The surface area of the water inside the harbour, or west of a line extended through Point Allerton, Lovell's and Deer Islands, covers some 46 square miles, over 13 of which there is a depth of 18 feet at mean low water, and 8 square miles of the 13 give a depth of 24 feet and over. Near the city the anchorage is wholly insufficient. The various outer roadsteads, however, are ample. Hingham Bay contains about 800 acres; Nantasket Roads, about 1,650; George's Roads, about 500 acres; President Road, about 960 acres; in all about 3,910 acres.

Business of Boston.

The series of annual Reports from Her Majesty's Consuls at Boston, which have been regularly issued by the Foreign Office for more than 40 years, may be referred to for details concerning the trade and commerce of this port. The following general notes on the business of Boston, which have been collected by the State Board on Docks and Terminals may, however, prove of some interest.

The total water-borne freight received and delivered at the port of Boston for the year ended December 31, 1895, was, in round numbers, 8,000,000 tons thus divided:—

	Quantity.
	Tons.
Coal cargoes* (mostly for railroad use)	3,500,000
Cargoes of coastwise line steamships	2,000,000
„ of foreign steamships	1,500,000
Cargoes, various (accounted for under the head of foreign and domestic business carried on in tramp steamers and sailing vessels)	1,000,000
Total	8,000,000

* Chiefly in barges towed to the port from the United States coal districts.

UNITED STATES.

The coastwise commerce of the city is large and growing, but of 11,372 vessels of all classes arriving here in 1895 over 9,000, the greater portion steamers, were engaged in this business. Increasing quantities of manufactured goods are shipped from this port to the West by water; goods to Lake ports, as far west as Duluth, are shipped by way of New York (during the open season), thence by river and canal to Buffalo, and thence to their destination by the lakes. Similarly goods are shipped hence to southern ports, and thence by rail to their destination. Not infrequently, it is stated, the best rates that can be obtained by rail are 50 per cent. more than all the water rates for the same class of goods. The coastwise business is done, to a greater or less extent, in competition with the railroads, and has a tendency, as noted above, to lower transportation charges. It represents a class of common carriers which, the Commissioners remark, it would be difficult to control by combination. By far the largest part of the coastwise business is carried on in steamships, running on established lines at regularly recurring intervals of time. The sailing vessels give cheap transportation with eastern and southern ports.

The business of the foreign steamship lines to and from this port has, at the same time, enormously increased. The managers of the Boston railroads, realising the importance of this traffic, have during the last two decades, and at great expense, built commodious terminals to connect with the ocean steamships. Boston is the third meat-packing port in the country, and largely so on account of superior transporting facilities. Shipments of manufactured goods by steamship lines are steadily increasing.

Some idea of the regular increase in the commerce of Boston may be obtained from the following figures, with which I close my extracts from the report under review.

In 1830 the value of the total exports and imports at Boston did not exceed 2,236,255*l.* (exports, 501,260*l.*; imports, 1,734,995*l.*). They had risen to 12,332,254*l.* (exports, 2,827,285*l.*; imports, 9,504,969*l.*), and had further increased in 1896 to 35,006,173*l.* (exports,* 19,170,200*l.*; imports, 15,835,973*l.*). A similar and necessary increase is noted in the registered tonnage entering and clearing from the port of Boston which, from 1,364,160 tons (entered, 793,927 tons; cleared, 570,233 tons) had risen in 1896 to 3,457,763 tons (entered, 1,843,134 tons; cleared, 1,614,629 tons) according to the returns of the United States custom-house.

In comparison with the other principal seaports of the United States Boston holds the second place for value of imports and exports, and for registered tonnage, being only surpassed, but it must be acknowledged very largely surpassed, by the great port of New York.

Failures. The business conditions prevailing in this Consular district during the year 1896 are shown by the record of mercantile

---

* In the returns from the United States Custom-house, published by the Boston Chamber of Commerce, the exports, as inserted elsewhere in this Report, are set down at 18,927,635*l.* I have retained here the Commissioners' figures.

failures, the list being the longest, and the liabilities the greatest of any year since the compilation of the relative statistics was commenced. "Bradstreet" reports the number of failures in business as follows :—

	Number in Business.	Number of Failures.
Eastern States	106,901	1,835
Total United States	1,079,070	15,094

The causes of failures in the Eastern States during 1896 are noted below :—

	Number.	Assets.	Liabilities.
		£	£
Incompetence	372	463,214	1,053,962
Inexperience	67	25,382	62,855
Lack of capital	355	194,857	462,053
Unwise credits	75	46,590	104,346
Failures of others	51	212,006	398,995
Extravagance	33	113,100	182,751
Neglect	83	49,360	131,990
Competition	205	70,508	218,616
Disaster	385	904,442	1,915,878
Speculation	25	39,400	157,867
Fraud	184	55,905	281,113
Total	1,835	2,174,764	4,970,426

Lack of capital, which is the primary obstacle to business throughout the whole of the United States, in the eastern States, takes the third place in the number of failures, while disaster, which includes commercial crises, fires, and floods, forms the primary obstacle in the eastern States, incompetence being the second.

In comparing the commerce of this port, it will be recalled that, as regards the year 1895, Boston showed an increase of 49·7 per cent. in its imports, while its nearest and largest competitor, New York, showed an increase of 17·8 per cent. only, and, while all other ports showed a decrease in the volume of exports, Boston made large gains over the previous year.*

Imports and exports.

The imports during 1896 reached a total of 13,198,179*l.*, a decrease of 2,791,376*l.* from the total of 1895, which was the largest in the history of the port. American gold coin was imported to the amount of 723,781*l.*, silver coin of 1,168*l.*, and gold bullion to the value of 27,100*l.* in addition.

The exports attained a record which has never before been surpassed, viz., 20,293,242*l.*, an increase of 2,489,268*l.* over the

* Foreign Office, 1896. Annual Series No. 1701. "Report for the Year 1895 on the Trade of the Boston Consular District."

UNITED STATES.

year 1895. The value of the gold and silver coin and bullion exported was 1,000*l*.

To the silver agitation may evidently be attributed the decrease in the imports at Boston, which was most apparent from June to October inclusive; the closing months of the year—November and December—showing a marked increase. The principal articles of import during the fiscal* year (July 1, 1895, to June 30, 1896) were:—

Articles.	Value.
	£
Wool	3,840,142
Sugar	1,371,398
Chemicals and drugs	1,026,960
Iron and its manufactures	1,092,410
Cotton	1,014,093
Hides	991,353
Leather	613,121

The following tables show the total values of the imports and exports, to and from Boston, for the fiscal year ending June 30, 1896, classed according to sources of production, and to degree of manufacture and uses respectively:—

Exports.

	Value.	Per Cent.
	£	
Products of agriculture	15,488,959	81·83
Manufactures	3,166,249	16·73
Forest	207,543	1·09
Mining	6,599	·03
Fisheries	7,240	·04
Miscellaneous	51,045	·27
Total	18,927,635	..

Imports.

	Value.	Per Cent.
	£	
Food and live animals	1,320,359	8·33
Raw materials	9,321,930	58·86
Articles manufactured for mechanical arts	2,197,892	13·88
Articles for consumption	2,359,169	14·89
Articles of voluntary use, luxuries, &c.	636,623	4·02
Total	15,835,973	..

* The statistics compiled locally and those issued by the United States authorities refer to different periods. The first are for the 12 months ending December 31; the second for the fiscal year, or 12 months ending June 30. Thus apparent discrepancies occur in the returns offered here, which have been taken from one or other authority as the required information could be obtained, and as is shown in the text.

The exports of butter increased in 1896 from 2,102,504 lbs. to 3,156,741 lbs., and of apples from 140,927 barrels to 747,106 barrels, being the largest amount ever shipped from a port in the United States in a single year.

The total in transit and transhipment trade amounted during the twelvemonths of this year to over 1,728,593*l.*

Boston still continues to lead all other ports in the United States in the shipments of cattle. Out of a total of 394,772 head of cattle exported in 1896 from all parts of the country, Boston exported 160,442, showing an increase of 45,558 head, or 40 per cent. over the shipments of last year. Owing to the admirable equipment of the cattle steamers, the rate of mortality of cattle shipped from Boston was below the general average for the United States—0·27 per cent., as compared with 0·32 per cent., according to the report of the Secretary of Agriculture.

Cattle.

The reduced crop has had a tendency to strengthen prices, but the heavy shortage abroad, inducing a large and increasing demand, was the chief cause of a considerable advance in the price of wheat, and shows, conclusively, that prices depend upon the foreign markets and their requirements.

Wheat.

The receipts at Boston were 13,427,724 bushels, as compared with 7,246,048 bushels in 1895. The exports amounted to 12,721,450 bushels, as against 7,216,709 bushels in 1895. Prices, owing, as has been said, to the foreign demand, rose considerably, and winter wheat has commanded a premium over spring of from 2*d.* to 6*d.* per bushel, due largely to the shortage of the winter crop, owing to continuous rain during harvest.

The crop of 1896 was enormous, exceeding the large yield of last year, which surpassed all previous records. Prices have, in consequence, been exceedingly low, the shortage of wheat having apparently no influence on the price of corn.

Corn.

Prices, on the Boston market, for steamer, yellow, ranged from 1*s.* 8¾*d.* in April, to 1*s.* 2½*d.* per bushel in September and December. Boston received 9,805,873 bushels of corn in 1896, as against 8,944,475 bushels in 1895, and exported 6,136,603 bushels, as against 5,664,192 bushels during the previous year.

Boston received 8,092,908 bushels of oats in 1896, nearly 2,000,000 in excess of 1895, and exported 2,147,673 bushels, as against only 83,000 bushels in 1895. Of this export all but 75,609 bushels was sent to Great Britain, being the first of such shipments for the past two years. The highest price reached per bushel was 1*s.* 2½*d.* in November, and the lowest 1*s.* in July.

Oats.

The flour market showed an improvement over previous years. Prices were low and trade dull during the first six months, but the last half of the year witnessed a heavy and increasing demand, and also a decided advance in price, the same as for wheat, and due, substantially, to the same causes. Boston handlers, holding large stocks when the advance occurred, reaped a good benefit. The export trade, however, still seems to suffer from the competition of English and French millers.

Flour.

Prices at the Boston market have ranged at about 16*s.* 1¾*d.*, spring patents bringing from 12s. 3½d. to 1l. 0s. 5d., and winter from 13s. 4d. to 1l. 1s. 8d. per barrel; 1,622,616 barrels were exported, against 2,384,719 barrels received.

Hay. The local receipts of hay were 15,605 car-loads, and the exports 50,711 bales. Medium and low grade hay overstocked the market most of the time, making the demand for the choice quality steady, at good prices. Choice to fancy ranged from 3l. 5s. to 4l. 2s. 6d. per bale, top prices being obtained in May.

Provisions. The features of the provision market during the past year have not been encouraging, as, although there has been a fairly steady demand, and the usual volume of receipts was maintained, the market has been lifeless, with low prices, and a downward tendency for the most part. Notably, in lard and mess pork, the low prices have not been equalled for years. The number of hogs packed in Boston during 1896 was 1,505,309 showing an increase over the previous year of more than 74,000.

Produce. The disagreeable features of tone and prices in the produce market that have been felt for some years past were repeated in 1896, but in a greater degree, the tendency being downward, until prices were reached that have hardly been equalled in the history of the trade. While 50,972,255 lbs. of home butter were received in Boston, only 3,156,741 lbs. were exported. The exports of domestic cheese were 21,566,448 lbs.

In the local butter market western currency extra was quoted at 1s. 0½d. per lb., but accumulations of stock broke the price to 10½d., again rising in February to 1s. Increasing receipts, however, with unseasonable weather, again lowered the price, in April, to the lowest point for the year, 7½d. The exceptionally hot weather kept prices low till the end of September, when they rose to 10d. in November, and to 1s. 1d. in December.

The butter handled in cold storage amounted to 270,000 tubs, as against 235,250 tubs in 1895.

The unprecedentedly low prices of 1895 were repeated this year in the cheese market, general dulness prevailing throughout the year. 80 per cent. of the cheese exported from Boston is Canadian cheese "in transit."

Eggs. In the egg market Western fresh opened at 11d. per dozen, but heavy increases in supply, together with a light demand, brought prices down to 7¾d., and lower still, to 6½d., with a continually dropping market, and slowly falling prices for all grades. This state of affairs was maintained during the summer on account of the great heat. It was not until late in August that a slow but steady improvement began, culminating, in early December, with prices up to 1s. for Western. Heavy receipts, however, and a light demand, soon brought a sharp reaction, and the year closed with prices at 9d. per dozen.

Poultry. The poultry market was better than during 1895, and prices were well sustained. The receipts were 192,236 packages in 1896, as against 198,237 packages in 1895.

Fruit. The fruit market during the past year met with exceptionally heavy losses, particularly in the case of citrus fruits. The demand, owing to the general depression, was very small, while the receipts were above the average, especially in the case of Mediterranean fruit, which, consequently, had to be sold at disastrously low prices.

In the banana trade the fruit arrived in good condition; the demand was also good, and prices being fully up to the average, the market showed a satisfactory result for the year. Owing to the trouble in Cuba, shipments from that island fell off, and the deficit had to be made up by increased shipments from Jamaica, chiefly in British bottoms. The total receipts of bananas amounted to 1,877,849 bunches.

Apples during the past year proved unprofitable both to producers and dealers, the crops having been unprecedentedly large. The receipts amounted to the unusual figure of 871,617 barrels, of which 747,106 barrels were exported, exceeding the exports from any other port in the United States. Prices in the local market have been lower than in any previous records, while shipments to foreign countries were so heavy as to overstock the markets, and, in many instances, they resulted in losses to the American shippers.

Cotton. The trade in cotton during the past year, as a whole, has been most unsatisfactory, but to the producing interests the shortage in crops has been nearly made up by the advance in prices. As a result of early conditions a period of active speculation ensued, during which prices rose until, in October, they reached to a fraction over $4\frac{1}{2}d.$ per lb., a gain of $2\frac{1}{4}d.$ over the lowest point touched during the season of 1895. A little over $4\frac{1}{2}d.$ per lb. for middling was the highest point touched, the lowest being $3\frac{3}{4}d.$ The average was a fraction over $4d.$ per lb. An average commercial value has been $8l.\ 5s.\ 6d.$ per bale, as against $6l.\ 2s.\ 6d.$ for the previous year.

Boston imported during 1896 some 49,430 bales of Egyptian cotton, and 4,107 bales from other places. The exports of cotton from this port to Great Britain amounted to 275,716 bales.

Wool. The imports of wool at Boston, as at other ports, show a large decrease in 1896, but while the comparative percentage is no larger, the actual volume of decrease is greater at Boston than at other ports on account of the importance of its dealings in this article. The receipts in 1896 were 442,054 bales domestic and 211,479 bales foreign.

The stocks of domestic wool in Boston, on December 31, 1896, were 50,906,900 lbs.; as against 44,878,000 lbs. a year ago. While the stocks of foreign wool in Boston, at the same date, were:—

(2400)

	Quantity.
	Lbs.
Australian, New Zealand, &c.	8,545,000
Cape	340,000
South Austrian	1,247,000
English and Irish	290,000
Pulled and scoured	2,482,000
Carpet	2,950,000
Total, foreign	15,854,000
,, domestic	50,906,900
On hand	66,760,900

Hides and leather.

"In hides the year opened with Western buffs at $3\frac{3}{4}d.$ per lb., prices declining to $3d.$ in April, tanners—in some cases—offering only $2\frac{3}{4}d.$ Prices rose $1d.$ until August, when they again dropped to a weak $3d.$ In September the demand became more active and prices advanced till the middle of November, when $4\frac{1}{2}d.$ was bid and $4\frac{3}{4}d.$ asked. December closed with a strong tone, at about $4d.$ bid.

For leather the year opened with a fair demand and a uniformly steady market. Manufacturers, generally, restricted their operations to actual needs, there being no incentive to speculation. In February prices declined, but large blocks were held, in all amounting to 500,000. The trade was almost stagnant until September, when the market resumed some activity under purchases which caused a firmer tone to prevail, and towards the end of October a sharp turn carried prices up $\frac{1}{2}d.$ to $1\frac{1}{2}d.$ per foot and per lb., which stopped buyers, except for actual needs. Prices remained steady and were firm through November and December.

The curtailment in the production of finished leather of all kinds made from Western and Eastern hides amounted to some 4,000,000 sides of upper, and 4,000,000 splits in 12 months.

The year closed with a greatly-improved situation. Leather held a very strong position, the sharp curtailment in the summer and autumn preventing any accumulation; while stocks in dealers' hands were small. The situation of hides was the same, tanners carrying limited stocks, dealers being bare of supplies and with no hides held back in the country. These conditions will insure a good market for both hides and leather in 1897, a demand practically equalling supply, so that good and probably higher prices may be expected to rule.

The following table shows the quotations of January 1 and December 31, 1896. Leather being that of No. 2:—

		January 1, 1896.		December 31, 1896.	
		From—	To—	From—	To—
		s. d.	s. d.	s. d.	s. d.
Rough leather	per lb.	0 9	0 10	0 10	0 10½
Rough splits, belt	,,	0 6	0 6¼	0 6½	0 6¾
Kip, dry	,,	0 5¼	0 6	0 5	0 5¾
Splits crimp	,,	0 7¾	0 10	0 8	0 9½
Plow grain	,,	0 5¼	0 5½	..	0 6¼
Glove, 3⅞-oz.	,,	0 4½	0 4¾	..	0 4¾
Calf, 15 to 25 S.	,,	2 11	3 1½	2 8½	2 11
,, Russia	,,	0 10½	0 11½	0 10	0 10½
Sole, Hemlock B.A.	,,	0 9½	0 10	..	0 9½
,, Union	,,	..	1 0	1 1½	1 2
Hides B.A.	,,	0 8½	0 9	..	0 9½
,, buff	,,	0 3¾	0 4	0 4	0 4⅛
,,	,,	0 5½	..	0 6¾	..
,,	,,	0 3⅛	..	0 3¾	..
Calf-skins, 9 to 12 S.	,,	3 4½	..	5 2½	..

Metals. While the fish trade, which will be considered later, may be, and is, the barometer of the business situation in the New England States, the iron and steel trade is the barometer of the business situation of the whole country.

The metal trade, in 1896, reflected the general dulness, this lasting till November, when an active movement followed the Presidential Election, only to fall back to a weak position, with a bright spot for this country, caused by a foreign demand for steel rails and bessemer ore and billets. The supply, however, was so large that the rates realised were very low. Prices have, generally, ruled low, owing—undoubtedly—to over-production, and there is a general fear that to relieve the situation an almost entire shut-down will be necessary. Southern iron is especially weak, that from the Virginia furnaces being the only quality to show any steadiness. Prices have not been so low for nearly five years; bessemer pig has been quoted at from 1l. 16s. to 1l. 18s. and steel billets at 3l. per ton f.o.b. The ore people, having failed to come to a pooling arrangement, has made the situation more acute, and, unless it is changed, there will be a large output for 1897. Finished steel has been, generally, very quiet during the year, the slight jump to higher prices after the Presidential Election having soon subsided. The same statement applies to steel rails. Structural steel is, generally, in quiet demand, though orders for building and bridge work in the New England States, and especially in this vicinity, have relieved the market somewhat.

New England manufacturers have little to report in the way of business, and, in point of fact, the New England States have ceased to be a dominant factor in the iron and steel trade, the middle States having almost completely absorbed the business, which was once so prominent a feature in this part of the country. The manufacture of nails and tacks, however, still remains, to a

(2400)

UNITED STATES.

large extent, in these States; and while there has been a noticeable failure in the trade for the past year, the margin of business promises to be fairly good for 1897. Cut nails were quoted in Boston at 2*l*. 16*s*. per ton, base nails at 5*s*. 8½*d*. to 6*s*. 1*d*., and wire nails at from 6*s*. 4*d*. to 6*s*. 7½*d*. per cwt.

Boiler tubes, Swedish iron, wrought-iron, pipe and bar iron have been and are in fairly satisfactory demand here in store, but concessions in price were the rule during 1896.

Copper has not been in large demand by manufacturers during the year, and, if left to them, prices would have ruled fairly low, but the export demand was large enough to run prices up to 6*d*. per lb. for lake and 5½*d*. per lb. for electrotype. The year ended with a fall in price of from ½*d*. to ¾*d*. per lb.

Fish.

The fish trade has been fairly good during the season of 1896, but prices have been low, in sympathy with those of most other industries. The present year, 1897, however, will—it is hoped—show an improvement, the higher prices which are being paid the American farmer for his wheat should give a stimulus to the fish business as well as to others. Boston holds an important position as a distributive point and as a great fishing port. As nearly as can be ascertained 275,000,000 lbs. of fish of all kinds and species are distributed annually. During the year 1896, 423 vessels and 9 steamers were engaged in supplying the Boston market with fish, and there were 4,214 arrivals of these vessels fully laden. The curing of codfish, hake, and haddock is a feature of the fish business, as is also the curing of "finnan haddies," 25,000,000 lbs. being cured on the wharves at Boston during the year. In consequence, this port is a leading place for the manufacture of nets, twines and seines, in which there was a fair trade in 1896.

Salt mackerel.

The Boston Fish Bureau, in its annual report for 1896, says: "Boston is the leading port in the world for the distribution of salt mackerel, and salt mackerel is the barometer of the fish trade." The quantity of mackerel salted here during the year 1896 was 160,714 barrels of good quality, being a large increase over 1895. The shore catch gave receipts of 41,125 barrels of bulls'-eyes timber mackerel (scomber collies) containing from 800 to 1,000 per barrel.

New salt mackerel from Nova Scotia, arriving in June, sold at from 1*l*. 18*s*. 1*d*. to 2*l*. 3*s*. 10*d*. per barrel. Irish mackerel, arriving on May 1, fetched nearly 3*l*. per barrel, while Prince Edward Island mackerel, arriving in July, sold at 2*l*. 12*s*. per barrel.

The following table shows the receipts of salt mackerel, in barrels, at Boston during the year 1896, as compiled by the Boston Fish Bureau:—

BOSTON.

Month.	Quantity.				
	Ireland.	Canada.	Norway.	Domestic.	Total.
	Barrels.	Barrels.	Barrels.	Barrels.	Barrels.
January	540	396	..	..	936
February	1,192	53	..	3	1,248
March	393	115	..	..	508
April	89	..	..	25	114
May	271	2	..	..	273
June	418	454	..	4,116	4,988
July	1,225	1,856	..	3,092	6,173
August	110	686	..	2,505	3,301
September	2,553	2,038	..	4,414	9,005
October	8,237	5,760	..	4,870	18,867
November	4,764	1,255	100	1,481	7,600
December	1,749	919	..	229	2,897
Total	21,541	13,534	100	20,735	55,910

Salt cod. There has been a fair distribution of salt cod-fish, but low prices have ruled. The market at Boston has chiefly been supplied from St. Pierre, the fish running about 28 per cent. of large size. The receipts of French cod-fish during the year were 4,140,443 lbs.

Smoked and barrel herring. Smoked herring is handled more on this market than elsewhere. During 1896 prices, ruling low, the receipts were 800,000 boxes. The imports of barrel herring are very important, as the fish caught on the American shores are not nearly equal to the foreign catches, either in quality or grade. This is worthy of note to our fishermen at home, as good prices can be obtained on this market for good fish. Over 150,000 barrels were imported last year, principally from Holland, Canada, Scandinavia, and Scotland.

Pickled salmon. The demand has been fair, and northern salmon fetched from 3l. 6s. to 4l. 2s. 6d. per barrel according to quality. Red trout fetched 2l. 1s. 1d., and white trout 1l. 19s. per barrel.

Canned lobsters. Canned lobsters have been in short supply, the pack from Canada being over 20 per cent. less than in 1895. Prices, consequently, should have ruled good, but the demand, owing to the hard times, was for small packages, and half-pound flats were in chief demand.

Fresh fish. Boston is, also, the principal centre for the distribution of fresh fish to all the States east of the Mississippi, and last year sent out over 110,000,000 lbs.

Considerable quantities of cod and haddock, of which there is no reliable record, arrive here, by train, from many small outports. The total receipts noted, however, during the year 1896, amounted to 56,968,150 lbs. On account of bad weather in the early part of the year, prices ruled the highest for many years. Later on they fluctuated greatly, according to supply and demand.

(2400)

Fresh mackerel showed an increase of 50 per cent. in receipts, largely from Nova Scotia, over 1895. The first arrivals fetched $5\frac{1}{2}d.$ each, gradually falling to $2\frac{3}{4}d.$

Smelts chiefly come from Canada. They showed such large importations in 1896 that prices ruled as low as $1\frac{1}{2}d.$ to $2\frac{1}{4}d.$ per lb.

Frozen herring is imported from Placentia Bay, Newfoundland. During the season 20 cargoes, aggregating 13,600 barrels, arrived, all of good size and quality. The question of assessing a duty on frozen herring has been referred to the United States Attorney-General for a proper construction of the law and the course to be followed, as arrivals here had been refused free entry, but the matter is still in suspense.

During 1896 the trade in live lobsters has been fair, but was affected in prices by the general depression. The receipts from Nova Scotia, from January to July, amounted to 32,805 barrels.

Fishing losses.

The past year, while having a greater loss in number of vessels than 1895, shows a less loss of life, a decrease in the value of ships lost, and a larger insurance to cover the losses.

In 1895 the total number of fishing vessels lost was 13, lives lost 104, and value of vessels lost 17,000*l.*, insured for 10,700*l.* The losses during the year 1896 were as follows:—

Ports.	Vessels Lost.	Lives Lost.	Value of Vessels.	Insurance.
	Number.	Number.	£	£
Boston	2	2	400	100
Gloucester	15	86	14,800	12,000
Portland	2	..	1,600	..
Total	19	88	16,800	12,100

The Boston Fish Bureau in its report for last year, says:—

"While it is by no means certain, it is possible that a new Tariff Law will be enacted at the present session of Congress, which will increase the duties on certain kinds of salt fish. The Bill differs from the existing (Wilson) Tariff in proposing an increase of $\frac{3}{4}$ c. per lb. on mackerel and halibut, $\frac{1}{4}$ c. per lb. on cod-fish, and a new duty of $1\frac{1}{2}$ c. per lb. on boneless fish. On all other kinds of fish the duty is the same. The increase in the duty on mackerel is aimed, especially, at the imports of Irish salt mackerel, while the new duty on boneless fish is aimed at the imports of these fish from Nova Scotia."

It, therefore, behoves catchers and curers of English and Irish mackerel to be careful in handling, curing, and packing their fish, also in selecting fish of good quality for export, in which case they need not fear the duty, as selected salt mackerel, well handled, cured and packed in strong barrels, not liable to leakage, will always find a ready sale at remunerative prices.

Foreign and

The ocean tonnage entering and clearing in the foreign trade in 1896 amounted to a total of 3,457,763 tons, as compared with 3,146,236 tons in 1895.

maritime trade.

The American tonnage shows an increase over the figures of 1895, but a less total of ships entered, the gain of tonnage being made by a larger entry of steamers. The foreign tonnage is the heaviest yet recorded. The total number of vessels of all nationalities which entered the port of Boston in 1896 from foreign ports was, according to the custom-house returns, 2,088, measuring 1,843,134 tons, as against 2,216 vessels, measuring 1,723,089 tons in 1895. Of the above 744 were British steamers of 1,461,973 tons, and 996 British sailing vessels of 156,942 tons. (See Annex B.)

Nationality.	Number of Vessels.	Tonnage.
British	1,740	1,618,915
American	245	146,276
Other nations	103	77,943
Total	2,088	1,843,134

The above table shows a decrease of 128 vessels for the year, as compared with 1895, but an increase of 120,045 tons. This is, probably, due to the fact, as stated above for American vessels, that, in general, steamers are taking the place of sailing vessels.

The number of British vessels from all ports, including those of the United States, entered at the Consulate, during the year 1896, was 1,787, of 1,632,583 net tons, as against 1,925 vessels of 1,493,506 net tons entered, in 1895, showing a decrease of 138 in the number of vessels and an increase of 139,077 net tons.

The vessels of other foreign nations show a decrease of nearly 20,000 tons, as compared with the previous year.

The above figures denote, conclusively, that British vessels continue to hold a preponderating position in the carrying trade of this port.

The year closed with a partial recovery from the effects of the so-called "War Panic" in December, 1895, respecting the Venezuela Boundary Question, but rumour of possible troubles among the nations of Europe were considered disturbing elements enough to make people in the monetary market uneasy, and a 7 and 8 per cent. rate was kept up at the clearing-house. This was followed, in February, by the great success of the United States Government in their issue of the 4 per cent., 29 years, 100,000,000 dol. loan. Still the Boston clearing-house kept the local rates up, even as high as 9 per cent. for call loans. Later, money ruled plentiful and easier until August, when disturbing elements again raised rates for a short period, to fall and rise again at every rumour till November 5 when the business world, generally, seemed reassured, and money soon began to be offered at quickly lowering rates.

Money and sterling exchange.

(2400)

The Boston bank clearings, in 1896, showed total exchanges of 899,624,870*l*., and total balances of 101,859,852*l*. The total sales for the year, at the Boston Stock Exchange, amounted to 4,205,678 listed shares, and 3,181,279 unlisted shares of stocks, also of 5,134,615*l*. of bonds. These figures show a large falling-off from those of 1895, and clearly prove the great distrust and fear the investing public had of the times. The sales of bonds decreased over 8,000,000*l*.

Bankers' sight bills of exchange on London were:—

| | Per 1*l*. Sterling. ||
	From—	To—
	Dol. c.	Dol. c.
In January	4 87½	4 89
April	4 86	4 89
July	4 87½	4 89
November	4 80½	4 84

In conclusion, the year 1895 closed with the general belief that business in all its branches was in a more healthy condition, and that confidence would soon be restored. The year just passed, however, did not bring to general business the improvement universally hoped for and expected. It must, however, be remembered that this was due to exceptional causes, such as the unusual features resulting from the war panic, and those which distinguished the Presidential Election Campaign.

The silver question, having been, at least, temporarily settled constitutes a distinct gain. Moreover, in its commercial record, the year has shown several encouraging features. Among the working class there has not been the stress that might have been expected from the general business conditions of the year, as the savings banks show that, during 1896, withdrawals have not been excessive, while deposits have, all things considered, been unusually good.

What effect the provisions of the New Tariff (Dingley) Bill, if they pass into law, may have upon trade and industry cannot be predicted.

Annex A.—ARRIVALS of Immigrants at the Port of Boston. (From the Report of the Boston Chamber of Commerce.)

STATEMENT showing the Number of Alien Immigrants from Foreign Countries who arrived at the Port of Boston during the Year ending December 31, 1896, with comparisons.

From—	Number.			
	1896.	1895.	1894.	1893.
Ireland	8,333	10,995	6,750	10,798
England	3,246	5,007	3,395	7,430
Scotland	741	1,161	686	1,794
Wales	31	60	34	57
Germany	90	316	959	377
France	42	40	31	31
Russia	377	2,019	1,158	94
Finland	934	479	111	580
Poland	15	34	32	72
Switzerland	4	4	15	4
Sweden	2,068	2,061	1,193	3,764
Norway	743	676	440	1,376
Denmark	48	114	63	137
Holland	5	11	10	3
Italy	24	32	26	39
Spain	9	6	16	7
Portugal	10	12	5	551
Hungary	6	73	31	12
Austria	43	320	149	119
Austria-Hungary (Bohemia and Moravia)	..	5	7	..
Austria-Hungary (Galicia and Bukowina)	10	95	12	..
Australia	2	..	..	1
Turkey in Europe	22	3	9	5
Turkey in Asia	..	1	2	..
Greece	22	6	65	51
Belgium	..	22	26	..
Roumania	8	19	2	..
Mexico	..	..	1	..
West Indies	33	24	18	..
South America	2	2	1	..
Japan	..	..	1	..
Africa	1	..	1	..
All other countries	78	40	19	91
Total	16,947	23,637	15,268	27,393

NOTE.—In addition to the above there arrived at the ports of Massachusetts from the Dominion of Canada, by water during 1896, 19,026 aliens, against 20,806 in 1895, 17,893 in 1894, and 26,982 in 1893.

Annex B.—TABLE showing Vessels of all Nationalities Entered at the Port of Boston from Foreign Countries during the Year 1896.

Country.	Steam. With Cargo. Number of Vessels.	Steam. With Cargo. Tons.	Steam. In Ballast. Number of Vessels.	Steam. In Ballast. Tons.	Sailing. With Cargo. Number of Vessels.	Sailing. With Cargo. Tons.	Sailing. In Ballast. Number of Vessels.	Sailing. In Ballast. Tons.	Total. Number of Vessels.	Total. Tons.
Great Britain and dependencies	740	1,456,475	4	5,498	996	156,942	..	..	1,740	1,618,915
Denmark	5	1,575	..	..	..	..	..	..	5	1,575
France	10	4,610	..	..	9	3,490	..	..	19	8,100
Germany	13	28,301	..	..	2	754	..	..	15	29,055
Haiti	..	..	..	..	1	126	..	..	1	126
Holland	..	..	..	..	1	1,418	..	..	1	1,418
Italy	..	..	..	..	5	3,123	..	..	5	3,123
Norway	52	30,426	..	..	5	4,120	..	..	57	34,546
Total foreign	820	1,521,387	4	5,498	1,019	169,973	..	..	1,843	1,696,858
" United States	50	55,773	5	2,416	190	88,087	..	..	245	146,276
Grand total	870	1,577,160	9	7,914	1,209	258,060	..	..	2,088	1,843,134

Annex C.—TABLE showing Vessels of all Nationalities Cleared from the Port of Boston for Foreign Countries during the Year 1896.

BOSTON.

Country.	Steam.					Sailing.					Total.	
	With Cargo.		In Ballast.		With Cargo.		In Ballast.			
	Number of Vessels.	Tons.	Number of Vessels.	Tons.	Number of Vessels.	Tons.	Number of Vessels.	Tons.	Number of Vessels.	Tons.
Great Britain and dependencies	598	1,251,221	45	39,455	553	67,786	433	63,313	1,629	1,421,775
France	10	4,610	..	..	7	1,012	..	..	17	5,622
Germany	1	2,334	..	..	..	..	..	..	1	2,334
Denmark	..	..	4	1,260	..	..	..	..	4	1,260
Italy	..	..	..	..	..	..	1	579	1	579
Norway	..	..	43	22,018	..	..	2	1,984	45	24,002
Total foreign	609	1,258,165	92	62,733	560	68,798	436	65,876	1,697	1,455,572
„ United States	35	40,170	12	8,907	92	35,321	196	74,659	335	159,057
Grand total	644	1,298,335	104	71,640	652	104,119	682	140,535	2,032	1,614,629

UNITED STATES.

Annex D.—RETURN of British Shipping at the Port of Boston during the Year 1896.

Direct Trade from and to Great Britain and British Colonies.

	Entered.							Cleared.						
Number of Vessels.			Total Tonnage.			Total Number of Crews.	Total Value of Cargoes.	Number of Vessels.			Total Tonnage.			Total Number of Crews.	Total Value of Cargoes.
With Cargoes.	In Ballast.	Total.	With Cargoes.	In Ballast.	Total.			With Cargoes.	In Ballast.	Total.	With Cargoes.	In Ballast.	Total.		
1,552	5	1,557	1,389,392	4,782	1,394,174	42,214	£ ...	1,136	466	1,602	1,310,562	105,971	1,416,533	45,380	£ ...

Indirect or Carrying Trade in British Vessels from and to all Foreign Countries.

	Entered.							Cleared.						
Number of Vessels.			Total Tonnage.			Total Number of Crews.	Total Value of Cargoes.	Number of Vessels.			Total Tonnage.			Total Number of Crews.	Total Value of Cargoes.
With Cargoes.	In Ballast.	Total.	With Cargoes.	In Ballast.	Total.			With Cargoes.	In Ballast.	Total.	With Cargoes.	In Ballast.	Total.		
202	28	230	233,858	4,551	238,409	4,330	£ ...	35	136	171	45,152	172,249	217,401	3,596	£ ...

Annex E.—STEAMSHIP Sailings from Boston to European Ports during the Year 1896 (from the Report of the Boston Chamber of Commerce).

BOSTON.

Month.	To Liverpool.	To London.	To Glasgow.	To Hull.	To Hull, via New York.	To Antwerp, via Baltimore.	To Hamburg, via Baltimore.	To Hamburg.	To Manchester.	Total.
January	15	7	2	1	1	1	..	..	1	28
February	15	6	2	1	..	2	..	1	..	27
March	15	9	2	2	..	2	1	1	..	32
April	18	6	3	2	..	2	1	..	..	32
May	17	6	2	1	1	2	..	..	..	29
June	19	7	2	2	..	2	..	..	..	32
July	17	8	2	2	..	2	..	..	..	31
August	16	6	3	2	..	2	..	..	..	29
September	17	5	2	2	..	2	..	..	..	28
October	17	8	3	2	..	2	..	..	..	32
November	15	7	2	2	..	2	1	..	..	29
December	18	7	3	1	..	2	1	..	..	32
Total, 1896	199	82	28	20	2	23	4	2	1	361
„ 1895	183	62	29	2	19	19	3	4	Bristol 5	326

Annex F.—FREIGHTS ruling from Boston to Liverpool during the Year 1896.

Months.	Grain.	Flour.	Provisions.	Cotton.	Cattle.	Apples.	Leather Finished.	Sole Leather.	Hay.
	Per Bushel.	Per Ton.	Per Ton.	Per Lb.	Per Head.	Per Barrel.	Per Ton.	Per Ton.	Per Ton.
	d. d.	s. d. s. d.	s. d. s. d.	d. d.	s. d. s. d.	s. d. s. d.	s. d. s. d.	s. d. s. d.	s. d. s. d.
January	3	10 0	12 6 to 13 6	$\frac{3}{32}$	35 0	1 6	12 6	20 0	
February	$2\frac{3}{4}$ to 3	5 0 to 6 0	6 0 12 6	$\frac{1}{16}$ to $\frac{3}{32}$	45 0	1 6 to 2 0	12 6 to 15 0	20 0	
March	$2\frac{1}{3}$ $2\frac{3}{4}$	4 7 5 6	3 8 6 6	$\frac{3}{64}$ $\frac{1}{16}$	35 0 to 45 0	...	7 6	15 0 to 17 6	
April	$\frac{5}{8}$ $1\frac{5}{8}$	4 0 5 0	5 0 6 3	$\frac{1}{32}$ $\frac{3}{64}$	30 0 45 0	1 3	7 0	12 6	
May	1 $1\frac{5}{8}$	5 0 6 0	5 0 7 6	$\frac{3}{64}$	30 0 40 0	...	7 0 10 0	12 0 15 0	
June	1 $1\frac{5}{8}$	6 9 7 6	6 3 7 6	$\frac{1}{32}$ $\frac{3}{64}$	40 0	...	7 6 10 0	15 0	
July	$1\frac{5}{8}$ 2	6 3 8 9	7 6 8 9	$\frac{1}{32}$	35 0	...	10 0	12 6	
August...	$1\frac{5}{8}$	8 9 10 0	8 9 10 0	$\frac{1}{16}$ $\frac{3}{32}$	25 0	1 6	12 6	12 6 17 6	
September	$1\frac{5}{8}$ 2	15 0	10 0 17 6	$\frac{3}{32}$ $\frac{9}{64}$	35 0 40 0	1 6 2 0	12 6 20 0	15 0 25 0	
October	2 $2\frac{1}{2}$	17 6	20 0 22 6	$\frac{1}{8}$ $\frac{11}{64}$	42 6 45 0	2 0 2 6	25 0 30 0	30 0 40 0	
November	$2\frac{3}{4}$ $3\frac{1}{2}$	15 0 17 6	22 6 25 0	$\frac{9}{64}$ $\frac{5}{32}$	47 6	2 0 2 6	35 0	45 0	
December	$3\frac{1}{2}$ 5	15 0 17 6	11 3 25 0	$\frac{1}{16}$ $\frac{7}{64}$	30 0 47 6	2 0 2 6	25 0 35 0	22 6 30 0	15 0 to 18 9

BOSTON.

Annex G.—TABLE showing the Principal Articles of Export from Boston, and the Quantities Exported during the Year ended December 31, 1896, compared with 1895.

Articles.		Quantity.	
		1896.	1895.
Cotton to Great Britain	Bales	275,716	290,137
Flour	Barrels	289,485	298,471
,,	Sacks	1,900,473	1,824,988
Wheat	Bushels	12,721,450	7,216,709
Corn	,,	6,136,603	5,664,192
Oats	,,	2,147,637	83,000
Peas	,,	155,212	14,996
Barley	,,	181,352	30,207
Rye	,,	167,316	..
Buckwheat	,,	28,560	..
Flax-seed	,,	75,445	..
Oatmeal	Barrels	49,773	21,358
,,	Sacks	57,259	56,948
Cornmeal	Barrels	66,637	66,189
Mill.feed	Tons	4,369	4,844
Butter	Lbs.	3,156,741	2,102,504
Cheese	,,	21,566,448	20,756,422
Olive-oil	,,	2,279,154	1,618,605
Apples	Barrels	747,106	140,927
Pork	,,	19,669	16,010
,,	Tierces	11,172	9,417
Beef	Barrels	11,982	9,615
,,	Tierces	10,542	91,378
Bacon	Boxes	429,642	400,945
Lard	Lbs.	83,607,417	89,456,444
Tallow	Barrels	12,111	254
,,	Tierces	15,904	1,557
Grease	Barrels	13,426	8,435
Hams	,,	134	360
,,	Tierces	786	1,106
Fresh beef	Quarters	493,930	417,583
,,	Rounds	3,270	..
Cattle	Head	160,442	114,884
Sheep	,,	120,182	181,620
,, dressed	Carcases	165	500
Horses	Number	5,112	Not compiled
Hay	Bales	50,711	210,205
Petroleum	Cases	76,316	34,538
,,	Barrels	5,379	3,732
Oil-cake	Sacks	81,282	60,270
Wool	Lbs.	3,572,991	..
Leather	Rolls	123,371	108,381
,,	Bales	64,079	50,914
,,	Bags	64,821	49,950
,,	Bundles	18,876	10,252
,,	Barrels	968	1,563
,,	Cases	5,261	5,538
,,	Packages	1,959	11,391
Staves	Pieces	995,855	1,084,560

UNITED STATES.

Annex H.—TABLE showing the Value of the Imports to the Port of Boston for the Fiscal Year ended June 30, 1896.

Articles.	Value.
	£
Wool	3,840,142
,, manufactures of	559,135
Sugar and molasses	1,731,398
Iron, and manufactures of	1,092,410
Chemicals, drugs, and dyes	1,026,961
Cotton	1,014,093
,, manufactures of	269,503
Hides and skins	991,353
Vegetable fibres	845,828
,, manufactures of	319,509
Leather	613,121
,, manufactures of	83,841
Fruit and nuts	400,832
Wood, and manufactures of	327,650
Fish	287,475
Paper stock	272,232
Crockery	240,601
Tobacco, and manufactures of	163,848
Indiarubber, crude	154,696
Cocoa and coffee	122,479
Oils, vegetable	107,379
Glass and hardware	100,041
Art, works of	93,556
Wines	82,928
Cement	65,857
Hair, and manufactures of	59,301
Stone, and manufactures of	57,633
Silk, and manufactures of	57,556
Grease and tallow	54,890
Spirits, distilled	50,659
Malt liquors	45,087
Books, &c.	44,190
Metal composition	37,387
Fur and fur skins	34,199
Toys	33,714
Paper, and manufactures of	31,170
Vegetables	29,103
Tea	22,856
Lead, and manufactures of	23,435
Tin	21,758
Spices	20,445
Tar	20,073
Salt	19,612
Coal	17,861
All other articles	347,175
Total	15,834,972

BOSTON.

Annex I.—TABLE showing the Value of the Exports from the Port of Boston for the Fiscal Year ended June 30, 1896.

Articles.	Value.
	£
Provisions	6,932,680
Live animals	2,871,387
Bread-stuffs	2,649,208
Cotton	2,237,915
„ manufactures of	160,593
Leather	1,789,903
„ manufactures of	73,784
Wood, and manufactures of	236,847
Spirits, distilled	233,920
Iron, and manufactures of	198,162
Machinery	157,040
Lumber	140,112
Glucose	114,846
Tobacco, and manufactures of	86,307
Oil-cake	64,402
Indiarubber, and manufactures of	58,045
Agricultural implements	52,431
Chemical dyes and medicines	59,935
Hay	52,816
Blacking	51,814
Fur and fur skins	41,031
Fruit and nuts	41,844
Wool, and manufactures of	39,702
Naval stores	33,726
Oils, mineral	39,992
„ all others	191
Flax, hemp, and jute, and manufactures of	34,581
Paper, and manufactures of	33,879
Paraffin and wax	29,913
Musical instruments	33,959
Books, maps, &c.	26,539
Hides and skins	29,363
Sugar and molasses	26,286
Builder's hardware	24,438
Bark for tanning	16,435
Seeds	15,552
Sugar meal	13,387
Paints	12,062
Fertilisers	11,183
Brass, and manufactures of	9,993
Cider	7,972
Fish	6,598
Hops	9,511
Hair, and manufactures of	4,970
Copper, and manufactures of	3,811
Soap	2,448
All other articles	161,635
Total	18,923,048

(2400)

UNITED STATES.

PORTLAND.

Mr. Vice-Consul Keating reports as follows:—

In view of the fact that no report has been made for several years past, it is difficult to compare the commerce of the year just ended with that of previous years. It is, however, generally conceded that the year 1896 closed at this port with a brighter outlook than even the most hopeful anticipated.

Population. The population of Portland, according to the last report of the City Auditor, was 41,156. The city has a tax valuation of 7,560,240*l*.

Manufacturing establishments. There are 662 manufacturing establishments, including locomotive and car works, rolling mills, tanneries, boot and shoe manufactories, machine shops, and foundries, and various other branches of manufacturing industries, employing more than 8,000 persons, to whom are annually paid 632,130*l*.

Harbour. Portland has a capacious harbour, easy of access at all seasons of the year, and situated as it is at the eastern extremity of the shortest railroad route, and about 12 hours nearer Europe than any other Atlantic port, it would seem that the city possessed all the advantages requisite to make it the pioneer distributing port for the west.

Ocean steamships. During the winter season of 1896 the number of ocean steamships was increased. There are now two lines to Liverpool (both calling at Halifax, N.S.), one line direct to London, one to Bristol, and one to Glasgow.

This improved service has enabled the exports to increase during the month of December, 1896, to 525,353*l*., from 196,704*l*. in December, 1895, a gain of 328,649*l*.

Grain elevator. During the past year a new grain elevator has been erected at a cost of about 20,000*l*. It has a capacity of 1,500,000 bushels of grain.

Exports. The principal exports to the United Kingdom are live-stock, corn, flour, apples, meat products, and wheat. The amount exported to December 1, 1896, showed an increase of 297,254*l*. over the total value of exports for 1895. The value of exports to the British West Indies was 21,049*l*., an increase of 3,650*l*. over 1895.

Cattle shipped. The number of cattle shipped has greatly increased during the past year. Additional facilities are now afforded by the completion, at a cost of 2,000*l*., of new stockyards at Deering, which furnish accommodation for 2,500 head of cattle.

Improvements. In the harbour a new lighthouse has been erected.

Congress, by an Act of June 3, 1896, adopted a project for dredging the harbour of Portland to a depth of 30 feet at mean low tide, the entire area of the harbour north of a line drawn from a point 250 feet at the inner end, to a point 800 feet at the outer end, north of the harbour line on the southerly side of the harbour, and also provided for the completion of the improvement of Back Cove. At the latter locality, where originally the channel had a depth of about 8 to 10 feet at low tide for about half its length, a project was in progress for dredging a channel 300 feet wide, and 12 feet deep at low tide, for a distance of about 5,600 feet.

At the close of the United States fiscal year for 1896, this channel had been dredged to its full width for about one-half its length, and to a width of about 215 feet for the remainder, all to a depth of 12 feet at mean low tide.

Before the improvement of the harbour was begun, the greatest depth at mean low tide across the bar, between the middle ground and Stamford Ledge, was 16 feet, while the depth on the middle ground itself was only from 8 to 10 feet. The depth in the inner harbour along the wharves was in places no more than 4 feet. The expenditures have resulted in removing the entire area of the middle ground up to the Harbour Commissioners' line, giving a wide and commodious entrance 29 feet deep at mean low tide; also in giving a depth of 16 feet at mean low tide within the inner harbour, along the wharves, and up to the Harbour Commissioners' line, with a breakwater to protect the anchorage.

Fisheries.

The fish brought to this port largely consists of hake, cod, haddock, pollock, herring, smelts, sword-fish, clams, alewives, and lobsters.

Lobster fishing in Maine forms an important industry, and the Commissioner of Sea and Shore Fisheries, in his report for 1896, presents the following interesting statement under this particular head:—

Number of men employed	2,708
Number of lobster cars	2,431
Value of lobster cars	4,306*l*.
Number of lobster boats	3,353
Value of lobster boats	438,366*l*.
Number of lobsters taken	7,825,575
Value of lobsters taken	153,055*l*.
Number of pots	172,865
Value of pots	38,886*l*.
Estimated number of pots used during the year	302,513

In the customs districts of this Vice-Consulate there are 512 vessels, measuring 10,122 tons, and 14,690 persons connected with the fisheries. The money value of the fisheries product in Maine for the year 1896 was as follows:—

Fisheries Product.	Value.
	£
Sardine	385,709
Lobster	158,451
Herring	50,233
Smelt	14,340
Sword	7,905
Alewives	3,241
Smoked herring	21,339
Clam	49,728
Salmon	2,457
Mackerel	16,913
Salt mackerel	40,506
Fresh fish	100,855
Shad..	5,143
Scallop	1,000
Eel	154
Sturgeon	141
Bass..	73
Fish oils	2,264
Scraps	4,000
Tom-cod	273
Total	864,725

During the year ended December 31, 1896, the Portland Market received—

	Quantity.
	Lbs.
Codfish	3,812,269
Haddock	5,158,416
Hake	2,212,223
Pollock	684,492
Cusk..	4,990,161
Halibut	518,928
Fresh mackerel	443,464
Total about	17,820,400

Representing in money value to the fishermen the sum of 75,895*l.* The total amount of this industry in the State for the year 1896 was 24,406,330 lbs. of fish, valued at 100,859 dol.

roads.

In considering the reports of the railroads having their centre in this city, it will be noticed that they show a decided increase all round. While 5,442 miles of the railroads in the other States have gone into the hands of receivers, involving 34,600,000*l.* worth of bonds and 20,506,600*l.* of stock, foreclosures also affected 1,373 miles of road and about 230,075,400*l.* worth of stocks and bonds. Maine on the other hand has constructed 92 miles of new road. The gross earnings of the various railroads increased from 1,522,225*l.* to 1,622,301*l.*; the passenger traffic showed a gain of 170,981 over the previous year, and the freight traffic a gain of 225,250 tons. In short, the railroads of this State made an increase of 5 per cent. in mileage, and nearly 7 per cent. in gross earnings.

In 1895, there were 15 vessels built at Bath, of a total tonnage of 8,485·02, an average of 566 tons per vessel. During 1896, 20 vessels were built, of a total tonnage of 16,242·05, an average tonnage of 812 tons per vessel. Shipbuilding.

The following constitute the principal industries of the State, the product of which, to a great extent, passes through Portland. Concluding remarks.

Granite, slate, lime, lumber, and ice are abundant. The manufacture of wood-pulp and paper forms an important industry. The canning of corn and farm products is also important, amounting to nearly 1,000,000 cases annually.

The plush, starch, cotton, and woollen mills afford employment for a large number of operatives.

The total number of manufacturing establishments in the State of Maine is 5,010. The value of the plants amount to 8,236,637l.

The number of employees average 75,780, and they annually receive in wages, 5,305,243l., in the following proportions:—

	Number Employed.	Amount Paid for Wages.
		£
Males over 16 years	40,714	3,096,743
Females over 15 years	11,923	633,821
Children	1,248	33,355
Male piece-workers over 16 years of age	6,167	468,711
Female piece-workers	9,128	344,391
Children	1,194	15,495
All others	5,406	712,727
Total	75,780	5,305,243

The operatives annually use materials valued at 10,304,118l., and they manufacture this amount into 19,137,900l. worth of finished products.

UNITED STATES.

TABLE showing the Total Amount of Capital Invested, the Value of Stock Used, the Greatest Number of Persons Employed, the Total Amount of Wages Paid, and the Value of Goods Made and Work Done in the Industries of the State of Massachusetts during the Year 1895, together with the Percentage of Increase or Decrease as compared with 1894.

Industries.	Number of Establishments Considered.	Capital Invested. Total in 1895. £	Capital Invested. Percentual + or − Compared with 1894.	Stocks Used. Total in 1895. £	Stocks Used. Percentual + or − Compared with 1894.	Greatest Number of Persons Employed. Total in 1895.	Greatest Number of Persons Employed. Percentual + or − Compared with 1894.	Amount of Wages Paid. Total in 1895. £	Amount of Wages Paid. Percentual + or − Compared with 1894.	Value of Goods Made and Work Done. Total in 1895. £	Value of Goods Made and Work Done. Percentual + or − Compared with 1894.
9 principal industries—											
Boots and shoes	544	4,452,062	− 6·31	9,577,735	+ 12·01	43,276	+ 4·96	3,487,333	− 0·23	15,376,542	+ 5·67
Carpetings	11	1,999,792	− 17·46	862,801	+ 19·12	4,740	+ 1·56	339,266	+ 27·61	1,433,803	+ 24·45
Cotton goods	157	23,047,261	+ 4·97	8,915,036	+ 1·76	80,926	+ 2·15	5,101,156	+ 12·22	17,337,816	+ 10·18
Leather	119	1,650,880	+ 8·35	2,793,390	+ 36·43	7,207	+ 9·93	574,988	+ 14·15	3,939,854	+ 35·94
Machines and machinery	292	4,940,016	− 12·72	1,803,964	+ 23·12	18,440	+ 19·86	1,633,045	+ 20·29	4,757,086	+ 19·77
Metals and metallic goods	278	3,234,753	− 3·25	1,784,730	+ 11·47	13,109	+ 11·06	1,168,695	+ 15·53	3,849,504	+ 14·57
Paper and paper goods	97	4,746,841	− 6·57	2,761,557	− 2·30	11,197	+ 1·91	855,147	+ 5·94	4,558,290	− 0·28
Woollen goods	110	4,518,770	+ 0·70	2,731,932	+ 11·00	16,719	+ 6·15	1,132,462	+ 21·98	4,726,186	+ 11·36
Worsted goods	21	2,991,403	+ 3·78	2,368,737	+ 43·84	12,475	+ 14·21	824,432	+ 48·33	3,751,892	+ 47·02
Other industries	2,000	24,393,256	− 9·22	24,402,419	− 0·15	105,813	+ 5·78	8,180,224	+ 9·95	42,628,466	+ 4·47
Total	3,629	75,175,034	− 6·39	58,002,301	+ 6·38	313,902	+ 5·83	23,296,748	+ 11·41	102,359,439	+ 9·18

NOTE.—In 1894 the total capital invested was 80,303,989*l.*; total stocks used, 54,522,983*l.*; greatest number of persons employed, 296,607; total amount of wages paid, 20,912,572*l.*; value of goods and work done, 93,729,835*l.* In 1895 the proportion of the sexes employed was: males, 64·91 per cent.; females, 35·09 per cent. In 1894 the proportion of the sexes employed was: males, 67 per cent.; females, 33 per cent.

The average number of days in operation was 291·42 in 1895 and 276·01 in 1894, showing an increase of 15·41 days, equal to 5·58 per cent. for 1895, as compared with the previous year.

FOREIGN OFFICE.

1897.
ANNUAL SERIES.

N⁰. 1935.

DIPLOMATIC AND CONSULAR REPORTS ON TRADE AND FINANCE.

UNITED STATES.

REPORT FOR THE YEAR 1896
ON THE
TRADE OF PORTLAND (OREGON).

REFERENCE TO PREVIOUS REPORT, Annual Series No. 1734.

Presented to both Houses of Parliament by Command of Her Majesty,
JUNE, 1897.

LONDON:
PRINTED FOR HER MAJESTY'S STATIONERY OFFICE,
BY HARRISON AND SONS, ST. MARTIN'S LANE,
PRINTERS IN ORDINARY TO HER MAJESTY.

And to be purchased, either directly or through any Bookseller, from
EYRE & SPOTTISWOODE, EAST HARDING STREET, FLEET STREET, E.C., and
32, ABINGDON STREET, WESTMINSTER, S.W.; or
JOHN MENZIES & Co., 12, HANOVER STREET, EDINBURGH, and
90, WEST NILE STREET, GLASGOW; or
HODGES, FIGGIS, & Co., Limited, 104, GRAFTON STREET, DUBLIN.

1897.

[C. 8277—153.]   *Price Threepence.*

New Series of Reports.

Reports of the Annual Series have been issued from Her Majesty's Diplomatic and Consular Officers at the following places, and may be obtained from the sources indicated on the title-page:—

No.		Price.	No.		Price.
1815.	Hamburg	1½d.	1875.	Trieste	1d.
1816.	New Orleans	1½d.	1876.	Curaçoa	1d.
1817.	Bengazi	½d.	1877.	Goa	1d.
1818.	Marmagao	½d.	1878.	Cagliari	1d.
1819.	Gothenburg	2d.	1879.	Guayaquil	1d.
1820.	Dar-al-Baida	3d.	1880.	Havana	1½d.
1821.	Erzeroum	½d.	1881.	Reykjavik (Iceland)	1d.
1822.	Munich	2½d.	1882.	Milan	1½d.
1823.	Samoa	½d.	1883.	Baltimore	1d.
1824.	Chinkiang	1d	1884.	Cettinjé	½d.
1825.	Jeddah	1d.	1885.	Bilbao	2½d.
1826.	Sofia	1½d.	1886.	Florence	1¼d.
1827.	Mexico	2d.	1887.	Brest	1½d.
1828.	Teneriffe	3½d.	1888.	Marseilles	1½d.
1829.	Batoum	1d.	1889.	Wuhu	1d.
1830.	Cadiz	1d.	1890.	Chinkiang	1d.
1831.	Martinique	1d.	1891.	Malaga	1d.
1832.	Odessa	1d.	1892.	Antwerp	½d.
1833.	Ghilan	1d.	1893.	Amsterdam	1d.
1834.	Old Calabar	6½d.	1894.	Galveston	2d.
1835.	Tamsui	1d.	1895.	Piræus	2½d.
1836.	Copenhagen	½d.	1896.	Stettin	2½d.
1837.	Salonica	1½d.	1897.	Martinique	1½d.
1838.	Honolulu	½d.	1898.	Corunna	2½d.
1839.	Buenos Ayres	2d.	1899.	Calais	1d.
1840.	Para	1d.	1900.	Honolulu	1d.
1841.	Bolivia	2d.	1901.	Riga	2d.
1842.	Washington	3d.	1902.	Tripoli	1d.
1843.	Berlin	2d.	1903.	Batoum	2d.
1844.	Uganda	1d.	1904.	Lorenzo Marques	2d.
1845.	Belgrade	1½d.	1905.	Batavia	2½d.
1846.	Dakar	½d.	1906.	Corfu	1½d.
1847.	Florence	1½d.	1907.	Foochow	1½d.
1848.	Copenhagen	2d.	1908.	Montevideo	5½d.
1849.	Havre	2d.	1909.	China	5d.
1850.	Serajevo	1d.	1910.	Philadelphia	1½d.
1851.	Madrid	2d.	1911.	Rio Grande do Sul	3½d.
1852.	La Rochelle	1½d.	1912.	Quito	1d.
1853.	Chicago	4d.	1913.	San José	1d.
1854.	Berlin	1d.	1914.	Dunkirk	1d.
1855.	Cherbourg	2½d.	1915.	Samoa	1d.
1856.	Beira	1d.	1916.	Bordeaux	2½d.
1857.	Charleston	2½d.	1917.	Porto Rico	1½d.
1858.	Saigon	½d.	1918.	Galatz	1½d.
1859.	Suakin	1d.	1919.	Christiania	½d.
1860.	Rouen	2d.	1920.	Copenhagen	3d.
1861.	Patras	1½d.	1921.	New York	2½d.
1862.	Barcelona	2d.	1922.	San Francisco	3½d.
1863.	Amoy	2½d.	1823.	Kiukiang	1d.
1864.	Trebizond	1d.	1924.	Harrar	½d.
1865.	Lisbon	2½d.	1925.	Berne	1½d.
1866.	Callao	2d.	1926.	Mannheim	1d.
1867.	Pernambuco	5d.	1927.	Fiume	1½d.
1868.	Naples	1½d.	1928.	Oporto	1d.
1869.	New Orleans	2½d.	1929.	Hangchow	1d.
1870.	Vera Cruz	2½d.	1930.	Boston	2½d.
1871.	Madeira	1d.	1931.	Tahiti	1d.
1872.	Jerusalem	1d.	1932.	Manila	1½d.
1873.	Ningpo	1d.	1933.	Caracas	1d.
1874.	Rio de Janeiro	2½d.	1934.	Hamburg	3d.

No. 1935.

Reference to previous Report, Annual Series No. 1734.

UNITED STATES.

PORTLAND.

Consul Laidlaw to the Marquess of Salisbury.

(Received at Foreign Office, May 19, 1897.)

My Lord,

I HAVE the honour to enclose my Report on the Trade and Commerce of Portland for the year 1896, with some Agricultural and other information touching other parts of this Consular District, together with the Annual Reports from the Vice-Consuls at Astoria, Tacoma and Seattle, and Port Townsend.

I have, &c.
(Signed) JAMES LAIDLAW.

Report on the Trade, Commerce, and Agriculture of the Consular District of Portland, Oregon, for the Year 1896.

TABLE of Contents.

	PAGE
Introductory remarks	2
British trade	3
Wheat	3
Flour	3
Barley	4
Bran	4
Fruit trade	4
Hops	4
Timber trade	4
Wool trade	4
Fish trade	5
Salmon	5
Import trade	6
Clearing-house	8
Banks	8
Exchange	9
Failures	9
Shipping and navigation	10
Freight	10

(2410)

UNITED STATES.

Table of Contents—continued.

	PAGE
Lights and buoys	11
Ports and harbours	11
Shipbuilding	11
Light vessels	11
Sailors	11
Mariners' home	12
Mining	12
Industries	13
Fisheries	14
Water and electric power	14
Labour	15
Warning to clerks, &c.	15
Wages	15
Population	15
Rivers and harbours	15
Canals	16
Railways	16
Agriculture	16
Irrigation	17
Orchards and fruits	18
Cattle	20
Taxation	20
Annexes—	
A.—Table of entrances and clearances of vessels	21
B.— ,, exports and imports by articles	21
C.— ,, total value of exports and imports by countries	23
Astoria Vice-Consulate—	
Trade report	23
Annexes—	
A.—Table of entrances and clearances of vessels	26
B.— ,, exports and imports by articles	26
C.— ,, total value of exports and imports by countries	27
Tacoma and Seattle Vice-Consulate—	
Trade report	36
Annexes—Tacoma—	
A.—Table of entrances and clearances of vessels	37
B.— ,, imports and exports by articles	39
Annexes—Seattle—	
A.—Table of entrances and clearances of vessels	41
B.— ,, exports and imports by articles	41
C.— ,, value of exports and imports by countries	42
Port Townsend Vice-Consulate—	
Trade report	43
Annexes—	
A.—Table of entrances and clearances of vessels	45
B.— ,, exports and imports by articles	46
C.— ,, value of exports and imports by countries	47

NOTE.—Calculations are made throughout this report at 5 dol. to the 1*l*.

Introductory remarks.

There has been a decided improvement in the trade of this port and district during 1896. Prices of produce, and particularly of wheat, were much higher, and during the last two months of the year were highly profitable to the holders. As a consequence many farmers have been able to pay off debts that have accumulated during the last few years, and are now in a better financial condition. There has been an increase in the production of gold throughout the district, and silver and lead mining, while not as profitable as some years ago, has been carried on to a greater extent than last year. The supply of labour is still in excess of the demand. Rates of freight have been very low and unprofitable to the shipowner.

The increase in the value of exports to foreign countries, as shown in Annex B attached to this report, was nearly 29 per cent., and in that of imports 34 per cent., exclusive of merchandise entered for transportation in bond to other districts and to Canada, the value of which is given in these tables. *Increased exports and imports.*

The improvement in British trade, as set forth in Annex C, is very marked, and exports of breadstuffs to Australia and South African ports were very considerable. Although the average quality of wheat was good, there was a good deal of shrunken grain in some sections of Eastern Oregon and Washington, consequent upon hot winds which prevailed in July when the crops were in the milk, and which materially reduced the crop. *British trade.* *Wheat.*

The year opened with Walla Walla wheat at 18s. 11d. per quarter, f.o.b.; prices advanced in February to 1l. 0s. 6d., and fell slowly to 17s. 5d. in July. In September prices advanced to 18s. 6d.; in October to 1l. 2s. 6d.; in November to 1l. 6s. 8d., closing at 1l. 6s. 9d. In December, 1894, prices were only 14s.

Shipments of wheat coastwise were 46,134 quarters, and the total shipments foreign and coastwise from the Columbia River, including clearances, were 972,992 quarters, valued at 1,075,993l., an average of 1l. 2s. 2d. per quarter.

The entire export of wheat from this Consular district to foreign countries was 1,279,665 quarters, only a small proportion of which went to South Africa, Australia, China, Japan, and the Hawaiian Islands, and the rest to Great Britain.

The export of flour has advanced largely of late years, and the trade to China and Japan is now very large, the steamers going full every trip. A cargo was shipped to Vladivostok during the year. *Flour.*

The shipments to foreign ports were as under:—

To—	Sacks of 280 Lbs.
Great Britain	56,536
Chinese ports	250,278
Japanese ports	30,214
Vladivostok	10,524
Honolulu	8,336
Australia	30,163
South African ports	36,605
British Columbia	3,584
Total	426,240

Total shipments, foreign and coastwise, were 555,871 sacks, valued at 481,992l. Average export value per sack, 17s. 4d.

The total shipments from this Consular district aggregated 760,799 sacks of 280 lbs.

In January patent roller extras sold at an average of 16s., and superfines at 11s. 8d. per sack. From February to end of September, 16s. 8d. and 12s. 7d. respectively. In October average prices were 1l. and 13s. 5d., and in November and December 1l. 5s. and 14s. 1d.

Barley. Very little barley was grown during the year, and only 13,820 centals were shipped to Bristol, valued at 3,000l., an average of 4s. 4d. per cental. No record has been kept of coastwise shipments of this and other grain except wheat.

Bran. 13,160 centals of bran were shipped to South Africa and to United Kingdom, aggregating 1,800l. in value.

Fruit trade. The yield of the larger fruits was very light, late frosts in April and May having destroyed a fine prospect. The loss was greatest in Western Oregon; in consequence the business was only profitable to those who, by location, escaped the almost general loss. Good prices were realised. This trade is capable of great extension.

Hop trade. Owing to the disastrous experience in prices during the last year a large number of hop yards were ploughed up, and others left uncultivated. Contrary, however, to expectations, a good demand was experienced after picking time, and prices were fairly remunerative. The yield in Oregon was about half of that of 1895, or 55,000 bales of 185 lbs. each, but quality and condition were better than for several years past. The year opened with a large stock of 1895 hops in the State, though not choice. In March and April prime and mediums sold as low as $1\frac{1}{2}d$. Picking began in September, and $2\frac{1}{2}d$. to 3d. was paid, and gradually prices were advanced till sales of new hops were made at $12\frac{1}{2}$ c. (6d.). Cost of picking and baling was $5\frac{1}{2}$ c. to 6 c. per lb. Stocks at the close of the year were light, and contracts have been made for 1897 hops at 8 c. (4d.) per lb. and over. Most of the hops were shipped by rail to New York and United Kingdom, but a small quantity sent direct to Australia. About 16,000 bales were picked in Washington.

Timber trade. The foreign lumber trade from this port is small, exports to Chile and South Africa being a little over 4,000,000 feet. Shipments coastwise are quite considerable, but of this no correct statistics have been obtainable. The demand has been better at improved prices.

A reference to the reports of the Vice-Consuls at Tacoma, Port Townsend and Astoria annexed to this report will show the magnitude of this trade.

Wool trade. The wool trade cannot be said to be in a satisfactory condition, but even at the low prices of the last two years growers have been able with economy to pay expenses. The staple of the Oregon clip was not so good as last year, but there was a perceptible increase in the quantity. The clip of Eastern Oregon is said to have aggregated about 18,000,000 lbs., and sold at from $4\frac{1}{2}$ c. ($2\frac{1}{4}d$.) to 9 c. ($4\frac{1}{2}d$.), according to quality and shrinkage. The clip of the Willamette and Umpqua Valleys (combing wools) was about 1,200,000 lbs., and sold at from 9 c. (4½d.) to 12 c. (6d.). During June and July there was a good demand. From July to September the market was stagnant, but demand set in again at an advance of 1 c. to 1½ c. from October to close of the year. The clip of Washington was about 2,500,000 lbs., and that of Idaho between 8,000,000 lbs. and 9,000,000 lbs. Most of the product is shipped by rail to the Eastern States. Consumption of the woollen mills in Oregon is estimated at 1,500,000 lbs.

Salmon, tinned.

Formerly the greatest proportion of the salmon tinned on the Columbia River was exported to the United Kingdom, but of late years most of the pack has been sold for consumption in the Eastern States. For details of the business, I refer to the reports of the Vice-Consuls at Astoria and Tacoma, annexed to this report, but the following is a summary of this business taken from the reports of the Oregon Fish and Game Protector and the Washington State Fish Commissioner.

	Quantity.	Value.
	Cases.	£
Columbia River (spring), Oregon side	297,655	292,092
,, (fall) ,,	52,919	34,976
,, (spring), Washington side	124,132	120,822
,, (fall) ,,	6,991	4,474
Other rivers and bays in Oregon	91,760	61,056
Puget Sound, Washington	195,664	140,000
Grays Harbour, Washington	21,274	13,598
Willapa Harbour, Washington	24,941	15,223
Total	815,336	682,241

The price paid for raw salmon was 4½ c. (2¼d.) per lb., and the business was not profitable.

The following were the average prices for good brands of Columbia River. Prices fell below these figures before the year closed.

	Per Dozen.	
	Spring Catch.	Fall Catch.
	s. d.	s. d. s. d.
Flat, 1-lb. tins	5 7	
Tall ,,	5 0	
Oval ,,	7 2	
Flat, ½-lb. tins	3 2	
Tall, 1-lb tins		3 0 to 3 7

Fresh fish.

In addition to local consumption of other varieties of fish, there was consumed locally or shipped East in refrigerator cars:—

(2410)

	Quantity.	Value.
	Lbs.	£
Salmon	5,042,141	46,857
Sturgeon	1,193,352	11,785

Import trade. Annex B attached to this report shows an increase in imports of earthenware, cement, sugar, sulphur, pig-iron, window glass, and bags, and quite a decrease in salt and chemicals. There is of course a large trade in finer goods, but as these come by rail it is impracticable to trace the amount of the trade.

Dry goods. Cotton. The high tariff checks the importation of anything but the finer cotton goods, such as printed lawns, percales, organdies, muslins, lace curtains, cretonnes, and such goods of the finer qualities are generally purchased through agents of British manufacturers in New York. In most of these goods the German manufacturers are strong competitors.

Domestics and calicos sold are nearly all of American manufacture.

Hosiery. American manufacturers are rapidly improving the quality of their goods, but seven-eighths of the hosiery now sold is of German manufacture. It seems to be acknowledged that British is the better in quality, but the German is cheaper, and the German manufacturer adopted earlier different methods of weaving the foot seam and so secured the trade.

Woollens. Of the cashmeres, tweeds, meltons, and worsteds sold in these markets, by far the largest portion is of Oregon or Eastern States manufacture in the cheaper grades, but there is a limited direct trade with Scotch and English manufacturers in these goods to supply the demand for better qualities. Some very high grade goods come from American mills. Italians and mohair serges are also imported. Dress goods are generally of American manufacture. It has been suggested that if manufacturers would put up worsted goods in smaller pieces, a much larger trade might be done.

Linen. Linen damasks, sheetings, towellings, and linen dress fabrics sold in these markets are generally imported from Great Britain, but German linen manufacturers are improving their qualities which have hitherto been of low grade.

Jute bags and bagging. There is a large market for grain bags, burlaps, and hop cloth, which is supplied from Calcutta either by sail or by steamer viâ Hong-Kong, but two sailing vessels brought full cargoes direct from Calcutta. Consumption was lessened by the shortage on wheat crop. Standard size wheat bags were bought at an average price of 2d.

Raw hemp. Imports of hemp were not much over half of those during 1895.

Cement. Of the cement imported during 1896, 35,298 barrels were Belgian, 12,022 English, and 10,759 German. Prior to 1883, quite a quantity of Rosendale and other Eastern cements was imported into this market, but since that time most of the cement used has been imported from foreign countries. In that year a small cargo was imported from Bremen, and although well spoken of the English held the market, and was considered the standard of excellence. In 1888, 5,000 barrels were received from Belgium, and in 1890 a further quantity. Since that time the Belgium and German manufacturers have been strong competitors for business. They undersold the British manufacturers, submitted their products to heavy tests as to fineness and strength, gave absolute guarantees as to quality, proved their best brands to be superior, and now hold the highest position in artificial cements. The British manufacturer refused for a long time to grind finer, but has now been compelled to do so; meanwhile the trade has been largely lost to him. Since 1894, 214,784 barrels of Belgian and German cement have been imported into this market, as against 121,527 barrels of British, and the artificial continental cements sell more readily than the British, though of course the natural cements do not, except for some purposes, on account of their lower cost. Market prices were lower than last year, artificial averaging about 10s. and natural 9s. per barrel.

Window glass. The Belgian window glass continues to monopolise the trade. I notice, however, that a small quantity was imported from Great Britain.

Tin-plates. Imports of tin-plate were less than last year, and some American plate was used, which is reported as very superior. Much lighter grades are now used than formerly for tinned goods trade, very little over 100 lbs. to the box having been imported, and a considerable quantity as light as 85 lbs. Standard weight B.V. grades of coke sold at an average of 16s. 4d., and lighter grades proportionally lower.

Roofing plates, Dean grade, 20 by 28, sold at 33s. From present appearances American plates are likely to monopolise the trade, if drawback allowances are discontinued, as seems possible.

Coal. Imports of foreign coal were about the same as last year, and Australian sold lower, averaging about 17s. A small cargo was received from Japan, but this coal is too pitchy, and not liked on that account. It contains a good deal of gas. The following were the receipts:—

From—	Quantity.
	Tons.
Australia	13,157
Japan	798
British Columbia	552
Great Britain	248
From coast mines, by sail and rail (about)	10,500
From Atlantic ports, by sea	1 600

Coke. Imports of coke were 2,016 tons from Belgium, and 1,303 tons from England, market prices about 34s. per ton.

Twine, hemp, and flax. Most of the twine used for net making is of Scotch and Irish manufacture. Imports of flax and hemp twine from the United Kingdom, both of netting and sacking, were quite large.

UNITED STATES.

Earthenware. Imports of chinaware from Germany seem to be increasing, and amounted to nearly 20 per cent. of entries at custom-house. One small vessel came from Belgium, but 70 per cent. of the entries of earthenware and glassware were British. Germany competes strongly with France in chinaware.

Cutlery. Imports of cutlery through the custom-house were small, but 50 per cent. came from Germany, and the rest from England.

Pig-iron. Imports of pig-iron were quite large in consequence of the local furnaces being blown out during the year, and enhanced railroad rates, but orders for next year do not seem to be obtainable.

Bar-iron. Some 60 tons of Belgian bar-iron were received, and a cargo of railway steel from the United Kingdom. The value of all imports and exports by countries is given in Annex C to this report.

Financial matters. Although the banks held plenty of money, the financial market was very stringent during most of the year prior to the presidential election, applications for loans were closely scrutinised, and few new enterprises were initiated, but the trade of the district has been put upon a sounder basis. The development in mining centres has been considerable, notably in Spokane Falls, Washington, where business is very active. Only one small bank in this port closed its doors, but there have been withdrawals from some of the Puget Sound ports.

Clearing-house. Transactions of the Portland clearing-house during the last five years were as under:—

	Amount.			
	1896.	1895.	1894.	1893.
	£	£	£	£
Clearances	12,481,779	11,768,457	11,316,504	1 5312,951
Balances	2,723,965	2,319,994	2,534,606	3,031,088

Banks. The condition of the national banks in Portland, Oregon, on December 17, 1896, and December 13, 1895, was as under:—

PORTLAND.

Resources.

	Amount. 1896.	Amount. 1895.
	£	£
Loans and discounts	679,301	753,073
United States bonds	305,060	250,000
Other stocks and bonds	225,226	298,338
Premium on bonds	24,862	16,538
Real estate, furniture, and fixtures	49,074	49,776
Redemption Fund, United States Treasury	6,075	2,250
Due from other banks	68,875	79,592
,, reserve agents	75,521	102,380
Cash on hand	399,217	188,549
Total	1,833,211	1,740,496

Liabilities.

	Amount. 1896.	Amount. 1895.
	£	£
Capital paid in	320,000	340,000
Surplus and profits, less expenses	163,740	172,368
Dividends unpaid	500	500
Circulation	120,920	41,310
Deposits and bank allowances	1,228,051	1,186,318
Total	1,833,211	1,740,496

There are five national banks, and besides these two British and seven savings and private banks, but only the national banks publish statements.

Exchange. During the first eight months of the year exchange varied little, averaging 4 dol. 84 c. per 1*l.* for 60 days' commercial drafts. As the election approached rates dropped, and in October went as low as 4 dol. 77 c. per 1*l.*, recovering towards the close of the year. The average for the last four months was 4 dol. 79 c. per 1*l.*

Failures. The following is a comparison of commercial failures in this district during the last two years, as compiled by Dun's Agency:—

UNITED STATES.

States.	1896. Number of Failures.	1896. Liabilities.	1895. Number of Failures.	1895. Liabilities.
		£		£
Oregon	178	332,880	216	351,714
Washington	149	378,389	160	315,815
Idaho	83	88,500	85	77,205
Total	410	799,769	461	744,734

British shipping. Of the tonnage employed in the foreign trade 88 per cent. was British, but the number of ships under the German flag trading to this port is increasing. Details of tonnage are given in Annex A attached to this report. The line of British steamers to Chinese and Japanese ports made regular trips, with generally full cargoes both ways. Cargoes inwards consisted principally of tea, raw silk and matting, and outwards of flour. One steamer cleared for Sydney, N.S.W.

Tonnage: engagements. Engagements of sailing tonnage exclusive of coasting voyages were as under:—

Cargoes.	Tons Register. 1896.	1895.	1894.
Grain and flour	131,381	138,356	129,055
Timber	14,976	8,419	1,764
Miscellaneous	3,516	843	5,808
Total	149,873	147,618	136,627

Freights. Charter rates for grain and flour cargoes to the United Kingdom were fairly good for these times of low freights, but at the close of the year a new steel ship was chartered at 17s. 6d. to United Kingdom, Havre, Antwerp, or Dunkirk, a rate never hitherto touched in the history of this port. The average rate for grain charters for iron vessels to the United Kingdom for orders, including Havre, Antwerp, and Dunkirk at the same rate, was 1l. 9s. 10d. The highest rates were paid prior to arrival, as high as 36s. 3d. having been paid. The following were the rates for arrived vessels during the year:—

Month.	Rates of Freight.	
	From—	To—
	s. d.	s. d.
January	26 3	32 0
February	..	25 0
April	..	25 6
May and June	..	25 0
July	..	26 3
August	..	28 9
September	..	31 3
October	28 9	31 3
November	..	25 0
December	17 6	20 0

Lights and buoys. There have been no changes of any consequence during the year in the lights and buoys of this district. Reference is made in the Astoria report annexed as to light in course of construction on the North Head Columbia river.

Ports and harbours. It appears from the report of the United States engineer in charge of this district, that the last survey made of the Columbia River Bar, in May and June last, shows a narrowing of the 30-foot channel mentioned in my last report, and that this channel is now only 29 feet in depth at average of lowest water, with a width of seven-eighths of a mile across the bar.

Dredging has been done on the various bars between Portland and Astoria, and the channels kept open, so that with the aid of the tides vessels drawing up to 23 feet could pass with little or no detention. During the summer months vessels of a much deeper draft can pass up at all times.

Shipbuilding. There has been but little shipbuilding done in this district during the year. Contracts were let by the United States Government to the Wolff and Zwicker Iron Works here for two torpedo boats, which are under way, and will be completed about August 1, 1897. Each is 146 feet in length, and $15\frac{1}{2}$ feet beam, and are intended to have a speed of at least $22\frac{1}{2}$ knots, with a draught of 5 feet 3 inches.

Light-vessels. The same firm is completing a light-vessel for the Umatilla Reef, Straits of Juan de Fuca, and is also building another for use on this coast. These last are composite vessels.

Sailors. Wages of sailors out of this port during most of the year were 4l., except in the summer months, when seamen could be had at 3l. Shipmasters continue to pay a bonus of 2l. per man, which is illegal under the United States Statutes, and in numerous instances have refused to engage good men, even when requiring no advance, and for whom no bonus was required. An independent seaman has often difficulty in getting employment, and men from crimps' houses are compelled to take an advance of 8l. whether they require it or not. Sometimes this reluctance proceeds from a mistaken fear on the part of shipmasters that the

Mariners' Home.

crimps will give them trouble. This is not the case at this port, as the law is strong enough to protect them, and a little firmness on the part of masters would reduce this disbursement account to some extent.

The Mariners' Home at this port has been closed for lack of support, and although the Seamen's Friend Society continues the work of the Seamen's Institute, better work is crippled for want of funds.

Changes in crews.

The following are the numbers and changes in crews of British vessels trading to this port during the year :—

	Number.
Total number of crews	2,681
Deserted	209
Discharged	148
Engaged	376
Deaths reported	3
Sent to hospital	21

The percentage of desertions to number of crews was 8 per cent., against 11 per cent. last year.

Mining.

During the year there has been a great development in gold mining, not only in Oregon, but throughout the rest of this Consular District. This is particularly the case in Southern Oregon, in Coos, Jackson and Josephine Counties, and in Union, Baker, and Grant Counties in Eastern Oregon. The Director of the Mint estimates the gold product of Oregon as 260,000*l.*, and silver at 75,000 ounces.

In Washington the six principal groups, each comprising several mining districts or camps, are St. Helens, Kittitas, Skagit, Okanogon, Colville, and Palouse. The Director of the Mint gives the approximate gold yield as 76,400*l.*, and silver 140,000 ounces.

Reference is made to the report on Tacoma, annexed, for product in Washington. The output of Tacoma's smelter for 1896 is given as 22,584 ounces of gold, and 436,504 ounces of silver, of average value 2*s.* 8*d.* per ounce.

The Cœur d'Alene districts of Idaho are the principal producers of silver and lead, and the State generally is rich in the precious metals. The United States assayer at Boise City has furnished me with a copy of his report on the product of Idaho for the year ending December 31, which is as follows :—

	Quantity.		Value.
	Fine Ounces.	Lbs.	
			£
Gold	112,409	..	464,740
Silver	5,007,940	..	1,294,953
Lead	..	98,445,986	590,676
Total	..	..	2,350,369

Coal in Oregon. Except the Coos Bay collieries, which produce between 50,000 and 60,000 tons, there are no others operated within the State of Oregon.

Coal in Washington. Statistics in Washington are carefully compiled by the coal mine inspectors, who make the following statement:—

	Tons of Coal Mined.	
	1896.	1895.
First district	773,236	715,786
Second „	429,288	447,951
Total	1,202,524	1,163,737

The number of men employed in the collieries of the first district was 1,851; the inspector of the second district does not give this data. There were no extensive accidents or disasters during the year, and the record of Washington collieries with respect to accident is good. The total number of accidents during the year was 37, of which eight were fatal.

Coke. From the coal produced, 35,967 tons of coke were made.

Iron. Although there are several iron furnaces in Oregon and Washington, the only one in operation was that at Ellensburg, Washington.

Other metals As yet not much attention is given to the base metals, but in course of time this will be done, the district being rich in minerals.

Lead. I am told the galena mines of Idaho are being now mined for the lead product more than formerly. The product and value is given above. The output of smelter at Tacoma, Washington, smelting ores from Idaho, Washington, Montana, British Columbia, and Alaska was 5,012,410 lbs., average value 11s. 2½d. per 100 lbs.

Industries. Although there has been some improvement in manufacturing business, trade in this respect was far from brisk during the year. There are seven woollen mills in this State, one of which at Oregon City is the largest on the coast, operating 14 strands, and employing 260 hands. All the product of this mill is sold in New York. These and other mills produce blankets of very fine quality, and flannels, tweeds, cashmeres, and worsted, generally of from cheap to good grades, finer qualities being bought from eastern mills, or imported from Great Britain. There is one woollen mill in Washington. I have no reliable figures at my command for 1896 of the product of these mills.

There are some 80 flour mills in the State, but many merely grind for local trade. The largest mills are located in Portland, and at Oregon City and Salem. These three mills have a capacity of 3,100 barrels per day. During the summer months mills were very generally shut down from scarcity of wheat.

Two large saw mills were burned at Portland during the year. Business was very light, and probably not much over 50 per cent. of that of 1895.

With the exception of one establishment having contracts for building Government machinery, all foundries and repair shops were very slack, and the same applies to furniture manufacturers and workshops generally.

There are two pulp mills at Oregon City utilising part of the enormous water power there, producing about 30,000 tons of news and wrapping paper. One of these mills making newspaper employs 250 hands, and the other which manufactures only straw and manilla wrapping papers employs 150 hands. There are also mills at Everett and La Camas in Washington. All these mills make their pulp from straw, cotton-wood, white fir, and spruce.

Meat-packing. There are two large establishments engaged in the slaughtering and packing of meat in and near Portland, which, during the year, slaughtered 15,000 cattle, 1,000 calves, 58,000 sheep and lambs, and 41,000 hogs. The largest packing company here employs 165 men, and the value of its products in 1896 was 180,000*l*. The following figures for the rest of the State are given me by a reliable firm. Cattle slaughtered, 17,000; calves, 2,000; sheep and lambs, 40,000; hogs, 45,000.

A large establishment at Tacoma employs 100 men, and the value of its product was 150,000*l*.

Fisheries. 35 fisheries were employed in packing salmon on the Columbia River, and on Oregon coast streams and bays, and during the season, 1,984 boats were employed, and 2,457 gill nets, besides traps and seines. There were 4,827 fishermen employed, and 2,373 shoremen and employés of the factories. Eight of these factories are on the Washington side of the Columbia. In addition to these, there are two factories on Grays Harbour, two on Willapa Harbour, and 11 in Puget Sound district, all in Washington.

Water power. There can be but very little doubt that in course of time the enormous water powers of Oregon and Washington, together with the supplies of raw material produced in these States, or which can be so readily and cheaply imported from abroad, will develop manufacturing industries to a great extent.

PORTLAND.

At Spokane, Washington, the falls of the river have a capacity of 30,000 horse power, and at Oregon City, 12 miles from Portland, Oregon, the capacity is 56,000 horse-power at the lowest stage of the water. Utilising part of this power, the Portland General Electric Company has constructed one of the most complete electric power stations in the United States, if not in the world. It provides power for the electric lighting of Portland, for street car traction, and for numerous shops and factories. *Electric power.*

I do not think the labour market is so congested as it has been for two or three years past, many having gone to the mines in British Columbia, but it is still in a depressed condition, particularly for skilled labour. *Labour.*

The chances for clerks, salesmen, and those who have no particular trade finding employment are very poor, and I would recommend such not to come here expecting to secure prompt employment, instances being numerous of their eventually becoming recipients of charity. *Warning to clerks, &c.*

Although wages here generally have kept up in those trades controlled by unions, plenty of men can be found who will work on almost any terms. Railway labourers are receiving 6s. a day. Farm labourers are to be had at 2l. a month, and often for their board and lodging. *Wages.*

I think it probable that the city has decreased its population during the year, in which there were registered 645 marriages, 1,160 births, and 884 deaths. *Population.*

There have been no epidemic diseases throughout this district. The rate of mortality in this city is estimated at 8·7 per 1,000. During the last four months of the year there were a large number of cases of diphtheria originating in a portion of the city where sewerage is deficient, but the number of deaths from this and other contagious diseases was surprisingly small.

The sanitary condition of the city is generally very good, and has been much improved in recent years by the plentiful supply of pure water, and the care exercised by the health department. *Sanitary.*

Works of improvement on river and harbours are being prosecuted at Coquille, Coos Bay, Umpqua, Siuslaw, Alsea, Yaquina, Nestugga, Tillamook, and on the Columbia and Willamette Rivers above Portland. With the exception of those named below, these have only a coasting trade. *River and harbour works.*

Coos Bay has some foreign trade, and may become an important shipping point. The jetty improvements noted in my last report are completed. Very little work was done on the jetties during the year. Nothing less than 20 feet at low water has been found on the bar during the year.

There has been no change in the condition of the Bar at Yaquina since my last report, but a new project has been adopted by the United States Engineers looking to an extension of the jetties at a further cost of 205,160l.

The following is extracted from the Annual Report of the United States Engineer in charge of the following river and harbour works:—Willapa Harbour, Grays Harbour, Puget Sound,

(2410)

Everett Harbour, Upper Columbia, and certain rivers in Idaho. Some of these works are merely of local interest.

Willapa Harbour, or Shoal Water Bay, has been improved by a system of dykes and dredging. The harbour has quite a large lumber trade, and has a comparatively easy entrance, with a depth of about 21 feet at mean lower low water. Average rise of tide, 8 feet.

Grays Harbour has a large lumber trade, some of which is foreign. Across the bar there is no well defined permanent channel, but several variable shifting channels having depths of 12 to 13 feet. The plan of improvement adopted is by means of a single jetty extending out to sea from the point on the south side of the harbour, a distance of about $3\frac{1}{2}$ miles, to control the ebbing and flooding waters to a sufficient extent to concentrate and direct upon the bar a much greater portion thereof than would naturally go there. The engineers expect to attain a depth across the bar of 24 feet at mean low water. The jetty to be of cobblestone, built above high-tide level, and estimated to cost 200,000*l*.

Everett Harbour is being improved by dredging a harbour basin and channel into the Snohomish River. Estimated cost of work just begun, 74,500*l*.

Canals.
Cascades.
The canal and locks at the Cascades of the Columbia River, which have been under construction since 1887, were completed and opened to the passage of river boats on November 5, 1896. The canal is 3,000 feet long, and the lock is 521 feet long between hollow quoins, 90 feet wide, and has a lift of 24 feet. Its total cost has been 710,000*l*., and it is now proposed to make a second lock by putting in side walls and concrete flooring between the upper lock gate and the upper guard gate, so as to extend the use of the canal up to a stage of 42 feet above high-water at its foot at an additional cost of 66,852*l*.

Lake Washington and Lake Union.
So far only preliminary work has been done on the great project referred to in my last report to connect the freshwater lakes of Washington and Union with the waters of Puget Sound. For this work Congress has so far appropriated 35,000*l*.

Railways.
With the exception of the Astoria Railway there is little railway work in progress throughout the district.

Boat railway.
The line of railway to carry river boats past the obstruction of the Columbia River at The Dalles has been definitely located. It has four curves, each of half a degree, and a maximum grade of 13·2 feet per mile. The Government is now surveying the right of way. Congress has so far appropriated 50,000*l*. for this work.

Agriculture.
The following figures relative to agriculture are taken from the Oregon Assessor's returns for the year 1896. It must be borne in mind that such returns are only comparatively useful, as they are always largely underrated:—

	Number.	Value.
		£
Acres of tillable land	3,422,685	..
Horses and mules	163,570	423,270
Cattle	382,852	732,263
Sheep and goats	1,654,851	334,715
Swine	115,365	43,328

Agricultural statistics from Idaho are very meagre, but the report of the State Engineer gives some interesting figures on irrigation works, from which it appears that the yield on irrigated lands in that State is very heavy. During the year 315,000 acres in 14 counties were irrigated, and the following table gives the result on 38,504 acres of irrigated and 3,960 acres of unirrigated land:—

Idaho irrigation.

Articles.		Average Per Acre.
Wheat	Bushels	31·08
Oats	,,	45·87
Corn	,,	35·23
Rye	,,	25·42
Barley	,,	41·75
Hay, timothy	Tons	2·26
,, alfalfa	,,	4·26
Potatoes	Lbs.	11,280
Beets	,,	25,430
Carrots	,,	18,247
Onions	,,	12,777
Apples	,,	15,487
Prunes	,,	17,633
Peaches	,,	14,124
Pears	,,	13,477
Cherries	,,	3,200
Grapes	,,	13,147

A large quantity of wheat comes to this market from the northern counties of Idaho.

There has been a great improvement in the conditions of agriculture in this district during the year, particularly in wheat growing and cattle rearing. Fruit growers were unfortunate in losing a large proportion of their crops through late frosts.

Agricultural conditions improved.

The following are the only approximate figures I have seen of the grain harvests of this Consular district, and they are largely guesswork, as no reliable statistics are kept:—

Cereals.

Articles.	Quantity.
	Bushels.
Wheat	25,000,000
Oats	11,000,000
Barley	3,500,000
Corn	550,000
Rye	120,000

(2410)

Wheat. A much larger acreage was sown for wheat than in 1895, and prospects for an enormous harvest were excellent until close to harvest time in July, when heavy damage was done by hot winds, as in 1895. The high prices realised compensated those farmers who had even a fair harvest. Statistics are given under another head in this report.

Oats. Oats were hardly half a crop, owing to dry weather of summer; quality poor generally. Prices averaged about 1 dol. 15 c. (4s. 7½d.) per cental, a highly profitable price to the farmer.

Barley. Barley is grown in Eastern Oregon, and Washington crop was small, not sufficient for home consumption for feed and brewing.

Potatoes. The yield of potatoes was rather light, partly because water stood too long on the lowlands, but principally owing to the damage done by early frosts before digging. The crop was very profitable, realising an average of 55 c. (2s. 2d.) per cental, though as high as 75 c. (3s.) was paid.

Flaxseed and fibre. There is considerable interest being taken in reviving the growth of flax both for seed and fibre, and I should not be surprised to see considerable development in this direction.

Hops. Under another head I have given market statistics of hops. Money was made by those who harvested their hops in good condition. 16,000 acres were cultivated in 1895, but growers were so discouraged by their experience that 10 to 12½ per cent. of the acreage was ploughed up and 30 per cent. more uncultivated. Farmers use kerosene emulsions and fish-oil soap, which they find very effective in spraying for lice.

Orchards and fruits. The Oregon State Board of Horticulture issued a very handsome and extensive report on horticulture, and the work of this Board has done much to improve the orchards of the State. There is a most noticeable advance in cultivation and methods of exterminating insect and fungus pests. The Board imported from California the "Vedalia cardinalis," which is doing effective service in destroying the scale insects. A cold and wet spring caused almost a general failure of fruit crops.

Cost of peach orchard. The figures given below of the cost of fruit raising in Oregon may be interesting. The following estimate of cost of a peach orchard is made by an experienced grower near Ashland, Oregon, taking the ground in the brush until it comes in profitable bearing the fifth year after setting out:—

	Amount.	
	Dol.	c.
Land per acre (a high valuation)..	100	0
Clearing and grubbing	30	0
Ploughing and subsoiling..	5	0
Laying-out and digging holes	8	0
Cost of trees and setting-out	20	0
Pruning and shaping 1st year	1	0
Fencing estimated at	16	0
Cost at end of 1st year	180	0
Cultivating and interest, 2nd year	31	0
,, ,, 3rd ,,	33	0
,, ,, 4th ,,	34	40
,, ,, 5th ,,	43	90
Total cost	322	30
Equivalent in sterling	64l. 9s. 3d.	

At this time each tree should produce 20 lbs. of marketable fruit, which at 160 trees per acre is 3,200 lbs. at 2½ c. (1¼d.) or 16l. per acre. After the eighth year each tree should produce 80 lbs. of fruit, and if properly cared for, the trees should bear for 20 years thereafter.

The following figures on cost of an apple orchard are given as the result of 15 years' experience by a grower near Grant's Pass, Oregon. The figures are up to the seventh year after planting:— *Cost of apple orchard.*

	Amount.		
	£	s.	d.
Ploughing and preparing ground	0	12	0
69 trees 2 years old at 12½ c. (25 feet by 25 feet apart)	1	14	6
Planting and laying-off ground	0	8	0
Cultivating and pruning for 7 years at 6 dol. per acre	8	8	0
Total cost on 1 acre to 7th year	11	2	6
Less 69 boxes of apples produced at 50 c. per box..	6	18	0

The eighth year, if in good ground, the trees should produce four boxes for each tree, and after 9 years of age the average product should be not less than ten boxes per tree. The maximum cost for cultivation is not greater than 2l. per acre as the trees grow older.

The cost of the land is not taken into account in the above. 10l. per acre would be full value of cleared land at present. As apples sold the last year at from 4s. to 6s. a box and there is a steady demand for good fruit it would appear there is money in the business.

Similar estimates give the cost of setting out a prune orchard and caring for same till the sixth year not including cost of land at 8l. 18s., 9l. 18s., and 10l. 3s. 4d. in different parts of the State, *Prunes.*

(2410)

but the produce of the fifth year should more than pay the cost of cultivation. The sixth year the productive capacity of the prune tree will increase nearly 100 per cent.; the seventh year 75 per cent., the eighth year 40 per cent., and at the ninth year it has reached its maximum.

The winter of 1895 was open and the losses on ranges of cattle and sheep were not exceptionally heavy.

Horses. Horses are not in demand, though I am told there is more enquiry now for good animals. The average range horse has at present very little value.

Cattle. There has been a growing scarcity of beef cattle and some improvement in prices with a tendency to increased values. The average price of fat steers on the ranges was about 27 dol. (5*l.* 8*s.*).

Sheep. Oregon is said now to rank third in the wool-producing States, and although the assessor's returns seem to show a diminished number of sheep as compared with 1895, other accounts state that the number increases yearly. Statistics of the wool trade are given under that head in this report. Sheep-owners seem to have done fairly well last year as prices of mutton have advanced. The average price paid on the ranges was about 2 dol. (8*s.*) with fleece, and 1 dol. 50 c. (6*s.*) after clipping.

Cashmere goats. The number of Cashmere goats in the State is increasing and they are quite profitable, there being a good demand for their hair at full prices.

Swine. Swine are always in demand for packing purposes. Packers paid an average of 7 dol. (1*l.* 8*s.*) per head.

Taxation and finances. Assessed value of all property in the State was 28,889,085*l.* in 1895, and 28,635,394*l.* in 1896. Within this city the valuation was 9,271,410*l.* in 1895, and 9,295,183*l.* in 1896.

Taxes were levied at the rate of 1·63 per cent. including State, county, and road taxes. The city tax was ·87 per cent.

The total revenue of this city including balances carried over from 1895 was 101,633*l.*, and the total expenditure 88,245*l.* This does not include street and sewer assessments, nor receipts and expenditure of water commission.

The receipts from water during the year were 43,214*l.*, and the expenditure 36,180*l.* Total cost of water system 969,936*l.*

The bonded indebtedness of the city of Portland including 580,000*l.* of water bonds is now 984,414*l.*, of which 865,000*l.* bears interest at 5 per cent. and the remainder at 6 per cent.

Business in real estate has been small, and the total transfers and sales recorded in the county of Multnomah amounted to 802,313*l.*

PORTLAND.

Annex A.—Return of all Shipping at the Port of Portland, Oregon, during the Year 1896.

Entered.

Nationality.	Sailing. Number of Vessels.	Sailing. Tons.	Steam. Number of Vessels.	Steam. Tons.	Total Number of Vessels.	Total Tons.
British	84	132,088	16	25,562	100	157,650
American, from foreign countries	2	1,619	13	5,096	15	6,715
American, from Atlantic ports	2	3,564	...	...	2	3,564
American coasting	50	15,267	154	153,049	204	168,316
German	4	6,152	...	...	4	6,152
French	1	1,235	...	...	1	1,235
Danish	1	1,327	...	...	1	1,327
Russian	1	2,153	...	...	1	2,153
Total	145	163,405	183	183,707	328	347,112
,, for the year preceding	151	172,623	182	154,117	333	326,740

Cleared.

Nationality.	Sailing. Number of Vessels.	Sailing. Tons.	Steam. Number of Vessels.	Steam. Tons.	Total. Number of Vessels.	Total. Tons.
British	81	125,984	16	25,562	97	151,546
American, to foreign countries	8	8,196	15	5,880	23	14,076
American coasting	59	16,373	153	155,919	212	172,292
German	10	15,108	...	...	10	15,108
French	1	1,235	...	...	1	1,235
Russian	1	2,153	...	...	1	2,153
Danish	1	1,327	...	...	1	1,327
Total	161	170,376	184	187,361	345	357,737
,, for the year preceding	159	182,147	176	155,336	335	337,483

Annex B.—Return of Principal Articles of Export from Portland, Oregon, during the Years 1896–95.

Articles.		1896. Quantity.	1896. Value. £	1895. Quantity.	1895. Value. £
Wheat	Quarters	862,185	1,002,547	988,553	832,790
,, flour	Sacks	426,240	370,020	342,812	230,753
Timber	Feet	4,036,000	7,052	2,937,700	4,193
Barley	Bushels	31,384	3,093	121,018	11,115
Canned salmon	Lbs.	97,598	2,066	96,600	2,380
Other articles	...	...	17,715	...	7,820
Total	...	...	1,402,493	...	1,089,051

(2410)

UNITED STATES.

Return of Principal Articles of Import to Portland, Oregon, during the Years 1896-95.

Articles.		1896. Quantity.	1896. Value.	1895. Quantity.	1895. Value.
			£		£
Coke	Tons	3,319	1,911	...	...
Coals	,,	14,755	5,446	14,587	6,621
Tin and tin-plate	Lbs.	1,788,732	8,715	1,909,913	9,297
Rice and rice flour	,,	1,626,416	4,178	1,666,569	4,931
Earthenware and glass	...	...	12,721	...	6,825
Salt	Lbs.	7,505,600	3,446	12,797,630	6,374
Cement	Barrels	58,079	13,621	49,470	12,136
Tea	Lbs.	400,874	10,628	424,185	10,969
Coffee	,,	151,499	5,284	180,707	6,414
Hemp and jute	Tons	350	5,992	3,141	11,666
Window glass	Lbs.	1,322,462	4,101	287,421	887
Bags and bagging	...	...	47,503	...	40,015
Sugar	Lbs.	2,310,292	11,908	503,258	2,808
Caustic soda	,,	169,879	594	388,592	1,393
Soda ash	,,	259,669	389	312,630	460
Chloride of lime	,,	69,197	221	140,036	584
Soda	,,	157,982	192	360,398	408
Sulphur	Tons	1,737	5,035	885	1,884
Manufactures of flax and hemp, including fishing twine	...	...	7,410	...	8,121
Pig-iron	Tons	2,138	5,275	...	...
Bar and railroad iron	,,	2,225	8,940	...	...
Raw and waste silk	Lbs.	57,664	12,937	...	...
Matting	...	...	3,224	...	...
Oils	...	...	2,951	...	...
All other articles	...	...	35,744	...	33,966
Total	...	...	218,366	...	165,759
Entered for transportation to other districts and Canada—					
Tea	Lbs.	3,813,777	102,450	5,134,122	123,537
Other articles	...	...	113,750	...	92,073
Grand total	...	...	434,566	...	381,369

Note.—The above returns do not include coastwise trade.

Annex C.—TABLE showing Total Value of all Articles Exported from and Imported to Portland, Oregon, from and to Foreign Countries during the Years 1896–95.

Country.	Exports. 1896.	Exports. 1895.	Imports. 1896.	Imports. 1895.
	£	£	£	£
Great Britain	1,002,681	959,032	58,262	49,875
Belgium	..	..	14,079	8,029
British Columbia	6,319	2,318	2,681	1,980
China and Japan	244,218	114,202	60,624	30,550
China and Japan in transit	..	..	211,017	215,610
Australia	43,004	2,348	4,552	7,405
Cuba	..	..	1,106	896
India and East Indies	..	..	65,675	56,512
India and East Indies in transit	..	..	1,167	..
Philippine Islands	..	..	5,992	2,500
Germany	..	..	8,967	5,634
Hawaiian Islands	13,744	6,088	138	630
South Africa	79,480	..	..	..
Chile	4,420	..	..	..
Asiatic Russia	8,200	..	102	..
All other countries	427	5,063	204	1,748
Total	1,402,493	1,089,051	434,566	381,369

ASTORIA, OREGON.

Mr. Vice-Consul Cherry reports as follows:—

General remarks. The seaborne business of this district as shown in the returns, when compared with that of last year is not satisfactory. The exports have fallen-off materially, the principal loss being in the item of salmon.

Real estate in all parts of the States of Washington and Oregon has found, or is finding, very rapidly its true value, after the inflated prices of past years.

Imports. Value of imports has increased altogether on account of the arrivals of 6,000 tons of steel rails and railway materials. The usual imports of tin-plates, coal, salt, and cement are to be noted.

Exports. As before stated exports have diminished, chiefly in salmon, both in quantity and price, and in wheat which is much lower in quantity but higher in price.

Shipping and navigation. An increase in the number of vessels entering this river is to be noted, but I find the average tonnage to be somewhat smaller. The proportion of vessels under the British flag shows a slight increase in number and tonnage, the latter being 91 per cent. The increase of steam tonnage under the British flag is very noticeable.

UNITED STATES.

Pilot service.

A second pilot schooner with a corps of pilots belonging to the neighbouring State of Washington went into commission on the Columbia River Bar in opposition to the Oregon pilots, but afterwards an agreement between the two sets of pilots was brought about, and this arrangement gives a first-class pilot service, one boat being always outside.

Disasters to shipping.

I have to mention the stranding of three vessels on the coast to the north of this port, all occasioned by the strong northerly set of the current. They were the British ship "Glenmorag," on March 19; the British barque "Zinita," on November 10; and the German barque "Potrimpos," late in December.

The "Zinita" was re-floated in a few days, and had the unusual experience of being off her port, driven off, going ashore, taken off, taken to a dry dock away from her destination and brought back to her port, all within three weeks, thereby saving her charter and being none the worse.

Since then a long continued run of unfavourable weather has prevented the re-floating of the other two vessels, and I daresay it will be found to be advisable to leave them till the fine weather.

Coast currents.

In connection with the above strandings, I cannot too urgently call the attention of hydrographers, and of shipmasters bound to this port, to the strong northerly set of the coast current, especially inshore where it has approached 3 knots an hour during the winter months after a long continuance of southerly weather. The great majority of disasters have occurred north of this river and all are more or less attributable to this current. Those wrecks that have occurred to the south have always been found to have overrun their distance.

Industries: Salmon-fishing.

The salmon fishing industry received a severe check owing to a very bitterly conducted strike of the fishermen against a proposed reduction of 20 per cent. in the price offered for salmon by the cannery men, resulting in the loss of several lives and of half the fishing season, the result being a compromise of 10 per cent. reduction, *i.e.*, of ½ c. (¼d.) from 5 c. (2½d.) to 4½ c. (2¼d.).

Salmon-canning.

Under the above circumstances salmon canning was unusually successful, the total spring pack being but little under that of 1895.

The direct export to Great Britain was much smaller, only 51,000 cases being shipped from here.

The total pack in the Columbia River and adjacent rivers within the limits of this Vice-Consular District amounts to 514,246 cases as follows:—

	Amount.
	Cases.
Columbia River spring catch	368,000
„ fall „	64,900
On the coast north of Columbia River	41,000
„ south „	40,346

ASTORIA.

Sturgeon-fishing. There is a continual falling off in sturgeon fishing, owing to over-fishing and no protection. I can hear of no combined effort to protect or propagate this fish.

Logs. The price of logs has fallen considerably, owing to over-supply and little demand. Another large raft of logs, spars, and piling was successfully taken down the coast to San Francisco making a handsome profit to the operator, and which will no doubt stimulate him to further efforts this season.

Sawn lumber. A decided increase in foreign shipments of sawn lumber is to be noted, but is absolutely nothing compared to what it should be; four vessels were ordered off the river, and one from here, to British Columbia and Puget Sound, to load lumber for the United Kingdom and British colonies, all of which could have had their cargoes out in this river. I understand that the chief market for lumber in this district, i.e., San Francisco, is over-supplied, and the shutting down of several of the mills is in contemplation.

Factories. The various small factories of box making, paper pulp, tanning, are all holding their own, but at no great increase of output.

Can-making. This has now become quite an industry, and the factory is doing a great deal of work outside supplying the salmon canneries, and is importing direct a great deal of British tin-plates. This plate is landed direct at the factory wharf, which has steamboat connection with the interior, and will shortly have a rail connection on the other side of the factory.

City waterworks. The total cost of the waterworks plant, as reported by the Water Commission, amounts to 57,000*l.*, and besides giving admirable service is now used in hydraulic grading of streets and lots. At a trial, grading work that would have cost 25 c. (1*s.*) per cubic yard by labour and cartage was done for less than 3 c. (1½*d.*) by water. The commission has made a tender to the city to furnish the lighting of the streets at a very much reduced cost.

Improvements. The contractor who undertook the construction of a railway line "from Astoria to a transcontinental connection" made a commencement; large grading contracts were given out, and lately bids for bridge work and trestles have been sought. It is doubtful if the line will be finished this year, but there is absolutely nothing to prevent it, as there are no great difficulties to overcome, as the steel rails for the full distance arrived from England last summer and now lie stored waiting to be laid. The rails weigh 77 lbs. to the yard, and are equal to the heaviest in use on the Southern Pacific Railroad, under whose auspices this line is supposed to be built.

Government improvements. The construction of a lighthouse on North Head has been going on since last summer, and was very much retarded by the exceptionally wet winter. The light is to be of the first order, and is to be removed from the present position on Cape Disappointment; its arc of visibility will be 220 degrees, as compared with 155 degrees on Cape Disappointment. Its approximate position will be 46° 17′ 48″ N. and 124° 4′ 46″ W., and it will be

UNITED STATES.

Population and health.

of great benefit to vessels coming down from the northward, especially along the coast, in which position the light at Cape Disappointment was shut out.

I see no record of any diminution of the population, notwithstanding the cry of hard times and the glittering prospects of wealth in the British Columbian gold fields.

There are but few of the permanent population that have left. The health of the district remains good, nothing but the "influenza," or as it is known here the "grippe," has shown itself beyond the usual run of infantile troubles.

Annex A.—RETURN of all Shipping at the Port of Astoria, Oregon, during the Year 1896.

ENTERED.

Nationality.	Sailing. Number of Vessels.	Sailing. Tons.	Steam. Number of Vessels.	Steam. Tons.	Total. Number of Vessels.	Total. Tons.
British	88	137,271	19	28,782	107	166,053
American coasting	125	34,780	386	306,889	511	341,669
,, foreign	7	5,435	4	1,568	11	7,003
Danish	1	1,325	...	...	1	1,325
French	1	1,235	...	...	1	1,235
German	4	6,790	...	...	4	6,790
Total	226	186,836	409	337,239	635	524,075
,, for the year preceding	230	239,377	352	299,434	582	538,811

CLEARED.

Nationality.	Sailing. Number of Vessels.	Sailing. Tons.	Steam. Number of Vessels.	Steam. Tons.	Total. Number of Vessels.	Total. Tons.
British	31	48,113	5	7,815	36	55,928
American coasting	123	34,190	361	306,291	484	340,481
,, foreign	8	6,224	4	1,568	12	7,792
Nicaraguan	1	351	...	...	1	351
Total	163	88,878	370	315,674	533	404,552
,, for the year preceding	215	220,262	301	295,222	516	515,484

Annex B.—RETURN of Principal Articles of Export from Astoria, Oregon, during the Years 1896-95.

Articles.		1896. Quantity.	1896. Value. £	1895. Quantity.	1895. Value. £
Salmon	Cases	53,158	59,213	81,583	105,882
Wheat	Bushels	45,422	6,881	263,171	27,868
Flour	Barrels	8,258	5,084	...	...
Seal-skins	...	...	...	...	769
Lumber	Feet	3,652,000	8,537	1,344,000	1,918
Sundries	...	...	1,600	...	182
Total	...	...	81,315	...	136,619

TACOMA AND SEATTLE.

Return of Principal Articles of Import to Astoria, Oregon, during the Years 1896-95.

Articles.		1896.		1895.	
		Quantity.	Value.	Quantity.	Value.
			£		£
Tin-plates ... Boxes ...		82,862	39,824	49,365	25,659
Salt ... Lbs. ...		22,400	16	...	...
Coal ... Tons ...		3,725	1,924	2,866	1,566
Steel rails ... Lbs. ...		14,560,563	30,542	...	...
Cement ... Barrels ...		5,420	1,439	...	...
Sundries		...	4,556	...	1,366
Total		...	78,301	...	28,591

Tacoma and Seattle.

Mr. Vice-Consul Alexander reports as follows:—

General remarks relative to the State. It may be pointed out that, owing to the undeveloped condition of the country, the productions of this State are principally those derived directly from the soil, such as wheat, timber, flour, and minerals—general manufactures being comparatively insignificant; while the high customs tariff, taken in connection with the freight rates, is a great hindrance to the importation of British manufactures, particularly to the ports of the Pacific North-West, such commodities only being imported as are absolutely necessary and unobtainable in this part of the country, notably cement, tin-plates, salt, sodas, liquors, fancy groceries, and glassware.

Tacoma has maintained its position during the year 1896 as the chief shipping centre of the foreign trade of the State, and it is a noteworthy fact that more than two-thirds of this trade has been carried on in British vessels.

Health, births, and deaths. Generally speaking, the health of the State has been good, there having been practically no cases of epidemic or infectious diseases, only one case of small-pox being reported in the State. The Secretary of the State Board of Health reports that there were, during the year 1896, 6,145 births, 2,811 deaths, and 2,138 marriages.

Cattle disease and losses of stock. An unusually long and severe winter has delayed the growth of the early spring grass and had a most disastrous effect on the various animals on the ranges in Eastern Washington, they having been unable to obtain sufficient food during the winter to enable them to withstand the less nutritive qualities of the spring grass. As a consequence, over 50 per cent. of these animals—mostly horses—have perished, it being estimated that in all over 100,000 horses have succumbed. Little regret, however, is felt at this result, as the value of horses has depreciated so much of late that it was becoming a serious problem to dispose of them, and they are regarded as almost in the nature of a pest. Stock suffered but slightly from the want of food, as those of any value were taken under shelter and fed with hay, and stock-owners are congratulating themselves on the now plentiful supply of bunch grass for their cattle, which would otherwise have been eaten by the horses. The horses were not worth 4s. a-piece, there was absolutely no market for them, and vast numbers have already been shot down on the ranges to get rid of them.

The great moisture in the spring in the eastern part of the State almost completely exterminated the ground squirrels, which have done immense damage in the past to the grain, and farmers are rejoicing at the excellent prospects for their crops.

Within the year, new regulations regarding the importation of cattle has become law, one of which is that "all cattle brought into this State must have been, within three months prior to their importation, submitted to the tuberculin test, from which no reaction occurred, certified to by a competent veterinarian. All sheep brought into the State must have been dipped within 30 days prior to, or must be dipped within 30 days after, having been brought into the State. All pigs imported into the State must be quarantined by their owners 30 days, after their arrival in this State.' Attention is drawn to these regulations on account of the proximity of British Columbia.

Industries. Timber.
The railway shipments to Eastern points, viâ the Northern Pacific, Great Northern, and Canadian Pacific Railways, amounted during the year to 6,486 truckloads of timber, and 14,194 truckloads of shingles, as compared with 5,662 of timber and 13,776 of shingles in 1895. The shipments consisted of 96,890,000 feet of timber, as compared with 90,984,000 feet in the preceding year, and 2,129,100,000 shingles, as against 2,181,240,000; thus showing an increase in timber and a slight decrease in shingles. The cargo shipments for 1896 from the State were 37,127,360 feet of timber and 6,697,159 of lath. The price of shingles was about the same as last year, 3s. 6d. per 1,000, to 4s. 6d. towards the close of the year.

Railways.
It does not appear that any notable extension of mileage has been made by the railway companies during the year, but the roadbed of the Northern Pacific has been steadily improved and grades reduced, more especially in the eastern part of the State. Enormous damage was sustained at various points towards the close of the year from high water in the rivers, particularly in Western Washington. Several wooden bridges which were destroyed have been replaced by steel on stone and concrete foundations, making them almost permanent structures. 120 freight cars of 70,000 lbs. capacity each, for specially heavy timber shipments, are being built at Tacoma. This company has also completed during the year a most extensive system of warehouses at Tacoma, besides constructing coal bunkers with a capacity of 12,000 tons, at a cost of 70,000 dol. (14,000l.), where vessels are now loaded by electric conveyors, and inaugurating numerous other undertakings with a view to the improvement of the wharves, thus giving this port the greatest facilities for despatch in the loading and discharging of steamships. These wharves being lighted by electricity, the work can be carried on by night, should occasion require.

There has been a renewal of interest in mining during the year 1896, and while the ore is mostly of low grade, averaging less than 40 dol. (8*l*.) to the ton, it appears to be abundant, 382,000 ozs. of gold having been produced, as against 30,000 in the previous year, besides 140,000 ozs. of silver. Although it is well known that iron exists in large quantities in the State, but little effort has been made to utilise it, the average prospector refusing to trouble himself with an iron find. The manufacture of iron is certain, however, to become one of the most profitable industries of the State. Marked improvements have been made at nearly all the coalmines during the year, the works at Roslyn especially having been much enlarged, rendering an increased production possible. The production of coal for the various mines of the State has been during the year 1,250,311 tons, valued at 3,000,777 dol. (600,156*l*.), and 3,469 men have been employed.

Mining.

It may not be out of place in this connection to give the value of the business of the sub-port of Northport in this State, this being the entrepôt for the ores imported into this country for reduction from the newly-discovered mines in the Kootenai district in British Columbia. The imports amounted to 48,406*l*. (242,030 dol.), and the exports to 236,013*l*. (1,180,068 dol.), making this sub-port the second export port of the State.

Although the run of salmon in the Puget Sound district has been unusually light, the amount tinned has been in excess of any previous year. Six new canneries have been erected, making a total of 11 now in operation in this district. The total pack of salmon was 195,664 cases, valued at 140,000*l*. (700,000 dol.). There were, in addition, 500,000 lbs. of fresh salmon sold, valued at 25,000*l*. (125,000 dol.); 1,000 barrels of salted salmon, valued at 800*l*. (4,000 dol.); 160,000 lbs. of smoked salmon, valued at 3,200*l*. (16,000 dol.); and 381,997 salmon shipped fresh to British Columbia, valued at 15,465*l*. (77,326 dol.). There are two factories in this district for preparing codfish, only one of which however, has been in operation during the past season. The fish are taken in the waters of Behring Sea, and shipped to these factories for drying. The amount dried this season has been less than last year, amounting to 171 tons, valued at 2,040*l*. (10,200 dol.). The sardine cannery mentioned in the last report has been abandoned, owing to lack of necessary capital.

Fisheries.

The excellent work commenced in the artificial propagation of fish has been judiciously continued during the past year. Early in the summer the State Fish Commission decided that it was advisable to extend its sphere of operations to the streams that empty into Puget Sound, and, after much difficulty and delay, a suitable site was selected on Baker Lake at the head of the Skagit River, almost on the borders of British Columbia, for a salmon hatchery, where a building has now been erected and stocked with 6,000,000 eggs of the nerka or sockeye salmon. The Commission recommends the early construction of at least two more hatcheries in this district, in order to maintain the supply of

Agriculture.

salmon annually coming into these waters, and again urges the amendment of the inadequate laws relating to fisheries. It is especially suggested that fishing should be absolutely prohibited on streams on which a hatchery is situated and within 1 mile of the mouth of such streams, and that a heavy penalty should be fixed for violations of this law. 268 licences have been granted for various fish-catching appliances to be used on Puget Sound, but no fish-wheels are in operation in this district.

The following table gives the estimated acreage and yield of the different crops for the whole State during the year 1896:—

Crops.	Acreage.	Average Yield Per Acre.	Total Yield.
		Bushels.	Bushels.
Wheat	495,000	12	5,940,000
Oats	75,000	30	2,250,000
Barley	75,000	30	2,250,000
Rye	3,000	20	60,000

The average net price of wheat to the farmers was 2s. 1d. per bushel; of oats, 4s. 2d. per cental; of barley, 2s. per cental; of rye, 3s. 1d. per bushel. The average freight from the grain districts to tide-water was 18s. per ton. The wheat crop was of good quality, but considerably under the average, owing to the grain being shrivelled by hot winds and drought during the filling stage. There was, probably, not more than half an average crop, but 90 per cent. of the grain graded No. 1 wheat. It is believed that the great bulk of the grain grown during the year which could be spared for export purposes has already moved, the balance being required for flour, feed, and seed purposes. The high prices obtained towards the close of the year induced farmers to dispose of all grain they could possibly spare, and they have consequently run themselves short of seed wheat, which may prove a hindrance to an increased crop for the coming year.

Grain inspection and grading.

The importance of the inspection of grain in this State has now been fully recognised, and little more may be said in addition to what was reported last year under this head. Some changes in the grades have been made, which are hereby reported—notably, in the case of wheat—as follows: all wheat in this State is divided into three grades, known respectively as grades No. 1, No. 2, and No. 3. All below grade No. 3 ranks as rejected wheat. No. 1 Bluestem and No. 1 Club are required to weigh not less than 58 lbs. to the measured bushel; No. 2 Bluestem and No. 2 Club are required to weigh not less than 56 lbs., and No. 3 Bluestem and No. 3 Club not less than 54 lbs. to the measured bushel

The following table shows the number of carloads of grain received at the three inspection stations for the year ending December 31, 1896:—

Articles.	Quantity.			Total Cars.
	Tacoma.	Seattle.	Spokane.	
Wheat	6,190	2,059	2,606	10,855
Oats	437	611	36	1,084
Barley	58	221	19	298
Total	..	..	..	12,237

Taking an average of 634 bushels, or 38,040 lbs., of wheat to a car we have approximately 6,882,070 bushels of wheat inspected; oats at 679 bushels, or 24,444 lbs., give 736,036 bushels inspected, and barley at 664 bushels, or 33,200 lbs., give 197,872 bushels, making a total of 7,815,978 bushels of grain inspected during the year. Wheat is reckoned at 60 lbs., oats at 36 lbs., and barley at 50 lbs. to the bushel. A very large percentage of the wheat crop in this State went to Portland, Oregon, and very little wheat went out of the State to eastern points.

Dairying. The State Dairy Commissioner, in his report, says that there were 78 creameries and cheese factories in operation, the total production of butter for the year being 1,838,657 lbs., which, at an average of 10d. per lb., represents a value of 76,610l. Of cheese there was produced 554,123 lbs., which, at an average of 5d. per lb., amounts to 11,544l. The value of milk is estimated at 60,000l. (300,000 dol.), of calves killed at 8,000l. (40,000 dol.), and of pork 12,000l. (60,000 dol.).

Horticulture. There is little to be said under the head of horticulture in addition to what has been said in previous reports. The area planted with fruit trees in the State is estimated at 53,810 acres. The apple crop was rather below the average, while other fruits were about the same as last year. The cold weather at the close of the year damaged peaches in some localities, while others apparently escaped unhurt. So far as can be ascertained, indications point to a good fruit crop in the coming year.

Hops. Very few hop yards were cultivated, on account of the low prices offered during the early part of the season. The advance which took place later in the year will probably revive the industry somewhat, and the acreage already in hops will be more carefully cultivated in hopes of still better prices being obtained. The whole stock is now pretty well disposed of.

Flax. The experiments with flax continue to be made with gratifying results, farmers in various parts of the State taking sufficient interest to sow small areas and forward the seed and fibre to the Government Commissioner. A small appropriation has been made by the State for the encouragement of these experiments.

Agricultural statistics. The following figures are taken from the returns of the State Board of Equalisation for 1896 for the State of Washington:—

	Number.	Value.
		£
Acres of improved land	2,211,162	13,666,321
Valuation of improvements	..	1,616,581
Horses, mules, and asses	155,485	472,258
Cattle	211,009	508,731
Sheep	446,989	102,808
Pigs	113,631	40,907

Commercial relations. China and Japan.

The Northern Pacific Steamship Company, which operates a line of British steamers between Tacoma and Japan and Hong-Kong, has a fleet consisting of four steamships, while during this year two others of large tonnage were chartered for the eastward voyage only, bringing full cargoes from the Orient, and both taking cargoes of grain from San Francisco to St. Vincent for orders. No sailing vessels have been chartered in connection with this company's service this year, for the first time since the opening of the line, and it is probable that in future the business will be entirely confined to steamships. In addition to the company's regular steamers, it is now employing an extra one, which will make several voyages during the course of the next year. The company's new time-table, just issued for the coming year, shows a sailing from Tacoma for every third Saturday throughout the year. There has been a steady increase in the cotton and timber shipments by these steamers, and also in the quantity of domestics carried forward to Shanghai; these come principally from the Southern States by way of the Northern Pacific Railway and connections. The timber, however, is all sawn at the mills locally situated. There has been a large export of flour during the past year, the greater portion of which has been manufactured in this State, although a considerable quantity has come from Oregon mills.

A new feature of the Trans-Pacific business this year is the export of steel rails, which came from the Eastern States by way of the Northern Pacific Railway, and were shipped to Japan in the month of December, 3,000 tons having gone forward in two vessels. There has been an increase throughout the year in all other staple articles of export, but owing to the increased price of flour towards the end of the year, the export of this commodity has somewhat fallen off for the present. The company has now opened connections, and is taking cargo on through bills of lading for Australia and also to South African ports. Four steamers are leaving China this year for South African ports direct, and the company is prepared to take cargo on through bills of lading by those steamers. Freight rates have remained steady throughout the year, the first-class passenger fares being as follows: to Japan, 20*l*. (100 dol.); to Shanghai and Hong-Kong, 25*l*. (125 dol.).

Japan.

Since the last report, the Nippon Yusen Kaisha, the Japanese Mail Steamship Company, has extended its ocean commerce to the port of Seattle, communication being established between

Yokohama and this port as a terminus, viâ the Sandwich Islands. This company was encouraged to make this venture through arrangements with the Great Northern Railway, which made the company its ocean carriers, thus securing it a certain amount of assured business, to the mutual benefit of both companies. The business seems not only to have held its own, but indicates by each shipment a steady increase, both in imports and exports. The chief commodities for export have been flour, timber, cotton, rails and other manufactures of iron; while the imports have consisted mostly of the usual Oriental merchandise, tea, silk, matting, sugar, rice, &c. To indicate the growth of this trade, it may be mentioned that only 185 tons were actually discharged at Seattle on the first voyage, while the last steamer brought in 1,170 tons, the balance of the cargoes being discharged at the Sandwich Islands. Full cargoes were taken out, destined for the most part for Japanese ports, no stop being made at the Sandwich Islands.

South Africa. The trade with South Africa, both British and Portuguese territories, has shown steady increase, shipments of wheat, flour, and other breadstuffs, as well as timber, having been carried both by sail and steam vessels, wheat being a new article of import this year, and the demand for flour having enormously increased. This trade is likely to become permanent in these particular commodities.

Central America. The trade with Central America is becoming more varied in its character, embracing the several kinds of liquors, oats, hay, timber, coal, iron manufactures, barbed wire, agricultural implements, cement, lime, building materials, oils, and indeed almost all the necessaries for the field and home.

Alaska. The Alaskan trade is of a general character, relating more particularly to the wants of miners and mining camps, including for the most part mining machinery, building materials, and provisions.

Dry dock. Among other items of interest may be noted that during the year the Government dry dock at Port Orchard has been completed, and several vessels, including some belonging to the United States Navy, have been successfully docked, everything working in a very satisfactory manner. It is expected that machinery and other appliances for the more complete repairing of vessels will be erected in due course of time, making this one of the most complete docks on the coast.

Exportation of cattle. During 1896, several head of milch cows have been exported to Japan and China, the animals arriving in even better condition than when they started. It would seem that Canada should pay some attention to this particular business, her facilities for this trade being equally as good as those of the United States.

Commerce of Tacoma. It may not be out of place to mention that the reports of the United States Treasury Department show that the port of Tacoma ranks second amongst the ports of the whole United States in the number and value of packages "without appraisement" passing through its custom-house in the past year, being preceded only by

(2410)

UNITED STATES.

New York and followed by San Francisco, thus clearly indicating the growing importance of this Puget Sound district as a competing route for Asiatic commerce.

Shipping. By referring to Annex A, it will be seen that the number of sailing vessels entering the port was 4 more than in 1895 but with decreased tonnage, while there was a decrease by 5 in the number of steamships but an increase in tonnage. In British vessels there was a decrease of 2, with about 6,500 tonnage. The clearances show an increase of 18 in sailing vessels and 5 in steam vessels, with an increase of about 20,000 tons in each case; in British sailing vessels the increase over the preceding year was 14, with about 20,000 tonnage, while the steamships increased by 10 in number with about 17,000 tonnage. It will be noticed that in the entrances of vessels there is a decrease in the registered tonnage of about 500, while the clearances indicate an increase of about 25,000 tons.

The harbour-master reports that during the year 1896, 428 vessels, with a total of 649,818 registered tons, entered the sub-port of Tacoma, being an increase in both number and tonnage over the year 1895. The inward cargo tonnage was, however, only 78,714 tons, being a decrease. During the same period, 414 vessels left the port, the registered tonnage of which amounted to 1,257,743 tons, being double that of last year, while cargo tonnage is reported as 640,851, showing a slight falling-off. These statistics do not include the local vessels which ply up and down Puget Sound.

Exports and imports. By referring to Annex B, the exports and imports for the last two years will be seen. Among the other articles in the export trade are included those chiefly to Chinese and Japanese ports, consisting of tinned meats and fruits, butterine, oil, beer, tobacco and cigars, hoofs and leather. A large part of the merchandise landed here from Oriental ports comes through in bond for immediate shipment to eastern points, this port receiving no credit for such shipments, as the duty on such merchandise is paid at the port of destination; consequently only a rough estimate can be made of the value of such consignments, which during the year amounted to about 493,480*l*. free of duty, and 120,250*l*. dutiable, aggregating 613,730*l*.

The exports show an increase of 797,155*l*. as compared with 1895, while the imports exhibit a falling-off of 502,379*l*. Taking the articles separately, we notice a steady increase in each of those enumerated, textile manufactures, iron manufactures and electrical supplies and appliances being especially noticeable. Among the iron manufactures is included the shipment of 3,200 tons of steel rails. While the quantity of wheat exported has not been so very much larger than last year, the high prices ruling towards the end of the year have raised the value almost one-third, which also affected the value of the flour exported. Four vessels with full cargoes of flour left this port during the past year, two going to the United Kingdom and two to South Africa, the remaining shipments having been made to Oriental ports. The markets for wheat, flour, and other breadstuffs in Cape Colony and the settlements in South Africa, particularly in British and Portuguese territory, are growing steadily, seven cargoes of merchandise of this character having left during the year 1896, one being partly loaded at Seattle, four cargoes of timber also having gone to these ports.

Turning to the imports for the year, we find a falling-off in the articles imported of over one-half, rather greater in the dutiable goods than in the non-dutiable. In the free list, we notice the difference in silk and tea by comparing the two years; there is a slight increase in the value of jute as well as ore, both of which commodities are supplied from British territory, chiefly India, British Columbia, and Canada. Among the articles paying duty there is no increase over the year 1895, with the exception of cement, more than half of which was supplied from Germany.

No account is taken in Annex B of the articles landed in bond, nor of the domestic trade, the foreign trade alone being represented. The harbour-master's statement shows that during the year 1896 there were 3,511,440 bushels of wheat shipped from this port, of the approximate value of 494,000*l.* (2,470,000 dol.); there were 382,674 barrels of flour, valued approximately at 234,449*l.* (1,172,247 dol.); the timber shipped was over 86,444,400 feet, with a value of about 155,049*l.* (775,247 dol.); the coal shipments amounted to 318,806 tons, having an estimated value of 190,499*l.* (952,494 dol.). The value of merchandise to China and Japan is estimated at 625,206*l.* (3,126,032 dol.), and that to British Columbia at 66,246*l.* (331,232 dol.); making a total of 1,765,454*l.* (8,827,270 dol.). His statement further shows that there were 20 cargoes of Oriental merchandise imported hither, to which is assigned a value of 1,161,495*l.* (5,807,478 dol.). Large quantities of local merchandise pass over the wharves of which no account is taken. The total value of all exports from this port for the year amounts to 2,093,478*l.* (10,467,389 dol.), and of all imports to 744,484*l.* (3,722,420 dol.), according to the statement of the Collector of Customs.

Annex C shows the commercial relations between this port and foreign countries. Under the export column, in order to indicate the trade with our own country, her colonies and dependencies more clearly, such countries have been bracketed together, making up the aggregate in the regular column. This plan has also been followed in regard to the South and Central American Republics. It will be noticed that Great Britain has received almost four times the value of commodities, made up of wheat cargoes, and one cargo each of flour and timber; and if we take this country in connection with her colonies, she easily assumes first place in the rank of exports, closely followed by China. It is only fair to assume that many of the wheat cargoes "for orders" will find their way to British ports, which will still further swell the amount of exports. Turning to the colonies, &c., we find South Africa has increased her exports from this port very considerably, cargoes of flour, wheat, breadstuffs, and timber being

(2410)

carried by steam as well as sailing vessel. India received the full cargo of wheat of the Norwegian steamship, "Tyr," while Australia is credited chiefly with timber. The trade with Hong-Kong consists mainly of flour, timber, condensed milk, liquors (malt), and tobacco. The trade with China and Japan shows great increase, China receiving the largest amount of exports; these countries taking all the cottons, textile and iron manufactures, including steel rails, electrical supplies, &c., also a large quantity of flour, timber, tobacco, condensed milk, and malt liquors. The trade with Central and South American countries consists principally of timber from this port. France and her possessions in Tahiti each received timber.

In looking over the import column we notice that there is a gratifying increase in imports from Great Britain; this is accounted for by cargoes made up of Portland cement, salt, tin-plates, pig-iron, bleaching powders, sodas, and liquors (malt, spirits, and mineral waters). The cement has been taken by the Northern Pacific Railway Company, while the several canneries take the salt, tin, and soda for preserving fish. The imports from Canada consist principally of ore and liquors, with a little coal and cedar timber, and Oriental goods transhipped to this port, viâ Vancouver, B.C., by the Canadian Pacific Railway. India imports jute for the manufacture of grain bags. The only other countries making importations to this port, with the exception of Germany, whence some cement was received, were Japan and China, which countries sent over silk, tea, sugar, rice, matting, and curios. There is a marked falling-off in the imports from these two countries in comparison with the preceding year.

The following table shows the number and nationalities of vessels which entered and cleared during the last year:—

Annex A.—RETURN of all Shipping at the Port of Tacoma during the Year 1896.

ENTERED.

Nationality.	Sailing. Number of Vessels.	Sailing. Tons.	Steam. Number of Vessels.	Steam. Tons.	Total. Number of Vessels.	Total. Tons.
British	23	39,914	38	49,773	61	89,687
American	7	5,616	15	7,813	22	13,429
Norwegian	4	3,885	2	3,400	6	7,285
German	2	3,492	...	...	2	3,492
Danish	1	1,651	...	...	1	1,651
Total	37	54,558	55	60,986	92	115,544
,, for the year preceding	33	55,499	60	60,455	93	115,954

TACOMA AND SEATTLE.

CLEARED.

Nationality.	Sailing. Number of Vessels.	Tons.	Steam. Number of Vessels.	Tons.	Total. Number of Vessels.	Tons.
British	38	65,012	42	54,384	80	119,396
American	17	12,632	7	3,846	24	16,478
Norwegian	4	2,608	1	1,417	5	4,025
German	4	5,934	...	...	4	5,934
Danish	1	1,651	...	...	1	1,651
Italian	1	1,246	...	...	1	1,246
Chilian	1	1,035	...	...	1	1,035
Total	66	90,118	50	59,647	116	149,765
,, for the year preceding	48	69,446	45	55,303	93	124,769

NOTE.—The entrances and clearances of American vessels do not include the domestic trade.

The following tables show the exports and imports for the past two years:—

Annex B.—RETURN of Principal Articles of Export from Tacoma during the Years 1896-95.

Articles.		1896. Quantity.	Value.	1895. Quantity.	Value.
			£		£
Wheat	Bushels	2,954,904	432,965	2,045,627	197,078
Flour	Barrels	355,670	210,372	301,657	143,786
Timber	Feet	31,159,000	72,678	34,574,000	62,688
Cotton	Lbs.	3,636,300	59,293	...	34,564
Textile manufactures	...	...	358,556	...	...
Milk, condensed	Lbs.	688,200	10,753	...	8,915
Fish, tinned, salmon	Cases	14,753	15,043	...	...
,, ,,	Lbs.	...	...	40,800	500
Iron manufactures	...	...	51,052	...	...
Electrical supplies	...	...	18,030	...	...
Other articles	...	...	57,298	...	41,354
Total	...	...	1,286,040	...	488,885

(2410)

UNITED STATES.

Return of Principal Articles of Import to Tacoma during the Years 1896–95.

Articles.		1896. Quantity.	1896. Value.	1895. Quantity.	1895. Value.
			£		£
Free—					
Silk, raw	Lbs.	775,000	429,756	2,188,000	874,917
Tea	,,	899,000	15,104	1,000,000	18,734
Matting	Rolls	846	779	...	...
Household effects	...	...	1,936	...	765
Jute	Lbs.	...	3,008	411,500	2,631
Ore	...	...	26,130	...	15,027
Other articles	...	...	5,745	...	18,004
Total	...	...	482,458	...	930,078
Dutiable—					
Sugar	Lbs.	2,748,000	18,189	10,290,000	44,537
Rice	,,	186,000	653	1,105,000	3,386
Cement	,,	8,458,000	5,630	6,178,000	3,882
Ore	...	...	4,797	...	13,897
Liquors (malt, spirit, &c.)	...	...	1,126	...	...
Other articles	...	...	8,605	...	28,822
Total	...	...	39,000	...	94,524
,, free and dutiable	...	...	521,458	...	1,024,602

Note.—Exchange has been converted at 5 dol. to the 1*l.*

Annex C.—TABLE showing Total Value of all Articles Exported from and Imported to Tacoma to and from Foreign Countries during the Years 1896–95.

	Exports.		Imports.	
Country.	1896.	1895.	1896.	1895.
	£	£	£	£
Great Britain	131,645	36,508	14,013	4,478
Queenstown and St. Vincent for orders	272,189	191,276	..	..
British colonies and dependencies—				
Hong-Kong .. 115,503		97,683	23,213	..
Africa .. 105,149		3,086	..	..
Australia .. 33,321		21,601	..	..
India .. 14,797		..	3,014	8,599
Canada .. 2,820		3,451	39,527	57,125
Other countries .. 505		..	..	..
	272,095			
China	369,402	24,269	171,833	285,421
Japan	205,539	76,126	268,818	688,780
South America—				
Peru .. 5,497		1,784	..	..
Ecuador .. 5,400		..	..	..
Chili .. 2,800		10,235	..	..
	13,697			
Central America—				
Mexico ports .. 5,625		4,281	..	..
Central America .. 3,201		..	..	..
	8,826			
France	2,040	..	..	..
French possessions—				
Tahiti	2,442	..	..	..
Africa, Portuguese	8,165	16,815	..	..
Germany	..	..	976	..
Other countries	..	1,770	64	199
Total	1,286,040	488,885	521,458	1,044,602

NOTE.—The domestic trade and goods for immediate transportation are not included in this table.

Seattle. General remarks.

Seattle still maintains its position as the business town of the State, and since the last report has become the ocean terminus of the Nippon Yusen Kaisha, the Japan Mail Steamship Company, in the Pacific Coast of the United States, this company being the ocean carrier of the Great Northern Railway. Seattle's trade with Alaskan territory is increasing, its business houses sending up most of the supplies to that country. It is from this port that the majority of the miners and prospectors start, and make their purchases for "outfit" and transportation upon arrival, the numbers starting for that territory from here being largely in excess of any previous year. Here, again, the Puget Sound and Central

Shipping and navigation.

American Steamship Company makes its headquarters, and reports increasing business.

By referring to Annex A at the end of this report, it will be seen that there was a decrease in the sailing vessels of 12, and an increase of 6 in the steam vessels; and a decrease of 6 in the total number of vessels that entered this port in 1896 over the year 1895, the registered tonnage being increased by about 8,000 tons. This annex also shows that there was an increase by one in the number of British vessels entering and in their registered tonnage of about 6,000 tons.

In turning to the clearances for the same period, there is found a falling-off of 21 in the sailing vessels, and 24 in the steam vessels, and in the total number of vessels clearing a decrease of 45, making a difference in the tonnage of 15,000 tons. In the number of British vessels clearing there was a decrease by 9, with a registered tonnage of almost 10,000 tons.

Exports and imports.

By referring to Annex B it may be noticed that the exports show an increase of 68,398*l.*, while the imports have also increased by 16,974*l.* The increase in the exports is due to the cargoes going to the Orient, principally made up of flour, cotton, and iron manufactures. The wheat shipments declined very greatly, while the shipments of timber showed a marked improvement, more than double the amount shipped last year. The importation of free goods shows a slight decline, while the dutiable goods exhibit a similar increase, chiefly in sugar and cement.

By referring to Annex C, it will be seen that the bulk of the export trade, consisting of wheat, still goes to Great Britain. The trade with the Orient, including Hong-Kong, has increased very greatly, in consequence of the new steamship line. A similar increase is noticeable in the trade with the Central American ports, on account of another line of steamships now running directly to these ports. Australia and the Sandwich Islands still take large amounts of timber, the trade with the latter country showing marked improvement.

The increase in the imports is also due to the connections by steamship with Oriental and South American ports, the bulk of the imports, however, coming from Hong-Kong. There appears to be a decrease in the imports from Great Britain. Canada remains the same, and Belgium and Germany contribute to the general increase of this column mainly from cargoes of cement and glassware. The imports from Great Britain consist mainly of cement, tin-plates, and other materials for preserving fish. These tables take no account of the domestic trade, of which it is impossible to give an estimate, vessels leaving here not only for the Puget Sound country, but also for Alaska, California, and British Columbia.

TACOMA AND SEATTLE.

Annex A.—RETURN of all Shipping at the Port of Seattle during the Year 1896.

ENTERED.

Nationality.	Sailing. Number of Vessels.	Sailing. Tons.	Steam. Number of Vessels.	Steam. Tons.	Total. Number of Vessels.	Total. Tons.
British	11	19,968	4	367	15	20,335
American	7	2,281	81	87,713	88	89,994
Japanese	...	...	6	12,249	6	12,249
Norwegian	...	...	3	2,520	3	2,520
German	1	1,407	...	...	1	1,407
Total	19	23,656	94	102,849	113	126,505
,, for the year preceding	31	18,367	88	100,339	119	118,706

CLEARED.

Nationality.	Sailing. Number of Vessels.	Sailing. Tons.	Steam. Number of Vessels.	Steam. Tons.	Total. Number of Vessels.	Total. Tons.
British	5	9,959	3	1,817	8	11,776
American	22	7,536	27	7,547	49	15,083
Japanese	...	...	6	12,249	6	12,249
Norwegian	...	...	4	3,360	4	3,360
Total	27	17,495	40	24,973	67	42,468
,, for the year preceding	48	33,662	64	23,563	112	57,225

NOTE.—The entrances and clearances of American vessels do not include the domestic trade.

Annex B.—RETURN of Principal Articles of Export from Seattle during the Years 1896–95.

Articles.		1896. Quantity.	1896. Value. £	1895. Quantity.	1895. Value. £
Wheat	Bushels	478,181	68,402	1,050,096	106,887
Flour	Barrels	83,160	54,343	...	...
Fish, tinned salmon	Cases	...	28,667	17,323	11,870
Timber	Feet	10,437,000	22,040	9,645,000	19,822
Cotton	Lbs.	213,826	19,683	...	...
Iron manufactures	...	...	7,978	...	...
Electrical supplies	...	...	1,570	...	...
Liquors (malt, spirit, mineral)	...	...	1,011	...	...
Other articles	...	...	16,180	...	12,897
Total	...	...	219,874	...	151,476

UNITED STATES.

RETURN of Principal Articles of Import to Seattle during the Years 1896–95.

Articles.		1896. Quantity.	1896. Value. £	1895. Quantity.	1895. Value. £
Free—					
Salt	Tons	659	695	712	975
Bleaching powder	Lbs.	499,000	1,773	...	...
Tea	...	...	351	...	...
Other articles	...	...	1,024	...	3,205
Total	...	...	3,843	...	4,180
Dutiable—					
Sugar	Lbs.	1,287,000	10,733	425,000	2,907
Rice	,,	1,618,000	2,424	739,000	1,693
Cement	,,	12,311,000	7,874	...	1,989
Liquors (malt, spirit, mineral)	...	...	3,597	...	2,790
Coal	Tons (2,240 lbs.)	888	527	624	416
Glass (empty bottles)	Lbs.	109,882	234	...	...
Caustic soda	,,	73,000	223	...	...
Other articles	...	...	6,828	...	5,334
Total	...	...	32,440	...	15,129
,, free and dutiable	...	...	36,283	...	19,309

NOTE.—Exchange has been figured at 5 dol. to the 1*l*.

Annex C.—TABLE showing Total Value of all Articles Exported from and Imported to Seattle from and to Foreign Countries during the Years 1896–95.

Country.	Exports. 1896. £	Exports. 1895. £	Imports. 1896. £	Imports. 1895. £
Great Britain	96,954	120,468	4,819	7,297
Colonies, dependencies:				
Hong-Kong	22,950	..	12,207	..
Canada	4,898	3,522	7,789	7,030
Australia	4,889	4,612	..	..
Japan	50,530	..	2,877	} 4,165
China	3,332	4,268	..	
Central American ports	20,831	11,284	..	..
Mexico	1,567	731	..	..
Sandwich Islands	7,174	1,752	..	..
Belgium	..	..	4,343	..
Germany	..	..	3,765	..
Other countries	6,749	4,839	483	817
Total	219,874	151,476	36,283	19,309

NOTE.—The domestic trade and goods for immediate transportation are not included in this table.

PORT TOWNSEND.

Mr. Vice-Consul Klöcker reports as follows:—

Lumber. The export to foreign and domestic ports, and to eastern cities by rail, indicate a healthy increase in the lumber interests. Although the volume of lumber exported from the lower Puget Sound to foreign countries shows a small decrease, yet the trade is in a more healthy condition than heretofore. Australia, China, Hawaii, west coast of South America, and South Africa, have been steady buyers, and to the latter country and to China and Japan increased orders have been received.

Shipping and freight. Lumber freights are dull, and have not improved from last year, as will be seen from annexed list of rates. Several big British ships have been laid up in this harbour from 6 to 12 months waiting for freights to improve, but are still here, and will now wait for the next wheat season.

| | Per 1,000 feet. ||
	Highest.	Lowest.
	£ s. d.	£ s. d.
Sydney, N.S.W.	1 15 0	1 10 0
Melbourne, Port Pirie, and Adelaide	2 2 6	1 15 0
Brisbane, Freemantle	2 5 0	2 0 0
China, Shanghai	2 7 6	2 2 6
Africa, Delagoa Bay	3 0 0	2 12 6
West Coast, South America	2 5 0	1 10 0
United Kingdom	3 7 6	2 17 6

The rates as quoted are for sailing ships, steamers having received about 5s. in addition per 1,000 feet.

Shipbuilding. A revenue steam cutter and a modern equipped torpedo boat were built at Seattle last year for the Government by private parties. At Port Blakely two steamers and four large-sized schooners were built, including the five masted schooner "Inca," which carries between 1,400,000 and 1,500,000 feet of lumber. The steel shipyard plant at Everett did not turn out any vessels last season.

Dry dock. The Government dry dock at Port Orchard has been finished, and is in complete working order. It has been thoroughly tested, and can accommodate the largest sized steamers visiting the Pacific coast.

Pilotage. A strong effort was made at the last sessions of the Washington State Legislature to pass a compulsory pilot law; it was opposed, however, by the local lumber and grain shippers, as well as European shipowners through their representatives here, and was defeated.

Steamship lines. A Japanese steamship company has established a regular line of steamships between Japan and Seattle, and in connection with a trans-continental line of railroad is securing a large amount of

Stevedoring.

Towage.

Fur sealing.

Fortifications.

Cement.

the Oriental business, which seems to be steadily increasing. This company has now building in Europe three modern steamers, which will be put on this run as soon as finished.

Owing to reliable and active opposition stevedoring rates have been greatly reduced this year, and it seems almost certain that if this work is supported by shipowners in England, by next season the rates will be on a par with those charged in British Columbian ports.

The British Columbian tug "Lorne" is now under the management of the Puget Sound Tug-Boat Company, of this city, which virtually does away with all opposition, and under the existing management good service at reasonable rates is maintained.

The fur-sealing industry has greatly diminished in the last year or two. The sealers aver that the recent regulations jointly adopted by Great Britain and the United States has practically caused the business to become thoroughly unprofitable.

The Government have surveyed the sites for the erection of proposed fortifications on Points Wilson, Marrowstone, and Admiralty, an equilateral triangle abreast of Port Townsend. Considerable land on these points has been purchased by the War Department, and semi-official announcement is made that preliminary work will be commenced this year. It is also proposed to connect Point Wilson with Point Marrowstone by a military road circling around Port Townsend Bay. During the progress of the work of construction it is proposed to re-station two or three companies of troops at Fort Townsend, two miles from this city.

Importation of cement for this year into the Puget Sound Custom-House District (said district besides Port Townsend as headquarters includes eight additional sub-ports) was 42,065 barrels, a slight increase, I believe, over the previous year. During the building boom on Puget Sound in the years 1888, 1889, and 1890, quantities of British cement were used. Since 1891, however, the German and Belgian cement has been introduced into this market, a little coming directly from Belgium and Germany, but the main bulk coming from Californian ports. From the annexed list the total importation will be seen of British and foreign cement from the year 1887 to 1896, inclusive.

TACOMA AND SEATTLE.

Year.	Quantity. English.	Belgian and German.
	Barrels.	Barrels.
1887	2,056	..
1888	7,594	..
1889	24,325	..
1890	70,811	..
1891	42,928	13,888
1892	15,940	2,000
1893	53,732	8,592
1894	33,492	..
1895	20,146	..
1896	18,708	23,357

The import trade shows an increase of 3,364*l*., and the export trade an increase of 287,359*l*., as compared with last year. *Imports and exports.*

The health of the city has been good, with no infectious or contagious diseases. *Health.*

I append the several annexes marked A, B, and C, to show the commerce and trade in this district.

Annex A.—RETURN of all Shipping at the Port of Port Townsend during the Year 1896.

ENTERED.

Nationality.	Sailing. Number of Vessels.	Tons.	Steam. Number of Vessels.	Tons.	Total. Number of Vessels.	Tons.
British	54	88,890	7	914	61	89,804
American	127	78,096	1,693	766,655	1,820	844,751
German	7	9,736	...	...	7	9,736
Norwegian	8	7,737	...	...	8	7,737
Chilian	12	13,118	...	...	12	13,118
Hawaiian	5	8,299	...	...	5	8,299
Italian	3	3,954	...	...	3	3,954
Nicaraguan	2	1,842	1	840	3	2,682
Total	218	211,672	1,701	768,409	1,919	980,081
,, for the year preceding	126	108,629	1,396	685,453	1,522	794,082

CLEARED.

Nationality.	Sailing. Number of Vessels.	Tons.	Steam. Number of Vessels.	Tons.	Total. Number of Vessels.	Tons.
British	54	89,132	7	914	61	90,046
American	154	109,028	1,768	843,533	1,922	952,561
German	8	11,563	...	...	8	11,563
Norwegian	6	6,921	...	...	6	6,921
Chilian	11	11,263	...	...	11	11,263
Hawaiian	5	6,512	...	...	5	6,512
Italian	1	1,462	...	...	1	1,462
Nicaraguan	4	3,776	...	...	4	3,776
Total	243	239,657	1,775	844,447	2,018	1,084,104
,, for the year preceding	134	121,988	1,442	775,619	1,576	897,607

Annex B.—RETURN of Principal Articles of Export from Port Townsend during the Years 1896-95.

Articles.		1896. Quantity.	1896. Value.	1895. Quantity.	1895. Value.
			£		£
Coals	Tons	4,113	11,503	...	...
Flour	...	...	20,040	...	...
Timber	Feet	128,450,135	154,718	144,409,000	180,731
Iron and manufactures of iron	...	...	55,216	...	40,640
Oils	...	...	11,203	...	7,634
Furs and hides	...	...	3,550	...	41,620
Provisions, meats	...	...	43,531	...	28,124
Cattle	...	...	19,011	...	24,060
Liquors and wines	...	...	10,870	...	4,165
Wood and manufactures of wood	...	...	46,052	...	...
Cotton	...	...	129,654	...	...
Fish	...	...	32,043	...	5,013
Tinned fruits and vegetables	...	...	18,927	...	7,312
Chemicals	...	...	8,125	...	...
Wool and manufactures of wool	...	...	1,600	...	11,553
Leather	...	...	5,690	...	...
Oil	...	...	4,560	...	...
Other articles	...	...	187,534	...	125,626
Total	...	...	763,827	...	476,478

RETURN of Principal Articles of Import to Port Townsend during the Years 1896-95.

Articles.	Value. 1896.	Value. 1895.
	£	£
Cement	2,604	554
Coal	2,534	3,117
Iron and manufactures of iron	252	412
Steel-wire rods	3,605	941
Tin-plates	641	115
Lead and ore	8,476	17,405
Zinc	20	..
Liquor	125	..
Sugar	3,035	1,724
Rice	697	5,041
Tea	3,554	5,498
Raw silk	42,075	1,532
Fish	826	16,630
Chemicals	4,820	..
Other articles	13,236	10,167
Total	86,500	63,136

Annex C.—TABLE showing Total Value of all Articles Exported from and Imported to Port Townsend from and to Foreign Countries during the Years 1896–95.

Country.	Exports. 1896.	Exports. 1895.	Imports. 1896.	Imports. 1895.
	£	£	£	£
Great Britain	64,787	12,136	..	248
British colonies and Canada	432,076	300,674	53,411	47,490
Australia	63,901	44,580	1,059	..
Germany	3,990	..	6,335	1,099
Salvador	8,957	..	..	..
Japan	5,169	..	672	1,898
Samoa	1,250	..	..	..
Belgium	..	..	3,852	..
Hawaiian Islands	41,255	26,480	6,055	499
Chili	24,711	31,510	..	..
China	8,956	4,612	2,900	5,633
Peru	18,950	4,517	..	..
Mexico	7,154	1,651	..	..
Africa	53,149	35,454	..	..
India	4,827	134	697	4,102
Guatemala	3,669	2,660	..	..
New Caledonia	2,611	6,610	..	..
Fiji Islands	3,188	3,510	..	..
Netherlands	..	1,430	..	..
Hong-Kong	2,570	..	8,404	..
Other countries	12,657	520	3,115	2,167
Total	763,827	476,478	86,500	63,136

(2410)

LONDON:
Printed for Her Majesty's Stationery Office,
By HARRISON AND SONS,
Printers in Ordinary to Her Majesty.
(75   6 | 97—H & S   2410)

WITHDRAWN